Content Reading and Literacy

Succeeding in Today's Diverse Classrooms

Third Edition

Donna E. Alvermann
The University of Georgia

Stephen F. Phelps
Buffalo State College

Allyn and Bacon
Boston   London   Toronto   Sydney   Tokyo   Singapore

Series Editor: Aurora Martinez-Ramos
Senior Vice-President and Publisher, Education: Paul Smith
Editorial Assistant: Beth Slater
Production Coordinator: Susan Brown
Editorial-Production Service: Matrix Productions
Cover Administrator: Linda Knowles
Composition Buyer: Linda Cox
Manufacturing Buyer: Julie McNeil
Electronic Composition: Omegatype Typography, Inc.
Designer: Glenna Collett

Copyright © 2002, 1998, 1994 by Allyn & Bacon
A Pearson Education Company
75 Arlington Street
Boston, MA 02116

Internet: www.ablongman.com

Between the time Website information is gathered and then published, it is not unusual
for some sites to have closed. Also, the transcription of URLs can result in unintended
typographical errors. The publisher would appreciate notification where these occur so
that they may be corrected in subsequent editions.

Library of Congress Cataloging-in-Publication Data

Alvermann, Donna E.
    Content reading and literacy : succeeding in today's diverse classrooms / Donna E.
Alvermann, Stephen F. Phelps.—3rd ed.
        p.   cm.
    Includes bibliographical references and indexes.
    ISBN 0-205-32742-7
    1. Content area reading—United States.   2. Reading (Secondary)—United States.   3.
Multicultural education—United States.   4. Reading (Secondary)—Social aspects—United
States.   5. Teenagers—Books and reading—United States.   I. Phelps, Stephen F.   II. Title.

LB1050.455.A47 2002
428.4´071´2—dc21   2001022393

Photo Credits: Chapters 1, 2, 3, 4, 5, 6, 8, 9, 11, Will Hart; Chapter 7, 10, 12, Will Faller.

Printed in the United States of America

10 9 8 7 6 5 4 3   05 04 03

For Jack, Sarah, Nick, and Bekah

▼▼▼▼▼▼▼▼

Contents

▼▼▼▼▼▼▼

Preface

▼▼▼▼▼▼▼

This, our third edition, has been the most fun and challenging to write. We found it fun to revise along the lines that both our readers of previous editions suggested and our reviewers for this edition pointed out in their thoughtful commentaries. The third edition also presented the challenge of blending the printed page with the electronic page. We hope that in doing so we have opened wide the Internet spaces in which your students will be able to explore the topics presented in *Content Reading and Literacy: Succeeding in Today's Diverse Classrooms*. We also anticipate some quality on-line communications with our readers through the book's companion website at http://www.ablongman.com/alvermann3e.

The third edition builds on the strengths of the second edition. We have increased the emphasis on English language learners and the literacy needs of students from diverse cultural backgrounds. Continued emphasis on how to teach English language learners the academic literacy strategies and skills they need to comprehend their subject matter texts becomes increasingly important as the diversity of students in schools also increases.

We have added special tips for teaching readers who struggle to comprehend the texts they are assigned to read. These tips are integrated throughout the book, with each chapter having one or more of them. We have also added a new chapter on writing across the curriculum. In previous editions, writing strategies were included in various chapters. Now, they are tied together in a single chapter. Based on the recommendations of those who have used this book in the past, we decided to write separate chapters on responding to reading and study strategies.

One of the most noticeable changes in this edition is our expanded coverage of teaching with the computer. Integrated throughout the book are World Wide Web links and strategies for using technology that are drawn from real classroom contexts. Since the first edition in 1994, there has been an astonishing increase in the use of technology, especially the Internet, both in schools and in society as a whole. Although it seems certain that informational technology will continue to grow, we believe that "book technology" will remain an essential aspect of academic literacy in the foreseeable future. Given the evolving landscape of technological innovation and the ephemeral nature of many Internet sites, it is impossible for a textbook such as this one to remain current. Consequently, we have chosen to include selected examples of how teachers have used technology to reinforce and expand students' literacies, along with a judicious listing of Internet sites. Those who wish to learn more about teaching with technology may follow any of a number of leads provided in this edition. Another option is to visit our companion website at http://www.ablongman.com/alvermann3e, which features additional resources and is regularly updated.

Another new feature is one we call "Responses from our Readers." This feature allows us to highlight how readers of previous editions have adapted strategies and materials for use in their own classrooms. We believe teachers appreciate knowing how others are trying new ideas and adapting them for use with their particular students.

In this edition, we offer a variety of perspectives in which to ground literacy instruction in the content areas, including those perspectives that draw from cognitive, sociocognitive, and sociocultural theories of learning. We also provide examples of literacy instruction that differentiate a social constructionist framework for learning from an information processing or schema theoretic framework.

Finally, as in previous editions, strategies and materials used in *Content Reading and Literacy: Succeeding in Today's Diverse Classrooms* have been field-tested with preservice and inservice subject matter specialists who view themselves as active facilitators of students' learning. Thus, once again, we are indebted to the many prospective and practicing teachers in our classes who have contributed in substantive ways to this book. Their stories about literacy-related events that have made a difference in their instruction, as well as their suggestions for strategies that appeal to a wide range of student abilities and interests, have given a practical bent to this book.

ACKNOWLEDGMENTS

We are deeply grateful to Dennis Mike of Buffalo State College for providing guidance and feedback on the use of computer technology in content area classrooms, to Josephine Peyton Young of Arizona State University for encouraging her students to reflect on the content of the second edition in order that we might make it more relevant to a culturally and linguistically diverse group of readers, and to our many students and colleagues who have challenged our thinking and contributed to our enthusiasm for teaching students to engage with print and nonprint texts at the middle and secondary school levels.

To our reviewers, Janet Busboom of Mercer University, Juan R. Lira of Texas A & M International University, Victoria Gentry Ridgeway of Clemson University, and Rose Mary Scott of the University of Wisconsin–Parkside, we say thank you for providing the kind of thoughtful critiques and useful suggestions that make this third edition what it is. Your expertise and investment of time are greatly appreciated.

Finally, we thank everyone who played a role in the editing and production of this book. Specifically, we acknowledge the expert guidance we received from our editors, Arnis Burvikovs and Aurora Martinez. We also thank Linda Bieze, Beth Slater, and Patrice Mailloux, who made sure that we received answers to our questions on a timely basis and clarified procedures when we were uncertain. To Joy Fulmer, we express appreciation for serving as the conduit for the exchange of materials between Athens, Georgia, and Buffalo, New York. Without her patience and good cheer, we would have been hard pressed to keep up with each other's many recommendations and requests for journal articles, chapters, and other such materials.

Content Literacy and the Reading Process

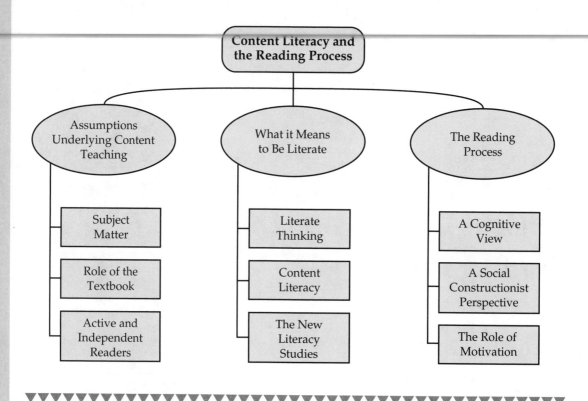

In the anecdote that follows, Melissa McFarland, a prospective high school English teacher, writes reflectively on her first few days as a teacher intern in one of the county school systems of rural northeast Georgia.* (Melissa wrote this piece while she was at the University of Georgia and enrolled in Donna's content reading course.) As you read the anecdote, try to imagine yourself in Melissa's place. Do you share her perspective on reading, or have your experiences led you to adopt a different perspective? Does the picture Melissa paints of her students remind you of your own? If you have not taught yet, does this anecdote ring true for you as a former high school student? What is the same about your experiences and Melissa's? What is different?

▼▼▼▼▼▼▼

Well, here I sit. Another day behind this great big desk at the front of the room. This is where I always dreamed of being but now that I'm here, what do I do? Am I doing all of the things I should be doing? Do they [my students] like me? Are they enjoying the reading we are doing? I wish I could tell.

I want them to feel as passionately about this thing called reading as I do. Some pipe dream, huh? Why can't they cry out loud when Othello kills

---

*Adapted with permission of Melissa McFarland.

Desdemona? Why don't they laugh at the witty cracks of Tom and Huck? It is the hardest thing in the world to do—teach something that you feel so strongly about.

There is so much housekeeping to be done in the course of the day that I have to devise a way to creatively handle it. I want to take the guy in the back row who probably has never read a whole book and spark a fire for books in him. Maybe a little Cormier or Golding for him. What about those students throughout the class who are going to college? Have I covered enough with them to prepare them for their SATs and college? Then there are those avid readers who I share a little karma with. But they are few and far between, and they don't need my help—only my guidance.

Balancing it all and making sure no one slips through the cracks is a tough job. I love to read as much as I love to breathe. So how do I teach them to breathe? Reading is so natural to me. I must remember to make it interesting and new each day. I must come up with new innovations in our reading assignments—never just assign a story and then test them over it.

Being a good teacher is not getting every student to score an A on the test, but being a good teacher is helping them to open their eyes to new interests and to think about things in a different way. I want them to believe that they have the power to control their own minds and not just regurgitate information I have assigned. I want them to find their own meanings in each literary work.

▼▼▼▼▼▼▼

We think Melissa's perspective on literacy instruction is filled with a passion that comes from her own love of reading. She shows concern for her students and expresses hope that they will learn to appreciate and enjoy literature on their own terms. Although Melissa worries about "covering" content and the ubiquitous assessments her students face, she plans to establish a proper instructional balance so that no one need fall through the cracks. Finally, Melissa recognizes the proactive role she must take in creating the kind of learning environment she wants her students to experience. In sum, we think Melissa understands the *why* of content area reading instruction quite well. She personally knows the value of being an active and independent reader, and she wants her students to experience the same.

Periodically throughout this chapter, we will return to Melissa's reflections on content teaching and the reading process. First, however, it is important to examine some of the assumptions underlying such instruction.

ASSUMPTIONS UNDERLYING CONTENT TEACHING

Most content area teachers assume it is their responsibility to cover their subject matter in a timely, accurate, and effective manner (Alvermann & Moore, 1991; Moore, 1996). They also assume, for the most part, that textbooks are necessary for teaching and learning content (Wade & Moje, 2000). Finally, content area teachers tend to assume that by the time students enter middle school and high school, they are strategic in their approach to reading and learning (Dole et al., 1991). These assumptions influence teachers' instructional decision making, their use of textbooks, and their perceptions of active and independent readers.

Subject Matter

The historical roots of content area reading instruction go back several decades. Prior to the Twentieth Century, the predominant mode of instruction in American secondary schools was one of imitation and memorization. In the early part of the twentieth century, the work of humanist educators such as John Dewey and developmentalists interested in individual growth factors began to emphasize child-centered curricula over rote memorization (Moore, Readence, & Rickelman, 1983). With the cognitive revolution in psychology in the early 1970s came the notion that reading and writing should be taught as thinking processes rather than in the mechanical manner advocated by the behaviorists, who had preceded the cognitivists. Although other writers at that time were beginning to publish books on reading at the secondary school level, Herber's (1970) text, *Teaching Reading in the Content Areas,* is generally regarded as the first to demonstrate how teachers can simultaneously teach content and process (reading). It is also one of the first content area methods texts to emphasize the importance of teachers' decision making.

Content area teachers take pride, and rightfully so, in knowing the subject matter they teach and how best to engage students in learning the same. They also recognize that they are responsible for monitoring students' learning and pacing their instruction accordingly. If these were the only two factors teachers had to take into consideration when making instructional decisions, it would be a relatively simple task to decide what to teach, when, and at what pace. Unfortunately, instructional decision making is complicated by what Newmann (1988) refers to as the addiction to coverage:

> We are addicted to coverage. This addiction seems endemic in high schools . . . but it affects all levels of the curriculum, from kindergarten through college. We expose students to broad surveys of the disciplines and to endless sets of skills and competencies. . . . The press for broad coverage causes many teachers to feel inadequate about leaving out so much content and apologetically mindful of the fact that much of what they teach is not fully understood by their students. (p. 346)

Melissa's concern for the college-bound students scattered throughout her class shows that she has justifiable worries about covering content: "Have I covered enough with them to prepare them for their SATs and college?" Addiction to coverage, however, is dangerous because it tends to produce a false dichotomy between content knowledge and process knowledge. When *knowing what* takes precedence over *knowing how,* as it typically does when preparing students for standardized tests pressures teachers to cover a wide variety of topics in an inadequate space of time, students are deprived of the opportunity to learn how bits of knowledge fit together and generalize to other areas of the curriculum or to real life. In short, students are denied the kind of instruction that leads to active and independent learning.

Role of the Textbook

Textbooks and other learning materials provide a focus for several chapter sections in this book. For example, in Chapter 3, we explore how hypertext and other forms of electronic media have led to a new relationship between text and reader. In Chapter 4, we consider the decision making involved in choosing appropriate materials to use in planning content literacy lessons or longer units of instruction. Here, however, we focus on three assumptions underlying the use of textbooks. One is that textbooks will help to structure loosely coupled curricular goals and objectives. By most estimates, textbooks do indeed structure from 67 to 90 percent of all classroom instruction (Woodward & Elliott, 1990), but this varies according to the type of instructional approach—transmission or participatory—that teachers espouse (Wade & Moje, 2000). This structuring can take several forms. For example, in one study of 24 middle-grade classrooms representing various content areas and student ability levels, teachers were observed using textbooks to refocus class discussions that had begun to stray, to verify information, and to cue students as to where to find answers to study guide questions (Alvermann, 1987).

A second assumption is that students will use their textbooks to learn course content. This assumption may or may not be borne out. It depends on whether students view their textbooks or their teachers as the ultimate source of knowledge. Some researchers (Hinchman & Zalewski, 1996; Ratekin et al., 1985; Smith & Feathers, 1983a, 1983b) have found that students perceive their teacher, not the textbook, as the primary source of knowledge. Students generally find their teacher easier to understand than the textbook, especially if they believe they will be tested on what the teacher says in class (Hinchman, 1987). Other researchers (Applebee, Langer, & Mullis, 1987; Goodlad, 1984; Stake & Easley, 1978) do not agree with findings that point to the teacher as the source of information. These researchers found evidence that teachers put the responsibility for acquiring the information contained in the text squarely on their students' shoulders. Still other researchers (Davey, 1988; Ratekin et al., 1985) have reported that in some content area classrooms it is the custom for teachers to use the textbook as a "safety net"—something to fall back on—rather than as a vital link and a basis for class discussions. When teachers use texts as safety nets, more often than not they substitute lecturing for discussions of assigned readings.

A third assumption is that textbooks will present the content in a coherent and unbiased fashion. We know from experience that this is not always so. In fact, the literature is filled with critiques of poorly structured texts (Commeyras

& Alvermann, 1996; Tyson-Bernstein, 1988), and Jean Anyon (1979) pointed out more than two decades ago that textbook authors cannot escape the fact that they, like all of us, hold certain ideological perspectives. When those perspectives appeal to our common sense but serve the interests of particular social groups at the expense of other less favored groups, teachers find it necessary to intervene (Lemke, 1995). Given appropriate planning strategies, even the most biased of texts can lead to excellent classroom discussions in which students learn to look at both sides of an issue for sources of possible misunderstanding. We firmly believe that in today's diverse classrooms, opportunities for students to respond to biased texts should be welcomed. Taking advantage of such opportunities can contribute toward building appreciation for individual differences.

Recalling Melissa's self-perceived need to be an active participant in her students' learning, it is difficult to conceive of students in her classroom ever relying totally on their textbooks or totally on her as their primary means for understanding course content. A balance is likely to be struck between the two means. It is also likely that Melissa will structure her lessons to integrate content and process. She appears to view content knowledge (knowing what) and process knowledge (knowing how) as being inextricably tied. This approach is one we favor, but success in implementing it depends to a great extent on the willingness of students to become actively and independently engaged in reading their content area texts.

Active and Independent Readers

Melissa's reflections on her first few days as a teacher intern suggest that she was keenly aware of the need to encourage students to become active and independent readers. In her words, "I want them to believe that they have the power to control their own minds . . . to find their own meanings in each literary work." Melissa also recognizes the necessity, but insufficiency, of simply immersing students in a literary environment; she knows that if her goal is to develop active and independent readers, its achievement will require a careful balancing act on her part. Through carefully weighing different instructional decisions, she will have to demonstrate her commitment to integrating content and process—to motivating students' love for literature while at the same time showing them how to acquire power and control over their own thinking and learning. Assuming that Melissa succeeds, what might her students look like as active and independent readers? What role will the textbook be likely to play in Melissa's classroom? What instructional decisions might support her commitment to integrating content and process?

Active readers.   Readers who engage in an active search for meaning use multiple strategies, including self-questioning, monitoring, organizing, and interacting with peers. In each instance, researchers believe, it is the cognitive processing that is induced in the strategic reader—not the strategy itself—that is responsible for promoting active reading (Dole et al., 1991; Pearson & Fielding, 1991).

Active readers *generate questions* before they read, as they read, and when they have finished reading. Before reading a chapter in a social studies book, for example, active readers ask themselves what the selection is likely to cover, whether they know anything about the topic or are interested in it, and what they intend to do with the information presented. As they read, they question the meanings of unfamiliar words or ask how a certain event is likely to trigger a reaction. After reading the chapter, active readers ask whether their prediction of what the chapter would cover was accurate, whether they learned anything new, and how they might apply what they learned to something they already know.

A fairly robust finding by researchers is that teaching students to generate their own questions leads to active learning and improved comprehension of text (Haller, Child, & Walberg, 1988; Palincsar & Brown, 1984; Wade & Moje, 2000; Wong, 1985). In one self-questioning study (Singer & Donlan, 1982), high school students were shown how to generate story-specific questions from a more general set of story grammar questions (e.g., "Who are the main characters?" "What problem did they encounter?" and "How did they attempt to solve the problem?"). Students in the self-questioning group comprehended complex short stories better than students in the control group, who answered teacher-generated questions. The researchers concluded that the experimental students' active involvement in generating questions caused them to select, organize, and subsume specific story events in a way that was superior to the control group's more passive processing of text.

Active readers *monitor,* or periodically check, their understanding of what they have read. Although monitoring can include self-questioning, it is used here to describe the two-part process that readers go through when they (1) become aware of a breakdown in comprehension and (2) apply fix-up strategies to regain understanding.

ACTIVITY   To experience monitoring for yourself, read the question first, followed by the short paragraph.

> *Question:* Why would a love of french fries ruin a marriage?
> *Three-sentence paragraph:* The hamburger chain owner was afraid his love for french fries would ruin his marriage. He was worried. He decided to go on a daily exercise program.*

---

*Adapted from C. J. Gordon, "Modeling inference awareness across the curriculum," *Journal of Reading,* 29 (444–447, 1985).

When you read the paragraph for the purpose of monitoring your comprehension, you might have called to mind what happens to people when they overindulge in fried foods. Thus, you might have inferred that the hamburger chain owner's love of french fries had caused him to put on weight, which in turn threatened his marriage—if, of course, it can be assumed that the owner's wife disliked overweight men. Suppose, however, that the owner did not eat any french fries; maybe he simply worked long hours and went home with the smell of fries on his clothes. Might this have contributed to the man's fear that his marriage was in trouble? In fact, any number of inferences could be drawn, depending on the knowledge and past experiences a reader brings to the task.

The point is, you are now aware from monitoring your reading that there is more than one plausible interpretation. Consequently, if you are like most active readers, you will try to resolve the ambiguity and potential loss of understanding by selecting from an array of fix-up strategies. What are some strategies that you could apply in the exercise involving the hamburger chain owner? You could ask to see the remainder of the text, in the anticipation that forthcoming information would provide some clue as to which inference is correct. Or, you might reread the three-sentence paragraph to see if there is any evidence to suggest one inference over the other. As you can see, the third sentence ("He decided to go on a daily exercise program.") lends support to the "overweight" inference, although students have argued that a daily exercise program would keep the hamburger chain owner away from home even more, and that it could conceivably add to the objectionable-odor problem.

Some researchers (Raphael & McKinney, 1983; Reis & Spekman, 1983) have demonstrated that average and below-average middle-grade students can profit from instruction in comprehension monitoring, especially if they are informed ahead of time of a strategy's potential value and if they are taught to verbalize their reasoning processes. Other researchers (Dole et al., 1991; Pearson & Fielding, 1991; Wade & Moje, 2000) have found that good comprehenders monitor their reading by using different strategies in response to different situations. Students who experience difficulty in comprehending their reading assignments do not demonstrate this kind of flexibility.

Active readers attempt to make sense of the large body of facts, interpretations, and principles presented in their various textbooks by *organizing* such information into meaningful units. They may do this in one of several ways: by graphically organizing the information so as to form a semantic map or structured overview, by writing summaries, by constructing outlines and taking notes, or by elaborating on the text by drawing from their background knowledge and past experiences whatever associations seem most helpful in bridging from the *known* ("in the head") to the *unknown* ("on the page").

Regardless of which organizing strategy they choose, active readers are skilled in separating important information from unimportant information. When students experience difficulty in organizing what they have read, it is quite often because they are insensitive to what is important. Sometimes this insensitivity is due to a reader's inability to identify information that an author deems important; at other times it is due to a reader's strong sense of personal relevancy. For instance, Winograd (1984) found that eighth graders who were having difficulty reading tended to identify importance on the basis of what held high personal interest for them (such as sentences containing rich visual detail), whereas good readers tended to identify important information on the basis of its superordinate or subordinate placement within the text structure. Young adolescents have difficulty organizing large bodies of information partially because they rely on personal relevance as a criterion for attributing importance.

Although we recognize that readers often reflect on what they have read and actively construct meaning from texts without the benefit of *peer interaction*, there is growing support for placing a greater emphasis on socially constructed meaning (Bloome & Green, 1992; Gee, 1996). Truly engaged readers, whether from the gifted, regular, or basic-level classes, enjoy opportunities for open-forum discussions, in which a free-flowing exchange of ideas enriches and refines their understandings of what was read and heightens their motivation to read further (Alvermann, O'Brien, & Dillon, 1990). Discussions of this type, unlike lecturing and recitations, provide learners for whom English is a second language with excellent opportunities to practice English and learn content simultaneously (Met, 1994). Interactions with peers also enable students from diverse cultural groups to learn from one another.

When active readers co-construct their thinking with peers, their collectively organized way of thinking is referred to as *exploratory talk,* or talk that is in the making, that is tentative and changing. Exploratory talk can also reflect thinking that was independently generated but that is being collectively refined or enriched (Barnes, 1976; Gavelek & Raphael, 1996; Palmer, 1991; Wade & Moje, 2000).

By participating in different kinds of classroom discourse, active readers are exercising a variety of ways of thinking. It is this diversity in thinking and speaking patterns that contributes to a truly interactive classroom environment, one in which independence in reading and learning can take root and grow and in which respect for ideas that differ from one's own can be fostered.

Independent readers.   Independent readers typically are independent learners, and vice versa. We agree with Herber and Nelson-Herber's (1987) claims that the similarities between the two are numerous and that independence can be developed by capitalizing on the following five principles:

1. *Independence comes from practice.* Readers develop independence when they have sufficient opportunities across the curriculum to establish their own purposes for reading, to make connections between their own experiences and

those they read about, to use valid criteria in making judgments about the quality and value of what they read, and to apply what they have learned in one content area to another. We can visualize students in Melissa's classroom using these skills while simultaneously immersed in the content deemed appropriate to her subject area.

2. *Independence develops by design, not chance.* As Melissa's students grow in their independence, they will require less and less in the way of structured learning activities. In the beginning, however, they will be quite dependent on Melissa as she models and guides them through activities designed to *show them how* to apply the reading and reasoning processes necessary for understanding the concepts she has identified as important to her content area. As time goes on, Melissa will gradually release more and more of the responsibility for modeling and guiding in order to encourage her students to assume some responsibility for applying what they have learned to new areas of study and new materials (Pearson & Gallagher, 1983).

3. *Independence is a relative state.* Do you recall Melissa's thinking as to the approach she would take "to spark a fire for books in . . . the guy in the back row who probably has never read a whole book"? Contrast that with her thoughts on the students in her class who were independent ("avid") readers: "They are few and far between, and they don't need my help—only my guidance." What we see here is an awareness on Melissa's part that the maturity level of the student must be matched with the appropriate resources if independence is to be developed and nurtured.

4. *Independence can be achieved in groups.* Herber and Nelson-Herber (1987) advocate small-group learning experiences to develop students' independence in reading. We agree with their view "that students can be as much in charge of their reading and reasoning processes and their use of ideas when interacting in cooperative groups as when working individually" (p. 586). There is also ample research to support this view on cooperative learning, which we discuss in Chapter 3. Although we find no mention of her stance on small-group learning in Melissa's reflections, we suspect that students in her classroom will find numerous opportunities to work with their peers as they practice and apply the reading and reasoning processes they are learning.

5. *Independence means forever "becoming."* No one is ever totally independent as a learner. Occasionally, we all rely on others to help us interpret, clarify, or elaborate on what we read. Melissa, too, demonstrates an awareness that helping her students become readers will require time, skill, and patience on her part.

In summary, content area reading instruction involves much more than covering the subject matter in a particular specialty area. It includes dealing with assumptions about the role of the textbook and developing active and independent readers in culturally diverse classrooms. Students who self-question, monitor their reading, organize information, and interact with their peers possess some of the strategies necessary for becoming independent learners. However, their overall sense of themselves as learners will depend to a large extent on how they see themselves as readers and what it means to be literate in a fast-changing world.

WHAT IT MEANS TO BE LITERATE

As individuals, we tend to approach literacy with our own agendas: we are in pursuit of *something*. Depending on our ideological frameworks, our educational backgrounds, and our social, economic, and political status in life, we may hold quite different perceptions of why we are in pursuit and what it means to be literate. For many, literacy is something to value for its intrinsic worth; for others, it may be a symbol of achievement or a means for social change; and for still others, it is something to profit from. In each of these perceptions, there is the underlying assumption that being literate means having a special capacity of one kind or another.

However, as Knoblauch (1990) pointed out, this is not necessarily the case. In observing that "literacy is one of those mischievous concepts, like virtuousness and craftsmanship, that appear to denote capacities but that actually convey value judgments," Knoblauch (p. 74) reminds us that individuals who have the motivation and status to enforce literacy as a social requirement are often the same ones whose value judgments count. Failure to take note of the power relations surrounding such judgments is tantamount to buying into the idea that literacy is a "neutral" or innocent concept. Recognizing the political nature of what it means to be literate is important to our work as educators. It may keep us from falling into the trap of equating a student's innate worthiness with her or his competence in reading and writing. It may also prevent us from being blinded by ideological leanings that sometimes propel us to act as if our own literacy agendas were innocent or pure.

During times of controversial education reform movements, such as those experienced in the United States in the late 1990s, people's literacy agendas are especially visible and open to inspection. For instance, in an article that examined this nation's pursuit of scientific literacy through education reform, Eisenhart, Finkel, and Marion (1996) found the guidelines for implementing such reform to be lacking in many ways. Among the limitations they noted was that relatively little attention was given to implementing strategies that would encourage minorities and girls to participate in science education programs leading to careers in science.

Writing from a similar perspective, Lee (1997) faulted the science education reform agenda for failing to take into account that implementing Western scientific literacy, with its emphasis on argumentation, skepticism, questioning, and criticism, would cause conflict for some students, especially those who come from cultures in which cooperation, consensus building, and respect for authority are highly valued. What seems clear from both these examples is the potential for misunderstandings to occur when people's personal, institutional, and societal agendas for literacy conflict or, worse, remain indifferent to each other. Issues surrounding still other literacy agendas and their relation to literate thinking, content literacy, and the new literacy studies are discussed next.

Literate Thinking

From Langer's (1989) perspective, reading and writing are "tools that enable, but do not insure, literate thinking" (p. 2). She argues vigorously against the tendency to equate literate thinking with the ability to analyze or synthesize large chunks of print.

ACTIVITY   Langer (1989) provides an example to highlight the distinction she draws between print literacy and literate thinking:

> When a group of American students read a social studies textbook and then discuss the contents and the implications, most people would say that the students are engaging in literate thinking (within the norms of this culture). But, what if the discussion had occurred after the students had seen a television news report about the same topic? I would still want to claim that the students had engaged in literate thinking even though they had neither read nor written. Now, imagine a group of students who do not know how to read or write in English or another language engaged in the very same conversation about the television news report. I would claim that they too would have engaged in literate thinking. In contrast, imagine that the students had read the same social studies text and then completed end-of-chapter questions by locating information in the text and copying the information the questions asked them to itemize. I would claim that the kinds of literacy in this activity do not reflect the kinds of school literacy that, based on the many reports and articles in both the professional and public press, are needed and valued by American society today. That activity does not involve culturally useful literate behavior, even if the students get the answers right. (p. 2)

Do you agree or disagree with Langer's argument? Why?

The 1980s spawned a rash of reform movements, most of which focused on erasing illiteracy as a threat to the economic well-being and worldwide competitiveness of the United States. A characteristic of most of the reforms has been their emphasis on a print- or book-focused literacy, which is not unlike the focus of this book. Schools in general are concerned with students' abilities to read and write—to demonstrate what is understood—regardless of grade level. The attention educators give to functional literacy, according to Greene (1991), leaves little time for asking some difficult, but important, questions:

> [Teachers] scarcely ever ask [themselves] about the difference literacy makes in various lives. Does it overcome alienation or confirm it? Does it reduce feelings of powerlessness or intensify them? How much, after all, depends on literacy and how much on social arrangements? How much on trust? On love? On glimpses of the half-moon? On wonderful ideas? On feeling, as Dickinson did, "a clearing" in the mind? (p. 130)

Similar concerns have been raised by Heath (1986b), whose research has shown that in many families and communities, being a competent reader and writer is not viewed as being a ticket to equality, a good job, or social mobility. In short, being literate has different meanings for different cultural groups, or as Langer (1989) so aptly puts it, "there is no right or wrong literacy, just the one that is, more or less, responsive to the demands of a particular culture" (p. 1).

Content Literacy

Generally, content literacy is defined as "the ability to use reading and writing for the acquisition of new content in a given discipline" (McKenna & Robinson, 1990, p. 184). To that we add the importance of oral language (e.g., small- and large-group discussions) in mediating students' ability to learn from reading and writing activities in their subject matter classes. Students' prior knowledge of a particular subject and their interest in learning more about it also mediate their ability to use their content literacy skills.

ACTIVITY

To give you a better sense of how one's discipline area tends to affect one's view of content literacy, we present a case that builds on the work of O'Brien and Stewart (1990). In their study, they sought to catalog and interpret preservice teachers' perceptions of content literacy instruction. The prospective teachers were students enrolled in content area reading and literacy classes taught by O'Brien and Stewart at Purdue University—classes much like the one in which you may be enrolled.

Learning from cases involving people much like ourselves at various points in our educational careers can be instructive on several levels. First, such learning lets us see firsthand how others view a situation. Second, it enables us to sort through our own perceptions as we "follow" the thinking of others. Finally, case learning (or case teaching, as it is frequently called) is a powerful motivator and a potential change agent; it may even lead us to question some of our own beliefs and practices.

The so-called "facts" of the case are presented in Figure 1.1. We organized them according to the content areas represented in O'Brien and Stewart's (1990) classes and on the basis of the prospective teachers' perceptions of whether or not (and why) content literacy instruction would be part of their practice once they were in their own classrooms. After you have read the case facts, try jotting down answers to the following questions. If you are enrolled in a content literacy class, you may want to find someone with whom you can share your reactions in preparation for sharing with the whole class.

Case questions.   In answering the following questions based on the case presented in Figure 1.1, try to make a mental note of what is informing your responses. Developing this kind of awareness may help you discover whether or not your cumulative school experiences continue to inform your beliefs and practices (Britzman, 1987).

Question 1: Why might biology, chemistry, English, and social studies majors, as a group, find content literacy instruction potentially more useful than the other majors represented?

Question 2: As a teacher or prospective teacher in one of the content areas listed in Figure 1.1, how do you feel about the sample reason given for using or not using content literacy instruction in your area? Why do you feel as you do?

Question 3: Has your reading of this case (and any discussions that may have resulted from it) motivated you to think differently about content literacy instruction? Why or why not?

Content knowledge.   Content literacy is not to be confused with content knowledge, although the two concepts do share some common ground. For example, as McKenna and Robinson (1990) pointed out, the more knowledge students have about the content they are assigned to read in their textbooks, the more that knowledge facilitates their reading and writing—a situation which in turn sets up a cyclical pattern such that still more knowledge is acquired and applied to other tasks requiring content literacy skills.

This cyclical pattern should come as good news to content area teachers. In effect, what it says is that teachers who instruct students in a subject matter specialty are helping to improve students' abilities to read and write in that subject area by simply providing some of the necessary background information. Providing background information however, is, only half of the task. The other half involves helping students acquire content literacy, or the ability to use reading and writing strategies to learn new content. Students who have the literacy skills necessary for supplementing their knowledge of the content by reading beyond what the teacher introduces through lectures, demonstrations, and so on are well on their way to becoming independent learners.

Disciplines Represented	Total Enrollment	Percent Expecting to Provide Content Literacy in Their Own Classrooms	Examples of Reasons Given for Using/Not Using Content Literacy Instruction
Art	3	0	*Art Major:* "Relating reading to art has been very taboo until recently. The school systems are just now beginning to incorporate books into the art department."
Biology	6	50	*Biology Major:* "I am more aware of new teaching methods to use and aware of students' reading abilities."
Chemistry	6	67	*Chemistry Major:* "But I don't think requiring *Secondary* teachers to remedy the problem is wise. The problem begins in late elementary when students are faced with science, history, and math textbooks. It would be much wiser to require elementary teachers to have classes in content reading. Having secondary teachers clean up the mess is like putting a Band-Aid on a severed pulmonary artery."
English	10	40	*English Major:* "The whole idea of 'content reading' seems useless to an English teacher. When dealing with literature or composition, none of the methods, techniques, or procedures seem particularly credible."
Foreign Language	7	0	*Foreign Language Major*: "There aren't any long reading passages in foreign language texts."
Math	26	15	*Math Major:* "I will be more conscious of how I introduce topics that may contain difficult vocabulary or material. It will also help me to better judge the textbooks I will use."
Physical Education	7	13	*Physical Ed. Major:* "In P.E. people are not taught skills by books and formal lectures. They are taught with hands-on experiences and progressive skills."
Social Studies	13	54	*History Major:* "I hope to use it [content literacy instruction]. I like a lot of the ideas, but I really don't expect to use any my first year or two. It'll be just straight lecturing. That's because that's what they're expecting me to do."
Vocational Education	13	15	*Vocational Ed. Major:* "I feel that in Voc. Ed., it is hands-on experience more than reading. Most people can do hands-on because it is demonstrative and not a sit down, read and write. Yes, you do have some reading, but nothing in a large amount."

FIGURE 1.1 A case involving preservice teachers' perceptions of usefulness of content literacy instruction (*Source:* D. O'Brien & R. A. Stewart, "Preservice teachers' perspectives on why every teacher is not a teacher of reading: A qualitative analysis." *Journal of Reading Behavior, 22,* 101–129, 1990.)

Special Hints for Struggling Readers

Hints for helping readers who struggle to learn the content of their subject matter classes abound. For example, Ivey (2000) has developed what she calls her "working generalizations" on teaching adolescents who struggle with reading. Based on her research and experience as a classroom teacher, these so-called generalizations include the following advice:

▸ Provide students with access to materials that hold personal interest for them and that span a wide range of difficulty levels.
▸ Make room in the school day for students to have time to share their reading experiences with others through small group discussions, buddy reading, and choral reading activities.

▸ Plan activities that require students to use reading and writing to complete a task that is content related and highly motivating, such as performing hands-on science experiments or communicating through e-mail with classmates who found novel ways to complete a math assignment.
▸ Take into account struggling readers' desires to improve their reading and help them do so through initiating the reading and writing workshop concept as a part of the regular classroom routine. (See Chapter 3 for an example of the reading and writing workshop adapted from Allen (1995) for high school use.)

The New Literacy Studies

In the 1980s and 1990s, an interdisciplinary group of scholars (Bloome & Green, 1992; Cazden, 1988; Cook-Gumperz, 1986; Gee, 1996; Heath, 1983; Luke, 1988; Street, 1995) began to ask questions such as "What is literacy?" "Who benefits from being literate?" and "What specific cultural meanings and practices are involved in becoming literate?" The point of asking these questions, all of which deal in one way or another with the differing contexts in which people read and write, was a growing mistrust in the more conventional view of literacy as a "neutral" or technical skill. No longer willing to think of reading as primarily a psychological phenomenon—one in which individuals who can decode and have the requisite background knowledge for drawing inferences are able to arrive at the right interpretation of a text—this interdisciplinary group of scholars began to document how the "right" interpretation of a text rarely holds for different individuals reading in different contexts. Their work and that of others who are similarly focused on students' multiple literacies has become known as the New Literacy Studies (Willinsky, 1990).

In addition, related work in the area of social cognition (Lave & Wenger, 1991; Tharp & Gallimore, 1988) and cultural studies (Lewis, 1998) has contributed to the growing sense that reading and writing are shaped by (and in turn help to shape) multiple sociocultural practices associated with becoming literate. Describing these practices as "deeply political," Gee (1999) has gone on to show

Technology Tip

▼▼▼

For additional information on the New Literacy Studies and James Paul Gee's discussion of this movement's role in a larger "social turn" away from a focus on individuals and their "private" minds and toward interaction and social practice, see this book's Web site: http://www. ablongman.com/alvermann3e.

how they also "fully integrate language, both oral and written, with nonlanguage 'stuff,' that is, with ways of acting, interacting, feeling, valuing, thinking, and believing, as well as with various sorts of nonverbal symbols, sites, tools, objects, and technologies" (p. 356). In summary, the New Literacy Studies encompass ways of behaving, knowing, thinking, and valuing which give meaning to the uses of reading and writing that go far beyond simply mining a textbook for its literal or inferential meaning.

Rethinking content literacy practices.   The New Literacy Studies are beginning to affect the ways in which teacher educators and classroom teachers think about content reading and writing instruction and how students learn from such instruction. This is especially the case among educators who subscribe to the so-called natural approaches to literacy instruction. Labeled typically as process writing and reader response, these approaches are being examined closely by individuals interested in critical literacy and critical language awareness—an awareness, that is, of why writers or speakers choose to write about certain topics, what content they include and leave out, whose interests they serve, and who is empowered (or disempowered) by the language they choose.

Some teacher educators (Kamler, 1999; Kamler & Comber, 1996), for instance, are beginning to reflect on how personal written response and other expressivist pedagogies such as reader response are teaching students to think about themselves and others in particularly naive ways—ways that rarely move them to social action and a critique of what they read or hear. Others (Lewis, 2000; Lewis, Ketter, & Fabos, 2001) are learning how to work around certain reader response approaches that emphasize personal identification at the expense of textual critique. Although there is much to admire in these natural approaches to literacy instruction, they have come under criticism of late for what they leave out (Moje, Willes, & Fassio, 2001; Patterson, Mellor, & O'Neill, 1994).

For instance, critics say that these approaches have major flaws, but they are flaws that can be corrected so as to enable important gains realized through student-centered instruction to move forward. One of the identified flaws is an overemphasis on promoting what critics refer to as an "inside-out" perspective. For example, they say that educators who teach from a reader response perspective put too much emphasis on personal experience and individual interpretation. This leads, they say, to a naive view of the reading process, one in which it would appear that texts could somehow be neutrally produced and read. What they propose is a drawing in of the view from "without" (Green, 1991; Lemke, 1995). For example, Annette Patterson and colleagues (1994) believe it is their responsibility as literacy educators to teach students to take up a range of reading positions—some that may lead to resistant readings of what have become dominant or "mainstream" texts.

Helping students develop a facility and an interest in reading resistantly is an idea that has taken on increasing significance since its introduction in the late 1970s (Fetterly, 1978; Scott, 1990). Although some literacy educators might argue that resistant reading is just another name for critical reading, we disagree. A characteristic of resistant reading that we find absent in conventional descriptions of critical reading is the notion of "reading subtexts" as "a way of distancing ourselves and gaining some control over the reading experience" (Commeyras & Alvermann, 1996, p. 45).

The importance of reading subtextually is highlighted in Sam Wineburg's (1991) study in which he compared how historians read historical texts and how talented high school students read the same texts. Wineburg found that the students were quite good at identifying the main ideas and answering the comprehension questions that went with the readings, but they failed to see how the authors of the texts had constructed them as social instruments "masterfully crafted to achieve a social end" (p. 502). The historians, on the other hand, read two types of subtexts. They read the texts as rhetorical artifacts, which involved reconstructing the "authors' purposes, intentions, and goals" (p. 498). They also read the texts as human artifacts, which involved identifying "elements that work at cross-purposes with the authors' intentions, bringing to the surface convictions the authors may have been unaware of or may have wished to conceal" (p. 499).

Some thought questions

1. Think back to a time when you taught students to read using a so-called natural language learning approach. Or, perhaps you were taught to read by someone who favored one or more of those approaches. Do you agree with the criticism leveled against such approaches? Why? Why not?
2. Are you a resistant reader? When and under what conditions?
3. If you do not read resistantly yourself, do you see any reason for teaching others to read in that fashion? Why? Why not?

Tips for working with English language learners.   Knowing the social functions of oral language within various cultural groups and how such language cues can be used to foster learning is vitally important, especially for teachers whose sociocultural background differs from that of their students. For example, knowing that adults in some groups ask questions of children for playful and teasing reasons, rather than to obtain information, may lead a teacher to avoid

Professional Growth

▼▼

The amount of information available on critical literacy is growing by leaps and bounds. To stay current with the professional literature on this topic, we recommend that readers of this text also consult an on-line journal devoted to the theory and practice behind critical literacy. A good starting place is the *Journal for Pedagogy, Pluralism and Practice.* A special themed issue of that journal, which was edited by Ira Shor, can be found at the following Web site: http://www.lesley.edu/journals/jppp/4/shor.html

recitation-like instruction in which questions are meant to elicit information already known to the teacher. Furthermore, accepting the reality that some students will interrupt and talk over one another as they jointly construct an embellished version of the text they were assigned to read may lead a teacher to value such exchanges, particularly if they contribute to productive discussions and active learning (Au, 1980). Finally, viewing positively the fact that in some cultural groups members need not perform all tasks equally well to be valued members of the community (Heath, 1991) may cause a teacher to opt for alternatives to whole-class instruction, such as cooperative learning and peer tutoring.

THE READING PROCESS

In recent years, developments in cognitive psychology, sociolinguistics, and cultural anthropology have drawn attention to the need for explanations of the reading process that take into account a broad view of the everyday world of students and their families, teachers, schools, and communities. This section focuses on three aspects of the reading process: a cognitive view, a social constructionist perspective, and the role of motivation in the reading process.

A Cognitive View

A cognitive or psycholinguistic view of the reading process assumes "an active reader who constructs meaning through the integration of existing and new knowledge and the flexible use of strategies to foster, monitor, regulate, and maintain comprehension" (Dole et al., 1991, p. 242). Students who take a personal, adaptive view of reading understand that knowledge is constructed by them and that the experiences they bring to texts shape in large part what they will comprehend (Brown, Collins, & Duguid, 1989).

One of our favorite articles of all time dates back to our days in graduate school at Syracuse University. Dr. Margaret Early, one of our professors at the time, introduced us to Cooper and Petrosky's (1976) "A Psycholinguistic View of the Fluent Reading Process." The authors of the article make the point that "in reading, the brain supplies more information than it receives from the eye about the text" (p. 191). The following activity is designed to demonstrate Cooper and Petrosky's point. See if you agree with their view of the fluent reading process.

ACTIVITY   Try your hand at using a little common sense and some prior knowledge of language and content to comprehend two paragraphs from a selection titled "The Kingdom of Kay Oss" (Roskos & Walker, 1994, p. 5).

The Kingdom of Kay Oss

Once in the land of Serenity there ruled a king called Kay Oss. The king wanted to be liked by all his people. So one day thx bxnxvolxnt dxspot dx-cidxd that no onx in thx country would bx rxsponsiblx for anything. Zll of thx workxrs rxstxd from thxir dzily lzbors. "Blxss Kzy Oss," thxy xxclzimxd.

Now thx lzw mzkxrs wxrx vxry wvsx. But zs wvsx zs thxy wxrx, thxy dx-cvdxd thzt thx bxst form of govxrnmxnt wzs nonx zt zll.

If you made sense of all or most of these two paragraphs with relative ease and little frustration, it might be said that you are the type of person who reads to obtain meaning rather than to identify letters or words per se. According to Frank Smith (1971), a prominent psycholinguist whose work builds on that of E. B. Huey (1908/1968):

The ability to put letters together to form words has very little to do with the actual process of [fluent] reading (as opposed to learning to read) and . . . even the ability to identify words loses its importance when one "reads for meaning." (Smith cited in Cooper & Petrosky, 1976, p. 186)

Simply put, reading is more than the linear sum of words. Think about this claim in relation to your reading of "The Kingdom of Kay Oss," and then answer the following questions:

1. Did you find that you needed only a minimum of visual cues from the printed text to understand it?
2. What prior knowledge did you call on to make sense of the selection?
3. To what extent did your knowledge of stories, in general, influence your understanding and reduce the uncertainty of the task?
4. How often did you rely on your knowledge of:

   Letter-sound associations (graphophonics)?
   Spelling patterns (orthography)?
   Relationships of words to each other (syntax)?
   Contextual meaning (semantics)?

5. Did you risk being "wrong" in your attempt to derive meaning? That is, did you use context to guess unfamiliar words or just skip them?

6. Did you maintain sufficient speed when reading the selection to overcome the limitations of visual processing and short-term memory?

If you find yourself agreeing with Cooper and Petrosky's (1976) claim that "in reading, the brain supplies more information than it receives from the eye about the text" (p. 191), then you will probably feel right at home when you read about the top-down model of text processing discussed later in this chapter. If you have doubts about this claim, you may feel more comfortable with the interactive model of reading, also discussed later in the chapter.

Prior knowledge and schema theory.   Prior knowledge can cover a wide range of ideas, skills, and attitudes. When we use the term, we are focusing particularly on a reader's previous or existing knowledge of the subject matter of the text. What a person already knows about a topic is probably the single most influential factor with respect to what he or she will learn.

Cognitive psychologists use the word *schema* to describe how people organize the raw data of everyday experiences into meaningful patterns. A schema is a collection of organized and interrelated ideas or concepts. Schemata (the plural form) are fluid; they overlap and intertwine, and they are constantly modified to assimilate or accommodate new information. Schemata enable people to draw generalizations, form opinions, and understand new experiences (Anderson, 1984).

Schemata are frequently explained using the example of restaurants, probably because everyone has had some experience in going out to eat. Your schema for going to a restaurant might include the following: Someone will ask you what you would like to eat; that person or another will bring food, usually the food you asked for; you will pay for this food; you will not have to wash the dishes. Depending on actual experiences with dining out, individual restaurant schemata will vary. If your culinary adventures are mostly at fast-food outlets in your hometown on the East Coast, you would know just what to do at a Burger King in Cody, Wyoming, but you might not be sure which fork to use or which wine to order in a fancy restaurant. If your experiences were more varied, however, you would probably know about such things as making reservations, tipping, à la carte menus, and the specialties at different kinds of ethnic restaurants. You would not expect to order chicken wings at the Russian Tea Room in New York City, even if you had never been there before.

Schemata operate similarly in reading. They act as a kind of mental filing system from which the individual can retrieve relevant existing knowledge and into which new information can be filed. As you read, your schema for a topic helps you to anticipate, to infer, to decide what is or is not important, to build relationships between ideas, and to decide what information merits close attention. After reading, you use your schema as a topic to help you recall what you have read and put it into your own words.

Schemata, which are sometimes referred to as prior knowledge structures, play a large role in the reading process. They determine which of several interpretations of a text is the most probable. For example, this famous sentence taken from the work of Bransford and McCarrell (1974) illustrates how one's culture can influence the meaning that is made of print:

The notes were sour because the seam split.

Although they may be familiar with all of the words and the syntax or ordering of those words, readers in the United States typically have difficulty constructing meaning for this sentence until they are provided with clues such as *bagpipe* or *Scottish musical instrument.*

According to Anderson (1984), schemata serve six functions in the reading process (Figure 1.2). Although researchers do not agree on their importance, these functions illustrate how readers use their prior knowledge to construct their meaning of a text. As indicated by these six functions, prior knowledge structures play a powerful role in text comprehension—so much so, in fact, that the concept of critical reading has had to be redefined. Instead of thinking of critical readers as those who simply apply higher-level thinking skills to evaluate the adequacy of a text, researchers have come to view them as those readers who also apply criteria that enable them to evaluate the adequacy of their own schemata. In short, "schema theory . . . [has] implicitly redefined critical reading by expanding it from a text-based activity to a text- and reader-based process" (Lyman & Collins, 1990, p. 59).

Making connections between theory and practice.   Victoria Ridgeway, a professional colleague of ours at Clemson University, likes to remind students in her content literacy classes of the importance of applying in their own classrooms what they know about prior knowledge and schema theory. She uses a series of three short passages to make her point. We include those passages here, along with several self-reflection questions aimed at helping you make connections between theory and practice.

The first passage illustrates the fact that prior knowledge must be *activated* to be of use. Note that no title is provided in order to demonstrate the difficulty in comprehending material for which prior knowledge, although available, has not been activated.

Passage:

The procedure is actually quite simple. First you arrange items into different groups. Of course one group may be sufficient depending on how much there is to do. If you have to go somewhere else due to lack of facilities, that is the next step; otherwise, you are pretty well set. It is important not to overdo things. That is, it is better to do too few things at once than too many. In the short run this may not seem important but complications can easily arise. A mistake can be expensive as well. The manipulation of the appropriate mechanisms should be self-explanatory, and we need not dwell on it here. At first,

1. *A schema provides ideational scaffolding for assimilating text information.* The idea is that a schema provides a niche, or slot, for certain text information. For instance, there is a slot for the main entree in a dining-at-a-fine-restaurant schema and a slot for the murder weapon in a who-done-it schema. Information that fits slots in the reader's schema is readily learned, perhaps with little mental effort.

2. *A schema facilitates selective allocation of attention.* A schema provides part of the basis for determining the important aspects of a text. It is hypothesized that skilled readers use importance as one basis for allocating cognitive resources—that is, for deciding where to pay close attention.

3. *A schema enables inferential elaboration.* No text is completely explicit. A reader's schema provides the basis for making inferences that go beyond the information literally stated in a text.

4. *A schema allows orderly searches of memory.* A schema can provide the reader with a guide to the types of information that need to be recalled. For instance, a person attempting to recall the food served at a fine meal can review the categories of food typically included in a fine meal: What was the appetizer? What was the soup? Was there a salad? And so on. In other words, by tracing through the schema used to structure the text, the reader is helped to gain access to the particular information learned when the text was read.

5. *A schema facilitates editing and summarizing.* Since a schema contains within itself criteria of importance, it enables the reader to produce summaries that include significant propositions and omit trivial ones.

6. *A schema permits inferential reconstruction.* When there are gaps in memory, a [reader's] schema, along with the specific text information that can be recalled, helps generate hypotheses about the missing information. For example, suppose [John] cannot recall what beverage was served with a fine meal. If he can recall that the entree was fish, he will be able to infer that the beverage may have been white wine.

FIGURE 1.2   Six functions of schemata   (*Source:* R. C. Anderson, "Role of the reader's schema in comprehension, learning, and memory," in R. C. Anderson, J. Osborn, & R. J. Tierney (Eds.), *Learning to read in American schools: Basal readers and texts*, p. 248, 1984, Hillsdale, NJ: Erlbaum. Used with permission of R. C. Anderson and Lawrence Erlbaum Associates, Inc., Hillsdale, NJ.)

the whole procedure will seem complicated. Soon, however, it will become just another facet of life. It is difficult to foresee any end to the necessity for this task in the immediate future, but then, one never can tell. After the procedure is completed, one arranges the materials into different groups again. Then they can be put into their appropriate places. Eventually they will be used once more and the whole cycle will then have to be repeated. However, that is part of life. (Bransford, 1979, pp. 134–135)

Self-reflection questions

1. If we had provided a title, such as "Washing Clothes," would the passage have made more sense immediately?

2. Would simply providing a title be adequate for activating your students' background knowledge about topics you regularly assign them to read? What else might you want to do to activate their knowledge more fully?

The second passage illustrates the importance of activating *appropriate* prior knowledge. Failure to do so can lead to confusion and misinterpretation of the text. For example, read the following passage twice: first, from the perspective of a *prisoner,* and then from a *wrestler's* perspective. After each of the readings, choose the best answer from the four possible ones that follow the question "How had Rocky been punished for his aggressiveness?"

Passage:

Rocky slowly got up from the mat, planning his escape. He hesitated a moment and thought. Things were not going well. What bothered him most was being held, especially since the charge against him had been weak. He considered his present situation. The lock that held him was strong but he thought he could break it. He knew, however, that his timing would have to be perfect. Rocky was aware that it was because of his early roughness that he had been penalized so severely—much too severely from his point of view. The situation was becoming frustrating; the pressure had been grinding on him for too long. He was being ridden unmercifully. Rocky was getting angry now. He felt he was ready to make his move. He knew that his success or failure would depend on what he did in the next few seconds. (Anderson et al., 1977, p. 372)

Comprehension question: How had Rocky been punished for his aggressiveness?

A. He had been demoted to the "B" team.
B. His opponent had been given points.
C. He lost his privileges for the weekend.
D. He had been arrested and imprisoned.

Self-reflection questions

1. Have you ever read something only to find out later that you had activated inappropriate background knowledge? How did it affect your comprehension? How did it make you feel?

2. As a teacher, or prospective teacher, what might you do instructionally to ensure that students activate appropriate background knowledge for reading the materials required in your content area?

The third passage demonstrates why prior knowledge must be *sufficient* to be of use in comprehending text. For example, you may have had experience playing baseball—even bowling—but the batsmen and bowlers in "Today's Cricket" do not play by the rules you might expect. In short, if you grew up in the United States, it is likely you are as "lost" as we are when it comes to comprehending a sport played mainly in England and other parts of the Commonwealth.

Passage:

"Today's Cricket"

The batsmen were merciless against the bowlers. The bowlers placed their men in slips and covers. But to no avail. The batsmen hit one four after another along with an occasional six. Not once did a ball look like it would hit their stumps or be caught. ("Wood's 100 Helps," 1978)

Self-reflection questions

1. Would knowing that "bowl" (as used in cricket) means "to put a batsman *out* by bowling the balls off the wicket" (*Webster's New World Dictionary*, 1991, p. 166) improve your understanding of the game? Why? Why not? What prior knowledge do you still lack?
2. If you were teaching a class in which your students were expected to read a story about cricket, how would you provide them with sufficient background knowledge?

In summary, as illustrated previously, it is one thing to develop a theoretical understanding of prior knowledge; it is quite another to apply that understanding in an actual classroom situation. However, we contend (and believe you would agree) that looking for ways to bridge theory and practice is well worth the effort.

Three models of the reading process.   The bottom-up, top-down, and interactive models of the reading process are all concerned with a reader's schemata, but to varying degrees (Ruddell, Ruddell, & Singer, 1995). The bottom-up model, sometimes referred to as the automaticity model (LaBerge & Samuels, 1976), is based on the idea that one can focus attention selectively on only one thing at a time. By this line of reasoning, until a reader can decode the words of a text automatically, he or she will be unable to devote a sufficient amount of attention to comprehending the text. That is, decoding requires that so much attention be paid to the pronunciation and meaning of individual words that there is little or no time left to concentrate on comprehending larger chunks of print such as sentences and paragraphs. As its name implies, the bottom-up model of the reading process assumes that meaning resides primarily in the text and that pieces of information are chunked incrementally to produce comprehension. Letters and their associated sounds are chunked to make words, words are chunked to make sentences, and so on. Of course, a reader's perceptual processes, such as visual and auditory memory, play a role in this model, because print must be perceived in order to be processed. Previous experiences and prior knowledge, or one's schemata, also play a role, but not to the extent that they do in the top-down model.

According to the top-down model of the reading process, what the reader already knows is thought to determine in large part what he or she will be able to comprehend. For example, even if *triskaidekaphobia* is pronounced accurately, the reader may not be able to comprehend its meaning in text:

Claudia's bout with triskaidekaphobia prevented her from ever staying on the thirteenth floor of a hotel.

In order for comprehension to occur, the reader would have to associate the meaning of the word *triskaidekaphobia* (fear of the number 13) with some previous experience or knowledge that linked the number 13 with unlucky. Proponents of the top-down model of reading argue that meaning resides largely in one's head, and it is the reader's schemata more than the print on the page that account for what is comprehended and what is not. As its name implies, the top-down model assumes that comprehending begins when a reader accesses appropriate background experiences and knowledge to make sense of print. In other words, unlike the bottom-up model, in which the reader incrementally chunks bigger and bigger pieces of information, the top-down model proposes that the reader makes educated guesses to predict the meaning of the print.

The interactive model of the reading process incorporates features of both the bottom-up and top-down models. Proponents of this model argue that the degree to which a reader uses print or prior knowledge will depend largely on the familiarity of the topic being read, how interested the reader is in the topic, and the purpose for which he or she is reading. For example, if you have read about different models of reading in the past and have an interest in learning more about them or reviewing what you know, you may be reading this section of the chapter using somewhat of a top-down process approach. However, if your purpose in reading is to prepare for a quiz on the chapter's contents, you may be applying some of the processes associated with the bottom-up model.

Alternatively, you may be reading along at a pretty good clip, making predictions about what you will find on the printed page, and slowing to examine more closely words such as *automaticity* and *triskaidekaphobia*. Perhaps you decoded a large word or looked for a familiar word part (such as *automatic*) in it. If you processed the information in this fashion, you were reading interactively. That is, you were using, alternately, what you knew from prior knowledge and what you were able to infer from your knowledge of the English language and the conventions of print. Sometimes your understanding was more conceptually driven (top-down) than text driven (bottom-up); at other times the reverse was true.

Along with a majority of other literacy educators, we believe the interactive model of the reading process is a good descriptor of how students typically read their content area texts. They connect what they know about language, decoding, and vocabulary to their background experiences and prior knowledge. They also take into account the demands of the reading task or the reasons for which they are reading. However, when decoding is not automatic or when insufficient prior knowledge prevents readers from conceptually making sense of print, they resort to a more text-driven model of reading.

Metacognition.   Metacognition, simply put, means knowing about knowing. It is a term used to describe students' awareness of *what* they know, their understanding of *how* to be strategic readers, and their knowledge of *when* (i.e., under what conditions) to evaluate the adequacy of their comprehension (Paris, Lipson, & Wixson, 1983). Metacognition is an awareness of what resources (materials, skills, and knowledge) one can call up to meet the demands of a particular task (Baker & Brown, 1980; Flavell, 1979). For example, before reading a textbook chapter on the Holocaust, students might take a mental inventory of the information about the topic they have gleaned previously from books, films,

Hints for Struggling Readers

It is helpful to keep in mind Stanovich's (1980) interactive-compensatory model when working with readers who struggle to decode texts. According to this model, they will tend to rely more than good readers on context for word recognition and hence have less freed-up capacity for comprehension than good readers. The instructional implications of the interactive-compensatory model for content area teachers include the following:

- Provide readers who struggle to decode their assigned texts with opportunities to hear those texts read aloud, perhaps through tape-assisted instruction.

- Give readers for whom word recognition is a problem supplemental materials that include visual clues to word meaning. Also consider the use of manipulatives in science and math areas.

- Allot extra time for readers who struggle to complete their assignments. Consider assigning fewer pages, perhaps concentrating on the key ideas in a passage or chapter.

- Encourage struggling readers to use the Internet. Sometimes the symbols and icons that are bothersome to good readers are the very means through which struggling readers make meaning.

and magazine accounts. They might also assess their interest in pursuing the topic further, their ability to read strategically, and/or their understanding of the purpose for the assignment. Developing such an awareness, however, does not ensure that they will succeed in comprehending the portion of text on the Holocaust. They will also need to monitor their reading.

Monitoring involves evaluating the trustworthiness of certain assumptions or inferences one makes while reading. It also involves applying any of a number of fix-up strategies when comprehension falters or breaks down completely. Moving backward and forward in text searches, concentrating on only the important information, making mental images, and contrasting new ideas with previous experiences are some of the most common fix-up strategies (Brown & Campione, 1994).

The importance of monitoring one's reading cannot be overstated. However, recent developments in understanding the reading process point to the difference between knowing something is not making sense and doing something about it. Knowledge that is treated as separate and distinct from the situations in which it is learned and put to use is less helpful than knowledge that is situated. Brown, Collins, and Duguid (1989), for example, argued that when students see no real-world purpose for what they are asked to read and write, they are unable to situate their learning.

ESL cognitive reading processes.　Among educators in the United States there is considerable disagreement over whether second-language learners use the same cognitive processes as native English speakers when reading (Garcia,

2000). Some theorists believe that English-as-a-second-language (ESL) readers use the same processes as their native-English-speaking peers (Heath, 1986a; Krashen, 1988); others (Bernhardt, 2000; Cowan, 1976) believe that findings from first-language literacy research fall short of explaining the second-language reading process. There is also disagreement as to whether proficiency in one's native language and oral proficiency in the second language are prerequisites for ESL reading instruction. Partial answers to these questions have come from Fitzgerald's (1995) comprehensive review of the literature on ESL learners' cognitive reading processes in which she reported these findings:

> On the whole, the studies reviewed in this article support the contention that the cognitive reading processes of ESL learners are *substantively* the same as those of native English speakers. . . . They used similar metacognitive strategies and monitored their comprehension when reading. . . . At the same time, some of the studies suggested that while the same basic processes may be used, a few selected facets of those processes may be used less or may operate more slowly for ESL learners than for native English readers. . . . Findings from the studies suggested a relatively good fit to the preexisting native-language reading theories, models, and views many of the studies were grounded in, most specifically to a psycholinguistic view, schema theory, an interactive view of reading, and views of metacognition in reading. (pp. 180–181)

As to the questions regarding whether proficiency in one's native language and oral proficiency in English are prerequisites for ESL reading instruction, the research is less clear. According to Fitzgerald (1995), the studies she reviewed supported "a prominent current view that native-language development can enhance ESL reading" (p. 181); however, as she noted, "the data were unclear on the separate issue of whether ESL oral proficiency is a prerequisite for ESL reading" (p. 182). In interpreting these findings for your own use, it would be wise to keep in mind that they apply only to one second language (English) and one country (the United States).

A Social Constructionist Perspective

The term *social constructionism* is frequently used synonymously with *social constructivism*, although there are many good reasons for not conflating the two concepts (Hruby, 2001). For purposes of this chapter, we concentrate on social constructionism. Both concepts are theories of learning; they are not theories of teaching per se. Hence, it makes sense to talk about the teaching practices that embrace these two theories of learning.

Constructivist learning theory.   Constructivism has become a catch-all term for a collection of theoretical approaches to learning that rely for their explanation on the cognitive developmental processes individuals use in deriving conceptual (abstract) understanding from their lived experiences. At the same time, the term has been used in very specific ways, thus creating a situation that invariably leads to much confusion (Phillips, 2000). Literacy educators generally limit their attention to four versions of constructivism: Piagetian constructivism, radical constructivism, sociohistorical constructivism, and social constructivism (Eisenhart, Finkel, & Marion, 1996; Phillips, 2000). Piagetian constructivism holds that conceptual development results from an individual's ability to assimilate and accommodate new information into existing knowledge structures. To count as learning, however, this newly assimilated (or accommodated) information must correspond with an authoritative body of knowledge external to the individual. Motivation for such learning rests in the individual and in the materials (content) to be learned.

Radical constructivism also situates motivation for learning in the person and the content to be learned. However, unlike Piagetian constructivism, radical constructivism assumes that evidence of new learning rests on an individual's ability to make personal sense of her or his own experiences; that is, radical constructivists have no need to apply some sort of external litmus test to determine the "correctness" of a student's personally constructed knowledge. In summary, educators who adhere to either Piagetian or radical constructivism view students as "autonomous actors who learn by building up their own understandings of their worlds in their heads" (Eisenhart, Finkel, & Marion, 1996, p. 278).

In contrast to these two perspectives are sociohistorical constructivism and social constructivism. Sociohistorical constructivism embraces Vygotsky's (1978) activity theory, whereas social constructivism is more closely associated with Bruner (1986), at least among literacy educators. Both sociohistorical and social constructivism are concerned with how factors outside the head, such as the culture of a classroom, the structural characteristics of schooling, and issues of social justice, form (rather than merely affect) what teachers and students do in the name of teaching and learning. Educators whose belief systems resonate with sociohistorical constructivism and social constructivism also believe that how students perceive themselves in a particular context (e.g., a content area class) mediates their motivation to learn (or not learn) the content of that class.

Social constructionist learning theory.   The centrality of language in mediating what people come to understand about their lived experiences is the feature that most readily distinguishes a social constructionist perspective from a constructivist perspective. In accepting a social constructionist perspective, we are saying that we believe knowledge is based on conventions of language that members of a particular community (e.g., a history class or a professional organization of reading educators) have constructed and agreed on. Gavelek and Raphael (1996) explain a social constructionist perspective as follows:

> This perspective has the potential to shift our focus on talk about text away
> from seeking "facts" or "truths" toward constructing "interpretations" and
> offering "warranted justifications" for interpretations. From this perspective,
> the teacher's role would shift from asking questions to ensure that students
> arrive at the "right" meaning to creating prompts that encourage students'

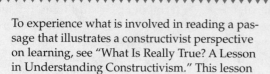

Technology Tip

To experience what is involved in reading a passage that illustrates a constructivist perspective on learning, see "What Is Really True? A Lesson in Understanding Constructivism." This lesson was developed by Lloyd Rieber, one of Donna's colleagues at the University of Georgia, and can be accessed at http://it.coe.uga.edu/~lrieber/constructlesson.html.

exploratory talk. . . . Teachers would encourage talk that elicits a range of possible interpretations among individuals reading and responding at any given time. Teachers would also encourage talking about previously read texts because individuals construct different readings at different periods in life or within different contexts. . . . Textual meaning is not "out there" to be acquired: It is something that is constructed by individuals through their interactions with each other and the world. In classrooms, these interactions take the form of discussions, and the teacher helps guide and participates in them. Underlying the processes of interpretations and justifications in discussions is language. (p. 183)

The fact that social constructionism can be traced through at least three historical periods of time, complete with their accompanying models of the process, means that it is a concept that defies attempts to "fix it" in space and time. Its fluidity as a concept is not surprising given the continual flux and development of language, culture, knowledge, and self (G. Hruby, personal communication, July 3, 2000). In an attempt to make this orientation to reading meaningful in the brief space of this chapter, we have included a short story by Richard Brautigan (1971) and an accompanying small group activity.

Story: "It's very hard to live in a studio apartment in San Jose with a man who's learning to play the violin." That's what she told the police when she handed them the empty revolver. (Brautigan, 1971, p. 197)

ACTIVITY   Gather a group of three or four individuals, and respond to the following prompts after someone in the group has read aloud Brautigan's story:

‣ Explain what happened.
‣ Elaborate on why it happened.
‣ Defend why you know you're right.

After completing the activity, reflect on the process. As you discussed your responses to the story, did you notice the role that language played in mediating your own and other people's interpretations? How would you explain your choice of language in constructing your interpretation? Why is your interpretation as viable as other people's interpretations? What previous experiences have you had that might possibly account for your interpretation of the story? Reflecting on questions such as these will help you understand how individuals go about socially constructing the meanings of all sorts of texts, not just short stories.

Such reflections will also illustrate Brock and Gavelek's (1998) point that although our cultural histories do not determine how we experience or respond to texts, these histories do in fact channel or help to frame our responses. In fact, the very idea that reading is a socially constructed practice draws on some of the most basic assumptions from cultural anthropology and sociolinguistics (Cook-Gumperz, 1986; Gee, 1988; Heath, 1983). One such assumption is that "students of different races, different social classes, and different genders may produce readings which challenge dominant or authoritative meanings because they have available to them different sets of values and beliefs" (Patterson, Mellor, & O'Neill, 1994, p. 66). However, it should come as no surprise that students who share common cultural backgrounds and who are contemporaries of one another may still respond to and interpret the same text very differently. This is to be expected given that each student will have had unique life experiences and different ways of using language to interpret those experiences.

Like Gee (1996) and Moll (1991), we believe it is almost impossible to think about literacy practices apart from the larger social and cultural milieu in which they reside. That the routines and rituals which develop to form the culture of classrooms influence how the different cognitive strategies introduced in this book will be perceived, implemented, and assessed is a given. It is also a given that conceptions of literacy as critical social practice do not deny the cognitive or behavioral aspects of reading, writing, and speaking, but instead portray them as attendant processes in a much larger social context—one that is institutionally located in the political structures of society in which power is at stake in people's social interactions on a day-to-day basis. Issues of gender, race, class, age, and other identity markers are historically part of these interactions (Alvermann et al., 1999; Luke & Freebody, 1997).

The Role of Motivation

Listening to the voices of students is key to understanding what motivates them to learn. Based on her review of research on student motivation, Barbara McCombs (1995) of the Mid-Continent Regional Educational Laboratory writes:

> The support is overwhelmingly on the side of learner-centered practices that honor individual learner perspectives and needs for competence, control, and

belonging. The voices of the students themselves provide even more support for this perspective. . . . When students are asked what makes school a place where they want to learn, they report that they want (a) rigor and joy in their schoolwork, (b) a balance of complexity and clarity, (c) opportunities to discuss personal meanings and values, (d) learning activities that are relevant and fun, and (e) learning experiences that offer choice and require action. (p. 10)

Middle-grade students' motivations for reading as measured by the *Motivations for Reading Questionnaire* extend and complement this view of the importance of intrinsically appealing learner-centered instruction. Approximately 600 students in a large mid-Atlantic city school system (55% African American, 43% Caucasian, and 2% Asian and Hispanic) said they do not avoid difficult reading activities. Motivational dimensions related to enjoyment, curiosity, and a sense of efficacy were the best predictors of the frequency with which they read (Wigfield et al., 1996).

When students are positively motivated, they view themselves as competent readers who are in control of their comprehension processes; they are said to be strategic in their approach to reading. Sometimes, however, students adopt tactics that result in an avoidance of reading or of spending time on assignments. When this occurs, they are said to be using strategies in a self-serving, or negative, fashion. Both positive and negative types of motivation for reading are present among students, regardless of ability level, socioeconomic status, or racial and ethnic background. Knowledge of how both types of motivation manifest themselves in subject matter classrooms is vital to understanding the reading process and to planning for instruction.

Positive strategies.   Strategic readers take pride in what they are able to learn independently from text. They view reading as a means of gaining control of their academic environment. They also develop feelings of self-worth and confidence in their ability to achieve desired goals (Weiner, 1986). This sense of control can lead to increased achievement in their subject matter classes; it can also lead to better peer relations.

As young adolescents move from the middle grades into secondary school, their perceptions of their control become stronger. According to Paris, Wasik, and Turner (1991), greater "perceived control leads to greater effort in the use of particular learning strategies. Successful students persist in the face of failure and choose appropriate tactics for challenging tasks more often than students who do not understand what controls learning outcomes" (p. 626).

For students to experience a sense of control in becoming competent readers, they must believe four things. First, they must believe that they are capable of assuming responsibility for their own learning and have the ability to complete their assignments. Second, they must believe that they have a voice in setting their own objectives for reading and in determining suitable standards of excellence. Third, they must be convinced of the usefulness of certain strategies for accomplishing specific objectives. Finally, they must believe that their successes as readers are contingent on the effort and skill they invest in becoming strategic readers (Paris, Wasik, & Turner, 1991).

Avoidance strategies.   Giving up on, or withdrawing from, situations that involve learning from text is a tactic students may use when the material they are assigned to read seems too difficult or uninteresting. This tactic may even be used by students for whom the material is neither too difficult nor uninteresting. Why? To the best of our knowledge, disengaged readers for one reason or another devalue reading; they tend to invest their time in other endeavors. Their attention is focused elsewhere, perhaps on a subject requiring less reading, a part-time job, or extracurricular activities. Another avoidance strategy students use involves shifting the blame for reading difficulties from themselves to someone or something else. For example, students may complain that their teachers dislike them, that they are distracted easily, or that other teachers load them up with homework. The least desirable avoidance strategy is the one used by students who free themselves of the responsibility for reading text to learn by copying assignments, cheating on tests, or repeatedly seeking the assistance of a friend or family member (Paris, Wasik, & Turner, 1991).

Each of these avoidance strategies shares certain attributes with the others. First, they all help to preserve students' positive self-perceptions because "passing the buck" leads to short-term success at preserving self-esteem. Second, they eventually lead to the *passive failure syndrome* (Johnston & Winograd, 1985),

A Response from Our Readers

Marlene Willis,* a middle-grades teacher and graduate student enrolled in Donna's content literacy methods course at the University of Georgia, wrote the following response after reading the section on students' use of both positive and avoidance strategies in Chapter 1 of this book:

I, as well as many students of my generation, persisted and felt that hard work would pay off; however, too many students today lack the drive to succeed. I felt that I was in control of my destiny. Students I encounter daily seem to leave their fates to chance. Clearly, an understanding of what controls learning outcomes is important.

That successful students persist when faced with failure and have a repertoire of tactics for challenging tasks is not surprising to me. How to instill in adolescents the four things that Paris, Wasik, and Turner (1991) say students need to believe remains the million-dollar question for me. . . . The real challenge as I see it is to first halt the fears adolescents (all of us) have of being labeled over- or underachievers (as well as a myriad of other revolting things) and then to find ways to propel students to become independent learners.

*Adapted with permission of Marlene S. Willis.

in which students, over time, fail to learn the necessary content and skills that make regular advancement in school an attainable goal. Third, students' sense of "beating the system" may lead to a false idea of what it takes to succeed in any endeavor, whether reading or something else.

Self-motivation.   The idea that teachers can cultivate within students the will, or self-motivation, to use their reading and writing skills in all areas of the curriculum is a central theme of this book. In fact, the underlying goal of most literacy instruction in middle and secondary schools is to enable students to use reading and writing as tools for learning the content of their coursework. However, teachers know that all too often adolescents do not make the effort that is necessary for this learning to take place (Bishop, 1989). Why this apathy?

Here are some answers to that question from the students' perspectives, as published in an announcement from the U.S. Department of Education (1992):

1. Students believe their ability and effort are the main reasons for school success. But if asked whether they would prefer to be called smart or hard-working, they will choose smart almost every time. They believe that hard-working students risk being considered excessively ambitious or of limited ability, both of which are embarrassing.
2. To avoid unpopular labels, students—especially the brightest—believe they must strike a balance between the extremes of achievement, not too high and not too low.
3. Many low-achieving students deny the importance of learning and withhold the effort it requires in order to avoid the stigma of having tried and failed. (p. 1)

Other answers to the apathy question come from teachers. For example, Janis Gabay, the 1990 National Teacher of the Year, argued that adolescents (especially minorities) are often labeled as "unmotivated" when actually it is a matter of their having no sense of ownership and no incentive to participate in classroom activities. To Gabay's (1991) way of thinking,

> Teachers can help their students become self-motivated in a number of ways: by tapping students' prior knowledge; setting forth clear expectations and goals so students know what they are aspiring to in a specific lesson, unit, or semester; conveying to students the difficulty of the challenge but emphasizing the supports the teacher will provide to ensure their success; giving lots of genuine praise for the incremental, tentative steps students take; holding students accountable in a way that includes self-evaluation of their progress; acknowledging each student through a significant nod, a smile, or an encouraging comment (not always in front of the whole class)—especially for that student at risk of "disconnecting"; and by modeling the enthusiasm that teaching and learning engender so students can see a tangible example of self-motivation, commitment, and effort. (p. 7)

Perhaps one of the most useful things to bear in mind as we work to increase our students' self-motivation is a statement attributed to John F. Kennedy.

Speaking on the importance of developing each child's potential to its fullest, Kennedy (cited in Inos & Quigley, 1995) said, "Not every child has an equal talent or an equal ability or equal motivation, but children have the equal right to develop their talent, their ability, and their motivation" (p. 1). We think this statement and its implications for classroom practice go a long way toward promoting the kind of literate environment that is at the heart of this book.

SUMMARY

A pervasive and legitimate concern of middle and high school content area teachers is how to help students learn from texts. In the English language arts curriculum that concern is broadened to include an emphasis on how to help readers evaluate the connotations and associations evoked by the experience of transacting with texts. In all areas of the curriculum, the goal is to support adolescents' literacy growth by providing them with access to materials they can and want to read (Moore et al., 1999). Ensuring that all students, including those who struggle with reading and who are learning English as a second language, become active and independent learners is a primary goal of content area educators. Teachers' pedagogical subject matter knowledge and their understanding of the role that textbooks and the Internet (through its various websites) play in classroom instruction are vital links to reaching that goal.

Traditional definitions of what it means to be literate have given way to a broadened view of literacy—one that includes cultural, civic, computer, media, scientific, and technological literacies. These multiple literacies require skills that extend far beyond the conventional reading and writing competencies associated with print literacy. They also require that teachers attend to more than a cognitive view of the reading process. Constructivist and social constructionist perspectives of that process, as well as students' motivations for becoming literate, must be taken into account as important mediators of students' ability to learn in various content areas.

SUGGESTED READINGS

Barton, D., Hamilton, M., & Ivanic, R. (2000). *Situated literacies: Reading and writing in context.* New York: Routledge.

Christie, F., & Misson, R. (Eds.) (1998). *Literacy and schooling.* New York: Routledge.

Cope, B., & Kalantzis, M. (Eds.) (2000). *Multiliteracies: Literacy learning and the design of social futures.* New York: Routledge.

Freebody, P., Luke, A., & Gilbert, P. (1991). Reading positions and practices in the classroom. *Curriculum Inquiry, 21,* 435–457.

Kipke, M. D. (Ed.) (1999). *Risks and opportunities: Synthesis of studies on adolescence.* Washington, DC: National Academy Press.

Spivey, N. N. (1997). *The constructivist metaphor: Reading, writing, and the making of meaning.* San Diego: Academic Press.

Language, Diversity, and Culture

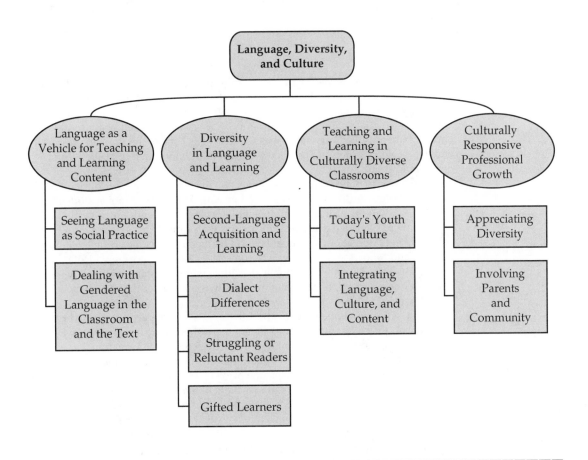

We open this chapter with a thumbnail sketch of Katya, one of several students who participated in a year-long study of adolescents' perceptions of classroom talk about their assigned reading materials. The sketch, compiled by Steve Phelps, a researcher in the study (Alvermann et al., 1996b), evokes images of why we believe teaching and learning in today's culturally diverse classrooms must entail more than simply attending to the assigned literacy tasks. Important as those tasks are, they cannot be isolated from the influences affecting students' everyday lives. As you read Steve's description of Katya, which he assembled from observing her in class and interviewing her in private, think of questions that you would like to ask her or her social studies teacher, Mr. Williams (pseudonyms are used throughout).

▼▼▼▼▼▼▼

Katya had come to the United States with her mother and three siblings from the Ukraine two years before the time of the study. They were members of the local Ukrainian Pentecostal Christian community. Katya said she attended church daily. Because her English was limited, both in vocabulary and in syntax, Katya had enrolled in two classes of English as a second language (ESL) as well as an after-school English program. She said she spoke Ukrainian at home. In her high school, Katya was referred to as "one of the Russian students," seemingly because the faculty and staff did not differentiate between the Ukraine and Russia.

Katya was very reserved and shy in class. To help overcome her difficulties with the language, Mr. Williams paired her with Ahmed, an Arabian student she had known the previous year in a biology class. Although Katya rarely uttered a word in class discussions, she (along with Ahmed) was one of the more diligent and attentive students in class when it came to reading, note-taking, and following the teacher's lectures. The only instances in which Katya attempted to enter into public discourse were occasional and nearly inaudible one-word responses when the class was going over the answers to a worksheet.

Although it would be easy to attribute Katya's lack of participation to her shyness or difficulty with the English language, there were brief flashes of evidence that suggested she was willing to share interesting information. For example, when she spoke with Steve about her life in the Ukraine and when she and Ahmed paged through a magazine prior to the start of class, Katya was animated and insightful. Katya's grades were in the low 90s, and on the final state Regent's Exam, which was part multiple choice and part essay, Katya got a 76. Although she did relatively well in her other subjects as well, she was unable to graduate at the end of the year because she did not have enough physical education credits. (Phelps & Weaver, 1999)

▼▼▼▼▼▼▼

What questions came to mind as you read this sketch? For us, one nagging question was, "What might Mr. Williams have done to create spaces for Katya's private voice in the public discourse of the classroom?" However, as we ask it, we think back to other studies of student voice in which researchers have found that attempts to empower others is not something one can do *to* or *for* another person (Alvermann, 1996; Orner, 1992; Perry & Delpit, 1998). In fact, some educators have begun to ask themselves, "Whose interests are served when students speak?" The answers, as you might expect, are layered and complex. It is this complexity, along with others, that we invite you to explore in the following pages.

The chapter is divided into four major sections, which reflect its four purposes. The purpose of the first section is to explore issues concerning language as a vehicle for teaching and learning in culturally diverse classrooms. The purpose of the second section is to describe issues regarding the various needs of English language learners (ELLs). The purpose of the third section is to examine the need for integrating language, culture, and content given today's youth culture. The purpose of the fourth section is to suggest ways of synchronizing professional growth opportunities so that they focus on culturally responsive teaching.

LANGUAGE AS A VEHICLE FOR TEACHING AND LEARNING CONTENT

A major influence on how we currently view the teaching and learning of content literacy is the work of Lev Vygotsky, a Russian psychologist. Although Vygotsky's (1978) ideas about the sociocultural approach to mind took shape in the early years of the twentieth century, educators in North America did not learn of them until edited translations of his work appeared in English in the 1960s and 1970s. In a nutshell, Vygotsky believed that "mental functioning in the individual originates in social, communicative processes" (Wertsch, 1991, p. 13), which are embedded in an array of cultural, historical, and institutional contexts. In other words, a Vygotskian perspective on learning does not assume that students will learn independently but rather that they will benefit from having someone more knowledgeable than themselves guide their learning (Vygotsky, 1978). The influence of a Vygotskian perspective on this book will become evident as you read and discuss Chapters 6, 7, 9, and 10, which include numerous strategies for guiding students' comprehension of content area texts.

This emphasis on the sociohistorical and cultural aspects of language as a mediator of even the most private forms of thinking has had a profound influence on how we view the reading process, as described in Chapter 1. Its influence is highlighted again here: first, in our look at language as social practice, and next in our discussion of ways to deal with the gendered nature of classroom language and text.

Seeing Language as Social Practice

Envisioning language as social practice requires that we think of language as both a social process and a socially conditioned process. What do we mean by this statement and why should you be concerned? Briefly, there was a time in the early twentieth century when educators believed that language had little to do with how people organized their lives and made sense of their surroundings. They concentrated instead on people's language proficiency in terms of vocabulary knowledge, word pronunciation, and syntactic patterning. Gradually, however, thinking changed, and by the late 1970s attention turned to viewing language as indistinguishable from the social practices that embed one's every move and thought. In short, language is a social process in that it is used to exchange meaning among people. What a person says and what other people hear will vary greatly depending on social and cultural factors. Language is socially conditioned in the sense that people learn language in social settings and continually modify it in their attempt to adapt to varied situations.

Consider, for example, the following story told by James Gee (1996), a sociolinguist whose work informs much of what we believe about the multiple literacies underlying subject matter learning. In this story, Gee illustrates how language in the social context of a biker bar (or pub) reveals much more about the narrator (himself) than his proficiency in using English:

> Imagine I park my motorcycle, enter my neighborhood "biker bar," and say to my leather-jacketed and tattooed drinking buddy, as I sit down: "May I have a match for my cigarette, please?" What I have said is perfectly grammatical English, but it is "wrong" nonetheless, unless I have used a heavily ironic tone of voice. It is not just *what* you say, but *how* you say it. And in this bar, I haven't said it in the "right way." I should have said something like "Gotta match?" or "Give me a light, wouldya?"
>
> But now imagine I say the "right" thing ("Gotta match?" or "Give me a light, wouldya?"), but while saying it, I carefully wipe off the bar stool with a napkin to avoid getting my newly pressed designer jeans dirty. In this case, I've still got it all wrong. In *this* bar they just don't do that sort of thing: I have *said* the right thing, but my "saying–doing" combination is nonetheless wrong. It's not just what you say or even just how you say it, it's also who you are and what you're doing while you say it. It is not enough just to say the right "lines." (p. viii)

What you have just read is an example of a Discourse, with a capital *D*. Briefly defined, Discourses are ways of speaking, thinking, and behaving in the world. Whether in biker bars, such as the one discussed previously , or in schools and other community sites, Discourses operate as ways of integrating and sorting individuals and groups. Gee (1996) describes how such integrating and sorting processes may affect us as teachers, and especially the expectations we hold for students:

> Each Discourse incorporates a usually taken for granted and tacit "theory" of what counts as a "normal" person and the "right" ways to think, feel, and behave. These theories crucially involve viewpoints on the distribution of social goods like status, worth, and material goods in society (who should and who should not have them). The biker bar "says" that "tough guys" are "real men"; the school "says" that certain children—often minority children and those from lower socioeconomic groups—are not suited for higher education and professional careers. (p. ix)

Some questions to get you thinking

1. What are some Discourses in which you claim membership?
2. How would others recognize you as a member of these Discourses?
3. Do you change your ways of speaking, thinking, and behaving when you move from one Discourse to another? Why?
4. What connections can you make between the example of the Discourse of the biker bar and the Discourses you are apt to find in various school settings?

Developing an awareness of how different Discourses construct the social realities of the classrooms in which we teach is an important first step in understanding how students organize their lives and construct meaning of their surroundings. A necessary second step is dealing with some of the social realities thus constructed.

Dealing with Gendered Language in the Classroom and the Text

Currently, there is a great deal of emphasis placed on student-centered literacy practices, such as personal response to texts in book clubs, literature circles, and cooperative-learning groups. However, little attention is being paid to the dynamics of classroom language that both constitutes and derives from such practices. This is curious, especially given what we know about adolescents' preoccupation with peer approval and acceptance.

We agree with Barbara Guzzetti (2000) that personal response to texts, as a literacy practice, can sometimes lead to gender divisiveness among students. We found instances of this in a classroom study of how social and cultural practices shared by a group of young adolescents shaped responses to texts that they had read in common (Alvermann et al., 1996a). In the two sections that follow on the language of classroom and text, we provide anecdotal evidence of what we mean.

Language of the classroom.

> I think the girls, we're like, we dominate, we rule the class.
> —*Jamaica*

> Since we've been talking about sexism [in books], the girls got their own point of view and the boys got their own . . . [and] we're always against each other.
> —*David*

Spoken passionately and with conviction, these statements reflected attitudes that existed in David Hinson's seventh-grade language arts class following a class reading of a play about a girls' soccer team that defeats a boys' soccer team. The discussion of this play eventually led a student to ask, "Should boys be allowed to join an all-girls' softball team?" Although a few students said yes, most of them flatly rejected the idea.

The proverbial battle lines between the sexes were drawn when Cherie announced: "An all-girls' team talks about 'girl talk' so boys would ruin everything." The boys, sensing they were being cast as the outsiders, retorted with statements like, "It just shows the stupidity of women." As the name-calling escalated, the students seemed bent on excluding each other's ideas along sexist lines rather than questioning the source of those ideas and why they might hold currency among their peers.

We believe that incidents such as this one can lead eventually to patterns of discourse that students internalize and act on in a variety of ways. When language of the classroom centers on the meanings boys and girls attach to being male or female, as in the example just given, gender becomes something students *do*—a way of being in the world. Over time, as stereotypes form and become more firmly inscribed each time gender is socially constructed through classroom talk, students shape their identities to fit the language they hear.

ACTIVITY   Record on a sheet of paper for three consecutive class sessions any language you hear that treats males and females in stereotypical ways. Keep notes on who uses that language and how the persons to whom it is directed tend to react. Share your findings on how gendered classroom language affects the way individuals think and feel about themselves.

Language of the text.   Reading texts in which an author's language socially constructs gender can also inscribe stereotypes. However, gender is but one of several filters through which readers experience texts. Social class, race, ethnicity, and culture are others. Consider, for instance, the overlapping filters that are operating in the following examples from Sally Randall's eighth-grade language arts classroom:

Example 1: Rather than assign the questions at the end of an excerpt from *The Pearl* (Steinbeck, 1989) in the class anthology, Ms. Randall asked the students to consider a series of quotations from the selection. One quotation helped students consider how an author's gendered way of writing can influence the language they use in discussing the text.

> Kino had wondered often at the iron in his patient, fragile wife. She, who was obedient and respectful and cheerful and patient, she could arch her back in child pain with hardly a cry. She could stand fatigue and hunger almost better than Kino himself. In the canoe she was like a strong man. (p. 677)

After students had read this quotation aloud, Ms. Randall asked them to consider why Steinbeck wrote the description of Kino's wife in this way. The first student to respond said Juana (Kino's wife) had the physical characteristics of a man but still gave Kino the honor and respect he deserved because he was a man. Ms. Randall then underlined the word *almost* and the phrase *like a strong man.* She asked the class to think about what those words implied. A student spoke up to say that Juana may have had qualities like a man but they were also women's qualities. Exchanges such as these allow students to explore multiple perspectives.

Example 2: *The Pearl* became the focus of another discussion in Ms. Randall's class. This time the students were asked to consider who was the more dominant character—Kino or Juana. Most of them concluded it had to be Kino because he was the man, and he made all the decisions for his family. Ms. Randall asked, "Do you think this is pretty common in literature for the man to be the dominant one?" Heads nodded in agreement, with Paula explaining it this way:

> Well, it kind of just started in the beginning. Adam was made first, and that was kind of like the man was the head of the family. And so it was just kind of in all the stories. That's just like in real life. That's just the way.

With this example, it is easy to see how the language of the classroom and the language of the text conspire to socially construct what it means to be male and, by implication, what it means to be female. Here, the weight of religion, literary

A Response from Our Readers.

▼▼

Elizabeth Armstrong-Yazzie,* a student enrolled in Josephine Young's content literacy course at Arizona State University, wrote the following response after reading Paula's interpretation of male dominance in Steinbeck's story.

I could see how many European American students might think in that way but what about students from other cultures? For example, what would Navajo students think of the quotations? The Navajo tribe is a matrilineal society. Traditional Navajos do not believe in the Adam and Eve creation story. They have their own creation story. Some Navajos may not have even heard of the Adam and Eve creation story.

This is a reminder that you should not assume that your students will understand everything you discuss in class. Be prepared to explain a lot and ask if your students are familiar with what you're talking about and if they understand it. I can't help but wonder how different the Navajo students' interpretations would be of the excerpt.

*Adapted with permission of Elizabeth Armstrong-Yazzie.

history, and culture combine to leave little doubt in Paula's mind that this is just the way life is, has always been, and will always be.

Interrupting the status quo.   Creating spaces for students to explore multiple perspectives and interpretations of their texts is a starting point, as in Example 1 and Example 2. However, as evidenced in the second example, the filters through which they often experience and discuss such texts may perpetuate the status quo and, in the process, reinforce the very stereotypes that the discussion was originally designed to examine and possibly challenge. Interrupting the status quo, therefore, requires a vigilance on the part of teachers. Strategies that support students as they begin to question the source of the ideas or the values expressed in the texts they read and hear discussed in class are most effective when they call into question inequities associated with gender bias (Alvermann, 2000).

For example, Wayne Williams, a physics teacher who collaborated in a two-year action research project with Barbara Guzzetti, a literacy teacher educator (Guzzetti & Williams, 1996), employed a simple but effective strategy for intervening in a gendered interactional style that favored boys' voices over girls' voices in his classroom. Briefly, Mr. Williams had been unaware during the first year of the study that the boys in his class generally believed that the girls' questioning style indicated an inability on their part to learn difficult concepts. In the second year of the study, Mr. Williams presented his subject matter in a way that demonstrated science involves an active questioning and exploring of ideas. In doing this, he was able to communicate that females' ways of talking should be viewed positively, rather than negatively, and that questioning is the first step in scientific inquiry.

DIVERSITY IN LANGUAGE AND LEARNING

We begin this section on second-language learning, dialect differences, struggling readers, and gifted learners with a cautionary note. It is easy to fall into the trap of generalizing about an individual based on one aspect of that person's group membership. How many times, for example, have you heard or taken part in conversations that narrowly define someone on the basis of their race, gender, age, ability, religion, and so on? Generalizing group characteristics to an individual is misleading in other ways as well. A case in point is Katya. If you were her teacher, why would it be important to identify her in more than one way?

Although Katya's nationality is Ukrainian, this is only one of her multiple group memberships. Katya, the individual, is simultaneously a woman and a member of the Pentecostal Christian community. Although she did not disclose information related to her social class or racial makeup, we do know she has at least one exceptionality—Katya is multilingual. She speaks Ukrainian, Russian, and English. Thus, if you were Katya's teacher, you would want to consider her multiple group memberships when planning for instruction, facilitating group discussions, devising assessments, or making any number of other instructional decisions. Without knowledge of the different norms, values, myths, traditions, and symbols that have meaning for different cultural groups, you will find it difficult to access or build on your students' rich and diverse backgrounds when introducing new concepts and strategies for learning from texts.

Although developing an awareness of your students' cultural backgrounds is important, it is not enough. Too often we think of "other" people as having a diverse set of beliefs and values and yet remain blind to our own. It is as if we simply do not see what looks and feels so "normal" to us. Try the following activity to gain insight into your own cultural norms.

ACTIVITY   Fold a sheet of notebook paper in half the long way. On the left side, state the values and beliefs you hold most dear. On the right side, briefly state how you practice or "live out" each of them. For instance, give examples of how you practice them. Then review both sides, noting as you go any statements that seem particularly narrow or finite. Inspect your more "absolute" ways of believing and valuing to see if you have a blind spot that may interfere in teaching a culturally diverse group of students. Think of how you might compensate for that blind spot.

Second-Language Acquisition and Learning

The distinction between second-language acquisition and second-language learning is not simply a dichotomous matter. It is more like a continuum, with the two terms serving as the imaginary poles. However, the distinction is useful in drawing attention to Krashen's (1989) claim that second-language development is more a matter of acquisition than of learning through formal methods.

According to Gee (1996), "acquisition is a process of acquiring something (usually subconsciously) by exposure to models, a process of trial and error, and practice within social groups, without formal teaching" (p. 138). For example, first-language development for native English speakers is primarily a matter of acquisition, though as most of us remember from classes in English grammar, some formal schooling was also involved. Like Gee (1996), we believe that we are better at performing what we *acquire* than what we *learn*:

> For most of us, playing a musical instrument, or dancing, or using a second language, are skills we attained by some mixture of acquisition and learning. But it is a safe bet that, over the same amount of time, people are better at (performing) these activities if acquisition predominated during that time. (p. 139)

We also believe language differences should be more than tolerated; they need to be celebrated and affirmed. As teachers, we need to help students appreciate that having two or more languages or dialects at their command gives them the prerogative to choose from among them as circumstances dictate. To literacy educator David Bloome's (1992) way of thinking,

> We need to replace the LEP (limited English proficiency) mentality with the LTEP (limited to English proficiency) mentality. Bilingualism and multilingualism need to be viewed as normal, healthy, and prevalent states of life (both for individuals and for communities). Monolingualism needs to be viewed as the aberration. (p. 7)

To appreciate the implications of Bloome's thinking for teaching and learning, it will help to become conversant with some of the major approaches to educating second-language learners. Advocates of various approaches to teaching English language learners (e.g., sheltered English, content-based ESL, bilingual/bicultural, and two-way bilingual) express strong rationales for preferring one type of instruction to another. However, with California's passage of Proposition 227 decreeing English-only instruction in the waning years of the past century, educators have had to rethink what it means to teach students whose primary or native language (L1) is something other than English. Because sheltered English instruction is increasingly the approach of choice in school districts throughout the United States (Echevarria, Vogt, & Short, 2000), we devote a proportionately greater amount of attention to it here. We include briefer descriptions of other approaches, however, because of their viability and presence in the research literature on bilingual education (Cummins, 1999; Fitzgerald & Cummins, 1999).

Sheltered English instruction. We are living in a time when adolescents' language backgrounds are becoming increasingly diverse but those of their teachers are not. What happens to students who come to school without the proficiency in

English to keep up with their peers in the various subject matter areas? How are such students expected to meet the high standards set by state and national reform movements? More and more frequently, schools are turning to sheltered English instruction as an approach that prepares ELLs to comprehend the content of their subject matter classes at the same time that they receive instruction in reading, writing, speaking, and listening in English.

Through various adaptations in their instruction, English-speaking teachers are able to make adjustments in the language demands put on students who are not yet fluent in English but who, with supportive teaching techniques, can understand grade-level content standards and concepts (Echevarria, Vogt, & Short, 2000). These adjustments may include scaffolding their instruction (e.g., modeling teacher thinking, providing analogies, and elaborating on student responses), providing necessary background information and experiences, and organizing their lessons in ways that simplify syntactic structures (e.g., using more active than passive verbs). Teachers in sheltered classrooms may also employ strategies that emphasize visual cues and other concrete means for helping students apply what they know in their primary language to the English language. Chapters 4 and 6–10 offer specific suggestions and strategies for working with ELLs in a variety of subject matter classrooms.

The downside of sheltered English instruction is that "many ELLs receive much of their instruction from content area teachers or aides who have not had appropriate professional development to address their second-language development needs" (Echevarria, Vogt, & Short, 2000, p. 4). The demand for teachers knowledgeable in the implementation of sheltered English instruction simply exceeds the supply. Although the sheltered approach to teaching involves many of the same instructional methods and strategies that regular classroom teachers use, most teachers who have not had coursework and experience in second-language acquisition lack the skills necessary for linguistically and culturally responsive instruction. Without knowledge of the ELL's second-language development needs, a teacher is at a distinct disadvantage, as is the learner who is the recipient of such instruction.

However, in schools that have initiated systemwide sheltered instruction taught by appropriately educated staff, the story is quite different. In these schools, it is highly likely that students whose first language is other than English will acquire academic literacy through instruction that shows them how to pool their emerging knowledge of English with what they know about the content and the tasks necessary for comprehending that content. The Sheltered Instruction Observational Protocol (SIOP) model (Echevarria, Vogt, & Short, 2000) is one example of a well-researched tool for planning and implementing sheltered English instruction in subject matter classrooms. Originally designed as an observation instrument, the SIOP is also used as a source of concrete examples of the features of sheltered instruction that make it possible for ELLs to acquire a second language and academic content simultaneously. Other strategies that take into account sheltered English instruction can be found in Chapter 4.

Content-based ESL.   This instructional approach uses academic content (sometimes packaged thematically) as a vehicle for second-language learning. Unlike sheltered English instruction in which ELLs work alongside their native-English-speaking peers, students enrolled in content-based ESL classes are all ELLs. Also, unlike sheltered instruction in which content learning and language development are merged, the primary goal of content-based ESL instruction is to prepare ELLs for regular English-medium classrooms (Echevarria, Vogt, & Short, 2000). The two approaches, however, do share a common problem: the demand for ESL and sheltered teachers far exceeds the supply.

ESL teachers, who typically are monolingual English speakers, often serve as "cultural brokers" by introducing learners to the mainstream culture as well as to the English language (Adamson, 1993). Critics of ESL programs charge that students are unable to keep up with their mainstream peers because they are pulled out of their content area classes and taught by teachers who emphasize English as a second language over subject matter learning.

Bilingual/bicultural programs.   Currently, Hispanics constitute the largest minority-language group in the public schools of this country, and according to one estimate (Waggoner, 1999) their numbers will grow through at least 2050, when this group will represent 30% of the school-age population. Bilingual/ bicultural (or sometimes, multilingual/multicultural) programs vary in the amount of native language used or the number of years that language is supported (Moran & Hakuta, 1995). Students enrolled in bilingual programs spend a portion of each day learning English, but they are taught content area subjects in their native language. Critics of this approach say that ELLs may be separated from their English-speaking peers for several years at a time and that this results in their becoming too reliant on native-language teaching. Advocates, on the other hand, claim that bilingual/bicultural programs instill a high level of self-esteem in students and enable them to maintain their native language. Advocates also claim that students who understand how their native, or first-language (L1), works will have an easier time making the transition to a second language (L2) (Greene, 1998).

Two-way bilingual education.   There is no isolation of second-language learners from first-language learners in two-way bilingual education programs. Instead, non-English-background learners and students who are monolingual in English attend classes together and study the same content in each other's language (Minami & Ovando, 1995). Two-way bilingual education programs enable language minority students to maintain positive feelings about their ethnicity and language. These programs also develop second-language skills in English-speaking students. Just as important, they offer the hope of better cross-cultural understanding and appreciation in an increasingly diverse society (Christian, 1994).

Some critics of two-way bilingual education claim that it is not economically feasible given the large numbers of ELLs in U.S. schools today. Other detractors of this approach point to the shortage of bilingual teachers. Although the research on bilingual and two-way bilingual programs is mixed, certain conclusions can be drawn. In their review of *Improving Schooling for Language Minority Children: A Research Agenda* (August & Hakuta, 1997), Fitzgerald and Cummins (1999) concluded that "the theory and supporting data suggest that certain cognitive abilities learned through reading instruction in either a new language or a native language will transfer to the reading in the other language" (p. 388). Fitzgerald and Cummins went on to add that the research shows that minority-language instruction will have no adverse effects on English-language or literacy development.

Dialect Differences

In the classroom communities in which we work, dialect is frequently the most salient feature of cultural diversity, and it is often a contentious issue. The dilemma is twofold. How does one teach the codes of power while at the same time respecting students' culture and language? How does one disentangle form and meaning in language? Dialect can be a very powerful way of expressing meaning; at the same time, it can be a powerful barrier to communication. Bidialectical speakers—that is, individuals who are facile in using both dialect and "standard" forms of English—recognize this dilemma, but they also know how advantageous it is to "own" more than one language.

We think Gloria Ladson-Billings (1994) presents a useful way of thinking about dialect differences in her book, *The Dreamkeepers*. Ladson-Billings describes the classroom practices of eight teachers who differ in personal style and methods but who share an ability to teach in a manner that affirms and reinforces African American students' belief in themselves and their cultural identities. Patricia Hilliard, one of the eight teachers in Ladson-Billings's book, is an African American teacher who has taught in both public and private schools in a large urban area. Like Lisa Delpit (1995), Hilliard is wary of instructional approaches that fail "to make students cognizant of the power of language and the language of power" (Ladson-Billings, 1994, p. 82). In Hilliard's words (cited in Ladson-Billings, 1994),

> I get so sick and tired of people trying to tell me that my children don't need to use any language other than the one they come to school with. Then those same people turn right around and judge the children negatively because of the way they express themselves. My job is to make sure that they can use *both* languages, that they understand that their language is valid but that the demands placed upon them by others mean that they will constantly have to prove their worth. We spend a lot of time talking about language, what it means, how you can use it, and how it can be used against you. (p. 82)

One way that Patricia Hilliard affirms and reinforces her students' cultural identities while she simultaneously teaches them the value of knowing both dialect and "standard" forms of English is through an activity that involves what she calls the "translation" process. Placing a transparency of the lyrics of their favorite rap on the overhead projector (double-spaced so she can write between the lines), Hilliard proceeds to engage her students in a translation activity. In talking with students about the process, she compares it to what interpreters do when they translate from one language to another. Hilliard (cited in Ladson-Billings, 1994) explains her objective for doing the activity as follows:

> I want the children to see that they have some valuable knowledge to contribute. I don't want them to be ashamed of what they know but I also want them to know and be comfortable with what school and the rest of the society requires. When I put it in the context of "translation" they get excited. They see it is possible to go from one to the other. It's not that they are not familiar with Standard English . . . they hear Standard English all the time on TV. It's certainly what I use in the classroom. But there is rarely any connection made between the way they speak and Standard English. I think that when they can see the connections and know that they can make the shifts, they become better at both. They're bilingual! (p. 84)

The point that Patricia Hilliard is making is one that linguists also make; that is, we are all speakers of one dialect or another. Whose dialect counts is often a matter of politics, however. Addressing this issue, Wayne O'Neil (1998), head of the Department of Linguistics and Philosophy at the Massachusetts Institute of Technology, wrote the following in response to the public's outrage over a school board's resolution to teach Ebonics in Oakland, California, in 1996:

> We assume . . . that there are standard versions of [all] languages, the pinnacles that each dialect speaker is supposed to aspire to, but that which normally—for reasons of class, or race, or geography—she or he is not able to reach. On this view, dialects are diminished varieties of a standard ("legitimate") language, a value judgment that has no standing in linguistics. For, on the scientific point of view, all . . . languages are rule-governed systems of equal complexity and interest—instantiations of the capacity for language that each infant enters the world with. (p. 41)

Ebonics, commonly known among linguists as Black English or African American Vernacular English (AAVE), was the term used in the Oakland school board resolution. Although members of the board never intended for Ebonics to replace Standard English, the media's distortion of the resolution led to this interpretation (Perry & Delpit, 1998). Amid much furor and heated debates through the press and TV talk shows, African Americans appeared divided on the issue. In addressing this divisiveness and the implications of Ebonics for teachers, the well-known African American educator Lisa Delpit (1998) stated,

> I have been asked often enough recently, "What do you think about Ebonics? Are you for it or against it?" My answer must be neither. . . . It exists. It is the language spoken by many of our African American children. It is the language they heard as their mothers nursed them and changed their diapers and played peek-a-boo with them. It is the language through which they first encountered love, nurturance, and joy. (p. 17)

Technology Tip

▼▼

To learn why the Linguistic Society of America passed its own resolution on the Ebonics debate, which stated that characterizations of Ebonics as "slang," "mutant," "lazy," "defective," "ungrammatical," or "broken English" are incorrect and demeaning, locate this information on the book's Web site (http://www.ablongman.com/alvermann3e.) To obtain further information on vernacular dialects in U.S. schools, use this e-mail address: *eric@cal.org*.

Delpit went on to add, however, that she, like most teachers and parents, believes that children who are not taught the power code of Standard English will not have equal access to good jobs and leadership positions. Therefore, Delpit recommends the following: help children who speak Ebonics learn Standard English so that through acquiring an additional form of linguistic expression they are able to code switch when necessary and still retain pride in the language with which they grew up.

Struggling or Reluctant Readers

We are all struggling or reluctant readers at times. Reflect for a moment on the type of text you struggle with or are reluctant to put much effort into understanding. Perhaps it is the owner's manual for your new computer, the technical jargon in the latest consumer price index, or the symbolism in a much touted film that all of your friends are wild about. Whatever your struggle or reluctance, it typically consists of more than an ability to decode text, broadly defined. The same is true for adolescents who struggle with reading or are reluctant to approach a task that reminds them of past struggles and perhaps even failure.

Even with the best literacy instruction in the early grades, some adolescents will enter secondary school with numerous and debilitating reading difficulties. These difficulties may be associated with poor motivation, low self-esteem, inadequate cognitive processing strategies, underdeveloped technical vocabularies, boredom with a curriculum that seemingly has little relevance to their everyday lives, and so on. For the purposes of this book, we are less interested in the causes of reading difficulties than with the instructional strategies and activities that teachers can use in working with struggling readers.

Staying focused on what adolescents who struggle with reading bring to their course is an important instructional principle—one that is backed by years of research and practice (Moore, Alvermann, & Hinchman, 2000; Readence, Moore, & Rickelman, 2000). In fact, many of the teachers we know take struggling readers' prior knowledge into consideration when planning instruction, teaching content, and assessing learning. Examples of how they do this can be found in Chapters

4–6. Here, we focus on some of the other principles of instruction that we believe are helpful when working with adolescents who struggle with reading.

For example, we believe that scaffolding instruction through appropriate comprehension monitoring, self-questioning, and small-group discussion strategies (Palincsar, 1986; Rothenberg & Watts, 2000) provides struggling readers with the support they need to comprehend the content of their subject matter classes. We also believe that direct instruction in vocabulary (Harmon, 2000), summarizing, using text structure, and certain information processing strategies such as those outlined in Flood and Lapp (2000) can make a difference in struggling readers' comprehension of their assigned readings. Finally, we believe struggling adolescent readers benefit from instruction that facilitates writing across the curriculum (Andrews, 2000), provides access to a range of reading materials (Bintz, 1993; Ivey, 1999b), and encourages them to participate in their own assessment, such as engaging in portfolio conferences (Young et al., 2000). These strategies, as well as others, are highlighted in the chapters that follow, along with examples of their application in actual classroom practice and how to teach them, taking struggling readers' needs into account.

Before concluding this section, a caveat is in order. We believe, like Ivey (1999a), that "whereas terminology or categories such as problem, average, superior, or low, middle, high may provide a general sense of how much students have developed as readers, they offer limited information about the complexities of individual experiences" (p. 188). Thus, planning instruction based on how a student has been labeled as a reader (e.g., struggling, low, and disabled) is a practice that lacks pedagogical soundness.

Gifted Learners

The nation's response to educating the gifted has historical underpinnings that are perhaps best captured in Richard Hofstadter's (1970) *Anti-Intellectualism in American Life*. Extending Alexis de Tocqueville's (1833/1983) characterization of American democracy in antebellum times, Hofstadter wrote,

> Again and again . . . it has been noticed that intellect in America is resented as a kind of excellence, as a claim to distinction, as a challenge to egalitarianism, as a quality which almost certainly deprives a man or woman of the common touch. (p. 51)

In short, intellect is viewed as "foreign to a society built on practicality and consensual understandings" (Resnick & Goodman, 1994, p. 110). In such a culture, gifted young people tend to stand out as special. This label of exceptionality has brought with it a host of tensions tied to issues of social and economic inequality. For example, placements in gifted and talented classes reflect an underrepresentation of minority and poor children (Mehan, 1991). They also reflect the misguided practice of automatically assigning ELLs to basic or general-level classes, rather than gifted classes, because their proficiency in the dominant

Technology Tip

▼▼▼

For more information on a similar view of gift-   www.ed.gov/pubs/TalentandDiversity/
edness, visit the following Web site: http://   talent.html.

language (English) fuels the perception that they are incapable of handling a challenging curriculum.

Of late, however, there has been a movement among educators of gifted and talented learners to expand their definition of giftedness; some, in fact, have moved away from the term entirely, favoring instead a curriculum that provides enrichment experiences for all students. This movement, sparked largely by Gardner's (1999) theory of multiple intelligences, has resulted in an increasing number of educators arguing that the ability to speak two or more languages is itself a special "gift."

Regardless of how restrictive or flexible one's definition of giftedness, adolescents who are highly creative and insightful will benefit from literacy instruction that offers opportunities for independent inquiry using the Internet, innovative problem solving, and expressive writing—activities that should be a part of all classrooms, but especially those in which gifted and talented students live and work (Ruddell, 1997). Keeping in mind that students of high ability who come from different cultures or from backgrounds of extreme poverty have the same potential to succeed as those students from the dominant culture will ensure that they have equal access to all literacy practices, not just those of a basic nature.

TEACHING AND LEARNING IN CULTURALLY DIVERSE CLASSROOMS

Although we weave suggestions for teaching culturally diverse students throughout this book, we focus here on the importance of integrating language, culture, and content in teaching culturally diverse students. However, first we invite you to consider the range of cultural diversity present among today's youth and the implications of this for you as a classroom teacher. Such consideration will no doubt heighten your awareness of the need to gear up to teach content reading and literacy in ways that are culturally relevant for all students, not just those who are most like you.

Today's Youth Culture

Each moment that teachers spend interacting with adolescents in content area classrooms is embedded in what social anthropologists Vered Amit-Talai and Helena Wulff (1995) refer to as "a range of cultural possibilities" (p. 231). They use this term to express the view that youth culture cannot be localized (and taught to) as if the classroom were a separate world of its own. Youth culture is produced at home, in school, on the streets, with friends, in malls, among siblings, through TV, music, and the Internet, and so on. To ignore this fact is to teach as if "teachers and students relate to one another undistracted by the classism, racism, and sexism that rage outside the classroom" (Brodkey, 1989, p. 139).

Although we discussed diversity issues that dealt with language, reading ability, and achievement motivation in the previous section, we barely touched the surface of the diversity present in today's youth culture. Consider, for example, the differences in working-class youth's discourse and school discourse. Patrick Finn (1999), an educator born into a working-class Irish Catholic family on the south side of Chicago, has devoted a lifetime exploring these differences and what they mean for literacy teaching and learning. According to Finn, there are two kinds of education in the United States:

> First, there is empowering education, which leads to powerful literacy, the
> kind of literacy that leads to positions of power and authority. Second, there is
> domesticating education, which leads to functional literacy, or literacy that
> makes a person productive and dependable, but not troublesome (pp. ix–x).

Arguing against the second kind, which is a conspiracy theory, Finn places the responsibility on schools for educating all youth in ways that are empowering, not simply domesticating.

Differences also abound in how adolescents view themselves in terms of ethnic identity. For example, among Hispanics (a label given to diverse groups of people by the federal government 30 years ago), popular youth culture has proclaimed a "Latino/Latina Revolution" led by Ricky Martin, Jennifer Lopez, and Christina Aguilera (Trujillo, 2000). According to Trujillo, a poll taken by the vice president of *quepasa.com* revealed that of 5,000 people responding, 37 percent chose Latino, 31 percent chose Hispanic, and the remaining 32 percent wanted to be identified as Mexican, Cuban, Puerto Rican, or whatever their national origin. Among Native Americans, as well as among Asian and Asian American youth, there is also the problem of being grouped together as if there were no differences among tribal groups or countries of national origin. Teachers who take the time to understand the differences between the Hopis and the Apaches or between Vietnamese and Chinese youth, for example, are on the road to achieving a more equitable and culturally responsive pedagogy (Henze & Hausser, 1999).

In matters of sexual orientation, differences also exist among heterosexual, gay, lesbian, bisexual, and transgender communities of people. Although sexual orientation is not typically a category to which authors of content area reading texts devote space, we include it here because of its place in the wider spectrum of multicultural education and because of the increasing number of publications dealing with homosexuality (Allan, 1999; Greenbaum, 1994; Young, 2000) that are appearing in professional journals focused on literacy teaching and learning. Whether coming from homes with gay or lesbian parents or embracing their own issues of sexual orientation, teenagers today need teachers who

Technology Tip

▼▼

Data from the National Assessment of Educational Progress on Long-Term Trends in Reading Assessment show that scores for overall student reading performance, as tested at age levels 9, 13, and 17, reflected an overall increase since the first assessment in 1971 for 9- and 13-year-olds in most racial/ethnic and gender subgroups. Black 17-year-olds were the only members of that age group to achieve an increase, and they did so while black drop-out rates were declining. For more information and updates, visit http://nces.ed.gov/pubsearch/search.asp.

are as accepting of them and their literacy needs (e.g., appropriate reading materials and informational texts) as they are of students from various racial, ethnic, socioeconomic, linguistic, and religious backgrounds.

Finally, among youth identified as being at risk of dropping out or youth who have cognitive and physical disabilities, there is much that can be done to help them see that their differences can be overcome or compensated for in productive ways. For example, sharing with students who traditionally have not performed well on reading tests the information contained in the Technology Tip at the top of this page might encourage them to stay in school and graduate.

Similarly, sharing the list of famous people with disabilities of one kind or another shown in Figure 2.1 with youth who have a particular learning, physical, or emotional disability can lead to better and fuller understandings of the human spirit and what it can accomplish under seemingly adverse situations.

Integrating Language, Culture, and Content

Being able to adjust one's lesson in the midst of teaching is part of a teacher's repertoire of instructional decision-making skills. Fred Genesee (1994), who researches second-language immersion programs in the United States and Canada, cites studies showing that teachers make as many as 1,300 instructional decisions each day. These decisions are most effective when teachers integrate their subject matter expertise with what they have learned about their students' language and culture. In the example that follows, a middle school teacher, Martie Menzel, uses e-texts with her eighth-grade ELLs to support their second-language learning and literacy development. Her decision to do so rests with her belief that the more ELLs are talking, the more language and content (in this instance, science) they are learning.

Ms. Menzel's class.   As a teacher in the Indian River School District of upstate New York, Ms. Menzel is accustomed to many languages being spoken by her students, many of whom are from military families. Her school serves a transient

Famous people with dyslexia

Thomas Edison	Inventor, scientist
Albert Einstein	Scientist, philosopher
Whoopi Goldberg	Actress
Magic Johnson	Professional athlete
George Patton	Military general
Nelson Rockefeller	Former vice president of the United States
Jackie Stewart	Race car driver
Woodrow Wilson	Former president of the United States

Famous people with movement differences

Muhammad Ali	Former professional athlete
Johnny Cash	Singer
Robert Dole	Former U.S. senator
Billy Graham	Religious leader
Pope John Paul II	Religious leader
Janet Reno	Former U.S. attorney general
Franklin Delano Roosevelt	Former president of the United States

Famous people with mood disorders

Patty Duke	Actress
Ernest Hemingway	Author
Mike Wallace	Journalist

Famous people with speech differences

Ludwig von Beethoven	German composer
Lewis Carroll	Author
Bill Clinton	Former president of the United States
Winston Churchill	Former prime minister of Britain
Walter Cronkite	Journalist
Helen Keller	Author
Marilyn Monroe	Actress

Famous people with dementia

Rita Hayworth	Actress
Ronald Reagan	Former president of the United States

Famous people with Tourette syndrome

Mahmoud Abdul-Rauf	Professional athlete
Jim Eisenreich	Professional athlete

Famous people with mental retardation

Chris Burke	Television actor
Gretchen Josephson	Poet

FIGURE 2.1 **Famous people with disabilities** (*Source:* Adapted from ERIC Clearinghouse on Disabilities and Gifted Education, copyright 1999; *http:/ericec.org/fact/famous.htm.* This list was compiled from various sources, including *Everyday Heroes* by Jeanne Lagorio Anthony, published by Empowerment in Action, P.O. Box 3064, Carlsbad, CA 92009; and *Understanding and Changing Our Reactions to Disabilities: Everybody's Different* by Nancy B. Miller and Catherine C. Sammons, published by Paul H. Brookes Publishing Co., Inc., P.O. Box 10624, Baltimore, MD 21285-0624.)

population. In this particular class, she had students who spoke Spanish, German, Korean, Tagalog, Hawaiian, Samoan, French, and Japanese. Her students often work in pairs at a computer that has only one mouse, and because the only common language of her multilingual students is frequently English, there are numerous opportunities for negotiating meaning in their second language. Although her students demonstrate fairly good oral language skills in their second language (English), they are limited in what they can comprehend from their academic or content area texts. Their limited knowledge of academic, or technical, vocabulary also limits their ability to write about what they are learning in their content classes.

To help her students improve their comprehension skills (in this instance, following written directions) and the use of comparisons (e.g., slow, slower, and slowest), Ms. Menzel introduced them to *Widget Workshop*, a software program that displays electronic text (e.g., information on the heart beat rates of different animals) at the same time that it allows access to a message board for taking notes on what they are learning. Working in pairs, students engage orally in comparing the heart rates of the animals. As they do, they practice choosing among the words slow, slower, and slowest.

According to Ms. Menzel, e-texts provide unique features that simultaneously foster her students' language and literacy development. These features include

1. A real need to communicate with a peer partner
2. A sense of ownership in the task
3. A certain "publicness" about the learning situation that makes it easy for her to monitor who is on task, who needs her help, and who is ready to move to the next level of difficulty

In summarizing the lesson and the effectiveness of using e-texts to work with ELLs, Ms. Menzel pointed out that during the entire lesson, her students' practice of science vocabulary and language forms (the comparatives) was authentic in that it arose from a real need to communicate with a peer about a common task (Meskill, Mossop, & Bates, 2000).

What's to be gained from this type of instruction?   More common than bilingual or two-way bilingual programs, Ms. Menzel's ESL class is focused chiefly on helping students learn to function in English-only classrooms. As noted earlier, critics of ESL instruction often charge that students are unable to keep up with their mainstream peers because they are pulled out of their content area classes and taught by teachers who emphasize English acquisition over subject matter learning. In Ms. Menzel's classroom, this does not seem to be entirely the case. In her class, at least as illustrated in the sample lesson using e-texts, students learned science vocabulary at the same time that they practiced English comparisons (slow, slower, and slowest). In some ways, Ms. Menzel's class is more like a sheltered English classroom than a traditional ESL class.

Technology Tip

▼▼

To find out more about e-texts and literacy development among ELLs, read the full report of the study that involved Ms. Menzel's class by Meskill, Mossop, and Bates (2000) at http://cela.albany.edu.

With their emphasis on preparing ELLs to function in English-only environments, ESL and sheltered English classrooms are considered by some educators as being the only viable means for reaching large numbers of second-language learners. For example, according to Cummins (1994), "upwards of five years may be required for students to reach a level of academic proficiency in English comparable to their native-English-speaking peers" (p. 40). This fact alone calls for long-term commitment to academic support in the second language (English).

Russian psychologist Lev Vygotsky's (1978) notion of the zone of proximal development (ZPD) is helpful in planning for this kind of support because it envisions ESL instruction as scaffolding—a temporary prop that helps move students from what they know (their native language) to what they need to know (English). Stated in more technical terms, the ZPD is the distance between a speaker's ability to handle English without guidance and his or her level of potential development under the guidance of more English-fluent adults or peers. The ZPD takes on added significance when one considers that ESL learners often experience "a pattern of insecurity or ambivalence about the value of their own cultural identity as a result of their interactions with the dominant group" (Cummins, 1994, p. 45). Teachers who plan instruction with the ZPD in mind increase their chances of helping students learn to use elements of their own culture to understand those of the dominant culture.

CULTURALLY RESPONSIVE PROFESSIONAL GROWTH

Appreciating Diversity

Allan Neilsen (1991) made the interesting observation that "while we often talk about differentiated curriculum and instruction for younger learners, we tend to act as though teachers, as learners, are 'all grown up' and all the same" (p. 67). That such is not the case is clearly the message Irvine (1990) hoped to get across when she wrote

> Teacher education appears to be suspended in a serious time warp, training future educators in the pedagogy of decades past and pretending that . . . graduates will teach . . . highly motivated, achievement-oriented . . . middle-class students from two-parent families. . . . By the Year 2010, 38 percent of all

children will come from a minority group. Demographic data confirm that working mothers, poor single mothers, teenage mothers, declining fertility rates among white middle-class women, increasing fertility rates among poor minority women, the influx of immigrants, and the growing underclass will dramatically change how we will administer schools and teach students.

Teacher education professionals must hastily respond to this problem of the growing, at-risk, minority student population, decreasing minority teacher pools, and increasing numbers of majority teacher education students. The profession must respond with the expectation that, at least in the near future, the majority of minority students' teachers will be white females who are unfamiliar with minority students' language, lifestyle, culture, family, and community. (p. 18)

Synchronizing professional growth opportunities so that they take into account the ever-widening gap between the number of minority students enrolled in school and the number of minority teachers available to instruct them in content literacy is a complex task. It involves educating all teachers—minority and nonminority—in a manner that helps them to understand the central role of culture in their lives and the lives of their students. Architects of such professional growth opportunities, Ladson-Billings (1994) argues, must ensure that teachers come away with more than a "foods-and-festivals" approach to understanding culture. She also maintains that it is foolhardy for any group to believe that "culture is what other people have; what we have is just *truth*."

Creating safe environments that foster classroom appreciation of diversity does not mean engaging in "neutral" discussions in which feelings of conflict or issues of power are submerged in teachers' and students' making-nice talk. On the contrary, according to Henzer and Hauser (1999), such issues can (and should) be raised. They offer the following strategies for engaging in this kind of talk:

In order to foster discussion about issues such as conflict or power, along with less emotionally charged topics relating to cultural values and practices, teachers need to establish an environment in which students feel comfortable expressing their views. Several strategies can be employed. For example, teachers can validate the knowledge of students at the outset through an activity where they create shared understandings of topics to be addressed, such as culture or ethnicity [see Give One/Get One handout in Figure 2.2]. Teachers can use self-disclosure as a way to humanize themselves and model the process of honest reflection. Another way in which many teachers establish safe conditions for dialogue is by setting up ground rules at the outset. For example, the class might agree that no individuals should dominate the conversation, that students have a right to pass if they do not want to share certain things about themselves, and that the opinions of others should be respected even if they disagree. (p. 3)

Involving Parents and Community

Synchronizing professional growth opportunities so that they focus on culturally responsive teaching strategies includes recognizing the need to develop parent and community partnerships in secondary literacy learning. In the past, a

---

Give One/Get One: Sample handout

A. Write (or draw) by yourself for _____ minutes putting down three answers to the following question:

What do you think of when you hear the term "culture"?

1. _____

2. _____

3. _____

B. Now get up and walk around. Give an idea from your list to another person—preferably someone you don't know very well—and get an idea from that person's list to add to your own. Write down the other person's name next to his or her idea. You have _____ minutes.

1. _____

2. _____

3. _____

FIGURE 2.2   **Give one/get one: sample handout**   (*Source:* Adapted with permission from R. C. Henze & M. E. Hausser (1999). *Personalizing culture through anthropological and educational perspectives,* Educational Practice Report No. 4, p. 24. Santa Cruz, CA: Center for Research on Education, Diversity and Excellence.)

deficit model of home–school relations assumed inappropriately that schools needed to exert a good deal of influence on certain low-income parents' literate interactions with their children in order to "make up" for perceived inadequacies in the home. This manner of thinking has largely given way to one of mutual understanding in which each party (parents and teachers) develops an awareness of the other's specific cultural practices. As Cairney (2000) noted, "In this way schooling can be adjusted to meet the needs of families. Parents, in turn, can also be given the opportunity to observe and understand the definitions of literacy that schools support" (p. 59).

With this change in focus has come an increased appreciation of intergenerational literacy programs (Gadsden, 2000), which are rich with implications for culturally responsive teaching if we pay attention to what we can learn from them as teachers. There is also room in this new reciprocal way of thinking about home–school partnerships for students to see their cultures reflected in a positive light through both the school curriculum and culturally responsive teaching. In short, no longer is it necessary for students to endure what Rosalinda Barrera refers to as the "culturalectomies" that children of her generation experienced growing up under the deficit model of home–school relations (Jimenez et al., 1999, p. 217).

However, we do recognize that communicating with parents representing a culture different from one's own can present challenges at times. For example, we are reminded of a research study that Lee Gunderson (2000) conducted in which he interviewed teenagers from various immigrant groups (refugees, landed immigrants, and entrepreneurs). What he learned about himself as a culturally responsive educator, in the process of doing this study, is worth repeating here because it illustrates what all of us—firmly established citizens and newly landed immigrants alike—share in our background of experiences. In Gunderson's words,

> I am an immigrant, a Norwegian-American-Canadian. Like millions of native English-speaking individuals in Australia, Canada, New Zealand, and the United States, my parents' first culture and language, in my case Norwegian, has withered away. . . . First- and second-generation immigrants remember their struggles learning a new language and a new culture. Most often, however, they are convinced that their losses were a consequence of their heroic or pioneer-like efforts to forge new lives for themselves and their families. They view their losses as part of the price they have paid to become members of a new society. Their willingness to sacrifice signifies in their minds their dedication to family and to the democratic ideals of their new country. They are members of the most recognizable diasporas. . . . The individuals of the third, fourth, and fifth generations are the lost ones whose first cultures like unsettled spirits haunt their angst-filled reveries. Becoming an American, an Australian, or a Canadian means the surrender of first languages and first cultures. Children and grandchildren have little sense of what has been lost.
>
> Perhaps in recognizing this loss in our own lives, we will be one step further along the path to becoming culturally responsive educators. At the very least, we will have stopped a moment to consider what it might be like to walk in the shoes of the adolescents who come to our classes each day speaking a different language, holding on to cultural practices that still make sense to them, and wishing for a teacher or two who will understand all of this. (p. 693)

SUMMARY

Envisioning language as social practice opens the door to new ways of thinking about content literacy teaching and learning in culturally diverse classrooms. With this envisioning comes an awareness of students' different ways of dialoguing with the world. Listening to students' views, and especially to the views of those who come from linguistic and ethnic minority backgrounds, can provide important clues about what is valued or devalued in the curriculum and why (Nieto, 1994). Just as the sorting practices of the school present their own special set of challenges, so too do the demographic changes in the U.S. student population. Experts predict that by 2008, the secondary education population will have increased 16 percent over what it was at the turn of the century (U.S. Department of Education, 1998). The makeup of that population is also expected to change. Unlike the two-thirds white (non-Hispanic) majority in our schools today, by 2010, approximately 4 of every 10 students in grades kindergarten through 12 will represent minority groups (Hodgkinson, 1992; Hoffman, 1999). At the same time, the number of minority teachers is expected to decline. These trends point to the need for all teachers to sharpen their instructional skills in the area of integrating language, content, and culture.

SUGGESTED READINGS

Bernhardt, E. (2000). Second-language reading as a case study of reading scholarship in the 20th century. In M. L. Kamil, P. Mosenthal, P. D. Pearson, & R. Barr (Eds.), *Handbook of reading research: Vol. 3* (pp. 791–811). Mahwah, NJ: Erlbaum.

Davies, B. (1993). *Shards of glass: Children reading and writing beyond gendered identities.* Cresskill, NJ: Hampton Press.

de la Luz Reyes, M., & Molner, L. A. (1991). Instructional strategies for second-language learners in the content areas. *Journal of Reading, 35,* 96–103.

Finders, M. (1997). *Just girls: Hidden literacies and life in junior high.* New York: Teachers College Press.

Garcia, G. (2000). Bilingual children's reading. In M. L. Kamil, P. Mosenthal, P. D. Pearson, & R. Barr (Eds.), *Handbook of reading research: Vol. 3* (pp. 813–834). Mahwah, NJ: Erlbaum.

Godina, H. (1999). High school students of Mexican background in the midwest: Cultural differences as a constraint to effective literacy instruction. In T. Shanahan & F. V. Rodriguez-Brown (Eds.), *48th Yearbook of the National Reading Conference* (pp. 266–279). Chicago: National Reading Conference.

Rickford, J., & Rickford, A. (1995). Dialect readers revisited. *Linguistics and Education, 7,* 107–128.

Creating a Favorable
Learning Environment

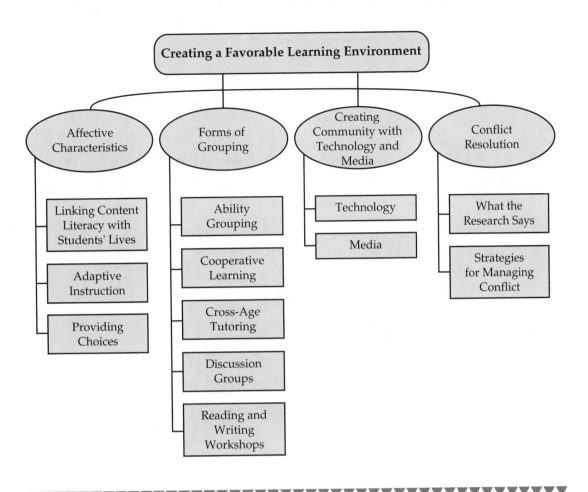

Creating a Favorable Learning Environment

- Affective Characteristics
  - Linking Content Literacy with Students' Lives
  - Adaptive Instruction
  - Providing Choices
- Forms of Grouping
  - Ability Grouping
  - Cooperative Learning
  - Cross-Age Tutoring
  - Discussion Groups
  - Reading and Writing Workshops
- Creating Community with Technology and Media
  - Technology
  - Media
- Conflict Resolution
  - What the Research Says
  - Strategies for Managing Conflict

▼▼

Creating a favorable learning environment involves generating contexts in which teachers and students are free to interact. Often this environment is informed by "those small moments in learning" that come to each of us but that at the time may seem insignificant, as in the following example:

▼▼▼▼▼▼▼

When I sense that the ways of learning are too mysterious in my classroom, I often find myself looking back on my own education. Such reminiscing always reminds me that in teaching and learning "big things often come in small packages." It also tells me that I neither learned everything that was presented to me nor fully understood what I had learned. Thus, my remembrances are not of whole books or papers, but rather of bits and pieces of my education. I realize that much of my learning has been in slivers and slices. I call these the small moments in learning. These are times that, like the light of the firefly, are experienced for only a short while. They come and go, and it is impossible to tell when they will appear, disappear, or reappear.

Once in graduate school, I was sitting in my class on adolescent psychology when some children were heard running through the outside hallway. A student in the first row rose to close the door, but the professor motioned for her to sit down. The professor then proceeded to make a point about the children and the student trying to shut the hallway door, instead of continuing with his lecture as I thought he would. He said that the children were only being children and that the noise would go away. It did. He then observed that educators . . . too often . . . [feel] that they must control and manipulate all situations involving children. He argued that this is a mistake, because if more adults would allow children to solve their own affairs, the children would learn to be more independent. . . . This whole little incident lasted all of 90 seconds and was highly unexpected, but I will always remember it.

Another time, in another graduate school course on the teaching of reading, the professor stopped . . . and told us about a television show in which a doctor explained that he used x-rays to confirm or disprove his predictions about a patient's condition. The professor used this story to argue that teachers need to use their own observations about a student's reading ability before passing judgment based on a standardized test. This was another off-the-cuff moment that was set off from the normal and expected flow of the class.

When I was a student teacher, I asked one of my students to read her paper out loud for the class to hear. As she started to read, I moved across the room to close the door. Afterwards, my supervising teacher told me that when I ask a student to read out loud, I should listen attentively. Otherwise, turning my back and moving away may unconsciously give the student and the class the message that I do not value what is being read. Ever since this small incident, I never move away when I ask a student to read out loud.

These few small moments of learning are sprinkled throughout my education. For both teacher and student, they are incidents and situations that cannot be predicted or planned. They will pop up as a surprise, as a treat, when one least expects it. . . . They are the odd and quirky moments that spin off from a teacher's love of the moment and willingness to improvise, to go on a hunch, to take a risk, to deviate a little, to go with one's teaching intuition. For the student, such moments are . . . short and concise and have a certain pithiness of language. They are quickly absorbed and, being pocket-sized, are easily carried away. They can be hidden in the cracks and crevices of one's education and brought out for reference as one needs them.*

▼▼▼▼▼▼

Can you recall any "small moments in learning"? What were they? Were they connected to your current class? To your own past teaching and learning experiences? In this chapter on creating a favorable learning environment, we

---

*Meier, D. "Learning in Small Moments," *Harvard Educational Review, 56,* 298–300. Copyright © 1986 by the President and Fellows of Harvard College. All rights reserved.

may instigate some "small moments of learning" in the affective practices we examine, in the close look we take at tracking and alternative forms of grouping, and in the issues we raise about technology and conflict resolution. Practically speaking, though, we realize that small moments of learning are more likely to occur when one is actually involved in working with students or in reflecting on one's own past teaching and learning experiences. Consequently, you should read this chapter with your classroom experiences in mind.

AFFECTIVE CHARACTERISTICS

A favorable learning environment supports students as they grapple with issues of affect that influence how they feel about school and their willingness to engage in academic activities. Affective characteristics of instruction that concern teachers in this kind of environment include those of linking content literacy with students' lives and providing students with choices. In advocating that classrooms become places in which the integration of heart, head, voice, and hand is the norm rather than the exception, Shelby Wolf and colleagues (Wolf, Edmiston, & Enciso, 1997) remind us of the need to teach in a manner that joins the different domains of knowing. As Vygotsky (1986) has written,

> Thought is not begotten by thought; it is engendered by motivation, i.e., by our desires and needs, our interests and emotions. Behind every thought there is an affective-volitional tendency, which holds the answer to the last "why" in the analysis of thinking. A true and full understanding of another's thought is possible only when we understand its affective-volitional basis. (p. 252)

We know, from our own experiences as teachers, the validity of Vygotsky's thinking. Time and time again, we have learned to rely on the affective currents in our classrooms as guideposts to what is possible in the cognitive domain. Working hard not to separate the cognitive from the affective is a way of life. It is an approach to teaching that we find both challenging and rewarding.

Linking Content Literacy with Students' Lives

The learning cycle.   Creating a favorable learning environment, to our way of thinking, should involve helping students link content literacy learning to their own lives. One way of assisting them in this process is to think of learning as being "controlled as much by experiences students bring to the learning situation as it is by the way the information is presented" (Marshall, 1996, p. 81). This view of learning, which Marshall calls *the learning cycle* (Figure 3.1), rests on the notion that students' earlier learning experiences tend to dictate in large part their attitude and willingness to engage in new learning.

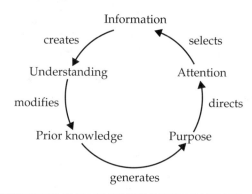

FIGURE 3.1   The learning cycle   (*Source:* N. Marshall (1996). The Students: Who are they and how do I reach them? In D. Lapp, J. Flood, & N. Farnan (Eds.), *Content area reading and learning,* p. 82.) Copyright 1982 by Allyn and Bacon. Reprinted by permission.

Like the schema-theoretic view of the reading process described in Chapter 1, the learning cycle is heavily dependent on prior knowledge. In Marshall's (1996) words,

> To understand [the learning cycle], it is easiest to begin with *prior knowledge.* Since all new learning is based on existing knowledge, the previous experiences of the students are central to the complete cycle. Furthermore, prior knowledge helps [generate] reasons for learning or not learning. Depending on *purpose* for learning, attention is directed differently. . . . *Attention* is limited; we cannot pay attention to everything in a new situation. For learning to be efficient, therefore, attention must be directed to the most important *information.* Once the information is encountered, it needs to be *understood.* . . . Finally, to be able to use new information as the basis of subsequent learning, students must use the new understanding to *modify* existing knowledge. (p. 82)

We see the learning cycle as a useful heuristic for thinking about ways to link content literacy with students' lives. First, it suggests that teachers need to take students' prior knowledge into account when planning their instruction—a theme that is central to Chapter 4. Second, it implies that students will have their own purposes for engaging in (or avoiding) certain learning activities. A closer look at the learning cycle suggests that teaching and learning are not simply mirror processes. As Wenger (1998) pointed out, instruction itself does not cause learning; instead, it creates the conditions and context in which learning can take place:

> Learning and teaching are not inherently linked. Much learning takes place without teaching, and indeed much teaching takes place without learning. To

the extent that teaching and learning are linked in practice, the linkage is one not of cause and effect but of resources and negotiation. . . . Learning is an emergent, ongoing process, which may use teaching as one of its many structuring resources. In this regard, teachers and instructional materials become resources for learning in much more complex ways than through their pedagogical intentions. (pp. 266–267)

We like to think of teachers and instructional materials as offering opportunities for engagement in learning. Thought of in this way, teaching involves creating a favorable learning environment, one in which students become invested in their own learning. Moreover, in this kind of environment, it is often the case that the things students learn extend beyond what the teacher is hired to teach. Such learning is sometimes referred to as "stolen knowledge" (Brown & Duguid, 1996, p. 49). In other words, a literate environment contains the resources and opportunities students need to participate in a community of learners who are legitimately free to "steal" the knowledge they need to make sense of the content and social practices they are expected to acquire. As Brown and Duguid explain, the need to steal knowledge arises from the fact that "relatively little of the complex web of actual practice [in this case, content literacy learning] can be made the subject of explicit instruction" (p. 50). Much remains implicit, where it is always available to be stolen as needed.

A strategy for linking content literacy to students' lives.   Short warm-up activities can demonstrate to students the usefulness of determining what they know and do not know about a certain topic prior to reading about it. Such activities also can shed light on how willing (or unwilling) students may be to engage in learning about the topic. For example, a strategy called Creative Thinking–Reading Activities (CT-RA) (Ruddell, 1996), which takes no more than 10 or 15 minutes to complete, offers students a chance to brainstorm solutions to the topic at hand using their everyday knowledge. This kind of activity rewards students for using ideas from their practical store of knowledge to solve textbook-related problems. The CT-RA includes the following steps (Ruddell, 1996, p. 103):

1. Develop with students the rules for brainstorming:
    a. Think of as many ideas as you can.
    b. No criticism of any ideas—even your own.
    c. Go for any freewheeling thought—the wilder the idea the better.
    d. Build on others' ideas and combine ideas when you can.
2. Give students the creative thinking task (only one) and allow five minutes for brainstorming. For example, a task might be to estimate the amount of industrial toxins that seep into their local waterways or reservoir.
3. Share ideas in large group.
4. Announce single criterion for students to evaluate and select an answer; for example, "Which of [the solutions to the problem] do you think is the wildest?"
5. Share these responses.

We like the CT-RA strategy because it provides spaces for ESL students and students who are less academically inclined to contribute their ideas—ideas that might otherwise be overlooked or dismissed. We also like it because we have observed students asking their peers for clarification in the small-group brainstorming portion of the strategy. According to Canales (1996), "asking questions for clarification is particularly critical for ESL students" (p. 7).

Teaching and learning subject matter in culturally diverse classrooms places special demands on teachers and students. Because there is a potential for misunderstandings among young adolescents to lead to feelings of alienation and lowered self-esteem, it is important to help them find ways of communicating effectively and in a free and open manner (Carnegie Council on Adolescent Development, 1996). We think the CT-RA strategy is a step in the right direction. Conflict resolution is also useful in creating a favorable learning environment. Strategies for building positive classroom attitudes by helping students work through some of their communicative differences can be found in the section on conflict resolution.

Adaptive Instruction

Creating a favorable learning environment in which students learn to respect and listen to each other is without doubt much easier to write about than to do. As Linda Christensen (1994), an English teacher at Jefferson High School in Portland, Oregon, notes,

> A sign in our hallway reads: No Racist or Sexist Remarks. I've often said, "I just don't tolerate that kind of behavior." But this year, it was like saying, "I don't tolerate ants." I have ants in my kitchen. I can spray chemicals on them and saturate the air with poison and "not tolerate" them, or I can find another solution that doesn't harm my family or pets in the process. If I just kick kids out of class, I "don't tolerate" their actions, but neither do I educate them or their classmates. And it works about as well as stamping out a few ants. I prepare them for repressive solutions where misbehavior is temporarily contained by an outside authority, not really addressed. Sometimes, I am forced to that position, but I try not to be. (p. 56)

We know that in the role of teacher one's tolerance level is sometimes exceeded. While not a panacea in such instances, letting students know that you expect them to assume greater responsibility for their own learning may stave off needless challenges to your authority as the teacher.

Teaching students how to assume responsibility for their own learning involves adapting one's instruction to fit the needs of various types of learners. Adaptive instruction is particularly germane to teaching students who are members of special populations, such as ESL students, gifted students, slower learners, and students with learning disabilities. As defined by Corno and Snow (1986), adaptive teaching is student-centered:

> [It] arranges environmental conditions to fit learners' individual differences. As learners gain in aptitude through experience with respect to the instructional

goals at hand, such teaching adapts by becoming less intrusive. Less intrusion, less teacher or instructional mediation, increases the . . . need for more learner self-regulation. (p. 621)

Generally, adaptive instruction follows five principles (Strother, 1985):

1. Students should receive instruction based on their assessed capabilities, not their weaknesses.
2. Materials and methods should be chosen on the basis of flexibility and appeal to students' interests.
3. Students should play an active role in setting goals and evaluating their progress toward those goals.
4. Alternative activities and materials should be available for students who require additional assistance.
5. Cooperative, rather than competitive, approaches to learning should be stressed.

As you proceed through this book, you will find numerous suggestions that take into account the five principles just listed. You will also find opportunities to adapt the strategies presented here so that they have practical application in your own classroom.

Providing Choices

Students find that being provided with choices, such as having a say in what they learn, adds to their willingness to cooperate in the schooling process. For example, Penny Oldfather and Sally Thomas (1996) found in their longitudinal study of Sally's fifth-grade class that students appreciate being involved in their own education, as do Kyle Gonzalez's students at Lakeview Middle School in Florida (Allen & Gonzalez, 1998). However, before she began teaching, Gonzalez says she tended to look at student choice as a surefire way to undermine authority in the classroom—a view she no longer holds. According to Gonzalez,

It all boils down to trust. The students have to trust me, and I have to trust them to make good choices. I also have to trust my ability to guide their decisions so that we can live with the choices they make. (p. 24)

Lynn Rhodes and Nancy Shanklin (1993), two experts in assessing literacy learning in grades K–8, say that providing students with choices in materials, activities, and time lines for finishing an assignment increases a teacher's chance of communicating genuine purposes for reading and writing. Rhodes and Shanklin also recommend that teachers follow students' leads whenever possible. Sometimes these leads are more subtle than direct, but when teachers pick up on them, they demonstrate a willingness to meet the student halfway.

Providing choices can extend to the kinds of questions teachers are willing to entertain. This is an area of particular interest to us. In our multicase study of five school sites throughout the United States, we were well aware of the questions that students and teachers considered "safe" to ask (Alvermann et al., 1996). We are uncomfortable with this kind of self-censoring behavior. We also found evidence in our research that supports Kathe Jervis's (1996) observation that "even in schools which seek to create diverse and integrated school communities, silence about race prevails" (p. 546). A willingness to hear the hard questions that children ask, Jervis argues, is basic to exploring issues of discrimination and equity.

Self-censorship of these hard questions leads to what Dwight Boyd (1996) calls the " 'munch, stomp, and dress up' view of multiculturalism" (p. 612). That is, when students and teachers limit themselves to asking safe questions, they are left with a superficial approach to understanding differences—one that leads to discussing a culture's food, dance, and clothing style preferences rather than its moral values and beliefs. In moving away from so-called safe discussions, teachers would provide students with choices regarding what is talked about in the curriculum. Given the litigious nature of our society, it is not a move that we expect to see in the near future. However, we agree with Jervis and Boyd that in failing to address the hard questions students might ask, we limit our ability to understand how they see the world. In turn, this places a limitation on the success that might be had in creating open and viable learning environments.

Professional Growth and the Learning Environment

To keep up with new developments in creating favorable learning environments for today's culturally diverse classrooms, content literacy teachers often take advantage of one or more types of professional growth opportunities. For example, they may elect to attend local miniconferences or the large annual conferences sponsored by the major organizations for literacy practitioners, such as the International Reading Association and the National Council of Teachers of English. Organizers of these conferences, whose programs offer a wide range of topics related to content teaching and learning, often fly in literacy experts from great distances to speak to teachers.

One such expert, Lorri Neilsen (1991), thinks of this type of arrangement as the "parachute model" of professional growth. In her words, the parachute model conjures up several clichés, one of which is "an image of the teacher as stoic survivor, in a remote community known as the classroom, consumed with the challenges of children and learning, waiting patiently for—and gratefully accepting—the periodic arrival of intellectual supplies parachuted in from the civilized world" (p. 65). Although this model offers expertise, we, like Neilsen, believe it must be supplemented by approaches that involve teachers in personal exploration, in which knowledge can be homegrown and shared locally through loosely knit professional alliances—for example, through informal teacher study groups, writing groups, mentoring programs, and professional development schools staffed by school and university personnel whose mission is to refine their own teaching practices through inquiry.

FORMS OF GROUPING

Tracking is but one, though still very common, way of grouping students for instruction at the middle and high school level. A system for deciding who should learn what and at what pace, tracking remains a controversial issue in the United States. Despite legal attempts to end or limit the amount of tracking in secondary schools, it is a system that has proven "extraordinarily resilient and resistant to change" (Welner & Oakes, 1996, p. 466). Nonetheless, in many reform-oriented school districts throughout the country, alternative forms of grouping, such as cooperative learning groups, cross-age tutoring, small-group discussions, and reading and writing workshops, are gaining in popularity.

Ability Grouping

In general, schools group students for instruction according to one of three types of tracking: curriculum, ability-group, or within-class. *Curriculum tracking* involves scheduling students' courses so that they follow a particular sequence and prepare students for life after high school. This gives rise to the familiar college preparatory, general, and vocational tracks of secondary schools.

Ability-group tracking, or between-class grouping, involves assigning students to a particular class section (such as history honors or general math) based on their past performance in that subject area. Such grouping is intended to reduce the heterogeneity of an instructional group and thus make the teacher's job more manageable. At the high school level, ability-group tracking is often synonymous with curriculum tracking. A special kind of tracking, called block scheduling, is found in some schools and consists of homogeneously grouping students for a large block of time each day.

Within-class grouping, which is more common at the elementary level than at the middle and secondary levels, consists of separating students into smaller instructional groups once they have been assigned to a particular class; for example, an English teacher might do within-class grouping to accommodate differences in students' reading or writing abilities (Glatthorn, 1991).

Arguments for.   Traditionally, those who favor ability-group tracking do so on the grounds that it affords teachers the opportunity to adapt their instruction in a way that challenges the faster learner and supports the slower learner. Proponents say that high-ability students become bored with schooling when the pace of instruction is slowed down to accommodate less able students. According to Feldhusen (1989), "grouping gifted and talented youth for at least part of the school day and offering a differentiated curriculum leads to higher achievement, engenders better attitudes and motivation, and does no harm to less able youth" (p. 4).

Arguments against. Those who argue against tracking by ability point to differences in (1) the type and quantity of knowledge high- and low-track students acquire, (2) the quality of teaching they receive, (3) the learning environments of the classrooms in which they are expected to spend six or more hours each day, and (4) their attitudes (Oakes, 1985). Hargreaves (1967) concluded that higher-track students feel more positively toward school than lower-track students do, partly because they are exposed to more competent teachers and teachers with better attitudes. Reading practices also seem to vary according to tracks, with higher-track students receiving instruction that allows them to exercise critical thinking skills and lower-track students being held more to factual recall.

A Response from Our Readers

▼▼▼

Abel Hernandez, a student in one of Professor Josephine Young's content literacy classes at Arizona State University, wrote the following reflection after reading the section on the pros and cons of ability grouping in the second edition of our text, *Content Reading and Literacy: Succeeding in Today's Diverse Schools*. With Mr. Hernandez's permission, we quote from his written reflection:

> As an affected member of a minority group who was impressed upon at an early age the effects of grouping, my feelings on this issue run deep. When I was in grades first through sixth I attended a segregated school that consisted of Hispanics/Mexicans. I was happy at that school and really did not mind being in such a school. It was not until I moved from Texas to Arizona that I began to appreciate the blatant discrimination that I had experienced as a child.
>
> Upon transferring, I, as well as the rest of my family, met with the principal of the [new] school. He strongly advised, encouraged, and suggested that I be placed in the special education classes at the school until the administration determined what level of education I had. My sister vehemently dis-

> agreed and informed the teacher that if I was placed in a special education class she would have no problem with filing a lawsuit against the school on the theory of alleged bias and discrimination because of my ethnicity.
>
> During my first day in class I happened to meet the special education students, and what a coincidence that all of them were Hispanics. To this day, I find it amazing the effects that tracking and grouping had on those children's lives. I can imagine what effect this would have had on me had my sister not championed my right to an education based on equal opportunity and not on my ethnicity or similarity to others like me.
>
> I believe there is a place for tracking and grouping but when it is done solely based on the color of one's skin, then it becomes intolerable. Grouping for the sake of the students' education is commendable, but when it is done for the convenience of the school, that is when the line has to be drawn.*

*Courtesy of Abel Hernandez.

Cooperative Learning

In cooperative-learning groups, students work together in small groups (of four or five individuals) to set goals and to learn from one another, with the incentive being a group reward for combined individual efforts. "The principal idea behind cooperative learning methods is that by rewarding groups as well as individuals for their academic achievement, peer norms will come to favor rather than oppose high achievement" (Slavin, 1984a, p. 54).

In cooperative-learning groups, students come to rely less on the teacher and more on one another. Acting as peer tutors, they learn more because they are actively engaged with the text or other instructional materials. Slavin (1984b) demonstrated the value of cooperative learning in culturally diverse classrooms and with students who have disabilities that could potentially interfere with their learning. By engaging students in cooperative learning, teachers set the stage for acceptance of diversity and valuing of individual contributions. Linguistically diverse students are known to benefit from cooperative learning because they become more actively involved and spend more time in meaningful exchanges with their peers than they otherwise would (Reyes & Molner, 1991).

Three widely used cooperative-learning techniques developed by Slavin and colleagues at the Johns Hopkins Center for Social Organization of Schools are Student Teams–Achievement Divisions (STAD), Teams–Games–Tournament (TGT), and Jigsaw II. As indicated in Figure 3.2, the three techniques share certain features: there are four or five members to a team, and each team is heterogeneously grouped according to ability, gender, ethnicity, and race. The three cooperative learning techniques are described by Lehr (1984) as follows:

> In STAD . . . team members study worksheets on material that the teacher has presented through lecture or discussion. Students may use any means of mastering the material, and they are given answer sheets so that it is clear that they are to master concepts, not merely fill in blanks on the sheet. They are told to study until all team members understand the subject. The students are quizzed individually, and the team's overall score is determined by the extent to which each student improved his or her performance over past efforts. A base score is set 5 points below each student's average, and [students] earn points up to a maximum of 10 for each point that exceeds their base score. This system allows low-performing students to contribute maximum points to the team by showing improvement or completing a perfect paper. Teams with the highest scores are recognized weekly in a class newspaper, as are students who exceed their own past records.
>
> The same procedures are used in TGT. However, rather than taking quizzes, students play academic games with other class members with similar past performance records. In preparation for the tournaments, which are held once or twice a week, teams hold regular practices when teammates help each other review skills taught by the teacher. Each student is then assigned to a tournament table to compete with representatives of two other teams with similar performance records. At the end of each game, the players at each table compare their

Student Teams-Achievement Divisions	Teams-Games-Tournament	Jigsaw II
TEACH	**TEACH**	**TEXT**
TEAM STUDY	**TEAM STUDY**	**TALK**
		TEAM REPORT
TEST	**TOURNAMENT**	**TEST**
TEAM RECOGNITION	**TEAM RECOGNITION**	**TEAM RECOGNITION**

FIGURE 3.2   Basic schedule of activities for STAD, TGT, and Jigsaw II   (*Source:* From R. E. Slavin, *Student Team Learning: A Practical Guide to Cooperative Learning,* © 1991, National Education Association. Reprinted with permission.)

scores to determine the top, middle, and low scorers at the various tables. Top scorers receive 6 points, middle scorers 4, and low scorers 2. Team scores are determined by adding the results for teammates, and these scores are then added to previous game scores in the tournament for a cumulative score. The games involve answering questions presented on cards or sheets and pertaining to the subject being studied. As in STAD, high-scoring teams and tournament winners receive recognition in a weekly class newspaper.

As originally developed by Aronson and his colleagues at the University of California, Santa Cruz, Jigsaw involves teams of five or six members, each of whom is given one segment of the day's lesson and made responsible for teaching it to others. Students who get the same segment meet in counterpart groups to help each other work out the best ways of teaching it and to anticipate the kinds of questions they might have to answer. Since the only way students can gain information about lesson segments other than their own is to listen to their teammates, the Jigsaw technique also becomes a method for enhancing listening and questioning skills. In Jigsaw II, a modification, students work in four- to five-member teams. Instead of receiving different lesson segments, all read a common text from which each is given a topic on which to become an expert. Students with the same topics meet, discuss, and return to their teams to teach what they have learned. After this, the entire class is quizzed for individual and team scores, as in STAD.*

Cooperative learning of a more informal nature than that prescribed in STAD, TGT, and Jigsaw II is generally defined as any collaborative act that involves two or more students working together to accomplish specific pedagogical tasks (Gumperz, Cook-Gumperz, & Szymanski, 1999). This type of grouping arrangement, when used in conjunction with content literacy instruction, has been found to be a highly effective means for improving students' understanding of academic subject matter (National Reading Panel, 2000). For example, Heather Thomas (1999) describes a tenth-grade biology class in which the teacher made extensive use of cooperative learning groups. In these groups, students helped each other complete various tasks at workstations throughout the room while "talking science" (Lemke, 1990)—that is, while using scientific vocabulary to formulate and test task-related hypotheses. Cooperative learning groups, as described by Thomas (1999) and others (Anderson, 1992; Gumperz, Cook-Gumperz, & Szymanski, 1999), also challenge students to think deeply about academic content, to draw on each other's prior knowledge, and to engage actively in learning communities composed of their peers.

Cross-Age Tutoring

The middle grades, in particular, lend themselves to the use of cross-age tutoring because of the school-within-a-school concept that most restructured middle schools espouse. The physical setting and the emphasis on the concept of

---

*Lehr, F. (1984). ERIC/RCS: Cooperative learning. *Journal of Reading, 27*(5), 458–461. Reprinted with permission of the International Reading Association.

community within the middle school support older students' teaching younger students to deal with their assignments. As the authors of *Turning Points* (Carnegie Council on Adolescent Development, 1989) note,

> Cross-age tutoring could take place . . . during the part of the day reserved for activities outside the core instructional program for younger and older students. Cross-age tutoring has shown consistent positive effects on achievement outcomes for both tutors and tutees. Tutors encounter opportunities to review basic skills without embarrassment, gain experience in applying academic abilities, and develop insight into the process of teaching and learning. Tutees receive individualized instruction and work with positive role models. (p. 52)

Cross-age tutoring differs from cooperative learning on several counts. First, cross-age tutoring usually occurs in dyads as opposed to small groups of four or five members. Second, cross-age tutoring is characterized by the transfer of very specific information and usually involves some form of basic skills practice, whereas cooperative learning tends to focus on higher-order thinking. Third, cross-age tutoring focuses on rewarding the individual, whereas cooperative learning rewards the group (although, certainly, individuals are also rewarded as members of the group) (Indrisano & Paratore, 1991).

Guidelines from the research on cross-age tutoring offer insights on how to pair the student partners. Generally, these guidelines hold for peer tutoring as well—that is, for partners who are approximately the same age but with varying achievement levels (Rekrut, 1994).

1. The age level of the tutor and learner may vary depending on the situation. Although older, more accomplished students typically serve as the tutors, they may not always be superior achievers. For example, we know of instances in which low-achieving high school students have served as successful tutors to struggling readers at the elementary level.
2. Same-sex pairs are preferable, but if such pairings are impossible, research has shown that older girls can successfully tutor younger boys.
3. Tutors need to be taught to work with their partners without making value judgments.
4. Post-tutoring debriefings should be ongoing and should give attention to both content and process skills.
5. Affective objectives, such as self-confidence and self-esteem building, are as important in cross-age tutoring as concept mastery and skill reinforcement.

Discussion Groups

As teachers we have always valued classroom discussion as a means for enriching and refining students' understandings. Recently, we had the opportunity to learn how students feel about this form of classroom communication. Findings from a multicase study involving adolescents at five culturally diverse sites throughout the United States (Alvermann et al., 1996) indicate that students perceive discussions as helping them understand what they read. They know what they like and dislike about large- and small-group discussions; they also know how various topics and tasks influence their participation. In sum, students told us that classroom discussions provide them with opportunities for testing their own ideas while learning to respect the ideas of others.

Definitions of discussion.   Multiple definitions exist for what discussion is or should be, but we prefer one developed largely from David Bridges's work with classroom teachers in Cambridge, UK:

1. Discussants should put forth multiple points of view and stand ready to change their minds about the matter under discussion.
2. Students should interact with one another as well as with the teacher.
3. Interactions should exceed the typical two- or three-word phrases common to recitation lessons. (Alvermann, Dillon, & O'Brien, 1987, p. 7)

These three criteria are helpful in distinguishing between a true discussion and what sometimes passes as one—a recitation in disguise. Recitations are rarely more than fast-paced exchanges between teachers and students in which teachers elicit answers to a series of preplanned questions. Little room is left for the substantive exchange of ideas because the teacher's evaluation of a student's answer is the signal to move on to the next question.

ACTIVITY   Consider the following excerpt from a fictionalized account of an interaction between Lennie and his teacher in Betsy Byars's well-known book, *The TV Kid* (1976). Is it an example of a discussion or a recitation? Why do you think so?

> "Do you think he was just talking about *one* year passing?" the teacher went on. "Or do you think, Lennie, the poet was seeing his whole life as a year, that he was seeing his whole life slipping past?"
>   "I'm not sure," Lennie's hand was still on his chin as if ready to stroke a long gray beard.
>   "Class?"
>   "His whole life slipping past," the class chorused together. They had had this teacher so long that they could tell, just from the way she asked a question, what they were supposed to answer. (p. 70)

Purposes.   Small-group discussions, like whole-class discussions, should stimulate students to think for themselves rather than rely solely on their teachers or their texts for ideas. The old notion that thinking must originate within the individual before it is ready to be shared with others has given way to the belief

Technology Tip

▼▼

Discussion groups need no longer be limited to in-class interactions. Lively discussions of teen writing, including feedback to published teen writers, can be accessed through http://www.TeenLit.com. Another website designed to meet the informational, educational, and recreational needs of young adults ages 12–18 is Teen Hoopla, which is updated regularly by a division of the American Library Association. Teen Hoopla (http://www.ala.org/teenhoopla/submcrit.html) features original material created by and for adolescents. Its purpose is to provide teenagers with an opportunity to express themselves about books, reading, and other issues affecting their lives.

that some of the best thinking may result from a discussion group's collective efforts (Sternberg, 1987). In fact, there is empirical evidence to suggest that "student-led small-group discussions of nonfiction are superior to both lecture and whole-class discussion in helping students recall and understand essays . . . [and] in preparing students to write analytic, opinion essays" (Sweigart as cited in Nystrand, Gamoran, & Heck, 1992, p. 3).

Discussion groups can take many forms. Common interests, problem solving, subject mastery, and current issues are but a few of the possible foci for small-group discussion. Regardless of the focus, one thing remains constant—the need to keep in mind that as group size increases, proportionately fewer members participate. A rule of thumb is that a discussion group should consist of no more individuals than are essential for completing the task the group has taken on.

Reading and Writing Workshops

The reading and writing workshop is a form of grouping most often associated with Nancie Atwell's first edition of *In the Middle* (1987). This book is often credited with changing the way middle school language arts teachers structure their classrooms to make them more inviting as literate environments. A few high school teachers have also used the concept of reading/writing workshop to break through some of the barriers that struggling readers have constructed after experiencing years of frustration with classroom literacy activities. For example, Janet Allen (1995), working with a group of ninth-grade "basic" students—all struggling readers—in rural Maine immersed them in a year-long encounter with all types of reading materials. Through daily read alouds, independent reading and writing time (including computer access), group sharing, journaling, conferencing, portfolios, and minilessons involving strategies and

Reading/Writing Workshop and the Struggling Reader

Creating a safe environment for readers who struggle with school literacy tasks involves the following:

▸ Providing sufficient time for students to complete reading and writing activities.

▸ Building in student choice, not only in types of literacy materials and equipment available but also in types of assessments and classroom routines.

▸ Supporting students by teaching them the strategies they will need to make connec-

tions between what they know and what they are expected to learn.

▸ Having a variety of resources from which to choose: for example, young adult literature collections; class sets of paperbacks for whole-group shared reading; multiple copies of single titles for guided reading and literature circles; and access to computers and recorded, unabridged books.

skills, by the end of the year the 15 struggling readers in Janet's reading/writing workshop realized that it is never too late to experience the joy of reading.

Taking what she had learned in her own classroom from working with adolescents who either could not (or would not) read, Allen helped to launch the Orange County (FL) Literacy Project for students who were previously unsuccessful in school. This project involved setting up literacy workshop classrooms (patterned after Allen's reading and writing workshop) in several pilot schools in Orange County. The concept has since spread to all middle schools in Orange County as well as to other middle schools and high schools in Florida and beyond (Allen & Gonzalez, 1998). Although quick to point out that the reading/writing workshop is no magic formula or recipe for success in working with struggling readers (meaning that teachers must adapt, not adopt, the concept), Allen and Gonzalez describe four components of a literacy environment that are crucial to a workshop's success. (See boxed inset above).

CREATING COMMUNITY WITH TECHNOLOGY AND MEDIA

Technology, and in particular the Internet, is revolutionizing how adolescents relate to print and nonprint media. Changes are occurring rapidly in what counts as reading and writing—so much so in fact, that entire books (Cope & Kalantzis, 2000; Reinking et al., 1998; Sefton-Green, 1999), as well as research reports from major foundations (Kaiser Family Foundation, 1999), and policy documents (National Reading Report, 2000), are focused on exploring the challenges of the digital arts for young people's literacy needs. Some literacy scholars, such as the late Alan Purves (1998), have theorized how the advent of hypertext—print and nonprint texts interlinked by the mere click of a computer mouse—has led to a new relationship between reader and text. These developments strongly suggest that technology and media use in schools must be taken into account in any discussion of how to create favorable learning environments for adolescents in the twenty-first century.

Technology

According to an international study of the trends in investment in information and communication technologies (ICT) by the Centre for Educational Research and Innovation (1999), "In the United States, more is now spent on ICT in schools than on books and other printed materials" (p. 47). Teaching with technology, and especially the Internet, is now an integral part of many teachers' school days, but before examining how such instruction lends itself to creating a community of learners, it is important to take stock of some issues related to teacher and student access. As might be expected, teachers' use of computers and the Internet in school varies according to their access to such technology, and especially along the following lines: number of years of teaching experience, grade level taught, and socioeconomic level of the school in which they teach.

Teacher access and use.   In response to a national survey conducted by the National Center for Education Statistics (U.S. Department of Education, 2000), 99 percent of full-time public school teachers in the United States reported they had access to computers or the Internet in the buildings in which they taught. In terms of usage, 39 percent of those teachers indicated they used computers or the Internet "a lot" to create instructional materials, and 34 percent said they used computers "a lot" for record keeping. Less than 10 percent reported using them to download lesson plans or to access the research on best practices—a somewhat disappointing statistic, given the rich source of content literacy materials available for instructional planning on the Internet (see Chapter 4).

Teachers new to the field (i.e., those with nine or fewer years of teaching experience) were more apt to use computers or the Internet to create instructional materials (49 percent) than were teachers with 20 or more years of experience (35 percent). Secondary teachers used computers or the Internet to create instructional materials (44 percent) and keep records (47 percent) more often than did elementary teachers (37 and 29 percent, respectively). Finally, teachers who taught in schools with a low poverty level (as determined by the number of youngsters eligible for free or reduced-price lunches) were more likely to use computers or the Internet "a lot" for creating instructional materials (52 percent) than were teachers in high-poverty schools (32 percent). The same patterns held for teachers who used computers for administrative record keeping.

ACTIVITY   To derive a profile of secondary school teachers and their reported use of computers or the Internet for classroom instruction, look at Table 3.1 and then answer the following questions:

> ‣ What percent of secondary school teachers say they assign students to use the computer or Internet for word processing? For practice drills? For research using the Internet? To solve problems and analyze data? To produce multimedia reports? For demonstrations? To correspond with others?
>
> ‣ What is the relation of teacher use of computers or the Internet for practice drills and the percent of students in a school who are eligible for free or reduced-price lunches? Why might this difference exist?
>
> ‣ How does a teacher's hours of professional development in the use of computers or the Internet affect the type of assignments he or she gives students?

Student access and use.   According to the U.S. Department of Education (1999), "students from high-income families are more likely to report using a computer at home or at school than students from low-income families" (p. 1). This inequity plays out in other ways as well. Students in schools serving primarily low-income families of color also have less access to CD-ROM equipment, to multimedia software, and to videodisc technology than do students in more affluent schools (Coley, Crandler, & Engle, 1997). Inequities such as these have implications well beyond the schoolhouse door because without access to the same kinds of experiences as their wealthier classmates, students of low-income families are less likely to gain access to high-paying jobs after they graduate.

In their article titled "Teaching English across the Technology/Wealth Gap," Charles Moran and Cynthia Selfe (1999) ponder the implications of this gap for literacy educators. One of the arguments they make is the need to keep our priorities focused on the principles we hold dear to creating a literate environment for all students. For example, Moran and Selfe question the assumption that as writers, we always need the latest technology. They argue for thinking more creatively about ways to ensure that we concentrate on teaching effectively and providing the best learning opportunities available using the technology we already have. Although this approach will not solve the access problem, it may at least stave off feelings of despair at having only low-end technology with which to work. Also, Moran and Selfe argue,

> We need to recognize that we can no longer simply educate students to become technology users—and consumers on autopilot—without also helping them learn how to understand technology issues from socially and politically informed perspectives. When [teachers] require students to use computers to complete a range of assignments—without also providing them the time and opportunity to explore the complex issues that surround technology in substantive ways—we may, without realizing it, be contributing to the education of

TABLE 3.1 Percent of teachers reporting using computers or the Internet for instruction and the percent assigning various uses to students to a moderate or large extent, by school and teacher characteristics: 1999

School and teacher characteristics	Teacher uses for classroom instruction	Teacher assigns to a moderate or large extent								
		Computer applications[1]	Practice drills	Research using the Internet	Solve problems and analyze data	Research using CD-ROM	Produce multimedia reports/ projects	Graphical presentations of materials	Demonstrations/ simulations	Correspond with others[2]
All public school teachers with access to computers or the Internet at school	53	41	31	30	27	27	24	19	17	7
School instructional level										
Elementary school	56	41	39	25	31	27	22	17	15	7
Secondary school	44	42	12	41	20	27	27	23	21	7
Percent of students in school eligible for free or reduced-price school lunch										
Less than 11 percent	61	55	26	39	25	32	29	26	22	7
11–30 percent	52	45	29	35	29	27	23	18	16	9
31–49 percent	53	39	33	29	26	30	23	16	17	11
50–70 percent	47	33	33	25	27	24	25	19	13	5
71 percent or more	50	31	35	18	27	19	22	19	16	3
Hours of professional development										
0 hours	30	21	19	20	14	16	16	10	8	4
1–8 hours	46	36	26	28	24	24	20	16	13	7
9–32 hours	61	47	35	32	30	31	26	21	19	8
More than 32 hours	71	55	43	42	41	34	37	31	29	9

1. Use computer applications such as word processing and spreadsheets.

2. Correspond with experts, authors, students from other schools, etc. via e-mail or Internet.

NOTE: Less than 1 percent of all public school teachers reported no computers or Internet access were available to them anywhere in their school. These teachers were not included in the estimates presented in this table.

SOURCE: U.S. Department of Education, National Center for Education Statistics, Fast Response Survey System, "Public School Teachers Use of Computers and the Internet," FRSS 70, 1999.

citizens who are habituated to technology use but who have little critical awareness about, or understanding of, the complex relationships among humans and
machines and the cultural contexts within which the two interact. (p. 52)

Moran and Selfe's call for developing within students a critical stance toward
technology is discussed in Chapter 9. There, also, we provide strategies for teaching critical literacy using popular media and the Internet.

Classroom example.   Linda Hardin, a veteran language arts teacher at Beck
Middle School in Greenville, South Carolina, used the Internet to build a sense of
community within her eighth-grade classroom as part of a history project to put
Greenville's history on the Web. This interdisciplinary project involved all sections of her language arts class—80 students in all. The class, becoming what
Hardin (1999) described as "tourists in their own town" (p. 7), documented parts
of Greenville's history, including the controversy surrounding the Reedy River,
which the Cherokees had fought to keep prior to the Revolutionary War. Initially
conceiving of their project in linear fashion, the students soon learned one of the
advantages of the Web. With the help of an Internet tool called WebQuest, they
soon learned how to organize the information they were obtaining from interviews with longtime residents of Greenville, from Web surfing, from hometown
library searches, and from e-mailing messages to historians across the United
States in a "hyperbranching" rather than linear manner. In effect, the students in
Ms. Hardin's language arts classes were learning how to publish their history on
the Internet in a way that allowed endless revisions and invited future links as
newly discovered maps, photos, or updates to a story came in. As Hardin (1999)
noted, "for us, it was like putting the index at the beginning of a book and allowing the reader to jump around from page to page rather than reading the entire text first" (p. 9).

Media

The degree to which mass media and technology affect how young people
spend their leisure time in the United States was the subject of a national survey
conducted and reported by the Kaiser Family Foundation (1999). Titled "Kids &

Technology Tip

▼▼▼

For information on the design of a WebQuest
and a design template, access the following article: "The History and Development of Web-
Quests" in *Learning and Leading with Technology*
(April 1999) at http://www.edweb.sdsu.edu.

Media," the report includes findings from a nationally representative sample of more than 3,000 children, ages 2–18, of which more than 2,000 were in grades 3–12. Youth in these grades reported spending an average of 6 hours and 43 minutes a day using media outside of school. In this study, media use was defined as watching TV; surfing the Internet; playing video games; listening to music on CDs, tapes, or the radio; going to the movies; and reading books, magazines, and newspapers for pleasure.

Contrary to popular perception, kids are not spending long hours surfing the Internet or playing video games. Less than 1 in 10 kids (9 percent) reported spending an hour a day on these two activities. In contrast, nearly 64 percent of the kids reported watching TV for more than an hour a day, with 17 percent saying they spent 5 or more hours daily watching TV. After TV, listening to music is the next most popular pastime. According to the survey, kids spend an average of almost an hour and a half each day listening to CDs, tapes, or the radio. Finally, although the study confirms that electronic media dominate young people's lives, it also shows that kids still read for pleasure. More than 8 in 10 kids (82 percent) reported reading "for fun" an average of 45 minutes daily (excluding the time they spent in free reading activities at school).

Although this is encouraging news, still, as the Kaiser Family Foundation (1999) staff writers point out, it is the case that young people are spending more than five times as much time each day in front of a TV, computer, or video game screen than they are with a book. We believe, however, that this comparison needs to be examined more fully. Based on a Spencer Foundation research project that Alvermann and colleagues (2000) conducted on adolescents' media use outside of school, it is evident that at least some of the time spent in front of computer and video game screens is time spent reading. Although different from book reading, we contend that surfing the Web for the next episode of a Japanese comic or skimming a video game magazine for hints on winning plays are just different ways to describe reading "for fun."

Teachers may find it useful to take adolescents' out-of-school media interests into account when planning ways to build a community of learners within their classrooms, being careful, of course, not to appropriate for school purposes the very things students find most pleasurable in their out-of-school pursuits (Luke, 1997, 2000). Teachers we know who have done this successfully have been ones who have built on their students' interests in computers and video.

For example, Marcella Kehaus (2001) developed a teen writers' on-line community (http://www.TeenLit.com) for students interested in writing for audiences beyond their classroom peers and teacher. Frustrated by the limited number of publishing opportunities for her own students, Kehaus, along with one of her teacher friends, developed the *TeenLit.com* Web site. This site, which receives on average 1,500 visitors a week, provides a forum for teens to publish and discuss their work, review books they have read, and engage in discussions with other teen writers.

Another teacher, Pat Egenberger (1999) of Ustach Middle School in Modesto, California, transformed a required class research project into a community-

Technology Tip

▼▼

TeenInk offers a similar on-line writing community. Published by the Young Authors Foundation, *TeenInk* started as a magazine. Now in its 11th year, the magazine reaches more than 350,000 readers nationwide every month. *TeenInk* has published 25,000 students' work since its inception. Now on-line, you and your students can access this magazine at http://www.TeenInk.com. For more links to Internet sites featuring on-line writing communities that extend beyond the classroom, see this book's companion Web site at http://www.ablongman.com/alvermann3e.

building activity. Students in Egenberger's eighth-grade English class created a 20-minute video that not only integrated language arts, science, and social studies but also led them to new understandings and appreciation of Pam Conrad's (1985) *Prairie Song,* a novel they had previously read. Using questions that they generated from their reading of Conrad's novel (e.g., "What was it like living in a soddy?" and "Were there really grasshopper storms?"), the students divided into teams of two or three to research the answers to their questions. They relied on resources from their school library and from the Internet. After writing short scripts about the information they had located, students formed video crews and took turns taping each other as they shared this information. Reflecting on the project, Egenberger wrote,

> In general, the students were surprised that what we had just done was a form of research. It didn't have to be frustrating, dreary, and solitary. Creating a class video gave them an audience for their work. A necessary school task was transformed into a community effort and celebration. (p. 57)

CONFLICT RESOLUTION

Resolving conflicts that arise among adolescents is central to the process of creating and maintaining a favorable learning environment, one in which students are free to express themselves as long as they show respect to others and take responsibility for their own actions. Often easier to write about than to do, conflict resolution is a process that requires some special skills on the part of teachers and students alike. In content literacy classrooms in which collaboration is encouraged, it is especially important that students have some understanding of this process. Best introduced by the teacher in preparation for independent group work, conflict resolution may include one or more of the following strategies: problem solving, listening to negative feedback or criticism and responding appropriately, mediating the conflicts of others,

Professional Growth in Teaching with Media

Sometimes teachers hesitate to engage their classes in media projects because they are simply unsure about how to assess students' work. A well-known Canadian media literacy figure, Chris Worsnop, addresses this concern in his book, *Assessing Media Work: Authentic Assessment in Media Education.* An especially helpful feature of this book is a set of assessment rubrics to guide you in performance-based evaluations of video, audio, and other media formats. Examples from across the curriculum, easy-to-understand directions, and sample forms for self-assessment as well as peer and teacher feedback are provided. This resource is available through the Center for Media Literacy in Los Angeles at http://www.medialit.org/Catalog/assessment.htm#top. For other Web sites on creating a favorable learning environment using video and the Internet, see this book's companion site, http://www.ablongman.com/alvermann3e.

compromising, accepting the answer "no," and coping with failure (Warger & Rutherford, 1997).

What the Research Says

A review of the research on understanding peer conflict (Laursen, Hartup, & Koplas, 1996) suggests that "classmates with no history of rewarding exchange and no emotional investment in one another [will] appear unconcerned about future interaction" (p. 94). This is unfortunate but all the more reason for teachers to work toward creating a learning environment in which all students have reason to feel valued for their contributions, regardless of race, ethnicity, class, gender, ability, physical size, sexual orientation, religious background, and other identity markers that set individuals apart and open them to unfair ridicule.

That bias exists in our classrooms, as well as in teachers' lounges, will come as no surprise to anyone who has taught. Most educators who responded to a nationwide survey in the magazine *Teaching Tolerance* (and reported by the National Council of Teachers of English in *The Council Chronicle*) rated race relations at their schools as "good." Paradoxically, they also responded that bias is an issue in their schools. According to the report ("Survey Finds Students, Teachers Show Bias," 2000),

> The results indicate that students make sexist and homophobic comments often and use racial epithets and slurs toward particular religious groups somewhat frequently. Respondents also reported dramatically high levels of intolerance among their teaching peers, who make statements of racial or religious intolerance almost twice as often as students. (p. 13)

Having to endure the bullying behaviors of others is the consequence most often cited by those who are the target of school bias. Interestingly, bullying,

Technology Tip

▼▼

To keep abreast of the latest antibias instructional practices, visit the Web site of the magazine *Teaching Tolerance* (http://www.teachingtolerance.org) or access our book's companion Web site (http://www.ablongman.com/alvermann3e) to learn about additional resources for teaching conflict resolution.

which has been defined as "repeated oppression, physical or psychological, of a less powerful person by a more powerful person or group" (Rigby cited in Koki, 2000, p. 1), is more of a problem in mainland United States than it is in Hawaii and other Pacific Island schools under U.S. jurisdiction. Thought to be a result of the Western ideal of rugged individualism, bullying is less evident in cultures in which peer/family/community support are traditionally valued over one's personal goals (Koki, 2000).

Strategies for Managing Conflict

Some of the best suggestions for managing classroom conflict that results from bullying comes from William Kreidler's book *Creative Conflict Resolution* (1984). Although written nearly two decades ago, this book offers practical and easy-to-initiate strategies for resolving problems before they become more serious. We include two of those strategies here, adapted to fit our notion of what would work in the classrooms with which we are most familiar—our own.

Negotiating a solution to a problem.   This strategy, which is easily adapted across content areas, consists of the following steps:

1. Write "negotiate" and "negotiating" on the board and ask students to brainstorm meanings for the two words.
2. After 5 minutes of brainstorming, invite individuals to share their definitions with the whole class. If the idea that negotiating is a way of solving problems between people so that everyone can win does not come out in the discussion, suggest it and seek student feedback.
3. List the following procedure for negotiating a problem:
   ‣ State what you think the problem is.
   ‣ Say what you want.
   ‣ Tell what the limits are (what can or cannot be changed).
   ‣ Work out an agreement.
   ‣ Ask if everyone is able to live with the negotiated outcome. If not, address individual concerns privately, in a small group, or as a whole class, depending on the case.

4. Walk students through the process using the following situation:

Jill, one of the students in your TGT cooperative learning group, is not summarizing correctly the assigned readings in the social studies text. This is causing you and other students to answer test questions incorrectly during the tournament. Resentment is building.

5. After the class has negotiated a solution to the problem, ask students to describe a situation in which this type of negotiation would not work. Then ask them to explain what they would do in such a situation.

Building respect and community.   This strategy for managing classroom conflict that stems from general disrespect toward others and little sense of community is best introduced early in the school year and revisited occasionally so that students can gauge for themselves whether or not any change has occurred in their learning environment. The procedure consists of the following steps:

1. Engage students in a discussion of the actions, words, and body language that signal respect or disrespect for others. Point out that you need not like someone to behave respectfully toward him or her.

2. Ask class members to think about their learning environment and the things they would like to change (as well as those aspects of the environment they would like to keep the same).

3. Give each student an index card and pencil and request that individuals describe what they would change (and would not change) about the class learning environment. They may choose to sign their cards or remain anonymous. Post the cards on the bulletin board.

4. After a few days (having allowed enough time for students to read and think about the cards on the bulletin board), open a class discussion focused on the following questions:

   ‣ How would it feel to learn in the environment that you envision?
   ‣ Is it a vision worth working toward?
   ‣ If so, how would we begin working toward it?

In following up on any progress the class is making, you would need to ensure that discussions focus on both the positives and the negatives associated with change. For example, you might ask individuals to recall situations in which respect was shown, how it made them feel, what events tended to derail good intentions, how those derailments were addressed, and where the class currently stands in relation to its goal of creating a more favorable learning environment. Time spent in teaching conflict resolution to adolescents is time well spent, as Van Slyck and Stern (1999) noted. According to these experts on youth-oriented conflict resolution, research has shown that "learning conflict resolution principles and techniques increases social support and decreases victimization" (p. 179)—changes that ultimately lead to higher self-esteem and less depression or anxiety among adolescents.

SUMMARY

Creating a favorable learning environment—one in which the "small moments of learning" help to create contexts in which teachers and students feel free to interact—is easier to write about than to do. A favorable learning environment supports students as they grapple with issues of affect that influence how they feel about school and their willingness to engage in the academic activities that are part of the schooling process. Although tracking by ability level is not likely to disappear in the near future, there are numerous alternatives for grouping, including cooperative learning, cross-age tutoring, discussion groups, and reading/writing workshops.

The use of technology and various media forms to create a community of learners is a literacy practice that increasingly more teachers are choosing as they strive to motivate student interest and learning in their content area classes. This practice requires that teachers be sensitive to the pleasures young people draw from the media and not appropriate them for school use in ways that would cause students to abandon their interests in reading and writing outside of school. It also requires that teachers take time to help adolescents express their dislikes and disagreements in ways that resolve or manage conflicts before they become serious threats to classroom life and beyond. Treating conflict resolution as a necessary and natural part of creating a favorable learning environment is a first step toward ensuring that students will have opportunities to express themselves freely as they read, write, speak, and listen to others discuss the content of your classroom.

SUGGESTED READINGS

Barton, D., Hamilton, M., & Ivanic, R. (Eds.) (2000). *Situated literacies: Reading and writing in context.* New York: Routledge.

Brozo, W. G., Valerio, P. C., & Salazar, M. M. (2000). A walk through Gracie's garden: Literacy and cultural explorations in a Mexican American junior high school. In D. W. Moore, D. E. Alvermann, & K. A. Hinchman (Eds.), *Struggling adolescent readers.* Mahwah, NJ: Erlbaum.

Forcey, L. R., & Harris, I. M. (Eds.) (1999). *Peacebuilding for adolescents: Strategies for educators and community leaders.* New York: Lang.

Golub, J. N. (2000). *Making learning happen: Strategies for an interactive classroom.* Portsmouth, NH: Boynton/Cook.

Zorfass, J. M. (with Copel, H.) (1998). *Teaching middle school students to be active researchers.* Alexandria, VA: Association for Supervision and Curriculum Development.

Planning for Content Literacy

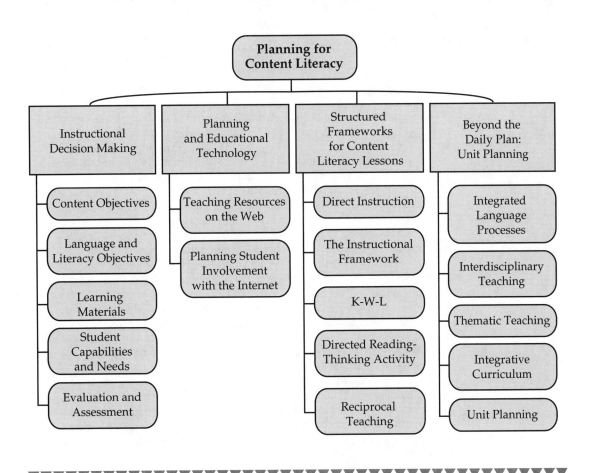

In a graduate class, Steve and his students read an article by Susan Ohanian (1985) in which she criticized gimmicky formulas or recipes for teaching. Kathryn Willoughby, a teacher in an urban elementary school, wrote the following reaction:

▼▼▼▼▼▼▼

I was looking over the latest secondhand clothes at a local consignment shop when I overheard two clearly educated and "upper-socio-ec" ladies debating the reasons for problems in the schools today. Naturally, I couldn't keep my mouth shut and right away identified myself as a teacher. It took all my restraint to keep from screaming when one of them, a former rural teacher of 30 years, said, "All a good teacher really needs is a chalkboard and piece of chalk." Popular attitudes and beliefs pervade the educational system; they stultify and repress change and improvement. "Teachers are glorified baby-sitters, teachers should be accountable for every growing pain and perceived injustice of the child's life, schools should teach every skill to mastery, teachers should instill values, but without making judgments." And my own brother, at a family reunion, was puzzled why I wasn't home from work at 2:30!

True, competent teachers have taught and inspired students with very little in the way of supplies, support, and technology. I'm not saying that teachers must have state-of-the-art equipment in order to do their job. We don't need to constantly reinvent the wheel, either. But save me from deluging my students with dittos, with one quick and dirty "activity" after another. I'm not interested in seatwork to keep my gifted kids out of trouble. If it's extra, then it's also nonessential. There is too much out there to learn and experience that is essential.

There's something to be said for cardboard cutouts, for ready-made bulletin boards, for those dittos. My neighbor down the hall was ready on the first day of school, her room neat, colorful and "finished looking." My bulletin board was still bare, awaiting the decision of the students on how to use it. I'm still gathering ideas and materials for my unit on Renaissance Life, having just found out what the kids want to read and know about. My plans tend to be "global" rather than one slot for each day, because events of learning don't always fit into neat time slots. I don't want to be handed all four corners of the box; I'm eager to set my own parameters and shape my own understandings.

Fresh is best, just like bread. If we are indeed the master chefs in the kitchen of learning, we already know there aren't many "stir-and-serve" recipes that are worth eating. Really good food takes time, preparation, a certain knack, and a little pinch of this and that. Have you every tried to get your grandmother's old family recipe that's not written down? Even when you make it to the letter of the recipe, it never quite tastes the same. That's what makes it special, worth eating.*

▼▼▼▼▼▼

Observing an effective and well-organized teacher can be deceptive. When a class is actively engaged in some kind of learning activity, whether it is instruction on how to graph a math equation, discussion of a poem, a chemistry experiment, or a conversation in Spanish, teacher and students can make learning seem logical, purposeful, almost effortless. Even when students become confused or ask for help, the teacher appears to know just what to do, how to ask the right question or rephrase instructions in a way that gets everybody back on track. Classroom veterans such as Kate Willoughby know, however, that good teaching is far from effortless. Rather, effective instruction is usually the result of thoughtful planning, careful preparation, and "a little pinch of this and that."

Like Kate, we too recognize that there is no one best way to plan for teaching. How a teacher prepares for the classroom will vary according to the particular style or preference of the teacher, the subject matter, the materials available, and, of course, the students. Experience is also an influential factor in the planning process. New teachers and those who are preparing for a new curriculum or a new topic are more likely to explicitly lay out objectives and teaching strategies,

---

*Used by permission of Kathryn B. Willoughby, Olmsted West School, Buffalo, New York.

whereas veterans can draw on previous lessons and classroom experience, updating and adapting as needed to maximize effectiveness.

We also acknowledge, as Robert Burns says, "The best-laid schemes o' mice an' men gang aft a-gley." Teaching can always be something of an adventure, and what actually happens in the classroom will usually be different from what one planned. An idea that seemed wonderful while sitting at the dining room table on Sunday afternoon may turn out to be a turkey on Monday morning. Most teachers can also relate instances when they abandoned a planned lesson to pursue a "teachable moment," an idea that evolved in the classroom and became more immediate, more important, more instructive than whatever had originally been on the agenda. With experience, teachers learn to anticipate both the potential problems and the opportunities for serendipity, and they learn how to adjust instruction as they meet the needs of the moment.

Nevertheless, most good teaching and learning happen by design. What occurs in a classroom is usually the result of a complex decision-making process that begins well before the bell rings, evolves throughout the class period, and continues even after the class has ended as the teacher evaluates how students reacted and what they learned and also thinks about what to do next. In this chapter we discuss some of the ways in which teachers design their instruction; we examine some of the decisions involved in planning for content area instruction and describe some frameworks for structuring content area literacy lessons.

INSTRUCTIONAL DECISION MAKING

Lesson planning, whether for a single day's activities, for a two- or three-week unit, or for an entire marking period, involves many complex and interrelated decisions. We have said that there is no single best way to plan, and a teacher may begin the planning process from any number of points. A chemistry teacher may begin by previewing chapter objectives in a teacher's manual. The French teacher may decide that students need more practice with translation from French to English. The geometry teacher may plan a day of review for a unit test on triangles. A language arts–social studies team may center their planning on a medieval faire, complete with costumes, games, entertainment, and food. Whatever their starting points, these teachers will need to consider what they want students to learn, the learning materials that are available, the capabilities and prior knowledge of students, and the specific instructional strategies and evaluation options that would be most effective. This section describes some of those factors that must be considered in teacher decision making.

Content Objectives

What do students need to learn? On the surface, this would seem like a simple question. However, if we were to examine a topic such as the American

Revolution, we would see that the answer is far from simple. What is important for students to know about the American Revolution? When it occurred? Who the principals were? Why it was fought? What the outcomes were? Any or all of these might arguably be essential.

Taken as a collection of isolated facts, the American Revolution can be pretty confusing: Townsend Acts, 1776, Washington, Boston Tea Party, Jefferson, Cornwallis, Give me liberty or give me death! This information will be easier to learn, and ultimately more meaningful, to the extent that the various parts can be related to each other. Therefore, it would be useful to organize a topic such as this around one or two key ideas. For instance, the history teacher may decide to organize his or her class's study of the Revolution around a theme as follows: "The American Revolution came about because people wanted the opportunity to make their own decisions." This central idea, or *organizing concept* (Phelps, 1984), could help the teacher to focus the various events, personalities, and ideas in the unit. Furthermore, it introduces a theme that may be revisited throughout the U.S. history curriculum as the class studies Jacksonian democracy, the Civil War, the rise of labor unions, or the suffrage movement. Figure 4.1 shows a planning web for the American Revolution centered on this organizing concept.

Our American Revolution example is broad and pertinent to a unit of study that may take a matter of weeks to complete. However, single class sessions may also be organized around a key idea. For instance, a high school geometry teacher may plan a lesson around the computation of the area of a circle, centered on the mathematical expression $A = \pi r^2$. That single mathematical sentence contains all the essential components of the lesson: multiplication, area, radius, π. If students learn those components and the relations between them they will have achieved the teacher's content objective; they will be able to compute the area of a circle.

An organizing concept may be broad or narrow. It may express a theme such as "the difficulty of making personal choices" when a class is reading Robert Cormier's novel *The Chocolate War* (1974), or it may be a more functional concept such as "vegetative propagation and sexual reproduction in plants" in a biology class. A teacher's primary objectives may also include content processes. That is, teachers want to help their students to think like a writer, a mathematician, a scientist, a historian, or a linguist. Good teaching should be grounded on clearly articulated content objectives, however they may be defined or articulated. Learning will be more meaningful when teachers (and students) see the big picture, and the overall point of classroom activity. Individual facts, ideas, or skills will be easier to learn when they can be related to each other and to a central concept or process. It will make it less likely that students will be involved in busywork such as filling out worksheets or copying down notes with no apparent pedagogical purpose other than to give the appearance of meaningful activity.

We want to stress that we are not talking about behavioral objectives. Nor do we believe it is necessary for teachers to laboriously write down objectives for every lesson using a particular formula or taxonomy, although this may be

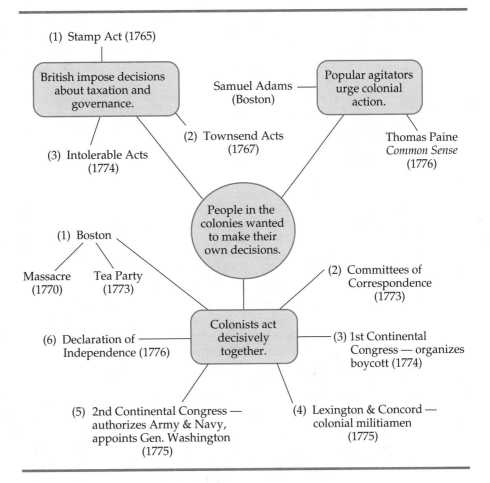

FIGURE 4.1 **Planning web for the American Revolution**

required in some schools and may have some utility in a methods course as a way to get teachers to think systematically about what they are doing. Content area teaching is based on a curriculum of ideas that students are expected to learn, and it is sufficient that teachers have some part of that curriculum clearly in mind as they plan what they are going to do and what they are going to have students do in class.

Language and Literacy Objectives

In addition to the content that teachers intend students to learn, certain skills will be required. For example, basic computational skills, using a calculator, and working with protractor and compass are needed in the study of geometry. Working with laboratory equipment, including setup, cleanup, and safety procedures, is an important component of science study. In this text, our emphasis is on the language and literacy skills that students will need in order to be effective learners.

Particularly when working with students from diverse backgrounds, who may have less access to the conventions and forms of discourse commonly accepted in mainstream academic settings, teachers may need to provide frequent explicit skill instruction (Au, 1998; Delpit, 1988). In the course of planning, teachers will want to think about the reading and writing activities that go along with learning and decide how their teaching will help students achieve those objectives.

The term *skills* has fallen into disfavor, especially among advocates of a natural language approach to literacy instruction, who object to attempts to fragment and isolate so-called literacy subskills and teach them individually through direct instruction and drill (Goodman, 1986; Weaver, 1988). Therefore, we use the term *literacy skills* advisedly. We do not mean to imply that there is a finite list of discrete skills, many unique to particular content areas, that should be systematically taught. However, we recognize that reading a chemistry chapter to prepare for a quiz, reading a short story and writing a personal response, or using the Internet to search for information for a history project each requires some special skills, and that these skills must be learned, usually through explicit instruction, in order for students to be successful.

As experts in their content specialties, teachers generally have a good deal of experience with reading and writing science, literature, social studies, mathematics, technology, and so on, but they may not be consciously aware of these abilities. The purpose of reading a text such as this one and taking a course on content area literacy is to increase teachers' sensitivity to the literacy requirements implied in a content area lesson. As teachers plan, they make decisions about what students will read and write; they analyze the literacy skills inherent in the subject and the reading material. They ask themselves, "How is this reading selection organized? What is there about the selection that makes it easy to understand or that is likely to be difficult? In order to complete this written assignment, what will students need to know or understand? How can I help them with this?"

Good teachers anticipate which skills may be difficult for students and plan to assist with those skills within the context of content area learning. If the biology chapter has an unusually heavy load of technical vocabulary based on Latin and Greek roots, the teacher may wish to use one or more strategies for helping students to master vocabulary. If students are likely to have difficulty giving voice to their personal reactions to fiction, the teacher may devise a way to guide student reflection and writing. If students need some assistance with note taking and report writing, the teacher could include appropriate instruction in daily plans as students gather information and begin drafting their written products. Other language- and literacy-related abilities that will be useful in content area classes include speaking and listening skills, working effectively with peers, preparing for tests, and abilities such as critical thinking, analysis, or prediction. (In the following chapters, we describe many teaching and learning strategies that integrate literacy learning with content learning.) Deciding what kinds of talking, listening, reading, and writing students will do and determining ways to assist students with those processes are important components of the planning process.

Learning Materials

While planning, teachers also consider what materials are at hand and what will be needed. Such things as laboratory equipment, math manipulatives, audio and video recordings, and various teacher-made materials may be used to demonstrate concepts, create interest, involve students, or provide essential background information. Regarding reading materials, teachers will think about textbooks, possible complementary readings from trade books or periodicals, worksheets and directions, exams, charts and diagrams, and reference materials.

Students of all cultural backgrounds will benefit when teachers introduce readings that authentically present diverse cultures, especially when the authors come from diverse cultural groups (Au, 1998). Writing assignments imply basic materials such as pen or pencil and paper, as well as journals, notebooks, computers and printers, and the possible formats for final written products such as newspapers, student-made books, formal reports or essays, posters, letters, electronic transmission, or bulletin boards.

Student Capabilities and Needs

Another important aspect of planning is accommodation of student needs. Teachers will try to anticipate what students already know, what strengths or aptitudes they may have, and what difficulties they are likely to encounter. In Chapter 2 we considered some of the factors that contribute to classroom diversity. In our mobile, diverse, and rapidly evolving society, it is impossible to talk about a "typical" classroom. Students bring varied cultural understandings, varied language backgrounds, and a wide variety of previous experiences to school. Students will also range widely in their interests, in their aptitudes for a particular subject, and in their reading and writing abilities. In addition, many students with identified learning difficulties or disabilities are included in regular classrooms, sometimes with the support of specialists and sometimes without.

The growing diversity in classrooms presents both challenges and opportunities for teachers. Traditional instruction based on textbook readings, lectures, memorization, and formal academic expository writing will simply not serve the needs of all learners.

Many African American and Hispanic students, for instance, tend to be field-independent, active learners who prefer group work, a student-centered environment, learning related to their personal experience, and frequent interaction with peers and teachers (Kuykendal, 1992). Finding alternatives to traditional instruction does not mean that learning should be any less rigorous and challenging, however. Rather, teachers can look for ways to help all students to become actively engaged. For instance, Pamela Adams's (1995) students in an untracked classroom were able to successfully read and enjoy *Romeo and Juliet*, and Bill Bigelow (1994) helped bring the U.S. history curriculum to life for an untracked high school class by having students play the roles of longshoremen, employers, farmers, unemployed workers, and union officials in a 1930s labor dispute. Throughout this textbook, you will find teaching and learning strategies that are especially suited for accommodating the individual differences among students in your classes.

One way in which teachers are able to successfully meet the needs of diverse students is through *instructional scaffolding*. Just as a construction crew may erect a scaffold to support them as they work and then gradually dismantle the scaffold as the work is completed, so a teacher can plan a supportive framework for student learning and then gradually withdraw it as students take over more responsibility for their own learning. For example, Randi Reppen (1994/1995) describes how she taught different genres of writing to students in a fifth-grade social studies class who were learning English as a second language. Students learned each style of writing by reading and discussing examples, with the teacher explicitly pointing out the features of the genre and comparing it with other genres. Then the teacher modeled by writing at the overhead projector for the whole class, asking students for input and describing what she was doing and why. Control over learning was gradually turned over to students, first by having them write in the particular style with peers in a small group and finally by having each student produce an individual piece of writing.

A group of high school and middle school teachers in the San Francisco Bay area, organized under the umbrella of the Strategic Literacy Network, implemented a scaffolded approach to content area instruction that they call *reading apprenticeship* (Schoenbach et al., 1999). The primary goal of reading apprenticeship is to show adolescent readers that expert reading is a complex, problem-solving process by engaging them in "metacognitive conversations" about what they are reading and learning. Reading apprenticeship involves four key dimensions that are necessary to support adolescent reading development (Schoenbach et al., p. 22):

- Social dimension: community building in the classroom, including recognizing the resources brought by each member and developing a safe environment for students to be open about their reading difficulties
- Personal dimension: developing students' identities and self-awareness as readers as well as their purposes for reading and goals for reading improvement

▸ Cognitive dimension: developing readers' mental processes, including their problem-solving strategies
▸ Knowledge-building dimension: identifying and expanding the kinds of knowledge readers bring to a text and further develop through interaction with that text

Content-area teachers in the Strategic Literacy Network have successfully shown their students how to use many strategies that are described in this book, including reciprocal teaching (this chapter), questioning strategies (Chapter 7), student-generated summaries (Chapter 10), and graphic organizers (Chapter 6–8). A key to their success is the ongoing conversation among students and teachers about literacy and learning processes, which serves to make the nature of those processes visible and accessible. Results of both formal testing and qualitative surveys indicate that network students made significant gains over the course of a year. In general, students who had the most need of literacy development, such as struggling readers, ELLs, and special education students, made the most gains (Schoenbach et al., 1999).

Instructional scaffolding is admittedly easier said than done. In order for scaffolding to be successful, a teacher must be committed to a view of education as more than simply transmitting facts and concepts. Scaffolding demands a thorough knowledge of the curriculum and various reading and learning processes, detailed understanding of students and their learning abilities and difficulties, and the ability to explain cognitive processes to students clearly and explicitly (Pressley et al., 1996).

Planning to use flexible and varied patterns of in-class grouping can also help a teacher capitalize on diverse student backgrounds and meet varied student needs (Au, 1998). Alternating among whole class instruction, various small-group activities, paired-learning tasks, and individual assignments allows students to assist each other, provides more opportunities to participate, and generally creates a learning environment based on student activity rather than passivity. We described grouping alternatives in Chapter 3, and you will find that many of the teaching suggestions in other chapters lend themselves to varied grouping patterns.

Another theme you will find throughout this book is the importance of linking students' background to new content. As teachers plan, they should look for potential points of congruence between what students know or believe and what they are going to be learning. For example, a biology teacher may realize that the study of DNA will be more meaningful if he or she highlights the role of DNA in certain hereditary diseases, such as sickle-cell anemia, which is prevalent among African Americans and people of Mediterranean heritage (Offner, 1992). This linkage of students' prior knowledge with new information implies that teachers will need to make an effort to learn something about their students and the community from which they come. The effort will be well worth it if a teacher can plan to draw on students' experiences, supplement sketchy prior knowledge, or anticipate points of conflict between students' conventional wisdom and new material to be learned.

Bill Bigelow (1994) suggests several interlocking components that have allowed him and his colleagues to work successfully with students of diverse ability and background. His recommendations include the following:

- Students need to experience ideas, not just hear about them. Bigelow recommends role-playing and simulations.
- Assignments need to be flexible and take into account students' interests and abilities.
- The classroom environment must be encouraging, even loving.
- Students need to understand how the ideas and skills they are learning can make a difference in their lives.
- Evaluation of students should be flexible and equitable.

Bigelow readily admits that teaching in an untracked classroom is easier said than done. Students may get off-task, miss assignments, and experience failure. However, when a teacher believes that all students can learn and plans to meet the needs of all students, the result can be a classroom that is lively, stimulating, and actively devoted to the pursuit of knowledge.

Planning content area instruction for ELLs.   Many of the general suggestions we have made are especially appropriate for students who are learning English, including flexible grouping, linking new content to prior knowledge, and instructional scaffolding. English language learners add a new dimension to teacher planning, however. In addition to knowledge of content and academic skills, they also need teachers who can help them develop their knowledge of the English language. Therefore, teachers who use a sheltered English approach scaffold their instruction by making adjustments both in the instructional tasks they plan and by adjusting their speech (Echevarria, Vogt, & Short, 2000). Teachers should also explicitly and clearly communicate both content and language objectives to students orally and in writing.

Sheltered English teachers adjust their speech by using simple subject–verb–object sentences, avoiding complex embedded constructions, and by accompanying their spoken presentations with visual representations in the form of charts, diagrams, demonstrations, real objects, or pictures. Such visual aids are also part of adjusting instruction to meet the triple goals of expanding ELLs' vocabulary and language skill, their content knowledge, and their ability to perform increasingly complex academic tasks. Additional instructional adaptations include (Echevarria, Vogt, & Short, 2000):

- Preteaching vocabulary
- Reviewing previous instruction before introducing new material
- Explicitly modeling language and literacy skills

- Planning simulations, role-playing, and hands-on experiences
- Giving ELLs support in their native language through the use of L1 reading materials, dictionaries, or bilingual peers and classroom aides
- Providing supplemental materials to support English language texts, including trade books, audiovisuals, pictures, computer-based information, audiotaped books, and specially designated textbooks with key concepts and vocabulary highlighted
- Creating graphic organizers, outlines, and study guides
- Allowing ELLs to demonstrate what they have learned through multiple channels, including hands-on activities, group projects, oral reports, and informal discussions, in addition to more formal quizzes and written assignments

A final component of sheltered English is engaging ELLs in instructional conversations that help them to improve their functional language skills. Specifically, students need opportunities to use academic language, not just social language. Peer interactions can facilitate this practice, but sheltered teachers also directly elicit elaborated responses from ELLs. This means suppressing the instinct to compensate for students' lack of English language facility by not calling on them, speaking for them, or completing a partial response. Instead, Echevarria, Vogt, and Short (2000) recommend using prompts such as "Tell me more about that," "What do you mean by . . . ," "What else . . . ," or "How do you know?" It is also very important to provide the ELL sufficient wait time to formulate a response after a question is posed.

Although accommodating the needs of ELLs requires some specialized planning and instructional modifications, most of the specific teaching strategies recommended for ELLs are derived from those designed for mainstream classes. You will find these strategies and methods described in this and subsequent chapters.

Evaluation and Assessment

As teachers plan, they also think about how they will evaluate students' learning. Quizzes and exams, homework, worksheets, journals, essays, projects, in-class presentations, and observation of student performance are among the tools that teachers use to make both formal and informal judgments about what students have accomplished. Decisions about evaluation may come near the end of the planning process, after teachers have worked out the content objectives, materials, and learning activities for a lesson or a series of lessons in a unit. Other times, evaluation may actually be a primary influence in planning, as it is when teachers must prepare students for a departmentalized exam or other testing at the district, city, or state level. Evaluation and assessment will be treated in detail in Chapter 5.

All the decision-making factors that we have cited here are interrelated, and the interrelation is more weblike than linear. There is no single best sequence for lesson planning. Knowing something about students' reading ability will influence what kinds of reading materials they will be able to use successfully as well as the kinds of literacy objectives that might reasonably be achieved. Determining content objectives will help a teacher think of ways to draw on student background and will also determine what will be emphasized in evaluation. Individual teachers will have their own preferred styles. Some will depend on external sources such as teachers' manuals, curriculum guides, or unit tests to help them formulate content objectives and teaching strategies, whereas others will draw on their own ideas of what should be emphasized. Some teachers may be student centered in their planning, whereas others are more content-oriented.

Teachers at elementary, middle school, and high school levels will all take into account the developmental characteristics of their students as well as the relative degree to which the content areas are either distinct or integrated at each level. Specific subject matter will also make a difference; teachers in different subject areas have very different notions of what they can and cannot do in their classes, and the various subject area subcultures have a strong influence on actual instructional practices (Grossman & Stodolsky, 1995; Stodolsky, 1988).

PLANNING AND EDUCATIONAL TECHNOLOGY

We are neither expert nor foolhardy enough to attempt detailed predictions of where technology may take us in the future. Nevertheless, it is safe to say that computer literacy, with emphasis on the Internet, will command continued importance as an integral part of students' literacy learning. Consequently, teachers will be increasingly expected to draw on computer resources in their planning and in the delivery of instruction. As they plan, teachers will also need to consider the technological skill and sophistication of their students.

The International Society for Technology in Education (ISTE), in collaboration with the U.S. Department of Education and other sponsors, has developed recommended technology standards for students at all grade levels (ISTE, 2000; http://cnets.iste.org/). Students should be able to

1. Demonstrate proficiency with basic operations and concepts
2. Understand social, ethical and human issues (including issues of copyright, plagiarism, and citation)
3. Use technology productivity tools to enhance learning and to collaborate in constructing models, preparing publications, and producing other creative works
4. Employ technology communication tools to collaborate, publish, and interact with peers, experts, and other audiences; use a variety of media and formats to communicate information and ideas effectively

5. Apply technology research tools to locate, evaluate, and collect information; use technology tools to process data and report results; evaluate and select new information resources
6. Use technological resources to make informed decisions; employ technology to solve real-world problems

Notice the explicit and implicit literacy abilities embedded in these standards. In order to use a technology resource such as the Internet, students will need basic reading and writing skills and an understanding of how they transfer to computer environments. They will also require keyboarding abilities, an understanding of computer terminology, flexible comprehension strategies, critical and analytical facilities, research skills (including Internet search strategies), and the ability to effectively combine print, audio, and visual media in order to communicate their ideas. Although some of this can be learned in technology classes, teachers in all content areas need to take into account the literacy ramifications as they guide students to use technological learning and communication tools.

Planning with the Internet involves two aspects. First, teachers can find lesson plans, unit plans, and many other kinds of instructional resources on the Web. Many sites welcome postings from teachers who wish to share successful ideas with colleagues. E-mail, listserves, bulletin boards, and chat rooms make it possible to communicate with other teachers or content area specialists and get specific planning suggestions. There is also a wealth of up-to-date information relative to almost any facet of any content area that one could imagine, available in an ever-expanding and ever-changing Internet environment.

The second facet of planning with the Internet is incorporating Internet activities and other technology uses into instruction. Teachers will want to plan what students will do with computers, how the Internet can complement the curriculum, and what students will need to know and do in order to have successful experiences with the Web and other technology.

Teaching Resources on the Web

There are numerous sites that give sample lesson plans and suggestions for teaching activities—many more than we could suggest here. Some good starting points include the following:

Teachers Net
Many different resources for teachers, including lesson plans, links to other useful sites, chat rooms, and message boards.
http://teachers.net/

Education World
Lesson plans; subject centers for history, science, social studies, and technology; links to other sites; features a search engine for the site's data base.
http://education-world.com/

Internet Literacy and Struggling Readers

The Internet can be a welcome change from textbooks and a motivating environment for struggling readers, but it will also present them with some special challenges (Balajthy, 1990). The very vastness of the Web can prove frustrating for readers who are not particularly adept at finding useful information quickly and easily. The disjunctive nature of hypertext environments (where the viewer can jump from screen to screen or site to site in any order) may make it difficult for some students to keep in mind the overarching structure of a site or lose track of their purpose; they may become "lost in hyperspace" (Nielsen, 1990). Also, much of the information that students may access will be conceptually challenging, with a good deal of difficult technical vocabulary.

The following suggestions can provide support for struggling readers as they use the Internet:

- Pair struggling readers with more able peers.
- Steer them to sites that have been previewed and found to be appropriate.
- Select sites that include helpful site maps and navigation tools.
- When the site does not provide navigational aids, prepare a graphic of the site's structure and explain it to students.
- Scaffold Internet searches by providing specific questions, directions, or explicit guidance.
- Preteach potentially difficult vocabulary that may be found at a site.
- Use "talking" software, such as eReader or textHelp, that gives the user a spoken version of the text on the screen.

Kathy Schrock's Guide for Educators
Features links to other sites, organized into categories, including subject areas; also has a wealth of Web Quest information, including examples.
http://discoveryschool.com/schrockguide/

The Global Schoolhouse
This site focuses on using information technology to support students' learning.
http://www.gsn.org/

International Society for Technology in Education
Technology suggestions for all subject areas, lesson plans, and information on the national technology standards.
http://www.iste.org/

Classroom Connect
Promotes educational use of the Internet; includes links to other worthwhile sites, lesson ideas, and many tips on using the Internet.
http://classroom.net/

Youth Net
A place where youth of all ages can meet, discuss, and participate in learning projects; many student projects, school Web sites, and student home pages can be accessed through this site.
http://youth.net/

The Suggested Readings at the end of this chapter recommend many other sites featuring lesson planning ideas, as does the companion Web site to this text (http://www.ablongman.com/alvermann3e).

In addition to lesson planning ideas, teachers will also find information on the Web to share with students. This might include useful background information, expanded coverage of a topic featured in the text, application of an important concept in some authentic context, or other information that is not included in the textbook. This is especially useful in the sciences and social studies, for which the limitations of textbook technology make it impossible for texts to include the most recent developments in science, politics, or world affairs.

For instance, a biology teacher leading his or her class in a study of genetics would not find the most recent details on mapping the human genetic code in the textbook. However, the teacher could "capture" a series of Internet pages related to this topic, including text and graphics, using Web-capturing software such as Web Whacker. This would allow the teacher to access the sites he or she had selected even if there were no on-line links in the classroom. By using multimedia authoring software such as HyperCard or HyperStudio and by linking his or her computer to a large-screen display, the teacher could develop a presentation that interspersed scientific data from the Human Genome Project or other scientific agencies with Web-based news articles on the latest developments, predictions of the future benefits of genetic mapping, and perhaps some thoughtful considerations of the social and ethical issues involved in genetic science. Such a presentation could easily be a starting point and a model for hands-on student Internet projects as well.

Planning Student Involvement with the Internet

Content area teachers plan a variety of student hands-on experiences with the Internet that involve collecting, synthesizing, organizing, creating, and presenting information. Student activities include

- Collecting hot lists, a list of sites related to a particular topic
- Evaluating Web sites using criteria provided by the teacher or developed collaboratively in class
- Other higher-level responses to selected sites, including interpretation, relation to personal experience, or synthesis with what they are learning in the classroom
- Conducting a treasure hunt in which they find answers to specific questions tailored for specific web sites

▸ Downloading items for a scrapbook, a collection of photos, maps, text, and audio or video clips that can be pasted into a multimedia presentation, a Web page, or other project

▸ Undertaking a Web Quest—a challenging task, scenario, or problem to solve in which student groups become experts on one aspect of a topic and then recombine and synthesize what they have learned with other groups either in their classroom or in other classrooms linked through the Internet

▸ Collaborative Internet projects (Mike & Rabinowitz, 1998) get students to communicate with peers in distant schools or experts in various fields, gather and synthesize information, and make their work public through electronic or other media.

The Internet and English language learners.   The Internet can be an especially useful tool for ELLs (Leu & Leu, 1999). E-mailing back and forth between English-speaking peers or teachers, either in their own school or in remote schools, gives ELLs authentic communication contexts for reading and writing English. If students enter into an Internet project with a school in which a student's native language is spoken, that student can become a resource for translating back and forth between languages. This helps to illustrate the practical advantages of students' dual-language competency and helps to integrate ELLs socially and academically with their monolingual peers. A second-language learner can use the Internet to access sites in his or her home country and share information with peers as part of an Internet activity. There is also an Internet site especially for ELLs, Dave's ESL Cafe (http://www.eslcafe.com), that features idioms, student and teacher links, and an e-mail exchange, among other things.

Internet planning guidelines.   Planning Internet activities can be difficult and, for a beginner, somewhat daunting. One Internet resource that would be a helpful starting point is Filamentality (http://www.kn.pacbell.com/wired/fil/into.html), a site that guides teachers in topic selection and searching the Web for relevant information. Filamentality also has templates for creating Web activities and allows teachers or students to post their own Web page describing their Web-based project. Mike & Rabinowitz (1998) suggest many Web sites that offer help to teachers planning Internet activities for students. The Global Schoolhouse network is an especially useful resource, including a Projects Registry (http://www.gsn.org/gsn/proj/index.html) that administers collaborative projects that bring together students and teachers from all over the world. All of the sites listed under Teaching Resources on the Web feature Internet-based learning activities, and our companion Web site will lead you to additional sites that can help you plan Internet activities.

The sheer volume of information available on the Internet, as well as the difficulty of finding just what you want, means that the Internet can consume a lot of planning time, especially for someone just beginning to explore the possibilities of the Web. Martha Rekrut, a high school English teacher in Rhode Island, describes her own initial experiences with using the Web as well as some successful Internet applications by teachers in other disciplines. She shares some guidelines for Internet beginners (Rekrut, 1999):

‣ Determine instructional objectives and do some preliminary research to decide if the Internet is going to be helpful.
‣ Integrate the Internet into the context of ongoing instruction.
‣ Be aware of the literacy demands of the Web.
‣ Develop specific objectives for each Internet session.
‣ Include a written component or product to be handed in at the end of each session.
‣ If possible, help students disseminate their findings on the Internet via e-mail, on the school's Web site, or through displays and public presentations.
‣ Help students evaluate their Internet experiences in discussion or in writing.

To this, we add a few other general suggestions for planning Internet activities. First, be aware of varied student expertise with computers and the Internet. It would not be surprising if you had students who were much more knowledgeable about computers and the Internet than you are, but you may need to offer basic "how-to" instruction to others. You will also want to make sure that the more tech-savvy students do not monopolize the available workstations or dominate an activity. Second, it is usually helpful to preselect sites for students to visit, especially if class computer time is limited and students are at the beginning or intermediate stages of Internet experience. This will save time and allow you to steer students toward sites that are reliable, reasonably well organized, and accessible at busy times of the day.

Finally, we encourage you to link book literacy with computer literacy. For instance, if students are working on a research project, you could require that they consult a certain number of book or periodical resources as well as the Internet, or you could use textbook selections as starting points for Internet exploration. Student projects should also include a student-composed written component. At the end of this chapter, we give an example of an interdisciplinary thematic unit that incorporates earth science, English, student use of the Internet and traditional print resources, student publication, and state assessments.

The Internet and other applications of computer technology have quickly become ubiquitous components of contemporary education. Although computers have many impressive applications in teaching and learning, there are also facets of technology that require some caution and critical evaluation on the part of teachers and students. Computer technology remains an unequally distributed resource across communities and schools, as noted in Chapter 3. Students of diverse background or ability are especially likely to be short-changed in the technological economy. Students and teachers will differ greatly in their expertise and interest for computers; not everyone needs to lead a logged-on life. Computer hardware and software and Internet applications and locations evolve with dizzying speed—much too fast for many (most?) busy teachers to keep up with. At the same time, much of what is available as software or on the Internet is of questionable utility, value, or verity. These are issues to bear in mind when planning.

STRUCTURED FRAMEWORKS FOR CONTENT LITERACY LESSONS

Many structured lesson-planning approaches have been proposed, and they may be effectively adapted to a variety of classroom circumstances. As you read, think about how you might use each framework in your own content specialty. In all probability, you will find useful ideas within each of the frameworks described. Rather than adopting any one particular framework in its entirety, you may decide, like Kate Willoughby in our opening anecdote, that good teaching is not necessarily built on formulas or "recipes." Rather, you may wish to select those ideas that you feel best fit your content specialty, your students, and your own preferences.

Direct Instruction

Direct instruction is useful for teaching a specific skill or process. In this approach, the teacher first states explicitly what is to be learned and models the skill or process. For example, a social studies teacher who wants students to learn how to write a summary might begin by explaining what a summary is, why it is useful, and how one is written. The teacher would then read a short passage from the history textbook and compose a summary on the overhead projector, explaining to the class the specific processes he or she was using.

After the process has been modeled for students, the teacher should involve them in guided practice. To continue our summary-writing example, the teacher could direct the class to read further from the text. The teacher then would compose another summary, but this time base it on input from the class. As an alternative form of guided practice, the teacher could have students work cooperatively in groups of two or three to compose summaries while the teacher walked around the room and offered assistance. Then the groups could compare their summaries and the teacher could help them analyze the merits of including or excluding certain information, their various choices for wording and syntax, and the accuracy with which the summaries captured the important ideas in the text.

In the direct instruction model, guided practice is followed by independent practice in which students use the skills on their own. In the case of summary writing, the teacher could ask students to read and summarize a selection from their text as a homework assignment.

The direct instruction model is most useful when there is a single, relatively straightforward content or literacy objective that can be initially modeled and taught within a one- or two-day time frame. Direct instruction can be effectively applied to such activities as computational skills in math, map reading and interpretation in geography, paragraph structure in English class, or grammatical constructions in a modern language class. Literacy skills such as using context as a vocabulary aid or understanding question–answer relationships can also be taught by direct instruction. However, as the content or literacy objectives become more complex or abstract, direct instruction may need to be followed by extended reinforcement and guided practice, especially for struggling readers (Swanson & de la Paz, 1988).

The Instructional Framework

Harold Herber (1978) describes an instructional framework for content area literacy lessons that takes into account both the content objectives and the literacy objectives of a lesson. It incorporates some of the elements of the direct instruction model. Unlike the direct instruction model, however, the Instructional Framework lends itself to conceptually complex topics that may evolve over longer periods of instruction. Herber's model consists of three major components: preparation, guidance, and independence.

During the *preparation* phase of instruction, a teacher may choose one or more means to get students ready to learn:

- Employ motivational techniques to pique students' interest and encourage them to make a personal investment in learning.
- Activate students' background knowledge.
- Where prior experience is lacking, help build up background for the new concepts that are to be studied.
- Help students anticipate what they will be learning and be purposeful in their efforts.
- Give clear and careful directions about what needs to be done, especially when the assignment involves novel processes or ideas.
- Introduce technical or difficult vocabulary that otherwise might interfere with learning.

Useful strategies for working with students' prior knowledge and building anticipation for learning are provided in Chapter 6, and Chapter 8 focuses on vocabulary development.

In the *guidance* phase of the Instructional Framework, teachers need to provide structured opportunities for students to develop both their learning processes, including their reading and writing abilities, and the concepts that constitute the subject area. The teacher helps students learn by structuring and guiding the interaction between reader and text or between writer and written product. According to Herber, such guidance "must be sufficiently structured to give purpose and direction, but sufficiently open to allow personal strengths, preferences, and discoveries to emerge" (p. 220). Teachers can provide this kind of guidance through thoughtful questioning, by preparing reading or study guides, or by developing cooperative-learning activities in which students can work together on tasks with teacher assistance. A variety of guided learning strategies are described in Chapters 6–11.

Independence is the final phase of Herber's Instructional Framework, and student independence, ideally, is the ultimate goal of instruction. As teachers, we want our students to be able to use both the learning processes and the concepts of our discipline. Math teachers want their students to apply math concepts and operations to authentic, real-life situations. The earth science teacher would hope students could apply their knowledge to local issues of environmental quality. The history teacher hopes that students will use their understanding of the past in order to more intelligently understand their positions as citizens in their communities and in the nation. Such independent applications of skills and knowledge require instruction that transcends rote memorization and perfunctory "coverage." Instead, teachers need to plan instruction that allows students to guide their own learning. This happens over time in classes in which teachers provide instructional scaffolding, where guidance is highly structured and explicit at first but then gradually withdrawn as students become increasingly capable of learning on their own. Reciprocal teaching, described later, is one good example of how this works. Throughout the following chapters, we offer other suggestions for how teachers can turn the responsibility for learning over to students.

K-W-L

K-W-L is a technique suggested by Donna Ogle (1986). Students first identify what they *know* about a topic, then decide what they *want* to find out about it, and finally discuss what they have *learned.* (Some teachers, when their students profess that there is nothing they *want* to find out about the topic, use the term *need* to find out instead—K-N-L). In the first phase of a K-W-L lesson, students brainstorm and discuss the ideas they have on a topic they will be reading about in their text. They can jot down their own ideas on worksheets or in their learning logs. With teacher guidance and modeling, they categorize the information they have discussed and anticipate other categories of information that they may find as they read.

Figure 4.2 shows a K-W-L worksheet developed by a high school self-contained special education class during a lesson on the U.S. Constitution. The students in this class ranged from 13 to 16 years old, and formal testing suggested their academic functioning levels ranged from second to sixth grade. The teacher, Michelle Beishline, began by reviewing the previous chapter; she asked the class to recall why the Colonists were unhappy with Great Britain. Then she asked who had heard of the Constitution and distributed a blank K-W-L worksheet. She told students to fill out everything they could think under the K (*Know*) column, first individually and then in a small group. Then she called on

K (Know)	W (Want to Know)	L (Learned)
—It was an important paper.	—How many people wrote it?	—55 men wrote it—farmers, merchants, and lawyers. They were called Framers.
—It had to do with freedom.	—When was it written?	
—A lot of people involved (John Hancock, George Washington, Ben Franklin)	—Who wrote it?	—Written in Philadelphia, summer 1787.
	—Why was it written?	—Kept secret so Framers could speak freely.
—It happened a long time ago.	—How long did it take to write?	
—Secret	—Where was it written?	—Nation needed a better government.
—Had to do with Boston Tea Party.	—Were there any women in on it?	—6 ideas:
—Was written with feather pen.	—How long was it?	1. protect rights of people
	—Why was it kept a secret?	2. powers controlled by law
	—What was it all about?	3. power is from people—voting
		4. power of government divided into 3 branches
Categories:		5. checks & balances
What was it all about?		6. federalism—a central gov't that shares power with the states
When?		
Who?		—Problems solved through compromise
How?		

FIGURE 4.2   **K-W-L worksheet for "Writing the Constitution"**   (*Source:* Michelle Beishline, Stanley G. Falk School, Buffalo, New York.)

students to share what they had written. As students volunteered, Michelle wrote their responses on a large chart on the board and interspersed some general questions: What is the Constitution? Why is it important? When do you think it was written? Who wrote it? She filled in more information under the K column as students elaborated on their answers.

Ms. Beishline then asked students what they would want to find out about the Constitution, and she asked them to list their questions under the W (*Want to Know*) column, first individually and then again in their groups. Once more, she called on students and filled in their responses on the chart on the board. Before students read the text, Michelle asked them what the most important categories of information were going to be, and the students responded with the categories in the lower left-hand corner of the chart: What was it all about? Why was it written? When? Who? The text selection on writing the Constitution was assigned as homework, and students were told to fill in the final column of the worksheet, L (*Learned*). Later in the day, a teacher aid read the text aloud for a few of the students with severe reading difficulties and helped them fill out the L column. The following day, students first compared what they had written in their small groups, and then the class completed the master chart with the help of the teacher.

The basic K-W-L activities may be extended by adding semantic mapping and summarizing activities. This is what Eileen Carr and Donna Ogle (1987) call K-W-L Plus. Michelle and her class developed a semantic map of the information they had learned (Figure 4.3.) After reading, they refined their semantic map. Using this map as an outline, the group then dictated the summary in Figure 4.4 as Michelle wrote on the overhead projector. Finally, the students copied their summary into their notebooks.

K-W-L lends itself to several variations. Students who have had several experiences with K-W-L could devise their own K-W-L lists in small groups, pairs, or individually. Teachers can add columns to the basic K-W-L format. For example, a "*How*" column could be added after the "*Want to Learn*" or "*Learned*" columns, and students could list ways of finding answers to their initial questions or new questions that arise after reading and discussing the textbook. Also, the *Learned* column could be divided into two sections, one for what was learned from books and another under which students could list what they have learned from other sources, from their personal experience, or from in-class activities such as role-playing or lab projects.

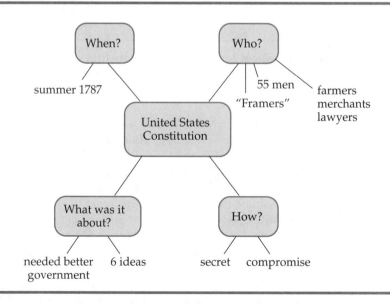

FIGURE 4.3   **K-W-L Plus concept map on the U.S. Constitution**

The Constitution of the United States

The Constitution was written because the nation needed a better government. It needed a government where the people would be protected.

The Constitution was written in 1787 in Philadelphia. It was written in the summertime. The men who wrote it were farmers, business owners (called merchants), and lawyers. There were 55 of them. These men were called "Framers" because they helped frame the Constitution. They met in secret so they could talk things out without worrying about anyone hearing them talk and argue. They solved problems by compromising.

The men came up with 6 ideas in the Constitution. The important ideas were to protect the people, to make sure that the government doesn't get too strong, that the power is gotten from the people by voting, that there are laws, that there are 3 parts to the government so no one gets too strong, and the parts check up on each other so no one gets too strong.

FIGURE 4.4   Student-dictated summary   (*Source:* Michelle Beishline, Stanley G. Falk School, Buffalo, New York.)

Directed Reading-Thinking Activity (DR-TA)

Russell Stauffer (1969, 1976) first proposed the Directed Reading-Thinking Activity as an alternative to the highly structured and teacher-directed basal reader lesson. However, this strategy quite naturally adapts to content area reading assignments as well. The content area DR-TA consists of four steps (Haggard, 1985):

- Activate prior knowledge.
- Predict what will be covered in the text.
- Read the text.
- Confirm, revise, or elaborate predictions with information from the text.

To illustrate how a DR-TA works for a reading assignment in a content area, we will use as an example a chapter on liquids from a high school physics text. In the first step, the teacher asks students to brainstorm briefly on the general topic, in this case "liquids." Once students have suggested a few things that come to mind, the teacher announces the specific topic of the lesson. Major sections of the chapter deal with pressure, buoyancy, and flotation. The teacher might write these three words on the board or direct students to glance quickly through the chapter, looking at major headings and illustrations.

Students discuss any other ideas engendered by this survey, and the teacher leads them in the second step of a DR-TA, to predict what will be covered or what they will learn in the chapter. These predictions are jotted down on the board. Because it promotes active involvement in reading, the prediction activity is the heart of a DR-TA. Students, in effect, generate some curiosity for the topic and set purposes for reading.

Purposeful reading is the third step: students read, and as they do so, they look for items on their list of predictions. The fourth step is to discuss what was read, with specific attention to what was predicted. Some predictions will be confirmed, some will require elaboration, and others will need to be revised. Students are also likely to find other information, not covered in their predictions, that they feel is important. As they discuss their reading, students should make specific reference to the text. The teacher can leave most of the discussion up to students, referring to the list of predictions, asking questions, and pointing out essential information as necessary.

The DR-TA is a flexible strategy. The essential steps of discussing prior knowledge, predicting, reading, and discussing what was learned can be approached in many ways. For instance, initial brainstorming and predicting can be done as a small-group activity or in pairs. Each group or pair adds to the list of predictions and then is responsible for discussing its predictions after reading. The reading itself can be assigned as homework, with the discussion and follow-up activities to be done the next day. There are also many ways to follow up a DR-TA. Martha Haggard (1985) suggests a group mapping activity and student selection of important vocabulary.

Two cautions about the DR-TA are in order. First, teachers should avoid putting words into students' mouths during the prediction and discussion phases. The value of the DR-TA is that it teaches readers to think for themselves. If the teacher asks specific questions prior to reading ("What do you predict Archimedes' principle is about? Do you think a brick could float?"), student involvement is stifled.

Second, DR-TA should not become a contest to see whose predictions are "correct." Although it is a laudable instinct to praise students for a job well done, praise for correct predictions gives the impression that the only good prediction is a right one. Many good predictions are possible, and divergent thinking should be encouraged. Good readers make predictions based on the best available knowledge but find that their knowledge is expanded or altered as they read, thus causing them to revise their original predictions. When a prediction is not verified in the text, teachers should encourage students to figure out why not or to articulate what was learned instead. Thinking actively and flexibly and using text information to expand one's knowledge are the truly praiseworthy accomplishments in a DR-TA. Good predictions are those that are creative, thoughtful, or plausible, given the available prior knowledge.

Reciprocal Teaching

In our discussion of accommodating diverse student capabilities, we used the term *scaffolding* to describe how teachers initially guide and support student learning and then gradually give students increasing responsibility for guiding their own learning. We described how teachers in the Strategic Literacy Network engaged students in reading apprenticeships, including explicit discussions of thinking and learning processes as students were initiated into new learning experiences (Schoenbach et al., 1999). This is a variation of *cognitive apprenticeship.* Content area teachers who use cognitive apprenticeship as their approach to instruction adhere to the principle that *knowing* cannot be separated from *doing.* That is, they believe that what students are taught in school must not be different from the real-world use of such knowledge. For example, teachers who believe in this approach would argue against teaching students to memorize facts about U.S. history because it is not the way historians use such facts. In the real world, historians interpret so-called facts about certain events and people's actions surrounding those events; they do not simply read and "neutrally" record in rote fashion what they recall from their reading. Why, then, proponents of cognitive apprenticeship argue, should students be expected to learn in a school culture that separates *what* is learned from *how* it is learned and used in the world outside the classroom (Brown, Collins, & Duguid, 1989)?

The term *apprenticeship* is used here to emphasize the central role of meaningful, authentic activity in any learning task. There is no room for activity that is not meaningful and authentic in traditional apprenticeships (in trades such as shoemaking or in professional apprenticeships such as medicine and law). However, students in middle and secondary schools are required daily to participate in activities that bear little if any resemblance to what practitioners do in the real world.

What can be done? John Brown and associates (1989) propose a cognitive apprenticeship approach to instruction "whereby [teachers] promote learning, first by . . . modeling their strategies for students in authentic activity . . . then [by supporting] students' attempts at doing the task . . . and finally [by empowering] students to continue independently" (p. 39). This instructional practice, which gradually releases responsibility to students for their own learning, has considerable research support, including Annemarie Palincsar and Ann Brown's work with reciprocal teaching of reading comprehension (Brown & Palincsar, 1989; Palincsar & Brown, 1984).

Reciprocal teaching has two major features. The first is instruction and practice of four comprehension strategies—predicting, question generating, clarifying, and summarizing. The second feature is a special kind of cognitive apprenticeship in which students gradually learn to assume the role of teacher in helping their peers construct meaning from text. Teachers teach and model the four comprehension strategies, often using some variation of the direct instruction model. Students learn the four strategies through dialogue among themselves. At first the teacher leads the dialogue, but as students become more proficient with the four strategies, the teacher gradually fades out of the dialogue and allows students to assume leadership.

Examples of the four strategies and a reciprocal teaching dialogue are given in Figure 4.5. We have included them in the order recommended by Brown and Palincsar (1989). However, it may be that the activities of predicting, summarizing, questioning, and clarifying may not always be undertaken in a rigid order. When students stop to question, clarify, and summarize partway through

Strategies for Reciprocal Teaching:
Sample Questions

Predicting

What are we going to learn about the role
of religion in Latin American society?
What kind of problems could the sine
and cosine ratios be used to solve?
What is likely to happen next?

Questioning

How are dicots and monocots different?
What were the results of the
Compromise of 1850?
What do you think is the main theme of
"A Good Man Is Hard to Find?"

Clarifying

Are there any parts that are not clear?
Are there any words you were unsure of?
Is there anything you think other readers
might misunderstand?

Summarizing

What did we learn?
What is/is not important in this chapter?
What is the main idea of this section?

Excerpt from a Lesson on Reading Titles and Lead
Paragraphs Using Cultural Literacy *by Hirsch (1987)*

Predicting

Teacher: Look at the chapter title, "What Every
American Needs to Know." What might the
author expect you to know?
Student 1: Things like the Founding Fathers,
Plymouth Rock, geography, five basic food
groups.
Teacher: Good predictions! Now, read paragraph
one.

Questioning

Student 2: What does Hirsch mean by "cultural
literacy"?
Student 3: World knowledge . . . that's what it
says in paragraph one.

Clarifying

Student 2: I'm still not sure what "cultural literacy" means exactly. I need some concrete examples.

Summarizing

Student 4: "Cultural literacy" is the common
background information we have stored in our
minds in order to understand what we read.
Student 2: Okay, so background information
means I already have ideas like the ones in the
book.

Predicting

Teacher: Good. Now, look at the subheading,
"The Decline of Teaching Cultural Literacy."
Student 5: I think this section will probably explain why students aren't becoming culturally
literate.

FIGURE 4.5 **Strategies for reciprocal teaching**

---

a selection, for instance, predicting may actually be the last thing they do before
they resume reading the next part of the text.

Successful use of reciprocal teaching with varied student populations has
been widely reported in professional literature. A review of 16 separate empirical studies indicated that reciprocal teaching generally yielded positive results

with students ranging from fourth grade through adult (Rosenshine and Meister, 1994). This review also suggested that reciprocal teaching was effective with students who had developed some decoding skills but who were poor in reading comprehension. Reciprocal teaching has been successfully adapted for social studies instruction of seventh- and eighth-grade learning disabled students who were learning English as a second language (Klingner & Vaughan, 1996). Reciprocal teaching has also been effective with a culturally diverse group of eighth-grade New Zealand students, many of whom had reading comprehension difficulties (Westera & Moore, 1995).

Two fundamentals of reciprocal teaching, supported by a substantial body of educational research, would appear to account for its effectiveness: direct strategy instruction and the gradual shift of responsibility for "teaching" from the teacher to the students (Pressley, 1998). Many of the teaching ideas described in this book would complement the four basic reciprocal teaching strateies, such as prereading prediction strategies (Chapter 6), questioning techniques (Chapter 7), vocabulary clarification (Chapter 8), and summarizing techniques (Chapter 10). The cognitive apprenticeship represented by reciprocal teaching could also be used to shift responsibility to students for activities such as discussion, checking the results of reading guides and homework assignments, revising and editing writing, or problem solving in math or science.

Obviously any implementation of reciprocal teaching requires the commitment of time and effort on the part of the teacher. The process of strategy instruction itself is time-consuming, especially when multiple strategies are taught. The process of fading responsibility from teacher to students also implies long-term practice of the strategies. To suggest a general time frame, Westera and Moore (1995) found that students with low reading comprehension scores who received 12 to 16 training sessions made significant gains on standardized tests, whereas similar students who had only 6–8 sessions made no gains.

Four important instructional practices are imbedded in reciprocal teaching (Rosenshine & Meister, 1994):

- Direct teaching of strategies, rather than reliance solely on teacher questioning
- Student practice of reading strategies with real reading, not with worksheets or contrived exercises
- Scaffolding of instruction; students as cognitive apprentices
- Peer support for learning

Reciprocal teaching involves a high degree of social interaction and collaboration, as students gradually learn to assume the role of teacher in helping their peers construct meaning from text. In essence, reciprocal teaching is authentic activity because "learning, both outside and inside school, advances through collaborative social interaction and the social construction of knowledge" (Brown, Collins, & Duguid, 1989, p. 40).

BEYOND THE DAILY PLAN: UNIT PLANNING

Teachers' instructional decisions clearly transcend the question of "What shall I do tomorrow?" Teachers also need a long-term view of teaching and learning. Reciprocal teaching, for instance, requires an ongoing commitment to the beliefs that students need to learn certain literacy strategies or processes and that students can learn from each other. We see this as part of a trend toward making schools more student centered and classrooms more socially interactive.

Teachers who understand the socially constructed nature of knowledge will plan to involve students in discussion, collaboration, and problem solving related to their content area studies. Also implied in this trend is a view of the curriculum as comprising meaningfully interrelated concepts and themes, not simply as isolated bits of information to be learned by rote. All of this implies that teachers will plan activities that enable students to make connections between content areas, between the real world and the world of the classroom, and between "knowing what" (facts and concepts) and "knowing how" (using facts and concepts in authentic ways).

In the following sections, we describe four frequently recommended approaches to integrating curriculum and accommodating the inherently social nature of learning: integrated language processes, interdisciplinary teaching, thematic teaching, and integrative curriculum. From these labels alone, it would seem that these approaches have much in common. Indeed, in the literature on integrated curricular practices, there is "inconsistency in use of terms and definitions" (Gavelek et al., 2000, p. 589). Nevertheless, there are some important distinctions.

Integrated Language Processes

Teachers who recognize the importance of the language in learning will plan to use some combination of reading, writing, listening, and speaking experiences as a tool to achieve a content area learning goal (Gavelek et al., 2000). Such integration has become common among teachers in the elementary grades, in which literacy instruction often includes reading and writing about science, social studies, and mathematics. Integrated language arts has also been institutionalized in many middle schools through the teaming of language arts teachers with teachers from other disciplines.

Integration of language arts may be initiated by an English teacher, or it may grow out of a content teacher's desire to go beyond the standard textbook and a traditional worksheet approach. For instance, a science or history teacher might assign complementary readings in trade books, an English teacher might coordinate an inquiry writing project with a colleague from another discipline, and teachers from any discipline may elect to have students write regularly in a learning log or journal. Spoken language is integrated into the curriculum through activities such as role-playing, small group discussion and projects, panel presentations, and debates.

In Chapters 1 and 2, we discussed the role of literacy and language in content area learning. If you have read those chapters you will understand our assertion that teachers in all disciplines have a responsibility to infuse practice with content-related literacy and language into their content area instruction. In that sense, integration of language arts is what this book is all about, and subsequent chapters will detail many strategies for accomplishing this.

Interdisciplinary Teaching

In the middle grades, it is quite common to assign students to interdisciplinary teams of teachers in order to create a school-within-a-school climate or the feeling that each student is special and belongs to a particular school "family" (Muth & Alvermann, 1999). Typically, interdisciplinary teams include teachers from each of the core academic areas (language arts, mathematics, social studies, and science), plus some representation from special education, physical education, music, art, and reading. Each team teaches the same group of students all year long so that teachers and students become well acquainted in their school-within-a-school. In addition, the team typically has a common planning time so that teachers can jointly construct lessons that will enable students to see how concepts learned in one discipline can apply in another. By teaming across disciplines, teachers create a learning environment that is intellectually stimulating for themselves as well as for their students. Teams can also help first-year teachers and experienced teachers who are new to a school more readily feel at ease and a part of the school community.

Although the built-in constraints of traditional high schools—such as subject matter specialization, inflexible scheduling, and large numbers of students—make interdisciplinary teaming difficult, special programs have been successful in even the largest of these schools. For example, the Humanitas program is an interdisciplinary, team-based approach to humanities teaching in the Los Angeles Unified School District. Because of the interdisciplinary nature of the program and its emphasis on building conceptual understanding of issues that have relevance for urban youth, teachers can frequently bypass textbooks in favor of primary source materials, newspapers, and novels. Essay questions rather than multiple-choice tests develop students' abilities to think and write in a critical vein about what they have read. For example, the following is an essay question from a ninth-grade interdisciplinary unit on culture and tradition (Aschbacker, 1991):

> The cosmology of a traditional culture permeates every aspect of that culture. This is illustrated in the following three cultural groups: the Eskimos, the Southwest Indians, and the Meso-Americans. Specifically, discuss the spirit world that each group believed in, and explain how it influenced [that

group's] culture and values. Include examples from your reading in art history, literature, and social studies to illustrate and substantiate your analysis. Finally, to what extent, if any, does the spirit world affect us today? (pp. 17–18)

Although interdisciplinary teaching can bridge all disciplines, there are also many opportunities for teachers from two or three disciplines to take an interdisciplinary approach. English and social studies teachers often work together, with the English teacher guiding the reading of literature relevant to a particular time period or cultural group that is being studied. Social studies and English teachers also cooperate frequently in helping students to conduct inquiry projects. They may share the responsibility for helping with topic selection, information searches, organization, writing, and editing. At the end, students may receive two separate grades for an inquiry project, one from each teacher representing his or her content specialty.

Harriet Cholden and Barbara Gertz (1996), fifth-grade teachers at Francis W. Parker School in Chicago, describe a unit they developed on the theme of "freedom and oppression" that combined elements of the social studies and language arts curricula. During the unit, each student read a biography of a historical figure such as Martin Luther King, Jr., Anne Frank, or Nelson Mandela. They also interviewed a person outside the school who had experienced significant freedom or oppression. As a culminating activity, students produced one-act historical fiction plays based on their accumulated knowledge and understanding.

English teachers may also team up successfully with their counterparts in science. Amy Schimberg and Heidi Grant, eighth-grade science and English teachers at John Jay Middle School in Cross River, New York, found that their disciplines had many natural connections in a mystery thematic unit designed to build on students' interest in recent high-profile crimes (Schimberg & Grant, 1998). In English class, Ms. Grant's students engaged in a mystery genre study. They read and discussed several types of mysteries and learned about the literary devices used by mystery writers. At the same time, a member of the local police force visited science classes to explain and demonstrate fingerprinting. Then, students were plunged into a simulated murder investigation. The crime scene was set and clues were left for the student investigators. Students applied previously learned skills in analyzing chemical and physical properties in the authentic context of the "forensic lab," in which stations for analyzing fingerprints, ink, fiber evidence, a handkerchief smelling of mysterious perfume, and poisons were set up. Student teams observed the crime scene, interviewed suspects (portrayed by school staff members), conducted forensic analyses, and kept all their notes and results in investigator's notebooks and a case file. At the end of their investigations, student teams presented their conclusions to the whole class. Schimberg and Grant recommend that "for a unit to be successful, subject area connections need to be natural; they should relate to one another and be meaningful to students" (p. 29).

Science and math also share natural affinities that make them good candidates for an interdisciplinary approach. Mathematics and science are compatible for integration in at least six ways (Berlin & White, 1994):

- *Ways of learning.* To learn science and math, students must be actively involved in exploratory learning.
- *Ways of knowing.* Both disciplines rely on inductive and deductive ways of knowing.
- *Process and thinking skills.* Science and math both involve classifying, collecting and organizing data, making hypotheses, measuring, observing, communicating, and other skills.
- *Content knowledge.* Many "big ideas" are common to math and science: probability, balance, conservation, systems, variability, scale, and others.
- *Attitudes and perceptions.* Scientists and mathematicians must learn to accept change, base decisions on data, have a desire for knowledge, work cooperatively, and be skeptical, honest, and logical.
- *Teaching strategies.* Both disciplines need to employ a mix of cooperative and individual activities, problem-solving and inquiry-based activities, use of technology and laboratory tools, and authentic assessments.

Technology is another content area that shares many fundamentals with science and math and therefore lends itself to three-way interdisciplinary teaching. Traditionally, technology teachers have worked in isolation from their colleagues in math and science, using a technological problem-solving method. Designing a car powered by a mouse trap or a balsa wood bridge-building contest are typical examples. Although such activities can be motivating, the scientific and mathematical principles underlying these projects are too frequently overlooked (Sanders, 1994). Students simply are not led to understand why one bridge is better than another or how to improve inherently weak designs.

As an alternative, Sanders (1994) suggests activities that are intended to be used by science, math, and technology teachers in concert. For example, students might be challenged to design and construct an electromagnetic device for moving junk automobiles, a generator that produces electricity from wind, a hydroponic plant-growing system, a hydraulic system for transporting hazardous materials, or a model rocket that maximizes height, velocity, and payload capacity. Teachers from all three disciplines would need to provide instruction that would enable students to complete a project. Each of these integration activities could be incorporated into existing curricula in three phases—a design phase, a construction phase, and an evaluation phase.

The latter phase, evaluation, is especially important because this is where students analyze data they have collected, test their solutions, and redesign the solutions, thus beginning a second pass through the design–construction–evaluation cycle. In the process, students are "doing science" in the sense of testing and reformulating hypotheses, and they are using mathematics in the design and evaluation of their projects.

Thematic Teaching

Distinctions between interdisciplinary teaming and thematic teaching are becoming increasingly blurred. Sometimes the two terms are even used synonymously. For us, the major distinction is that thematic teaching can be implemented successfully within a single content area classroom (e.g., a civics class), but the success of interdisciplinary teaming often depends on special organizational school structures, such as flexible block scheduling and common teacher planning periods. We think that this distinction has practical significance since so few schools throughout the United States have implemented interdisciplinary programs of study.

The single-discipline thematic unit allows teachers to incorporate a variety of materials and instructional groupings to meet the reading interests and needs of their students. History instruction can be transformed from an encyclopedic stream of names and dates to something more manageable and comprehensible for students. To do this, teachers must identify fundamental ideas or organizing concepts within the subject and selectively abandon less important material that might have been emphasized if the goal were to cover a certain amount of content by the end of the year. For example, Rodney White (1995) suggests organizing the study of world history around a thematic unit on religion. Rather than taking a strictly chronological approach to history, with the topic of religion given brief attention in disparate chapters, students could undertake a comparative study of the historical evolution of the world's religions. This would allow them to understand both the commonalties and differences among people and to explore issues such as the separation of church and state in the United States, the contrast between Eastern and Western worlds, and relationships among Judaism, Christianity, and Islam. Such a unitary approach to world history would be especially appropriate in a culturally diverse classroom. White also suggests a culturally sensitive study of U.S. history that could be developed around the theme "What is an American?" with students thinking about and discussing questions of cultural unity versus diversity.

In science as in history, there is a movement away from teaching a collection of isolated facts. Ellen Metzger (1992) suggests that the study of earth science is especially effective for promoting scientific literacy because it integrates biology, chemistry, physics, history, and mathematics. She proposes an organization of the earth science curriculum around the theory of plate tectonics, or the formation, movement, and geologic activity associated with the layers of the earth and the lithospheric plates that compose the earth's surface. Other earth science topics, such as climate, geology, energy resources, and evolution, can all be related to plate tectonic theory. Similarly, Susan Offner (1992) proposes a biology unit founded on the theme of human heredity that would tie together concepts of protein structures, enzymes, DNA, genetics, and hereditary diseases. Understandings that students consolidate in this unit would carry over to the study of the various systems of the human body, evolution, and other diverse units of the biology curriculum.

Thematic teaching within a single discipline helps students see the larger picture. It also makes instructional decision making and learning a process shared between teachers and students. Perhaps, most important, there is the allure that thematic teaching holds for students, who are frequently the last ones consulted when it comes to choosing what they will read and how they will be assessed in the traditional content area classrooms described by Goodlad (1984) and others.

Integrative Curriculum

Richard Powell and colleagues (Powell & Skoog, 1995; Powell, Skoog, & Troutman, 1996; Powell, 1997) describe an integrated, theme-based curriculum for middle schools that emphasizes student discovery and ownership of learning. Rather than being based in traditional linear subject matter curricula, an integrative curriculum is organized around themes, often selected with input from teachers, community members, parents, and students. The various subject areas are drawn on as resources that can contribute to the development of a given theme.

Where traditional multidisciplinary approaches maintain disciplinary boundaries and an emphasis on coverage or mastery of a predetermined set of curricular objectives, integrated curriculum promotes "uncoverage" of content through "a generative and inductive process that leads to student understanding" (Powell, Skoog, & Troutman, 1996, p. 10). Instead of learning the facts and principles of photosynthesis as part of a biology unit on plants, for instance, students would "uncover" the biochemistry of photosynthesis as part of their study of global warming or ecology. Untied from traditional linear coverage of a subject, the role of the teacher changes in an integrative curriculum. Teachers are likely to do less "dispensing" of information and instead do more facilitating and managing of learning, in part by directing students to resources in the library and on-line (Powell, 1997).

Powell and associates describe middle schools that have adopted an integrated curriculum. In addition, proponents of the theory of multiple intelligences have documented similar kinds of integrative curricula across all levels, from elementary to high school (Campbell & Campbell, 1999). Psychologist Howard Gardner (1983, 1991) proposes that intelligence is more complex than the traditional view would have us believe. He has identified nine forms of problem-solving capacity, or intelligence, in humans: linguistic, logical-mathematical, visual-spatial, bodily kinesthetic, musical, interpersonal, intrapersonal, naturalist, and existential. Using Gardner's work as a theoretical foundation, many teachers and schools have developed curricula that allow students to develop all facets of their intelligence.

In middle schools and high schools that have adopted a multiple intelligences perspective, students and teachers engage in interdisciplinary, project-based learning that gives each student an opportunity to contribute and learn using his or her strengths. Many of the projects that students undertake have a community-based component as well. Campbell and Campbell (1999) describe high schools in Washington and California that have adopted elements of integrative curriculum despite the obstacles of scheduling, short class periods, staff turnover, and high-stakes state testing. In these schools, students work on extended projects under the guidance of an interdisciplinary team of teachers. At one school, seniors must complete a 24-week application project in order to graduate. Developed with the mentoring of community experts and teachers, application projects might involve planning an event, learning a new skill, designing a product, offering a service, or conducting a special investigation. As part of the project, students must do research and give a final presentation to a group of informed adults.

Integrative curriculum requires a special dedication from administrators and teachers. Because of the complexity of integrating curriculum, schools need to provide a good deal of staff development and planning time. Some staff members, as well as people in the community, may see integrative curriculum as a threat to the status quo of traditional disciplinary structures and instruction. Indeed, it could be argued that a knowledge of disciplines and the cultural, historical, and epistemological influences which have shaped them are themselves important aspects of education (Gavelek et al., 2000). A movement toward an integrative curriculum, with its emphasis on student decision making, problem solving, critical thinking, and investigation of local, national, or global issues, may also occasion political or religious opposition. Although not appropriate for every school, advocates of integrative curriculum point to the broad range of student competency, motivation, and achievement that can result.

Unit Planning

Whether a thematic unit integrates learning across content areas or is developed within a single discipline, careful planning and preparation are required. The steps in planning a thematic unit follow the decision-making process described at the beginning of this chapter. The first step would be to select a unifying theme or organizing concept for the unit (Goerss, 1996). The possibilities both within and across disciplines are enormous. It may help to think of three categories of themes (Fogarty, 1994): topical themes, such as dinosaurs; conceptual themes, such as systems; and problematic themes, such as "How do humans survive?"

Timothy Shanahan (1995) warns against picking topical themes that do not allow students to inquire deeply into meaningful ideas. For instance, if a unit on dinosaurs meant reading *Jurassic Park* (Crichton, 1990), writing some dinosaur poems or science fiction, and printing out dinosaur graphics with the classroom computer, students might get some useful reading and writing practice, but they would not be learning much about dinosaurs, about science (beyond the considerably fictionalized concepts in the novel), or about math. However, a dinosaur unit that led students to explore concepts such as extinction, climatic change, evolution, chaos theory, DNA, geologic time, habitat, classification of species, and measurement would represent much more substantial learning.

Earlier in the chapter, when we discussed cognitive apprenticeship, we said that learning will be more meaningful if students are engaged in authentic activity—if they can discern meaningful purposes in what they are doing. Bette Bergeron and Elizabeth Rudenga (1996) propose an interrelated five-part framework for evaluating the authenticity of learning activities in a unit plan:

- *Purpose.* Literacy activities intended primarily for practice or evaluation will be less meaningful than those designed to communicate or share ideas.
- *Choice.* To the extent possible, students and teachers should negotiate curricular goals, activities, and materials rather than having all choices made by the teacher.
- *Audience.* Reading and writing are less purposeful if the only audience is the teacher. Learning can be shared with peers and audiences outside the classroom.
- *Resources.* Contrived learning materials are inherently less motivating and meaningful than real-life resources. Students benefit from using a variety of resources, print and nonprint.
- *Relevance.* Activities should meet relevant curriculum requirements and the development of meaningful learning.

Of course, meeting each criterion for authenticity with every learning activity would not be practical. A framework such as this, however, does give you a means to focus your planning on genuine learning rather than simply covering curriculum or keeping students occupied.

Once a thematic focus or organizing concept has been selected for a unit, teachers will begin listing overall goals, related concepts and skills, available materials, possible activities and teaching strategies, and ways to evaluate students' learning, all with the particular needs and abilities of their students in mind (Goerss, 1996). This will take some time as resources are located, materials such as study guides and handouts are developed, Internet sites are located, and new ideas for the unit come from reflection, research, and conversations with students and colleagues. To keep the ideas for a unit organized, teachers often use a web or graphic organizer to map out concepts, resources, or activities. In Figure 4.1, we illustrated a completed concept planning web for a unit on the American Revolution, and Figure 4.6 shows two generic variations of planning webs.

The final stages of unit planning involve planning activities, developing assessment procedures, and constructing a time line for the unit. To enhance student interest, engagement, and learning, it is best to plan a variety of activities, including whole-class, small-group, and independent activities, some that are teacher assigned, and some that are self-selected by students. J. D. Cooper (1997) suggests the use of three chronological categories of activities. *Initiating activities*

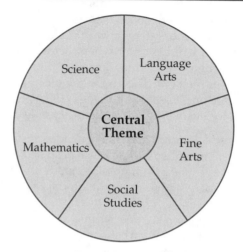

Cross-Disciplinary Planning Web

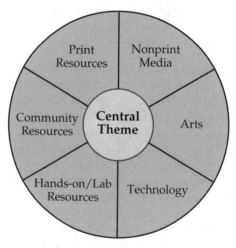

Resource Planning Web

FIGURE 4.6   Planning webs for thematic teaching

should motivate students, activate prior knowledge and build background, and help students take responsibility for their own learning. *Developing activities* involve students in reading, writing, discussing, problem solving, and hands-on experience with making something, creating, or experimenting. *Culminating activities* allow students to share their learning, reflect on the ideas in the unit, and evaluate their own efforts.

Teachers as Researchers

▼▼

Recently, many teachers have included systematic and thoughtful inquiry in teaching and learning as part of their overall planning. Through this teacher research (sometimes called action research), they have shared their professional lives with wider audiences through presentations to district, local, state, or national conferences or publication in the Internet, in books, or in journals. The main purpose of most teacher research is "to *teach better*, to act or understand something differently so that their students' learning is enhanced. . . . The purpose is not to 'do research,' but to observe, document, and analyze the daily work of . . . teaching and learning as it occurs in and out of classroom and school contexts" (Lytle, 2000, p. 702). For example, Bob Fecho (1998) wrote about his experiences as a white teacher grappling with issues of language and dialect with his African American high school students in Philadelphia. Some teachers also collaborate with university researchers to conduct classroom investigations; both of us (Alvermann, Olson, & Umpleby, 1993; Alvermann et al., 1996; Phelps & Weaver, 1999) have learned a great deal from such collaborations.

The questions that teachers research are often highly personal, arising from some "discrepancy, nudge, problem, curiosity, desire, surprise, contradiction, and/or 'felt need' that is directly tied to their particular setting" (Lytle, 2000, p. 696). Teacher research takes many different forms, sometimes quite different from the standard conception of "research" as something involving variables, control groups, treatments, and sophisticated statistical analyses. Often, teachers' inquiries are reported as carefully considered narratives, personal accounts, case studies, or other versions of what is considered qualitative research (Grady, 1998). Teacher research is disseminated by such national groups as the Breadloaf Rural Teachers Network and the National Writing Project as well as in the journals of various national teacher associations, *Harvard Educational Review*, and *New Advocate*.

Because of their involvement in the instructional process, content area teachers are in a unique position to conduct meaningful research. By defining the questions, choosing the procedures, analyzing the results, and applying their findings, teachers can find specific answers to specific problems in ways that no "outsider" could. Although teacher research is sometimes criticized for lack of rigor or for being too personalized, we believe that teachers' voices are an essential element in our efforts to better understand teaching and learning.

Putting it all together.   Recently, Steve participated in a conference on using technology in education at which he heard a presentation by Gene Kulbago, an English teacher at Niagara Middle School in Niagara Falls, New York. Gene and his colleague, earth science teacher Mary Marcinkowski, have collaborated on an earth science research project that illustrates many of the ideas presented in this chapter. Niagara Middle is an urban middle school that serves a diverse population of students. It features a schoolwide technology program in which all students learn to use word processing, desktop publishing and presentation software, Internet browsers, digital cameras, and scanners. Although sixth-graders learn basic skills in a ten-week introductory technology course, the entire three-year curriculum of the school is infused with applications of technology in virtually every content area.

Gene and Mary are experienced teachers, both professionally active in state and local teacher organizations. (Mary was recently president of the Science Teachers Association of New York State.) They teach approximately 50 eighth-grade students in an honors program, all of whom are taking Mary's earth science course for New York State Regents high school credit. In order to receive credit for this course (and as part of state high school graduation requirements), students take a statewide earth science examination at the end of the year. Ten percent of the examination is awarded for completing a research project on an appropriate earth science topic.

The seeds of the earth science research project are sown in seventh grade, in which students learn basic research skills and the format for a research paper and then apply them to a short paper on a student-selected science topic. Then in eighth grade, Mr. Kulbago and Mrs. Marcinkowski and their students embark on earth science research projects that will occupy much of their time, especially in the second half of the school year. Figure 4.7 shows a planning web for this project. After the teachers have outlined the general parameters of the project, students begin to think about topics they would like to pursue. Students have investigated a wide range of topics, such as the formation of hurricanes or tornadoes, dinosaur extinction theories, the geology of the Niagara River gorge, New York State oil and natural gas reserves, evidence for global warming, and the causes and effects of the Buffalo blizzard of 1977.

With guidance from their teachers, students begin collecting information for their projects. They are required to gather information from both electronic and traditional print resources. To get students started, the teachers have selected 18 sample Internet sites that feature reliable and useful earth science information along with links to other sites. Gene posts these on his own Web site, which students access for reference during their projects. Gene's Web site also includes specifications for writing a research paper and a summary of MLA guidelines for style and citations. On-line, students branch out to a great variety of Web sites, due to the diversity of their topics. Gene says that most students would prefer to conduct their searches entirely on-line, but he and Mary believe that it is important that students be facile with traditional print resources as well, such as science encyclopedias, scientific journals, and science trade books. Throughout their research, students are guided to make critical judgments about the credibility of the information they are collecting, especially from the Internet, by considering the authors' knowledge, purpose, and affiliations or other credentials.

By February, students are expected to begin drafting their research papers. When students have a final draft completed, Mr. Kulbago evaluates them for adherence to MLA guidelines and other standard writing conventions. Students are then expected to revise as needed, after which Mrs. Marcinkowski evaluates the papers for their scientific content. This evaluation is followed by a conference with Mrs. Marcinkowski, and then the research papers are revised and finalized during language arts class time.

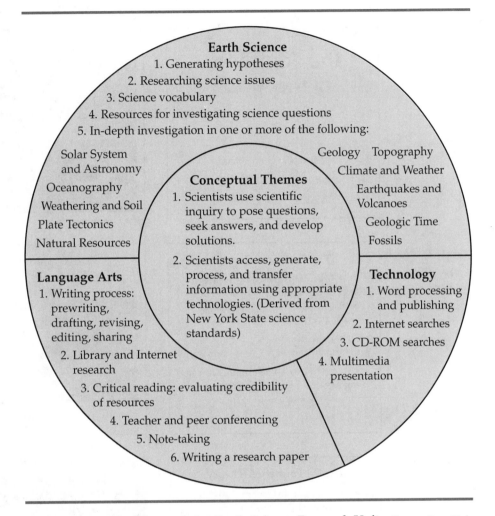

Earth Science
1. Generating hypotheses
2. Researching science issues
3. Science vocabulary
4. Resources for investigating science questions
5. In-depth investigation in one or more of the following:

Solar System and Astronomy
Oceanography
Weathering and Soil
Plate Tectonics
Natural Resources

Geology   Topography
Climate and Weather
Earthquakes and Volcanoes
Geologic Time
Fossils

Conceptual Themes
1. Scientists use scientific inquiry to pose questions, seek answers, and develop solutions.
2. Scientists access, generate, process, and transfer information using appropriate technologies. (Derived from New York State science standards)

Language Arts
1. Writing process: prewriting, drafting, revising, editing, sharing
2. Library and Internet research
3. Critical reading: evaluating credibility of resources
4. Teacher and peer conferencing
5. Note-taking
6. Writing a research paper

Technology
1. Word processing and publishing
2. Internet searches
3. CD-ROM searches
4. Multimedia presentation

FIGURE 4.7   **Planning web for Earth Science Research Unit**   (*Source:* Gene Kulbago and Mary Marcinkowski, Niagara Middle School, Niagara Falls, New York.)

As students are completing their research papers, they begin preparing a Power Point multimedia presentation of their findings. These presentations are designed to highlight the major findings in a creative way that will hold audience interest, along with a concluding statement of the importance of the topic. Students share the completed multimedia presentations at a special parent night. Figure 4.8 shows sample "slides" from student Frank Accardo's multimedia presentation.

Together, the research paper and Power Point presentations constitute the "research" portion of the state earth science exam. Ms. Marcinkowski calculates

The Formation of the Moon

Frank Accardo
Earth Science 8
Mrs. Marcinkowski
Mr. Kulbago
June 2000

The Collision Theory

The Collision Theory

- This theory's main idea says that a large body in space collided with the earth in its early development stages causing parts to shatter.

- Later those same parts came together to form the moon.

- This can be proved believable because samples of the earth's rock were the same as the moon's.

The Capture Theory

The basis of this theory states mainly that the earth and moon were formed separately and the moon revolved around the sun. But on one special occasion the earth's gravity caught the moon and pulled it into its own region, hence making it the earth's moon.

The Co-Formation Theory

The main idea of this theory says that the earth and moon were formed as a double-planet system and that they were both formed from a cloud of dust. Some experts believe that our whole universe was formed from a cloud of dust. If they were both formed from this so-called cloud of dust then it's only logical that since they were formed together they stayed together, hence their position now.

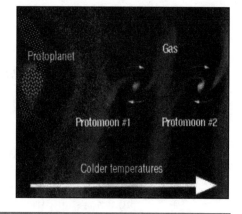

FIGURE 4.8   Multimedia slides for Earth Science Research Presentation
(*Source:* Frank Anthony Accardo, Niagara Middle School, Niagara Falls, New York.)

The Escape Theory

The English mathematician George H. Darwin suggested in 1879 that the earth and moon were literally formed together. Because of the earth's attraction to the sun a great bulge began to form on the side of it. At this time the earth's rotation had a much greater speed than it does now and spun a great amount faster. As the bulge grew, it began to break away from the earth. As soon as the bulge was large enough and the earth was spinning fast enough, the bulge just broke off into space. But since the newly formed moon wasn't strong enough to escape the earth's gravity, it was caught and has stayed there ever since as the earth's moon.

My Conclusion

There are so many theories on how our magnificent moon was formed and information backing each one, who knows which is actually true? Hopefully as science and mankind progress into the future we will have a better idea of the moon's actual formation and maybe we'll even know for sure how it all really happened. Until then all we can do is study the theories we have today and try and choose for ourselves which is true.

Bibliography

Bill Arnett. "The moon" Last updated: 1/5/00. 1/20/00 http://seds.lpl.arizona.edu/nineplanets/luna.html.

Gamow, George. Moon. New York. Abelard-Schuman. 1959.

Johnson. "Moon making." 2/01/00. http://www.kidsnspace.org/moon.htm.

Bibliography

"Moon." 1995 Microsoft Encarta. Version 95. CD-ROM. 1995.

University of Michigan. "The Formation of the Moon." 1/20/00 http://www.windows.umich.edu.

World Book. "How the Moon was Formed." 1/25/00. http://www.worldbook.com/fun/moon/html/formed.htm.

FIGURE 4.8   continued

a final grade for the two projects by evaluating the depth of the research, the variety of resources used, the expression of students' understanding of the topic, and the appropriateness of the topic to the earth science curriculum. This then becomes 10% of students' earth science exam grade, added to 15% for a practical hands-on laboratory activity and 75% for a traditional pencil-and-paper examination.

It is important to note that for experienced teachers such Gene Kulbago and Mary Marcinkowski, planning is usually ongoing and cumulative. They have developed different aspects of the earth science research unit over the three years that they have presented it, and at the end of the current school year they were already making plans for what they would add to the project next year to make it more meaningful and broad reaching. One addition will be student oral reports in order to strengthen the speaking and listening aspects of the projects.

Another facet they would like to add is a social studies component so that students can also consider the historical and social contexts of scientific issues. For instance, students who chose to research the Niagara River gorge might investigate the social, political, and economic issues surrounding the development of tourist attractions at Niagara Falls, the generation of hydroelectric power, or the shared border between the United States and Canada. Considering such aspects of a topic would incorporate a social constructionist aspect to the project as students learned that science is not just "neutral" facts but rather has ramifications that are socially shaped and contested and which call on learners to construct and defend their own interpretations.

This earth science unit exemplifies good applications of integrated language processes and interdisciplinary teaching. Teachers from two disciplines, science and English, have collaborated to integrate technology, reading, writing, speaking, and listening as fundamental tools in extending student understanding of several earth science topics. In this case, the unit theme encompasses the broad topic of scientific investigation and is specifically keyed to one of the state requirements for successful completion of the earth science course. Although the disciplinary boundaries of English and science are maintained, the unit is designed to have students learn and apply skills and strategies that overlap between the two subject areas. This unit meets all the criteria for authenticity suggested by Bergeron and Rudenga (1996). Specific topics and a variety of print and nonprint resources are chosen by students. Major purposes of the project are for students to investigate meaningful topics and to communicate their findings in multiple formats to an audience of their peers. Also, the activities are all directly relevant to both local and state curriculum requirements.

SUMMARY

As you read about the various ways that teachers can plan lessons and units, we are sure you found some ideas attractive, others impractical or incompatible with your situation, and thought of ways to modify other ideas to suit your style, your students, and your content area. We would not be so presumptive as to prescribe a particular planning approach for any teacher. However, we have tried to emphasize four points that will influence your planning. First, we encourage you to think about how students will use language and literacy in your content area. Second, you can look for ways to help students take charge of their own learning. Third, learning will be more meaningful and long-lasting if your students can make connections among the concepts they learn, connections between content areas, and connections to what they know and experience outside of school. Finally, there are no short-term "fixes" for the difficulties many students encounter with their content area studies, but when teachers commit to integrating literacy learning with the learning of content over a period of time, there will be visible gains in student achievement. This has been clearly demonstrated by teachers in the Strategic Literacy Network with their diverse urban population (Schoenbach et al., 1999).

SUGGESTED READINGS

Au, K. (1998). Social constructivism and the school literacy learning of students of diverse backgrounds. *Journal of Literacy Research, 30,* 297–319.

Echevarria, J., Vogt, M., & Short, D. (2000). *Making content comprehensible for English language learners.* Boston: Allyn & Bacon.

International Society for Technology in Education (2000). *National Educational Technology Standards for Students: Connecting Curriculum & Technology.* Eugene, OR: International Society for Technology in Education.

Leu, D., & Leu, D. (1999). *Teaching with the Internet: Lessons from the classroom.* Norwood, MA: Gordon.

Lounsbury, J. H. (Ed.) (1992). *Connecting the curriculum through interdisciplinary instruction.* Columbus, OH: National Middle School Association.

Miller, E. (1998). *The Internet resource directory for K–12 teachers & librarians.* Englewood, CO: Teacher Ideas Press. [Updated annually; see Libraries Unlimited Web site for most recent version: http://www.lu.com/Internet_Resource_Directory]

Schoenbach, R., Greenleaf, C., Cziko, C., & Hurwitz, L. (1999). *Reading for understanding: A guide to improving reading in middle and high school classrooms.* San Francisco: Jossey-Bass.

Sharp, V., Levine, M., & Sharp, R. (1998). *The best web sites for teachers,* 2nd ed. Eugene, OR: International Society for Technology in Education.

Weaver, C., Chaston, J., & Peterson, S. (1995). *Theme exploration: A voyage of discovery.* Portsmouth, NH: Heinemann.

SOFTWARE REFERENCES

eReader
Center for Applied Special Technology
Peabody, MA

HyperCard
Apple Education
Cupertino, CA
http://www.apple.com/education/

HyperStudio
Knowledge Adventure
Torrance, CA
http://www.KnowledgeAdventure.com/

Power Point
Microsoft Corporation
www.microsoft.com

textHelp
textHELP Systems Ltd.
Antrim, N. Ireland
www.texthelp.com

WebWhacker
Forest Technologies
Cary, IL
http://www.ForestTech.com/

Assessment of Students and Textbooks

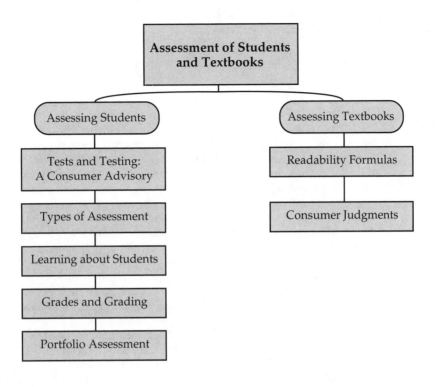

The past decade has brought many changes in the nature of educational assessment. There has been a marked proliferation of assessment options and requirements; students are being assessed in schools for varied and often conflicting purposes. Various constituencies look to assessment for different reasons and engage in an ongoing and sometimes rancorous debate over how student assessment should be conducted. The issues that have been raised are far from being resolved. Given the limitations inherent in educational assessment, many of them never will be resolved. In this chapter we address many of the issues surrounding student assessment, but because of their complexity and intractability, we do not presume to settle the many theoretical and philosophical questions that exist. Instead, we concentrate on the practical day-to-day assessment decisions that teachers make.

How well can students read, write, think, and study? Can they apply what they know? How can teachers fairly and accurately reflect student knowledge through the grades they award? How difficult, interesting, and useful are available texts? This chapter explores some ways to find answers to these questions.

In the following reminiscence, Dawn Voelker, a math teacher at West Seneca (New York) Central Schools, reflects on what it was like to be on the receiving end of teacher assessment. We think it captures many of the difficulties experienced by students and teachers.

▼▼▼▼▼▼▼

I can clearly remember my friend Kathy and I working on a project in high school. It involved research, reading, and an interview. We chose the same topic, so we decided to do the paper together. It started off great. We met every night possible and helped one another out. As time went on, she wasn't doing any of the reading and research. On the other hand, I was working my tail off. I got to the point where I didn't care because I knew we were getting separate grades anyway.

When the interviewing part came up, she made the whole thing up. I told her that she had better work harder, but she insisted she would do fine. I continued to do my project and put forth more effort than on any other paper. Kathy's laziness inspired me to work even harder. I wanted to do better than she did.

The projects were handed in, graded, and returned to us within a week. As the papers were being passed back, I glanced over at Kathy. I was expecting disappointment. Instead, she gleamed, held up her paper, and said, "I got an A minus." I thought to myself, "Great! This means I at least have an A."

When I got my paper back, there on the front was a huge C+. Below the grade was a note: "Misspellings, grammatical errors and run-ons." I felt like crawling under my desk. My face got red-hot as Kathy stared at me, waiting for me to announce my grade. Instead, I just stuck the project in my folder and stared straight ahead.

I couldn't understand why I had put forth all the effort and gotten an average grade. Just because I had misspellings and run-ons? That was completely unfair. Kathy put down anything and made it sound good and got an A. I didn't have the nerve to confront my teacher and tell him that I had worked so hard and deserved a better grade. I wanted to tell him that Kathy practically made hers up. I just didn't say anything because I trusted that he knew more about grading than I did.*

▼▼▼▼▼▼▼

Most of us can commiserate with Dawn's dismay and confusion, yet we would be reluctant to criticize the teacher too harshly. After all, he saw only the product of Dawn's and Kathy's work, not the process of producing them.

There are many variables in a teacher's day, many things to consider as decisions are made about what will happen in the classroom. There are, of course, students. Middle-grade and high school teachers often see from 100 to 150 or more students in a day. Like Dawn and Kathy, each of these students has his or her own personality, aptitudes, interests, and effect on classroom dynamics. They represent at least 100 energetic bundles of human variability. Teachers must somehow plan instruction that meets their disparate needs and must make periodic judgments—in the form of grades—of how well individual students have learned a subject. Textbooks and other text and nontext materials represent

———

*Used with permission of Dawn Voelker, West Seneca Central Schools, West Seneca, NY.

another set of variables for teachers. Text materials especially will vary greatly in their levels of difficulty, interest, and utility. They may be well suited to students' needs; they may be quite inappropriate. The more you know about these variables—students and texts—the more effective you can be as a teacher.

ASSESSING STUDENTS

Experts on educational evaluation talk about two purposes for assessing students. *Formative assessment* is intended to help "form," or develop, a student. Formative assessment helps a teacher to draw conclusions about the various strengths and weaknesses of the individual, those things that might help or hinder learning. *Summative assessment* is intended to make a "summarizing" judgment of what a person has learned or done. Grades on tests, assignments, and report cards are examples of summative assessments.

Whatever the purposes of assessment, we believe that good assessment practices have certain characteristics:

1. *Good assessment draws on multiple sources of information.* No single test—whether it is a standardized, norm-referenced, commercially published test of student achievement or a teacher-made, ten-item multiple-choice pop quiz on last night's homework—can tell a teacher the "true" state of a student's knowledge.
2. *Good assessment results in information that is useful to both students and teachers.* Students need to know how they are doing, what they are doing right, and what they can do to improve. Teachers need to know about students' attitudes, interests, background knowledge, and aptitude for reading, writing, and other academic tasks.
3. *Good assessment gives students optimal conditions for showing their capabilities.* Varied assessment procedures, fairly introduced and interpreted, give students the chance to show their individual strengths.
4. *Good assessment involves students in self-assessment.* In the long run, the judgments that students make about themselves are just as important as—if not more important than—the judgments teachers make about students. Self-evaluation is an essential component of learning how to learn.
5. *Good assessment admits the potential of fallibility.* After all is said and done, teachers must acknowledge that some students will remain enigmas and that some judgments, no matter how carefully considered, will be inaccurate.

Tests and Testing: A Consumer Advisory

There are many stakeholders in the debates over student assessment, and their demands frequently conflict (Pearson, 1998). Community members have numerous concerns: Are tax dollars being well spent? Do our schools compare favorably with those in other districts or states? Are the values and culture of the community being fairly represented? Is my child learning as well as I would like? Politicians at the local, state, and national levels try to represent the many voices of their community, but they frequently view assessment as a means to further their political agendas as well. Test results may be used by politicians to promote funding for educational programs or to further attacks on public schools, teachers' unions, or particular aspects of the curriculum.

School administrators view assessment as a way to demonstrate accountability and program effectiveness, yet they must also consider how cost-effective various assessment techniques may be. Teachers are looking for ways to find out how well students are progressing, both so that they can report to other stakeholders and so that they can devise effective instruction. At the same time, teachers know that their own performance will be judged by how well their students do on statewide or district testing. Of all the voices in the assessment debate, the one least often heard is that of students, yet they have perhaps the most important stake of all.

The professed purposes of testing are as varied and contradictory as the stakeholders. Reformers of all political stripes may see tests as a means to drive school reform. Some may look to state or national assessments as a way to raise student achievement, whereas others see alternative assessment procedures as a way to complement curricular reforms and increase students' participation in their learning. Some people see assessment as a means to ensure equity for students of diverse backgrounds, whereas others point out that assessment procedures often reinforce or even create an unequal playing field for children of different economic, linguistic, or cultural backgrounds. Many teachers argue that assessment should be a professional tool that they can use to evaluate and improve instruction. However, for state boards of education, college admissions officers, and employers, assessment may provide a gatekeeping function, determining whether an individual can graduate from high school, enter college, engage in certain professions, or hold a particular job.

The conflicting demands and claims surrounding educational assessment present several very real problems to classroom teachers. Among them are

- *Validity.* How can we be sure that a particular assessment tool is really telling us what we want to know?
- *Credibility.* How well will other stakeholders—parents, administrators, taxpayers, etc.—accept the results of assessment?
- *Time.* Demands on a teacher's time are daunting. How can we get useful information without taking too much valuable instructional time? Will teachers be given adequate time to expand and develop their knowledge of assessment strategies?
- *Influences on curriculum and teaching.* How can we deal with the pressure to "teach to the test," to alter what and how we teach in order to increase student performance on externally imposed assessments?

‣ *Teacher knowledge and training.* Will we have the requisite knowledge of assessment, the curriculum, and students? Will there be opportunities for inservice training and reflection in order to design assessments and collect, analyze, and report results?

‣ *Equity.* Will assessment fairly reflect the abilities of all our students, especially those from diverse linguistic, social, or cultural backgrounds? Do we promote fairness by asking all students to take the same test in the same circumstances, or do we provide students with alternatives so that each can show what he or she is capable of doing in optimal circumstances?

While reading the following discussion of tests and testing, you should keep in mind the limitations of testing. You might think of tests as being like snapshots: some may be flattering, and some may be downright dreadful. Your friends or family might like a photo you think makes you look goofy, whereas *you* might prefer one that makes you look sleek, athletic, or intellectual, even though others say it looks nothing like you. No photo, not even a portrait by a talented photographer, is the real you. It is at best an image of you at a particular time that, by skill or accident, may communicate something of your essence.

So it is with almost any instrument or procedure designed to evaluate or assess students. A student may do well or poorly on a particular test, but the test alone cannot tell definitely why the student performed that way or whether that is typical of the student's performance. It is at best a suggestion of what was going on inside the student's head at that particular moment. However, over a period of time, after experiencing the student's oral and written output, scores on tests and assignments, and participation (or lack of it) in classroom activities, you can form a composite judgment of how well he or she is doing in your subject and of his or her general aptitude as a student. The best decisions about students will be made after carefully considering many sources of information.

Teachers who work with students of diverse cultural backgrounds must especially be aware of the cultural biases that can influence tests and testing. Tests (and the curricula they are designed to assess) are generally devised by members of the dominant culture and may be inadequate for evaluating the knowledge, achievement, and ability of students from other cultures. There are several sources of cultural bias in standardized tests (Garcia & Pearson, 1994; Helms, 1992) and in more innovative forms of testing (Au, 1998); many of these biases apply to teacher-designed tests as well:

1. *Content and conceptual bias.* Test content is most likely to reflect the knowledge and values of mainstream society. Test content may be more or less familiar to members of different cultures, who may therefore assign different meanings to the same concept. Even though some concepts may have been covered by the instructor, other concepts that are unfamiliar may appear in the wording of test questions or multiple-choice responses. Standardized tests also predominantly emphasize isolated skills, literal-level facts, and low-level thinking.

2. *Linguistic bias.* Lack of familiarity with academic English, with specific vocabulary, or with familiar synonyms (e.g., *canine* for *dog*) may influence test scores for students whose primary language or dialect is not standard English. Time limits will be especially problematic for bilingual students. It is difficult to decide whether bilingual students are better off being tested in English or in their native language, and a test in either language may not demonstrate what a student knows in both languages.

3. *Functional bias.* The mainstream conventions of testing, where adults request known answers to questions that have no apparent functional goal, may be perceived as foolish or nonsensical to members of other cultures. Some cultures may also prize answers that are imaginative or elaborative as opposed to literally true. Many tests are not flexible enough to fully assess the capabilities of English language learners.

4. *Consequential bias.* Results of testing are often used as graduation requirements or to place students in remedial or lower-track classes. Unfortunately, students of color and low-income students are disproportionately impacted, and this is due in part to the biases inherent in test content and procedures. To compound this problem, students in remedial programs are subjected to further testing, most of which focuses on discrete skills and isolated, literal-level facts. This results in fragmented, skills-based instruction for these students.

We take the final point in our advisory from Georgia Garcia and David Pearson (1994), who remind us of the position of power we assume as teachers:

> Assessment is a political act. Assessments tell people how they should value themselves and others. They open doors for some and close them for others. The very act of giving an assessment is a demonstration of power: One individual tells the other what to read, how to respond, how much time to take. One insinuates a sense of greater power because of greater knowledge (i.e., possession of the correct answers). The political dilemma is a problem for all students, but it is particularly acute for students from diverse cultural, linguistic, and economic backgrounds whose cultures, languages, and identities have been at best ignored and at worst betrayed in the assessment process. (p. 381)

It is our responsibility to exercise our power ethically, carefully, and compassionately.

You can minimize cultural bias in several ways (Garcia & Pearson, 1994; Helms, 1992). First, you can devise a variety of assessment forms to give all students an opportunity to demonstrate their competence. Assessments can be oral or written, timed or untimed, individual or group, subjective or objective. Practical, hands-on tasks may be more effective than pencil-and-paper tests. You can also include test and evaluation procedures that reflect diverse cultural content and values. Finally, you can follow up on apparent "wrong" answers by asking students for elaborated explanations or justifications for their responses. These may reveal more about students' actual knowledge of a concept than the test results indicate.

Types of Assessment

The professional lexicon describes several different kinds of student assessment. Some of the terms used are relatively new, and many of them seem to be used interchangeably or in such a way that their meaning is unclear or confusing. Consequently, we will give a brief definition and description of some of the more common types of assessment used in schools.

Standardized tests.   Standardized tests are commercially prepared tests used to assess the achievement of large numbers of students in reading, math, and other academic areas. They are designed so that their administration, scoring, and interpretation are uniform, or standard, across all settings. Many schools require that standardized tests be administered once or twice a year, and standardized test results are usually included in a student's cumulative school record.

Standardized tests are norm-referenced. This means that an individual's score on a test is compared with a large, demographically representative cross section of American students, called a norming population. Comparisons are made possible by converting raw test scores to derived scores such as percentiles or stanines, which indicate the position of an individual score relative to the scores of the norming population.

Standardized tests have been the target of considerable criticism. In a review of assessment policies, Valencia and Wixson (2000) conclude that "high-stakes standardized basic skills tests led to narrowing of the curriculum; overemphasis on basic skills and test-like instructional methods; reduction in effective instructional time and an increase in time for test preparation; inflated test scores; and pressure on teachers to improve test scores" (p. 915). Standardized reading tests are especially antithetical to the beliefs of natural language teachers, who "find them synthetic, contrived, confining, and controlling, out of touch with modern theory and research. The tests reduce reading and writing to trivial, decontextualized, abstract skills to be tested with multiple-choice questions" (Goodman, 1989, p. xi). These critics argue, among other things, that standardized tests actually assess a narrow and artificial set of reading abilities. The test scores, on the other hand, render those abilities into global categories of "comprehension" and "vocabulary" and a composite "total reading" score, none of which really indicates much about what a student actually can or cannot do. Critics also point out that a student's performance on standardized tests is influenced by nonreading factors such as prior knowledge, test-taking skill, physical and emotional status, and cultural background.

Standardized test results are probably not particularly useful to the content area teacher. They can give a preliminary estimate, or rough sorting, of students into "high, medium, and low ability" categories, but this estimate must be tempered by the understanding that an individual student's scores are not very precise. A difference of a few raw score points is not very significant, even though it may affect the derived percentile or stanine score. Schell (1988) points out that comprehension is very often text-specific: a reader may comprehend very differently in two texts at the same reading level. Therefore, a student who scores very high on a test of reading comprehension may still have considerable difficulty with a particular text or subject. Standardized tests are no substitute for informed teacher observation and judgment.

Authentic assessment.   The term *authentic assessment* is used to describe a broad range of assessment tasks and data that are based on everyday situations or realistic applications of content knowledge and concepts. Much of what students learn cannot be adequately assessed through multiple-choice or other objective test formats. Therefore, in order to demonstrate how well they can use what they have learned, students must engage in tasks that approximate real-world situations (Wiggins, 1998). Teacher observations, teacher–student conferences, student journals, portfolios, inquiry projects, exhibitions, hands-on activities, open-ended problem solving, essay questions, and performances are some means of authentic assessment. Although the term is used differently by many people, authentic assessments are usually teacher designed and closely related to the context of the actual teaching and learning that go on in the classroom. Teachers frequently include students as partners in the authentic assessment process.

One middle school science department culminated a semester-long, lab-based study of physical science with an authentic assessment called the "sludge lab." Small groups of students were given three days to analyze the contents of a vial of murky water and sediment. (Some proponents of authentic assessment would argue that this task would be more authentic if students actually collected and analyzed a sample of water taken from a source in or near their community rather than receiving a specially concocted sample from the teacher.) Students used practical lab skills, concepts of chemistry and physical science, cooperative learning strategies, and reading and writing abilities to successfully complete the sludge lab reports. Students were graded both for the actual results obtained and reported and for the way in which they went about producing those results.

Authentic assessment tasks are complex and challenging and frequently have several possible outcomes. Grading such tasks is also complex because several variables must often be evaluated. Both teachers and students should evaluate not just the end product but also the processes that are used to complete the task. Although authentic assessments are usually more work for students and teachers, they yield a better picture of student achievement and place a premium on application, not just rote learning.

In addition, authentic assessments have many potential advantages over traditional kinds of testing for students of diverse cultural backgrounds, especially for bilingual students (Garcia & Pearson, 1994). Authentic assessment is more amenable to adaptations that include cultural content and values of diverse students. When students are asked to use what they have learned in more realistic settings, they are better able to relate new learning to their own cultural-specific understandings. Bilingual students have the opportunity to show what they know in both languages and how both languages interact in the learning process. Teachers have much more flexibility in collecting and interpreting information on how students are learning and developing, and students are more likely to be judged in terms of their individual progress rather than according to externally imposed criteria.

In a case study of a fifth-grade student who had recently moved to the United States from Korea, Kim and Pearson (1999) found that using a portfolio for assessment purposes enabled the student, the teacher, and the parents to engage in a concrete discussion of the student's academic abilities and progress, whereas discussions without the portfolio tended to be more general and focus on the student's social uses of language.

At the same time, authentic assessment poses some potential difficulties. There is a question regarding who defines "authenticity" or what counts as "real" (Alvermann & Commeyras, 1998). When teachers define authentic tasks and the parameters for analyzing performance on those tasks, there is no guarantee that the assessment has relevance to the reality of students, or that the assessment will be free of cultural biases. Authentic assessment with culturally and linguistically diverse students requires a good deal of unbiased knowledge about student culture and language on the part of the teacher.

For example, an English teacher might work with African American students on descriptive writing. To decide what constitutes an "authentic" descriptive writing task for these students, the teacher would need to know not only something about their interests and experiences but also something about how writing is valued by the students, the purposes for which students use writing and language, and the linguistic and rhetorical conventions of students' vernacular. In evaluating students' written products, the teacher would also need to decide if dialect features in the writing should or could be considered separately from the persuasive power of the writing.

Both decisions—what counts as "authentic writing" and how dialect features can influence the effectiveness of the writing—might best be arrived at through discussion and negotiation with students. Therein lies what many consider to be the primary advantage of authentic assessments: student involvement. When assessment grows out of the everyday activities of the classroom, assessment becomes an integral component of instruction. Students can become active partners in determining what will be learned, how it will be learned, and how learning can best be demonstrated and evaluated.

We will expand on the potential advantages and disadvantages of authentic assessment later in this chapter when we discuss the use of student portfolios.

Performance assessment.   Standardized tests are still used by many states and school districts to make decisions about program effectiveness and student competence. However, as of 1997, 36 of the 50 states had statewide testing programs that "included extended responses typical of performance assessments" (Valencia & Wixson, 2000, p. 916). Performance assessment overlaps in many ways with authentic assessment, and some educators may use the terms interchangeably. Indeed, many performance assessment tasks would look identical to what we have described as authentic assessment. The difference is that performance assessments are graded according to externally established criteria and students usually are expected to achieve some benchmark score as an index of competency in the area being tested. Performance assessments of writing, for instance, have been commonplace for more than 20 years. In a typical writing competency test, students are given one or more actual writing tasks and their written products are then given a holistic "pass/fail" by trained raters.

Performance assessments are designed to simulate real-world tasks, and they require the active participation of students in the creation of an answer or product that shows application of the student's knowledge and understanding. Performance assessment and authentic assessment may be based on the same techniques, including projects, essays, problem solving, experiments, demonstrations, or portfolios. However, performance assessments involve some sort of benchmarks or criteria for judging student performance, often called *rubrics*. Although a teacher may develop a rubric for evaluating or assigning grades to authentic assessment data such as portfolios, rubrics for evaluating performance assessments are designed to allow for comparisons across classrooms or even across schools or districts. The development and dissemination of rubrics make assessment public; all stakeholders, including parents, teachers, and students, have access to the criteria for successful performance.

In order to achieve comparability and fairness across different settings, those who rate performance assessments must undergo systematic training. For example, if a group of science teachers were selected to score the results of districtwide performance assessments, they would likely receive in-service training in which they would learn about the standards or rubrics, study benchmark responses illustrating various levels of achievement, and practice scoring sample responses.

The use of performance assessment to judge the performance of students, teachers, or programs has some advantages over traditional standardized testing and multiple-choice exams. Performance assessments are by their very nature more closely tied to what actually happens in the classroom. When the criteria for success can be clearly stated up front, both teachers and students have a better idea of what they are doing and why, and learning may take on more relevance. Instruction is likely to focus more on practical application and less on rote learning of isolated skills and information. Performance assessments also have many of the advantages of authentic assessment for students of diverse backgrounds. Performance assessments allow for more teacher scaffolding, more freedom to work in a variety of settings and without time constraints, and more acceptance of diverse responses than do traditional tests.

On the other hand, research on performance assessment is still at "a primitive stage" (Garcia & Pearson, 1994), and many questions about its utility remain unanswered. Technical problems of validity and reliability must be resolved (Spalding, 2000; Valencia & Wixson, 2000). If teachers provide assistance with performance tasks and students work in groups, there is a question of how much an assessment can tell us about the performance of individual students (Gearhart & Herman, 1995). There is always the possibility that results will be inflated if teachers "teach to the test." As with authentic assessment, there is also the question of who decides what counts as "real" and what constitutes mastery. If performance assessments are designed exclusively to reflect the knowledge and values of mainstream culture and if they rely heavily on the ability to read and write standard English, they will continue to marginalize students from diverse backgrounds (Garcia & Pearson, 1994). Finally, performance assessments represent a significant increase in time and cost over traditional multiple-choice assessments.

National assessments.   When we wrote the first edition of this text, there seemed to be increasing agreement among politicians, teachers' unions, and school officials that national curriculum standards and testing procedures had the potential to reinforce equity among schools and clarify what students throughout the country should be expected to attain. The National Council of Education Standards and Testing, established by Congress, had called for national standards in mathematics, science, history, geography, and English. A national coalition of several states and urban school districts, called the New Standards Project, sponsored hundreds of meetings during the 1990s to attempt to develop national standards-based performance assessments that would have credibility for teachers and other stakeholders. Now, however, the outlook for national standards and testing is quite different. The 1990s brought about political changes, public criticism of some of the proposed standards, disagreement among and within some professional organizations, and questions about the reliability, generalizability, and utility of large-scale performance-based assessments. It appears that "the once bright promise of subject area standards, born from a desire to improve the rigor and effectiveness of American education, has faded under a wide array of criticisms, and the movement itself has bogged down under its own weight" (Marzano & Kendall, 1996, p. 7). Instead, individual states and school districts have developed their own standards and assessments, borrowing freely from the work done by various organizations to develop national standards.

In fact, national assessment of students has been a reality since 1971. The National Assessment of Education Progress (NAEP) is a congressionally mandated program that has sampled the reading and writing abilities of 9-, 13-, and 17-year-old students since then. Student reading achievement has generally remained steady, with slight overall increases and comparatively greater improvement for African American and Hispanic students, from 1971 through 1998. The national average for twelfth graders had declined from 1992 to 1994, but the national average twelfth-grade score returned to approximately the same level as

1992. At eighth grade, the national average was higher in 1998 than in 1994 and 1992 (Donahue et al., 1999).

At grade 8, score increases were observed among lower- and middle-performing students. At grade 12, score increases were observed among middle- and upper-performing students; however, the score for lower-performing twelfth graders was not as high in 1998 as it had been in 1992. Among all eighth graders in 1998, only 33 percent achieved the "proficient" level or higher; 40% of twelfth graders were at or above this level. At both eighth and twelfth grades, higher scores were reported for students who were assigned more academic reading, who were asked to explain their understanding of their reading in class, who wrote long answers on tests, and who watched three or fewer hours of television daily.

Writing was also assessed by NAEP in 1998 (Greenwald et al., 1999). Students in fourth, eighth and twelfth grades completed three types of writing tasks: informative, persuasive, and narrative. Sixteen percent of eighth graders and 22 percent of twelfth graders scored below the "basic" level, and only about one-fourth of the students at these grade levels scored at the "proficient" level or above. There was also a large gender gap favoring girls in the writing assessment; twice as many girls as boys were "proficient" or better.

Careful analysis of NAEP data and other test data suggests that there has been no dramatic change in reading status for grades 1–8 in the past 30 years, and until 1994, NAEP reading assessments showed continual increases for twelfth graders from 1970 to 1990 (Kibby, 1993). Although the level of literacy among U.S. students is far from satisfactory, there is little evidence of a precipitous decline in ability as is often decried in the media. In fact, there is growing evidence that the so-called "crisis in education" is more myth than reality (Berliner & Biddle, 1995).

State assessments.   As mentioned previously, the development of content area standards and assessments has largely shifted from the national to the state and local level. Currently, 36 of the 50 states have some form of statewide assessment, and nearly half the states have high school exit exams (Columbia University Teachers College, 2000). Many states have tried to develop more authentic types of assessments, especially of literacy. Statewide performance assessments of reading and writing "include longer and more complex reading selections from a variety of genres, higher-level comprehension questions, extended written responses, and cross-text analyses" (Valencia & Wixson, 2000, p. 917).

This movement toward establishing and assessing higher standards appears to be driven by two related assumptions. One is that raising the bar for high school graduation can accomplish systemic reform of teaching and learning at the classroom level (Valencia & Wixson, 2000). The second argument is economic: ensuring higher levels of achievement will prepare students for productive roles in the labor force (Levin, 1998). The validity of these arguments has been questioned, however. Levin suggests that although education does indeed affect economic outcomes, the specific aspects of education that make a difference are not clear. Indeed, he counters that

> "[Y]ears of education provide a much better prediction of earning and occupational success than any specific attribute of education such as test scores. . . . It is generic skills with face validity that are likely to be more valuable and that can be molded through training and job experience to the specific needs of different jobs, different workplaces, and different times as technology, products, and services change over the lifetime of the worker" (p. 7).

There is also reason to question whether higher standards and more rigorous assessments have the desired effects on teaching and learning. Standards and tests alone cannot influence what happens in the classroom unless teachers are given sufficient professional development opportunities to implement meaningful changes and sufficient time to assess students' progress. For example, John McVay, a middle school math teacher in a suburb of New York City, estimates that if he were to do a culminating performance assessment at the end of six math units during the year and spend 15 minutes on each of his 187 students' work, he would need about 35 eight-hour student-free workdays (or 18 weekends) (Focused Reporting Project, 1999). High-stakes performance assessments are relatively intrusive, inefficient, costly, time-consuming, and difficult to administer (Madaus & O'Dwyer, 1999) and are subject to persistent questions about their reliability and validity (Pearson, 1998; Valencia & Wixson, 2000). There are also serious concerns that high-stakes performance assessments may further disadvantage ELLs and other students of diverse backgrounds (Au, 1998; Madaus & O'Dwyer, 1999). In their review of the research on standards and assessment policy, Valencia and Wixson (2000) summarize the issue of systemic reform:

> "[I]t is clear that literacy standards and assessment do have an influence on teachers' beliefs and practice, but the influence is not always in the expected or desired direction. The effect is mediated by a large number of factors such as teachers' knowledge, beliefs, and existing practices; the economic, social, philosophical, and political conditions of the school or district; the stakes attached to the policy; and the quality of the support and lines of communication provided to teachers and administrators. It is equally clear that policy by itself is not sufficient to promote desired change; simply implementing new assessments or creating new standards does not insure improved teaching or learning." (p. 930)

Regardless of the arguments over standards and assessment policy, the reality is that statewide assessments do pose both challenges and opportunities for teachers. One persistent issue is whether or not to "teach to the test." For example, New York State is in the process of implementing new standards and assessments for all content areas. By 2004, all New York State students will need to pass five statewide high school Regents exams, and students are being assessed in elementary and middle school to determine whether they are on track to meet the rigorous new requirements.

The English language arts exams in New York include listening and reading comprehension, taking notes, synthesizing ideas from readings on the same subject in two or more different genres, application of literary criticism, and extended written responses. The social studies and history exams, in response to the trend in social studies education to use primary sources, require students to provide extended written responses to questions based on samples from documents. The earth science exam, as described in Chapter 4, includes research and lab-based components as well as a more traditional exam that combines multiple-choice and essay responses. Math exams feature multiple-step problems that require students to provide a written explanation of their solution. The new standards as well as the tasks in all these exams are challenging and imply a constructivist curriculum that emphasizes "knowing how" as well as "knowing what."

Struggling Readers And State Assessments

High-stakes testing can be especially problematic for struggling readers. For them, the pressure of passing a state-mandated test can result in an excess of skill-and-drill instruction. Such was the case for Kathy Bussert-Webb (1999, 2000), who describes her experiences as the teacher of ninth-grade remedial reading in a south Texas high school in which 98 percent of the student body were Mexican American, mostly native speakers of Spanish. Because the school had a poor pass rate on the Texas Achievement of Academic Skills assessment (TAAS), a high school graduation requirement, the school administration began to focus on intense, structured teaching of the skills covered on the test. For Bussert-Webb and her students, this meant a lot of reading of short passages and answering multiple-choice questions.

After becoming increasingly dissatisfied with this approach, Bussert-Webb abandoned it and did what her instincts and training led her to believe was best for her students. She focused instead on making personal connections with students, increasing their connections with reading, and having more class discussions instead of covering the curriculum. Students began reading things they cared about, such as low-rider truck magazines, young adult novels, and stories by Latino/a authors. As a result, she found her students had fewer discipline problems and off-task behaviors. Most important, they did more reading—50 percent more than her previous students—and enjoyed it. Her students had the most library points of any class in the school.

What about the TAAS? Overall, the pass rate for sophomores at the school improved dramatically, from a 59 percent pass rate in 1995 to 82 percent in 1999. All but three of Bussert-Webb's struggling readers passed, a success rate of 88 percent. The three who did not pass just missed the passing score of 70 percent, with scores of 69, 67, and 65 percent, compared to a mean score of 59 percent for the other students at the school who failed. Although it would be a mistake to read too much into these data, it is clear that Bussert-Webb's student-centered, holistic curriculum did not negatively affect her students.

In an effort to prepare teachers and students for these new requirements, districts throughout New York have invested heavily in staff development. In many cases, school districts or individual teachers have made up parallel assessment tasks that mirror the state exams, and students have been given (sometimes extensive) practice. Practicing for the state exam is not by itself necessarily a bad thing, especially if teachers carefully deconstruct the tasks by explaining what is expected and giving guidance on how to accomplish it. However, we caution that time spent on extensive practice in test-taking might be better spent by involving students in more authentic and meaningful experiences with reading and writing, mathematical problem solving, examination of primary sources, laboratory activities, and research; in fact, many districts and individual teachers have used the implementation of the new standards to do just that. Rather than focusing solely on devising, administering, and scoring practice tests, they have worked on ways to change curriculum and instruction to align more closely with the new standards.

Learning about Students

In Chapter 1, we said that students should receive instruction based on their capabilities, not their weaknesses. In order to plan effective instruction, we need to learn as much as we can about students' norms, values, traditions, language, and beliefs as well as their reading, writing, and study skills. All these factors may affect their performance in a content area classroom. The following sections consider practical ways of assessing these variables.

Interest and attitude inventories.   Many teachers find it helpful to find out what students think about a content area or a specific topic. Knowing that several students like science fiction will help an English teacher plan the reading selections for the whole class or decide to include science fiction as a topic for small-group book talks. On the other hand, if significant numbers claim a distaste for poetry, the teacher knows that introductory poetry selections will have to be chosen carefully and that it will be necessary to do a little sales promotion on behalf of the genre. An interest, or attitude, inventory can be given at the beginning of the year or at the introduction of a new unit. A sample inventory for high school English is shown in Figure 5.1.

A content area learning log or journal is another good source of information about students' attitudes and interests or their backgrounds. Teachers can ask students to jot down "what I liked best this week," "something I'd like to know more about," or "what I thought was hardest this week." By periodically reviewing students' log entries the teacher can get helpful feedback on what students are thinking, learning, and feeling.

Effective teaching starts with what students already know and leads them to new understandings. Therefore, it is helpful to know not only what students feel

INVENTORY OF ATTITUDES AND INTERESTS

1. **Rate each item from 1 (least) to 5 (most). I like to read:**

    _____ Science fiction   _____ Plays
    _____ Poetry   _____ Short stories
    _____ Fantasy   _____ Biographies
    _____ Romance   _____ Adventure
    _____ Novels   _____ History
    _____ Sports   _____ Current events
    _____ War stories   _____ Mysteries
    _____ Other :_____

2. **Rate each item from 1 (least) to 5 (most). I like to write:**

    _____ Letters to friends   _____ My opinions
    _____ In a diary/journal   _____ Poems
    _____ Short stories   _____ Humorous stories
    _____ Plays, scripts   _____ Nonfiction
    _____ Other: _____

3. **Rate each item from 1 (hardest) to 5 (easiest). When I write, this is what I find hard and easy about it:**

    _____ Getting started   _____ Changing what I have written
    _____ Finding ideas to write about   _____ Letting someone else read my
    _____ Organizing my ideas   writing
    _____ Putting the words on paper   _____ Proofreading

Rate the next items using this scale:

1 = Strongly disagree
2 = Disagree
3 = Not sure
4 = Agree
5 = Strongly agree

    _____   4. I am a good writer.
                 Why do you say this?

    _____   5. I am a good reader.
                 Why do you say this?

    _____   6. I have a good vocabulary.
    _____   7. I am good at spelling.
    _____   8. English is difficult for me.
    _____   9. English is a useful subject.
    _____   10. I think English is interesting.

FIGURE 5.1   **Attitude/interest inventory for high school English students**

about a topic but also what they know about it. Some of this may come out in an interest inventory or in class discussions. There are also many instructional strategies that begin with what students already know or believe. You will find several such strategies discussed in later chapters, especially Chapter 6.

Kidwatching.   Advocates of a constructivist approach to literacy learning believe that externally imposed testing does not adequately assess what students are taught or what they can do (Cambourne & Turnbill, 1990; Goodman, 1989). More important, they maintain that the best assessment comes from the people who know most intimately what students can do in school—teachers (Johnston, 1987). The informed judgments that teachers make by observing students has been called *kidwatching* (Goodman, 1985).

Kidwatching practices are similar to what is known as diagnostic teaching, or the cycle of teaching, assessing, and further teaching. A middle school teacher describes that cycle as follows (Dalrymple, 1989):

> Assessing and evaluating learning . . . are considered part of the teaching cycle; they are ongoing; and they are curriculum based. . . . Planning, teaching, and evaluating are continually intermingled as three interwoven cycles. . . . As the classroom teacher observes and interacts with the students, he or she is making decisions about lesson plans and teaching strategies. Once those plans are enacted, the teacher observes and interacts and makes more educational decisions. (p. 112)

The list of things a teacher might want to observe is a matter of individual choice, especially when one considers the variety of concepts and activities across content areas. Therefore, some teachers develop their own observation checklists. Dalrymple (1989) suggests using a class roster as a convenient recording form for observations. The teacher makes up class lists with the names of all students. Multiple copies of each class list can be made on a word processor or copy machine. The teacher can then add column heads across the top of the blank rosters to identify the project and activities to be observed, and the space after students' names can be left blank and used to record the teacher's observations. The roster can be filled in using a coding system of checks or pluses and minuses, a numerical system, or brief descriptions. Some of these data may later be converted to gradebook credit.

Cloze passages.   Cloze passages (Bormuth, 1968; Taylor, 1953) can be used to estimate how well students will fare with a particular text. The cloze procedure is based on the idea that humans instinctively try to bring about closure to unfinished or incomplete patterns. A cloze passage is constructed by deleting words from a text passage. Readers' success with filling in the blanks suggests their relative potential for comprehending that reading material.

The passage should be reasonably complete and coherent on its own. The length of the passage will depend on the number of words to be deleted. Although many authorities recommend that approximately 50 words be deleted, we have found this to be frustrating for many students, especially younger students and struggling readers. Because scores are ultimately converted to percentages, we have found deletion of 25, 33, or 50 words to be most convenient, as each item is then worth either four, three, or two points. Many teachers include a practice passage with five to ten items, which they use to model the cloze procedure.

Figure 5.2 presents a short cloze passage from a middle school science text. Try filling in the blanks yourself. (The deleted words are listed below the figure. Cover them while completing the passage.)

The following are instructions for constructing, administering, scoring, and interpreting a cloze passage:

1. Construction
   a. Select a passage. Copy it on a word processor with no typographical errors.
   b. Delete a word at random from the second sentence of the passage. (The first and last sentences should be left intact to give additional context to

---

ORES

Minerals from which metals and nonmetals can be removed in usable amounts are called ores. Metals are elements that _____(1)_____ certain special properties. Metals _____(2)_____ shiny surfaces and are _____(3)_____ to conduct electricity and _____(4)_____. Metals also have the _____(5)_____ of malleability. Malleability is _____(6)_____ ability of a metal _____(7)_____ be hammered into thin _____(8)_____ without breaking. Another property _____(9)_____ metals is ductility. Ductility _____(10)_____ the ability of a _____(11)_____ to be pulled into _____(12)_____ strands without breaking. Iron, _____(13)_____, aluminum, copper, silver, and _____(14)_____ are metals. Most metals _____(15)_____ found combined with other substances, or impurities, in ores. After the ores are removed from the earth by mining, the metals must be removed from the ores.

Deleted Words

1. have	6. the	11. substance
2. have	7. to	12. thin
3. able	8. sheets	13. lead
4. heat	9. of	14. gold
5. property	10. is	15. are

FIGURE 5.2   **Sample cloze passage**   (*Source:* Passage taken from Charles Coble et al., *Earth Science*, p. 159. Englewood Cliffs, NJ: Prentice Hall, 1993.)

the beginning and end of the passage.) Beginning with the first deletion, every fifth word is deleted until the desired number of words have been left out. To make the task somewhat easier, delete every sixth or seventh word. It is important, however, that a specific interval be selected and maintained throughout the passage. In no circumstances should words be avoided because they seem too hard or too easy.

   c. Leave a blank space for each deleted word. All blanks should be of equal length so as not to give any clues about word length.

2. Administration
   a. Give students a copy of the cloze passage and instruct them to read through it before they do anything else.
   b. Instruct students to go back and fill in the blanks with words that they think make sense. They should be encouraged to make a guess at each blank. There should be no time limit for completing the passage.

3. Scoring
   a. Count only words that are exact replacements for (or intelligibly spelled facsimiles of) the deleted words.
   b. Figure the percentage of exact replacements. For instance, if you have left 25 blanks, each is worth four points. A student who gets 14 exact replacements scores 56 percent ($4 \times 14 = 56$).

4. Interpretation
   a. A score above 60 percent suggests that the text material is at a student's *independent level.* That is, the student should be able to read that material on his or her own with excellent understanding.
   b. A score between 40 and 60 percent suggests that the material is at the student's *instructional level.* The material would be challenging, but with appropriate help from the teacher it would be useful.
   c. A score below 40 percent suggests that the material is at the student's *frustration level.* It may be too difficult for that student.

Teachers who are used to encouraging good guesses and giving students the benefit of the doubt often feel it is unduly stringent not to count good synonyms when scoring a cloze passage. However, what constitutes a "good synonym"? Take the sentence "John got in his _____ and drove downtown," from which the word *truck* is deleted. If a student wrote *van* in the blank, a reasonable person might count that as a synonym. However, what about *car* or *Chevy* or *Trans Am*? Some teachers would accept those; they are vehicles. How about *suit*? That is not a vehicle, but it fits the sentence. The point is that teachers will vary in what they will accept as a synonym, and that variance will affect the reliability of assessments using cloze passages. If only exact replacements are counted, the task is simpler and more objective.

Instead of penalizing readers for good guesses, the suggested scoring criteria for a cloze passage account for the many synonyms that good readers are likely to use. Although a score of 65 percent would be barely passing on most exams, it is an excellent score on a cloze passage.

A teacher may avoid emphasis on "right" or "wrong" answers by letting students score their own papers. When all students have completed the passage, the teacher shows them the list of deleted words. They can write the words above their "inexact" guesses. This gives students immediate feedback on their efforts and allows for a discussion of why some words did or did not fit the context. The teacher should make it clear that many of the students' guesses would make sense in the passage, even though they are not the words used by the author. That is, good synonyms are not wrong.

We need to emphasize that cloze results are only estimates and must be interpreted with caution, especially for individual students. When a class or several classes of students are sampled, however, cloze passages give practical insight into the question "How will these students do with this reading material?"

Informal content text inventories.   Teachers can also use textbook passages to devise short, informal assessments. At the beginning of the school year, students can be asked to read a two- or three-page selection from the text, followed by questions that emphasize vocabulary, comprehension at various levels, and the ability to interpret graphs and visual aids. (Chapter 7 discusses in detail the art of designing good comprehension questions.) Sharon Walpole (1998/1999) suggests asking students to write a summary of what they have read to determine which ideas they select and how they organize them. She also interviews students to assess their understanding of the structures and features of textbooks. In her interviews, she poses three general questions:

- What is that? (With reference to a particular textbook feature, such as section titles, emphasized words, glossary, or end-of-chapter activities)
- Why did the author put it there?
- How could you use it?

The results from such informal assessments can reveal a good deal about students' capabilities as readers.

Much can also be learned by privately having a student read a short passage aloud and then retell what was understood. Although multiple class sections with large numbers of students may make this impractical for many teachers, it can be especially useful with struggling readers who have learned many strategies to mask their difficulties with the printed page.

Grades and Grading

Giving grades to students is an almost universal reality for teachers and is almost universally ignored in reading methods textbooks. This neglect may be due in part to reluctance to confront one of the primary contradictions in the

Technology Tips

▼▼▼

The following Web sites feature additional information on various aspects of assessment, as noted.

NAEP Reading & Writing reports:
http://nces.ed.gov/nationsreportcard/reading/reading.asp
http://nces.ed.gov/nationsreportcard/writing/writing.asp

Consortium for Equity in Standards & Testing
http://www.csteep.bc.edu/ctest
Focus on how standards and assessments can be used more fairly; news and research articles, links to other Web sites.

Relearning by Design
http://www.relearning.org/
Grant Wiggins' organization; information on assessment, standards, curriculum, and rubrics.

Explorasource
http://www.explorasource/com/educator/index.htm
Links topics to standards (national, state, and some local) and to resources for teaching to the standards.

Center for Research on Evaluation, Standards, and Student Testing
http://www.cse.ucla.edu
Funded by U.S. Department of Education; part of UCLA Center for Study of Evaluation; features many research studies on assessment- and standards-related topics.

teacher's role—the conflict between maintaining standards and respecting individual students. Thomas (1986) illustrates this contradiction in his discussion of the use of the grade F. He suggests that the two extremes might be stated as follows:

> Students should get an F regardless of effort if they do not meet minimum standards for the subject.
> Students should not get an F if they have made their best effort in the subject.

This dilemma applies to all of a teacher's decisions about assigning grades to students. Should the bright student who rarely cracks a book get the same grade as the average student who diligently spends hours on assignments? Should spelling and grammar "count" toward the grade on a history project, and if so, how much? What should end-of-term grades be based on? How much should homework count? What about class participation? Should grades be used as weapons to discourage unwanted behavior?

The traditional system of giving letter grades has many significant drawbacks (Willis, 1993). First, a single letter grade gives no hint of what a student can actually do or not do, or what an individual's strengths or weaknesses might be. When letter grades are stringently applied, only a few students do well (i.e., receive an A), and less able students are demoralized by constant negative reinforcement. On the other hand, if most students receive A's and B's, the underlying meaning of grades as indices of ability becomes even less clear. Finally, letter grades may actually undermine some teaching strategies such as cooperative learning or writer's workshop, in which the emphases are less on product and more on process, less on individual accomplishment and more on achievement of the group, shared learning, and confidence building.

Despite calls for more student-centered teaching and alternative means of assessment, determining grades in high schools continues to follow largely traditional and narrow formulas. In a survey of grading practices and policies in seven high schools, it appeared that grades were based largely on tests and quizzes with projects and homework contributing a less significant portion (Agnew, 1985). Teachers believed that they controlled grading practices, and each teacher's system was highly subjective. Similarly, a study of the grading preferences of 91 high school science teachers determined that traditional labs, quizzes, and tests were by far the most frequently used determinants of grades (Feldman, Alibrandi, & Kropf, 1998). The teachers reported that they rarely used portfolios or journals, two forms of authentic assessment frequently recommended by reformers. Another study of high school grading practices (Stiggins, Frisbie, & Griswold, 1989) also found that grading was variable, subjective, and often at odds with the recommendations of researchers and methods textbook authors.

The dilemma of grading is especially sharp for those who work with students outside the middle-class academic mainstream. Students from diverse ethnic or cultural backgrounds, students with limited proficiency in standard English, and students with identified learning problems often find themselves in an academic game with long odds; their chances for success seem to be diminished by the very system that is supposed to bring them into the mainstream (Oakes, 1986). The national drop-out rate among African American and Hispanic high school students is a depressing indication that too many of these children simply give up in the face of repeated failure. However, Agnew (1985) found that in the school with the highest percentage of students of minority and low socioeconomic status, grades were based on behavior, attendance, and effort more than on achievement. In assigning grades, teachers must be sure that their standards and procedures are rigorous; they do students no favor by rewarding them for learning little or nothing. However, teachers also want to encourage all students and give each one a chance to show his or her capabilities.

Objectivity or teacher judgment?   Even though a teacher tries to design an objective grading system, it is impossible to avoid using judgment in arriving at grades. Take, for example, multiple-choice tests, which are often referred to as "objective tests" because they supposedly have clear-cut right and wrong answers and teacher judgment does not enter into the scoring—students either know the material and answer correctly or they do not. However, anyone who has ever made up a multiple-choice test knows how difficult it is to write good, unambiguous questions that reflect important content and that have answers that are clearly "right." In selecting what will be tested and how test items will be worded, a teacher is making subjective decisions. Still other subjective decisions must be made if students challenge some questions because they were too hard or because more than one answer might be right. Teachers cannot escape professional subjectivity.

Schools or districts often adopt uniform grading systems (e.g., 90–100 = A and 80–89 = B) in an attempt to attain objectivity across classes and grade levels. However, individual teachers must still decide what will be evaluated, how much each such activity will be worth, and how a final grade on the 0–100 scale will be computed. It is a well-known fact that within every school that uses such a system, some teachers are known as "hard" markers and others "easy." This creates "a situation in which grades given by one teacher might mean something entirely different from grades given by another teacher" (Marzano & Kendall, 1996, p. 10).

It is no wonder, then, that students are often confused about grades. Many students do not know how grades are determined or why they got a particular grade. Low achievers especially tend to attribute poor grades to external factors, to things beyond their control (Evans & Engelberg, 1985).

High school students and most middle-grade students do not receive a grade in reading, but most of their grades, especially in academic subjects, have a large reading–writing–language factor built in. For example, suppose a ninth-grade social studies teacher relies heavily on lectures and recitation to present course material. Textbook reading is almost never assigned, although the teacher may read aloud from the text occasionally. Grades are based on worksheets and chapter tests. Even though students are not doing much reading and writing, they must be able to follow, organize, and remember the information presented in class. They must be able to read the worksheets and write out answers. Also, they must be able to read the items on the tests. When teachers use academic jargon or technical vocabulary in the wording of test questions, students are less likely to give good answers than if everyday terms are used (Cunningham & Moore, 1993).

Every teacher comes to terms with the dilemmas of grading in his or her own way; it would be foolish and presumptuous of us to suggest that any uniform approach would be possible or desirable. However, the following subsections suggest some strategies that might help you avoid some of the pitfalls of assigning grades to students.

Tough but fair.   "Old Smitty's tough but fair. She makes you work hard, but you learn a lot in her class." We have always admired teachers with reputations like that, for whom grades are not just final marks on a report card but more indicative of a process of teaching, learning, assessing, and communicating. Barbara

(*Source:* Used with special permission of North American Syndicate.)

Walvoord and Virginia Anderson (1998), college English and biology teachers, respectively, describe the power of grades to influence learning. For them, grading is only one element in the overall planning process:

> Grading . . . includes tailoring the test or assignment to the learning goals of the course, establishing criteria and standards, helping students acquire learning over time, shaping student motivation, feeding back results so students can learn from their mistakes, communicating about students' learning to the students and to other audiences, and using results to plan future teaching methods. When we talk about grading, we have student learning most in mind. (p. 1)

We suggest five guidelines that will help you develop a "tough but fair" grading system:

▸ Select assignments, tests, or projects that reflect and measure what you value most as a teacher. For example, a math teacher who was interested in *how* his students solved problems might ask students to provide a written explanation of what they did and why as well as the answers to problems (Walvoord & Anderson, 1998).

▸ Provide a variety of opportunities to earn credit. Diverse students have diverse ways of learning and showing what they have learned. Figure 5.3 lists some possible credit-bearing activities that involve some combination of language and literacy ability. You might also consider extra-credit activities or revisions so that students can make up for less-than-optimal performances.

▸ Be clear about your grading system and standards. Begin a new year by describing clearly what must be done for credit, how different activities will be weighted, and what must be done to earn a grade of A, B, C, and so forth.

Peer conferences	Creating a display, poster, graph, etc.
Teacher conferences	Math word problems
Participation in group work	Photographs
Writing in journal or log	Audio or video recordings
Responding to another student's journal or log	Vocabulary puzzles, analogies
	Self-selected vocabulary list
Attending selected out-of-school events	Writing, performing, or producing a dramatic piece
Reporting to class	
Panel presentation	Sharing a book or poem with classmates
Debate	Self-evaluation
Hosting a guest speaker	Extra reading
Demonstrating an experiment or process	Book review, oral or written

FIGURE 5.3 **Opportunities to earn course credit**

> ▸ Be clear about how you will assess specific assignments and tests. Many teachers develop *rubrics,* itemized lists of criteria that are distributed when an assignment is made and filled out and returned when the assignment is graded.
> ▸ Collaborate with students to set and achieve goals and to deconstruct the language of both official and teacher-devised standards. In Chapter 1, we suggested that students should play an active part in setting goals and evaluating their progress. This is especially important when working with culturally diverse students, who may not be familiar with the nuances of school discourse and who may feel that academic tasks are arbitrarily assigned and evaluated. In a collaborative study of how portfolios could be used as part of the grading process (Sarroub et al., 1997), university researchers and eighth-grade teachers found that students were particularly interested in decoding the "secret world of assessment," recrafting the official standards into language they could understand, and generating their own standards for assessment.

Grading systems.   A social studies class of bilingual seventh-graders collaborated in setting up a grading system for a four-week unit on the theme "How does where you live influence how you live?" (Freeman & Freeman, 1989). Through brainstorming and class discussion, they developed a list of questions to research in pairs or groups of three. They kept records of their research methods, materials, and conferences and presented their reports to the class. Credit for activities and class participation was negotiated at the beginning of the unit. Among other things, students received credit for their participation in brainstorming and research, for completing the various components of the project, for their oral and written reports, and for how well they listened to others. More credit could be earned for unusual or creative work. Also, the possibility existed for making up lost credit or redoing unsatisfactory work. The teachers tried to direct students' focus toward the content of the unit and the research processes rather than to grades. The system was negotiated at the beginning of the unit and referred to infrequently while students were working on the topic.

Contracting is another grading system that involves some collaboration and negotiation with students. Teachers spell out criteria for different grades or negotiate with individual students what they hope to earn and what work they will complete. Students "contract" to complete the requirements for an A, a B, and so on. Although contracting is more time-consuming for teachers, it can have the effect of making students feel more responsible for fulfilling their contracts.

Most traditional grading systems are based either on weighted averages or total points. In a weighted-average system, teachers average such factors as quiz grades, unit tests, homework, and class participation. A typical weighted-average arrangement for a marking period might be as follows:

Homework average:	15%
Weekly quiz average:	20%
Unit test average:	40%
Project:	15%
Class participation average:	10%

In this case, the teacher would be saying that unit tests are the most important part of the grade, whereas class participation carries a relatively small value. Students would know that a single low grade on a weekly quiz would not be disastrous, but those whose homework was always completed and of good quality might still not get A's if they did not do well on unit tests.

A straight point system is similar, but in this case there is a set number of points for various factors, and students must achieve a certain number of points for different grades. Here is an example for a science course:

Homework:	0–75 pts.	
Tests:	0–200 pts.	A = 460–500 pts.
Lab activities:	0–100 pts.	B = 410–459 pts.
Lab journal:	0–50 pts.	C = 350–409 pts.
Research project:	0–75 pts.	D = 300–349 pts.
Total possible:	500 pts.	

Again in this example, test grades comprise the single largest factor. However, instead of an average of all test scores, the grade is based on the actual number of points scored on the tests. Teachers who use point systems claim that they are more quantitative and objective than other means of grading, but they are nevertheless making subjective decisions about what kinds of tests and assignments are given and how they are evaluated and weighted.

Both weighted-average and point systems can easily be set up on a computer using spreadsheet software or specially designed gradebook software, which make record keeping and report cards easier to manage. The growing ubiquity of computers in schools, however, may actually work against grading reform if the relative convenience of grading software entrenches point and averaging systems and discourages alternatives that are not readily quantifiable (Feldman, Alibrandi, & Kropf, 1998).

Grant Wiggins (1998), a recognized assessment authority and researcher, argues that single-letter grades at the end of a marking period provide little useful feedback for students or other stakeholders. Instead, he urges the adoption of multidimensional grading systems that would report subscores for various categories of accomplishment. Specifically, Wiggins proposes that students should be given both grades and performance indicators. Grades would be an index of expectations for an individual student—his or her ability, effort, and what Wiggins calls "habits of mind and work." Thus, struggling readers might achieve good grades for a subject, even though they do not do as well as many of their peers. However, performance indicators would measure a student's progress against grade level or exit criteria. Performance indicators would give an idea of how well a student had progressed relative to standards for a particular subject and grade level. Such a system obviously would be more complex and time-consuming than single-letter grade systems and would likely have to be adopted by an entire school or district rather than by an individual teacher.

Rubrics.   Rubrics help students to know "what the teacher is looking for," make grading a large number of assignments easier for the teacher, and make grading more uniform. There is no set format for developing rubrics (Wiggins, 1998). They may be holistic, giving a single descriptor for a whole performance, or they may be trait analytic, with multiple descriptors for various dimensions of a performance. Rubrics can be generic, as when an English teacher uses the same rubric for evaluating all student writing, or they may be event specific, as in the case of a rubric designed for a single project.

Usually, rubrics feature a scale of possible points to be earned, the dimensions of the task, and the criteria that must be met. An example of a rubric for Gene Kulbago and Mary Marcinkowski's earth science research project (described in Chapter 4) is given in Figure 5.4. In this case, the dimensions of the task include organization, information, and adherence to MLA and standard language conventions. The points and criteria for each dimension are also indicated.

Content area quizzes and tests.   Probably the most frequently used means of evaluating middle-grade and secondary school students are tests made up by teachers or provided by textbook publishers. Any test—true/false, multiple choice, short answer, or essay—must be readable in order for students to be able to respond to it. This may seem a simple requirement, but it is often overlooked. The result is that some students perform poorly not because they did not know the material but because they misunderstood the questions. Rakow and Gee (1987) devised a checklist for test items, which may be used to minimize student confusion (Figure 5.5).

Student Name _____

Date _____

Title of Paper _____

	Concern	Possible Points	Points Earned
Organization	Paper contains an Introductory Statement which clearly defines the hypothesis.	5	
	Information is organized in such a way to make it understandable to the audience.	10	
	Paper contains a concluding statement which evaluates the hypothesis based upon information (data) discovered during research.	10	
Information	Student used a variety of informational sources, including both electronic and published (written) sources.	10	
	Student has selected appropriate sources and has evaluated them for credibility.	5	
	Student has included sufficient information in the report necessary to make a valid conclusion.	20	
MLA and Language Conventions	Paper contains a proper title page.	5	
	The paper contains a bibliography which follows the MLA style.	10	
	The paper demonstrates proper use of parenthetical documentation.	10	
	Paper demonstrates proper use of language conventions: spelling, capital letters, paragraphing, gramatical usage, etc.	10	
	Paper is reasonably neat and demontrates effort on the part of the writer.	5	
	Comments		Final Score

FIGURE 5.4   Rubric for earth science research report   (*Source:* Gene Kulbago, Niagara Middle School, Niagara Falls, New York.)

_____ 1. Students are likely to have the experiences and prior knowledge necessary to understand what the question calls for.

_____ 2. The vocabulary is appropriate for the intended grade level.

_____ 3. The sentence complexity is appropriate for the intended grade level.

_____ 4. Definitions and examples are clear and understandable.

_____ 5. The required reasoning skills are appropriate for the students' cognitive level.

_____ 6. Relationships are made clear through precise, logical connectives.

_____ 7. Content within items is clearly organized.

_____ 8. Graphs, illustrations, and other graphic aids facilitate comprehension.

_____ 9. The questions are clearly framed.

_____ 10. The content of the items is of interest to the intended audience.

FIGURE 5.5   Checklist for evaluating test item readability   (*Source:* S. Rakow & T. Gee, "Test science, not reading," *The Science Teacher, 54,* 28–31, February 1987. Used with permission from NSTA Publications, National Science Teachers Association, 1742 Connecticut Ave., NW, Washington, DC 20009.)

It is difficult to write "foolproof" test items. Students often see good reasons, unanticipated by teachers, why more than one of the possible responses for a multiple-choice question could be correct. They may feel frustrated by true/false answers because they know that under certain conditions a statement could be either true or false. In fact, the constraints of so-called objective test items frequently penalize students who are divergent thinkers or are good at inference and interpretation; they see subtleties where others see only right or wrong. Therefore, teachers sometimes use a *quiz qualifier*—simply space at the end of an objective test where students can qualify their answers. If a student feels that the answer to question number 23 could be either a or c, he or she explains why in the quiz qualifier. If the student gets the answer wrong, the teacher reads the qualification, and if it is convincing, the student gets credit for item 23.

Testing students in the manner in which they have been taught requires some thought. A teacher may reinforce vocabulary by using analogies and categorizing activities. The purpose of these exercises is to help students go beyond dictionary-type definitions and see the relationships between ideas. If that is how the teacher has taught vocabulary, then it only makes sense for him or her to test students by using similar analogies and categorizing activities.

It is also reasonable for a teacher to give students help in preparing for tests. Teachers should make it clear what will be tested and what the test will look like. Often, teachers give students practice tests or test items, especially when students are faced with departmentalized, district, or state exams. This is sometimes criticized as "teaching the test." Although such preparation should not take an inordinate amount of time away from actual content-based instruction, guided practice in test taking shows students what to expect, allows them to make a trial run and critique their results, and can result in improved performance.

Portfolio Assessment

Some time ago, Barney, an out-of-town friend and professional photographer, came to visit and brought his portfolio. In fact, Barney brought three portfolios. One was his professional portfolio, which included photos of buildings, food, manufactured products, and people. There were color prints, transparencies, and samples of actual brochures, magazines, and books that he had illustrated. It gave an impressive overview of his best work and his capability as a commercial photographer. The second portfolio was a selection of black-and-white landscapes and portraits and a series of photographs of a model, which had evolved over several years. This was a highly personal and expressive collection that showed Barney's thoughtful and artistic side. The third portfolio was a selection of Barney's newspaper photos, which he had assembled especially for a trip to New York City and meetings with newspaper photo editors.

Two aspects of Barney's portfolios are relevant to our discussion of assessment and grading: the work was self-selected, and a variety of items were included. The pictures in each portfolio were carefully selected for different purposes and indeed made very different impressions. Barney selected pieces that displayed a range of subjects, techniques, and moods, and he included finished work as well as work in progress.

Students can prepare similar portfolios of their work in content area courses. Kenneth Wolf and Yvonne Siu-Runyan (1996) define a student portfolio as "a selective collection of student work and records of progress gathered across diverse contexts over time, framed by reflection and enriched through collaboration, that has as its aim the advancement of student learning" (p. 31). They identify three portfolio models, each with a different primary purpose:

- *Ownership portfolios.* These collections of student work emphasize student choice, reflection, and self-assessment. The main purpose of an ownership portfolio is to allow students to display and reflect on their accomplishments.
- *Feedback portfolios.* These are co-constructed by the teacher and the student. They give an overall portrait of a student's development, strengths, and needs. The purposes of feedback portfolios are to guide student learning and to communicate with parents.
- *Accountability portfolios.* These are portfolios that are used as performance assessments. They typically contain student work, teacher records, and standardized performance assessments. Accountability portfolios are assembled according to structured guidelines and are often evaluated by people other than the classroom teacher with reference to an established rubric. The purpose of these portfolios is to demonstrate student achievement for accountability or program evaluation.

There is an especially important distinction between accountability portfolios and those designed purely for classroom use, as the two uses of portfolios are in many respects at odds (Tierney et al., 1998; Valenica & Wixson, 2000; Wiggins,

1998). Classroom-based portfolios are assembled and evaluated according to criteria established by teachers, often in collaboration with students. Their purpose is to help teachers, students, and parents understand learning, and they are often important factors in guiding teachers' instructional decisions. Interpretation of classroom-based portfolios is nuanced and sensitive to individual students and their instructional settings. Accountability portfolios, on the other hand, must meet externally imposed criteria and may form the basis for high-stakes conclusions about students, teachers, or schools. Measurement researchers have voiced serious reservations about the reliability and validity of accountability portfolios (Tierney et al., 1998; Valencia & Wixson, 2000). Although accountability portfolios certainly have the potential to influence instruction and learning, their net effect may be disruptive and counterproductive if external demands displace a teacher's professional judgment of what is best for students. In the discussion that follows, our emphasis is on classroom-based portfolios.

Sarah Drake (1998) describes a portfolio project she initiated during her second year as a history teacher at Naperville North High School in Illinois. At the beginning of the year, she told her ninth-grade ancient history and eleventh-grade U.S. history students that they would be building a portfolio that would showcase their best work and their understanding of the vital themes and narratives of history. Together, she and her students developed criteria for selecting ten items that represented their learning of history over the semester. Students included group projects, Venn diagrams, journal entries, essays, research papers, political cartoons, posters, and maps in their portfolios. They needed to write a brief explanation of why each item was chosen and a summary in which they explained the most important concept(s) they had learned.

With student input, she developed a rubric for the portfolio that evaluated students on the dimensions of historical knowledge, reasoning, and communication. Students held peer-evaluation sessions three times during the semester to help them organize their portfolios and develop their selection rationalizations. At the end of the semester, each student had a 10-minute individual conference with Ms. Drake in which they discussed the portfolio. Although students were dubious at first, Sarah found most of her students were able to recognize vital themes and narratives of history, and that their summaries expressed personal examinations and insightful reflections. She was especially pleased with the results of the portfolio interviews, during which she learned new information about students and built on relationships she had established.

A middle school science teacher, Kathie May, describes a lab activity in which her students tried to find out how much sugar was in their favorite brand of chewing gum (1994). She prepared a lab activity and had the students work in groups, hypothesizing, weighing chewing gum samples before and after they were chewed, comparing their results, and drawing conclusions. When each group was finished, they turned in a portfolio that included their initial hypotheses for the experiment, a list of dependent and independent variables, materials needed for the experiment, their experimental procedures, a data table of their results, an accurately labeled graph of the whole class's data, a list of possible experimental errors, and ideas for a new experiment based on what they had learned. Kathie had prepared a scoring rubric that listed how many points each of the items in the portfolio was worth and the criteria for earning points. She had students exchange portfolios and use the rubric to score each other.

A final example shows how portfolios can be used to evaluate interdisciplinary learning. In a project that involves math, science, and technology, teams of students are given the task of designing a strong, lightweight construction beam by reinforcing concrete with one or more recyclable materials: aluminum cans, plastic milk jugs, soda bottles, or newspaper (Sanders, 1994). Students design and construct their beam, weigh it, and test its ability to support a load. They document their work with a portfolio that would be evaluated by the science, math, and technology teachers. The portfolio would include

- Sketches of all the solutions they thought of
- Notes made during the project, including hypotheses, brainstorming, or questions
- Descriptions of the science and math principles involved in their project
- Information they gathered from resources
- Graphic illustrations of how their beam performed (graphs, tables, and photos)
- A final self-assessment of the project, including a critique of their processes, the final product, and suggestions for redesign

Portfolio assessment may be adapted in many ways. In science classes, students might be asked to pick their two best lab sessions and present their procedural and observational notes along with the finished lab reports and a statement of why these labs were chosen. In social studies, students could be asked to go to their learning logs and assess their before-and-after knowledge of a subject, including examples from their work that were instrumental in changing their attitudes or understandings. In French, students might collect tape recordings of conversations from early, midway, and late in the term or the notes and drafts that led to the completed translation of a poem or piece of prose. In any course, students might include their best and worst tests, with an "improved" or corrected version of the poor test and a self-evaluation of the difference in performance. Other suggestions for portfolio contents are given in Figure 5.6.

Research indicates that portfolio assessment can be more effective than single, static measures of student achievement. Simmons (1990) reports that for middle-grade students, "self-selected portfolios of their best work are significantly better than timed tests in estimating students' writing abilities" (p. 28). In another study (Garcia et al., 1990), two groups of teachers were asked to assess students with limited English proficiency. One group was given standardized test data, and the other was given portfolios of observational data with samples of student reading and writing. In all cases, the teachers who looked at the portfolios gave more complete evaluations and recommendations and more detailed requests for additional information.

Math

Story problems written for others to solve
Written report of strategies used to solve a problem
Pictures or graphs illustrating problem and solution
Examples of how math concepts are applied
Computer spreadsheets

Science

Drawings
Lab notes
Photos of projects or labs
Anecdotal stories of field work
Science reports with notes and drafts

Social Studies

Charts, graphs, and maps
Oral histories
Time lines
Written reports or essays with notes and drafts

Travel brochure for region, state, or country
Creative writing
Audio or video tapes of debates, panels, speeches, or presentations

All Subjects

Homework assignments
Exams or tests with self-evaluations
List of self-selected vocabulary
Content-area biographies: "My life as a scientist"
Semantic maps
Log or journal entries
Record of teacher and peer conferences
Brainstorming lists
Photographs
Record of outside reading related to content area
Audio or video tapes
Movie or television reviews

FIGURE 5.6   Suggestions for items to include in content area portfolios

Another advantage of portfolios is their potential to inform and improve instruction. In a conversation about the possibilities of portfolio assessment among researchers and teachers, Tierney et al. (1998) assert that portfolios can "serve an important role in helping teachers customize teaching and learning to the students' needs, interests, background, and circumstances" (p. 478).

Student involvement.   A second oft-cited benefit of portfolio assessment is student involvement in self-evaluation and discourse about what, why, and how they are learning (Bauer & Garcia, 1997; Kim & Pearson, 1999; Sarroub et al., 1998; Tierney et al., 1998). To guide students' self-evaluation of their portfolio work, teachers could use questions similar to the following, adapted from Reif (1990):

What makes this your best work?
How did you go about producing it?
What problems did you encounter?
How did you solve them?
What makes your most effective work different from your least effective work?
What goals did you set for yourself?
How well did you accomplish them?
What are your goals for the next marking period?

Portfolio assessment allows students to be active participant–observers of their own growth and development. When they are asked to select, polish, arrange, and analyze their own work, they have a chance to see that learning is not haphazard or incidental to any efforts of their own. They also have more direct input into what ultimately goes on their report cards. Each student can state his or her best case to the teacher.

Pat Frey-Mason, a math teacher in an urban high school, has her students keep portfolios. When students have difficulty with certain types of problems, they are asked to work similar problems and write short reflections of what was learned in the second attempt. The problems and reflections are included in their portfolios. Excerpts from two student reflections are shown in Figure 5.7.

Implementing portfolio assessment.   Using portfolios as assessment tools represents a significant shift from traditional ways of teaching and testing. If you have not used portfolios, getting started with them will take some time, patience, and trial and error.

Because much of the effectiveness of portfolio assessment is derived from students' increased awareness of their own learning, it is not surprising that students' perspectives and expectations are crucial to successful implementation of portfolios (Moje, Brozo, & Haas, 1994). Therefore, you will want to involve students from the very beginning. You will need to explain what a portfolio is, what it will include, why it is being assembled, how it is related to the curriculum, and how it will be evaluated. Although you may retain final authority over these issues, it will

---

Jennifer Z.: I feel that doing another problem similar to the first one helped me in a few ways. One, I got more practice at doing those types of problems. Two, the more I do those types of problems, the more used to them I become. Finally, by reading the corrections and trying the problems over, I have become more aware of my mistakes. Basically, I have become more conscious of each particular section of a problem situation. Though I still get a rush of adrenaline when working with math, I must admit after doing things over I do feel a bit more confident to get down and attack the problem.

Kelly R.: When first approaching the problem, I went through the directions and just graphed what

they gave me. For example, for part (a) it said to make a graph symmetric with respect to the X axis. The easiest way I saw of doing this part of the problem was to imagine the X line being folded down the middle and just flipping the image over the line. Luckily, this method worked for parts (a) and (b) but this method didn't work for parts (c) and (d). Problems occurred when I didn't follow the methods, according to the directions. When referring to "symmetric to the origin" it requires a different method. Because I did this problem so poorly, I was given a similar problem. With this problem instead of just graphing the graphs I used a sure method to graph each one. I FOLLOWED THE DIRECTIONS!

FIGURE 5.7   **Sample self-analyses from student portfolios for precalculus math**   (*Source:* Supplied by Patricia Frey-Mason, Chair, Math Department, Buffalo Academy for Visual and Performing Arts, Buffalo, NY.)

be helpful if you let students negotiate them with you. Students are more likely to take responsibility for their learning and to reach higher levels of achievement if they know clearly what is expected and have had a voice in determining it.

Portfolios are also likely to be more successful if you provide guidance and modeling for students as they put them together. You may wish to start with short and simple activities and group efforts before you have students undertake a complex individual portfolio project. Students will need assistance with selecting, arranging, and evaluating their portfolio contents. As students prepare their portfolios, you could use class time to demonstrate and discuss these processes. Class time can also be used to work on portfolios and get advice and assistance from peers or from you. Your feedback will be as important during portfolio preparation as it will be at the end of the process. It will also help if you negotiate incremental steps and deadlines for major portfolio projects.

Tracey Wathen describes how she implemented a two-tiered portfolio system with her middle school ESL class (Smolen et al., 1995). On Mondays, she distributed index cards to the class on which they wrote their literacy goals for the week. As the students worked on various reading and writing activities, they kept their notes, drafts, reflections, and other literacy-related materials in a working portfolio. On Fridays, students used the blank side of their goals cards to reflect on how well they had achieved their weekly goals, and they selected pieces from their working portfolios to include in a showcase ownership portfolio that displayed their growth in literacy and English language proficiency. Because students initially tended to write relatively simplistic goals ("I will read four books this week"), Tracey led the class in brainstorming good reading and writing strategies and classifying these behaviors. She modeled various strategies such as predicting and visualizing story settings and emphasized them with poster charts. As a result, students began to set more strategic goals, and their achievement of these goals was reflected in their portfolios.

Portfolio pros and cons.   As with other forms of assessment, portfolios have both advantages and drawbacks. On the plus side, we have repeatedly emphasized the value of portfolios in increasing students' awareness and involvement in their own learning. Portfolios can also provide detailed, authentic representations of what students have learned and what has taken place in a classroom for parents, colleagues, and administrators. Finally, portfolios can give us an opportunity to reflect on our practice as teachers. More than numeric scores on a test, portfolios allow us to take stock of what has worked, what has been learned, and what is important to learn.

By now, it is probably apparent to you that portfolios also require considerable time to introduce, create, and evaluate. That is indeed a potential drawback. Portfolio assessment takes much more teacher time and effort than simply giving a multiple-choice unit test from the teacher's manual. However, because portfolios intimately integrate assessment and instruction, many teachers believe that the time and effort are well spent.

Although portfolios can help to inform teachers' instructional decisions, that potential may not always be realized. Eurydice Bauer (1999) reviewed 19 classroom studies of alternative literacy assessments, 13 of which featured portfolios. She found that some teachers had difficulty moving from assessment to instruction. She also reported few indications that alternative assessments led to more equitable instruction for struggling readers. Portfolio assessment is probably more prevalent in elementary grades and English classes, whereas teachers in other disciplines may be more resistant to any departure from traditional assessments. Indeed, teacher training, knowledge, and beliefs are all essential determinants of whether portfolios will be used, how they will be implemented, and what ultimate effects they may have on teaching and learning (Bauer, 1999; Sarroub et al., 1997; Valencia & Wixson, 2000).

There is a final negative potential in portfolios that should be considered—the possible infringement of students' personal privacy (Hargreaves, 1989). If we were to substitute the term *dossier* for *portfolio*, very different images might be conveyed—images of aberrant behavior, surveillance, and control. However, when we assemble portfolios that include teacher observations and comments, results from standardized tests and students' permanent records, and a broad range of students' work, we are including some of the very things that might be found in a police dossier or mental health record. When we ask students to engage in self-evaluation, to open up their thought processes and personal reflections for scrutiny, or to include their social relationships as part of an assessment of group projects, we are collecting very sensitive information. The information in a portfolio may be stored for future reference, subjected to interpretation according to standards imposed by a teacher or external authority, and used to make high-stakes decisions about students, all of which create a potential "threat to individual liberty, personal privacy, and human diversity" (Hargreaves, 1989, p. 138). When accountability portfolios are used in a performance assessment, teachers are subject to similar threats.

We do not mean to suggest that portfolios should not be used. We believe that the potential benefits of portfolio assessment far outweigh any potential harm. Rather, we return to a point we made when discussing the potential biases that are inherent in assessment: assessment involves responsibility. Because we are in the position of making important judgments about students, we must take special care of how judgments are made and the possible consequences.

ASSESSING TEXTBOOKS

Although less than perfect, no doubt, textbooks are still a fact of life in most content area classrooms. Teachers often have little choice of texts; a single text is available for each subject. Sometimes a department chooses more than one text for a subject, assigning different books to different tracks. Many times teachers participate with school administrators in deciding which of several competing texts should be adopted. What teachers need in any of these situations are ways to look at textbooks, to see their strengths and weaknesses and their suitability for students.

Earlier, we discussed the cloze procedure, which was originally developed to assess the difficulty of text (Taylor, 1953). It applies a kind of Goldilocks test, which suggests whether students will find the book "too hard," "too easy," or "just right."

There are two other general approaches to judging textbooks' suitability: readability formulas and consumer judgments. Readability formulas are quantitative yardsticks for estimating differences in difficulty among texts. They can be tedious to apply, but they are relatively objective and useful if a large number of texts must be formally compared. Teachers and students make consumer judgments when they look through a text, sample a few passages, and identify features they feel make the book easy or hard, interesting or dull. If teachers collaborate with one another and with students to develop a checklist of predetermined criteria, group judgments of a textbook can be quite reliable and closely correlated to the scores of readability formulas (Klare, 1984).

Readability Formulas

Most readability formulas rely on two assumptions. The first is that longer sentences on the average are more difficult to read than shorter ones. Theoretically, sentence length gives an estimate of syntactic complexity. The longer the sentence, the more likely it is to have imbedded clauses, passive constructions, and other features that can cause difficulty for readers. The second assumption is that unfamiliar words make text harder to read. These assumptions and the way they are applied in the use of readability formulas are not without controversy.

Fry (1977) takes the second assumption a step further and asserts that on average, long words are more likely to be unfamiliar or difficult to understand than short words. The Fry readability formula is one of the most popular methods for estimating text readability. It is useful for our purposes because it provides estimates over a wide range, from primary to college level. The procedures for using the Fry formula are given in Figure 5.8. Several microcomputer programs are available that will compute Fry estimates for text samples entered via the keyboard. Persons with adequate typing skills might find them more convenient than a manual count.

The use of readability formulas has caused considerable debate. First, formulas perpetuate a common but erroneous impression that educators can mechanically and precisely match student reading levels to text difficulty levels. The whole concept of "reading level" is subject to question, whether it is applied to people or to texts (Cadenhead, 1987; International Reading Association, 1982). Reading level is at best a metaphor for certain observable facts: some people read better than others; some books are harder to read than others. Two books at the "tenth-grade level" may vary considerably in the difficulties they

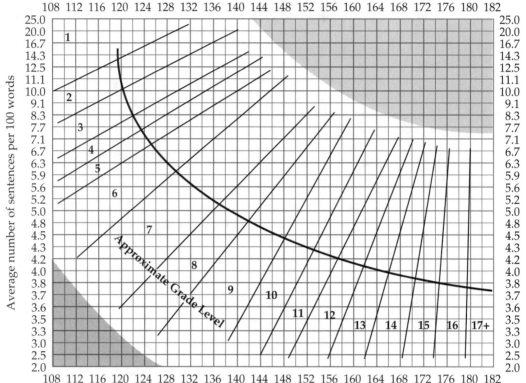

Average number of syllables per 100 words

FIGURE 5.8   **Fry readability graph**   (*Source:* Edward Fry, Rutgers University Reading Center, New Brunswick, NJ 08904.)

Directions for Computing Readability

1. Randomly select three 100-word samples from the text. A word is any group of symbols with a space on each side. A number such as 1776 counts as a word; so does an initialization such as USA.

2. Count the number of sentences within each 100-word sample. If a 100-word sample ends in the middle of a sentence, figure the decimal fraction of the sentence that is included.

3. Count the number of syllables in each 100-word sample. A syllable is defined as a phonetic syllable. In numerals and initializations, each symbol counts as a syllable. For example, 1776 counts as

four syllables, and USA as three. Hint: A 100-word sample has at least 100 syllables. Make a light tic mark above each additional syllable, count the total number of tic marks, and add to 100.

4. Compute the average number of sentences and the average number of syllables per 100 words.

5. Plot these two averages on the graph. They should intersect either above or below the curved line within one of the numbered segments. The number in the segment is the approximate grade level of the text. A few books may fall in the shaded gray areas; their grade-level scores are invalid.

present to readers; two readers at the tenth-grade level will vary widely in their aptitude for reading different kinds of texts. Reading level is hardly a precise metric.

Critics such as Cullinan and Fitzgerald (1985) and Sewall (1988) charge that formulas consider only a very narrow range of text characteristics and completely ignore student variables such as interest and prior knowledge. Short sentences can be hard to read, especially if important connecting words are omitted. Many short words are unfamiliar to most students, and many multi-syllabic words are commonly understood. When authors and publishers try to make textbooks fit readability formulas, the resulting prose is frequently lifeless and hard to read.

Fry (1989) defends the simple two-variable formula. He acknowledges some limitations but points to the utility of readability formulas for those in schools, publishing firms, libraries, and businesses who must have some yardstick for estimating the difficulty of books. He contends that even though sentence length and word length are not absolute indicators of difficulty, they are valid when considered in the average. He also argues that formulas are not intended to be writers' guides, and that the mindless application of formulas in producing text is in fact blatant misuse.

We take a pragmatic stance on readability formulas. These formulas can be useful adjuncts to teacher judgments, especially when teachers must survey a large number of books. However, the formulas also have obvious limitations. We doubt that many experienced teachers would place unreserved trust in results based solely on formulas. Common sense suggests that teachers consider many factors when deciding which books to use.

Consumer Judgments (or Don't Judge a Book by Its Cover)

In practice, most teachers assess textbooks by using them. They preview the text while planning, they observe students interacting with the text, and they see how students react to reading assignments. From these practical observations, they form judgments about how good the text is and how they should use it.

If a group of teachers are working on textbook adoption and need to screen several texts, they can decide among themselves what is important and possibly devise their own checklist. Science teachers are interested in what sort of laboratory activities are included in a textbook and how they are explained and illustrated. Writing style is important in a social studies text, but it would be impossible to judge style in an English anthology containing the work of many authors. Math teachers want to know what kinds of problems are featured in a text and how many problems focus on each kind of math concept. When we consider the unique content and instructional problems of foreign languages, health, industrial arts, and computer science, we must conclude that no single checklist could cover all of them.

Whatever the content area, there are some general factors to consider when judging a text. Instead of a checklist, we offer a framework that you can use to develop your own checklist for assessing text materials (Figure 5.9).

It is rare for all teachers of the same subject to agree that they are using the best available text and rarer still to find a teacher who claims to be using a perfect text. Also, considerable criticism has been aimed at texts from outside of faculty rooms. Content texts are too often written in a way that is "inconsiderate" to the reader (Anderson & Armbruster, 1984). Schallert and Roser (1996) contend that even though modern content texts have improved, they are often pointless and "contentless." They cite the lavish illustrations interspersed with incessant short, unanswered questions in many early grade texts and the frequent lack of coherent examples or explanations that tie information together in more advanced texts. Social studies texts have been attacked for their "ahistorical" bias, distracting formats, and lifeless writing (Sewall, 1988). The content of textbooks in science, social studies, and literature has been the subject of religious and political controversy. People from diverse cultures are often ignored, underrepresented, or misrepresented.

Content

Does the content complement the curriculum?
Is the content current?
Is there balance between depth and breadth of coverage?
How many new or difficult vocabulary terms are included and how are they introduced and defined?
How dense are the new concepts in the text?
Is the content generally appropriate to students' prior knowledge?

Format

Are there good graphic aids and illustrations? Are they distracting or irrelevant to the content?
How are chapters set up? Are there introductions, summaries, heads and subheads, and marginal notes?
Are layout and print attractive and easy to read?
How useful are the index, glossary, etc.?

Utility

How good are the activities at the end of the chapters?
Do text questions call for interpretation, evaluation, and application as well as literal recall?
Is there a teacher's manual? Would it be helpful?
Are quizzes or test questions provided? How good are they?
Does the text or manual suggest additional readings or related trade books?

Style

Is the writing lively and interesting to read?
Is the syntax at a suitable level of complexity?
Is the writing coherent and clear?

FIGURE 5.9   **Framework for assessing texts**

SUMMARY

There are many variables in a teacher's day—variables that require countless decisions about students, teaching methods, materials, and assessment. The more information a teacher has, the better the quality of those decisions will be. This chapter offered many suggestions for collecting and interpreting information on students' reading and writing abilities and for utilizing that information when planning instruction and assigning grades. It also looked at ways of deciding how difficult or useful textbooks might be. All of these decisions are ultimately professional judgments. As a profession, teaching is more art than science. The teaching art has many legitimate forms of expression, and good teachers, like good artists, are constantly evolving. There is no "right" way to assign grades, no "best" test of reading ability, no "perfect" text for any subject, but good teachers keep looking and experimenting.

SUGGESTED READINGS

Glatthorn, A., Bragaw, D., Dawkins, K., & Parker, J. (1998). *Performance assessment and standards-based curricula: The achievement cycle.* Larchmont, NY: Eye on Education.

Rhodes, L. (Ed.) (1993). *Literacy assessment: A handbook of instruments.* Portsmouth, NH: Heinemann.

Strickland, K., & Strickland, J. (1998). *Reflections on assessment: Its purposes, methods, and effects on learning.* Portsmouth, NH: Boynton/Cook.

Valencia, S., Hiebert, E., & Afflerbach, P. (Eds.) (1993). *Authentic reading assessment: Practices & possibilities.* Newark, DE: International Reading Association.

Walker, B. (2000). *Diagnostic teaching of reading: Techniques for instruction and assessment,* 4th ed. Upper Saddle River, NJ: Merrill.

Walvoord, B., & Anderson, V. (1998). *Effective grading: A tool for learning and assessment.* San Francisco: Jossey-Bass.

Wiggins, G. (1998). *Educative assessment: Designing assessments to inform and improve student performance.* San Francisco: Jossey-Bass.

Preparing
to Read

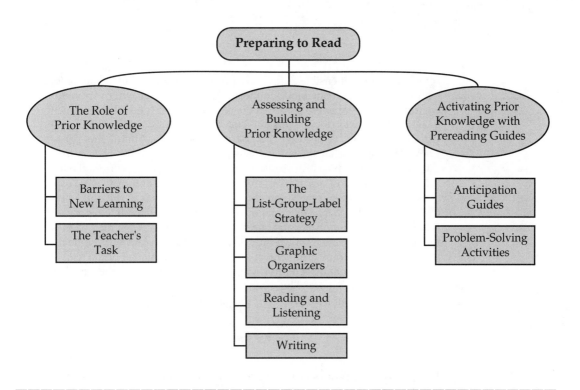

In previous chapters, we discussed the importance of helping students make connections between their own knowledge, values, and concerns and the ideas in their texts and coursework. In this chapter, we elaborate on these suggestions by describing ways to activate and build prior knowledge, create interest and motivation for reading, and focus students on their reading and learning activities.

The following scenario illustrates what can happen when students are *not* focused on a reading assignment. It is based on events that have been reported to us by teachers and students and that we have observed ourselves in many classrooms. As you read it, ask yourself how the teacher might have helped students connect with the reading assignment.

▼▼▼▼▼▼▼

The tenth-grade class had finished a short film on the geography of Japan with 20 minutes left in the period. Mr. Gregory told them to use the time to begin reading "Traditional Japan," the second chapter in the new unit. He wrote on the board: "Read Chapter 16, pages 252–257. Answer question 1, p. 255 and questions 1 and 3, p. 257 for tomorrow."

As Felicia began to read, her mind was on the track meet. In a little less than two hours, she would be running the mile relay for the first time. A series of incomprehensible dates and unpronounceable names swam before her eyes as she read. She plodded through a long passage on government written by some Japanese prince in the seventh century. Finally she came to question 1, "What principle did the Shotoku constitution stress?" Her eyes wandered back to the heading "Shotoku's Constitution." In the first paragraph, she found what she needed. She put her name and the page and question number on a clean sheet of paper and began to copy from the text: "Confucian values of orderly society and obedience to authority were especially stressed." Wasn't there something about Confucius in the unit test on China? Maybe he was an emperor or something. Oh, well. Mr. Gregory would explain it tomorrow, and she had done the first part of the assignment. If she could finish this in class, she could go get pizza with some of the girls after the track meet. She ought to do well on her leg of the relay; her quarter-mile times had been improving. Felicia thought of all their drill on the exchange of the baton. She rehearsed it in her mind . . . be sure to get a firm grip on the baton before starting to sprint . . . her eyes moved across more names and dates.

▼▼▼▼▼▼▼

Felicia's difficulty was not that she *cannot* read but that she was not *ready* to read. Before a person begins to read, whether for work, for pleasure, or for school, several interrelated factors influence how and what will be understood and remembered:

1. *Interest.* If students want to know more about a topic, curiosity will help to guide their reading. Students are more likely to recall something of interest to them.
2. *Motivation.* Reading done for pleasure is different from reading done for work or school. Reading will be less labored in a class students enjoy, more purposeful and serious when they are trying to get a good grade.
3. *Purpose.* Purpose can be either long term or short term. One purpose may be to do well on a test or in a class discussion. A student may also have a more immediate purpose, such as the need to answer a question, solve a problem, or find a particular piece of information. If students' main purpose is simply to get through the reading, their efforts will be less fruitful.
4. *Attention.* If a student's mind is on the reading, without distractions from the immediate surroundings or competing thoughts, he or she will probably comprehend more.
5. *Strategy.* Having an effective plan or strategy increases the likelihood of success, and the anticipation of success also increases motivation. Anyone may conduct reading methodically, whether it is a particular order for reading the Sunday paper or a plan for studying a difficult chemistry chapter.
6. *Prior knowledge.* In some ways, this factor is a composite of all of the above. Students' knowledge of language, of reading and study, of the world, and particularly of the topic at hand will influence how they proceed through a

text. Prior knowledge helps students set purposes, direct their attention, fill in gaps, make connections or inferences, monitor their progress, and recall what they have read.

Students vary widely in the knowledge, skill, and enthusiasm they bring to a reading assignment. Like Felicia in the previous scenario, they may frequently read without interest, motivation, or attention, without adequate purpose or strategy, and without full awareness of their pertinent prior knowledge. Good teachers recognize this and realize that preparing students well will go a long way toward making their reading successful. Most of the teaching strategies in this chapter not only help to prepare students for reading but also carry over into the reading itself. Furthermore, most of them are designed for cooperative learning, or small-group interaction, or can be so adapted.

THE ROLE OF PRIOR KNOWLEDGE

Prior knowledge can cover a wide range of skills, ideas, and attitudes. When we use the term, we are focusing particularly on a reader's background knowledge of the subject matter of the text. What a person already knows about a topic is probably the single most influential factor in what he or she will learn.

Barriers to New Learning

In Chapter 1, we discussed how people use schemata to organize and collect their thoughts and synthesize their experiences. Many research studies have demonstrated how inappropriate or missing schemata can influence learning from reading (Anderson, 1984). Distortions or misinterpretations may result when readers attempt to make sense of unfamiliar ideas by drawing on their cultural schemata. For example, Steffensen, Joag-Dev, and Anderson (1979) asked Americans and natives of India to read two letters, one about an American wedding and the other about an Indian wedding. Both the Americans and the Indians needed less time to read the letter that had culturally familiar content and recalled more information from the familiar material. Each group interpreted the same information differently, depending on its cultural perspective. For instance, some American readers thought that the dowry described in the Indian passage referred to an exchange of gifts between the families or favors given to the attendants by the bride and groom. Because the American bride was wearing her grandmother's wedding gown, one Indian reader inferred that the dress was badly out of fashion.

Problems also arise when a reader has no relevant schema or an insufficient schema, if relevant schemata are not recalled, or if an existing schema is inconsistent with information in the text. A reader will often ignore ideas in a text or discussion that conflict with conventional wisdom or supposed real-world knowledge (Alvermann, Smith, & Readence, 1985; Guzzetti & Hynd, 1998; Hynd et al., 1995). Students with reading difficulties appear to have particular trouble using their prior knowledge to modify misconceptions or to learn new information from reading. Often, a reader who is struggling to understand a difficult text will fasten on isolated details in the text, call on an inappropriate schema to fill in the gaps, and consequently make unwarranted inferences (Pressley, 2000).

We should not underestimate the tenacity with which students will hold onto their beliefs, even in the face of conflicting evidence. Watson and Konicek (1990) discuss a class of students in Massachusetts who were studying heat transfer. All of them knew from experience that hats, sweaters, and blankets made them warm in winter. They conducted a series of experiments in which they wrapped thermometers in various articles of warm clothing and waited for the temperature to rise. Even when this failed to happen, they maintained their belief that the clothing made them warm. According to Watson and Konicek, several barriers make it difficult for students to change previously developed concepts. The first is stubbornness, or "the refusal to admit one's theory may be wrong" (p. 682). Second, language itself gets in the way of changing old beliefs: sweaters are "warm clothes." Third, perceptions can reinforce beliefs: when you put on a sweater, you feel warmer.

Factors such as cognitive, social, and moral development also influence the ease with which students can accommodate new ideas that conflict with everyday experience and conventional wisdom. Anyone who has ever tried teaching the difference between fact and opinion to middle-grade students will sympathize with this because the typical middle schooler will tell you, "If I agree with it, it's a fact!" Students are much too canny to accept an idea simply because a textbook or teacher says they should.

A factor that has strong potential to affect conceptual change is culture. The misinterpretations of American and Indian readers in the study by Steffensen, Joag-Dev, and Anderson (1979) resulted from cultural differences. In another study, black and white teenagers were asked to read a passage that described "sounding," a kind of verbal duel frequent in African American communities (Reynolds et al., 1982). The white readers tended to interpret the episode as dangerous, even violent; the black readers were more likely to see it as a nonthreatening contest of wits. Although cultural schemata determine in part how students perceive what they read, making culturally based assumptions about what students will or will not understand holds the danger of devolving to stereotypes, which may themselves create barriers to learning.

The effects of culture are much more subtle than is indicated by common stereotypes such as "Italians/Irish/Hispanics are emotional," "students from single-parent households lack discipline," and "yuppie children are achievement motivated." Shirley Brice Heath (1983) details the complex and subtle interplay of family, neighborhood, economic circumstances, and religion that influences what children learn about language and literacy. She describes how children from two small working-class communities came to school with quite different

Technology Tip

▼▼▼

Certain aspects of youth culture also need to be taken into account when considering the barriers to new learning. For updates on what educators should know about today's teenagers, their expectations, and the challenges they present teachers who are charged with preparing them to read, search the Educational Resources Information Center data bases (http://www.accesseric.org/) for resources on youth culture.

ideas about what language, reading, and writing are, how they should be used, and what should be thought about them. The culture of the school reflected yet another set of ideas—the mainstream values and attitudes of the town. What often resulted was a conflict of expectations between school and student—to the detriment of the student.

The Teacher's Task

How can a teacher possibly prepare students for new or conflicting ideas when there are so many potential differences in their backgrounds and experiences? First, you can recognize where students' cultural values and beliefs may conflict with elements of the curriculum. If you are not sure what conflicts may exist, it is especially important to plan classroom activities that will allow students to call forth and discuss their schemata. You should recognize the validity and strengths of students' cultural experiences and look for points of congruence between what they know and what you are teaching. You should be ready to explain the unfamiliar and discuss apparent inconsistencies. Whenever possible, you should encourage students to resolve contradictions, but you should also recognize that resolution or compromise may be impossible. For instance, there are legitimate differences in interpretations of literature, history, and politics, and these may be argued endlessly but never resolved.

We draw three broad implications from our understanding of how schemata affect the reading process:

1. What the reader brings to the page in the way of prior knowledge is more important to comprehension than what is actually on the page.
2. What teachers do before reading to prepare students can be more effective in promoting comprehension than what is done after reading.
3. Before reading, teachers should try to activate students' prior knowledge, assess the sufficiency and accuracy of that knowledge, and build appropriate background knowledge when necessary.

Good teachers have long understood the necessity of preparing students, and this is reflected in the teaching practices commonly used in content areas. New material is often introduced by a review of what has already been covered, by presenting essential background information via a lecture or media such as films and pictures, and by brainstorming and class discussion. Vocabulary instruction, which is another way to prepare students for reading or studying new topics, is discussed at length in Chapter 8.

ASSESSING AND BUILDING PRIOR KNOWLEDGE

This section presents some teaching strategies that help students build a schema before reading a selection. Each strategy is designed to "bridge the gap between what the reader already knows and what the reader needs to know before he/she can meaningfully learn the task at hand" (Ausubel, 1968, p. 148). Each of these techniques is relatively easy to plan and introduce in the classroom. As you read about these strategies, keep in mind how students' different sociocultural backgrounds and the varying knowledge they bring to a task will need to be taken into account.

The List-Group-Label Strategy

The strategy called List-Group-Label (Taba, 1967) is a variation on brainstorming that can be done with a whole class, in small groups, or by individual students. Students first list all the words they can think of that are associated with a new topic; then they group the words they have listed by looking for words that have something in common. Several variant groupings are usually possible, and a particular word often fits into more than one group. Once groups of words are established, students decide on a label for each group. An important part of List-Group-Label is the discussion of why words belong in a certain group.

If students' background is fairly extensive, a List-Group-Label session should be sufficient to help them activate and organize what they already know. Students will learn from one another; only where significant gaps or misconceptions exist will the teacher need to fill in additional background. List-Group-Label is also effective as a review activity after students have read about a topic.

Graphic Organizers

When a teacher and students diagram their labeled groups of ideas, they are in effect creating what Barron (1969) called a *graphic organizer,* or structured overview. Barron suggested that important vocabulary terms can be arranged in a diagram that illustrates the relationships between ideas. A typical graphic organizer, with coordinate and subordinate ideas arranged in a branching pattern, is shown in Figure 6.1. Other formats for graphic organizers are presented in Figure 6.2. Like the List-Group-Label strategy, graphic organizers can also be used to review information at the end of a unit or chapter.

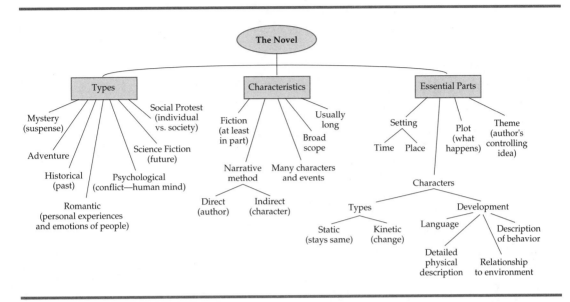

FIGURE 6.1   **A graphic organizer with a branching format for a high school English class on the novel**

A teacher may prepare a graphic organizer ahead of time and explain it to the students while displaying it on the chalkboard or with the overhead projector. However, a graphic organizer is more effective when students participate in its development. The example in Figure 6.1 was designed to introduce a unit on the novel as a literary form. If the teacher prepared this organizer ahead of time, he or she might have included only the title and top three labels on an overhead transparency. The teacher could have introduced the new topic by asking students to discuss what they know about novels—characteristics, authors, novels they have read, and so on. The teacher could then have displayed his or her partial graphic organizer and begun to fill in some of the ideas that students generated. Where students did not volunteer essential information, the teacher could have filled in the blanks.

Reading and Listening

For mature readers, much of the background for reading a particular selection comes from previous reading experiences. They have prepared for reading by reading (Alexander & Jetton, 2000). Similarly, a relatively simple method for building students' background for a reading selection is to have them first read another selection on the same topic. In a study with eleventh graders, Crafton (1983) found that reading two articles on the same topic improved students' comprehension of the second article. Specifically, those students generated more inferences, used

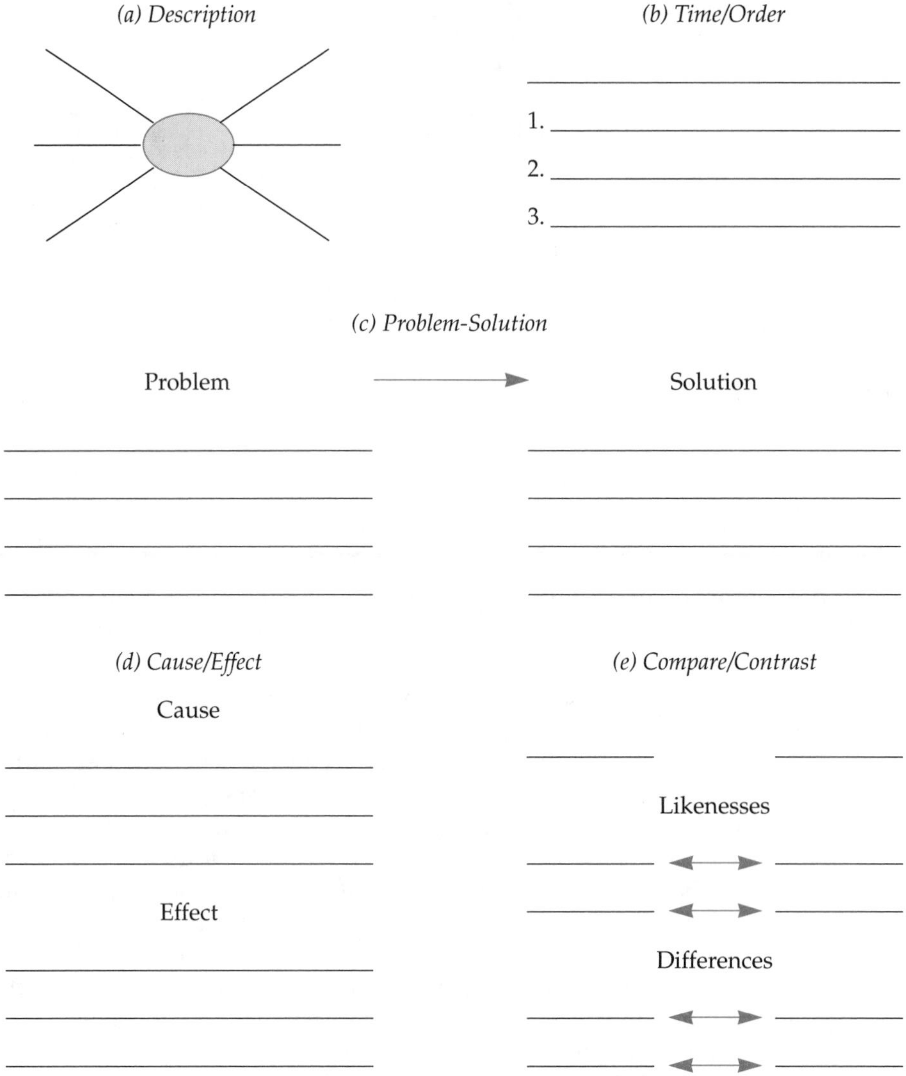

(a) Description

(b) Time/Order

1. _____
2. _____
3. _____

(c) Problem-Solution

Problem   ⟶   Solution

_____   _____
_____   _____
_____   _____
_____   _____

(d) Cause/Effect

Cause

_____

_____

_____

Effect

_____

_____

_____

(e) Compare/Contrast

Likenesses

_____ ⟷ _____

_____ ⟷ _____

Differences

_____ ⟷ _____

_____ ⟷ _____

FIGURE 6.2   Other formats for graphic organizers   (Dorothy McLeod, D.C. *Source:* Graphic Organizers, reprinted from PEER Classroom Activities by permission of D. C. Heath & Company.)

more outside information and personal involvement, and focused more on higher-level information than did students who read two unrelated articles.

Reading a pertinent selection from a different textbook, a trade book, or a magazine should help to activate and build background for subsequent reading of a targeted selection in a content area text. For instance, a biology teacher introducing a unit on biomes might give the class an excerpt on rain forests from *Scientific American*. An English teacher could intersperse the reading of *Huckleberry Finn* with relevant sections of Twain's *Life on the Mississippi*. If securing multiple copies of the preparatory selection is impossible or if having students read on their own is impractical for some other reason, a teacher can always read to students.

For example, a social studies teacher who plans to introduce a unit on intergenerational family relationships might begin by reading a short essay titled "My Name" by Sandra Cisneros (1989). If time is a factor, the teacher might choose to concentrate on a particular section of the essay, such as the part in which Esperanza, a young girl growing up in a Chicano barrio and the narrator of the essay, recalls how she was named after her great-grandmother:

> A wild horse of a woman, so wild she wouldn't marry. Until my great-grandfather threw a sack over her head and carried her off. Just like that, as if she were a fancy chandelier. That's the way he did it. And the story goes she never forgave him. She looked out the window her whole life, the way so many women sit their sadness on their elbow. Esperanza, I have inherited her name, but I don't want to inherit her place by the window. (p. 11)

As students listen, the teacher might ask them to pick out what Courtney Cazden (2000) calls their "strong lines"—especially memorable phrases or sentences—and be prepared to share them at the end. The idea of asking students to recall their strong lines comes from Cazden's work with Puente (Spanish for "bridge") teachers who conduct reading and writing workshops for Mexican American community college students.

Another strategy for using reading as a schema builder is called *Skinny Books* (Gilles et al., 1988). A teacher can collect several related and relevant readings from newspapers, magazines, trade books, and other sources and put them together in a folder or theme binder. For instance, for a class studying local elections, a teacher might assemble several "skinny books" with articles on various candidates, rules of voting, campaign literature, and a sample ballot (Gilles et al., 1988). Students should be given time to read and discuss these prior to reading the assigned text.

Technology Tip

For other suggestions on how to use reading and listening activities that will prepare students from diverse cultures to read their content area texts, visit the website of Education World® Where Educators Go to Learn at http://www.education-world.com/

Writing

Writing is really a special kind of thinking. When students write, they must reflect on what they know, select what they wish to use, organize the selected ideas, and commit them to written language with some concern that a reader will be able to understand what is meant. Writing what they *do* know can lead them to discover what they do *not* know or what they need to find out. Writing, therefore, can also serve as a bridge between prior knowledge and new material to be learned.

A growing number of content area teachers have their students keep a journal, or learning log, for their subject. A *learning log* is a notebook dedicated to jotting, reflecting, drafting, and sometimes doodling. (We discuss learning logs in depth in Chapter 10.) Students are regularly given five to ten minutes during a period to write in their logs, and teachers periodically collect and read the logs. If the teacher responds to a particular entry by writing a short note in a student's log, it becomes a kind of private dialogue between teacher and student. Students can use their learning logs for listing, speculating, or predicting before reading.

After a brainstorming session or some other preliminary organizing activity, a teacher might give students five minutes for *free-writing* on a topic ("Write whatever comes to mind on the topic of insects"). For free-writing, the only requirement is that students continue writing for the time period specified (Elbow, 1973). If students protest that they do not know what to write, the teacher can spend a few minutes brainstorming and jotting ideas on the blackboard to help focus the writing activity. Free-writing products are often rough and disjointed, but the object of free-writing is not polished prose. Free-writing promotes written fluency and helps writers to begin collecting and organizing their thoughts.

A teacher might also precede a reading assignment with a focused learning log entry. Nikki Assad used the prompts in Figure 6.3 to help her high school English students anticipate events in the novel *The Catcher in the Rye* (Salinger, 1951). Once or twice a week, she gave students ten minutes in class to respond in their learning log prior to reading specific chapters. Log entries were discussed,

---

What do you hate about school?

What is a phony?

Describe your most embarrassing moment.

Explain one moment or situation you could put in a glass case.

Have you ever said something you wish you could take back?

What are your favorite places away from home to go? Why?

Think of something you broke or damaged that did not belong to you. How did you feel when this happened?

Who is one person you can rely on? Why?

FIGURE 6.3   **Learning log prompts for *The Catcher in the Rye*** (*Source:* Nikki Assad, Kenmore East High School, Tonawanda, New York)

List everything you know about ancient Greece. What would you like to know about ancient Greece?

What would you do if you were left alone in a desert?

Guess how ancient people used the sun to help them tell time.

List all the animals or plants you believe may be endangered.

Pretend a new continent was discovered and you are going to settle there. What are five things you'll need to do?

What do you think matter is?

List all of the things you do or use every day that involve water.

What are your feelings about pollution?

What do you think will happen next? What would you like to happen next? (Asked after part of a story or book has been read)

How do you think poetry is different from prose?

List three things you'd like to know about the Constitution.

FIGURE 6.4   Examples of prompts for focused learning log entries   (*Source:* Adapted from Nancie Atwell, *Coming to know: Writing to learn in the intermediate grades.* Portsmouth, NH: Heinemann, 1990.)

sometimes before reading a chapter and sometimes after. Although the learning log prompts were designed to activate prior knowledge before students read a chapter, Nikki anticipated that some students would read the novel more quickly or would have read the novel previously. Therefore, students who had already read a chapter were encouraged to include their reflections on the chapter in their response to the learning log prompt.

To give an idea of other things students might write about, several learning log prompts are listed in Figure 6.4. Prereading learning log writing has many adaptations. Students could share their log entries in pairs or in small groups. They could write updated log entries after they have read. A teacher can assess students' prior knowledge and comprehension by quickly scanning the class's log entries.

Throughout the rest of this chapter, you will find other activities that involve writing, some used before reading and some used after. For instance, as you read the sections on prereading guides and problem solving you will see many possibilities for writing activities. Some of the strategies will stimulate learning log entries or even evolve into more formal written products.

ACTIVATING PRIOR KNOWLEDGE WITH PREREADING GUIDES

Like Felicia at the beginning of this chapter, most middle school and high school students have a lot more on their agendas than schoolwork. After all, in addition to their academic development, they are hard at work on social, physical, and personal growth. It should not come as a surprise that many are not particularly interested in using trigonometric ratios, reading *Julius Caesar*, conjugating

Spanish verbs, or learning how the valence-shell electron-pair repulsion model helps in predicting the shapes of molecules. We like to take a realistic view of this by paraphrasing Abraham Lincoln: you can interest some of your students all of the time, you can interest all of your students some of the time, but you will never get all of them excited about the valence-shell electron-pair repulsion model at the same time.

Interest is an important factor in learning, as we said at the beginning of this chapter. Many of you can probably remember teachers who, through their enthusiasm and commitment, brought to life subjects that you ordinarily dreaded. Student interest is relative, though; you might not expect great enthusiasm ("Golly, Ms. Trimble, I now realize that John Milton is the greatest writer who ever lived!"), but you would like to see some curiosity, commitment, and engagement on the part of students during the few minutes they are with you each day. Martha Ruddell (1996) suggests three principles that can serve as a basis for planning interest-generating instruction:

1. Learning occurs most rapidly and efficiently when new concepts and information build on what is already known.
2. The easiest way to gain and hold students' interest and attention is by engaging them in intellectually rich activities that require problem solving, critical thinking, and active participation.
3. Personal identification with and investment in an activity increases and sustains a learner's persistence and productivity.

A major purpose of prereading guides is to engage students' interest by focusing a lesson on their ideas and beliefs. The guides presented here are designed to involve students in discussions of what they know and believe, including ideas that may be contentious or contrary to the orthodoxy of the textbook and curriculum. A prereading guide should allow students to use the discussion as a platform for understanding and organizing new information.

Much of the teacher's effort with prereading guides takes place before class, in the designing of a guide. The teacher will not be as active in leading the actual discussion as with other strategies. Instead, copies of the guide are distributed after a brief introduction, and students are set to work, usually in small groups, on the tasks presented in the guide. The teacher becomes less a leader and more a facilitator or moderator.

Anticipation Guides

An *anticipation guide* (called a prediction guide by Harold Herber, 1978) is a series of statements that are relevant both to what students already know and to the materials they are going to be studying. As part of a well-planned lesson, such a guide serves as a catalyst for activating relevant schemata and leads students into reading with some personal investment in finding out what is in the text. Anticipation guides are useful tools for effecting conceptual change.

Hints for Struggling Readers

Prereading guides are especially helpful when working with students who struggle with their textbook assignments. We recommend using these guides in conjunction with various media formats and the Internet:

▸ Tape record relevant sections of a text to assist readers who struggle with decoding and need extra help in completing the guides. Signal on the tape where the information is to be used on the guide.

▸ Provide a list of Web sites for students to explore who do not have the requisite background knowledge to complete a prereading guide. Ask students to add to that list as they search the Internet for related sites.

▸ Encourage struggling readers to use the classroom or school media center collection of videotapes and CD-ROMs on topics that you assign for reading. Make sure that the directions and activities on the prereading guides are stated in such a way that students can use what they learn from the media to complete the guides.

▸ Make use of struggling readers' everyday knowledge—knowledge that comes from out-of-school experiences—to scaffold school literacy tasks on the prereading guide. For example, let adolescents use their interest in music CDs to scaffold text-based learning. This might involve letting them rap their answers to the guide material.

▸ Use sheltered English techniques that rely on visuals and manipulatives when designing prereading guides for students who speak a language other than English as their first language.

Dufflemeyer, Baum, and Merkley (1987) explain this function: "By virtue of [their] potential for provoking disagreement and bringing to the surface notions which represent a challenge to students' existing beliefs, anticipation guides serve not only as prior knowledge activators but also as springboards for modifying strongly held misconceptions about the topic" (p. 147). When students' prior knowledge is inaccurate, as is often the case, especially in math and science, confronting their misconceptions directly can be helpful in bringing about new understanding (Guzzetti et al., 1993).

Paul Mance, a teacher at a middle school in Angola, New York, a predominantly rural school district bordering on a Seneca Nation reservation, used an anticipation guide in his ninth-grade English class. The class was going to read *The Rising of the Moon*, a play about a rebel in the Irish Revolution. Paul began by writing on the board, "Thou shalt not kill, except . . ." and asking, "Is it ever right to take another person's life?" The students had many ideas. They discussed euthanasia (a word volunteered by a member of the class), self-defense, and war. He listed these on the board. Then he distributed the anticipation guide (Figure 6.5). After a minute or two, students began to compare responses within their small groups. The Native American students in the class had particularly telling insights on some of the issues in the guide.

ANTICIPATION GUIDE FOR THE RISING OF THE MOON

We are going to read a play called *The Rising of the Moon*. It is about a rebel on the run during the Irish Revolution. He tried his best to outsmart the police and avoid being captured. The play deals with many issues of basic human rights for all people.

Directions: Read the list of issues below. If you agree with a statement, make a check in column A. Be ready to explain why you agree or disagree with each item.

A (You)	B (Author)	
_____	_____	1. It is always wrong to kill.
_____	_____	2. Your country comes before your own belief.
_____	_____	3. Lying is always bad.
_____	_____	4. A person should be willing to die for his or her country.
_____	_____	5. The law is always right.
_____	_____	6. People who live in the same country usually think alike.
_____	_____	7. All men are brothers.
_____	_____	8. Police are cold and unsympathetic.

Once we have discussed these items in class, read the play. If you think the author would agree with you, make a check in column B. You must be able to cite evidence from the play to support your choices in column B.

FIGURE 6.5   An anticipation guide for a ninth-grade English class (*Source:* Paul Mance, Lake Shore Middle School, Angola, New York.)

When the groups had considered each of the items on the guide, Paul asked them to summarize their discussions for the rest of the class. The class weighed the pros and cons of each issue, bringing up many experiences and current events in support of their opinions. Then Paul asked the class, "Based on what you've discussed, and the little bit you know about this play, do you think the author would agree with you?" Again the students had a number of ideas, including some information about politics and conflict in Ireland, about police, and about life on the run as they imagined it. Several students wanted to know if the playwright was Irish, and if so, which side he was on. The teacher suggested this would be a good thing to try to figure out when they read the play for homework.

The next day students sat again with their working groups. They got out their anticipation guides and literature anthologies and began to go back through each of the issues on the guide. Students frequently turned to a particular section of the play and pointed out information that supported their interpretation. Once again, Paul called the class together to review and summarize. Although there was a high degree of consensus on what the author intended, a few students remained unpersuaded on particular points. All students had a chance to explain their point of view, however. Finally, Paul asked students to pick one statement from the anticipation guide and write in their learning log why they thought the author agreed or disagreed with them on that particular issue. This log entry became the basis of an essay that students polished and submitted for a grade.

Developing anticipation guides.   The use of anticipation guides requires some planning on the part of the teacher. We suggest the following steps in preparing and using an anticipation guide:

1. Analyze the reading assignment to identify key ideas and information.
2. Think of points of congruence between text ideas and students' prior knowledge. To do this, you may need to look beyond the facts and literal information in the text. Try to find the ideas underlying the facts.
3. Anticipate ideas that may be counterintuitive or controversial, especially any misconceptions that students might have about the material.
4. Devise written statements that address students' existing schemata. Although the number of statements will vary, five to eight is recommended for most one- or two-day lessons.
5. Write a brief background or introduction to the reading assignment.
6. Write directions for students. Be sure to provide a bridge between the reader and the author. Direct students to read the text with reference to their own ideas. (Note that the guide in Figure 6.5 says, "If you think the author would agree with you . . .")
7. Have students work on the guide after a brief introduction to the topic. (Refer to the section on building prior knowledge for some good introductory techniques.)
8. Small-group discussion of the guide, both before and after reading, is an effective means for generating student involvement.

There is one mistake that teachers sometimes make in developing an anticipation guide. When a statement on a guide is too passage dependent, that is, when it is too far removed from students' personal knowledge and experience, they can only make wild guesses about whether or not it is true. This discourages student investment and curiosity and instead reinforces the impression that the textbook is much "smarter" than the reader and is therefore unapproachable. For example, to prepare eighth-grade students for a science chapter on physical properties, a teacher might draft a guide that included the following definition from the text: "A physical property is a characteristic of matter that may be observed without changing the chemical composition of the substance." If this were the only introduction the students had to the topic, they might have difficulty activating schemata for the following statements:

> You can change a physical property of an object by applying heat to the object.
> Water has a lower boiling point than alcohol.
> We use physical properties to identify and describe objects.

The definition of a physical property is too abstract, and the statements contain potentially unfamiliar technical terms from the text, such as "boiling point." The following statements should be more accessible because they appeal more directly to students' experiences:

Heat can change objects.
Water and alcohol are different.
We use our senses to identify and describe objects.

Other factors that contribute to the effectiveness of anticipation guides (Dufflemeyer, 1994):

- Statements should reflect important ideas in the text.
- Statements that reflect common knowledge are less likely to stimulate thinking and discussion.
- Statements should be general rather than specific.
- Statements that challenge student beliefs will highlight discrepancies between what they believe and what is in the text.

An important element of the anticipation guide is the bridge between students' prior knowledge and ideas in the text. (Note that the guide in Figure 6.5 directs students to read the text and decide whether or not the author would agree with them. They must also be ready to support their decisions.) In what they call an *extended anticipation guide,* Frederick Dufflemeyer and colleagues (Dufflemeyer, Baum, & Merkley, 1987; Dufflemeyer & Baum, 1992) take this element a step further by asking students to paraphrase what they found in the text. In the example of an extended anticipation guide in Figure 6.6, students are asked to decide whether the text information is compatible with what they discussed before reading. Finally, students write their own paraphrase of what the text says.

Applications of the anticipation guide.   Anticipation guides can be created for a variety of subjects. Figure 6.7 shows a guide developed by Ray Kamery for tenth- and eleventh-grade students in an urban high school resource room who were going to read an excerpt from *The Autobiography of Malcolm X* (1965). In the selection, Malcolm X describes how he determined to educate himself by reading widely while in prison. Before working with the guide, Ray asked students to think about the last time they wished they were different or wished the world could be different. Students then discussed their reactions to the five statements on the guide. After reading the text selection, students again discussed the statements on the guide. Finally, the teacher had them write an essay on the question "How did reading change the course of Malcolm X's life?"

The guide in Figure 6.8 was developed for a first-year French class by their teacher, Beth Anne Connors. The students were going to be reading a dialogue in which a hotel clerk and a guest discussed hotel amenities, room rates, and reservations. Most of the new vocabulary in the selection was specific to travel and hotels. Several differences between hotels in France and in the United States

ANTICIPATION GUIDE: POPULATION CHANGES

Isle Royale National Park is a large island in Lake Superior. In 1900, a few moose found their way to the island. By 1920, more than 2,000 moose lived there. Between 1920 and 1970, the number of moose on the island went up and down several times.

Directions: Below are several things that influenced the moose herd. Decide whether each one would increase (+) or decrease (–) the number of moose in the herd. Be ready to explain your choices.

+/–

_____   1. There are approximately four moose for every square kilometer on the island.

_____   2. A forest fire burns over a quarter of the island. This land is then grown over with moss, lichen, and new trees (moose food).

_____   3. The birth rate of the herd goes up. The death rate goes down.

_____   4. A pack of wolves comes to the island.

Directions: Now read pages 453–455 in your text. If what you read supports your choices, place a check in the Yes column. If the text does not support your prediction, place a check in the No column. For each item, write in your own words what actually happened.

Support?

Yes	No		In Your Own Words
____	____	1.	_____
____	____	2.	_____
____	____	3.	_____
____	____	4.	_____

FIGURE 6.6   **An extended anticipation guide for a seventh-grade science lesson**   (*Source:* Based on W. Ramsey et al., *Holt Life Science.* New York: Holt, Rinehart & Winston, 1986.)

were implied in the passage. Beth Anne began by asking the class, "Combien parme vous est jamais resté dans un hotel pendant un voyage?" ("How many of you have ever stayed in a hotel during a trip?") She distributed the anticipation guide and asked the students to respond to Part I in groups. In Part II of the guide, they listed in English any words they thought would be used in the passage. As they read the text silently, the students jotted down the French equivalents of the words they had anticipated. Additional French words were written in the bottom section. They compared their postreading lists and discussed the terms, with assistance from the teacher. The students then reread the dialogue orally in pairs. Finally, they used their vocabulary lists to write a summary of the

ANTICIPATION GUIDE FOR *THE AUTOBIOGRAPHY OF MALCOLM X*

Directions: We have already discussed how people can change. You no doubt have your own ideas about how people can change their lives and change the world. Based on our discussions and your own opinions, put a check mark in column A next to those statements with which you agree.

A	B	
_____	_____	1. After people turn 18, they really cannot change their lives.
_____	_____	2. The actions of a single person cannot change the world.
_____	_____	3. Education is an effective way to change oneself.
_____	_____	4. Improving one's ability to read can be the single largest factor in changing one's life.
_____	_____	5. Racism is proof that the world can never really change.

You are going to read about the life of Malcolm X, an African American leader of the 1950s and 1960s. After you finish the reading, you will have a chance to look back at your responses. Place a check mark in column B for those statements with which Malcolm X would agree. Be prepared to explain why you think his opinions would agree with or differ from your own.

FIGURE 6.7   Anticipation guide used in a high school resource room
(*Source:* Raymond Kamery, South Park High School, Buffalo, New York.)

story, in which they described one similarity and one difference between hotels in the United States and France. The teacher found that the anticipation guide made students less dependent on her for help with new vocabulary. Because they had anticipated many of the ideas and words that were found in the text, they were able to attend more to the overall meaning of the passage and were less concerned with understanding every single word.

Jennifer Ostrach was presenting a new concept to her sixth-grade math class: "When integers with unlike signs are added, the sum will be the difference between the integers and will have the sign of the greater integer." To help her students understand this concept on their own terms, she prepared the anticipation guide in Figure 6.9, which featured everyday situations she knew her students would be familiar with. She began class with a preview of the previous lesson on adding integers with like signs. Then she placed the following problem sentence on the board and asked the class to brainstorm possible solutions: $+4 + -6$.

After they had talked about the problem, Jennifer distributed the anticipation guide and had them work on it in groups of three or four. Students talked about their responses, read the pertinent selection in the math book, and then

ANTICIPATION GUIDE: À L'HÔTEL

Part I: We are going to read a story about a man who is trying to make hotel reservations in France. Think about the types of things that people usually expect when staying in a hotel. Read each of the following statements and then mark the appropriate column stating whether you agree or disagree with each expectation. You must be able to explain your choices.

Agree   **Disagree**

_____   _____   1. Unless it is vacation season, you will have no trouble getting a room.

_____   _____   2. There will be a phone and a TV in the room.

_____   _____   3. There will be a bathroom in the room.

_____   _____   4. The hotel will have a pool and/or other recreational facilities.

_____   _____   5. The hotel will be reasonably priced.

Part II: In column A, list 10 words in English that will most likely appear in the text. Then read "À l'hôtel." If you find any of the words you listed, write the French word in column B. Write any other new words or phrases from the selection that you think are important at the bottom of the page.

A. Anglais   **B. Français**

1. _____   _____

2. _____   _____

3. _____   _____

4. _____   _____

5. _____   _____

6. _____   _____

7. _____   _____

8. _____   _____

9. _____   _____

10. _____   _____

Autres mots où phrases importantes:

FIGURE 6.8   An anticipation guide for a first-year French class   (*Source:* Beth Anne Connors, Royalton-Hartland Junior-Senior High School, Middleport, New York.)

reexamined their responses. Then Jennifer assisted them as they wrote their own problem sentences using the integers in the statements. As a concluding activity, each student designed a problem like those in the anticipation guide and gave it to the other students in the group to solve.

ANTICIPATION GUIDE FOR ADDING INTEGERS WITH UNLIKE SIGNS

Directions: Read each statement below and decide whether you agree with it or not. Write A (Agree) or D (Disagree) in the blank before each. Compare responses with others in your group. Be ready to explain your choices.

A or D

_____ 1. If a team wins 6 home games and loses 4 away games, they have won more games than they have lost.

_____ 2. If a football team gains 17 yards on one play and loses 9 yards on the next play, they have gained yardage.

_____ 3. If you spend $15 at the mall and find a $20 bill on the way home, you are ahead.

_____ 4. If you get a bill for $53 and a paycheck for $35, you have enough money to pay the bill.

_____ 5. If you have $8 and buy a movie ticket for $6, you will have enough to buy a supersize bucket of popcorn for $3.

_____ 6. You can add two numbers and still have less than zero.

Directions: Now read p. 408 in your math book. Note the rule for adding positive and negative integers and the examples. Go back to the statements above and see if you have changed your mind. In the space following statements 1 through 5, write an addition sentence using integers and solve the problem. After statement 6, design your own word problem like those in the guide, and give it to others in your group to solve.

FIGURE 6.9   **Anticipation guide for adding integers with unlike signs**
(*Source:* Jennifer Ostrach, Maryvale Middle School, Cheektowaga, New York.)

Problem-Solving Activities

John Arnold, a middle school teacher in one of Steve's classes, developed a combination prereading teaching strategy to use in introducing a seventh-grade unit on the American Revolutionary War. The combination prereading strategy included graphic organizers, an anticipation guide, and a problem-solving activity. Here, we focus on only the problem-solving activity. John introduced the organizing concept for this activity—that the American Revolutionary War was a conflict in which people with varying viewpoints had to make personal decisions and sacrifices—with a book talk. His talk featured five books: *My Brother Sam Is Dead* (Collier & Collier, 1974), *The Bloody Country* (Collier & Collier, 1976), *Johnny Tremain* (Forbes, 1943), *The Fifth of March* (Rinaldi, 1993), and *A Ride into Morning* (Rinaldi, 1995). Each student was required to select two of the five titles to read. Although students had been introduced to the concept of the American Revolutionary War previously, this unit was to be their first in-depth study of the war between the colonists and England.

Based on his knowledge of the students' backgrounds, John believed that war was still a very abstract concept for them. Consequently, he introduced students to a computer simulation that he had developed to teach them about the difficult choices people in leadership positions have to make in times of revolution. Materials for the simulation are illustrated in Figure 6.10 and Figure 6.11. Students divided up the advisors' roles and those of the governor, president, merchants, and rebels among themselves. The objective of the

---

THE SITUATION

Rebels in the province of Catalan are calling for independence from Democ. They complain of unfair taxes and unfair treatment by the national government.

Not everyone supports rebellion in Catalan. Many merchants feel strong ties to the mother country.

The President of Democ also rejects the revolution.

As the governor and his/her advisors, you are under the gun.

Which side will you support?

CAST OF CHARACTERS:

Democ—a large nation made up of several provinces in the West and one large province in the East

Catalan—the recently settled eastern province of Democ. Catalan is separated from the heavily populated western provinces by a vast open frontier. Catalan is rich in natural resources.

Governor—the governor of the province of Catalan in the country of Democ. The governor has a militia at his/her disposal.

The President—the elected head of Democ. She rules the country with a parliament, which makes laws. The parliament consists of representatives from each province, and it is dominated by the western provinces.

The rebels—people in Catalan who want to revolt against Democ and make Catalan an independent nation.

The merchants—people in Catalan who don't want to revolt against Democ. They have strong economic and emotional ties to the rest of the country.

THE ADVISORS:

Carmen DeSouza—Ms. DeSouza, the Chief of Staff, provides historical insight into the issues you must face.

Charles Zale—Because of the separation between Catalan and the rest of the nation, Mr. Zale was sent to the province as a special ambassador from Democ.

Clive Chaplain—A trusted advisor, Mr. Chaplain has been appointed a special liaison to the rebels to understand and report on their actions.

Natalie Barber—As special liaison to the merchants, Ms. Barber reports to you about the feeling and viewpoints of this group.

FIGURE 6.10 **The situation and cast of characters** (*Source:* John Arnold, Virtual Blackboard, Inc.)

DETERMINE YOUR GOALS

A. Maintain peace. Avoid bloodshed.

Avoiding violence as revolution looms ahead will be very difficult. How can you keep the peace while rebels are promoting a violent rebellion and the President is sending a national army? If you can't negotiate a settlement, you may have to use strong action to keep the situation from getting out of hand.

B. Help the rebels with their cause.

The rebels want independence. Helping them obtain it may mean sacrificing some of your other goals. The President will probably not give up control of Catalan without a fight. In addition, if you give support to the rebels, how will the merchants react? This goal means uniting people of your province in support of the rebel cause. Do you think you can? It certainly won't be easy.

C. Keep your position of power.

You are currently the governor or one of his/her trusted advisors. After a revolution, who knows what position you might have? To achieve this goal, you don't have to remain in your present position. If you emerged as the leader of a strong rebel movement, for instance, you would certainly be in a position of power. Be careful. Being a leader of the losing side won't leave you with much power, if you have any at all.

D. Unite the people of the province.

The rebels want a revolution; the merchants don't. Can't you bring the two sides together? Do they share any common beliefs, fears, or hatreds? You will have to act wisely and skillfully to achieve this goal.

FIGURE 6.11   **Determine your goals**   (*Source:* John Arnold, Virtual Blackboard, Inc.)

simulation was for students to analyze the situation, determine their goals, consider their options, make a decision, and examine the consequences (see Figure 6.12).

As a follow-up to this problem-solving activity, which took five days to complete, John introduced the class to Jigsaw, a cooperative learning strategy (Slavin, 1983) that involved students in searching the Internet for information about the people, events, and documents important to the American Revolution. He divided the class into groups of five, with each student taking one of the following five roles in every group: governor, merchant, ambassador, chief of staff, and rebel. Appropriate tasks that involved searches on the Internet were assigned to each role player. Students with the same role met in study groups. For example, the governors met to search for information that enabled them to compare the Declaration of Independence and the Resolves of the First Continental Congress; the merchants met to research events leading up to the revolution; the ambassadors met to learn about the people of the American Revolutionary War; the chiefs of staff met to study documents of that war; and the rebels were responsible for researching the battles of the American Revolution.

DECISIONS, DECISIONS: REVOLUTIONARY WARS

Welcome to *Decisions, Decisions: Revolutionary Wars*! You and your classmates will be role-playing different characters. Once group member will be the governor (on whose shoulders all decisions weigh) and the remainder will be advisors. These advisors will help the governor make decisions and choices during the simulation. You will be responsible for sharing information with your teammates. Decisions and choices you make personally—as an advisor—will be summarized in your learning log. The governor will summarize group decisions and choices and then share those with the group members. The following outline will help guide you during the simulation:

Analyze the Situation:
1. Watch the introduction on the computer.
2. Review the situation below.
3. If you are an advisor, read your letter and summarize your position. Report back to your group. If you are the governor, summarize all the advisors' positions and share with the group.

Determine Your Goals:
1. Read the goals on pages 11–12 of the advisor book. Governors will be supplied with this information.
2. Each individual will rank the goals. The rankings will be shared with the group. The group will arrive at a group ranking based on discussion.
3. The group rankings will be entered into the computer.

Consider Your Options:
1. The computer will give each advisor a keyword that matches one of the briefings found on pages 14–18. Each advisor will summarize and present his/her opinion to the group. The governor will summarize the positions.

Make a Decision:
1. Discuss all options with the group. When ready, enter your decision into the computer. The governor should do all inputting into the computer.

Examine the Consequences:
1. The computer will display the consequences of each decision and direct you back to the briefing book for more information.
2. Continue with the simulation until peace is reached or war destroys all.

GOOD LUCK!!!

FIGURE 6.12 **Decisions, decisions** (*Source:* John Arnold, Virtual Blackboard, Inc.)

John gave each study group a pair of worksheets on which students were to match the description of a document, person, event, or battle with the appropriate name for that document, person, event, or battle. Figure 6.13 illustrates the pair of worksheets that the merchants received (the group that was to research the events leading up to the American Revolution). So that students would have some guidance in searching the Internet for the descriptions needed in the matching activity, John gave each study group a Web Quest. The Web Quest, which was

Events Leading Up to the American Revolution

Match the description on the right with each event on the left. Cut out the descriptions and paste them next to the correct event. You will use the World Wide Web to help you find the correct descriptions.

BOSTON TEA PARTY	This act was to offset the cost of the French and Indian War by taxing products like molasses and placing levies on luxury items. 1764
BOSTON MASSACRE	A fiscal plan to balance England's budget, this legislation placed duties on products like paper, lead, glass, and tea shipped to America. 1767
BILLETING ACT	In a continued response to the Townshend Revenue Act, Boston colonists dressed as Mohawk Indians and ransacked crates of tea. 1773
COERCIVE ACTS	A series of acts designed to punish the people of Boston. These acts include closing the Boston port, limiting town meetings, and quartering soldiers. 1774
FRENCH AND INDIAN WAR	This act required colonists to provide housing and supplies for royal troops. 1765
STAMP ACT	Because of reaction to the Townshend Revenue Act, more British soldiers were in Boston. Because of antagonism, the British soldiers fired on the colonists, killing three. 1770
SUGAR ACT	This war was to determine French or English supremacy in North America. The English won but at a very high price. 1754–1758
TOWNSHEND REVENUE ACT	This act taxed paper products (like newspapers and pamphlets) and official documents that required a stamp. 1765

FIGURE 6.13   **Events leading up to the American Revolution**   (*Source:* John Arnold, Virtual Blackboard, Inc.)

titled "Events Leading up to the American Revolution," consisted of a map of British-occupied Boston and the surrounding countryside held by the colonists. It also included a list of eight events leading up to the Revolutionary War: Boston Massacre, Boston Tea Party, Billeting Act, Coercive Acts, French and Indian War, Sugar Act, Stamp Act, and Townshend Revenue Act. Each event was a hyperlink to an Internet site that discussed a particular event. In all, the students spent five days on the Jigsaw activity (three days searching the Internet for information, and two days reporting back to their original groups).

Following the computer simulation and Jigsaw activity, John gave each student an assessment rubric (Figure 6.14) and a rating sheet (Figure 6.15). These were used for determining how well individual members and the group as a whole worked together on the activity.

During problem solving, students use their prior knowledge, their analytical powers, and their creative thinking. Finding solutions to realistic problems validates previous experience and demonstrates its relevance to new learning. Problem solving can be especially useful in a culturally diverse classroom because it allows students to contribute from their unique vantage points, creating a mix of perspectives, which benefits all. Brown (1988) suggests that there are issues or concepts that are critical to individuals, regardless of culture, such as communication processes, counting and measuring, consumer economics, and conflict resolution. Discussion of these kinds of topics can highlight cultural

---

Using this rubric, you will assess how well your group performed and how well each member of the group performed. Be fair in your assessment, because you will be asked why you chose the assessment you did and remember your group members are assessing you at the same time!

SETTING GOALS:

Work well in a group:

3 points:　Participate in group and re-state other students' words and ideas (doesn't have to be in a supportive way).

2 points:　Participate in group, but no outward recognition of others' ideas.

1 point:　No involvement in group; inattentive.

0 point:　Disrupt group.

Good Arguments:

3 points:　All ideas and suggestions are supported with relevant and accepted information.

2 points:　Arguments mostly supported.

1 point:　Support is personal or unrelated to content of viewpoint.

0 point:　No support for points of view.

FIGURE 6.14　**Rubric for assessing group and individual members' performances**　(*Source:* John Arnold, Virtual Blackboard, Inc.)

Now use the rubric to rate each individual of your group and the group itself.

	Member #1	Member #2	Member #3	Member #4	Group
Goals: Working well in a group:					
Good arguments:					
Decisions: Work well in a group:					
Use of content:					
Fact and opinion:					
Correct information:					
TOTALS					

FIGURE 6.15   **Rating sheet**   (*Source:* John Arnold, Virtual Blackboard, Inc.)

differences and expand cultural boundaries. Discussion will also reveal "many commonalities among lifestyles [that] are impervious to ethnic, racial, and economic diversity" (p. 39). Figure 6.16 gives some problem-solving activities suggested by Brown for introducing these topics.

SUMMARY

Prior knowledge is a powerful determinant of reading success. Reading about something interesting and familiar seems effortless; the reader is not really conscious of reading at all. Plowing through difficult and unfamiliar reading material, however, can be a frustrating and fruitless task. A person may read and reread with little comprehension or retention of the ideas encountered.

This chapter described many strategies for activating and building students' prior knowl-edge before they read. These strategies can promote motivation, purpose, and confidence in readers. Students are more likely to be successful with challenging reading material when they can discuss what they know or believe, when they get a preview of what they will be reading, or when the teacher has stimulated a need to know—an itch of curiosity that can be scratched by reading.

COMMUNICATION PROCESSES

A shanty town in northern California became the temporary home for 75 migrant workers. The work force was composed of Haitian and Cambodian refugees who spoke only their native languages. How might the two groups communicate successfully?

COUNTING AND MEASURING

A family of 9 people received a donation of 13 ears of corn, which will become its evening meal. What suggestions would you have for dividing the corn equally among the family members?

CONSUMER ECONOMICS

What kind of information do you need to help you decide whether to make major food purchases from the neighborhood grocer or from one of the large supermarkets?

CONFLICT RESOLUTION

Threats of physical violence have been directed toward a black family that recently moved into a previously all-white community. Although things have gone smoothly at school for the two sons, both have suffered much verbal abuse on the weekends. This potentially explosive situation has resulted in several meetings among small groups of residents. You have been asked to serve as a consultant to the president of the neighborhood association. What measures would you recommend to bring about a resolution that could satisfy all parties?

FIGURE 6.16   **Problem-solving activities for introducing certain critical topics**   (*Source:* Adapted from T. J. Brown, *High impact teaching: Strategies for educating minority youth.* Lanham, MD: University Press of America, 1988.)

SUGGESTED READINGS

Anderson, R. C., & Pearson, P. D. (1984). A schema-theoretic view of basic processes in reading. In P. D. Pearson (Ed.), *Handbook of reading research* (pp. 255–292). New York: Longman.

Godina, H. (1999). High school students of Mexican background in the Midwest: Cultural differences as a constraint to effective literacy instruction. In T. Shanahan & F. V. Rodriguez-Brown (Eds.), *National Reading Conference Yearbook 48* (pp. 266–279). Chicago: National Reading Conference.

Herber, H. (1978). Prediction as motivation and an aid to comprehension. In H. Herber (Ed.), *Teaching reading in content areas* (2nd ed.) Englewood Cliffs, NJ: Prentice Hall.

Nuwash, C. F. (1999). Reading and listening in English as a second language. In T. Shanahan & F. V. Rodriguez-Brown (Eds.), *National Reading Conference Yearbook 48* (pp. 249–257). Chicago: National Reading Conference.

Readence, J. E., Moore, D. W., & Rickelman, R. J. (2000). *Prereading activities for content area reading and learning* (3rd ed.). Newark, DE: International Reading Association.

Reading to Learn

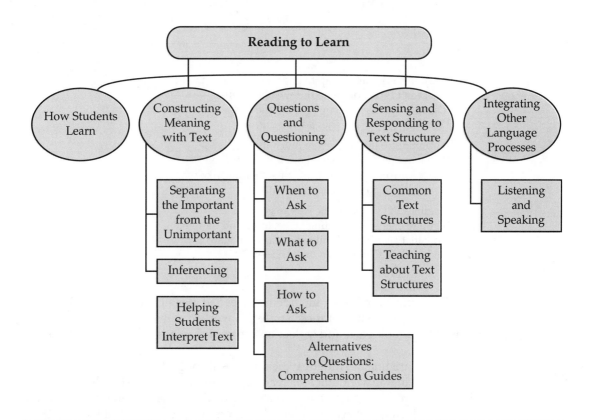

The following poem was written by Christine Woyshner, formerly a teacher in Lackawanna, New York, who was thinking back on her own days as a student. It raises some questions that are central to this chapter: What happens when a student sits down to read a content area text assignment? What strategies might the student use, and how effective are they?

▼▼▼▼▼▼▼

'Twas the night before English and to my dismay
I had not finished the reading due the next day.
My pencils were sharpened and laid on my desk.
As far as I was concerned, I'd do my best.

We were asked to read *Hamlet*. "No problem," I thought.
I cracked open my copy the school district just bought.
"Thee, though, thou" the words they did say.
Just what the heck does that mean, anyway?

Let's see . . . that Hamlet, he seems pretty wild.
I think I'll go see what's on TV for a while.
Now *E.R.* is over, I'll return to my book,
But first I'll open the fridge for a look.

Okay, this is great. I'm up to page ten.
I still can't figure out who did what and when.
It's too bad it's so late, or I'd go to the mall.
I'd better go give my friend Pat a call.

It's getting so late, there's so much more to read.
Pat mentioned a book she thought I might need.
It's by someone named "Cliff" or something like that.
Now I can be an A student, like Pat.

Reading *Cliff's Notes* is the way to go
If you're ever stuck reading "thee, thou, and though."
Now that *Hamlet*'s behind me, I really am glad,
And reading Cliff's *Iliad* won't be so bad.*

▼▼▼▼▼▼▼

Christine's strategies included sharpened pencils, TV and food breaks, and expert help. Some of these strategies worked, some didn't; in the end she was able to look back and reflect on the confidence she had gained from the experience.

Like Christine, a student typically goes through three interrelated phases when working on a content area reading assignment. The first of these, the subject of the previous chapter, is *preparing* for reading. The second phase is *reading to learn,* which has also been referred to as on-line processing (Jones et al., 1987) and information search (Estes & Vaughan, 1985). The final phase involves *reflecting* on what has been read, which means analyzing and evaluating ideas and perhaps extending learning by coming up with original ideas or products.

It is tempting to think of these phases in strictly chronological terms as occurring before, during, and after reading. Learning is not linear, however, and these three phases are not discrete. As students read and learn, they are constantly anticipating, processing, connecting, reflecting, and reviewing. That is why many of the strategies suggested in previous chapters, such as K-W-L, anticipation guides, and DR-TA, actually follow through all three phases of the reading process.

The focus of this chapter is reading to learn, or what happens when a student opens a book and reads. Ideally, what happens is that the reader learns something about algebra, chemistry, history, or whatever the subject might be. However, text content does not transfer directly and intact into the mind of the reader; it is not like loading a text file from a disk into your computer. Although this chapter may seem to emphasize the text, we have not forgotten the importance of the reader or the fact that reading is socially situated. What is learned from reading depends, among other things, on the reader's prior knowledge, attitudes, intention, and learning strategies as well as the social context in which reading and learning occur. Learning implies more than just rote mastery of facts, formulas, and "who did what and when"; it also means thinking about and using that information. Rather than seeing a particular text as having a sin-

---

*Reprinted with permission of Christine A. Woyshner, Temple University.

gle meaning that all successful readers must apprehend, it is more accurate to think of text as representing a range of potential meanings.

Students generally view their textbooks as sources of important information, necessary for success on tests and assignments. However, they are often unsure of their own ability to understand and think about text material. Some good students develop effective strategies for learning from their texts, but many others find the increased demands of learning from their texts overwhelming. Even though they may want to learn and try to learn, the complexity and abstraction of something like Shakespearean language or the laws of physics may pose seemingly insurmountable problems.

Although the content of their studies becomes more complex, the actual strategies that middle-grade and secondary students have for learning often remain relatively primitive. For instance, many readers will not go back and reread portions of a text to support their comprehension because they believe it is "illegal" or because it takes too much time (Garner & Alexander, 1989). After extensive observations and interviews with 13- and 14-year-old students as they worked in their content area classes, Nicholson (1984) described a "search-and-destroy" strategy used to answer assigned questions. This consists of going back to the text, finding the same words used in the question, and hoping an answer will be nearby. Search and destroy works when students know what they are looking for, but many students simply "pick out the bits"—finding answers without regard to whether or not they understand them. The opposite strategy to "picking out the bits" is "copying it all down"—simply writing down large chunks of text that seem to satisfy the assignment. Some students refine their technique by writing the "easy bits" in their own words and copying the "hard bits" directly from the text. Other coping strategies of unsuccessful readers have been identified by Brozo (2000). These include avoiding eye contact with the teacher, engaging in disruptive behavior, using listening skills to gain information, relying on classmates, "forgetting" books and materials, and trying to impress the teacher with manipulative techniques.

For content area teachers, experts in their subject matter, the difficulties of their novice students can be frustrating and perplexing. How can students learn when they seem to lack the necessary background and skills? There is no easy or quick solution, but there are several things a teacher can do that will help students read to learn.

HOW STUDENTS LEARN

Research supports several critical assumptions about learning, cited by Jones et al. (1987):

1. *Learning is goal oriented.* Learning goals may be global or task specific. Whatever the ultimate objective for undertaking a task, the immediate goals of the successful learner are to understand the task and to figure out a way to accomplish it.

2. *Learning means linking new information with prior knowledge.* Much of the difficulty that students have with learning in content areas arises when background knowledge is insufficient or inaccurate.

3. *Learning requires organizing knowledge.* Two kinds of organization are important. One is the way in which learners make connections and organize information in their minds. The other is the manner in which ideas and information are organized in text material.

4. *Learning is strategic.* A learner must have a strategy, or method, for approaching a task. Using *Cliff's Notes*, counting pages and dividing up the reading, and picking out the bits are examples of strategies. Many able learners develop successful strategies on their own. Less able learners can and do benefit from being shown how.

5. *Learning is influenced by development.* Some people have more aptitude than others for reading, studying, writing, and taking tests. Students develop at different rates and mature at different ages. Students in a single middle or secondary school classroom will have a wide range of abilities, but all of them will be capable of improving and moving ahead.

We add one other assumption: learning may be influenced by gender, social class, and culture. Some female students may be discouraged in math and science classes if they are led to believe by peers, family, or teachers that these subjects are too difficult or somehow unfeminine. Students who come to school without adequate nutrition, housing, or medical care are likely to find learning more difficult. Some students speak a language or dialect that is not accepted or readily understood by teachers, and lack of familiarity with the conventions of standard English may put these students at a disadvantage. Learning is also influenced by a student's expectations for the future—work, further education, or parenting. Finally, learning will be influenced by the context in which it takes place. A student's school experience will be shaped in part by the way in which his or her family and community view education and by the school setting. Is school seen as an opportunity or as one more element of social oppression? How is learning defined or valued, and what counts as learning for a student's family, peers, and teachers?

To accommodate a variety of cultural backgrounds in the classroom, Field and Aebersold (1990) make three recommendations to teachers. First, teachers need to evaluate students' "cognitive clarity" about reading and learning. What do students expect from the class? How do they view the subject matter and its relation to their everyday life? Second, teachers should clearly articulate their assumptions and expectations and plan ways to help students become proficient with the expected reading and learning tasks. Third, teachers need to learn as much as possible about the home environments and cultural backgrounds of their students.

We fully realize the difficulties of learning about the home and cultural backgrounds of 150 different students, but we are equally aware of the dangers inherent in making assumptions about students on the basis of limited or stereotypical conceptions of their cultural or socioeconomic circumstances. Taylor and Dorsey-Gaines (1988) studied several inner-city African American families that were struggling to give their children a good start in life. The researchers warn against the stereotypes that are popularized in the media and some social science research. They found that these families, although they demonstrated a variety of domestic arrangements and strategies, shared certain characteristics:

1. The parents were determined to raise healthy children.
2. Children were cared for with tenderness and affection.
3. Home environments were structured, with rules and expectations for cooperation and participation.
4. Literacy was used for a wide variety of social, technical, and aesthetic purposes.
5. Literacy did not guarantee economic success.
6. Some family members were highly literate even though they were not formally educated.

Danny, the teenage son in one of these families, ended up dropping out of school in the eighth grade and becoming entangled in the juvenile justice system. Although he was a responsible family member who took care of his little sisters and worked to earn money for the family, he found school to be an alien and hostile place, completely insensitive to the realities of his life.

We draw several conclusions from our understanding of how students learn. The first is that students need to be shown how to learn, not just what to learn (Pressley, 2000). Second, students need guidance and support in the learning process (Alexander & Jetton, 2000). Teachers must understand, too, that becoming an efficient learner is a long-term process. Mastering each new strategy requires continued practice and feedback. Third, teachers need to consider students' background, beliefs, and prior knowledge when introducing new ideas and information (Au, 1998). Teachers should consider the meaning of schooling for children and help them to build a sense of ownership and pride in their ability and their school community. Finally, the process of learning cannot be divorced from the content to be learned (Idol, Jones, & Mayer, 1991). Learning how to learn occurs most effectively in the context of real classroom content area instruction.

CONSTRUCTING MEANING WITH TEXT

Learning from text involves constructing meaning from the author's message. We do not mean to diminish the role of the reader; rather, we emphasize that in order for text to be a useful learning tool, a reader needs to be able to construct a mental representation of what is conveyed by it. In Chapter 1, we outlined a cognitive view of the reading process that emphasizes the mental operations of the reader in comprehension and a contrasting social constructionist view that recognizes the influences of language and social factors on a reader's understanding of text. From a cognitive standpoint (Goldman & Rakestraw, 2000), comprehension of text

> involves building coherent mental representations of information. It means processing the meaning of individual words and phrases in the text as well as how these individual words and phrases relate to one another, both within the text and within a larger, preexisting knowledge base. To accomplish this, readers rely on both text-driven and knowledge-driven processes." (p. 311)

A social constructionist would view the question of comprehension quite differently (Gergen, 1999):

> (C)onstructionists take meaning to be continuously negotiable; no arrangement of words is self-sustaining in the sense of possessing a single meaning. The meanings of "I love you," for example, border on the infinite. Such reasoning suggests that all bodies of thought are spongy or porous. Whatever is said can mean many different things; meaning can be changed as conversations develop. . . . (V)ocabulary is also porous, and every concept is subject to multiple renderings depending on the context. (p. 236)

These two viewpoints each have their merits, and they are continuously debated among researchers and theorists. (We have exchanged several faxes and e-mails regarding this passage, trying to reach a version that is satisfactory to both.) There appears to be some common ground between the two. Comprehension requires transaction between the text and the reader's prior knowledge. If we include a reader's socially constructed ways of speaking, thinking, and behaving (Gee, 1996) as part of prior knowledge, then these two views of the reading process become more complementary than contradictory.

A hypothetical example may help to illustrate the complementary roles of author, reader, and social context. Steve lives in a northern city with a more than 30-year history as a hockey town; he is an ardent, season-ticket-holding hockey fan. Donna lives in the South near a major city that has only recently reacquired a major league hockey team; she is mildly interested in the sport, mostly out of courtesy to her friend Steve. Imagine that we both read a news article on the decline of fighting as a part of the sport. Donna, reading from her position as a pacifist and a relative hockey "outsider," might see that decline as a good thing. Steve, although he shares many of Donna's understandings of the world, nevertheless might find fighting to be an acceptable facet of the sport. We could talk endlessly about our interpretations of the article, and our discussion would be grounded partly on what the author of the article actually said, partly on our prior experience and beliefs about such things as sports and violence in our society, and partly on our long-standing friendship and discussions of many varied topics and ideas. In other words, our different understandings of the article would be textually, personally, and socially constructed.

Sometimes, constructing meaning with text is easy, especially when the reading material is interesting and well written and the topic is familiar. However, even the most experienced and effective reader will encounter text that must be closely read, reread, and pondered before an approximation of the author's intended message can be teased out and an interpretation of that message formed. In this section, we try to balance the roles of text and reader as we focus on two interrelated components of constructing meaning: determining what is important in the text and drawing inferences.

Separating the Important from the Unimportant

One salient difference between effective and ineffective readers is the ability to determine what is and is not important in a reading selection (Winograd, 1984). Poor readers often perceive all the information in a passage as equally important or, more to the point, equally bewildering. Good readers, on the other hand, are able to see the *macrostructure* of a text. That is, they can perceive the relative importance and interrelation of the various ideas presented.

Determining what is or is not important is in part socially constructed. Alexander and Jetton (2000) distinguish between three categories of "importance." *Reader-determined* importance depends on the reader's internal criteria. *Author-determined* importance is derived from the author's choices in language and hierarchical structure of the text. Finally, *teacher-determined importance* refers to judgments that a reader might make about what the teacher values and what may be assessed. It is quite possible that three very different (but equally viable) judgments of importance could be made for the same textbook passage.

Determining important ideas has traditionally been one of the primary goals of reading instruction. In reading programs, in workbooks, and on skill sheets, students practice "finding the main idea" and "identifying supporting details." The implication is that these are discrete skills that can be taught in isolation and transferred to other reading situations. Readers are asked to find the topic sentence, identify the best title, or list three supporting details from short, specially constructed paragraphs or passages.

The problem is that naturally occurring texts are quite different from the contrived passages in skill exercises. The actual reading materials used in content area instruction are much more complex. Authors rarely write a series of paragraphs, each beginning with an explicit topic sentence followed by supporting details (Hare, Rabinowitz, & Schieble, 1989). In their research on main ideas in nonfiction, O'Hear and Aikman (1996) found main ideas in 88 percent of the paragraphs in 12 contemporary best-sellers. Nearly two-thirds (63 percent) of the main ideas in these books were positioned in the first sentence of a paragraph. However, in reviewing other research on main ideas, O'Hear and Aikman reported wide variation in the percentage of paragraphs with main ideas, depending on the writing being studied and also depending on researchers' definition of main idea. (The fact that researchers cannot agree on what constitutes a "main idea" should give you some clue as to why this can be difficult for elementary and secondary school students.) Because of the complexities involved in finding main ideas in naturally occurring texts, Hare, Rabinowitz, and Schieble, among others, recommend that instruction on finding main ideas should be based on the actual reading materials that students use in school.

The complexity of school texts can be illustrated by a paragraph from a tenth-grade global studies textbook. A three-page section of the text discusses family life in India (Hantula et al., 1988). One paragraph describes the roles of men and women:

> In an Indian family household, the oldest able male is considered the head. He has the authority to make family decisions, market crops, organize household labor for heavier agricultural tasks, and deal with strangers. The oldest able female is in charge of domestic affairs. Generally the mother of the sons or the wife of the eldest brother, she supervises the food, health care, raising of children, and cleaning. Young wives hold the lowest place in the household, especially before they have sons. They are given the least desirable jobs. Their mothers-in-law maintain control and often are quite strict with them. In a joint family, men and women tend to keep their daily activities separate. (p. 354)

A colleague of ours says that finding a main idea can be like trying to nail jelly to a wall, and this paragraph is a good example of what he means. There is no single, explicitly stated main idea. Within the paragraph, two superordinate ideas seem to have equal importance: the role of men and the role of women. Determining the importance of the subordinate ideas in the paragraph is largely subjective. Some readers might be interested in the status of the young wives, others in the idea that the daily activities of men and women are kept separate, and so on. All of these ideas are details that support the superordinate idea of the entire passage—the joint family. Who is to say that one is more important than another? It is hardly surprising that many students have difficulty judging the importance of ideas, even when they have mastered the skill of underlining topic sentences in their workbooks.

Inferencing

When main ideas are implied by an author, readers must fill in the connections between various details and construct their own idea of the author's message. This process of filling in and connecting is called *inferencing*. Among other things, readers make inferences about word meanings, an author's intentions, connections with their previous experience, connections within the text, and what will come next. Indeed, "inference is the heart of the comprehension process" (Dole et al., 1991, p. 245).

Inferencing develops naturally, and even young readers are capable of drawing inferences. However, Raphael and Pearson's (1982) research with question–answer relationships discussed in detail later, indicates that for middle-grade students inferential questions are more difficult to answer than literal questions. Although high school students might be expected to be more adept at drawing inferences, in keeping with their increased cognitive and conceptual maturity, secondary teachers with whom we have worked confirm that many of their students are uncomfortable and tentative when asked to make connections, reach conclusions, or otherwise go beyond what is right there in the textbook. This finding is supported by the research of Hare, Rabinowitz, and Schieble (1989), who found that eleventh graders had more difficulty with implicit than with explicit main ideas.

Students' difficulty may arise in part because inferences are neither equally important nor equally obvious. The third and fourth sentences of the paragraph on the Indian joint family offer an interesting example: "The oldest able female is in charge of domestic affairs. Generally the mother of the sons or the wife of the eldest brother, she supervises the food, health care, raising of children, and cleaning" (Hantula et al., 1988, p. 354). To understand these sentences, the reader must make the connection that the "oldest able female," the "mother of the sons," the "wife of the eldest brother," and "she" all refer to the same person— the female head of the joint family. This connection centers on the pronoun *she*, which ties the two sentences together. Experienced readers make this essential connection easily, but less facile readers may miss it. Many other inferences of varying importance and subtlety may be drawn from these two sentences: the meaning of "able," what is involved in "supervising the food," the importance of sons to the status of women, and so on.

Another reason students may have difficulty with inferences is that classroom activities often do not require them to draw inferences. Struggling readers especially tend to receive instruction that emphasizes lower-level skills and literal comprehension. Poor readers do not necessarily suffer from inadequate thinking strategies. Rather, they may lack the kinds of procedural knowledge that more able readers use to draw inferences (Winne, Graham, & Prock, 1993). Struggling readers especially may place undue emphasis on their own background knowledge and rely less on text information. With instruction and practice, however, readers can improve their ability to draw inferences from their reading.

When a text is densely packed with information, it is difficult for a reader to decide what should be remembered and what can be ignored. Important connections and implications may be overlooked. The paragraph cited previously is just one paragraph from a chapter of 17 pages. Constructing the author's message in this chapter will require making countless connections and decisions. How will a student know what to look for, what to consider? Simply telling students to "read Chapter 22 for Thursday" will not offer enough guidance.

Helping Students Interpret Text

The lesson formats described in Chapter 4 as well as the reading guides and questioning strategies featured later in this chapter are all effective means for helping students learn from reading. Textbooks may also have features that help students interpret the author's message. Headings and subheadings, highlighted vocabulary, and end-of-chapter notes and questions offer many cues to knowledgeable readers. In the past few years, publishers seem to have made an effort to produce more user-friendly texts. For instance, one recently published biology text (Schraer & Stoltze, 1993) presents key words and main idea questions at the beginning of each chapter, lists content objectives and review questions for each section, and provides an extensive chapter review that includes an outline, a fill-in-the-blanks semantic web, critical thinking questions, analogies, and problem-solving questions. Such features can be a great planning aid to a teacher who points them out to students and judiciously assigns questions and activities for homework and class discussion.

Not all teachers are blessed with up-to-date and well-written textbooks, however. Also, even the most "considerate" textbook may still be challenging for the majority of students, especially if they do not know how to use the features it offers. Thus, this section describes a few more strategies for helping students to "construct the message."

Direct instruction. It is useful to address a comprehension strategy squarely, through direct instruction (Alexander & Jetton, 2000; Pressley, 2000). We do not mean that students should be subjected to isolated workbook drill, divorced from any real interaction or natural context. Direct instruction of comprehension strategies is most effective in the context of the curricular content and actual reading materials of content area classes. This is especially true for students with reading and learning disabilities, who benefit from extra support and explicit instruction and feedback (Bulgren & Scanlon, 1997/1998; Swanson & de la Paz, 1998).

Baumann (1984) suggests a model for direct instruction on identifying main ideas in which the teacher introduces, models, and teaches the skill and then shifts the focus of the lesson to student application. This instructional model would be suitable for teaching inferencing and other comprehension skills as well:

1. *Introduction:* Tell students the purpose of the lesson and why the particular skill can be helpful to a reader.
2. *Example:* Direct students' attention to a section of text that clearly illustrates the skill.
3. *Direct instruction:* Lead the lesson by "telling, showing, demonstrating, modeling the skill to be learned" (Baumann, 1984, p. 98). Students are engaged through questioning and discussion.
4. *Student application:* Begin to shift the responsibility for learning from the teacher to the student. Present more text samples and give guidance, support, and feedback while students apply the skill.
5. *Independent practice:* Allow students to assume full responsibility. Assign further reading that requires application of the skill and that students complete on their own.

This basic design of teacher presentation, guided practice, and independent practice has been a bedrock of instructional design for a long time. We recognize the resistance that many content area teachers may feel to teaching reading strategies, and we are also aware of the tremendous curricular pressures that secondary teachers face. Finding time for reading strategy instruction, even when it is integrated into content curriculum, can be difficult (Scanlon, Deshler, & Schumaker, 1996). However, there is ample evidence that students can benefit from direct instruction, both in their literacy skills and in content acquisition. Using this model, Baumann (1984) taught sixth graders how to find both explicit and implicit main ideas, first in paragraphs and then in short passages. After eight lessons, these students were better able to recognize and produce explicit and implicit main ideas than a comparable group who had received instruction and practice in finding main ideas from a popular basal reading series. In a similar study, Sjostrom and Hare (1984) found that a group of African American and Hispanic high school students who received direct instruction following Baumann's model were better able to recognize explicit and implicit main ideas and to summarize science material than a control group that received vocabulary instruction. In these studies, students were actively involved in searching for ideas, answering questions, and discussing the concept of main ideas. According to Baumann, this active involvement of students accounts for the success of the direct instruction model. Other examples of direct comprehension instruction are described in the discussion of question–answer relationships and three-level comprehension guides in the following sections.

Sticky notes.   Sticky-backed notes can be used in a variety of ways to actively involve students in constructing the author's message. A teacher can jot down important ideas and supporting details on individual sticky notes and give one to each pair or small group of students in the class with instructions to find the noted information in the text. After students have had time to locate this, the teacher calls on them to volunteer one main idea. After a pair or group explains the idea on its note and shows where it occurs in the text, the teacher asks for supporting details from the other pairs or groups. As students add their contributions, they arrange the notes on the board to form an outline of the text passage. Important inferences can also be jotted down on sticky notes, and students can be instructed to explain the inference and find support for it in the text.

QUESTIONS AND QUESTIONING

Using questions to help students learn is at least as old as Socrates. Asking questions about texts is "perhaps the most common kind of academic work in comprehension instruction" (Dole et al., 1991). Good questions can guide students' search for information, lead them to consider difficult ideas, and prompt new insights. Long tradition and widespread use do not mean that questioning is always effective, however.

Too often, questions test what students have learned rather than helping them to learn. A high proportion of teachers' questions tend to be literal, "what's it say in the book" questions, asked after students have read (Durkin, 1978/1979). In Chapter 3, we considered the differences between discussion (which prompts thinking and learning) and recitation (which prompts memorization). In a traditional classroom recitation, the teacher dispenses questions and is at once the repository and arbiter of "correct" answers. Students are frequently given little time to formulate a reply before the teacher either calls on someone else or asks a new question. Although such recitations probably have their place in helping students to review and remember the vast curricular content they are expected to cover, they do little to help students learn as they read.

Although questioning is among the most common classroom activities, all students may not be equally prepared for question–answer situations. Responses to a teacher's questions may vary depending on a student's cultural background. Mainstream middle-class families prepare young children

Peanuts reprinted by permission of United Feature Syndicate, Inc.

for school by rewarding the kinds of language behavior that are also rewarded by schools (Heath, 1991; Gee, 1996). This behavior includes answering questions that focus on labels, on information known to the questioner, and on recounts of previously learned information. Such adult–child questioning situations usually require children to say what they mean.

The same kinds of language behavior are not necessarily prized in other cultural groups, in which labels and language may be learned cooperatively in functional settings, often from siblings rather than adults. In some communities, question–answer exchanges between adults and children take on a different form from what is routinely done in schools. Shirley Brice Heath (1991) found that in their home settings, young African American children in one community were frequently asked playful or teasing questions and questions that encouraged their interpretive or analytical powers. Students from diverse cultural backgrounds may also possess extraordinary language powers that can be utilized in school settings. Lisa Delpit (1995) notes that Native American children come from communities in which storytelling, featuring a wealth of meaning with an economy of words, is highly sophisticated. Delpit also notes the "verbal adroitness, the cogent and quick wit, the brilliant use of metaphorical language, the facility in rhythm and rhyme" (p. 57) that are developed and celebrated in the African American community.

These cultural differences in language use imply a need to modify the traditional recitation session with its emphasis on single correct, literal answers. Some students may need support and guidance in formulating answers to conventional classroom questions; they may perform better when responses are formulated in small discussion groups rather than in whole-class recitations. Equally important, the kinds of questions that are asked and the answers that are rewarded should reflect the verbal strengths of students. Higher-level questions and active give-and-take in discussion facilitate learning by culturally diverse students (Hill, 1989).

Research on questioning has suggested many ways in which teachers can make their questioning more effective. To use questions well, teachers need to know when to ask, what to ask, and how to ask.

When to Ask: The Right Time and the Right Place

Questions appear to have different effects depending on when they are asked (Just & Carpenter, 1987). Generally, questions asked before reading tend to help readers focus on the targeted information. Prereading questions in effect tell the readers what to look for and, by implication, what to ignore. On the other hand, questions that follow reading tend to improve understanding not only of the targeted information but also of information that is not covered by the questions. Furthermore, questions seem to be more effective the closer they are to the information in the reading material. Interspersing questions within text is sometimes called "slicing the task" because it reduces the amount of text that students must read and comprehend at a given time (Wood, 1986).

These findings have some practical implications for teachers. When students are especially in need of guidance—for example, when they must digest relatively long and difficult text assignments—prereading questions help them separate the important from the unimportant by alerting them to essential ideas and information. On the other hand, when selections are more manageable or when the teacher is aiming for a broader general understanding of a selection, postreading questions might be the best approach. In practice, many teachers use a mix of prereading questions to guide students' reading and postreading questions to assess their understanding and stimulate them to reflect.

The physical proximity of questions to text is more difficult to accomplish. Obviously, a teacher cannot insert questions in students' textbooks or be there in person to ask the right questions just as a student finishes a particular passage. One solution is to give students a question guide that is keyed to particular sections of the text, with instructions to complete the answers as they go. Anytime a teacher gives students a list of questions beforehand, though, there is the probability that some students will resort to the search-and-destroy method, simply reading the questions and skimming the text to match words in the questions to words in the text.

What to Ask: The Relation between Questions and Answers

There are many different types of questions. At one extreme is the factual question with a single correct answer: Who is buried in Grant's tomb? When was the War of 1812? Responding to some questions, however, requires a good deal of thought: How do the presidencies of Grant and Nixon compare? What were the causes and the immediate and long-term consequences of the War of 1812? Factual questions can be useful, but they are overused in too many classrooms. According to Just and Carpenter (1987), "questions that require high-level abstraction (such as the application of a principle) produce more learning than factual questions. High-level questions probably encourage deeper processing and more thorough organization" (pp. 421–422).

Many questions asked by teachers are necessarily extemporaneous reactions to classroom situations, but questioning is most effective when it is planned in advance. Teachers who develop a core of questions can target specific information or concepts and can encourage different kinds of thinking. It is easier to plan and ask effective questions if a teacher has some way to conceptualize or categorize questions.

When you are developing questions to stimulate or assess students' comprehension, it is useful to think about how a student will formulate an answer. Different questions may prompt answers from different sources, and so it is useful to think of question–answer relationships (QARs) (Pearson & Johnson,

1978). The answer to some questions may be *textually explicit*, or literally stated in the text. A reader might paraphrase the text, point to the exact words, or read them aloud to answer the questions. Other questions may call for a response that is *textually implicit*, not directly stated but suggested or implied by the text. To formulate an answer, a reader has to think about what the author has said and perhaps integrate information from several places in the text. Sometimes the answer to a question does not come from the text at all. The reader must call on prior knowledge or beliefs to answer the question. Pearson and Johnson call this prior knowledge a reader's "script" and say that such an answer would be *scriptally implicit*.

In a series of studies, Taffy Raphael further developed the concept of QARs and demonstrated their potential for helping students to comprehend their reading (Raphael & Pearson, 1982; Raphael, 1982, 1984, 1986). Raphael suggested that younger students, those in second grade or below, could most easily distinguish two main sources of information—the text itself and their own background knowledge. She coined the phrase *In the Book* to describe answers that were either textually explicit or textually implicit, and she used the phrase *In My Head* for answers that were scriptally implicit.

As readers become more conceptually mature, they are able to make finer discriminations between the kinds of answers they produce, and it is possible for them to think of four different QARs. Older readers are able to see that some answers are textually explicit, which Raphael (1986) labeled *Right There*. They are also able to understand that some answers are not directly stated but rather require inferences drawn from different parts of the text. These textually implicit answers are derived by the reader *Putting It Together*.

By the intermediate grades, students are able to make finer discriminations between kinds of questions. They can identify two different types of questions that call on their background knowledge. Some scriptally implicit questions require the reader to combine prior knowledge with information from the text to derive a response; hence, these are *Author and You* answers. Finally, some questions can be answered solely from the reader's knowledge base; they may even be answered without reading the text. As a reader, you are *On Your Own*.

Figure 7.1 gives a graphic representation of the various QARs, with sample questions and answers based on the story of *Goldilocks and the Three Bears*. To give you a further idea of how the four QARs might work with textbook material, we invite you to try the following activity.

ACTIVITY   Here is a short passage titled "Why the British Lost" from a high school American history text (Boorstin & Kelley, 1996). Following it are eight questions. The first four are answered for you and labeled Right There, Putting It Together, Author and You, and On Your Own. A brief rationale is given for each

In the Book

In My Head
(scriptally implicit)

Right There
(textually explicit)   Putting It Together
(textually implicit)   Author and You   On Your Own

SAMPLE QUESTIONS AND ANSWERS:
"GOLDILOCKS AND THE THREE BEARS"

1. **Right There:** What were the Three Bears eating for breakfast?
   Answer: They were eating porridge.

2. **Putting It Together:** Why was Baby Bear so upset when he came home?
   Answer: Because his breakfast was gone, his chair was broken, and there was a stranger sleeping in his bed.

3. **Author and You:** What kind of a person was Goldilocks?
   Answer: She was not very nice. She was bold. She was hungry and tired, and maybe she was lost or homeless.

4. **On Your Own:** Why is it a bad idea to go into a stranger's house when no one is home?
   Answer: It is against the law; it is trespassing. The people would not like it. They might be mean people and do something bad to you.

FIGURE 7.1   **Question–answer relationships**

relationship. See whether you can answer the last four questions and decide what the QAR is for each of them. (The answers are at the bottom of page 237.)

> The British were separated from their headquarters by a vast ocean. Their lines of communication were long. The British government was badly informed. They thought the Americans were much weaker than they really were. And they expected help from uprisings of thousands of Loyalists. But these uprisings never happened.
>
> The most important explanation was that the British had set themselves an impossible task. Though they had an army that was large for that day, how could it ever be large enough to occupy and subjugate a continent? The British knew so little of America that they thought their capture of New York City would end the war. After the Battle of Long Island in August 1776, General Howe actually asked the Americans to send him a peace commission, and cheerfully expected to receive the American surrender. But he was badly disappointed. For the colonists had no single capital that the British could capture to win the war.
>
> American success was largely due to perseverance in keeping an army in the field throughout the long, hard years. George Washington was a man of

great courage and good judgment. And Americans had the strengths of a New World—with a new kind of army fighting in new ways. Still, it is doubtful the Americans could have won without the aid of France.

Although many Americans opposed the Revolution, and some were luke-warm, it was a people's war. As many as half of all men of military age were in the army at one time or another. Each had the special power and special courage that came from fighting for himself, for his family, and for his home. (p. 100)

1. *Question:* What did the British expect from the Loyalists?
   Answer: They expected uprisings from thousands of Loyalists.
   QAR: Right There—the answer is almost a direct quote from the text.
2. *Question:* What evidence is there that the British were responsible for defeating themselves?
   Answer: The were badly informed. They were overly confident and made many poor judgments. They tried to fight a war that was too far away from their headquarters.
   QAR: Putting It Together—The reader must select information from several places in the text and make inferences about this information.
3. *Question:* What could Britain have done to win the war?
   Answers: They could have gotten better information. They could have had better generals who would have adapted to a new kind of warfare. They could have captured General Washington. They could have nego-tiated a treaty with France.
   QAR: Author and You—The reader must know many of the issues and events from the text, but the question also calls for the reader to use prior knowledge and reasoning to think of possible answers.
4. *Question:* What qualities are important in a leader during a time of crisis?
   Answers: During a crisis, a leader should have courage, good judgment, ability to inspire loyalty and confidence, intelligence, coolheadedness.
   QAR: On Your Own—The reader can rely entirely on prior knowledge; no knowledge of the text or the events of the American Revolution is required.
5. *Question:* In what way was the Revolution a people's war?
6. *Question:* If the United States were invaded by a foreign army, what might people in your community do?
7. *Question:* What did the British think would happen when they captured New York City?
8. *Question:* What lessons might we learn today from Britain's experience in the American Revolution?

In her work with intermediate-grade students, Raphael demonstrated that students can be taught about QARs and that this knowledge of where answers come from can actually improve students' ability to answer questions (Raphael &

Pearson, 1982; Raphael, 1982, 1984, 1986). There is also evidence that students maintain their use of QAR strategies over time, and that QAR training with narrative text transfers when students read expository text (Ezell et al., 1996).

A content area teacher might teach students about QARs using a procedure similar to that suggested by Raphael (1982):

1. Explain the four QARs and demonstrate them with relatively simple examples.
2. Once students appear to have grasped the relationships, give them several questions labeled Right There, Putting It Together, Author and You, or On Your Own, and have them develop answers.
3. As students become competent with this type of practice, begin posing questions without labels and instruct students to develop answers and decide which QAR applies.

Throughout this instructional sequence, discussion of questions, text, and answers is essential to help illustrate and reinforce the relationships. The emphasis should be on comprehension. What is important are the answers that students supply and the sources of those answers. QAR instruction should not become a task of simply "labeling" questions as Right There, Putting It Together, and so on.

David Dunbar, a teacher of a seventh-grade class that included several students with reading disabilities, followed a similar procedure to prepare his class for reading *The Hostage* (Taylor, 1984), a novel about a fishing family in the Pacific Northwest who are responding to a $100,000 prize offered for the capture of a killer whale, known locally as a "blackfish." Dave began by explaining the four QARs and illustrating them with questions and answers based on the *The Three Little Pigs*. Then he gave his students additional practice with questions and answers based on a short story they had read previously. Once he believed that his class had a good understanding of QARs, he gave them the question guide in Figure 7.2 and asked them to read the first two chapters of *The Hostage*. Students worked on the reading and question guide independently, although Mr. Dunbar gave assistance as needed to some of the struggling readers.

discussed in the text.

background knowledge and opinions, but a person must also have knowledge of the factors that are follow through whatever you start. *QAR:* Author and You—A number of answers are possible, depending on readers' away country when the people of that country are mostly against you. Be sure you have the means and the will to come involved in something. We shouldn't try to take on impossible tasks. It is imprudent to enter into a war in a far-Right There—The answer is stated explicitly in the text. 8. *Answer:* We should know what we are doing before we be-of the text is necessary. 7. *Answer:* The British thought the war would end once they captured New York City. *QAR:* Your Own—The question can be answered with background knowledge and the readers' suppositions; no knowledge war. Some people might become collaborators, though, depending on what they thought of the invaders. *QAR:* On *Answer:* People in our community might fight back. They would join the army or go underground and fight a guerrilla Putting It Together—The answer is not directly stated. The reader must infer the answer from what the authors say. 6. won because people were willing to sacrifice and keep fighting even though they met some early defeats. *QAR:* 5. *Answer:* Half of all the men served in the army. People were fighting for their own families and homes. America

---

THE HOSTAGE

CHAPTERS 1–2

Directions: Write complete answers to the following questions. Be ready to explain how you arrived at your answer.

Right There

1. In what country is Lumber Landing located?
2. What is gillnetting?
3. What is trolling?
4. What is a blackfish?

Putting It Together

1. What does it mean to "batten down the hatches"?
2. What happened to the boat that Jamie and his Dad heard on the CB radio during the storm?
3. How did Jamie's mom feel about his dad being a fisherman?

Author and You

1. Are fishermen wealthy people?
2. How could they catch a blackfish with a boat the size of the "Dawn Girl"?

On Your Own

1. Can people who aren't wealthy be happy?
2. How much would $100,000 change the way you live?

FIGURE 7.2 **QAR guide for Chapters 1 and 2 of *The Hostage*** (*Source:* David Dunbar, Alexander High School, Alexander, New York.)

At the next class meeting, Dave called on students to share their answers as he wrote them on the blackboard. As students volunteered their responses, he asked them how they had gotten their answers and reinforced the relationships between the questions and answers. Discussion of the Author and You and On Your Own questions resulted in a variety of responses and opinions from the class, including the students with reading disabilities. As the class proceeded through the novel, Mr. Dunbar prepared similar question guides to aid students' reading and discussion.

Instruction in QARs readily complements the kind of question–answer reading assignments and discussions often used by content teachers. All of the examples can be based on students' actual textbook reading assignments, and discussion of QARs requires minimal additional classroom time.

The QAR taxonomy is simple and intuitively easy to comprehend. In practice, however, teachers have found a few difficulties inherent in this very simplicity. Comprehension (in this case, the answers to questions) is too complex to be tidily classified by four relationships. The QAR taxonomy also implies a linear process that simply does not exist. Readers do not begin by comprehending information that is right there, then move on to putting ideas together, and end up being on their own. In fact, these kinds of comprehension occur simultaneously and interdependently. It could even be argued that all comprehension is scriptally implicit in the sense that people can comprehend only to the extent that they use their scripts, or prior knowledge, to make sense of the text.

The definitions of the four relationships are not precise. For instance, if a student answers a question with the exact words from two different paragraphs in the text, is the QAR Right There because the exact words were used or Putting It Together because the answer integrated information from different parts of the text? Often, a reader will answer a question using an Author and You or Putting It Together QAR when the information is actually Right There. The answer is not necessarily wrong just because it came from a source other than one the teacher had intended.

Despite these limitations, we believe that the four QARs provide a useful framework for teachers and students. First, there is a good argument for teaching students about QARs. When students are consciously aware of the different sources of information available to answer questions, they become more strategic in their reading and thinking, and their comprehension is improved (Raphael, 1984). Second, we have found that the four QARs are helpful in teacher planning. Teachers need to strike a balance between literal questions and more thought-provoking questions. Questions reflecting the Putting It Together, Author and You, and On Your Own QARs help students to see relationships within the text and connections between text ideas and other ideas in the subject area and to make associations with their own prior knowledge and experiences. Such questions frequently have more than a single good answer, which stimulates students to think rather than passively wait to be told the "right" answer.

How to Ask: Questioning Strategies

Teachers frequently devise prereading questions, assign end-of-chapter questions, or use questions to guide class recitations and discussions. This section offers some alternative questioning strategies that can help students become more actively involved in formulating and answering questions. In conjunction with instruction on QARs, these techniques can facilitate students' development of independent strategies for reading to learn.

Questioning the author.　Developing readers often accept uncritically the authority of the textbook without stopping to consider that texts are written by authors who have made decisions about what to include and how to present information. Questioning the Author (QtA) is an approach that helps students see that a "book's content is simply someone's ideas written down, and that this person may not have always expressed things in the clearest or easiest way for readers to understand" (Beck et al., 1997, p. 18). The researchers who developed QtA use the term "queries" to differentiate their questioning strategy from the usual teacher-dominated classroom routine of recitation in which the teacher asks questions and evaluates students' responses.

Material from content area textbooks can be classified as *expository text*, or writing that explains something. This is in contrast to *narrative text*, which tells a story, such as in novels, plays, or short stories. There are two types of QtA queries that can be used with either narrative or expository text (Beck et al., 1997). *Initiating queries* are used to begin consideration of important ideas in the text. The following are generic examples of initiating queries:

▸ What is the author trying to say?
▸ What is the author's message?

Follow-up queries are designed to guide students in evaluating and connecting ideas and constructing meaning. The following are sample follow-up queries:

▸ Does the author explain this clearly?
▸ Does the author tell us why?
▸ How does this connect to what the author told us before?

Whereas initiating and follow-up queries can be applied to expository or narrative text, *narrative queries* specifically help students to think about what an author is doing with character and plot:

▸ How do things look for this character now?
▸ What do you think this character is up to now, given what the author has told us?
▸ How has the author let you know that something has changed?
▸ How has the author settled this for us?

QtA strategies require thoughtful planning and implementation. The teacher must analyze the reading assignment carefully to determine key ideas (both explicit and implicit), anticipate concepts or connections that may cause comprehension difficulties for students, plan queries, and segment the text into meaningful sections to determine stopping points for discussion. QtA can be used selectively to introduce new selections that students will be completing as homework or to support students' reading of especially difficult segments.

When introducing QtA for the first time, it is a good idea to explain the purposes of QtA. Students should be told explicitly that comprehension difficulties are often as much the fault of the author as they are of the reader, and that part of the work of reading well is to question whether authors are making their ideas clear. When Doug Buehl, a high school teacher in Madison, Wisconsin, introduces QtA, he helps his students to identify the authors of their text by name and speculate on any biographical information that might be available (Buehl, 1998). After explaining the nature of QtA, students should read a selection from the text, followed by teacher queries to initiate discussion. In addition to posing queries, the teachers' role during discussion is to help students construct meaning by highlighting key points, returning students' attention to the text, and refining and interpreting student comments. Teachers also model their own thinking, fill in gaps left by the author, and guide students in summarizing and moving on through the text.

QtA obviously requires a good deal of teacher knowledge, preparation, and in-class practice. However, Beck and associates (1997) have found that QtA has resulted in more student talk, more student-initiated questions, and more emphasis on meaning and integration of ideas than in traditional question–answer sessions in which the focus is on evaluating student comprehension and recall of literal-level information from the text.

ReQuest.   Reciprocal questioning, or *ReQuest* (Manzo, 1969), is a relatively simple variation on classroom routine. Instead of the teacher asking questions, the students are given the opportunity to ask questions of the teacher. The ReQuest procedure works as follows:

1. Identify a text selection that has several obvious stopping points for discussion and prediction. Prepare a few higher-level questions for each section of the text.
2. Prepare students for the reading selection by previewing it, by discussing background information or selected vocabulary, or by instigating some other appropriate activity.
3. Tell students that they will be reversing roles with you. As they read the first part of the selection, they are to think of questions that they will ask you.
4. Let students read to a predetermined point. Then allow the students to ask you as many questions as they can think of. Respond without looking at the text.
5. When students have asked their questions, they close their books, and you direct questions to them. At this point, you should model higher-level questioning.
6. Repeat the reading–questioning procedure through successive segments of the text until a logical point is reached at which to make predictions about the rest of the material. Lead students to speculate on what they will find as they read, and continue the lesson along the lines of a DR-TA (discussed in Chapter 4).

In our experience, students are very eager to take on the role of teacher. The questions they initially ask are often factual, but, with teacher modeling, they quickly begin asking more complex and thoughtful questions. The ReQuest procedure combines very neatly with direct instruction in questioning or other comprehension strategies (Ciadello, 1998). If the class has previously learned about QARs, the teacher can think aloud about the sources of information used to formulate answers: "I know that information isn't right there in the book, but my previous experience would lead me to say that . . ." The amount of text covered between questioning episodes can be varied to meet the reading ability of the students and the difficulty of the material. Also, ReQuest can be a cooperative-learning activity if students are allowed to formulate their questions with a partner or in small groups.

Self-questioning.   One attribute of active readers is that they generate questions before, during, and after reading. Such active self-questioning can be taught. The ReQuest procedure would be one way of encouraging student self-questioning. Another approach to self-questioning was described by Singer and

Donlan (1982). A group of high school students were taught that short stories generally have several general attributes in common, such as characters, goals, obstacles, outcomes, and themes. As they read short stories, these readers considered model questions about these attributes and were guided to develop their own questions. On daily quizzes, the self-questioning group significantly outperformed another group that simply answered the teacher's questions.

Instruction in self-questioning can be adapted to other genres and other content areas. Students of poetry can be guided to ask their own questions about rhyme, meter, or imagery. Social studies teachers can show their students how to ask questions about causes and effects or comparisons and contrasts. When students encounter math problems, they can be shown how to ask their own questions about what is given and what is to be found. Students familiar with the QARs can formulate their own Right There, Putting It Together, Author and You, and On Your Own questions (Helfeldt & Henk, 1990). As homework, students can be asked to make up a certain number of self-questions and answers for the next day, and their questions can become the departure point for class discussion.

You could adapt a quadrant activity similar to one that Roni Draper used in her middle school math class (McIntosh & Draper, 1995). Over several class periods, she gave her students explicit instruction in QARs and demonstrated how they applied to their mathematics text. Once students had a good working knowledge of QARs, she gave them a sheet of paper divided into four quadrants labeled Question, Answer, Relationship, and Explanation. Working alone, in pairs, or in small groups, according to their preferences, students wrote their own question in the appropriately labeled quadrant. They made a note in their math logs as to which type of QAR they thought this question was and then traded papers with someone else. In the remaining three quadrants, they answered each other's questions, wrote down what type of QAR it was, and noted the explanation for this choice. They exchanged papers again and compared their responses. Where there was disagreement between those who wrote the questions and those who answered them, discussion continued until they agreed. Draper found that this procedure facilitated mathematical communication among her students, who were thus able to clarify and consolidate their understanding of mathematical concepts.

Self-questioning has a high level of success in improving comprehension, probably because it leads to more active reading and thinking. Self-questioning is also an effective strategy for students who are learning English (Jimenez & Gamez, 1996). Formulating questions and answers helps them to express their thoughts in English, often by borrowing and manipulating the language of the text. Self-questioning also allows bilingual students to actively monitor their own comprehension rather than passively responding to questions posed by the teacher. When students work on activities such as self-questioning in pairs or cooperative groups, it gives them an opportunity to practice their language skills while talking about the content they are learning, all in a less formal and less threatening atmosphere than whole-class recitation (Nelson, 1996).

Questions and the Struggling Reader

In a review of research on QARs, Raphael and Gavelek (1984) note that "classroom training in QARs appeared to make average- and low-ability students look much like high-ability students in their ability to answer questions" (p. 241). It is noteworthy that self-questioning seems to be especially beneficial to poor readers (Brozo, 2000; Gillespie, 1990). Nolan (1991) used a combination of prediction and self-questioning to boost the reading comprehension of middle-grade students, and he found that those with the most severe reading difficulties made the most gains. André and Anderson (1978/1979) also found self-questioning to be particularly effective with students having low verbal ability. They hypothesized that self-questioning gave these readers a strategy much more effective than their usual "plow through the words" approach and that students with high verbal ability may already have the component skills of selecting and organizing information. When teaching questioning strategies to struggling readers, teachers should begin with simple materials and provide ample practice, support, and feedback to help students gain confidence in using the strategies correctly across a variety of reading assignments (Swanson & de la Paz, 1998).

Alternatives to Questions: Comprehension Guides

Harold Herber (1978) suggests that students in content areas can benefit from being walked through a comprehension process similar to that used by expert readers. To accomplish this, Herber proposes that teachers devise a comprehension guide designed to support students in constructing meaning at three different levels. The *literal level* consists of specific facts and concepts that are explicitly stated. The *interpretive level* requires "reading between the lines" or drawing inferences about ideas that the author implies. The *applied level* represents comprehension that extends beyond the text to form new ideas or use ideas from the text in different contexts. Like QARs, these three levels of comprehension are neither

Technology Tip

For more suggestions on classroom questioning strategies, visit the University of Delaware's Center for Teaching Effectiveness Web site (http://udel.edu.cte/97book/question). As part of the university's handbook for teaching assistants, you will find a list of specific strategies for encouraging students to ask and answer questions.

discrete nor linear. That is, there will be a good deal of overlap among levels, and readers will move back and forth among these kinds of comprehension as they work their way through a text.

A levels of comprehension guide presents students with a list of declarative statements at each level before they read. This alerts readers to potentially important ideas and supports their search for meaning. As they read, students look for the ideas featured in the guide. After reading, the guide can be used as a departure point for discussion in small groups, as students compare their reactions to the guide and look back through the text to support their decisions.

ACTIVITY   To experience a levels of comprehension guide, first read the guide in Figure 7.3 and then read the following passage, which is the first chapter of Charles Dickens' *Hard Times* (1991). In this passage, the practical businessman Mr. Thomas Gradgrind is introducing a new schoolmaster to students in an elementary school. After reading the passage, return to the reading guide and respond to each item.

"Now, what I want is, Facts. Teach these boys and girls nothing but Facts. Facts alone are wanted in life. Plant nothing else, and root out everything else. You can only form the minds of reasoning animals upon Facts; nothing else will ever be of any service to them. This is the principle on which I bring up my own children, and this is the principle on which I bring up these children. Stick to Facts, sir!"

The scene was a plain, bare, monotonous vault of a schoolroom, and the speaker's square forefinger emphasized his observations by underscoring every sentence with a line on the schoolmaster's sleeve. The emphasis was helped by the speaker's square wall of a forehead, which had his eyebrows for its base, while his eyes found commodious cellarage in two dark caves, overshadowed by the wall. The emphasis was helped by the speaker's mouth, which was wide, thin, and hard set. The emphasis was helped by the speaker's voice, which was inflexible, dry, and dictatorial. The emphasis was helped by the speaker's hair, which bristled on the skirts of his bald head, a plantation of firs to keep the wind from its shining surface, all covered with knobs, like the crust of a plum pie, as if the head had scarecely warehouse-room for the hard facts stored inside. The speaker's obstinate carriage, square coat, square legs, square shoulders—nay, his very neckcloth, trained to take him by the throat with an unaccommodating grasp, like a stubborn fact, as it was—all helped the emphasis.

"In this life, we want nothing but Facts, sir, nothing but Facts!"

The speaker, and the schoolmaster, and the third grown person present, all backed a little, and swept with their eyes the inclined plane of little vessels then and there arranged in order, ready to have imperial gallons of facts poured into them until they were full to the brim.

"HARD TIMES"

I. Literal: Place a check mark next to the statement if you think it says the same thing that the author says. You should be able to show where you found this in the passage.

_____ 1. Mr. Gradgrind, the speaker, wants the students to learn facts.

_____ 2. The schoolroom was brightly decorated.

_____ 3. Mr. Gradgrind emphasized his remarks with a dry, dictatorial voice.

II. Interpretive: Place a check mark next to ideas you think the author implies. Be ready to support your decisions.

_____ 1. A person could tell a lot about Mr. Gradgrind's beliefs by the way he looked.

_____ 2. By "little vessels," the author means the students.

III. Applied: Check ideas you would agree with based on your own experience and what you have read. Make sure you can explain why you agree or disagree.

_____ 1. Schooling should appeal to the imagination as well as the intellect.

_____ 2. Education has changed considerably since Dickens' time.

FIGURE 7.3   **Levels of comprehension guide:** _Hard Times_

Note that in the guide in Figure 7.3, literal level statement 2 is intended as a distractor. It is literally *not* true according to the text. Similarly, teachers may include ideas in the interpretive or applied levels that have more than one legitimate response. These distractors are intended to generate thought and discussion and to keep readers from simply checking all the items on the guide without doing the reading.

A levels of comprehension guide designed by Amy Sanders for her class of seven 13- to 15-year-old special education students is shown in Figure 7.4. Previously, Amy had introduced the three levels of comprehension to her students and illustrated each level with a reading guide based on a short, familiar passage. Now Ms. Sanders and her class were going to be spending three days learning about the sense of taste. The key ideas for this lesson were presented in five pages of their science text, which included two experiments to be carried out in class along with exposition on how people perceive taste.

To begin the lesson, Ms. Sanders passed out the reading guide and read through the instructions and statements with students. She asked them to speculate what the reading passage might be about and what ideas they might be learning. Because most of her students had difficulty reading the science text on their own, she paired six of them to read the text and complete the

---

READING GUIDE: THE SENSE OF TASTE

I. Literal. Place a check mark next to the statements you think say the same thing the author says. (The words may be slightly different from the text.) Be prepared to show where you found this in the text.

_____ 1. Your sense organ for taste is your tongue.

_____ 2. Taste buds send messages to your tongue.

_____ 3. You don't taste food when it is dry.

_____ 4. Your tongue is sensitive to four tastes: sweet, sour, bitter, and salty.

II. Interpretive. Check the statements you think the author implies. Some thinking is required! Be ready to support your answers.

_____ 1. The front sides of your tongue taste the salt from a potato chip better than the back of your tongue.

_____ 2. Different parts of your tongue are sensitive to salt, bitter, sweet, and sour.

_____ 3. You can see your taste buds on your tongue.

_____ 4. Smell and taste work together.

III. Applied. Check the statements that you agree with, based on your experiences and what you learned from the passage. Choose _one_ statement and write why you did or didn't check it.

_____ 1. If something doesn't smell good, you probably shouldn't eat it.

_____ 2. Two can do better than one.

FIGURE 7.4 **Levels of comprehension guide, "The Sense of Taste"** (*Source: Amy Sanders, Baker Victory Day Treatment Center, Lackawanna, New York.*)

guide together, while the seventh student worked on his own. After they had finished reading, she brought the class together to share their responses to the guide. Together, the group listed key facts and ideas from the passage and then used their list to complete a graphic organizer. They then performed the first of the two experiments, which involved finding the parts of their tongues that were more sensitive to a piece of candy and a lemon slice. They reconfirmed their reading guide responses based on their findings.

On the second day, the class went to the computer lab, in which they accessed Neuroscience Resources for Kids (*http://faculty.washington.edu/chudler/tasty.html*). This site was used to reinforce and extend concepts that had been encountered in the text. Although some of the material here was a good deal more challenging and technical than what had been described in the text, Amy asked her students to review their reading guides and see if the Web site supported their responses or added any new insights. She also asked each computer pair to find at least two new technical vocabulary terms related to "taste," and to be prepared to explain them to the rest of the class.

On the third day, the class reviewed the reading guide and graphic organizer and then performed the second experiment described in the text as well as two others that Ms. Sanders found at a Web site called Experiments in Good Taste (*http://ificinfo.health.org/insight/exper.htm*). As a culminating activity, the students were given a quiz which consisted of filling in a blank version of the graphic organizer and writing a short essay that explained the relationship between taste and smell.

Selective reading guides.   Another way to support students' learning is to create a selective reading guide that points students to important information in the text. This is similar to the kinds of end-of-chapter review questions that are found in many textbooks. However, teachers may prefer to make their own decisions regarding which facts, ideas, and terminology are most important and devise a guide that directs students to specific sections of the text. When such a guide is given to students before they read, it makes their reading more purposeful and efficient. The expectation here is that students will not neccessarily need to read *all* the text but only those sections which contain essential information.

An example of a selective reading guide designed by Kim Miller, a high school health teacher, is shown in Figure 7.5. Kim introduced the guide to her class along with a brief introduction to the topic of cardiovascular disease. She explained that this is the number one killer in the United States, and asked how many students knew someone who had been affected by cardiovascular disease. Then she read through the reading guide with students, explaining the directions. She was careful to point out that some of the information asked for in the guide was explicitly stated in the text, but that there were also ideas which were implicit or which required them to use some of their prior knowledge. She suggested that students read the text through once and then go back and reread specific pages as needed to complete the guide. Students were asked to complete the reading and the guide for homework. The next day, students were put into groups of three or four to check over each other's responses, and then Mrs. Miller reassembled the whole class to compare responses, clarify any confusion, and provide additional explanations as neccessary.

SENSING AND RESPONDING TO TEXT STRUCTURE

A chapter in a history textbook, a poem, or a short story are not just a random collection of words, facts, and ideas. Within each type of text are structures that tie ideas together. Texts "have both a content and a structure, with the knowledge of both entering into the comprehension process" (Just & Carpenter, 1987, p. 241). Teachers can aid student comprehension both by teaching students about text structure and by using the structures inherent in texts to help students organize the information that is presented (Goldman & Rakestraw, 2000).

"CARDIOVASCULAR DISEASES"

Directions: Read pages 569–578 in your text, looking for answers to the following questions.

1. (P. 569) Define "hypertension." Can hypertension cause death? How?

2. (P. 570) Describe the difference between "atherosclerosis" and "arteriosclerosis." Which is more deadly? Why?

3. (Pp. 571–572) Explain how you could tell if someone were having a heart attack. List three ways to prevent a heart attack.

4. (P. 573) Explain how "cardiac arrest" is different from a heart attack.

5. (Pp. 573–574) Define "thrombus" and "embolus." Tell why these are dangerous.

6. (Pp. 569–574 and p. 578) Compare the *causes* of cardiovascular disease with ways of *preventing* it. The first one has been done for you.

Causes	*Prevention*
a. Eating foods high in fat.	a. Follow a low-fat diet.
b.	b.
c.	c.
d.	d.
e.	e.

7. Based on your comparison chart, make an overall conclusion about the relationship between the causes and prevention of cardiovascular disease.

FIGURE 7.5   **Selective reading guide: "Cardiovascular Disease"**   (*Source:* Kim Miller, Kenmore West High School, Kenmore, New York.)

Common Text Structures

Five kinds of structures, or organizational patterns, are commonly found in textbooks:

1. *Simple listing:* A collection of related facts or ideas, sometimes presented in order of importance. An example is the presentation of different types of bacteria in a biology text.

2. *Sequence or time order:* A series of events that occur in a particular order. An example is a discussion of early African societies, from ancient Egypt to Timbuktu in the 1500s, in a global studies text.

3. *Compare and contrast:* A description of similarities and/or differences among two or more things. An example is the explanation of mean, median, and mode in a mathematics text.

4. *Cause and effect:* A description of events and their causes or consequences. Often, a single cause will have more than one effect, and a single event may have more than one cause. An example is a discussion of how temperature, pressure, concentration, and catalysts affect chemical reactions.

5. *Problem–solution:* Similar to cause and effect, except that outcomes are a result or solution of a perceived need or problem. An example is an explanation in a history text of how New Deal legislation was passed during the first 100 days of Roosevelt's presidency in response to the Great Depression.

Authors rarely use one of these patterns exclusively. Instead, they use multiple patterns. Within a section of text, however, the essential content is often presented via a single pattern. A chapter on color in a physics text, for example, *lists* the complementary colors and the colors of the spectrum and *compares* color by reflection with color by transmission. However, most of the chapter is concerned with how humans perceive color, and this is explained in terms of *causes and effects,* such as what happens when colored pigments are mixed, why the sky is blue, and why sunsets are red.

We will not emphasize simple listing in our discussion of text structure. It is more familiar to most students than the other structures, and it does not present as much difficulty for readers. Teaching strategies for working with lists of examples or attributes can be found in the section on questioning and the one on constructing the author's message.

Although these five organizational patterns are commonly used throughout expository text, they are also found in narrative text and poetry. The plot of most fiction is driven by characters in search of a solution to a problem, as when Ahab seeks to destroy the white whale or Huck Finn tries to escape from his father. These problems set off chains of cause-and-effect events. Literature also makes frequent use of comparison and contrast, such as the comparisons of two lovers found in several of Shakespeare's sonnets.

Literature presents additional structural complexities, however. Although it is beyond the scope of this text to consider in detail the varied structures of poetry, drama, and novels, it is worth noting that narrative text generally follows a structure sometimes referred to as *story grammar.* Like the grammar or syntax of a sentence, a story is made up of certain components that fit together in a predictable sequence. The first common element in story structure is a *setting,* which establishes the time and place of the events. Authors also establish *characters* early in the story. An *initiating event* sets the plot in motion by establishing a problem or a conflict that one or more characters must try to resolve. What follows then are one or more episodes or *attempts* to resolve the problem, each with an *outcome.* The culmination of the plot is the *resolution* of the problem. The elements of story grammar are usually arranged in a predictable manner, although authors often manipulate story structures for literary effect. For instance, time and place may be purposely vague, the origins of a problem or conflict may only be implied, or an author might end a story without a definite resolution. Complex novels may feature numerous intertwined subplots with several characters, conflicts, attempts, and outcomes.

Teaching about Text Structures

There is evidence that text structure affects the reading comprehension of middle-grade and secondary students (Goldman & Rakestraw, 2000). In a study with fourth, sixth, and eleventh graders, Hare, Rabinowitz, and Schieble (1989) found "that both comparison/contrast and cause/effect texts (but not sequence texts) did pose greater difficulty for [students] than listing texts" (p. 86). Furthermore, awareness of text structures seems to have a positive effect on comprehension. Richgels et al. (1987) found that sixth graders had a high awareness of comparison/contrast structure and a low awareness of causation, and that structure-aware students were likely to use their awareness strategically as they read. Thus, the researchers believed that these students were "promising candidates for instruction in how to apply a structure strategy" while reading (p. 192). After studying fifth- and seventh-grade students' knowledge of text structure, Garner and Gillingham (1987) concluded that students benefit from direct instruction in the use of text structure. There is also evidence that students who are taught about text structures will use their knowledge to improve the structural coherence of their writing as well as to enhance their reading comprehension (Goldman & Rakestraw, 2000; Gordon, 1990; Miller & George, 1992).

Teacher modeling with Think Alongs.   To introduce students to text structures, the teacher should identify and describe a specific structure, drawing simple examples from the textbook. The teacher could read aloud short passages, pointing out words that signal a particular text pattern and modeling the thinking processes that those words trigger. (A list of words commonly used to signal text patterns is given in Figure 7.6.) This modeling of thinking processes is called a Think Along (Ehlinger & Pritchard, 1994).

For example, a biology teacher might demonstrate the pattern of comparison and contrast with the following passage, which serves as a transition between two major sections of a chapter (Schraer & Stoltze, 1993):

> The problems of life in aquatic biomes are different from the problems in terrestrial biomes. For one thing, in aquatic biomes, water is always present. However, in fresh water, organisms must excrete less water, and in salt water, excess salt may be excreted by organisms. Temperature changes in the course of a year are much less in aquatic environments than they are on land. Temperatures in the oceans show the least change, while those in lakes and ponds show more change. Other physical factors that affect living things in aquatic

Sequence/Time Order	Compare & Contrast	Cause and Effect/Problem-Solution
first, second, third, etc.	on the other hand	because
next	however	since
initially	less than, least	therefore
later	more than, most	if . . . then
following that	other	due to
finally	differently, difference	hence
before	similarly, similarity	thus
after	dissimilar	as a result
when	but	consequently
now	not only . . . but also	subsequently
in the past	either . . . or, neither . . . nor	accordingly
previously	while	eventually
presently	yet	initiated
	likewise	precipitated
	also	the outcome
	in comparison	the aftermath
	in contrast	
	conversely	

FIGURE 7.6   **Signal words for text structures**

biomes are the amounts of oxygen and carbon dioxide dissolved in the water, the availability of organic and inorganic nutrients, and light intensity. (p. 854)

As the teacher reads this passage with the class, he or she could point out the use of the signal words *different from, however, less than, least,* and *while.* The teacher might also show how the comparisons and contrasts are layered, with contrasts drawn between aquatic and terrestrial biomes, freshwater and salt water, and oceans and lakes. The passage helps to bridge the information in the two sections of the chapter, and the teacher can show how this passage helps to anticipate some of the new material. Students could be involved in a discussion of why the authors use comparison and contrast and how knowledge of that structure might help them comprehend the text. Calling on students to volunteer examples from earlier lessons or their previous experience is also helpful. Once attention has been drawn to a specific structure, one of the following teaching strategies can be used to help students work with further text passages in which that structure is predominant.

Graphic representations.   In Chapter 6, we gave an example of a semantic map that could be used to introduce students to key ideas in a reading selection. Semantic maps are also useful for giving readers a graphic representation of the structural relationships between ideas in a passage. According to Jones, Pierce, and Hunter (1988/1989), students can be taught how to construct their own graphic representations of text ideas through a five-step teaching process:

1. Students survey the reading passage to see which organizational pattern, if any, the author appears to use.
2. Students construct a predicted outline of the passage. At first, they will need guidance to do this, perhaps with the teacher modeling on the chalkboard or overhead projector. Over time, students will become increasingly able to construct their own outlines.
3. Students read the passage.
4. The outlines are revised and completed, again with help from the teacher if needed.
5. Students use their completed outlines to formulate a written or oral summary of the passage. This can be done independently or as a cooperative-learning activity.

Jones, Pierce, and Hunter (1988/1989) suggest a general graphic form for each of several text structures (Figure 7.7). Each graphic form has associated *key frame questions* that can be used to guide students as they read the passage.

Jones, Pierce, and Hunter (1988/1989) make several suggestions for teachers who want to work with graphic representations. As students begin developing their own outlines, teachers should be prepared to accept legitimate individual differences in interpretation. It is also likely that students will need repeated practice to develop useful graphic representations on their own. The researchers also recommend that students be tested on the ideas they have represented graphically. The time and effort spent on graphic representations will be especially beneficial to those low-achieving students who have few strategies for learning from text.

Guides to organizational patterns.   Just as a motorist uses a road map to plot a route, students can use a reading guide to help them navigate through a complicated text. The guide allows them to find the right intersections, avoid detours, recognize landmarks, and arrive at their destination with minimal delay. Teachers may design guides that can help students read assignments that feature potentially difficult organizational patterns or text structures. According to Herber (1978), an *organizational pattern guide* allows a student to "focus on the predominant pattern, using it as an aid to understanding relationships within the material and as an aid for recall after the reading has been completed" (p. 79).

For example, a sixth-grade science teacher is planning to spend a week working with a chapter on diseases. She knows from past experience that her students will have difficulty understanding the cause-and-effect relationships involved in the chapter. To help them, she devises a reading guide (Figure 7.8). On Monday, she reviews recent class discussions of cause-and-effect patterns in the text, introduces the topic of the chapter, and leads the class as they

(a) Series of Events Chain

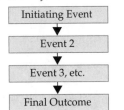

Key Frame Questions:
What is the object, procedure, or initiating event?
What are the stages or steps?
How do they lead to one another?
What is the final outcome?

(b) Cycle (This form could be used for either sequence or cause/effect structures.)

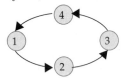

Key Frame Questions:
What are the critical events in the cycle?
How are they related?
In what ways are they self-reinforcing?

(c) Compare/Contrast Matrix

	Name 1	Name 2
Attribute 1		
Attribute 2		
Attribute 3		

Key Frame Questions:
What things are being compared?
How are they similar?
How are they different?

(d) Cause/Effect Fishbone Map (A single cause that has multiple effects can be represented by reversing the cause and effect labels.)

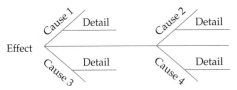

Key Frame Questions:
What are the factors that cause X?
How do they interrelate?
Are the factors that cause X the same as those that cause X to persist?

(e) Problem-Solution Outline

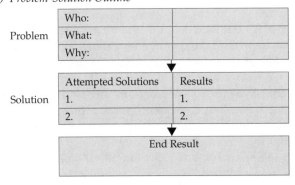

Key Frame Questions:
What was the problem?
Who had the problem?
Why was it a problem?
What attempts were made to solve the problem?
Did those attempts succeed?

FIGURE 7.7   Graphic forms for representing text structures   (*Source:* From B. F. Jones, J. Pierce, & B. Hunter, "Teaching students to construct graphic representations," *Educational Leadership, 46,* 20–25, 1988/1989, December/January.)

Technology Tip

▼▼

There are software programs such as Timeliner and Inspiration that can be used by teachers or students to prepare and print out graphic representations of ideas. Timeliner can be used to prepare time lines of historical events. It is available in a version that can switch back and forth between English and Spanish. Inspiration can create webs, diagrams, maps, or outlines with information provided by the user.

Timeliner 4.0
Tom Snyder Productions
Watertown, MA
http://www.tomsnyder.com

Inspiration 6.0
Inspiration Software
Portland, OR
http://inspiration.com

brainstorm about diseases and their causes and cures. The teacher then distributes copies of the guide and goes over the instructions for Part I, emphasizing that there will be several possible ways to match the causes and effects. She assigns the first half of the chapter as homework. During the next three days, the teacher refers to Part I of the guide as students work their way through the chapter and carry out a lab experiment on the effect of disinfectants in preventing bacterial growth. When students have read the whole chapter, she has them complete Part II of the guide and compare responses for both parts with their lab partners. The class reviews the guide, lab work, and important vocabulary terms on Thursday. On Friday, students take a two-part chapter test. The first part consists of multiple-choice questions. For the second part of the test, students must pick one of the four statements from Part II of the reading guide and explain in writing why they agree or disagree with it.

You have probably noticed that Part I of the guide leads students to work with ideas within the predominant organizational pattern—cause and effect. Part II is what Herber (1978) calls the "so what?" part of the guide. That is, it challenges readers to draw conclusions, refer to their own experience, and in effect answer the question "So what does this all add up to?" The science teacher could have omitted this part of the guide if she felt such tasks could be addressed in other ways. She could also have given students only the items in the effects column, with directions to find the causes. This activity would be more difficult but might be effective with students who have the ability to determine causes on their own.

To develop an organizational pattern guide, first determine whether essential information and ideas are conveyed through one of the common text structures and whether this is likely to cause difficulty for students. Sequence, for instance, is inherent in most fiction and historical writing, but it may not be problematical for students unless the sequence in the text is different from the actual chronological sequence, as when an author uses flashbacks or otherwise presents events in a

READING GUIDE

I. Directions: Read the list of possible causes and effects below. As you read Chapter 6, match the causes to the effects. Note: some letters (causes) will be used more than once, and there may be more than one cause for a single effect. Be ready to back up your answers with information from the text.

CAUSES

a. skin stops microorganisms
b. white blood cells "remember" how to make antibodies
c. viruses
d. microorganisms in water or air
e. disinfectants kill germs
f. malnutrition, heredity, chemicals in air or water
g. bacteria
h. white blood cells destroy germs and damaged tissues
i. direct contact
j. mucus traps germs
k. vaccine causes the body to produce antibodies that kill bacteria
l. animal carriers
m. fungi

EFFECTS

_____ 1. infectious diseases
_____ 2. strep throat
_____ 3. disease is stopped or prevented
_____ 4. a person becomes immune
_____ 5. polio
_____ 6. infection stops and healing takes place
_____ 7. noninfectious diseases
_____ 8. infectious diseases spread from one host to another
_____ 9. diseases in plants

II. Directions: Below you will find some ideas about catching or preventing diseases. Check the ones you agree with, based on your own experience and what we have read and talked about. You must be able to explain why you did or didn't check each one.

_____ 1. People get sick from many different causes.
_____ 2. What you can't see won't hurt you.
_____ 3. Even though the human body has many natural defenses against disease, it still can use some help.
_____ 4. A good offense is the best defense.

FIGURE 7.8   **A reading guide that reveals the cause-and-effect structure of a chapter on diseases**

nonlinear fashion. Figure 7.9 is an interesting example of a sequence guide that helps students to apply that pattern to math problem solving.

The example in Figure 7.10 shows a format for comparison/contrast guides. The teacher lists comparisons, some literal and some inferred, from a passage on feudalism. Students have to decide whether or not the author actually makes

SEQUENCE GUIDE: SOLVING MATHEMATICAL EXPRESSIONS

Directions: Your job will be to find the value of the following mathematical expression:

$$(2^2 + 11) - 6/3 \times 5 + 1$$

First, look over the steps listed below. Then read page 53 in your textbook. Using this information, place a number 1 next to the step you feel should come first in solving the problem, a 2 next to the second step, and so on.

_____ A. Divide by 3.
_____ B. Add 11.
_____ C. Find the value of 2^2.
_____ D. Add 1.
_____ E. Subtract 6.
_____ F. Subtract 10.
_____ G. Multiply by 5.

Now, perform the steps in the order you've placed them and solve the problem.

Answer: _____

Directions: Check those statements you feel are supported by what you know about math and what you learned from this exercise.

_____ 1. Be consistent.
_____ 2. Changing the order can change the answer.
_____ 3. Addition and subtraction are considered just as important as multiplication and division when solving a mathematical expression.

FIGURE 7.9   **Sequence guide for helping seventh graders learn to solve mathematical expressions**   (*Source:* Sharon Bauer, Edward Town Middle School, Niagara-Wheatfield Central Schools, New York.)

those comparisons. As they explain their decisions, they will discuss the similarities and differences between serfs and free peasants, the Middle Ages and the Renaissance, and so on.

Story maps.   Research on story grammar suggests that children as young as five or six have a well-developed sense of the elements in story structure (Mandler & Johnson, 1979; Stein & Glenn, 1979). Extensive teaching of story structure beyond early elementary grades, therefore, is probably not warranted. However, as literary offerings become more sophisticated or complex, some readers may have difficulty tracking a story's development (Goldman & Rakestraw, 2000). To help readers navigate through a complex or unusual narrative, teachers may employ a variation of a story map. When working with story maps, teachers should expect varied student opinions regarding the initiating event, main problem, and what constitutes "important" events. Figure 7.11 illustrates

---

COMPARE AND CONTRAST: THE MIDDLE AGES

Directions: Read the list of comparisons below and then read pages 152–158 in your text. When you have finished reading, check those comparisons you believe are made either directly or indirectly by the author.

_____ 1. hopeless/hopeful
_____ 2. military service by knights/taxes
_____ 3. serfs/free peasants
_____ 4. work for the lord/pay rent
_____ 5. feudalism/national governments
_____ 6. fields of crops/raising sheep
_____ 7. Middle Ages/Renaissance
_____ 8. knights in armor/guns and cannons
_____ 9. vassal of a lord/number in a nation

Directions: Once you have finished the first part of this guide, check those statements below that you feel can be supported by what you read or your own experiences. Compare your responses with those of other members of the class. Be sure you can support your choices.

_____ 1. You get what you pay for.
_____ 2. Advances in technology often bring about the need for social and political changes.
_____ 3. Necessity is the mother of invention.
_____ 4. Guilds of the Middle Ages were much like the unions of today.
_____ 5. It takes a woman to get the job done right.

FIGURE 7.10   Comparison/contrast guide for a sixth-grade social studies lesson   (_Source:_ Marilynne Crawford, Maya School, Guatemala City, Guatemala.)

a story map for _Romeo and Juliet._ Note that this story map does very little to involve readers in thinking about the theme of the play, Shakespeare's poetry, or the main characters and their dilemma. Outlining the structure of a story may help readers to follow the plot, but it is not sufficient engagement with a good literary work. A story map should be used as a foundation for other, more thoughtful consideration of the story.

INTEGRATING OTHER LANGUAGE PROCESSES

Many of the teaching strategies discussed in this chapter integrate oral language and reading. Small-group discussion of reading guides promotes listening and speaking ability, as do self-questioning and ReQuest.

"ROMEO AND JULIET"

Time & Place: **Characters:**

Middle Ages   *Romeo—a Montague*
Verona, Italy   *Juliet—a Capulet*
                                                      (Montagues & Capulets are
                                                      bitter enemies)

The event that starts the main plot:

Romeo sneaks into a Capulet costume party and meets Juliet.

Characters' Response and Main Problem:

Romeo and Juliet fall in love, but they can't do anything about it because their families
hate each other.

Major Events:

1. *Romeo goes to Juliet's at night; they pledge their love to each other.*

2. *Romeo and Juliet secretly get married.*

3. *In a street fight, Romeo kills Juliet's cousin. He has to leave town to avoid arrest.*

4. *Juliet's father tells her she has to marry Paris, a young nobleman.*

5. *Juliet arranges to fake her death so she can escape with Romeo.*

Resolution:

Romeo doesn't know the plan, sees Juliet "dead," kills himself.
Juliet wakes up, sees Romeo dead, kills herself.

Capulets and Montagues see the result of their hatred for each other.

FIGURE 7.11   **Story map for *Romeo and Juliet***

One other strategy that uses listening as a means of helping students learn from text is called *Listen-Read-Discuss* (Manzo & Casale, 1985), which is really a refinement of the traditional lecture–discussion format of many high school classes. The key component of Listen-Read-Discuss is what the teacher does before students read. Manzo and Casale recommend that the teacher take about 15 minutes to lecture on the material to be covered. The content of the lecture should include a clear presentation of important ideas in the reading assignment. The teacher can highlight facts, ideas, text structures, or vocabulary that might be problematic. This lecture will familiarize students with the material and help them to anticipate the demands of the assignment. Students then read the assigned pages in class or as a homework assignment. The final discussion can be guided by three questions:

1. What did you understand best from what you read and heard?
2. What did you understand least from what you read and heard?
3. What questions or thoughts did this lesson raise in your mind about the topic or related issues?

These questions can be discussed in small groups, which in turn share their conclusions with the whole class. Other language processes can also be integrated if students are asked to produce a brief written summary after the discussions.

Variations of Listen-Read-Discuss can be a welcome relief from the tedium of trying to attend to lengthy lectures. Lectures tend to yield diminishing returns the longer they last. Nevertheless, there are times when lecture is the most effective way to deliver content, such as when there are not enough reading materials available or if a particular topic is not covered or given insufficient elaboration in the text. As a general rule of thumb, it is a good idea to limit lectures to 15–20 minutes and to try to initiate some active participation on the part of students after the lecture. In addition to reading and discussion as a lecture follow-up, students might work in pairs or small groups to create a visual representation of ideas in the lecture, to make a decision based on the information they have heard, or to choose an important idea from the lecture with the reason for the choice. Writing can also be integrated if students are asked to produce a brief written summary or "position paper" after the lecture.

SUMMARY

Using textbooks as tools for learning can be a challenge for many students. Through instruction and support, teachers can help students develop useful strategies for learning from reading. Thoughtful questioning can guide students' learning, especially if they are shown how to ask their own questions as they read. Readers of textbooks also need to learn how to work with different text structures and how to interpret an author's message. When teachers model these strategies and lead students through meaningful practice with content area text materials, students become more effective learners.

SUGGESTED READINGS

Beck, I., McKeown, M., Hamilton, R., & Kucan, L. (1997). *Questioning the author: An approach for enhancing student engagement with text.* Newark, DE: International Reading Association.

Jones, B., Palincsar, A., Ogle, D., & Carr, E. (Eds.) (1987). *Strategic teaching and learning: Cognitive instruction in the content areas.* Alexandria, VA: Association for Supervision & Curriculum Development.

Raphael, T. (1986). Teaching question–answer relationships, revisited. *The Reading Teacher, 39,* 516–522.

Taylor, B., Graves, M., & van den Brock, P. (1999). *Reading for meaning: Fostering comprehension in the middle grades.* Newark, DE: International Reading Association.

Wood, K., Lapp, D., & Flood, J. (1992). *Guiding readers through text: A review of study guides.* Newark, DE: International Reading Association.

Increasing Vocabulary and Conceptual Growth

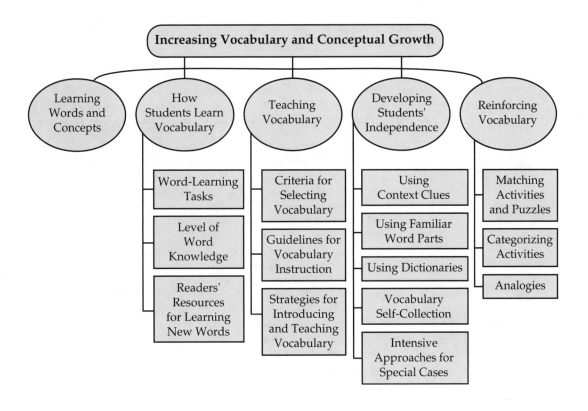

Polonious: What do you read, my lord?
Hamlet: Words, words, words.

If Hamlet is right and reading is just "words, words, words," then common sense suggests that a person who does not know the words is not going to have much success. In fact, it has long been recognized that vocabulary knowledge strongly influences reading comprehension (Nagy & Scott, 2000). Students need to learn the meanings of many new words, and to the extent that they can do this, they will be able to read and understand. Learning vocabulary is much more than memorizing words and definitions, however. In content areas, words are labels for important concepts and can only be mastered through repeated experience within meaningful context. The following anecdote from Lori Eframson, a rehabilitation counselor in Buffalo, New York, dramatically illustrates this point:

▼▼▼▼▼▼▼

On a September day in 1973, when I was ten years old, I dove into what I thought was a pile of hay in a barn. It turned out to be only a floor-covering of hay, and I broke three vertebrae in the cervical region of my neck. This left me paralyzed from my shoulders down. My dive into the hay had changed my life forever. It also forced me to learn a whole new language—the technical language of medicine.

I spent six months in traction in a teaching hospital in Syracuse, New York. When the doctor would come to see me on his daily rounds, he would bring ten or twelve students with him and talk about me and my body as if I weren't there. I listened intently to every word he said, but understood almost none of it. None of this technical jargon was explained to me, either. Being a very curious kid, I wanted to know what they were saying about me. This was information that was very important to me, and I absorbed it all. I began to put pieces of the puzzle together. After a month or so, I found it easier to follow what the doctor was talking about. He said almost the same thing every day!

One day, he came in with his group of curious students. Before he could open his mouth, I spewed out his usual phrases. He and his students stood with their mouths hanging open as I told them about my central nervous system, the compression of the cervical, thoracic, and lumbar regions of my spine, the contraction and spasms of my muscles, the loss of sensation, and the conditions of paraplegia and quadraplegia. From this point on, the doctor would come in and say, "This is Lori. I'm going to let *her* tell you what's going on with her." It was kind of a joke, but I began to understand and accept my condition as I spoke about it.*

▼▼▼▼▼▼▼

In this chapter, we first consider how readers learn vocabulary and then discuss several techniques for guiding and reinforcing students' vocabulary and conceptual growth. We emphasize ways to develop readers' strategies for learning vocabulary on their own.

LEARNING WORDS AND CONCEPTS

A close look at vocabulary development reveals several knotty questions: What exactly is a word? How many words are there that need to be learned? How are they learned? What do we mean when we say a person has "learned" a word?

On a simple typographic level, a word is a group of letters surrounded by white space. Such a definition hardly accounts for the richness of meaning that a word can represent, however. The word *fidelity*, for instance, represents a whole range of philosophical, psychological, and practical concepts in contexts ranging from ethics to matrimony to electronic sound reproduction. For our purposes, it may help to think of *word families*, or groups of words with clear relationships (Nagy & Herman, 1987). For instance, the words *specify, specifies, specific*, and *specification* are all members of the same family. Knowing the meaning of one of these words increases the chances of being able to infer the meanings of the others.

---

*Used with the permission of Lori Eframson.

Nagy and Herman (1987) estimate that there are about 88,500 distinct word families in the printed English used in grades 3–9 and that the average schoolchild learns approximately 3,000 new words each year through twelfth grade. That is approximately eight new words each day! It is important to remember that these are rough averages. Students from different backgrounds vary considerably in their learning of vocabulary (White, Graves, & Slater, 1990), and students who are having reading difficulties have more trouble learning new words (Shefelbine, 1990).

It is not likely that students are absorbing eight new meanings a day from direct instruction by their teachers or by old-fashioned rote memorization. Although direct instruction is effective in teaching new word meanings, students also learn new meanings from wide reading, from conversation, and from the rich language environment of school, family, community, and mass media.

What is meant by saying a person "knows" a word is not simple. Students might understand the word *order* as something one does in a restaurant and as a general term having to do with arranging things. However, they would find new and different meanings for this word in content areas. Within social studies, they would find many meanings: a military order, a religious order, the Order of the Garter, law and order, and a new world order. Would they "know" the word if they did not understand all these? In biology, order has a specific meaning in the classification of organisms. Would it be enough to know that an *order* is a way to classify living things, or would students also need to know where *order* comes in (between *class* and *family,* two other words that everybody knows)?

The point is that in content areas, words are more than marks on a page, more even than dictionary definitions. Content area vocabulary represents concepts, and learning the vocabulary means understanding the concepts well enough to apply them in a meaningful way. Although declarative knowledge (being able to define a term) may be sufficient for some technical vocabulary, much of the vocabulary learned in content areas requires procedural knowledge, or being able to do things with a concept, to apply it in combination with other ideas (Nagy & Scott, 2000). In Chapter 1, we discussed schemata, or the webs of experience and knowledge that people construct in order to make sense of the world. People use words to describe or label their schemata. Teaching vocabulary is therefore a matter of helping students apply new labels to existing schemata, build on existing schemata, and develop entirely new schemata.

HOW STUDENTS LEARN VOCABULARY

Every content area has a large collection of specialized or technical terms that denote important concepts. Sometimes these words and concepts are already familiar to students, for example, when high school seniors study *political parties.* Other words with commonly known meanings have specialized (and often different) meanings in a content area, as exemplified by the word *order* and by mathematical terms such as *proof, point, line,* and *root.* There are also technical terms that are specific to a particular content area, such as *abscissa, metaphor, photosynthesis,* and *archipelago.*

Word-Learning Tasks

When we talk of learning vocabulary, we are really talking of four different relationships between words and schemata or concepts (Graves & Slater, 1996; Herber, 1978). These four relationships, or word-learning tasks, are (1) known word/known concept, (2) new word/known concept, (3) known word/new concept, and (4) new word/new concept. These relationships are illustrated in Figure 8.1. In the first, a common or known word represents a concept that students understand. When seventh graders begin a unit on *weather,* they are using a familiar word to label familiar phenomena. This is more than review, however. In their study of weather, they will enlarge and refine their concept.

The second kind of word-learning task is to apply new words to familiar concepts. The teacher may introduce the terms *meteorology* and *precipitation.* Students will be familiar with rain or snow, but some may not know the generic term for "wet stuff that falls from the sky." Most have seen weather forecasts on television and heard the word *meteorologist,* but they may not know the meaning of *meteorology.*

The third word-learning task requires students to learn a new concept but use a familiar word. For example, students will have several ideas about what *pressure* means, but the concepts of air pressure (or barometric pressure) and how changes in pressure affect weather may be new. All students know the words *watch* and *warning,* but these terms have specific technical meanings when the National Weather Service issues a *storm watch* or *storm warning.* This third word-learning task may present some special difficulties when students have to unlearn or at least suspend a known meaning for a word in order to learn a new concept. A good example is the word *work.* In everyday usage this refers to a variety of things that people do: go to work, work out an agreement,

Words	Concept	Examples from a Science Unit
1. Known word	Known concept	weather
2. New word	Known concept	meteorology, precipitation
3. Known word	New concept	pressure, storm watch, storm warning
4. New word	New concept	humidity, hygrometer

FIGURE 8.1   **The four word-learning tasks**

work up a sweat, and work on a problem. In physics, however, *work* has a very precise meaning: it is the amount of force applied to an object multiplied by the distance the object moves. By this definition, studying for a chapter test or doing 30 math problems is no work at all! This seeming paradox can be very frustrating, especially for middle-grade students. However, every content area has many examples of this kind of word.

The final word-learning task is probably the most difficult. In this case, students must learn both a new concept and a new word to describe it. Although seventh-grade students may have heard the term *humidity* used in weather reports, the concept of moisture in the air will be new for many. The term *hygrometer* and the way in which this instrument measures humidity will almost certainly be novel. These students will be developing new concepts and vocabulary within the overall schema of weather.

Levels of Word Knowledge

The complexity of word-learning tasks is compounded by the varying levels of word knowledge that students bring to these tasks and the varying levels of word knowledge that teachers expect them to take away.

We have questioned what it means to know or learn a word. There is no easy answer. Words have many uses and meanings. Like people, they may be complete strangers or intimate friends, with many intervening gradations of acquaintanceship, from "Weren't we in an English class together once?" to "Hey, it's great to see you again!"

A word may be in a student's *receptive vocabulary* (recognized when seen or heard), yet may rarely or never be part of that person's *expressive vocabulary* (used in speech or in writing). Some words (and associated concepts) are learned so well in school that people never forget them. Other words are learned superficially, and all but a vague residue seems to evaporate from memory as soon as the student has taken a test or moved on to another subject.

Teachers require different levels of word and concept knowledge. To match a word and definition in a multiple-choice test, a student must recognize the word and associate it with the information given. For example, the following question could be answered even if the student had never seen a hygrometer:

A _____ is used to measure humidity.

a. thermometer   b. barometer
c. hygrometer   d. hydrometer

If the student were supposed to actually use a hygrometer to measure humidity and to explain how the hygrometer works, the task might seem much more difficult. Certainly the knowledge required would be deeper and more complex. However, if the student had practiced using a hygrometer and had been carefully taught how it works, the task might be easier than the rote memory retrieval required for the multiple-choice test.

The question of what it means to learn a word is relative. The answer depends on how the word is to be used, when it will be encountered again, how the word is taught, and how a person's knowledge is to be assessed.

Readers' Resources for Learning New Words

When a reader comes across an unfamiliar word, there are four ways he or she might approximate the meaning: context clues, morphemic analysis, expert advice, and the dictionary (Harmon, 1998; Nagy & Scott, 2000).

Context clues.   Written and spoken contexts are the richest resources for learning new words (Nagy & Herman, 1987). What other possible explanation is there for the rapid growth in vocabulary in children and the fact that adults are constantly learning new words and new meanings for old words? When proficient readers encounter an unfamiliar word, they usually read on, content to ignore that word or derive a partial understanding as long as their overall comprehension of the passage is satisfactory. Although initial exposure to an unfamiliar word in context may have limited usefulness, seeing or hearing the word again in different contexts may build a more complete meaning, until eventually the word becomes well understood (Nagy & Scott, 2000).

Context is not always helpful, however. Unfamiliar words often appear in contexts that offer few, if any, hints to the word's meaning (Schatz & Baldwin, 1986). In fact, the context may be misleading or confusing. To demonstrate just how little help context can be, read the following passage from *A House for Mr. Biswas* by V. S. Naipaul (1984) and try to figure out what the italicized word means:

> His tailless shirt flapped loose, unbuttoned all the way down, the short
> sleeves rolled up almost to his arm-pits. It was as though, unable to hide his
> *prognathous* face, he wished to display the rest of himself as well. (p. 244)

If you did not previously know the meaning of *prognathous,* you may have guessed something like "ugly" or "homely" because of the implication that the man's face should be hidden. However, nothing in the context suggests the actual meaning of the word, which is "having a protruding jaw."

Morphemic analysis.   Familiar word parts—roots and affixes—are another aid in wrestling with unfamiliar words. Using these parts to approximate meaning is sometimes called *morphemic analysis. A morpheme* is the technical term for the smallest unit of meaning in a language. The word *car* is a free morpheme; it can stand alone. The suffix *-s* is a bound morpheme; it has no meaning by itself, but when added to a word, as in *cars,* it carries the meaning of "more than one." *Cars* is therefore a word made up of two morphemes. Some morphemes are fairly consistent in the way they modify a root word, such as the prefixes *re-* in *reproduce* and *un-* in *unlikely*. Another large group of morphemes, many of Latin or Greek origin, combine with other morphemes to make up familiar or predictable words in science, math, and social studies (*biology, photosynthesis, centimeter, polygon, automation,* and *monopoly*).

We said at the beginning of the chapter that it is really more useful to think of words in families than as discrete entities. When a person learns one word, she or he may be able to generalize to other variations of the word. A person who knows the word *exist* will probably understand the words *existence* and *existent*. Morphemic generalization is not infallible, however. Knowing the variations of *exist* is not much help in understanding *existentialism,* and knowing *sign* does not help with *resignation*. White, Power, and White (1989) studied 1,700 words with the common prefixes *un-, re-, in-* (not), and *dis-*. They estimated that 20 percent of these words could not be reliably deciphered through analysis of morphemes.

Context clues and morphemic analysis can be complementary, as in the following example from a middle-grade social studies text (Rawls & Weeks, 1985): "Energy from the earth's core can be tapped through hot water or steam near the earth's surface. This *geothermal* energy can be used to generate electricity" (p. 727). The context clearly explains the concept, and familiarity with other words containing the roots *geo* and *therm* (*geography* and *thermometer*) will reinforce the meaning of the word.

Expert advice.   A reader who is stumped by a word can ask for expert advice. The "expert" can be a teacher, a parent or sibling, or the student at the next desk. Often, asking someone is the simplest and most satisfying solution. By asking and receiving a good answer, the reader gets the needed information while the motivation to learn is strong and with minimal disruption of the reading process.

Dictionaries.   When context or roots and affixes fail to help with the meaning of a word, a reader can consult a dictionary or glossary. In fact, when students ask for help with a word, many well-meaning teachers tell them, "Look it up in the dictionary." Although dictionaries are valuable tools, they are not always effective for learning vocabulary. Students may turn to the dictionary, read a definition, and come away no better informed than when they started. For instance, if you look up the term *radioisotope* in the dictionary, you will find the definition "radioactive isotope," which is not very useful unless you happen to know those words. Looking up *microtubule* in the glossary of a high school biology textbook yields "long, cylindrical organelles found in cilia and flagella." (Help!)

It is not that dictionaries, glossaries, and thesauruses are not useful tools or that students should never be told to look a word up. The point is that students must be shown how to use various resources for learning words. The following section on teaching strategies presents several ways to enhance students' use of context clues, morphemic analysis, and dictionaries.

TEACHING VOCABULARY

A teacher must decide how much attention to give to vocabulary, which words should be taught, and when and how they should be taught. There is an important cost–benefit ratio to consider (Graves, 1986; Graves & Prenn, 1986). Simply put, the harder the task and the deeper the knowledge expected of students, the more time that must be put into instruction, as illustrated by the earlier example about the word *hygrometer*. Given the necessity of covering much curriculum in too little time, teachers must try to keep the costs of instruction low and the benefits high. Because school reading materials present so many potentially unfamiliar words, this is quite a challenge.

To illustrate this problem, we examined two very different samples of content area text: a chapter from a sixth-grade science textbook and a short story from a ninth-grade literature anthology. We listed words from each selection that might be unfamiliar to a significant portion of students in the respective grade levels (Figures 8.2 and 8.3). Although each word is a candidate for special attention, no science or English teacher would be able to take time to teach all of the words on either list.

Examination of the two lists yields some important insights into content area vocabulary. First, it becomes easier to understand how students might encounter an average of eight unfamiliar words each day. There are some similarities between the lists. Both selections have common words used in uncommon ways (*cell, eye, runner, daughter, egg, rise, game,* and *lots*). Each list features terms made

trait*	potato eyes
reproduction*	strawberry runners
heredity*	fertilization*
inherited*	egg*
asexual reproduction*	sperm*
sexual reproduction*	pistil*
unique	stigma*
cell*	ovary*
amoeba	stamen*
nucleus*	anther*
clone*	pollen*
oyster	budding*
cell division*	sea anemones
daughter cells*	hydra
regeneration*	
organisms	
salamander	

*Printed in boldface and defined in the margin.

FIGURE 8.2   **Potentially unfamiliar terms from a chapter (about 3,800 words long) on reproduction in a sixth-grade science textbook**

catkins	deterred
preparatory school*	inconceivable
genial	quadruplicate
blueprints	sward
dormitory	grandeur
Shah of Iran	perplexity
asinine	resignation
game (a game woman)	incredulity
ambitious	foil**
reserve (lack of reserve)	conflict***
rise (waited for a rise on a remark)	third-person narration**
unrepentant	omniscient**
segregated	scholarship
lots (to draw lots)	

*Defined in a footnote.
**Defined in Skill Development section at the end of the story.
***Unit theme.

FIGURE 8.3   **Potentially unfamiliar terms from *The Lie* by Kurt Vonnegut (about 3,200 words long)**

up of two or more words (*third-person narration, preparatory school, asexual reproduction,* and *daughter cells*). The two lists are also indicative of some of the differences between expository and narrative text. Roughly two-thirds of the terms in the science chapter (Figure 8.2) are written in boldface, explained in context, and defined in the margins of the textbook. Most of them are repeated throughout the chapter as concept builds on concept. Clearly, the science passage is dense in new words and concepts, and to understand the chapter a reader will need a pretty clear understanding of each term. To teach the vocabulary is to teach the content.

Although the short story had almost as many potentially unfamiliar words, only four of them were defined in the text (Figure 8.3), and only three appeared more than once in the story. Most ninth-grade readers could follow the plot and understand the story even if they recognized less than half of the words on the list. Except for *preparatory school* (which is defined in a footnote), none of these words are essential for adequate comprehension, although each adds color and depth to the story. Spending an inordinate amount of time on learning this vocabulary would detract from the more important and interesting reactions to the plot, theme, and characters of the story.

Criteria for Selecting Vocabulary

Comparison of the word lists in Figures 8.2 and 8.3 suggests that the first step toward maximizing the cost–benefit ratio should be judicious choice of words with which to work. Harold Herber (1978) suggests four criteria to keep in mind when selecting vocabulary: relation to key concepts, relative importance, students' ability and background, and potential for enhancing independent learning.

Relation to key concepts.   There is little point in spending time with a word if it is not necessary to the comprehension of the selection. Many of the words in Figure 8.3 can be eliminated under this criterion. They are not crucial to getting the gist of the narrative or understanding the conflicts in the plot.

Relative importance.   A teacher must decide the relative importance of concepts and terms. For instance, in Figure 8.2, the terms *sexual reproduction* and *asexual reproduction* are the two central ideas in the chapter. Also, some terms have relatively high value outside the specific selection at hand. Since the next chapter in the science text is about genetics, the terms *trait, heredity,* and *clone* will be used frequently in the subsequent lessons. Many terms that students learn even have resonances beyond the school year and beyond a particular content area. Consider, for instance, the cumulative nature of the math curriculum and the importance of math concepts in biology, chemistry, and physics.

Students' ability and background.   Which words are likely to be familiar to most students? What experience will students from diverse linguistic, social, and cultural backgrounds have with the words and concepts? Students with limited proficiency in English may know the words in their native language but not in English. Have any of the terms been studied previously, and will a quick review be enough to refresh students' understanding? What resources or skills do the students have that might allow them to figure out the words themselves? If most students know a word or can easily associate it with something familiar, that word will require less attention. For example, in Figures 8.2 and 8.3, *oyster* and *segregated* might be familiar enough that they would not need much attention.

Potential for enhancing independent learning.   Sometimes when teachers teach specific words and concepts, they also develop strategies, such as context clues, morphemic analysis, or dictionary skills, that students can use to figure out the meanings of other words they may encounter. For instance, discussion of the prefix *re-* in *regeneration* and *reproduction* will help students understand those terms, but it will also give them a strategy for understanding words such as *reaction, recycling,* and *renewable.*

Guidelines for Vocabulary Instruction

Our understanding of the research on vocabulary instruction (Baumann & Kameenui, 1991; Blachowicz & Fisher, 2000; Graves, 1986; Kibby, 1995; Stahl & Clark, 1987) leads us to six guidelines for teaching vocabulary:

1. Start with what students already know, and build new terms and concepts on that.

2. Provide students with multiple exposures to new terms and concepts. A single presentation is rarely enough to convey complex meanings.
3. Involve students in varied activities using new terms and concepts. Active engagement creates interest and strengthens learning; varied contexts help to develop fuller meanings for words.
4. Teach to promote transfer. Concentrate on words and strategies that have the widest possible application to other subjects and other reading situations.
5. Include discussion as one of the vocabulary activities. When students know they may have to explain new terms in their own words, they tend to process the meanings of the terms more thoroughly.
6. Make your classroom a word-rich environment in which students are immersed in rich language and appreciation for the power of words.

The teaching strategies presented throughout the rest of this chapter were selected to meet these guidelines.

Strategies for Introducing and Teaching Vocabulary

This section discusses several strategies for introducing and teaching content area vocabulary. Depending on the number and difficulty of the vocabulary terms in a lesson, teachers may choose to use any of these strategies before students read, while they read and discuss the text in class, or after they have read an assignment as homework.

In-class presentation.   Perhaps the least costly strategy in terms of time, yet still beneficial, is simply presenting students with a list of important vocabulary and briefly discussing each term. For instance, a teacher in an eleventh-grade history class might quickly refer to the following six terms written on the blackboard: *free enterprise, monopoly, trust, holding company, Social Darwinism,* and *laissez faire.* The teacher asks the students if they know any of these terms, then briefly defines each, and finally tells them to pay careful attention to the terms as they read the section titled "The Age of Industry" for tomorrow's class. A simple presentation such as this may be all that is required if there are relatively few terms, if they are clearly explained in the text, and if students have sufficient ability.

Semantic mapping.   One strategy has attracted more attention than any other as a means of introducing new vocabulary, perhaps because it is so versatile and because nearly a decade of research has shown it to be effective (Baumann & Kameenui, 1991). The basic idea is to place key terms into a diagram, sometimes called a *semantic map* or semantic web (Johnson & Pearson, 1984). Key words are arranged in clusters that represent the way in which semantic information is organized in one's memory. The main topic is at the center, with related concepts radiating outward from it (Figure 8.4).

A semantic map is most effective when it is developed with students' input and discussion. The example in Figure 8.4 was constructed for a tenth-grade

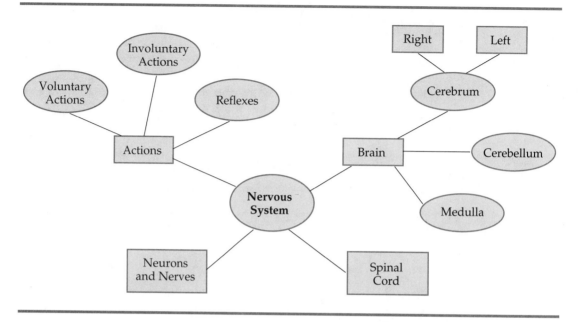

FIGURE 8.4   Semantic map of the nervous system for a tenth-grade biology unit

general biology class. The teacher told students they would be studying the nervous system next and wrote those two words on the blackboard. She then asked students what they knew about the nervous system—what its function was, what the various parts were, and how they were related. As students came up with terms like *brain* and *nerves,* she added them to the growing semantic map on the board, along with terms that she added and defined herself, such as *neurons.* Through questioning, students were able to give examples of *voluntary* and *involuntary actions* and *reflexes.* Finally, the teacher added the terms for the various parts of the brain and explained each one briefly. Students copied the resulting map into their notebooks and referred to it frequently as they worked through the chapter. Another version of the semantic map, called the *graphic organizer* (Barron, 1969), was introduced in Chapter 6.

Concept of definition map.   Readers often have trouble giving their own definitions for words because they do not have a fully developed concept of what a definition is. Word maps have been used to teach students about three types of information that together make up the concept of a definition (Schwartz & Raphael, 1985; Schwartz, 1988). As students discuss a particular term, they are asked to consider the *category* in which it falls ("What is it?"), its *properties* ("What is it like?"), and *illustrations* of the term ("What are some examples?"). A completed *concept of definition map* is shown in Figure 8.5. Using such a map, students should be able to write a full definition of the term. Once students are

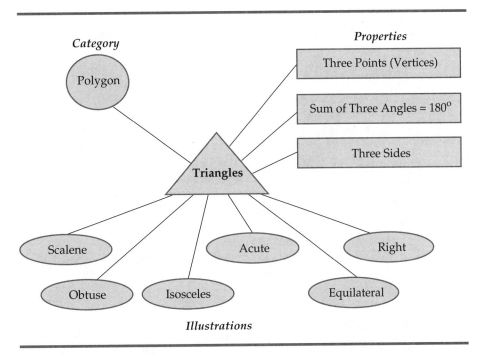

FIGURE 8.5   A concept of definition map on triangles for an eighth-grade math class

familiar with the concept of definition map, they can develop definitions for one or two words in small groups and report their work to the whole class.

Semantic maps and graphic organizers have been successfully adopted by many teachers, who see several advantages to them. When students are involved in discussing and developing a semantic map or graphic organizer, they are able to combine their prior knowledge with new information. The map or diagram also allows them to see the interrelation of the concepts they are studying—how one idea fits with another. These techniques have a solid research base. They have been shown to be particularly effective with students of diverse reading abilities and ethnic backgrounds (Baumann & Kameenui, 1991) because they allow students to use their background knowledge and experience in learning new vocabulary.

Semantic feature analysis.   Another strategy for teaching vocabulary that has been effective with diverse student groups is *semantic feature analysis* (Anders & Bos, 1986; Baumann & Kameenui, 1991; Bos et al., 1989; Johnson & Pearson, 1984). Semantic feature analysis helps students see relationships among key concepts and vocabulary, particularly the many dimensions of meaning that may be associated with a particular term.

The example given in Figure 8.6 was developed by Lavon Smith, a teacher of ESL in Athens, Georgia, for a reading assignment on health and diet. In the leftmost column of the grid, Lavon listed various foods and included spaces for students to fill in other favorites. Across the top of the grid, he listed several characteristics of foods that students were going to be reading about and discussing. He gave each student a copy of the grid and also displayed a copy on the overhead projector. First, the class went down the left-hand column and discussed each kind of food listed, practicing pronunciation and making sure that all students understood the terms. Then Lavon reviewed the words written across the top of the grid, briefly defining the terms *protein, cholesterol, ethnic,* and *gourmet.* The discussion of ethnic food elicited a lot of enthusiastic participation from this ethnically diverse group, and Lavon pointed out how many ethnic foods had become staples in the American diet. As they talked, the group marked each box on the grid. A plus (+) signified a positive relationship between two terms (e.g., beef has animal protein). A minus (–) meant a negative relationship (e.g., egg roll is not eaten raw). A question mark (?) indicated that the class was unsure of the relationship. Lavon left these decisions up to the

Food	Has animal protein	Has choles-terol	Fattening	Has added sugar	Very healthful	Often eaten raw	Ethnic food	Fast food	Junk food	Gourmet food
Beef										
Mars Bar										
Egg										
Carrot										
Salmon										
Apple										
Egg roll										
Hamburger										
Whole milk										
Whole wheat bread										

FIGURE 8.6   Semantic feature analysis grid for a reading assignment on health and diet for an ESL class (*Source:* Lavon Smith, Athens, Georgia.)

class. For some columns, such as "Fast Food" and "Junk Food," there were diverse opinions. After the students had completed discussion of the feature analysis grid, they were assigned a four-page reading in their ESL reader. As they read, the students verified or revised their responses on the feature analysis grid. The next day they discussed the grid again as a whole class, paying special attention to the previously unknown relationships.

Possible sentences. Possible sentences (Moore & Moore, 1992; Stahl & Kapinus, 1991) is a technique that requires relatively little preparation time but is quite effective for getting students actively involved in discussing, writing, and reading, all focused on key vocabulary terms. It works as follows:

1. Identify six to eight key vocabulary words and list them on the board. Pronounce each word for the students. For instance, as an English teacher you might select the words *game, deterred, preparatory school, resignation,* and *scholarship* from the short story "The Lie" (Figure 8.3).
2. Also list a few key words that are likely to be known by students. In this case, you might use *rich, education,* and *examination,* all words that are important in the story.
3. Ask students to make up sentences using at least two words from the list. This can be done in small groups or individually. Record the student sentences on the board until all the words on the list have been used at least once. It does not matter if some words are used incorrectly. The following are possible sentences using the examples listed previously:

   You can get a good *education* at a *preparatory school.*
   She thought the *examination* was just a *game.*
   He *deterred* his *education* until after he got out of the Army.
   After he won the lottery, he was so *rich* he submitted his *resignation.*

4. Ask students to speculate what the story might be about. Students then read the text, looking for the targeted vocabulary terms. They verify whether or not their sentences are "possible." That is, are the words used in the same sense in which they are used in the story?
5. Have students participate in either small-group or whole-class discussion to reach a consensus on whether their sentences are possible. If they are not, they are amended or refined as needed. A dictionary may be used if the context of the story does not yield a satisfactory meaning.
6. As a final step, ask for new sentences using at least two of the words. This reinforces the meanings of the words and gives students yet another exposure to them.

Visual associations. It is often easier to remember a new word and its meaning if one can connect it with a strong visual image. Verbal–visual associations are often recommended as particularly useful word-learning strategies for ELLs (Herrell, 2000; Echevarria, Vogt, & Short, 2000). Gary Hopkins (Hopkins & Bean, 2000) used a strategy he called vocabulary squares to teach roots and prefixes to junior and senior high school students at Lame Deer High School on the Northern Cheyenne Reservation in Montana. He drew a square and subdivided it into four panels. (An example of a vocabulary square is shown in Figure 8.7.) In the first panel, he wrote a root or prefix that he wanted students to learn. In the second panel, he wrote the dictionary definition. The third panel featured an example of how the root or prefix was used in a word. Then he drew a picture to illustrate the example in the fourth panel.

After modeling the vocabulary square for students, Hopkins had them copy it in their notebooks. Thereafter, he posted a new root or prefix each day and asked students to complete their own vocabulary squares. After some initial resistance from students who were used to more traditional vocabulary worksheets, he found that student interest began to increase. Students talked with each other about their choices of examples and drawings, thereby reinforcing their understanding of the target morphemes. The vocabulary squares appealed to different learning styles: some students liked the sequential, verbal aspect of the definitions and examples, whereas others preferred the drawing. Overall, Hopkins found a higher level of engagement in vocabulary learning which was verified when most of his high school students were able to score 90% or higher on a vocabulary quiz.

Instead of roots and prefixes, vocabulary squares could be modified to teach content area vocabulary terms. The first panel would contain the target word, the second square the dictionary definition, and the third square could feature a sentence using the word. Then an illustration would again go into the remaining space.

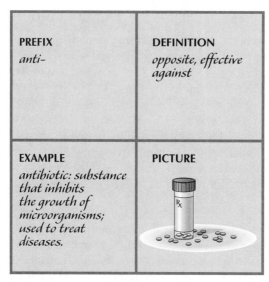

FIGURE 8.7   **Vocabulary square**

Selling words.   Teachers should be "wordmongers," or sellers of words. Learning vocabulary is not just a matter of strategies and instruction, costs and benefits. There is an affective dimension, too. Students need to have fun with words, to become "word-aware" and "word-curious." As good role models, teachers can nurture appreciation of words. Teachers can "sell" words by discussing connotations and ingenious usages, exploring word histories and derivations, and sharing new additions to their personal lexicon. Appendix A presents a list of books that deal with vocabulary in various content areas. Teachers might include some of these books in their classroom libraries and refer to them during class discussions. Looking up word histories, acronyms, and interesting or amusing words is a good activity for odd and idle minutes when the teacher is taking attendance or when a student has finished a test or seatwork assignment before the rest of the class. Teachers can also generate interest and appreciation for language by playing with words in riddles, puns, and language games. Several of the books in Appendix A illustrate the humor of language use and misuse. Other examples of the interest, power, and humor of words can come from newspaper clippings and cartoons.

DEVELOPING STUDENTS' INDEPENDENCE

Teachers should try to teach more than the terms needed on the next test; they should also emphasize strategies that readers can use to deal with unfamiliar words in other contexts. This section examines some vocabulary-teaching techniques that also reinforce word-learning strategies that readers can use independently.

Using Context Clues

When we discussed how readers learn vocabulary, we said that context clues are useful but sometimes misleading. Despite the potential difficulties in relying on context, there is ample evidence that instruction in using context clues is effective, both for learning the meanings of specifically targeted words (Buikema & Graves, 1993; Konopak et al., 1987) and for deriving the meanings of words generally (Jenkins, Matlock, & Slocum, 1989; Nagy & Scott, 2000). Instruction in using context clues is especially effective if it is combined with direct instruction in the meanings of specific words.

Target words in sentences.   A teacher can present target words in sentences that are either taken directly from the text or composed by the teacher. The sentences can be shown to students on the chalkboard, the overhead, or a handout. Some teachers initially cover or omit the target words and encourage students to predict the meanings of the words from the context. Students should talk about how they arrived at their predictions. That is, what in the context suggests what the target words mean? This kind of discussion helps make students more aware of how context can help with unfamiliar words.

When presenting words in sentences, the teacher must ensure that the context is rich enough to imply the meaning of the word. For example, of the following two sentences, only the second one suggests that a pinafore is an item of clothing:

1. Marcia had a new *pinafore.*
2. Marcia couldn't wait to wear her new *pinafore* to the party.

The teacher may use more than one sentence in order to fully convey the nuances of meaning in a word. Consider the following examples:

1. In England, the title of duke is *hereditary* and is normally passed on to the oldest son.
2. Many of your physical characteristics, such as skin, hair, and eye color, are *hereditary.*
3. Personality may be partly *hereditary* and partly a result of how a person is brought up.

Comparing the ways in which the word *hereditary* is used in the three sentences allows students to develop a more detailed understanding of what is or is not hereditary.

Target words in text.   A teacher can help readers use context clues by calling attention to specific words in the text. In a study with eleventh graders, Konopak et al. (1987) underlined difficult words in a passage on the Civil War taken from a social studies text. Students were told to look for these words as they read and to attempt to write a meaning for each, based on clues in the text. Another group of students read the same text that did not have the target words underlined. The group that was intentionally looking for the target words learned more than the control group.

Instead of underlining words, a teacher can provide a word list with page numbers. When the text gives relatively rich clues, this is a fairly quick and easy method of alerting students to important terms and helping them find the meanings. A postreading discussion then focuses on what students think the words meant and what clues from the text they used.

Knowledge rating.   To introduce a list of potentially unfamiliar words, teachers can use a strategy called *knowledge rating* (Blachowicz, 1986). Figure 8.8 presents a knowledge rating chart developed by Gretchen Bourdeau, a sixth-grade science teacher, as an introduction to a chapter on astronomy. Students who thought they could define a word checked the first column, "Know it well." Students who had heard or seen a word but were unsure what it meant checked the second column, "Heard of it." If the word was completely unfamiliar, students checked the "Clue-less" column. Students were told to jot down the meanings of "Know it well" terms on the backs of their papers. They were especially motivated by this activity because it was all right not to know an answer.

RATE YOUR SPACE KNOWLEDGE		
	Know it well	**Heard of it**	**Clueless**
aurora			
galaxy			
quasar			
big bang theory			
black hole			
pulsar			
neutron star			
supernova			
corona			
sunspot			
fusion			
prominence			
Milky Way			
telescope			
red giant			
nebula			
solar flare			

FIGURE 8.8   **A knowledge-rating chart for a sixth-grade science lesson**
(*Source:* Gretchen Bourdeau, Oglethorpe County Middle School, Georgia.)

After they had worked on their own for about 15 minutes, Ms. Bourdeau led the class as they developed a list of the terms they knew and discussed what these words meant. Of the 17 terms, there were only three for which all the students were "clueless": quasar, big bang theory, and prominence. Gretchen defined these for the class and noted that these three would need special attention as they continued their study of astronomy. At the end of the class period, students left the class with an awareness of how much they already knew about this new topic, a firm understanding of most of the vocabulary, and a significant investment of interest and attention. In the following days, as they read and discussed the chapter, the class confirmed, altered, or expanded on their understanding of these terms.

Wide reading.   If most vocabulary learning is a result of exposure in context, it follows that people who read widely and regularly will develop larger vocabularies than those who only crack a book under duress. For this reason, regular independent reading is frequently suggested as the most effective vocabulary-building strategy (Nagy, Herman, & Anderson, 1985). Many content area teachers encourage students to read beyond their textbooks by assigning projects that require outside reading and by frequently sharing content-related books and articles with students. (Using literature in content areas is the subject of Chapter 1.)

Using Familiar Word Parts

Students can learn many words by morphemic generalization, especially when they use it in conjunction with context clues (Blachowicz & Zabroske, 1990; Wysocki & Jenkins, 1987). Through the intermediate grades and into high school, the number of words in content areas that are built with common roots and affixes increases dramatically. Therefore, it makes sense to help students by teaching them the strategy of morphemic analysis and by teaching them directly many of the important building blocks of the English language.

Teaching morphemic analysis.   When a new term is made up of familiar or easily analyzable parts, students should be led to infer the meaning. Good examples are *reproduce* and *regeneration* from the list in Figure 8.2. Once attention has been drawn to the prefix *re-*, students can be asked for other *re-* words they know. A general meaning for the prefix can then be derived from words such as *rebuild* and *repay*. The next step is to ask what other familiar parts they see in the two new words, leading to a discussion of *produce* and *generate*. Finally, the class can derive possible meanings for the two words.

Not all words are made up of familiar parts, however. Teachers can still help students by directly teaching the meanings of selected morphemes, as Gary Hopkins did in the vocabulary squares activity discussed previously. If students learn that the root *gen* in *regeneration* refers to "birth" or "species," they will have a clue to the relationship among the various meanings of *generation* and related words such as *gene, genetics,* and *generic.*

Etymology.   When a teacher and students talk about the meanings of roots and affixes, they are essentially discussing the origin and history of words. This is called *etymology* (from the Greek word *etumen,* which means "the real or true sense of a word"). There is much more to etymology than the study of roots and affixes, however. Although it is not strictly an independent word-learning strategy, the study of word origins can help students remember word meanings and can create motivation for word learning. Figure 8.9 lists some examples of interesting word origins. Teachers might share these origins with students or ask students to investigate their histories in a good college-level dictionary or in one of the etymological dictionaries listed in Appendix A.

It is especially interesting to consider the contributions to American English that have been made by various nationalities and ethnic groups and to see how the language is constantly being enriched by borrowing from many vital language communities. For example, as English-speaking immigrants first encountered the Americas, they borrowed Native American words for the many places and things they were seeing for the first time. As a result, American English has more than 300 loan words from Native American languages, primarily those of the Algonquian language family (Carver, 1991).

Regional variations in language are another source of interest. In New England, for instance, a freshwater stream is called a brook. In the north or northwest, it is called a creek (which may rhyme with leek or trick, depending on regional preferences). In New York State, along the Hudson River, it may be called a kill, a Dutch derivation. In Kentucky it is called a branch. In Louisiana, it would be called a bayou, a word the French borrowed from the Choctaw natives.

"People" words:	Acronyms:	Borrowed words:			
chauvinism	snafu	*Spanish:*		*African:*	
watt	NATO	fiesta	alligator	banjo	yam
arachnid	radar	macho	patio	jazz	phony
		mesa	ranch	tote	zombie
"Place" words:		canyon	hammock	okra	
jersey		*Native American:*			
tweed					
madras		racoon	squash		
china		kayak	hickory		
		tomato	potato		
		moccasin	chocolate		

FIGURE 8.9   **Origins of a few English words**

Vocabulary on the Internet

The Internet provides many vocabulary resources. References, word origins, and word games suitable for all grade levels and content areas can be found at the sites listed here. For more vocabulary Internet applications, see our Web site at http://www.ablongman.com/alvermann3e.

Merriam Webster WWW Dictionary
http://www.m-w.com/dictionary.htm
Dictionary, thesaurus, word of the day, word games, and more.

OneLook Dictionary
http://www.onelook.com/index.html
OneLook Dictionary uses more than 3 million words from more than 600 hundred dictionaries; includes entries from dictionaries in English, French, German, Italian, and Spanish.

World Wide Words
http://www.worldwidewords.org
World Wide Words is devoted to the English language—its history, quirks, curiosities, and evolution; new words, weird words, questions and answers, and many articles on the English language.

Take Our Word for It, the Weekly Word-Origin Webzine
http://www.takeourword.com

Common Errors in English
http://www.wsu.edu/~brians/errors/errors.html
Includes a lengthy list of commonly misspelled words and misquoted phrases; a great quick reference guide for young writers.

Word Pitfalls
http://www.amherst.edu/~writing/wb_html/misused_words.html
A list of frequently misused words, usages "that make you look stupid," and words Faculty Say They Don't Want to Read Again, Ever.

Fake Out
http://www.eduplace.com/fakeout/
An interactive game that challenges students to correctly guess definitions. The game changes every week. For real word fanatics, there are archives of past challenges.

Vocabulary.com
http://www.vocabulary.com/index.html
A great place for games and puzzles that promote word power. The site includes thematic word puzzles on a range of topics set up by grade level.

In Arizona, it would be an arroyo, a Spanish word. Linguistic borrowing and variation are natural language phenomena; awareness of them helps students to appreciate the multicultural nature of American society and the fact that English is alive and perpetually changing.

Using Dictionaries

"Look these words up in the dictionary and write a sentence for each one." How many times do you think that assignment has been given in American schools? In many content area classes, it is the only vocabulary-teaching strategy ever employed. In desperation, students often respond to the "look 'em up and write" assignment by finding something familiar in the dictionary definition, inventing a sentence that includes the familiar term, and substituting in the word they are supposed to be learning. Here are some typical results (Miller and Gildea, 1987):

> I was *meticulous* about falling off the cliff. (meticulous: careful)
>
> Our family *erodes* a lot. (erode: to eat out, to eat away)
>
> Mrs. Morrow *stimulated* the soup. (stimulate: to stir up)

We believe that the teachers who made those assignments got pretty much what they deserved.

The best use of the dictionary is in conjunction with other strategies that encourage students to anticipate or predict word meanings. Strategies such as context clues, morphemic analysis, knowledge rating, and vocabulary self-collection are discussed in various sections of this chapter. The dictionary or glossary is a means for confirming guesses or clarifying meanings, and the dictionary definition is just one of the multiple exposures that students need in order to master a word. Information from the dictionary becomes a part of the class discussion, and the teacher can immediately help clear up any confusion over what the dictionary says.

Given that most middle-grade and secondary students have mastered the basic skill of finding a word in the dictionary, we suggest that content teachers enhance "look 'em up" assignments by modeling and giving students occasional guided practice in the following dictionary skills:

1. *Finding variant parts of speech:* For example, *incredulity* (Figure 8.3) is not a main entry in the *American Heritage Dictionary.* It is listed instead at the end of the entry for the adjective *incredulous.* Teachers need to show students how to find the word and lead them to "translate" from the adjective to the noun.
2. *Matching the dictionary with the context:* A character in the short story *The Lie* discusses a situation "with growing incredulity." If *incredulous* means "disbelieving or skeptical," what does this phrase mean? Why might the character be incredulous?
3. *Deciding which definition fits:* In one dictionary, the word *game* has 13 definitions. Which one fits the phrase "a game, ambitious woman"?
4. *Using the information and abbreviations in an entry:* In addition to definitions, dictionary entries may also give the part of speech of a word, variant spellings, the derivation, pronunciation, and synonyms or antonyms.

When students know *how* and *when* to use a dictionary, it becomes a natural adjunct to learning new words. Keep in mind that looking up a word in the dictionary is disruptive and time-consuming. Few adult readers run to the dictionary for every unfamiliar word, and it is unrealistic to expect students to do so. When a student asks for help with a word, telling him or her to "look it up" is probably less effective than simply providing a quick definition.

Vocabulary Self-Collection

Martha Haggard (1982, 1986) describes a simple but effective method for getting students to become more "word-aware." As they read, students identify words they think the class should learn. After reading, they compare and discuss the terms they identified. The procedures for *vocabulary self-collection* are as follows:

1. Each student team identifies a word that is important for learning content information. The teacher also identifies one word.
2. The teacher writes the words on the chalkboard as teams give definitions from context.
3. Class members add any information they can to each definition.
4. Teacher and students consult references for definitions that are incomplete or unclear. Final definitions are derived.
5. Students and teacher narrow the list to arrive at the final class list.
6. Students record the class list and agreed-upon definitions in their journals.
7. Students record any additional personal vocabulary in their journals.
8. Words from the class list are used in follow-up study activities.
9. Words are tested as they apply to content information.

These steps are suggested for small teams of students involved in reading content area textbooks, but they can be modified in several ways. Different teams may take responsibility for finding and teaching vocabulary on different days or in different sections of the text. Once they are familiar with the procedure, students may collect vocabulary terms individually in their content area notebook or learning log. The teacher can expand vocabulary self-collection outside the classroom and textbook by asking students to bring in and share content-related words collected from other sources.

Teachers should scaffold vocabulary self-selection by modeling their own strategies for selecting vocabulary as well as how they use context, morphemic analysis, or the dictionary to help determine word meanings (Blachowicz & Fisher, 2000). They can point out words that they have selected and explain to students how they decided the relative importance of the words. They can also demonstrate how to use textbook vocabulary aids such as bold-faced type, contextual or side-bar definitions, pronunciation keys, chapter vocabulary lists, and glossaries.

We think vocabulary self-collection is one of the most efficient and effective strategies for developing word knowledge. Preparation time is minimal and in-class time can be adjusted to meet students' needs. Self-collection shifts the responsibility for identifying and teaching vocabulary from the teacher to the students. This has several significant benefits. First, students are likely to identify different words from those the teacher might pick, ones they identify as unfamiliar yet important. Second, compared with teacher-compiled vocabulary lists, word study through self-collection is more motivational, more directly related to students' prior knowledge, and more actively involves students in their learning. Third, by selecting and discussing vocabulary on their own, students increase their sensitivity to words and develop new strategies for word learning. Vocabulary self-collection is recommended as an especially effective strategy for ESL students.

Intensive Approaches for Special Cases

The teaching strategies presented so far have been fairly economical in terms of preparation and presentation time. For some students, especially those who have reading difficulties or limited proficiency in English, a more elaborate approach may be appropriate.

Students with reading difficulties tend to be dramatically less "word-wise" than capable readers, and less adept with printed language in general (Blachowicz & Fisher, 2000). They often know fewer words and have a less complete understanding of the words they do know (Shefelbine, 1990). Poor readers also have difficulty reconciling differences when a word appears in varied contexts and are often unsuccessful in mastering a word in context, even when a definition is provided (McKeown, 1985). This is a classic case of "the rich get richer, the poor get poorer." Good readers know more words, are more adept at learning new words, and read more, thus learning even more words. Those with reading difficulties have less success with using context and read less, thus falling further behind.

Blachowicz and Zabroske (1990) describe an intensive year-long program developed for middle-grade remedial readers. Together, teachers and students compiled a list of the types of context clues that helped them with word meanings. Students were shown how to use a four-step process:

1. *Look* before, at, and after the word.
2. *Reason* about what is already known and what is in the text.
3. *Predict* a possible meaning.
4. *Resolve* by trying again or consulting a person or a dictionary.

The students worked with context clues throughout the school year. Activities included direct teacher modeling, class discussion, frequent practice, and writing. Although using context was the major focus of instruction, these students were actually involved in an intensive program of heightened word awareness. Words, word meanings, and ways of learning words were emphasized throughout the year. In addition to context, students also considered roots and affixes, dictionary definitions, and word histories. By the third month, student teams began to lead weekly vocabulary lessons, identifying words and leading their peers to use the strategies they had developed. They also invented a contest called "Mystery Word." A photocopy from a book, magazine, or newspaper on which a word was highlighted was posted. Students wrote down what they thought the word meant and what clues they used to figure it out. At the end of the day, the student team who had posted the word reviewed all the guesses with the class and consulted a dictionary if necessary to resolve uncertainty about the meaning.

Small Puppies, Big Dogs, and Real Reading

Alfred Tatum (2000) describes a multifaceted approach to teaching a class of eighth-grade struggling readers in a Chicago school. These African American adolescents, assigned to the class because of low reading test scores, were reluctant to read, seldom finished assignments, refused to respond, and equated "reading" with worksheets, assessment questions, and chronic inadequacy. This was Tatum's dilemma: subjecting students like these to isolated skill instruction only serves to deepen their sense of failure and alienation, but trying to engage them in meaningful reading experiences is frustrating because of their lack of skills.

Tatum identified three major barriers to student success: fear of embarrassment, lack of word attack ability, and limited vocabularies. To reduce the potential of embarrassment, he set about building a supportive classroom community in which the difficulty of reading could openly be acknowledged, miscues were considered part of learning, and students could be actively involved in teaching each other and assessing their own progress.

Within this supportive community, Tatum offered a balanced instructional program that featured skill and strategy instruction along with reading of fiction, nonfiction, and poetry relevant to the African American experience, materials that challenged students to think and talk about their social and cultural traditions. Students read and discussed each selection with a partner three times before whole-class discussions and written follow-up. The teacher guided class discussion and modeled comprehension strategies such as self-questioning and constructing graphic organizers.

Because the students had great difficulty decoding words, their attention was too often diverted from comprehension. To help with this, Tatum began an intensive study of syllables and phonogram patterns, what the students called "attacking the small puppies (syllables) to get to the big dogs (multisyllabic words)." Each day, he selected several multisyllabic words from their readings and taught students how to break them down into syllables and then blend them together into their correct pronunciations. Students were given varied activities to practice decoding and encoding these words.

Pronunciation and spelling were not the only goals, however. The meanings of the words were discussed, their use in the literature selections was highlighted, and students were encouraged to use them in writing and class discussion. The class thought up excerpts from songs to help them remember the meanings of some words. (For example, *reciprocate* was associated with "It's the big payback" from a song by James Brown.) The words on the word wall were continuously reviewed and vocabulary tests were given every other week. More than 450 multisyllabic words ended up on the word wall, and all but a handful of the students could recognize and spell words such as *ambitious, cognizant, mediocre,* and *indefatigable.*

The combination of intensive word study and culturally relevant literature brought about a dramatic shift in both students' attitude and competence. At the end of the year, 25 of 29 students, all of whom started the year several years behind grade level in reading, were promoted to high school by meeting the requirement of a grade-equivalent score of 7.0 on the Iowa Test of Basic Skills.

English language learners.   Vocabulary will present special challenges to students who are learning English as a second language. Students in ESL or bilingual education classes often have a difficult time making the transition to mainstream content area classes. Even when students appear to have developed English fluency in social situations, they may need more time to develop academic proficiency with the language. Some authorities estimate that it may take as long as five or more years for students to develop academic proficiency (Cummins, 1994). Students may nevertheless be expected to pass district or state examinations in content areas, with little or no accommodation made for their language status. Vocabulary has a particularly adverse affect on ELLs' performance on such testing (Fitzgerald, 1995; Garcia & Pearson, 1994).

ELLs are likely to have more difficulty than native speakers with deriving meaning from context (Lebauer, 1985.) They will need a substantial core vocabulary to facilitate contextual learning (Blachowicz & Fisher, 2000). Although English or bilingual dictionaries can be very helpful for ELLs, they may prove frustrating for some students who cannot find inflected forms of words or who find inadequate or confusing definitions (Gonzalez, 1999). Figurative or idiomatic usages and unknown connotations will be especially problematic. Marie Vande Steeg (1991) relates the problems her high school ELLs had with life science vocabulary such as *tissue* and *organ;* some thought tissues were for blowing noses and organs were played in church. A partial or incorrect understanding of a word may interfere with understanding an entire passage. As noted elsewhere, cultural differences may also underlie some misunderstandings.

On the other hand, students who are learning English have many strengths on which they can draw. Their basic reading processes are substantially similar to those of native speakers, although they may use certain strategies less effectively and more slowly. Among the strategies that bilingual students use in reading are the transfer of reading skills and background knowledge across languages, monitoring of comprehension, looking for cognate words, using context, and making inferences to determine word meanings (Fitzgerald, 1995; Jimenez, Garcia, & Pearson, 1996).

Teaching ELLs requires some general considerations in regard to vocabulary. Among these are patience and anticipation that there will be many unknown or confusing words, help with recognizing cognate vocabulary, and careful development of students' prior knowledge. To help students with limited proficiency in English succeed, many schools have established *sheltered English classrooms,* in which content is taught with the help of gestures, visual aids, and hands-on experiences. A sheltered English classroom operates on the following principles (Pierce, 1988):

1. The focus is on meaning rather than form. Students' language miscues are not overtly corrected.
2. Simplified sentences and controlled vocabulary are used.
3. Content area concepts are presented using a variety of clue-rich contexts, such as demonstrations, visual aids, maps, and experiments.
4. Students are involved in content-related conversational interaction.
5. New students are allowed a "silent period"; they do not have to speak until they are ready.

If you review our discussion of sheltered English teaching in Chapter 4, it will be apparent that vocabulary activities are particularly well suited to sheltered English classes. Sheltered English content classes should provide an environment in which ELLs get frequent and varied exposures to new words and concepts. Teachers can model correct usage of vocabulary terms and paraphrase difficult text passages. They can also tailor the selection of vocabulary to the needs of ELLs by focusing on a few key terms rather than a long list of words and by having students keep individual word study books.

In her life science class, in which nine different languages were represented, Marie Vande Steeg (1991) had her students use their senses to help them learn. When studying cells, they made gelatin cells using fruits and vegetables as organelles. As they ate their gelatin cells, they drew them on the board and explained them. Students ate carrots, sweet potatoes, and other root vegetables when they were studying roots. The teacher had a lab assistant make popcorn in the back of the room to illustrate the concept of diffusion. When students smelled the popcorn, the principle of diffusion became easier to understand.

For a review of important concepts, Vande Steeg printed scientific sentences on cards with one word to each card. She gave packets of these sentence strips to students, who arranged them to make scientifically (and grammatically) correct sentences. She also printed scientific vocabulary on index cards and gave them to cooperative-learning groups to discuss. After a designated amount of time, groups took turns sharing their words with the whole class.

Many of the teaching strategies suggested throughout this book are appropriate for sheltered English classes. Development of speaking and listening skills can be aided by engaging students in small-group work such as problem solving, science experiments, or preparation of skits. New material should be presented at a slow pace, with as much visual reinforcement of concepts as possible. Reading materials should be simplified or written at low readability levels, and reading assignments can be enhanced by strategies such as anticipation guides, reading guides, and discussion webs. Specific vocabulary strategies described in this chapter that are especially appropriate for ELLs include semantic webs, semantic feature analysis, concept of definition maps, word walls, sorting words, vocabulary self-collection, and vocabulary squares (Echevarria, Vogt, & Short, 2000; Herrell, 2000). Writing activities such as summarizing and taking dictation can reinforce the main points and vocabulary of a lesson. Learning logs serve as an excellent low-risk means for students to practice their English writing skills.

Mary Blake and Patricia Majors (1995) found that ELLs of intermediate proficiency can benefit most from holistic instruction that reinforces new vocabulary through reading, writing, listening, and speaking. They suggest a five-stage instructional process:

1. *Prereading activities:* The teacher presents selected vocabulary, leads students to practice pronunciation, and gives students definitions. Other activities, such as knowledge rating, semantic mapping, or semantic feature analysis, could be used as well.

2. *Oral reading and responses:* Students and teacher take turns reading aloud with periodic stops for comprehension. Targeted vocabulary is given special attention. Students may write about the selection in their learning logs.

3. *Focused word study:* Students work with individual study cards that include the target word, a meaningful sentence, a definition, and perhaps the word written in the students' first language. Students play word games. They could also use any of the various vocabulary-reinforcing activities that are described in the next section.

4. *Evaluating word knowledge:* Students are quizzed on their understanding through crossword puzzles, cloze passages with definitions provided, and other formats.

5. *Writing workshop:* The teacher models a written summary or short composition that uses as many of the target terms as possible. The final step of the process is for students to brainstorm, draft, and revise their own written pieces featuring the new vocabulary.

In content area classes with a large proportion of non–native English speakers or students reading significantly below grade level, intensive focus on vocabulary is beneficial. If such students make up a small portion of the population, a support program can be instituted by a reading specialist, special education teacher, or ESL teacher and coordinated with content area teachers. Motivating such students to think about and acquire new words may be one of the best strategies for helping them overcome reading difficulties, especially if the program is combined with ample opportunities to practice reading independently.

REINFORCING VOCABULARY

Whether vocabulary terms are briefly presented, discussed after reading, or form the focus of one of the more elaborate teaching strategies we have described, it is often desirable to give students additional independent practice to reinforce the words they are learning. This may be done through discussion, writing, pencil-and-paper exercises, or computer activities. This section describes several different kinds of vocabulary reinforcers.

Matching Activities and Puzzles

The simplest type of reinforcing activity requires students to match words with their definitions. Teachers often use matching exercises after vocabulary has been introduced, either before or after students read a text selection. Presenting matching activities in the format of a crossword puzzle or other type of self-correcting activity adds a motivational dimension. There are many computer programs that can generate word puzzles for duplication or completion at the computer.

One type of word puzzle, sometimes called a *bubblegram,* is illustrated in Figure 8.10. This exercise can be simplified by adding a word list from which students choose the appropriate terms. Word puzzles should be edited carefully to make sure that the clues yield words that match the spaces provided. For instance, the first clue in Figure 8.10 is "smallest blood vessels." Enough spaces should be provided for students to write the plural form, *capillaries.* Similarly, if the clue calls for a verb form (*digested*), the puzzle space should not require the noun or adjective (*digestion* or *digestive*).

Matching activities, in whatever format, are limited in that they only require students to associate a word with a definition. Although this may be useful, it does not by itself guarantee that students will master the concepts associated with the words, the possible variations in meanings, or the association between terms.

Categorizing Activities

In some vocabulary reinforcers, students are asked to consider the relationships among various terms by deciding how they might be categorized. In order to decide what words do or do not go together, students must know more than definitions.

In a particularly difficult chapter on geometry in an eighth-grade math text, more than 60 technical terms are introduced. The chapter is typical of much math material because the vocabulary is cumulative. Terms that are introduced at the beginning (*line, angle, point,* and *vertex*) must be thoroughly understood because they are used throughout the chapter. A math teacher could help students review for a chapter test by giving them the vocabulary reinforcer in Figure 8.11.

Sorting words is a very simple but effective categorizing activity that encourages active student involvement. In pairs or small groups, students are given a list of words to sort into meaningful categories. Using selected geometry terms from Figure 8.11, for instance, the teacher might tell students to sort words into the categories "angles," "polygons," "triangles," and "circles." For a more challenging activity which would result in a greater variety of responses, students could simply be given words to sort without predetermined categories. Each group would then have to explain their arrangements.

Analogies

Analogies are another powerful tool for helping students see relationships among vocabulary terms. The traditional form of the analogy sets up a parallel relationship between four terms: A is to B as X is to Y. Several types of analogous relationships, with examples, are presented in Figure 8.12. The key to these analogies is the various relating factors. The relationship on one side of an

BUBBLEGRAM

Directions: Use the clues on the lower half of the page to identify the words. The letters in the circles will spell out the Mystery word at the bottom of the page.

1. ◯ __ __ __ __ __ __ __ __ __ __
2. __ __ __ __ __ ◯ __ __ __ __
3. __ ◯ __ __ __ __ __ __
4. ◯ __ __ __ __
5. __ ◯ __ __ __ __ __ __
6. __ __ __ __ __ ◯ __ __ __ __
7. __ __ __ __ __ ◯
8. __ __ __ __ ◯
9. __ ◯ __ __ __ __ __
10. __ ◯ __ __ __ __ __ __ __ __
11. __ __ __ ◯ __

Clues:

1. smallest blood vessels
2. lower heart chambers that pump blood to the body
3. vessels to carry blood away from the heart
4. smallest living parts of the body
5. thin-walled upper chambers of the heart
6. combines with oxygen in the lungs
7. liquid portion of the blood
8. main organ of the circulatory system
9. food broken down into usable parts
10. another name for blood cells
11. vessels to carry blood to the heart

MYSTERY WORD: __ __ __ __ __ __ __ __ __ __ __

CLUE: What goes around comes around.

FIGURE 8.10   A bubblegram for reinforcing vocabulary on the circulatory system for a sixth-grade science class (*Source:* Arlene Giolando, Martin Luther King School, Buffalo, New York.)

VOCABULARY REINFORCER

Directions: In each group of words, there is one word that does not belong with the others. Cross it out. Then pick a word from the "Labels" list to describe each group of words. You must be able to tell how the words are related.

1. _____

acute
right
line
obtuse
vertex

2. _____

sphere
pyramid
polyhedron
cube
parallelogram

3. _____

prism
arc
chord
radius
diameter

4. _____

triangle
trapezoid
rhombus
circle
pentagon

5. _____

scalene
diameter
isosceles
equilateral
congruent sides

6. _____

complementary
perpendicular
90°
supplementary
right triangle

Labels

RIGHT ANGLE
LINES
ANGLES
TRIANGLES

POLYGONS
CIRCLES
CONGRUENT
3-DIMENSIONAL FIGURES

FIGURE 8.11   **Categorizing vocabulary reinforcer for an eighth-grade geometry lesson**

analogy must parallel the relationship on the other side. In order to be logically correct, term A must bear the same relationship to term B that term X has to term Y. Thus, the relating factor of "Places" in Figure 8.12 is that Sacramento and Springfield are the capital cities of their respective states. The relating factor between "Action : Object" is that the stomach digests food, while the lungs breathe air. Analogies can be fairly difficult for teachers to devise and students to complete, but they are quite effective for reinforcing thinking skills and conceptual understandings.

Figure 8.13 provides an example of the use of analogies to reinforce vocabulary for a high school biology assignment. After reading and discussing the chapter, students worked in small groups to complete the analogies. Then the

Part to Whole
noun : subject :: verb : predicate

Synonym/Antonym
obscure : vague :: potent : strong
affluence : poverty :: safety : peril

People
Gandhi : India :: Martin Luther King : America
Samuel Clemens : Mark Twain :: Theodore Giesl :
   Dr. Seuss

Places
Sacramento : California :: Springfield : Illinois
Fredericksburg : Confederates :: Gettysburg : Union

Dates
1776 : United States :: 1917 : Russia

Degree
hot : searing :: cold : frigid

Cause and Effect
virus : measles :: bacteria : food poisoning
drought : starvation :: flood : devastation

Characteristic
credit card : finance charge :: loan : interest

Action/Object
digest : stomach :: breathe : lungs

Function
legislature : make laws :: judiciary : interpret laws
keyboard : enter data :: disk drive : store data

FIGURE 8.12   Types and examples of analogies

VOCABULARY REINFORCER

Directions: Fill in the blanks with the word from the list below that best completes the analogy. Be able to explain your answer.

   Example: beagle : dog :: robin : bird
   Read the line as follows: Beagle is to dog as robin is to bird.

1. circulation : blood :: streaming : _____
2. capillaries : earthworm :: _____ : grasshopper
3. open circulatory system : grasshopper :: closed circulatory system : _____
4. protists : cyclosis :: hydra : _____
5. grasshopper blood : colorless :: earthworm blood : _____
6. single-celled : amoeba :: multicellular : _____
7. grasshopper : heart :: earthworm : _____
8. transport across cell membranes : _____ :: transport within a cell or organism : circulation
9. slow : fast :: open circulatory system : _____
10. earthworm : circulation :: protist : _____

Word List

earthworm	hemoglobin (red)	hydra
cyclosis	closed circulatory system	absorption
sinuses	aortic arches	cytoplasm
diffusion		

FIGURE 8.13   A vocabulary reinforcer using analogies for a high school biology unit   (*Source:* Ruth Major, School 81, Buffalo, New York.)

class went over the reinforcer, with groups taking turns explaining the reasons behind their responses and the relationship among the four terms.

Before students are asked to work independently with analogies, we suggest that teachers discuss analogies with them and give them several simple examples so that they become familiar with the format and the relating factors. It would also be helpful to work through the first item or two on an analogy reinforcer.

There are various ways to use analogies in content areas. The teacher might provide students with the entire analogy and ask them to explain the relating factor. Another possibility is to have students create their own analogies with vocabulary from their texts. James Middleton (1991) gives students a worksheet similar to the one illustrated in Figure 8.14 after they have had several exposures to the vocabulary terms. Notice that this worksheet requires students to look for analogous relationships but does not ask them to devise a formal analogy of the $A : B : : X : Y$ format. That could be done, however, once students have had sufficient exposure to formal analogies. The examples in Figure 8.14 would be

transpiration : water in plant : : suction : water in straw
nucleus : cell : : brain : animal

Vocabulary term	Is like: (everyday process, object, another biological term)	How? (Make a sketch or explain.)
1. transpiration	water in a straw	evaporation pulls water through xylem like suction pulls water through a straw
2. nucleus	brain	the nucleus controls the cell like a brain controls an animal
3.		
4.		

FIGURE 8.14   **Analogies worksheet**   (*Source:* Adapted from J. Middleton, Student-generated analogies in biology. *The American Biology Teacher, 53,* 42–46, 1991.)

Middleton also includes analogy items on quizzes and tests. For example, one test item might look as follows (Middleton, 1991, p. 44):

amino acid : protein

(a) speak : laugh
(b) hammer : nail
(c) flour : cake
(d) black : white

Here, the correct answer is c, because the relating factor is part : whole. Middleton notes that these types of questions are especially valuable for high school students because they are featured on standardized tests such as the SAT.

Using vocabulary in writing.   Several of the vocabulary teaching strategies we have described involve writing. Using a new word in writing helps to reinforce its meaning and also gives students a greater feeling of confidence in their understanding. Students can use new terms in their learning log jottings, in written summaries, or in other kinds of writing assignments devised by the teacher. Cindy Borowski, a math teacher, has her students use new math vocabulary to write their own word problems. An example from one of Cindy's students is given in Figure 8.15.

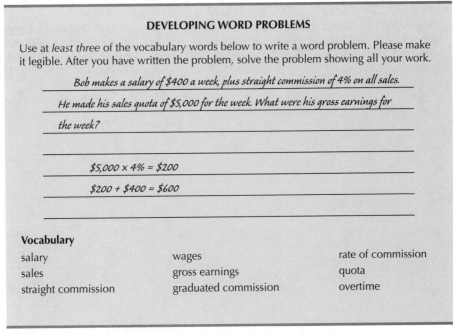

DEVELOPING WORD PROBLEMS

Use at *least three* of the vocabulary words below to write a word problem. Please make it legible. After you have written the problem, solve the problem showing all your work.

Bob makes a salary of $400 a week, plus straight commission of 4% on all sales.

He made his sales quota of $5,000 for the week. What were his gross earnings for

the week?

$5,000 × 4% = $200

$200 + $400 = $600

Vocabulary

salary	wages	rate of commission
sales	gross earnings	quota
straight commission	graduated commission	overtime

FIGURE 8.15   **Using vocabulary in writing**   (*Source:* Cindy Borowski, Frontier Central Schools, Hamburg, New York.)

SUMMARY

Content area texts introduce many new and difficult concepts, usually represented either by unfamiliar words or by familiar words used in new ways. The conceptual load of a single chapter or even a single page can be quite heavy, and the effect is cumulative. Mastering a term introduced on one page may be a prerequisite for grasping other terms presented on the next page. The demands of content area vocabulary can be especially daunting for students who are not very good readers or lack proficiency in English.

Given the pressures of extensive curricula, limited time, and a wide range of student abilities, teachers need vocabulary strategies that can yield the greatest benefit in student learning with the least cost in planning and instructional time. Many effective strategies for introducing and reinforcing vocabulary meanings have been presented in this chapter. Students learn best when they encounter new words in various contexts, when they can relate new words to their previous experiences, and when they have varied opportunities to use new words in discussion, in writing, and in practice.

SUGGESTED READINGS

Blachowicz, C., & Fisher, P. (1996). *Teaching vocabulary in all classrooms.* Columbus, OH: Merrill.

Blachowicz, C., & Fisher, P. (2000). Vocabulary instruction. In M. Kamil, P. Mosenthal, P. D. Pearson, & R. Barr (Eds.), *Handbook of Reading Research, Volume 3* (pp. 503–523). Mahwah, NJ: Erlbaum.

Nagy, W. (1988). *Teaching vocabulary to improve reading comprehension.* Newark, DE: International Reading Association.

Pittleman, S., Heimlich, S., Berglund, R., & French, M. (1991). *Semantic feature analysis: Classroom applications.* Newark, DE: International Reading Association.

Responding
to Reading

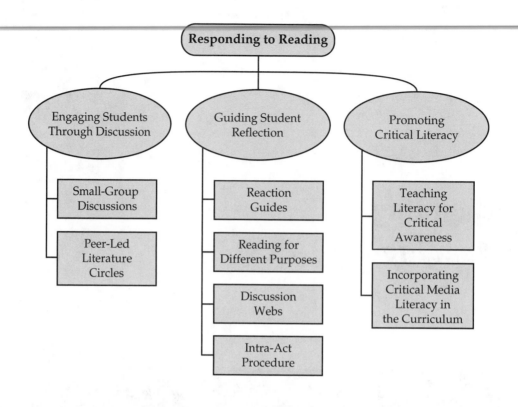

Responding to Reading

- Engaging Students Through Discussion
  - Small-Group Discussions
  - Peer-Led Literature Circles
- Guiding Student Reflection
  - Reaction Guides
  - Reading for Different Purposes
  - Discussion Webs
  - Intra-Act Procedure
- Promoting Critical Literacy
  - Teaching Literacy for Critical Awareness
  - Incorporating Critical Media Literacy in the Curriculum

▼▼

M ost of you can probably remember a teacher whose class you looked forward to because you knew you were going to have a chance to think, to talk, and to come up with new and sometimes surprising ideas. Maybe it was a history teacher who helped you see the relevance behind the dry dates and names of people and places. Perhaps it was a math teacher who helped you think like a mathematician for an hour or so each week. It might have been a science teacher who gave you a little shiver when you realized how complex, how systematic, and yet how mysterious our world really is. Whatever the subject, the memorable teacher was probably one who had high expectations and for whom you worked hard. That teacher may be the very one you keep in mind as you seek a model for your own efforts in the classroom. Perhaps it was someone like José Gonzalez, a teacher in an urban high school in which nearly 40 percent of the students come from Hispanic backgrounds.

▼▼▼▼▼▼▼

Mr. Gonzalez is leading a discussion of four stories that the class has read. The stories are quite different, written from the 1930s to the 1990s by authors from Argentina, Spain, Mexico, and Puerto Rico. Most of the 15 students are of Puerto Rican background, about half of them born in the United States. A few are recent immigrants from Central America. They have varying degrees of English proficiency, but in this class there are no language barriers to discussion, for the class is conducted entirely in Spanish. Mr. Gonzalez is particularly interested in preparing these students for success in college. As he tells a visitor, "I want them to think; I want to treat them like adults."

Mr. Gonzalez begins by asking questions about "El Cuento," the story most recently read. At first only two or three students respond as they talk about the basics of plot and character. But then they come to the most dramatic moment of the story—the death of a child—and more students become animated. Students begin talking to each other, and Mr. Gonzalez talks less, interjecting occasionally to arbitrate disputes, include other students in the discussion, or pose an alternative point of view. He asks students to reflect on similarities and differences in the social and political views of the several authors. The discussion also touches on contemporary social issues, especially those he knows are relevant to his students' lives.

During the 45 minutes of the class, the discussion ebbs and flows. At any one time, only a few students seem to be actively participating, but the individual discussants change as students engage in the conversation, argue their point of view for a while, and then drop out to reflect and listen. The atmosphere in the class is relaxed and informal, but the discussion is thoughtful, the participants animated, the listeners attentive. Nearly every student there has something to offer during the class, and it is obvious the students enjoy being treated like adults who have important thoughts to share.

▼▼▼▼▼▼▼

Mr. Gonzalez leads his students to make connections, draw conclusions, and extend their thinking in many directions. Although he shares many of his own ideas, the emphasis in this class is on what students think. According to many critics of education, too little of this sort of teaching is done in American schools. Middle and secondary schools too often place a premium on rote learning. Reading and writing assignments, class activities, and examinations too often require an accumulation of facts and largely ignore higher levels of thinking.

By placing an emphasis on what his students think as they discuss what they have read, Mr. Gonzalez is scaffolding their understandings of the four texts. Through discussion, he is helping them make connections between literature and their everyday lives. According to Judith Langer, a well-known researcher and teacher educator, many teachers find it difficult to let go of the traditional classroom response pattern in which they initiate a question, a student responds, and they in turn evaluate that response (the IRE pattern). Langer tells teachers with whom she works that learning new response patterns, such as the one Mr. Gonzalez uses, is like "getting new bones" (Langer cited in Allington & McGill-Franzen, 2000). Difficult as it may be, we believe that the effort spent doing so will pay dividends in the end. In fact, there is research to suggest that students at the middle and high school level view discussions which invite a wide range of responses as helping them comprehend what they read (Alvermann et al., 1996). This finding also seems to hold for ESL and bilingual learners as well as for students typically served through inclusion programs (Floriani, 1993; Goatley, Brock, & Raphael, 1995).

In this chapter we consider some ways that a teacher can encourage students to think beyond the facts in the text, to reflect on what they have read. What exactly is meant by "reflecting on reading"? What are the "higher orders" of thinking and reading? Different authorities give different and frequently confusing answers to these questions (Kennedy, Fisher, & Ennis, 1991; Kirby & Kuykendall, 1991). Rather than presenting an exhaustive list of reading or thinking behaviors, we echo Shirley Brice Heath (1991), who argues that true literacy goes beyond limited ends such as filling out worksheets and answering multiple-choice examination questions. She suggests that a truly literate individual "can compare, sequence, argue with, interpret, and create extended chunks of spoken and written language in response to a written text" (p. 3). A reflective reader can talk or write about what he or she has read and, in the process, come up with new meanings and new ideas, often quite different or even opposed to those intended by the author. Such a reader, Heath says, is "an individualist, a reflective skeptic, a questioner, a doubter, an arguer, and an observing bystander" (p. 12), roles very much like those taken on by students in Mr. Gonzalez's literature class.

The ability to read and think reflectively does not generally develop naturally; as with other learning, students must be given models, support, and continued practice. Cultural differences may be a factor in developing reflective thinking, and they should also be taken into account. Heath (1991) notes, for instance, that in many African American and Mexican American working-class communities, learning occurs through demonstration and apprenticeship, and there is a natural expectation that different people within the community will have different talents. There is less of a premium placed on individual effort and achievement and more reliance on the group itself. In the increasingly diverse classrooms of the present, teachers should try to incorporate what their students do know and can do. Specifically, teachers need to provide "expanded opportunities to interpret texts orally and to negotiate meanings in communal settings" (Heath, 1991, p. 19).

The strategies included in this chapter are generally designed to integrate reading, thinking, and oral language. Although a fair amount of writing is also involved, we have saved those strategies that focus primarily on writing as a means of reflecting, inquiring, and summarizing for Chapter 10. In this chapter, we first suggest some ideas for grouping that teachers might consider when engaging students in discussions of various types of texts. Later, we offer several classroom-tested strategies for guiding students' reflections and then discuss ways of promoting critical literacy, including critical media literacy.

ENGAGING STUDENTS THROUGH DISCUSSION

Important as they are to student engagement in general, cognitive and motivational factors alone cannot fully account for students' willingness to participate in academic tasks that require reading for meaning. The culture of the classroom clearly plays a significant role in how readily students are willing to engage in reading and follow-up discussion groups. Small-group discussions and peer-led literature circles are two aspects of classroom culture that hold promise for engaging students in reading and learning from texts.

Small-Group Discussions

In a whole-class discussion, only a few students can participate at any one time. In such a situation, it is difficult to avoid domination of the discussion by the teacher and a handful of articulate students. In Chapter 3, we discussed various ways to group students. Small-group learning complements many of the goals of teaching in culturally diverse classrooms. When students work on a task in small groups, more individuals have an opportunity to voice their ideas in greater detail. A greater diversity of views and beliefs on a topic can be expressed. Small-group discussion also reduces the competition between individual students and promotes group interdependence and a sense of community.

Students learning English as a second language have more opportunity to practice their language skills, to learn technical vocabulary, and to benefit from peer teaching. Finally, small-group discussion activities allow students to assume and practice a variety of important roles. They may be proponents, devil's advocates, mediators, researchers, summarizers, task-minders, monitors, or spokespersons. Sometimes these roles may be assigned, but more often than not they emerge as part of the natural processes of the group.

Roles, although important, are not the first things that students mention when they are asked what makes a good discussion. Based on our interviews from a multicase study of classroom discussions in middle and high school classrooms throughout the United States (Alvermann et al., 1996), we know that students are well aware of the conditions they believe are conducive to effective discussions. First is the importance of small-group discussion. The students we interviewed said that small-group, unlike whole-group, discussions provide them with greater opportunities to voice their opinions. For example, in their own words:

John: I kind of like those [small groups] because you don't have to fight over, you don't have to wait and wait and wait before you have a chance to talk. You only have like five people in the group and everybody is close enough to hear you, so you just kind of say your thing when you feel like it.

Alice: The small group is kind of nicer [sic] because it is more personal and people kind of listen to you more and get interested in it.

Christy: It seems like it takes forever for [the teacher] to call on me, and by that time we have gone on to another subject, by the time I get to say anything [in whole-class discussions].

Melanie: It [whole-group] gets me nervous to talk in front of a whole lot of people about, like, opinions and stuff. But then, small group, it's like me and my friends, so it is easier. (p. 254)

Classroom cultures that support students' perceptions of a good discussion have a second characteristic in common. According to the adolescents whom we interviewed, students should have a say in how small discussion groups are formed and the rules for participating in them. Students prefer to choose their own working groups and to make rules that will guard against off-track discussions due to members not having read their assignments in advance. Although characterizing effective small-group discussions in this way is hardly news, it is noteworthy that in the classrooms we observed in which students had a hand in setting discussion practices, peer-group pressure was an important factor in how the groups used talk to mediate their comprehension of assigned materials. Overall, they were adamant in their belief that they had a better understanding of what they read when they listened to their peers discuss a selection.

A particular form of small-group discussion that bears special mention here is the instructional conversation (IC), which offers teachers a way to engage students in the academic language of the various content areas (Tharp & Gallimore, 1989). Advantages of the IC include the opportunity to structure discussions so that student talk occurs much more often than teacher talk and focuses on the content language, concepts, and vocabulary of particular subject matter. The IC is especially beneficial to ELLs who may have achieved considerable proficiency in everyday language but need more time and instruction to gain competency in using academic language. By accepting students' preferred participation formats, teachers remain sensitive to variations in cultural background (Tharp, Dalton, & Yamauchi, 1994) while at the same time responsive to what students need to know about academic language in a specific content area. Teachers who are adept at using the IC are guided by what Dalton (1998, p. 30) describes as the "three-checks":

▸ *Clarification:* Teachers ensure students' understanding (e.g., Are we clear?).
▸ *Validation:* Teachers provide opportunities for students to explain their reasoning (e.g., How do you know?).
▸ *Confirmation:* Teachers encourage students to negotiate with each other about what meaning to construct from the text (e.g., Do we agree?).

Implementing small-group discussions. Some teachers worry about implementing discussion activities designed to limit their talk while increasing the number of opportunities for student talk. Generally, they are concerned that their classrooms will become noisy and unfocused and that students will spend too much time "off task," socializing instead of working. In an attempt to reassure teachers that this need not be the case and that the alternative—a virtual lack of student talk—is just as worrisome (especially for struggling readers), consider the following true story told by Janet Allen (1995), a veteran teacher of 20 years:

As Allen (1995) goes on to explain, initiating and sustaining "that sea of talk . . . didn't come naturally" (p. 112). She had to work hard at involving the struggling readers in her class who were long accustomed to suppressing their opinions for fear of being laughed at by peers or made to feel inferior in other

Immersing Struggling Readers in a "Sea of Talk"

In my 20 years of teaching I had found that students in lower tracks were often relegated to classrooms that had virtually eliminated talk. I certainly understood teachers' hesitancy about involving students in discussions. I have many memories of trying to build and sustain conversation in remedial classes—experiences that haunt my dreams to this day. In seconds one comment can spark another's anger, and fists compensate for an inability to disagree with words. I also knew that if I continued a practice based on silence and worksheets, I was denying students access to a system based on one's ability to use language. Whatever it took to help students become able to carry on conversations, whether about books or life, I was willing to try. . . . Jan Duncan, a New Zealand educator, says that in our classrooms, "Reading and writing should float on a sea of talk." (Allen, 1995, p. 112)

ways. That she did succeed, however, was in no small measure due to her ability to plan and involve students in their own learning. From our own experiences, we know that effective small-group discussions are the product of thorough preparation and deft on-the-spot facilitation by the teacher. Here are several things we recommend doing:

1. *Assign clear and manageable tasks.* Before they begin work, groups must have a clear idea of what they are to accomplish.
2. *Prepare and guide students for the task.* Be sure students have enough background information. It may be necessary to model, or walk them through, a similar activity before they try the task on their own.
3. *Set limits.* Tell students how long they have to complete their task and how much they are expected to produce. For instance, say, "You have ten minutes to come up with two different solutions to this problem." If a task has several steps, remind students occasionally how much time has elapsed and where they should be in the process.
4. *Monitor and assist group work.* As students talk, move around the room to observe, question, encourage, and, when necessary, to keep groups focused and progressing on their task. Draw out reticent group members and make sure that more voluble participants give others a chance to speak. It is especially important (but difficult) to avoid actively participating in groups yourself. When you contribute substantively to the workings of a group, you defeat the very purpose of cooperative learning, which is to have students develop ideas on their own.
5. *Moderate a whole-class follow-up.* Let the various groups share and compare their conclusions and reasoning.
6. *Be a model.* During both small-group and whole-class discussions, model thought processes, good listening, tolerance, and ways to handle conflict.

Peer-Led Literature Circles

A literature circle occurs when a group of youngsters come together to read and discuss a common book (Daniels, 1994). The discussion, which is peer led, typically is conducted by a discussion director whose job it is to prepare a list of questions for the group to answer. Others in the group assume roles such as the connector (responsible for connecting the text to everyday life experiences or to other texts), the word or phrase finder (responsible for locating language in the text that is colorful, unusual, funny, etc.), the literary luminator (responsible for identifying sections of the text the group might find interesting to read aloud), and the illustrator (responsible for visually representing his or her favorite part of the story, sharing it with other members of the group, and receiving their feedback). Students alternate in these roles so that everyone has responsibility for guiding the discussions in different ways over time.

An underlying assumption of peer-led literature circles is that young people will take responsibility for their own learning when they are given choices and sufficient structure in which to implement those choices. The teacher's role is one of facilitator and guide in getting the groups to function on their own, which includes deciding how much reading will be done for the next group discussion and the roles each member will play in the discussion. Although literature circles and "book clubs" (McMahon & Raphael, 1997) are similar in their goals and the procedures for implementing them, the two are distinct enough to require separate discussions. The book club program, for example, is particularly useful in integrating content knowledge and the language arts, whereas literature circles are more focused on responding to books from a literary perspective.

Recently, literature circles have been used to stimulate students' interests in reading in their second language. For example, Claudia Peralta-Nash and Julie Dutch (2000) initiated cycles of literature circles over an entire school year to engage Julie's bilingual classroom in reading and discussing books in both Spanish and English. What they discovered was that Spanish-dominant youngsters were more apt to take risks and join groups reading an English novel when they had the support of their group (self-chosen) to do so. Likewise, English-dominant students were more apt to choose books written in Spanish when they participated in discussions in which both Spanish and English were used to discuss a book selection.

Although peer-led literature circles may be slightly stilted at first, after students have had sufficient practice in making choices and assuming responsibility for organizing and carrying out discussions on their own, the creativity unleashed by these circles is considerable (Burns, 1998; Peralta-Nash & Dutch, 2000). For example, in the culminating book projects that are frequently a part of literature circles, students are encouraged to analyze a book's storyline for underlying assumptions, to imaginatively create alternative solutions to a protagonist's problems, and to make text-to-life connections by exploring a literary theme in relation to their own lives. This type of activity closely parallels the triarchic theory of intelligence (Sternberg & Grigorenko, 2000), which is steadily

Professional Growth Opportunity

To learn more about the triarchic theory of intelligence and how a working knowledge of multiple intelligences can be incorporated into instructional decision making and assessment that is fair to diverse types of students, subscribe to *The National Research Center on the Gifted and Talented Newsletter* (NRC/GT, 2131 Hillside Road, U-7, Storrs, CT 06269-3007) or check out the center's Web site at http://www.gifted.uconn.edu).

gaining empirical support for its thesis that an individual's abilities are not fixed but instead can be developed just like any other form of expertise. When applied to instructional practices, a triarchic theory of intelligence has been shown to support teaching practices that require students to analyze, create, and process what they read rather than merely memorize it.

GUIDING STUDENT REFLECTION

In our experience, students usually appreciate genuine opportunities to flex their thinking muscles. The results are not always predictable; adolescents can be quirky and extravagant in developing their opinions. The concept of cognitive apprenticeship is especially pertinent here. The teacher can be a model of reflective thinking, guiding and supporting students as they think about and beyond the text. With persistence and a measure of tolerance from the teacher, students can develop their independent reflective powers.

Content teachers have found a number of activities that promote reflective thinking, student interaction, and the application and extension of ideas. The strategies presented here are adaptable to various content areas and age levels. Each one encourages students to think and talk about what they have read, and each one has the potential to lead to thoughtful writing as well. Reflective thinking is not just for gifted and talented students or those who are academically proficient; there is ample research evidence suggesting that students of all intellectual ability levels can benefit from instruction in higher levels of thinking (Haney & Thistlethwaite, 1991; Kennedy, Fisher, & Ennis, 1991; Sternberg et al., 2000).

Reaction Guides

When class members have completed a reading assignment, watched a videotape or movie, or attended a dramatic performance, how does the teacher get them to talk about their reactions, with special attention to one or two issues, in small groups? To help focus the groups on such a task, the teacher could prepare a *reaction guide* similar to the reading guides discussed in previous chapters.

A reaction guide can be tailored to lead students' thinking along various paths. The teacher might want students to engage in an intensive analysis of the text or performance, or the goal could be to stimulate a more far-reaching reaction. In the guide shown in Figure 9.1, the teacher wanted students to respond to some of the specific incidents in the movie *Conrac*. He also wanted them to relate the ideas from the movie to the ongoing unit theme of prejudice, which they had been reading and talking about for the past two weeks.

To create a reaction guide, first identify a few key ideas or possible lines of thought you would like students to pursue. It is probably best to avoid crowd-

---

REACTION GUIDE: *CONRAC*

I. Directions: Identify the character in the movie who made each statement. We have talked about prejudice based on age, sex, social class or group, race, and religion. If you think the statement shows prejudice, write in the kind of prejudice you think is involved.

1. "Colored children need the whip."
   Character? _____
   Prejudice? _____
2. "We (teachers) are overseers, and things are tough on overseers."
   Character? _____
   Prejudice? _____
3. "You got that thin white skin. I don't have that advantage. So I just try to please the man."
   Character? _____
   Prejudice? _____
4. "Kids don't need trips; they need drill."
   Character? _____
   Prejudice? _____
5. "I'm white and I'm proud."
   Character? _____
   Prejudice? _____

II. Directions: Reflect on what you saw and heard in the movie, and your own experiences. Which of the following statements would you agree with? Be able to give examples to support your choices.

_____ 1. Anybody can learn if he or she is given the chance.
_____ 2. Prejudice is usually too strong for a single person to overcome.
_____ 3. Teachers can learn as much from students as students can learn from teachers.
_____ 4. Things like poetry and classical music are only for the upper classes.

FIGURE 9.1   Reaction guide on a movie for an eighth-grade English class

ing too much into the guide so that students can have time to really explore their reactions. Directions to students should make it clear that they must be able to support their responses. The actual format of the guide is flexible; it may feature questions, statements, or a checklist. Another possibility is to ask readers to respond to polar opposites along a semantic differential scale (Bean & Bishop, 1992). For instance, to guide students' reaction to *The Great Gatsby*, the teacher might ask them to respond on a five-point scale to statements such as the following (Bean & Bishop, 1992, p. 252):

> Nick Carraway _____ Jay Gatsby.
> despised   respected
>   1   2   3   4   5
>
> Gatsby was _____.
> selfish   giving
>   1   2   3   4   5

James Middleton (1991) describes a strategy he uses to promote problem solving and creative thinking among his biology students. He identifies a problem in biology, asks students to think of an analogous everyday problem, and then encourages them to find solutions to both the everyday and the biological problems. The following is an example of this analogical problem solving (p. 45):

> *Biological Problem:* How can we get rid of trapped heat from the greenhouse effect?
> *Everyday Problem:* How can we get rid of heat in a greenhouse?
> *Everyday Solutions:* Punch holes in the greenhouse. Turn on fans.
> *Biological Solutions:* Punch holes in the CO_2 cloud. Create storms in the upper atmosphere.

Reading for Different Purposes

To encourage students to move beyond surface-level understanding and to challenge them to extend and elaborate on the ideas of others, you might ask members of a class to read the same material for different purposes or from different perspectives (Dolan et al., 1979). The procedure works as follows:

1. Assign all students the same material to read. (News stories, editorials, and magazine articles on current issues are particularly well-suited to this activity.)
2. After students have read the material, break the class into groups and give each group a different task, such as the following:
   a. Name an obvious and a less obvious, or hidden, purpose the author may have had.
   b. Determine one relevant and one irrelevant sentence in the text.
   c. Look for evidence of biased reporting or emotive language in the text.

    d. List three fact statements and three opinion statements, and ask students to determine which is which.

    e. Present an alternative argument to one in the text, and ask students to choose the stronger of the two.

    f. Test the author's assertions by referring to other sources.

    g. Devise a set of questions that can be answered only by consulting additional sources.

3. When groups have completed their discussions, a spokesperson for each group presents its findings to the class for discussion. For instance, the first group might ask the class to decide which of the two purposes, obvious or hidden, seems more probable and why.

4. As a follow-up, students can write a summary of their group's issue or perhaps rewrite the text leaving out the irrelevant material or substituting different words for the emotive language.

ACTIVITY   Try reading for different purposes. If you are part of a group, have each person read the following abstract from a journal article for one of the purposes listed; then compare responses. If you are working alone, read the abstract for at least two of these purposes:

1. Read from the point of view of a nutrition expert. How would you critique the abstract?
2. Read from the point of view of an athlete in training for the Olympics. How would you critique the article?
3. Name an obvious and a less obvious, or hidden, purpose the author may have had in writing the article.
4. Find one statement of fact and one opinion.
5. Devise an alternative reason for why determination of the effectiveness of supplements has been hampered.

Active persons ingest protein supplements primarily to promote muscle strength, function, and possibly size. Currently, it is not possible to form a consensus position regarding the benefit of protein or amino acid supplements in exercise training. Determination of whether supplements are beneficial has been hampered by the failure to select appropriate endpoints for evaluation of a positive effect. Furthermore, studies focused at a more basic level have failed to agree on the response of protein metabolism to exercise. An additional complication of dietary studies that is not often taken into account is amount of energy intake. (Wolfe, 2000, p. 551)

This procedure can be adapted or modified to fit different types of reading assignments. To follow up on literature, students can be asked to react from the points of view of different characters. In social studies, groups can take different slants on social issues; they might be asked, for example, to assess the Chicago Haymarket Riot of 1886 from the point of view of the workers, the strikebreakers, the police, the anarchists, politicians, and the general public. Students can also be asked to look at events from different cultural perspectives. For instance, how might Native Americans, Hispanic Americans, and African Americans view the arrival of Columbus or the Emancipation Proclamation? A chemistry class might reflect on a chapter on air pollution from the standpoint of an environmentalist, a Los Angeles automobile commuter, and an employee and an officer of a major manufacturing firm. Members of a class can choose the most important perspectives, or points of view, during a brainstorming session after the initial reading, and these can be assigned to groups for discussion and presentation. As an alternative or a follow-up, different groups can read conflicting accounts of the same event taken from popular periodicals or books (Frager & Thompson, 1985).

Discussion Webs

When students consider more than one point of view, they have an opportunity to reflect and expand their understanding of what has been read. However, when whole-class discussions are monopolized by a few highly verbal students, those who are less glib may be unwilling or unable to think through and voice their opinions. Students who are learning English may have difficulty using their newly acquired language skills in academic settings. Female students especially may be at a disadvantage in classrooms in which male voices and male conversational styles are privileged (Alvermann, 1995/1996; Guzzetti & Williams, 1996).

A discussion web (Alvermann, 1992) can help to structure discussions in such a way that more students have an opportunity to contribute. Discussion webs make it easier to keep a discussion focused and to ensure that discussants support their assertions with relevant information rather than generalizations, emotional arguments, or conversational intimidation. A *discussion web* is a graphic aid that presents a central issue or question along with spaces in which readers can fill in evidence supporting opposing points of view. The example shown in Figure 9.2 has the central question "Was Athens a true democracy?" On either side of the web, there are spaces for students to list reasons for answering no and yes to the central question.

The discussion web is used to encourage discussion and reflection as part of a five-step procedure (Alvermann, 1992):

1. Prepare students for reading using any of the strategies suggested in Chapter 6.
2. After students have read, introduce the central question and the discussion web. Have students discuss the points of view defined by the web in pairs, and take turns jotting down reasons in the two support columns. To ensure that students consider both sides of the issue, instruct them to give an equal number of reasons in each column.

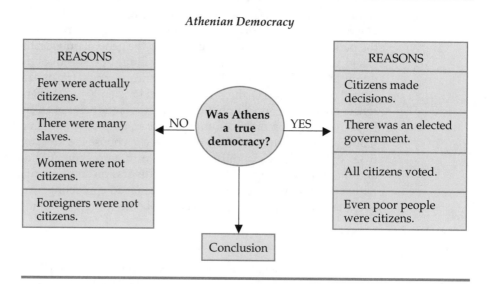

FIGURE 9.2   **Discussion web for sixth-grade social studies unit on Athenian democracy**

3. After students have jotted down a few of their reasons, pair one set of partners with another. To give all group members a chance to participate, ask each of the four to present at least one reason to the rest of the group. Have the new group of four compare their discussion webs and ask them to reach a group conclusion. If all members cannot agree, tell them to develop a dissenting opinion, or minority report, as well.

4. When the groups of four have reached their conclusions, give each group three minutes to present its conclusion, its single best reason, and any dissenting opinion. (If each group gives a single reason, it reduces the likelihood that the last few groups will have little to say.) Finally, open the discussion up to the whole class.

5. As a follow-up activity, have students use their webs and the ideas they have heard presented to write individual answers to the central question.

Many variations on the basic discussion web can be created by changing the labels on the basic structure. The web may be used to stimulate a prereading discussion of students' predictions by using a central "What do you think . . . ?" question and labeling the columns "Prediction 1" and "Prediction 2." In science, students who are preparing to conduct an experiment might generate hypotheses about the outcome and list their reasons in columns labeled "Hypothesis 1" and "Hypothesis 2." In social studies or literature, readers can compare two people or characters. For example, they might compare the positions of Lincoln and Douglas on slavery or think about who was the dominant character in the trip down the Mississippi—Huck or Jim. A discussion web can even help students decide what information is relevant in math word problems. The web shown in Figure 9.3 was designed so that pairs of students could decide which information is needed to solve three problems. Then the pairs were combined into groups of four to compare their decisions and work together to solve the problems.

Intra-Act Procedure

Easily adapted to guide reflection in most content areas, the Intra-Act procedure (Hoffman, 1979) spurs verbal interaction around a group problem-solving task. It derives its name from the inferred *intra*personal dialogue that takes place among individuals who are engaged in an exercise of self-*act*ualization

A Sappy Story

Vermont is one of the country's major producers of maple syrup. There are close to 2,500 maple growers in Vermont, each of whom taps an average of 1,000 trees. About 500,000 gallons of maple syrup are produced each year.

When the sap is running, growers collect it from their trees daily and boil it down to make the syrup. Traditionally, the season for "sugaring," as this process is called, begins on the first Tuesday in March. In reality, though, the sap runs only when temperatures rise to 40°F–50°F during the day and fall to 20°F–30°F at night.

A grower can tap 7,000 gallons of sap from 1,000 trees per season, yielding 200 gallons of syrup, which is then sold at $4.50 per half-pint.

1. On average, how many trees are there per grower?
2. How many gallons of sap are tapped per tree?
3. What is the ratio of the gallons of sap a grower taps to the gallons of syrup made from it, in simplest form?

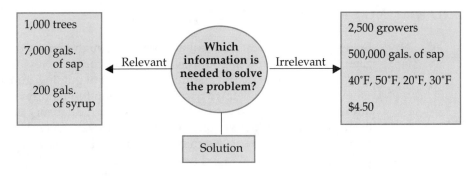

FIGURE 9.3   **Discussion web for eighth-grade math**   (*Source:* Problem from S. Chapin, M. Illingworth, M. Landau, J. Masingila, & L. McCracken, *Middle grade mathematics: Course 3.* Needham, MA: Prentice Hall, 1995.)

leading to concept formation. The Intra-Act procedure was developed during a time in education history when values clarification was at the forefront. Today, we see it being useful as a way to encourage students to reflect on what they read by predicting how the meaning that they construct of a particular text is likely to be the same, different, or some combination of how others in their peer group construct the same message.

The procedure begins with a comprehension activity. Students are asked to read a particular text. For example, they are to read an essay on how Martin Luther King prepared for his now famous "I Have a Dream" speech. After reading the selection silently, they are directed to discuss it with other members of their small group for approximately five to ten minutes. A peer leader starts the discussion by summarizing the selection as he or she understood it, and then others join in with their reactions. At the end of the discussion period, students work individually on a set of four value statements that the teacher has prepared in advance (Figure 9.4). On their copies of these statements, students record whether they agree (A) or disagree (D) with each statement.

In the example provided, Jesse recorded his initial reactions to the four statements by circling A or D next to each statement. Figure 9.4 shows that Jesse disagreed with all but the second statement. It also shows his predictions as to how other members in his group would respond to the various statements, based on how he remembers the discussion in which they were all involved.

In the final phase of Intra-Act, students share their responses to each of the four statements and reflect on whether or not their predictions square with their peers' actual responses. In this phase it is particularly important for teachers to stress that agreement (or lack of agreement) with a statement has nothing to do with that statement's validity as such. It is also important to give students time in this final step to reflect on why they responded as they did and to encourage discussion of their reflections.

PROMOTING CRITICAL LITERACY

Developing adolescents' critical awareness through literacy practices that engage them in interpreting and evaluating all forms of text (print, nonprint, image-based, and verbal) is an important aspect of guiding students in their response to reading. When we use the word *critical* to modify literacy, as in the title of this section, we do so with the notion of critical theory in mind. If critical theory is a relatively new concept for you, or even if you know a great deal about it and its premises, we think you will find Hinchey's (1998) retelling of the following Zen parable and her analysis of it quite helpful.

> In a Zen parable, a young fish asks an elder fish to define the nature of the sea. The young one complains that although everyone talks constantly about the sea, he can't see it and he can't really get a clear understanding of what it is.

SAMPLE SET OF STATEMENTS FOR INTRA-ACT

Date: January 15, 2001

Name: Jesse

Discussion Leader: Yolanda

Group Members

	Jesse		Yolanda		Chris		Kathy	
1 Martin Luther King probably knew the impact his speech would have on people.	A	(D)	A	(D)	A	(D)	(A)	D
2 The times in which MLK lived were similar to present times.	(A)	D	A	(D)	A	(D)	A	(D)
3 A speech writer, not MLK, was responsible for the "I Have a Dream" speech.	A	(D)	A	(D)	A	(D)	A	(D)
4 Any of a number of MLK's friends could have given the speech.	A	(D)	(A)	D	(A)	D	A	(D)

FIGURE 9.4   Sample worksheet for the Intra-Act procedure using an essay on Martin Luther King's "I Have a Dream" speech

The wise elder notes that the sea is all around the young one; it is where he was born and where he will die; it is a sort of envelope, and he can't see it because he is part of it.

Such is the difficulty of coming to understand our own cultural beliefs and how they influence our actions. Like the fish who has trouble understanding the very sea surrounding him, we have trouble identifying the influence of our culture because we are immersed in it and are part of it; we have been since birth and we will be until death—or until an experience with a different culture shows us that things might be other than the we way we've always known them to be.

It is in overcoming this difficulty that critical theory is especially valuable. It offers us a new perspective to use in analyzing our experiences, as the fish would get an entirely new perspective on the sea if he were able to consider it from a beach. The lens of critical theory refocuses our vision of the place we've lived all our lives. As is true of all theory, the usefulness of critical theory is that it helps open our minds to possibilities we once found unimaginable. (Maybe standardized tests aren't reliable. Maybe tracking promotes inequality rather than equality.) Once such heresies are imagined, we can explore them. And maybe in our explorations, we can change the face of the way things *are*, forever. (p. 15)

Indeed, it must be quite obvious by now that when we refer to critical literacy, we mean a form of reading that goes well beyond responding to words on a page. Among other things, "critical literacy makes possible a more adequate and accurate 'reading' of the world" (Lankshear & McLaren, 1993, p. xviii). It provides us, as teachers, with a way of looking at how textual knowledge is taken up and put to use for the benefit of some, but not all, people. It also gives us a way to engage students in analyzing media texts and the audiences for whom those texts are produced.

Teaching Literacy for Critical Awareness

The notion that literacy is on the verge of reinventing itself (Luke & Elkins, 1998) has become more than just a handle on which to hang our observation about the unprecedented and disorienting pace at which texts and everyday literate practices are changing. Increasingly, we find our lives changing in material ways as a result of major shifts in cultural practices, economic systems, and social institutions worldwide. This is a time when literacy educators from around the globe are speculating about the ways in which new technologies will alter our current conceptions about reading and responding to texts of various kinds.

At the center of much of this activity is the perceived need to assist students in their critical awareness of how all texts (both print and nonprint) position them as readers and viewers within different social, cultural, and historical contexts. However, a word of caution is needed here. To attribute a certain innocence to students—to suggest that they do not recognize the very influences we, as teachers, are trying to make them aware of—is to suggest that power is something that can be owned (a piece of property, of sorts) that we can give or withhold. This view of empowerment, although common, is nonetheless problematic, as Australian educator Wendy Morgan (1997) deftly notes in her description of the arrogance and self-defeating practices that can accompany such a view. In arguing that the best intentioned teachers can be misinterpreted, Morgan offers the following example:

> This issue is likely to be particularly pressing for teachers of first-world students, whether "working class" or "middle class," whose forms of life are very different from the illiterate and dispossessed in Latin America or elsewhere. A project to enlighten the former may be self-defeating if it does not take into account . . . their subordination to the teacher's authority within the school . . . [and] . . . their complex productive relationships within their culture. For while their teachers may aim to "emancipate" them from their thraldom to mass mediated culture and capitalist consumerism, such students may accumulate a kind of cultural capital, consisting of a capacity to play the intellectual game and mimic the terms and gestures of their teachers. Granted, all thought is learned and produced within a shaping, constraining context; nonetheless the risk remains that members of a "school of thought" may be merely thinkers similarly schooled. (p. 14)

So what would Morgan (1997) have us do differently? Espousing a postmodern view of critical literacy, she conceives of classroom practices that would abandon the search for villains or heroes in our texts, for the oppressors or the emancipators among us, and for the general labeling of oppositional categories such as "us" and "them." Doing away with these overly simplistic binaries, Morgan argues, would give teachers and students alike the opportunity to "develop a different view of how people may act, provisionally, at a particular time and within particular conditions" (p. 26). It would also give rise to challenging the notion that power is a possession to be distributed at will and substitute in its place the idea that power is negotiated in our social relations with others.

The implications of these different views for facilitating students' responses to what they read were described in Chapter 1 in our discussion of rethinking content literacy practices, multiliteracies (New London Group, 1997), and the New Literacy Studies (Willinsky, 1990). Briefly, and by way of review, when one teaches for critical literacy awareness, it is generally for one or more of the following reasons:

- To motivate students to explore the assumptions authors seem to have been operating under when constructing their messages.
- To facilitate students' thinking about the decisions authors make (and why) with regard to word choice, content (included as well as excluded), and interests served.
- To encourage multiple readings of the same text from different perspectives.

Here, we expand this list by considering how readers respond to hypertext and by inquiring into what critical literacy awareness might look like in this medium. An expert in hypertext literacy, Jay Bolter (1992) has observed that "above all, hypertext challenges our sense that each [text] is a complete, separate, and unique expression of its author" (p. 22). This observation, coupled

Technology Tips for Building Critical Literacy Awareness

▼▼▼

If you are concerned that your students lack know-how in critically evaluating Web sites, check out ways to develop this skill at http://www.anovember.com/articles.zack.html, or for other suggestions on how to teach students to critique the media for bias, access this book's companion site, http://www.abalongman.com/ alvermann3e. For information specific to educating girls to be tech-savvy in today's computing culture, visit http://www.aauw.org or e-mail the American Association of University Women (foundation@aauw.org) for a copy of *Tech-Savvy: Educating Girls in the New Computer Age.*

with the potential for readers to reconstruct an author's text while at the same time leaving tracks for subsequent readers to follow or revise, suggests that teaching for critical literacy awareness with hypertext might take into account the following questions:

- In manipulating the text to meet his or her own desire for information (or entertainment), what do we come to know about the hypertext reader that we would not otherwise know about him or her?
- Are hypertext readings of authors' messages privileged in ways that linear readings are not? If so, what might be the consequences of this privileging?
- How does the associative linking of materials in hypertext create spaces for thinking differently about issues of race, class, gender, ethnicity, sexual orientation, ability, age, wellness, and other identity markers?

Incorporating Critical Media Literacy in the Curriculum

Just as the word *literacy* is used differently in various contexts, so too is critical media literacy. Depending on one's perspective or theoretical frame, the term *critical media literacy* may be characterized as the ability to

- Reflect on the pleasures derived from popular media (e.g., TV, radio, video games, movies, music CDs, the Internet, and cyberpunk culture).
- Analyze how popular media texts shape and are shaped by youth culture.
- Map the ways in which individuals take up popular culture texts differently.
- Uncover the codes and practices that privilege some and silence others.
- Problematize the relationship between audience and mode of media production (Alvermann & Hagood, 2000).

It is important to note that in offering a range of defining characteristics for the term critical media literacy, we deliberately refrained from referring to it as simply visual or critical viewing literacy because both of these viewing practices are constrained by their reliance on the outdated notion that audiences are passive in relation to the media's messages. In guiding students' critical responses to the media, teachers would do well to point out that audiences (such as the students themselves) are typically neither passive nor predictable. In fact, as cultural studies scholars Hall and Whannel (1998) emphasized in their analysis of the entertainment media, "the use intended by the [media] provider and the use actually made by the audience never wholly coincide, and frequently conflict" (pp. 61–62). It is this potential for conflict—the oppositional reading of a media text—that makes it possible for some audiences to perceive Madonna as nothing more than a "boy toy," whereas others observe in her the personification of resistance to patriarchy's definition of what a woman should be, do, and say.

The extent to which school curricula can incorporate literacy practices related to TV, video, computer games, music, comics, and other popular culture forms is yet to be determined (Alvermann & Hagood, 2000). What we do know, however, is that when students are not required to leave their out-of-school literacies at the classroom door, they are eager responders to popular media texts, with a few offering critiques on their own that have surprised even the most seasoned of teachers (Lewis, 1998). Although some educators endorse this blurring of in-school and out-of-school literacies (Alvermann, Moon, & Hagood, 1999; Buckingham & Sefton-Green, 1994), others, although not opposed to the idea, offer a variety of caveats worth considering (Duncan, 1996).

For example, Australian educator Carmen Luke (1997), in alluding to one of the misconceptions that frequently envelops critical media literacy when it becomes part of the school curriculum, noted the following:

> [Asking students to critique the media texts they find pleasurable] is likely to cue a critical response which can often be an outright lie . . . [for while] students are quick to talk a good anti-sexist, anti-racist, pro-equity game . . . what they write in the essay or what they tell us in classroom discussion is no measure of what goes on in their heads. (p. 43)

In similar fashion, David Buckingham (1993) cautioned about the danger of asking young people to critique the very pleasures they derive from popular media texts. He suggests that teachers take time to engage with different media for which they have little or no background experience (such as computer games) in order to get a sense of what their students find so enjoyable. Doing so need not end up in some naïve celebration of popular culture, nor does it necessarily lead to an appropriation of students' outside interests in the service of schooling. Rather, it serves as an introduction to what students value and find motivational. Sometimes that can prove surprising.

For example, when literacy teacher educators Alleen and Don Nilsen (2000) took it upon themselves to investigate the controversial Gameboy version of Pokémon and the trading cards associated with the game, they found that kids were using many school-related literacy skills to improve their game playing. Banned in many schools throughout the United States for distracting kids of all ages from serious learning, the 150 Pokémon, all with their own names and descriptors for how they evolve (e.g., Bulbasaur evolves into Ivysaur, which in turn evolves into Venusaur), are providing much morphemic analysis and spelling practice on the side. The Nilsens also found evidence of literary allusions in the game cards (e.g., Geodude evolves into Graveller, who evolves into Golem, the creature in J. R. R. Tolkien's *The Lord of the Rings*).

Approaches to teaching critical media literacy.   Prior to incorporating critical media literacy into an already full curriculum, most teachers with whom we work want to know what it might look like in their classroom. Figure 9.5 pro-

Approaches to Teaching Critical Media Literacy

Approach	*Perspective*	*Example*
False-Consciousness Ideology	If students knew the detrimental effects of most popular media, they would be wiser consumers.	"Turn off the TV" week-long initiative to call attention to amount of TV young people watch.
Teacher-as-Liberating-Guide	Students are taught how to become "the ideal viewer" so as to avoid the thoughtless consumption of popular media texts.	Media texts are critiqued devoid of any concern about the pleasures that students might derive from them. Teaching becomes a process of demystification.
Pleasures without Parameters	All media texts are equally good. Views and voices from everywhere become views and voices from nowhere; the slippery slope of relativism prevails.	Concerns for students' pleasures override all else; teachers are careful not to require students to analyze and critique that which they like (or don't like).
Self-Reflexive and "Balanced"	Critical media literacy is not merely a cognitive experience; nor is it solely experiencing pleasures without challenges to extend students' learning. Teachers acknowledge several crucial points: the expertise students bring to the learning environment; the pleasures they derive from popular media texts; and the multiple readings students produce from these texts.	Teachers provide opportunities for students to explore how popular media texts position them socially, culturally, materially, and otherwise; the goal is not to spoil students' pleasures in the media but rather to extend their understandings of how things work.

FIGURE 9.5   **Approaches to teaching critical media literacy**   (*Source:* Adapted from D. E. Alvermann, J. S. Moon, & M. C. Hagood, *Popular Culture in the Classroom: Teaching and Researching Critical Media Literacy*, pp. 23–28. Newark, DE: International Reading Association and the National Reading Conference, 1999.)

vides a rough sketch of four different approaches, all of which have their advantages and disadvantages. In studying this figure, it will be helpful to picture a particular class or content area subject in which critical media literacy might seem a "natural" fit. It will also prove instructive to name the advantages and disadvantages of each approach for your particular situation.

It is not only the approaches to teaching critical media literacy that will vary among teachers. Also at variance will be the beliefs teachers hold about what counts as an appropriate response to assigned readings. For example, how much of a student's out-of-school literacy practices that are media related should get through the classroom door? Not sure? Try thinking through the following activity, and if circumstances permit, engage with a small group of your peers to address the issues raised in a reaction paper that Allison Hanson,* a graduate student in Donna's content literacy course, turned in as a class assignment.

ACTIVITY   **What Counts as an Appropriate Response to Assigned Readings?**
First, read the excerpt below in which Allison describes her teenage son's development as a reader and his passion for creating lists. Then, study carefully one of the media–related lists that her son, Paul, created. Finally, pretend that you are Paul's high school English teacher and decide whether or not you would think it appropriate to incorporate Paul's passion for creating media lists as a possible response to a reading assignment that you are planning to make. If you decide it would be appropriate, describe under what conditions you could imagine doing so. If you decide it would be inappropriate, explain why you think so.

EXCERPT FROM ALLISON'S REACTION PAPER

Paul began his quest for literacy in a way that would please any mother (I think). He literally taught himself how to read at four years of age. His choice of texts was a Golden Book story I had bought for him from Winn Dixie when we first moved to Conyers, Georgia. The book, *The Best Christmas Tree Ever*, was about forest animals living in a tree that was overlooked by Santa every year, and how they solved the problem. . . . I remember his second grade teacher talking about him with wonder as she explained how he enjoyed reading the encyclopedias from her class set. He felt compelled to write from encyclopedias for hours at his grandparents' house also. I loved feeding his love for books. . . . He participated eagerly in all of the summer reading programs at the library and was known to check out and devour large chapter books such as the Superman sagas. By middle school, however, his interest in reading books for pleasure fizzled out.

Books were clearly out in middle school, and magazines, catalogues, and video game manuals were in. Paul was also into baseball statistics from collectors' cards and newspapers. While reading a magazine or whatever, he

---

*Used with Allison Hanson's permission.

could be seen on the floor,with his writing journal or notebook paper. He would create lists for hours on end. Pages and pages of players' names and averages, special moves for video game goals, shopping lists complete with product descriptions and prices from mail order catalogues, etc., were spread around his room from corner to corner. His literacy habits have really not changed a lot since.

Although he's now a senior in high school, there is a clear difference between what Paul reads at school academically and what he reads at home for pleasure. He's reading Shakespeare and other "great" literary pieces at school. He tells me that he wishes he could go to a college where he wouldn't have to take English literature. . . . At home he still makes lists for CDs, special computer programming language codes, shoe and clothing catalogue numbers, etc.

Paul's Media-Related List*
Mass Destruction
Ace Combat
Ace Combat II
GPolice x
Street Fighter EX Plw
Soul Blade
Fighters Megamix
WCW vs. The World
WCW vs. Nitro
Dynasty Warriors
Street Fighter Collection
NFL Game Day '98
NHL '98
NCAA Football '98
NBA Action '98
PGA Tour '98
NBA Shoot Out '98
NBA In The Zone '98
NCAA Game Breaker '98
NCAA March Madness '98
Nagaro Winter Olympics
Here's Adventures
Blast Corps
Croc: Legend of the Gobbos
Arkanoid
Space Invaders
Desert Demolition
Ecco: The Tides of Time
Mega Bomberman

---

*Source: Paul Hanson, Senior, Loganville High School

By including this activity here, we are not implying that we think teachers will have the time and resources available for accommodating each and every-one of their students' out-of-school literacy practices, and in particular, those related to the media. However, we do think that the more teachers can learn about such practices, the more likely they will be to appreciate the impact of new technologies on current notions of what counts as reading and responding to texts of various kinds. If the foregoing activity has accomplished no more than that, it will have earned its place in this chapter.

SUMMARY

Teachers at the middle and high school levels are under intense pressure to cover their curricula. It seems that each year local or state authorities add new requirements regarding what should be included in a content area course. It is hardly surprising that some teachers, struggling to cover all the required topics by June, are skeptical when they are told they should also be teaching students how to apply thoughtful and critical strategies as they respond to what they read.

Yet, thinking critically, or the ability to go beyond the text or lecture and use information in productive ways, is arguably more important than much of the information itself. State and national assessments are increasingly focusing on the sort of thinking processes discussed in this chapter. Content coverage and higher-level critical thinking are not mutually exclusive in classrooms where students are involved in talking about what they are reading.

SUGGESTED READINGS

Alvermann, D. E. (2000). Classroom talk about texts: Is it dear, cheap, or a bargain at any price? In B. Taylor, M. Graves, & P. van den Broek (Eds.), *Reading for meaning: Fostering comprehension in the middle grades* (pp. 136–151). New York: Teachers College Press.

Gilbert, P. (1988). Stoning the romance: Girls as resistant readers and writers. *Curriculum Perspectives, 8*(2), 13–18.

Golub, J. N. (2000). *Making learning happen: Strategies for an interactive classroom.* Portsmouth, NH: Boynton/Cook.

Knobel, M. (1999). *Everyday literacies.* New York: Peter Lang.

Miller, S. M., & Legge, S. (1999). Supporting possible worlds: Transforming literature teaching and learning through conversations in the narrative mode. *Research in the Teaching of English, 34,* 10–64.

Muspratt, S., Luke, A., & Freebody, P. (Eds.). (1997). *Constructing critical literacies: Teaching and learning textual practice.* Creskill, NJ: Hampton Press.

Thornburg, D. (1991). Strategy instruction for academically at-risk students: An exploratory study of teaching "higher-order" reading and writing in the social studies. *Reading, Writing, and Learning Disabilities, 7,* 377–406.

Willis, A. I., & Johnson, J. L. (2000). "A horizon of possibilities": A critical framework for transforming multiethnic literature instruction. Available through Reading Online at: http://www.readingonline.org/articles/willis/index.html

Writing across the Curriculum

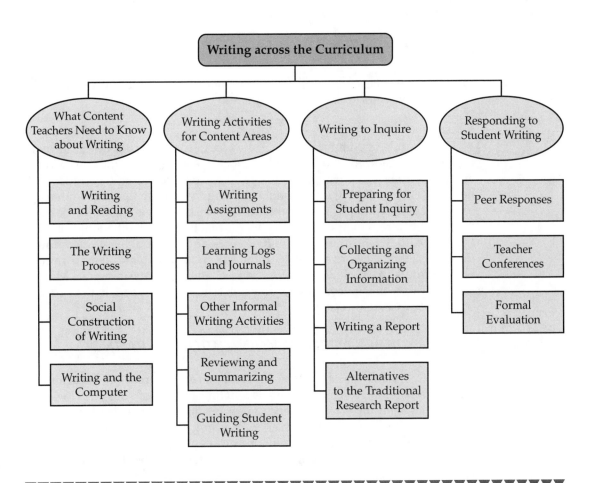

As a powerful tool for thinking, learning, and communicating, writing is an essential component of content area literacy. Donald Murray (1984), a Pulitzer prize-winning journalist and teacher of writing, explains it as follows:

▼▼▼▼▼▼▼

Writing is thinking. Writing, in fact, is the most disciplined form of thinking. It allows us to be precise, to stand back and examine what we have thought, to see what our words really mean, to see if they stand up to our own critical eye, make sense, will be understood by someone else. . . . The writer may write to inform, to explain, to entertain, to persuade, but whatever the purpose there should be, first of all, the satisfaction of the writer's own learning, the joy and surprise of finding what you have to say. . . . Writing can give you power, for we live in a complicated technological society, and those people who can collect information, order it into significant meaning and then communicate it to others will influence the course of events within the town or nation, school or university, company or corporation. (pp. 3–4)

▼▼▼▼▼▼▼

When students commit ideas and knowledge to writing, they must be more thoughtful, organized, and precise than when speaking. When they write for an audience (a teacher, their peers, the recipient of a letter, or the reader of a newsletter), they do so with the understanding that the reader cannot interrupt to ask for clarification or to say whether the message is coming across. Writers must abstract from their thinking the words that best express their meaning. As they write, they have the opportunity to look at their thoughts written down, decide whether they are adequate to their purpose, and alter them in various ways. Writers make choices, make changes, and make meaning. As Murray (1984) says, writing gives students power in school and beyond, in the world of work, politics, and everyday affairs.

WHAT CONTENT TEACHERS NEED TO KNOW ABOUT WRITING

For English language arts teachers, much of this chapter may be "preaching to the choir." After all, teaching writing is a significant part of your job. However, those of you who are teaching science, math, history, or other subjects may wonder why you need to know much about teaching writing. The short answer is that the more you know about writing processes and pedagogy, the more effective you can be in helping your students write in your subject area. The longer answer is. . . . Well, read on.

Writing and Reading

Research suggests that there is an especially beneficial effect to combining writing with reading activities. Tierney et al. (1989) noted that "reading and writing in combination have the potential to contribute in powerful ways to thinking" (p. 166). When Judith Langer (1986) compared the ways in which high school juniors completed short-answer questions, took notes, and wrote essay answers, she found that writing essays not only contributed the most to their topic knowledge but also seemed to improve their thinking about the content: "When writing essays, students seem to step back from the text after reading it—they reconceptualize the content in ways that cut across ideas, focusing on larger issues or topics. In doing this, they integrate information and engage in more complex thought" (p. 406).

In another study using social studies material with high school juniors, Martin and Konopak (1987) employed a relatively simple combination of brainstorming, writing, and reading. In a three-day trial, they found this procedure helped students synthesize information from several sources and integrate new information with their prior knowledge. The researchers got similar results when they tried the same procedure with sixth-grade students (Konopak, Martin, & Martin, 1990).

Writing, then, is a potent tool for learning and reflecting across the school curriculum. Many teachers have found that writing means much more than an in-class five-paragraph essay or a one-shot term paper. As you read the following examples, consider the kinds of thinking required as students read, talk, and write:

> At the end of the year, a sixth-grade teacher involves her class in a review of all they have studied in science, including the scientific method and famous scientists, the environment, electricity, the plant and animal kingdoms, astronomy, and meteorology. After reading *The Magic School Bus Inside the Earth* and *The Magic School Bus Inside the Human Body* by Joanna Cole, groups of students write and illustrate their own adventure stories about field trips to the labs of famous scientists, a forest ranger station, a nuclear power plant, and other places related to their studies. For three weeks, students converge on the media center with three-by-five index cards and buzz together in composing and editorial conferences. When their books are written, illustrated, laminated, and bound, they proudly show them off to visiting fifth graders who are getting a preview of their next year in school.

> An eighth-grade history class is considering the relative effectiveness of violence and nonviolence in conflict resolution. On the first day, each cooperative learning group receives two case studies to read. Following the instructions given in Figure 10.1, they collectively write brief comparisons of the two cases. On the second day, the groups report their interpretations to the class. Through questioning, the teacher helps the class focus on the long- and short-term effects, both personal and social, of conflicts between aboriginals and colonials in New Zealand and North America, between blacks and whites during the American civil rights movement of the 1960s, and between muggers and victims on city streets. The teacher lists these cases on the blackboard and students add other historical and current events to the list. The teacher makes an assignment: pick one event, research it, and write a position paper advocating violence or nonviolence. In the following two weeks the teacher devotes part or all of several classes to media center visits, drafting, and conferencing. When students have completed their inquiries and writing, the cooperative learning groups present their individual papers in the format of an academic roundtable. As a finale, students write individually about what they have learned from their study of conflict resolution and how this relates to their personal experience.

The Writing Process

The use of writing in schools has changed as teachers have broadened their understanding of how writers work. All writers, from beginners to professional authors, go through similar processes to produce a piece of writing:

1. *Prewriting:* This involves deciding on a topic, collecting one's thoughts, gathering data, organizing ideas mentally or on paper, and perhaps rehearsing in one's mind or in writing some of the things that will be said.

REFLECTIVE WRITING: VIOLENCE VERSUS NONVIOLENCE

Directions: Read the case studies given to your group. Each one includes acts of violence and nonviolence. Complete the chart below with information you find in the case studies.

	Case Study 1	Case Study 2
A. 1. Identify act(s) of violence.		
2. What was the intended goal/objective?		
3. Was the goal/objective achieved?		
B. 1. Identify act(s) of nonviolence.		
2. What was the intended goal/objective?		
3. Was the goal/objective achieved?		

C. Decide: How are these acts similar? How do they differ? Are they more alike than different, or vice versa? Why?

D. Write: As a group, draft a brief written comparison of your two cases, including essential information from A, B, and C above. You will be presenting this in class tomorrow.

FIGURE 10.1   A reflective writing activity for a tenth-grade history class
(*Source:* Reprinted by permission of Margaret Boykin, Buffalo Public Schools, #18, Buffalo, New York.)

2. *Drafting:* This is actually putting words, sentences, and paragraphs down on paper. The word *drafting* necessarily implies something unfinished or unpolished, for a piece of writing may go through many drafts before it reaches its final form. During drafting, the emphasis is on fluency and getting ideas onto paper.

3. *Revising:* Revision literally means "to see again." As a writer reads what has been written with the eyes of a reader, he or she can look for meaning and clarity. The writer may add, delete, or rearrange information at this point. During revision, it may also be helpful to have another person read the work and share his or her impressions.

4. *Editing:* The distinction between revising and editing is important. When revising, the focus is on content or meaning. When editing, the focus is on form, on things such as spelling, punctuation, grammatical conventions, and finding just the right word.

5. *Postwriting:* Sometimes this is called publishing, in the sense that when a piece of writing is finished, it is often "made public." For most student writing, this means handing it in to the teacher. However, there are other audiences and venues for student writing—classmates, parents, students in other classes and

grades, and school publications. Students often find opportunities to share their writing outside the school community as well. They may write letters to authors, politicians, newspapers, or students in another school. Local businesses, professionals, civic organizations, and community agencies may agree to sponsor student writing projects and respond to the final products.

Many students publish their work on the school's Web site or on their own Web sites. In Chapter 3, we described two Internet sites that publish student writing, TeenLit (*http://TeenLit.com*) and TeenInk (*http://TeenInk.com*). TeenInk is the on-line magazine associated with *The 21st Century*, a monthly periodical for adolescent writing published by the Young Authors Foundation. Fiction, nonfiction, and poetry may be submitted to The 21st Century, Box 30, Newton, MA 02461.

Having described these phases in numerical order, we must emphasize that the writing process is *not* strictly linear; a writer does not march through the process as if it were so many steps in a recipe for apple pie. Writing is recursive. At any stage in the development of a piece of writing, the author may go back or forward in the process. While drafting this text, for instance, we have frequently (more often than we like to think about) revised our outline, changed our focus, gathered more information, and rewritten. As part of this process, we have shared parts of the book with each other, with colleagues, and with friends. Even as we sit drafting at our word processors, we find ourselves continuously rereading, revising, and editing.

Another important point about the writing process, especially in the context of content area teaching, is that writing activities do not always have to culminate in finished products to be useful. A lot of writing is informal and never shared with a wide audience or intended for the evaluative eye of a teacher. This informal, unfinished writing is valuable because it promotes reflective thinking. It also gives the writer (and others) an opportunity to look back and trace changes and development in learning and thinking. For this reason, many content area teachers have adopted learning logs and other informal writing activities.

When teachers are familiar with the writing process, they find it affects their expectations and their teaching in at least five important ways. First, they realize that there will be a great deal of variability in students' writing. Within a single classroom, there will be writers who are fluent and confident as well as some for whom it will be a struggle to put a few words or sentences on the page. There will also be great variability in writing styles and approaches. Although the basic writing process is similar for all writers, each individual develops his or her own preferences and strategies for writing.

Second, process-oriented teachers know that developing writers need regular and frequent practice. Competence comes with experience. When students write regularly in a variety of modes, including unfinished writing, both their ability and their confidence increase.

Third, these teachers emphasize the writing process, especially prewriting and revising, in their assignments and instruction. Rather than overwhelming students with a multipage handout titled something like "Requirements for the History 11 Term Paper," they provide students with incremental modeling, guidance, and practice in the different phases of the writing process. These teachers also confer with students regularly as they work on their writing and provide structured opportunities for students to confer with each other.

Fourth, the more teachers know about writing processes, the more they understand that *writing well is hard work,* whether you are a student or a published professional writer. Teachers who are themselves writers are in an especially good position to communicate this important message to their students, as Anne Shealy (2000), a middle school teacher, learned in a graduate writers' workshop: "I discovered that writing was almost always a difficult process, but the exertion is a natural, acceptable step in becoming a better writer. My continued development as a writer informs my teaching of writing" (p. 11).

Finally, these teachers are likely to emphasize the content of students' writing over the form. They recognize that developing writers are not perfect. Even professional authors must rely on copy editors. It does not seem sensible to hold learners to a higher standard than that applied to experts. Rather, process-oriented teachers respond primarily to the meaning in students' writing and view the mechanics as a secondary, but important, consideration.

The results of the 1998 National Assessment of Educational Progress (NAEP) writing assessment support instructional strategies often associated with an understanding of writing processes (Greenwald et al., 1999). Students who actually planned their NAEP writing on blank spaces provided during the examination and students who said their teachers had them plan their writing in school scored significantly higher than students who made no prewriting plans. Eighth and twelfth graders who said they were consistently asked to write multiple drafts performed better than those who never or occasionally did more than one draft. Finally, students whose teachers talked to them about their writing outperformed those who said their teachers never talked to them about their written work.

Social Construction of Writing

Our description of writing processes has largely emphasized the individual cognitive aspects of writing, at least up to the point at which writing is shared with others. However, there are also important social dimensions to both the long-term development of writing abilities and the actual composition of a particular piece of writing. As with other facets of literacy, writing is socially constructed, and therefore involves (Schultz & Fecho, 2000)

> the historical, cultural, and social identities the individual brings to writing, the social world in which the writing occurs, the peer and teacher interactions that surround the writing, and the classroom organization, including the

curriculum and pedagogical decisions made by the teacher and the school. (p. 54)

Writing is more than a set of technical skills which can be taught and learned in a normative progression; rather, it is a complex interplay of writer, audience, language, and social context.

Language, culture, and writing.   Written words, as language made tangible and subject to public scrutiny, reveal the interrelationships of language, culture, and education. In a fundamental way, to be educated in our society means to be literate. Facility with writing, especially in the direct exposition of thesis and elaboration most often associated with school writing tasks, is a significant marker of an individual's mastery of schooled literacy as a primary discourse. Some features of written language, such as spelling, dialect, and "code-switching" miscues by ELLs, are especially apparent. However, the relation between culture and language is much deeper and more complex than what is revealed in these surface features (Gee, 1996; Heath, 1983; Delpit, 1995). *Pragmatics* is a term used by linguists to describe how people use language socially "for demonstrating intelligence, apologizing, asking for a favor, telling someone what to do, claiming allegiance with others, displaying status, getting one's point across, even telling a story" (Meier, 1998, p. 122). People from different cultural and linguistic communities have varied strategies for negotiating these situations, and pragmatics may often be a significant source of misunderstanding both within and across cultural groups.

For example, Chinese cultural traditions place more emphasis on collectivism and "fitting in" than U.S. traditions, which are more likely to prize individualism. Native Chinese who are learning to write English tend to favor a style that emphasizes contingency, avoids strong assertions, prefers the collective "we" to the individual "I," and relies on rhetorical devices such as proverbs and analog, in contrast to native English-speaking U.S. writers who are more direct, quicker to assert and defend polarized positions, and more likely to employ personal anecdotes (Wu & Rubin, 2000).

African American oral and written traditions also feature many unique patterns of style and pragmatics that are absent or not so richly developed in other North American language communities. These include (Meier, 1998a)

characteristic intonational patterns; metaphorical language; concrete examples and analogies to make a point; rhyme, rhythm, alliteration, and other forms of repetition, including word play; use of proverbs, aphorisms, biblical quotations, and learned allusions; colorful and unusual vocabulary; arguing *to* a main point (rather than *from* a main point); making a point through indirection. (p. 99)

These are highly prized and effective conventions in many contexts, although they may not be awarded points in the five-paragraph persuasive essay or the history term paper if standard rhetorical conventions are expected.

Social class is another factor that may denote writing styles. Hemphill (1999) found that working-class adolescents produced responses to poetry that prominently featured their own role as readers and elaborated on the characters' thoughts and actions in the narrative, whereas middle-class students were more likely to concentrate on abstracted meaning or "big ideas" and suppress explicit self-references.

Although our diverse language communities all have their individual styles and strengths, it is nevertheless important that students gain facility with standard academic English. The question is not *whether* students should learn Standard English spelling, grammar, and rhetoric, but *how* (Delpit, 1995). First, teachers of linguistically diverse students need to understand and appreciate language differences. When asked what advice she would give white teachers of Ebonics-speaking students, high school English teacher Hafeesah Dalji replied (Dalji & Miner, 1998)

> Respect the language of the students. Let them know that no language is inferior or superior. Give them examples. And of course you have to feel that way, too, because if you don't there is no sense in trying to teach what you don't feel, because students will see it. You also have to be knowledgeable about Ebonics before you are able to work with students in transferring their language to Standard English. . . . A European teacher has to recognize that there is a rhythm to the language, they have to recognize the cadence of the language, they have to recognize the rich metaphors, so they can draw upon this when they are trying to tell their students, "Now let's say this in another way, in Standard English." (pp. 114–115)

While acknowledging and appreciating language differences is an essential first step in teaching Standard English, it is not always a comfortable position for monolingual teachers who may be unfamiliar with other language forms. Teaching Standard English also has ideological and social implications that may cause discomfort for some teachers and students. To be blunt, "it is difficult to talk about black language/Ebonics in a meaningful way without simultaneously talking about racism" (Meier, 1998b, p. 120). English teacher Bob Fecho found this out when he read a poem by Nikki Giovanni with his African American students, who were initially offended that this writer whom they assumed to be white was making fun of their language (Fecho, 1998, 2000). Understanding that Giovanni was in fact an African American led Fecho and his students into a year-long study of language usage during which students investigated and debated language differences both within and across cultures.

Teaching Standard English forms to linguistically diverse students can best be accomplished by comparing and analyzing different uses of language and by explicitly modeling and teaching standard conventions. Authors such as Alice Walker, Amy Tan, or Judith Ortiz Cofer who effectively meld or switch between linguistic and rhetorical styles help to illustrate language differences at the same time that they validate the multicultural power of language. (In Chapter 12, we talk more about the uses of multicultural literature and suggest other resources for including diverse voices in the classroom.) It is much easier to explicitly compare language forms and make students aware of standard styles and conventions in an atmosphere in which language variation is celebrated rather than suppressed. Exercises in which students translate from one style to another, write in different voices or from different points of view and for different audiences, practice specific language forms or features, and read aloud from a variety of published and student-written text all help to increase students' metacognitive awareness of language and expand their language power.

Writing and English Language Learners.   Learning Standard English written forms is especially challenging for students who are still learning to hear and speak the language. However, ELLs are able to begin writing even as they are learning spoken English. Sarah Hudelson (1999) lists several widely accepted principles of second-language writing:

- Students need to be able to take risks and make mistakes.
- They need support through all phases of the writing process, including multiple drafts, revisions, and opportunities to share their writing with others.
- ELLs need practice writing for different purposes, including reflections on content learning, responses to literature, and inquiry writing.
- Reading different kinds of text, especially good expository writing, will have a positive influence on students' writing.
- Learning logs (described later) provide an excellent medium for ELLs to write informally about their content subjects.
- ELLs who have learned to write in their native language can transfer much of what they know about writing to English contexts. Writing development in both languages can be simultaneous and complementary.

Writing and the Computer

The personal computer gets our vote as the most useful tool for the writer since the invention of papyrus. Using a computer as a word processor, a writer can draft quickly, revise instantly, save and retrieve drafts in any stage of development, check for and correct errors, and print drafts or final copies in almost any format desired. Add to that the information-sharing and -gathering potential of the Internet and electronic databases, and we do not think our case is overstated. With a modem, students can link directly to students in other classrooms and other schools, to universities, and to professional information networks. Compact disk read-only memory (CD-ROM) systems allow users access to encyclopedic databases that include text, pictures, and sound. By typing in a single word, users can search quickly through the equivalent of 250,000 typed pages. The systems also allow users to take notes and store them in computer data files.

Because computers are now commonplace in schools—at all levels—and in many homes, increasingly more students are discovering new writing fluency and power as they become liberated from the physical constraints of paper and

Technology Tips—Writing Links

In Chapter 4, we described how English teacher Gene Kulbago had set up a website that his students could visit for help with their writing and literature study. Among the useful sites that Gene has included are the following:

On-Line English Grammar
http://www.edunet.com/english/grammar/index.cfm

Guide to Grammar and Writing (Capital Community College, Hartford, CT)
http://webster.commnet.edu/grammar/index.htm

Guide to Writing Research Papers (Capital Community College, Hartford, CT)
http://webster.commnet.edu/mla.htm

Modern Language Association Style Manual
http://www.mla.org/style/style_index.htm

pencil. This can be seen in the results of the 1998 NAEP writing assessment, in which moderate computer use was associated with higher average scores (Greenwald et al., 1999). Teachers should encourage students to use the computer whenever possible as a tool in prewriting, drafting, revising, editing, and publishing. Fluency is facilitated if students are taught basic keyboarding skills in middle school or earlier.

Students may work at the computer alone or in pairs. When students are preparing written products in cooperative learning groups, one or two individuals from each group can be assigned to do the keyboarding work. When access to the computer is limited, students commonly write a first draft longhand and enter it into the computer, revising as they go. Once a draft is available on the computer, it can be read by teachers or peers. Suggested revisions become much easier to incorporate; they can often be accomplished on the spot. Many word-processing programs include a spell checker, or the school may have a separate spell-check program. When the writers are satisfied with their drafts, they can print out a neat copy. We will consider other uses of the computer in writing later.

WRITING ACTIVITIES FOR CONTENT AREAS

Writing in content areas may range from informal notes and jottings to lengthy formal research reports, complete with footnotes and bibliography. In the following sections, we describe some of the useful writing activities that content teachers use.

Writing Assignments

A successful school writing experience begins with a good writing assignment. When an assignment is precise and specific and offers the writer ample guidance, the writer is more likely to produce a satisfactory product. Five elements of an assignment can be crafted to heighten student involvement and interest and to avoid frustration and confusion:

1. *Choosing a topic:* Writing is hard work, and enthusiasm can be especially hard to maintain when the topic is of little or no interest to the writer. The more discretion a student has in selecting what to write about, the more care and effort he or she is likely to invest in writing. In content area classes, it is usually necessary for the teacher to specify a general topic related to the area of study. However, there are still many ways to allow student choice. In the examples presented earlier, the sixth-grade scientists chose the topics for their adventure stories, and the writers in the high school history class chose the event and point of view they presented at the roundtable.

2. *Specify an audience and purpose for writing:* Writers need experience with writing for a variety of realistic purposes and for audiences other than the teacher. The sixth graders were writing to explain one area of science to a general, uninitiated audience and specifically to younger students who would be in sixth grade the next year. The high school students were writing as advocates of a particular point of view to an audience of their peers. If writers have a purpose and audience in mind, they can decide what information is needed, what voice or stance to take, and what will best meet the needs of their readers.

3. *Writing in varied modes:* There are many forms that content area writing can take. Students gain competence and avoid boredom when they have opportunities to write in different formats. (See Figure 10.2 for some possibilities.)

4. *Accommodating the writing process:* Students will need help and guidance with the various phases of the writing process. This means supporting students' prewriting decisions and data collection, allowing sufficient time for drafting and revising, and providing opportunities for teacher and peer conferences to aid revision. Supplying the necessary guidance implies that some in-class time will be used for working on the assignment.

5. *Guiding students' writing:* Students can be overwhelmed and dismayed by all the work and potential for frustration and failure built into a writing assignment that comes with a lengthy list of specifications and requirements. Instead of springing all this detail on them at once, the teacher can introduce a writing project in increments while offering guidance at each stage. Discussion, brainstorming, and semantic webbing facilitate student engagement and planning during the introduction of an assignment. Data collection, drafting, conferencing, and editing can be supported by the teacher-designed guides discussed in this chapter.

When we make a writing assignment, teach about writing, or assess what students have written, we are in effect making political choices, if we understand

Journals or diaries
Fiction:
   Fantasy
   Historical
   Adventure
   Science fiction
   Choose-your-own-adventure
   Children's books
Picture books
Dictionaries
Fact books
How-to books
Biographies
Letters to real or imaginary people
Dialogues and conversations
Thumbnail sketches of:
   People
   Places
   Important concepts
   Historical events
Requests
Job descriptions
Applications and resumés
Acceptance or rejection letters
Research reports
Science:
   Observations
   Notebook
   Lab reports
   Hypotheses
Interviews (real and imaginary)
Photos and captions
Recipes
Catalogs
Obituaries, epitaphs, eulogies

Memos
Poems
Scripts:
   Plays
   Radio
   Television
Prophecies, predictions, visions
Newspaper writing:
   Articles
   Editorials
   Features
Advertisements
Proposals:
   Social programs
   Grants
   Research
   Construction
Position papers and responses
Reviews of:
   Books
   Movies and TV
   Recordings
   Performances
Math:
   Word problems
   Problem solutions
   Practical applications
Cartoons
Debates
Songs and raps
Games and puzzles
Posters, displays, collages
Instructions or directions
Travelogues

FIGURE 10.2   Possible modes for content area writing   (*Source:* Adapted from S. Tschudi & J. Yates, *Teaching writing in the content areas: Senior high school.* Washington, DC: National Education Association, 1983.)

the term "political" in the broad sense that acknowledges the interrelationships among language, power, and culture (Kamler, 1999). Just as we sanction certain kinds of reading when we assign a particular text, so we are signaling to students what "counts" as writing through the kinds of writing we require and the kinds of writing we do not ask for (Freebody, Luke, & Gilbert, 1991). It is therefore useful to consider not just *what* students should be writing but also what their writing *implies* for them and their world.

R.A.F.T. assignments. The acronym R.A.F.T. can help a teacher plan successful writing assignments by varying some of the elements discussed previously (Santa, Havens, & Harrison, 1996). The letters stand for *Role, Audience, Format,* and *Topic.* A writer might take many roles: reporter, scientist, famous historical figure, a character from a story, an animal, or even an inanimate object. In a given role, the writer may address a variety of real or imaginary audiences. The format may be a poem, a letter, or any of the other modes listed in Figure 10.2. Finally, the topic should include a strong verb such as "persuade," "compare," "describe," or "explain," which will help the writer understand the tone and purpose of the writing. When studying fractions, for example, math students might write a want ad for an improper fraction or a letter from the numerator to the denominator explaining why it is the most important part of the fraction. Figure 10.3 illustrates how other R.A.F.T. assignments could be developed. Use the blank column to think of a role, audience, format, and topic that would be pertinent to your subject area.

A word of caution is necessary for developing R.A.F.T. assignments. The purposes of using a planning device such as R.A.F.T. are to increase student motivation and interest in a writing assignment and to devise writing assignments that vary from the traditional student essay written for the teacher. As we have said, good writing, especially good academic writing, requires hard work. Writers are likely to invest the most effort and motivation in topics that hold strong personal interest (Graves, 1983). A role or topic that may seem "creative" to one person may hold little attraction to another. Not every student will be eager to

Content Area	Health or Biology	Geometry	Global Studies	_____
Role	nutritionist	interior decorator/ contractor	rain forest animal (list several)	
Audience	members of football and volleyball teams	homeowner	farmer	
Format	presentation before practice	floor plan and written estimate	request	
Topic	compare and contrast the most effective and nutritious diet for each sport	explain cost to carpet four rooms	consider alternatives to cutting forest	

FIGURE 10.3 **Using R.A.F.T. to plan writing assignments**

write from the point of view of a rain forest animal, Captain Ahab's second mate, the unknown variable in a two-step equation, or a red blood cell traveling through the circulatory system. One possibility is to develop assignments that allow students to choose from more than one possible role, audience, format, or topic. Another idea might be to let students assist in determining possible roles, audiences, and so on.

Learning Logs and Journals

Learning logs or content area journals have been enthusiastically and effectively adopted by many content area teachers in both middle and secondary schools. For instance, eleven- to thirteen-year-old math students who wrote in their math journals for seven to ten minutes three times a week over twelve weeks showed improvement in their conceptual understanding, procedural knowledge, and math communication compared to a similar group that did practice problems instead of journal writing (Jurdak & Abu Zein, 1998). They are among the most frequently recommended strategies for helping students learn English as a second language (Ardizzone, 1992; Arthur, 1991; Dolly, 1990). As mentioned in Chapter 6, learning logs are notebooks that are dedicated to informal writing, note taking, and musing on content area subjects. Regular log entries give students opportunities for risk-free reflection. It is a place for students to try out ideas, to put their thoughts down on paper so they can see what is there, and to develop writing fluency that can transfer to other written assignments. Learning logs are good platforms for prewriting rehearsal and drafting. Some of what students write in their logs may eventually find its way into their more formal writing. They can be excellent resources when reviewing for a quiz or test, and students might even be allowed to consult their learning logs as "lifeline" resources during an examination. Learning logs also constitute a valuable record of student growth and learning over a marking period, a semester, or a year.

What students actually write in their logs varies widely. Entries can be specified by the teacher or left entirely to the student. Almost certainly, teachers will need to suggest topics or questions at first. Figure 10.4 lists some generic prompts that you could tailor to your subject area. *Process entries* generally ask students to reflect on *how* they have learned; *reaction entries* focus more on *what* they have learned. We think both kinds of prompts are useful, even though the distinction between the two may get blurred in students' writing.

The double-entry journal is another variation on content area learning logs (Bromley, 1993; Fretzin, 1992). In a double-entry journal, the writer either draws a line down the middle of the page or uses two opposing pages. The left-hand side is used to jot down a stimulus for thought. This could be a personal experience, a quotation from a book or something said in class, a new vocabulary term, or an important issue or concept. On the right side, the writer can enter his or her reactions, thoughts, and feelings. At first, teachers can provide prompts

Process Entries

What did I understand about the work we did in class today?

What didn't I understand? What was confusing?

What problems did I have with a text assignment?

How did I solve a problem with understanding, vocabulary, text, etc.?

At what point did I get confused?

What did I like or dislike today?

What questions do I have about what we did today?

Notes, lists, or jottings relevant to my upcoming assignments.

My reflections on cooperative learning group processes—what did or didn't work and why, my role, the role of other participants.

My predictions and expectations about a new topic.

Reaction Entries

If I were the teacher, what questions would I ask about this assignment/chapter, etc.?

Explain a theory, concept, vocabulary term, etc., to another person.

Free-writing: simply write for 5–10 minutes about a specific topic, whatever comes into the writer's mind.

Summarize, analyze, synthesize, compare and contrast, evaluate an idea, topic, event, person, etc.

Connection with prior knowledge or experience.

"Unsent letters" to people, living or dead, historical or mythical, about topic of study.

Doodles; words and pictures that reflect feelings or thoughts on a topic.

Response to higher-order questions posed by the teacher.

Reread a log entry from last week. Write a reaction to what was written.

FIGURE 10.4   Sample prompts for students' learning log entries

for the left side of the journal. When students become familiar with the double-entry format, they can be asked to find their own prompts.

The double-entry journal format can be used across all content areas. Math students could write out a particularly difficult problem on the left side and explain their solutions on the right. Physics students could state one of the laws of thermodynamics on the left side and describe one way in which it has practical application in their lives on the right. In literature study, readers could choose characters, plot events, figurative language, or specific quotations to include on the left side, with their personal interpretations or reactions on the right. The double-entry format could also be used to have students juxtapose pros and cons on an issue, causes and effects, or comparisons and contrasts.

Pamela Carroll (2000) suggests a triple-entry format for journal writing. Writers make three columns or divide the page into thirds horizontally. The first space is used to note specific parts of the text that caught their fancy—words, phrases, or sentences, along with page numbers. The second space is used to note reactions, questions, or elaborations to the passages they have cited. The final space is reserved for a peer who reads the first two entries and then writes a response. This is most effective when students are given a few minutes following writing to converse in reader–responder pairs.

Many students may initially resist the idea of writing in a learning log, especially in science or math classes, in which writing is not traditionally required on a regular basis (Berenson & Carter, 1995). It may help to begin learning log writing with "feeling"-type prompts that have no right or wrong answers and move on to more conceptually oriented prompts after students have gotten used to the routine of learning log writing. Learning log entries will be longer and more thoughtful if you talk with the class about what they might write, specify your expectations for their learning log writing, and model entries that have been written by other students. Finally, it will help to set a timer or to have a specific time period each day or week dedicated to learning log writing.

A learning log is an excellent repository for all sorts of miscellanea. Students may use their logs to take lecture notes, to keep procedural and observational notes during labs, and to jot down new or essential vocabulary. If they are assigned reading beyond their textbooks, reactions can be noted in their logs. They may jot down quotations from their reading, their classmates, or the teacher. They can copy discussion webs or other graphic representations from the board, or they can create their own webs in the log.

Teachers have worked out different strategies for keeping track of students' learning log entries. When one or two class sections are writing in logs, it is easy to review entries on a weekly or biweekly basis. Multiple sections can turn in their logs on a staggered schedule. If teachers regularly review student logs, they get a sense of what is or is not working, both for individual students and for a whole class, and students see that the logs are important to the teacher. Reading student logs does not have to be a Herculean task. Because learning logs contain unfinished writing, the teacher should not be assigning a qualitative grade or marking mechanics. Log entries can be a messy mixture of trash and treasure, so a quick, impressionistic reading is usually sufficient to ferret out the important parts and ensure that the writer is making the expected effort. Gradebook credit can be given on a pass/fail basis for making regular entries.

Responding to log entries is a matter of choice. A check mark or a word or two in the margin may be enough. A teacher who prefers not to write directly in the students' logs can use sticky notes. Occasional elaborated responses to questions or observations will motivate students and make the learning log a more meaningful tool. Teachers sometimes use logs to conduct ongoing dialogues with students, and they find that this promotes a type of teacher–student communication that otherwise would not occur in daily classroom exchanges (Atwell, 1998).

Martha Dolly (1990) points out that when teacher and students carry on a dialogue in this manner, the learning log becomes a reading activity as well as a writing one for students. She says that this intertwining of reading and writing is especially beneficial for students who are learning English as a second language since it makes literacy both active and functional. Students who struggle with formal reading and writing assignments find the exchange of questions, answers, and observations stimulating. One of Dolly's students, a young man from Sri Lanka, wrote in his final journal entry how relieved he was that there would be no more assignments. However, he concluded, "In the other hand, I am unhappy that there will be no one to correspond for my ideas" (p. 362).

Other Informal Writing Activities

Students can engage in informal, unfinished writing activities even if they do not keep learning logs. A teacher could use the first five minutes of class for a writing warm-up, based on one of the prompts listed in Figure 10.4. A teacher can assign brief "entrance visas" to be written outside of class and handed in at the beginning of the next class period. "Exit visas" can be written in class and collected from students at the end of the period. Free-writing is a simple writing-to-reflect activity that can be used at the beginning or the end of a unit. Students can compare their free-writing products in groups or free-write for five minutes as a follow-up to group work.

What students do after writing is an essential element in the success of an informal writing activity (Tierney, Readence, & Dishner, 2000). They need an opportunity to share their written responses so that they can see how others have interpreted the reading. This reinforces the understanding that a variety of responses are possible. When teachers write and share their responses with students, they add their experience to the discussion and serve as good reflective models.

Another informal writing activity, called *writing roulette* (Bean, 1992), can be used to reinforce content area vocabulary. The teacher provides a simple story structure consisting of three elements: a setting and a character, a problem or goal for the character, and a resolution. Students are told they must use and underline at least one word from their content unit in each section of the story. Students begin writing about the setting and character and continue for a specified time, perhaps five minutes. When the time is up, papers are exchanged within a small group, and a new time limit is set. Each student reads the paper he or she receives and writes the problem section of the story. Papers are exchanged a final time so that a third student writes the resolution. The finished stories are then returned to the original authors, who share them with the small group.

Reviewing and Summarizing

Many students believe that if they have read each page, they have conscientiously fulfilled an assignment to "read Chapter 12." If there are no questions to answer, no reading guide to complete, they are content to let the teacher tell them in class what it all meant, or at least what was important. Consequently, their efforts at reading and learning are passive and less effective than if they had actively sought to consolidate what they had learned. They have omitted the final, integrative step in reading to learn—taking the time to review the text and summarize what was learned. Summarizing reinforces and consolidates the many processes involved in learning from text, such as determining important information, perceiving text structure, and drawing inferences.

Numerous studies have shown that students of varying ages benefit from learning how to produce written summaries of what they have read (Armbruster, Anderson, & Ostertag, 1987; Taylor & Beach, 1984). Hare and Borchardt (1984) found that summary writing was effective with urban African American and Hispanic high school students. In order to write a summary, a reader must know how to perform three basic processes (Hidi & Anderson, 1986):

1. Select and delete information.
2. Condense information by combining or by substituting a general term for a group of specific terms (e.g., "farm animals" instead of "horses, goats, pigs, and sheep").
3. Transform the information into writing.

Although basic, these processes are hardly simple. As with other reading processes, students need to be shown how to summarize and need continual, long-term practice in order to effectively add summarizing to their repertoire of reading strategies.

Strategies for teaching students to summarize.   Hierarchical summaries, R.E.A.P., and G.I.S.T. are three formal procedures for teaching summarization. Each has several useful features. *Hierarchical summaries* are structured around the headings and subheadings found in most content area texts (Taylor & Beach, 1984). The procedure is as follows:

1. Students preview the reading selection with emphasis on headings, highlighted vocabulary, and other typographical cues.
2. Based on the preview, teacher and students together develop a skeleton outline that the teacher writes on the blackboard, overhead projector, or projected computer screen.
3. Students read the text using the outline as a reading guide.
4. After reading, students compose main idea statements for main points in the outline and add essential supporting details, again with teacher guidance.
5. Finally, students develop a "key idea" or summarizing statement for the entire passage, which becomes the first sentence of the summary.

The hierarchical summary is a strategy that students can learn to use independently. The strategy depends, however, on the heading/subheading format of textbooks, and it would not be appropriate for narrative or other material that did not have clear graphic signals for important information and text organization.

R.E.A.P. is an acronym for four stages in reading and understanding: *R*ead the text; *E*ncode into your own language; *A*nnotate by writing the message down; *P*onder, or think about, the message on your own and with others. Skilled readers make many different kinds of annotations. Sometimes they jot down a critical comment, a question, a note on the author's intentions, or, perhaps, a personal reaction. The simplest kind, though, is a summary annotation. Eanet and Manzo (1976) suggest that students be introduced to summary annotations of paragraphs through a four-step sequence:

1. Show students a sample paragraph and a summary annotation. Explain what an annotation is and why readers might use annotations to help them understand and remember what they have read.
2. Show students another paragraph, this time with three annotations. One is a good summary, and the other two are flawed. Lead students to select the best summary and discover the problems with the other two.
3. Show students how to summarize by modeling the process for them with a third paragraph.
4. Have individual students develop their own summary annotations. In groups, they analyze their summaries and combine ideas to come up with a concise and complete summary.

G.I.S.T. stands for *Generating Interactions between Schemata and Text* (Cunningham, 1982). Using the G.I.S.T. procedure, students produce progressively more condensed summaries of a text selection. To begin the G.I.S.T. procedure, you need a short, coherent expository paragraph. You then proceed as follows:

1. Show students the first sentence of the paragraph, and ask them to retell it in 15 words or less. Write their summary on the chalkboard or overhead as they dictate and edit it as a group.
2. Show students the second sentence of the paragraph. Erase their first summary statement and ask students to summarize both sentences in 15 words or less.
3. Continue this procedure, one sentence at a time, until the group has summarized the entire paragraph in 15 words or less.
4. Repeat this procedure as many times as necessary until students become adept. Then, lead them to summarize an entire paragraph at one time, rather than sentence by sentence.
5. Finally, when the group has built some proficiency with the G.I.S.T. procedure, have students produce summary statements individually.

All students need guided practice in summarizing before they can be expected to produce summaries independently. Initial efforts can be carried out in cooperative-learning settings to maximize student participation. Intermediate and middle-grade students and secondary students with lower reading ability will need several guided practice sessions, but they can take more responsibility for generating the outlines and summaries each time. Able high school readers should be able to summarize on their own after one or two instructional sessions.

Summarizing and the Struggling Reader

There are important developmental differences in the way students summarize (Anderson & Hidi, 1988/1989; Hill, 1991; Paris, Wasik, & Turner, 1991). The variability of summarizing skill within a single grade level is illustrated by the contrasting examples from two seventh graders in Figure 10.5. The students read an article, "Good-bye Communism," in a current events newspaper. The teacher placed the following list of key words on the board: communism, independence, coup, and economic crisis. Students copied these words in their notebooks to guide them in writing a short summary of important events in the article. Both summaries capture the key idea, but Adam's is short and features only two additional details, with no connections among the information in the summary. Jonathon, on the other hand, includes several key ideas with direct support and provides definitions of key terms.

Like Adam, younger or less able readers have difficulty combining ideas, rearranging information, and translating ideas into their own words. Although most students know that a summary should include important information from a passage, struggling readers are less adept than good readers at identifying what is important and are less likely to include important information in their summaries (Winograd, 1984). For Adam, including the main idea of the article in his summary is a good beginning. For his next summary, his teacher might give him a shorter selection of text to work with and model for him how to elaborate on his main point, perhaps by asking himself "who," "what," and "why" questions. She could also pair Adam with a more able student or enlist the help of a resource teacher who could give Adam more practice and support in summarizing. Even though his skill level is quite different from Jonathon's, Adam should be able to improve his reading ability through summarizing.

Teachers should not expect that students' independent efforts will be flawless, however, as the examples in Figure 10.5 demonstrate. Summary writing is a difficult skill that requires plenty of practice. Implicit information and text passages that are long and complex will be especially problematic, even for relatively advanced students.

Narrative text is generally easier to summarize than expository text, so it might be advisable to start inexperienced students with a short story in an English anthology or a chapter in a novel. If that is not practical, students will have the most initial success with relatively short passages of expository text, perhaps five or six paragraphs at most. Self-contained passages with explicitly stated main ideas and a clear structure will be the easiest to work with. For typical science, math, or social studies text material, this might mean working with a single important subsection of a chapter, perhaps a page or two in length. Able high school readers can be expected to work with longer selections of text.

ADAM'S SUMMARY

(Adam is classified as learning disabled.)

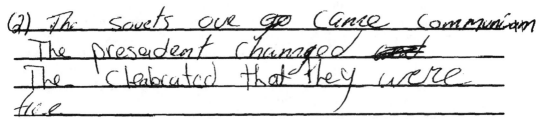

JONATHON'S SUMMARY

(Jonathon is in an honors class.)

GOOD-BYE COMMUNISM

COMMUNISM IS WHEN THE GOVERNMENT CONTROLS EVERYTHING. THE SOVIET UNION JUST GOT RID OF COMMUNISM. DURING THAT TIME WHEN COMMUNISM RULED MANY REPUBLICANS THREATEND TO LEAVE AND BECOME INDEPEND COUNTRES. THE GOVERNMENT CONTROLED WHAT YOU WOULD GROW WHAT JOB YOU GOT WHAT TO BUY AND SO ON, PEOPLE WANTED TO BE FREE, THEY WANTED TO BEABLE TO DO WHAT THEY WANTED TO. NOW THAT COMMUNISM IS OVER THEY ARE FACING PROBLEMS. THEY NEED MORE FOOD FOR THE PEOPLE OTHER COUNTRIES ARE GIVING SUPPORT SUCH AS FOOD SUPPLES AND SO ON

FIGURE 10.5   **Sample summaries of a social studies reading by two seventh graders**

The main ideas may seem obvious to us as expert readers and summarizers, but students learning how to summarize may pick out ideas that are personally important or interesting to them instead of trying to find the main ideas in the text. Therefore, it is helpful to point out that a summary should try to capture the ideas that would probably be important to the author (Anderson & Hidi, 1988/1989). Students who are learning how to summarize should also be allowed to work with a copy of the text to refer to. Summarizing requires careful consideration of the text, including rereading and checking for information. It is not an exercise in memorization.

In Chapter 4, we introduced K-W-L Plus, in which students generate a semantic web of key ideas from the text and use the web as an outline for writing a summary. A semantic web or graphic organizer can be a helpful first step in summarizing because it allows students to see the relationship between main ideas and supporting details (Hill, 1991). Graphic organizers that help students see how information is organized can help students learn to use different kinds of organization, both in reading comprehension and in the writing of summaries.

Summaries written for different purposes and different audiences produce different results. Anderson and Hidi (1988/1989) draw a distinction between reader-based and writer-based summaries. *Reader-based summaries,* not intended for formal evaluation, tend to be longer and easier to produce than *writer-based summaries,* which are written to hand in to the teacher. Shorter summaries require more condensation and synthesis than longer summaries and are thus the products of more complex thinking. Therefore, early efforts at summarizing should be kept informal. Students have less difficulty if they are asked to write summaries in their content area notebooks or learning logs. Summaries can be compared and checked with partners or in small groups. Students will see the practical value of summaries if these are used to review for quizzes, to initiate discussion, or to prepare for a written report or project. Formal summarizing assignments to be collected and graded are probably appropriate only for experienced high school students.

Guiding Student Writing

Some content area teachers say that they are reluctant to assign writing because students' written products are often not very good. When students are asked to write on a topic from a reading assignment, many simply do not have enough experience to know how to proceed. They end up churning out a vague paragraph or two that can be as hard to read as it was to write. Of course, if students do not write much, they will not get any better, and a vicious circle becomes established. If teachers can give some support and structure to students' writing, the writing will be easier and the products should improve.

Guided writing procedure.   The *guided writing procedure* (Smith & Bean, 1980; Konopak, Martin, & Martin, 1987) has six steps that can be implemented over two or three days:

1. Students brainstorm on their prior knowledge of a new topic.
2. As a class or in groups, students label their ideas and organize them into a semantic web or other graphic format.
3. Each student writes on the topic.
4. Students read the assigned text selection.

5. Based on their reading, students revise their original writing.

6. A brief quiz is given on the material.

As we mentioned earlier, this writing procedure has been successfully implemented with both middle-grade and secondary students. Writers in both age groups produced fewer text-explicit details and more higher-level ideas than their peers who did not write before reading (Konopak, Martin, & Martin, 1990; Martin & Konopak, 1987).

The guided writing procedure is also effective with students who are developing proficiency in English (Reyes & Molner, 1991). The combination of oral language, reading, and writing helps linguistically diverse students synthesize their thinking and go beyond the highly structured grammar exercises that are characteristic of many ESL writing programs. Reyes and Molner recommend modifying this procedure to include cooperative-learning formats in which second-language learners can achieve greater success. They also caution that teachers should not overemphasize form and mechanics when reading these students' drafts.

Writing guides.   When students write after studying a textbook chapter or unit or after reading a novel, they are able to pull many ideas together, see meaningful relationships, and consolidate what they have learned. When discussing writing assignments earlier, we said that a teacher can help students understand what and how to write by manipulating certain elements of the task. *Writing guides* constitute a good illustration of how this can be done.

In the writing guide shown in Figure 10.6, the teacher uses the format of a grant proposal to get students to write about what they have learned in their study of genetics. This format gives writers a clear purpose (to obtain a research grant) and a voice (formal and scientific) for their writing. The hints give students guidance about what should be included in their proposals. The teacher acknowledges the importance of revising and editing by asking each student to trade papers with a fellow scientist to make sure the proposal includes the important information and is free of errors in spelling or grammar.

The writing guide in Figure 10.7 was designed as a follow-up to an eighth-grade social studies unit on immigration. In this assignment, students are to take on the role of a recent immigrant to the United States who is writing to a relative or friend in the old country. Students may choose the country of origin. The teacher has suggested many topics that can be included in the letter, but the specific information and the tone of the letter are left to the individual writers. The writers are also told that they will be sharing their letters with the whole class as well as with the teacher.

Same facts, different audience.   Lawrence Baines (2000) describes an activity that can be adapted to most content areas. To begin with, students are given a fact sheet related to a "hot topic" in current events or their content area curriculum.

WRITING GUIDE: GENETICS

Imagine you are Gregor Mendel's lab assistant. Pretend that you are writing an explanation of your findings so that you can receive a grant to further your research. Write a well-developed explanation of your findings from your experiments with pea plants. You should have a clear explanation of Mendel's research and a description of a Punnet square.

Hint: Remember that you are writing a scientific paper. Be sure to include and explain the following terms:

heredity	genetics	dominant
pure	hybrid	recessive
genotype	generation	genes
	phenotype	

Hint: Scientists are thorough people. Don't forget to explain the outcomes of each of the pairs below.

1. Two dominant genes
2. Two recessive genes
3. One dominant and one recessive gene

Give an example of the genotype and phenotype that result from each of the above combinations.

Hint: Make sure you do not lose the grant because of silly grammatical errors or spelling mistakes. Trade papers with a friend. Ask him/her to be sure that you have clearly covered the necessary information.

FIGURE 10.6   Writing guide for an eighth-grade science unit   (*Source:* Reprinted by permission of Judith L. Stenroos, Buffalo Public Schools, #31, Buffalo, New York.)

After a class discussion of the fact sheet, students can be divided into groups of three or four and given a worksheet that lists different audiences and possible writing topics for each. (Figure 10.8 gives an example for facts related to the sinking and subsequent discovery of the wreck of the *Titanic*.) Each group should select three projects they would like to work on and make a plan for dividing up the labor. After a day or two of in-class writing time, groups present their projects to the rest of the class, which gives them feedback on the effectiveness of the writing. This should be followed by a whole-class analysis of the different kinds of appeals that were used in the writing. The number of audiences and writing projects can be varied, and this could also be an individual writing activity instead of a cooperative group task.

Creative writing.   You may believe that so-called "creative writing" is the exclusive province of the English or language arts teacher, but there are many forms of creative writing that lend themselves to other content areas. In fact,

WRITING GUIDE: IMMIGRATION

You are a member of a family that has only been in the United States about six months. You have been through many difficult times here. You are writing to an old friend or relative back in your home country. You are anxious to tell this person about your experiences here, both good and bad. Based on what we have read and discussed about the hardships that immigrants face, write this individual a personal letter.

Remember to include some of the ideas from our reading and discussion. Some possibilities:

Depict your new living area (including your neighbors and neighborhood).

Describe something typical of the United States. (For example, perhaps your reader has never seen a skyscraper; explain to him or her why they're called skyscrapers.)

Describe the different types of people you have met from all over the world.

Tell about language difficulties you have encountered. Explain how you learned English. Why is it important that your native tongue be spoken at home?

Describe your job and wages. Are you treated fairly? Why?

Explain the attitude of native-born Americans toward immigrants. Tell what it means to be called a "greenhorn." Do you think this is fair? Why?

Education is said to be the way to get ahead in America. Explain what is meant by this statement.

Tell how the children are adjusting to this new land.

What do you miss most of all about your homeland? Are you sorry that you left? Why?

What was the voyage to America like?

What are some of the benefits of living in the United States? What are some of the pitfalls?

FIGURE 10.7   **Writing guide for an eighth-grade social studies unit**   (*Source:* Reprinted by permission of Janyce M. Hepp, Williamsville Central School District, Williamsville, New York.)

SAME FACTS, DIFFERENT AUDIENCE

Directions: Select one project for each of the audiences.

1. Audience 1: Royal Maritime Commission appointed in 1912 to study the sinking.
   a. Write an investigative report that attempts to assign blame for the disaster.
   b. Write a series of recommendations for avoiding such accidents in the future.

2. Audience 2: Family members of victims.
   a. Write a letter from the steamship company expressing condolences.
   b. As an attorney, write a proposal for a lawsuit against one or more parties to the accident.

3. Audience 3: Contemporary *Titanic* fanatics.
   a. Write an advertising brochure for submersible trips to the wreck.
   b. Write a proposal to ban further exploitation of the *Titanic* wreckage.

FIGURE 10.8   **Same Facts, Different Audience guide: The wreck of the *Titanic***

entire genres of literature, such as science fiction and historical fiction, have been developed around concepts that come from those disciplines. You could use the R.A.F.T. planning guide (Figure 10.3) to develop fiction-based writing assignments around ideas in your content areas.

Jokes, riddles, cartoons, songs and raps, and advertisements are other examples of creative writing that can be adapted to various content areas. Several poetry formats lend themselves to content areas, too. An acrostic poem spells out a key word or phrase with the first letter of each line, as in the following example written for a geography class studying Africa:

Shifting sand dunes
Across a vast area.
Harsh landscape with
Ancient highways.
Rain is scarce
And temperatures are high.

The cinquain is another poetry format that lends itself to writing in content areas. It is a five-line poem with a set number of syllables in each successive line. The syllable pattern is two-four-six-eight-two. The following is an example that incorporates concepts from a middle school earth science lesson:

The moon
Reflects the sun,
Revolving 'round the earth,
Waxing and waning and pulling
The tides.

The biopoem is frequently used as a beginning-of-the-year exercise to unlimber the writing synapses and help students get acquainted with new classmates. The basic format can be adapted to include many facts and concepts focused on particular people, things, places, or events from various content areas. The autobiographical biopoem form and an adaptation for an historical personage are illustrated in Figure 10.9.

Brainstorming a list of key concepts and descriptive words will help students as they try to write poetry or fiction. You may also wish to share a model of your own writing or compose an example with the whole class before having students try creative writing on their own. Occasional creative writing activities add variety to content area studies, help students to consolidate new ideas, and serve as an important outlet for those whose aptitudes are more creative than academic.

The lighter side.   Not all content-related writing need be serious. Playing with language is another useful creative outlet that can lighten the classroom atmosphere and promote language development. Jokes, puns, and satire have always been used to critique leaders, highlight social issues, and score points in public

BIOPOEMS

(Auto) BioPoem	*Historical BioPoem*
Line 1: Your first name.	First name of subject.
Line 2: Four adjectives that describe you.	Four adjectives that describe subject.
Line 3: Resident of. . . .	Resident of. . . .
Line 4: Son or daughter of. . . .	Lover of. . . . (3 people, places, things)
Line 5: Brother or sister of. . . .	Who believed. . . . (1 or more ideas)
Line 6: Lover of. . . . (3 items)	Who used. . . . (3 methods or things)
Line 7: Who likes to. . . . (3 things)	Who wanted . . . (3 things)
Line 8: Who hates to. . . . (2 things)	Who said, ". . . ." (Give a quote)
Line 9: Who would like to. . . . (3 things)	Who gave. . . . (3 things)
Line 10: Your last name.	Last name of subject.

FIGURE 10.9   Biopoem formats

discourse. Humorous writing, then, can serve a more serious purpose of engaging students in critical thinking about a topic. Students can write short pieces that feature humorous repetition, exaggeration, or unexpected associations (Weber, 2000). A class can brainstorm content-related top ten lists or variations on Ten Things to Do With a Dead Cat. (Our apologies to cat lovers for this example; we are decidedly "dog people.") Students might create wacky advertisements or want ads based on content area facts or concepts. There are many other humorous variations possible among the modes of content area writing listed in Figure 10.2.

Sydeana Martin (2000) suggests a tabloid exposé format that can be used to write about literature, history, scientific developments, or current events. This would start by sharing some humorous headlines with the class, either real or teacher created, typical of tabloids such as the *National Inquirer.* The teacher then introduces the topic, and students brainstorm tabloid headlines. Finally, students take the role of tabloid reporter and write up the topic in tabloid style.

In chemistry, Ron DeLorenzo (1999) uses tongue-in-cheek mystery titles to engage student interest, build communication skills, and illustrate important science concepts. For example, he gives a detailed analysis of the temperature of hell (slightly above 246°F based on biblical reference and scientific fact, according to DeLorenzo). Other mystery topics include the following: Why do humans kiss? How can sand predict earthquakes? Why do ice cream and car batteries explode? Why is electricity free in the winter? (Essays on each of these topics can be found at the Internet site of the Greenwich Science Education Center, *http://www. educationcenter.org/.*) Given some hints and guidance, students could write their own solutions to these mysteries. They could also create their own science mysteries.

Teaching Struggling Writers

Too often, instruction for students with writing disabilities focuses heavily on drill with spelling and mechanics. This narrow concentration, added to the difficulties that struggling writers have with handwriting, organization, and sustaining fluency, means that they often do very little actual writing. Bernice Wong and associates (Wong et al., 1997; Wong, 1997) have shown that a three-phase instructional process can lead to significant improvement in the writing of adolescents with learning disabilities. The three phases are

1. Teacher modeling of specific expository genres combined with collaborative planning

2. Drafting at a word processor, which helps to attenuate handwriting, spelling, and fluency problems

3. Revising with peer and teacher conferences

In an instructional study, Wong et al. (1997) gave explicit instruction in writing compare-and-contrast essays to 21 struggling adolescent writers. After writing six compare-and-contrast essays, these students demonstrated significantly improved clarity and organization and utilization of facts and details to support comparisons and contrasts. Wong and associates credited this success to their explicit focus on a single genre, to the intensity of the instruction, and to the interactive dialogues among teachers and peers.

WRITING TO INQUIRE

We are living in what is sometimes called the Information Age and are witnessing the rapid expansion of knowledge across many disparate fields. What is taught in science, social studies, and mathematics will almost certainly change dramatically over the next decade. In an age of rapidly changing and expanding knowledge, a well-educated person must have the ability to inquire into a topic—to investigate it, read about it, think about it, and communicate about it. All too often we find that when students in our teacher education courses reflect on their own experiences in writing a report when they were youngsters, they recall a scenario not unlike that told by Amy Haysman below. As you read an excerpt from Amy's reflections, think about the problems she encountered and what specialized skills she needed to write her report.

The one research report that really impacted my life was due on January 30, 1984. I don't think I will ever forget that date or the term paper assignment I turned into Mrs. Hudson on that cold, dreary morning. When my ninth-grade teacher had first presented this assignment in class, I was excited. I was all grown up now! I was in high school and had finally been told to do the famous, dreaded task of writing a term paper. . . . I was given a slip of paper that said, "The characterization of Lady Macbeth in *Macbeth*." Was I supposed to know what this means?" I thought to myself. Suddenly, this coming-of-age assignment wasn't too appealing. Luckily, my teacher anticipated my panic attack and told everybody not to worry because she planned to teach us how to do the research step by step. Writing the paper was then up to us.

For the next few weeks, Mrs. Hudson led the class, page by grueling page, through a 38-page folder entitled, "The Term Paper: A Guide to Research, Documentation, and Format." We were then set loose in the school library. . . . After countless hours in several libraries, I had compiled a stack of note cards too big to fit in even a jumbo-size rubber band. I decided it was time to stop researching and start writing. As I read my note cards, I realized two problems. One, I didn't really understand what was written on these cards from the 13 books I had quoted, and two, I really had no idea how to write this paper. I had not learned anything about the characterization of Lady Macbeth in my frenzy to take notes and write bibliography cards in the correct form.*

Chances are, this scenario brought back vivid memories of the term paper, one of the most dreaded of all school projects for students and teachers alike. One obvious problem for Amy was her assigned topic. Perhaps if her teacher has considered aspects of an assignment represented by the R.A.F.T. acronym she might have had a better idea of why she was writing, what she was writing about, and for whom she was writing. When students are sent forth to "do research" for little more reason than it is ninth grade and the term paper is part of the ninth-grade curriculum, the results are too often exactly as Amy describes them.

One way to make writing to inquire more authentic and engaging is to consider how professionals in various content areas use writing. In a study of the writing of five research scientists, Debby Deal (1999) found that they used a progressive combination of expressive writing (personal, tentative, and meant primarily for themselves) and transactional writing (more formal, structured, and intended to communicate ideas to others) as they moved from the early stages of designing an experiment through data collection and analysis and the final preparation of a report to a funding agency or an article for a professional journal. Carolyn Keys (1999) argues that science students need to be engaged in authentic scientific writing, which she says should involve the production of new knowledge. Traditional scientific genres that promote scientific thinking include

1. Writing about experiments that are student designed or which may yield more than one data set
2. Writing explanations of scientific phenomena and processes
3. Writing reports based on secondhand sources
4. Biographies of one or a group of scientists
5. Persuasive expository writing on a controversial topic, such as whether dinosaurs are warm- or cold-blooded

Authentic historical inquiry should help students understand that history is not just a dry, noncontroversial recitation of facts, dates, and names of rich and powerful people but rather a frequently contentious interpretation of diverse

---

*Reprinted by permission of Amy P. Haysman.

perspectives and experiences with direct relevance to our contemporary lives. Therefore, students of history need to be guided to ask authentic questions, select and examine a variety of evidence, appreciate the context of historical events, evaluate divergent perspectives, and reach logical (albeit tentative) conclusions (Foster & Padgett, 1999).

Preparing for Student Inquiry

Asking students to embark on an extended inquiry project requires thoughtful planning and guidance. We suggest some general planning parameters here and describe more specific strategies in following sections.

Preparation should begin well before the assignment is explained and topics are selected. First, teachers need to decide on a conceptual framework within which students will select topics. By narrowing the scope of possible topic selection, teachers can do more advance preparation. They can alert media center colleagues and begin to identify resources. By placing some limits on the range of topics, teachers will be in a better position to provide resources and assistance as students pursue their research.

Establishing an overall theme for inquiry also makes it possible to build appropriate background through lecture, audiovisuals, read-aloud selections from literary works or nonfiction, primary sources, or guest speakers. For example, Cena and Mitchell (1998) describe how they began a research unit on the Middle Ages by showing a PBS video based on David Macaulay's book *Cathedral* (1973). After seeing the video and the book students were able to suggest several major themes related to life in the Middle Ages, including technology of building construction, social class distinctions, the arts, and the roles of religion, politics, and economics.

Once students understand the general issues related to their research theme, they can begin to brainstorm specific questions to investigate. Teachers should encourage reflection on the suitability of these topics—whether they are too narrow or too broad, whether the question is open or closed, and whether there are likely to be sufficient resources available for their inquiry.

As students embark on their inquiries, teachers may need to provide varied kinds of assistance. Directing students to appropriate resources, including people to interview, print sources, CD-ROMs, and Web sites, is a given. Students may also need guidance on how to evaluate their resources. Minilessons might cover any of a number of research skills that will facilitate inquiry, including

- How to take notes
- How to use indexes and tables of contents to pinpoint needed information
- Generating search terms for on-line indexes and the Internet
- How to read a "results" page from an Internet search
- How to organize information and begin writing
- Appropriate citation techniques
- Stylistic requirements for final reports

Throughout the inquiry process, from brainstorming topics to preparation of a final draft, teachers can encourage students to share their work with each other. This kind of peer collaboration and feedback was an important part of the inquiry process of the scientists interviewed by Deal (1999).

A final consideration in planning for student inquiry is time. Not only should teachers allow sufficient time for research and writing but also it is helpful to establish reasonable deadlines for various stages of the inquiry process, such as topic selection, identifying resources, developing an outline, beginning a draft, and completing a draft. Teachers can monitor student progress with a checklist or by periodically looking at student research logs. Meaningful inquiry takes a good deal of time for professionals, so it would be difficult to expect much less from apprentices. Although much of the inquiry process can be done outside of class, it is reasonable to expect that concentrated periods of class time will be devoted to students' research. For instance, the early stages of inquiry might require a few days to get everybody started. Then, a specified day each week might be devoted to student projects, with two or three days reserved for the final stages of preparation and presentation.

Collecting and Organizing Information

We think that the following two techniques for collecting and organizing information, when introduced to your students over a reasonable period of time, will keep them from experiencing some of the same frustrations Amy felt when it came time to write her paper.

Research or three-search?   Term papers can be as vexing to the teacher who has to read them as they are to the students who have to write them. For example, consider Terry Phelps's (1992) recollections:

> After years of grading research papers, I began to question their value. To begin with, I hated reading the wretched things. They were usually boring strings of quotes with none of the students' own thoughts. Most students fitted the papers to the quotes rather than vice versa. True synthesis was rare, and evidence that any learning had taken place was scant. (p. 76)

Phelps's dislike of grading term papers prompted him to look for alternatives to the traditional method of report writing. First, he wanted to develop a process that would enable students to rely more on their own ideas and interpretations and less on meaningless strings of quotations. To do this, he developed what he calls a *three-search paper* (Phelps, 1992). Named after the three search processes students must go through to produce a final written paper—reflecting, interviewing, and reading—the three-search paper discourages students from building their reports around quotations. It does this by engaging them in more personally and socially active kinds of research before sending them off to the library to find printed sources that support, expand, or explain what they have learned from personal reflection and interviews.

The three-search process for report writing begins with several reflective, or introspective, activities. Students examine sample papers that were written by former students to give them an idea of what their final papers may look like. Names are removed from the papers to preserve anonymity, and examples of both good and not-so-good papers are provided. Students also engage in a free-writing activity that encourages them to jot down whatever experiences they have had in relation to the topic on which they will write. Then, working in groups of three, students give each other feedback by focusing on what can be eliminated and what must be added to each person's list.

At the interview step, students examine the sample papers once more, this time for the purpose of noting how good writers incorporate specific examples and ask open-ended questions rather than questions that can be answered with yes or no. Then, each student interviews at least two people, including a peer and an authority on the topic he or she has chosen to research. For example, a student living outside Charlottesville, Virginia, who is planning to do a three-search paper on Thomas Jefferson might interview a representative of the Jefferson Memorial Foundation at Monticello as well as an African American peer. The interviews might focus on these persons' views about Jefferson, author of the Declaration of Independence and owner of more than 170 slaves. [For more information, see *Confronting Thomas Jefferson, Slave Owner* by James Blackman (1992).]

The final step—reading periodicals, books, pamphlets, and so forth—is usually the first step in the traditional approach to report writing. However, in the three-search process, printed sources are consulted only after students have had opportunities to reflect on previous experiences with the research topic and after they have interviewed at least two other individuals. As Phelps (1992) discovered, "by this time, students are fairly well immersed in their subjects; hence, a trip to the library for the third area of research is more focused and less odious" (p. 77).

I-charts.   An inquiry chart, or *I-chart* (Hoffman, 1992), capitalizes on what students already know about a particular research topic prior to reading. I-charts can be the basis for whole-class, small-group, or individual inquiry. A sample I-chart is illustrated in Figure 10.10. Students list their topic and an inquiry question about the topic, along with any information they already know on the topic. Then they consult various resources, noting bibliographic information and important ideas from each. Figure 10.10 has spaces for three resources, but I-charts can be expanded to include more. It is useful, however, to limit the amount of note-taking space to discourage wholesale copying of resource text. The I-chart has a place to list key words that students will want to use in their written reports, and it also provides space for the student to jot down any new questions that arise once their inquiry is under way.

Sally Randall (2000), a teacher at Oconee County Middle School in Watkinsville, Georgia, adapted the I-chart to make it fit her eighth graders' needs. She

---

I-CHART

Name: _____   Topic: _____

Subtopic: _____

What I Already Know: _____

Resource:	Important Ideas

Interesting Related Facts: _____

Key Words: _____

New Questions to Research: _____

FIGURE 10.10   **I-chart**

wanted to help her students build on prior knowledge and develop critical thinking skills as they collected and organized information for writing a research report. The I-chart provided a structure that suited her instructional goals.

First, Sally prepared her students for the eighth-grade interdisciplinary unit on the wilderness by teaching specific language arts skills that they would need in researching the topic. These skills included letter writing, paraphrasing, interviewing, and reference skills for use in looking up information in source materials and in constructing a bibliography of those materials. She relied on her colleague in science to prepare the class for topics related to the wilderness unit.

After students had chosen a topic that suited their interests, they wrote proposals, listing what they already knew about the topic, what they wanted to learn, and where they would look for the information. This step in the process helped the students to narrow their topics.

Next, students brainstormed questions they had about their topics—questions that could not be answered by a simple "yes" or "no." Following this brainstorming activity, they set up their individual I-charts. They turned their subtopics into questions. As they wrote their different subtopics/questions at the top of each of their multiple I-charts, the students also recorded what they already knew about a particular subtopic.

Then, turning to their source materials, they began to read for information that would help them answer their questions. They also wrote letters to people in the community who they thought would be knowledgeable on their topics of interest. This appeal to outside sources opened opportunities for meeting and talking with people who represented a diversity of interests and backgrounds.

Recording the information involved students in using what they had learned about note taking and paraphrasing. It also introduced them to an efficient way of recording bibliographic information. Briefly, they drew a line on their I-charts after they had completed writing down what they had learned from a particular source. Then, on a separate sheet of paper labeled "References" they wrote the complete bibliographical information about that source. From that point on, they only needed to refer to a source by its number when they wished to add information to their I-charts.

Writing a Report

Report writing calls for some specialized skills if students are to succeed in researching and writing about what they find. One of these skills is outlining, and another is paraphrasing.

Outlining. After Sally Randall's eighth graders had completed their I-charts, they were ready to begin the writing process. Each student had accumulated information on eight to ten subtopics (e.g., "What animals live in the rain forest?"), and they had organized their answers to the subtopic questions on their I-charts. By attaching a Roman numeral to each subtopic in their respective I-charts, the students had the beginnings of a formal outline. They added the details and interesting related facts found within their I-charts to complete the rest of their outline. As Randall (2000) noted in her discussion of the eighth graders' work, some used their outlines to create a visual display:

> The final product was a visual display for a wilderness convention much like the typical science fair. Students used the information they had learned to create a display of maps, charts, listings of facts, pictures, graphs, and timelines. They [also] created . . . a pamphlet informing the public of their expertise. These were showcased at an evening program to which we invited parents, experts who had been interviewed, and county librarians who had provided research assistance. (p. 540)

Paraphrasing.   Too often teachers assume students are able to paraphrase and find later, much to their dismay, that entire sections of a text have been copied verbatim with or without the use of quotation marks. Singer and Donlan's (1989) steps in teaching students how to paraphrase are easy to follow and demonstrate both *syntactic paraphrasing* (changing the order of the words) and *semantic paraphrasing* (substituting synonyms for the original words):

> *Step 1:* Present a passage from a text along with a paraphrased version. Lead students to discuss how the two differ.
>
> *Step 2:* Lead students to practice paraphrasing short passages from a text. Help them by identifying phrases to reword, using a dictionary to find synonyms, and modeling how long passages can be rewritten in shorter form.
>
> *Step 3:* Gradually introduce longer passages and eliminate or reduce your support.

Evaluating Web Sources

The Internet is largely unregulated, rapidly expanding, and continuously changing. Anybody with minimal technology skills can post a Web site and say whatever they wish. Therefore, one important Internet inquiry strategy is the ability to evaluate the reliability of what is found there. The following guidelines are adapted from suggestions made by Gardner, Benham, and Newell (1999) and Foster and Padgett (1999). Most of them can be applied to other inquiry resources as well.

1. Explain extension domains. Common extensions include

.com	commercial entity
.edu	educational institution
.gov	government agency
.mil	military
.net	network resource
.org	other type of organization, usually not-for-profit
.web	Web-related organizations

2. Is an author's name listed? Who is the author? What are his or her credentials? What is his or her affiliation and relation to the sponsors of the Web site? Is there an e-mail address, phone number, or other way to contact the author?

3. How accurate is the information? Are there references, links, or other ways to verify it? Is there any conflicting or supporting evidence?

4. How objective is the site? Why was this written? Do the language, graphics, or imagery reveal the author's perspective?

5. When was this written? Is there a date when the site was created and/or revised? Is the information current?

6. Does this site adequately cover the topic? How well does the information compare to other published resources? What is missing, hidden, or confusing? What additional information would be useful to know about this?

For more on evaluating Web sources, see our companion Web site at http://www.ablongman.com/alvermann3e.

Inquiry for Struggling Readers and Writers

Martha Rekrut (1997) recommends a collaborative approach to helping low achievers conduct inquiry. Inquiry topics should be of high interest to students and should be derived from questions that arise during the course of instruction. She recommends placing students in heterogeneous research groups of two, three, or four. She also says it is important to carefully teach and practice summarization or paraphrasing skills before students begin their research.

Alternatives to the Traditional Research Report

In earlier chapters, we featured several student inquiry projects which involved computer or media technology both in the research process and in the presentation of the results. In Chapter 3, we gave an example of a Web Quest project on local history in which students used the Web to gather information and then posted their results on the Internet. That chapter also described a class that presented their research in a 20-minute video that integrated language arts, science, and social studies concepts. At the end of Chapter 4, there were examples of student research in earth science taken from the Internet and displayed in a multimedia presentation. Chapter 6 culminated with a unit on the Revolutionary War which combined readings from historical fiction, a computer-based simulation, and a Web Quest. It is clear from these examples that the days are long gone when research meant little more than time spent with the *Reader's Guide* and stacks of index cards. New technologies have dramatically changed the ways in which inquiry can be conducted and reported. In the following sections, we take a closer look at some alternatives to the term paper.

Multigenre reports.   Inquiry results can be reported in genres and media other than the traditional expository research paper (Moulton, 1999). Students who have learned about the Curie family of scientists, for instance, might create birth, marriage, and death certificates in order to convey important details of their lives, along with newspaper accounts of the Nobel prizes won by members of the family in 1903, 1911, and 1935. Another possibility would be to create "laboratory notes" explaining one or more of the Curie discoveries. Students investigating Elizabethan theater might create posters and playbills for Shakespeare's plays. Inquiry results can also be incorporated into poems, skits or plays, and songs. Students might bring in short music clips that relate to some aspect of their research, along with a written explanation of the significance of their musical selection to their topic. Photos with captions, original artwork, and audio and video recordings are other media that can be used to present inquiry findings. These various genres and media can be motivating and provide a creative outlet for student learning, but still be based on significant data collection, synthesis, and evaluation.

Hypermedia.   Hypermedia software allows users to create computer-based files that may include text, sound, and visual images. Some hypermedia software, such as HyperStudio (Knowledge Adventure), Power Point (Microsoft), or Storyspace (Eastgate Systems), is designed for presentation of information. Other hypermedia software is designed specifically to create HTML (hypertext markup language) files or Web pages for the Internet. Many hypermedia programs and some word processor software also have the capability to save files as HTML so that the files can be posted to the Internet. Recent versions of Netscape Navigator and Microsoft Internet Explorer feature such Internet authoring software and there are also dedicated Internet authoring programs such as Home Page (Claris). Contemporary hypermedia software is generally user-friendly and can be easily learned by students in the upper elementary grades.

The contents of a hypermedia file may be original creations of the person who is making the file or they may be imported to the file from another computer file, a scanner, CD-ROM, the Internet, videodisk, or audio CD. The information within a hypermedia file is connected by hyperlinks, much like the Internet, so that anyone who accesses the file may move from link to link in whatever order may be of interest. For example, if a student were to create a hypermedia file on the jazz trumpeter Miles Davis, he or she might include photos of Miles, pictures of his album covers, a discography, reviews of his recordings, a biography, sound clips from his recordings or interviews, and pictures of a trumpet with a written description of the instrument and how it is played. With many hypermedia programs, he or she could also include links to Internet sites. The student could use this file to make a presentation of his or her research or it could be accessed on the computer by other interested people. If done as an HTML file, it could be posted to the Internet for an unlimited audience.

Teachers and students have found many uses for hypermedia. In Chapter 4, we described an earth science research project guided by biology teacher Mary Marcinkowski and her language arts colleague Gene Kulbago. One product of this research was individual hypermedia presentations. Nancy Patterson (1999) describes how her eighth-grade students began their research with Native American poems. Students highlighted words and phrases they were curious about in the poems and began searching for more information on the Internet. For example, a poem about the Spanish conquistadors led some students to learn more about the Spanish Conquest, which then led to Spanish galleons and Spanish weaponry of the sixteenth century. At the same time, they were also following leads to information on the Anasazi, the Navajo, and other Native Americans of the Southwest.

Typically, Patterson's students read dozens of on-line articles as well as other information they found in library reference materials. When they accumulated sufficient information on one of their subtopics, they created a "page" file which became part of a web of links from one topic to another. Their final hypermedia products opened with their selected poem. By clicking on high-lighted words in the poem, a reader could move to another page, which in turn would have links to other pages. Students created an average of 20 pages each for their final products. In contrast to the traditional research paper, Patterson found this project to be much more motivating. It also gave her students an ex-panded sense of what "text" is and how it can be manipulated. It allowed them to make choices about what to investigate, how to present information, and what organizational logic might link their varied findings.

Collaborative Internet projects.   The Internet makes it possible for collabora-tive inquiry to extend beyond a single classroom to different schools, states, and countries. E-mail communications, collaboration with experts in various fields, "virtual gatherings" in which on-line presentations introduce people from dif-ferent countries, electronic publishing, and shared data collection projects are a few of the collaborative Internet projects described by Mike and Rabinowitz (1998). One example is the Save the Beaches project, which involves students from throughout the world in pooled data collection and analysis in the process of solving environmental problems, specifically the cleanup of local beaches (*http://ednhp.hartford.edu/WWW/Nina/Beaches2.html*). Teachers can find other pro-jects or register a project of their own, along with an invitation to others to join, at the Global Schoolhouse Projects Registry (*http://www.gsn.org/gsn/proj/index.html*).

There are many more applications of technology for inquiry than we could possibly catalog here, and teachers and students are continuously finding new ways to use technological tools for conducting inquiry and disseminating the results. To learn more, you might consult some of the references we have cited here as well as the Suggested Readings at the end of Chapter 4.

RESPONDING TO STUDENT WRITING

We recently met a friend, who is an English teacher, for dinner at a sidewalk café. When we had told him we might be a little late, he said that would be no prob-lem. He was planning to spend a couple of hours there anyway, enjoying the pleasant spring weather and doing what English teachers do in the evening— reading student papers. Although English teachers may accept that as part of their turf, teachers in other disciplines usually do not. As you have been reading our recommendations for encouraging students to write, you might well have been wondering how you would read and correct all that writing. For high school teachers who have 100 or more students writing on a regular basis, that is something to consider. Fortunately, responding to student writing does not have to be an overwhelming chore for a teacher.

First, responding to writing need not be left entirely to the end of the writ-ing process, when papers are handed in and it is too late to do anything about problems of content, clarity, or form. Second, responding does not have to be the sole responsibility of the teacher. Much of what students write can be read and responded to while it is still in process, and students can be very effective reviewers of one another's work.

Peer Responses

Throughout this chapter, we have made many suggestions for peer collaboration on writing. Group brainstorming and composing, exchanges of drafts, and conferences for revision and editing all help students get feedback on their work, see that others have similar questions or problems, and enhance the quality of their final written products. Collaboration among student writers does not occur spontaneously, however. Teachers need to take a little time to model good responses and to set some ground rules.

The key to responding to a writer's work is what Donald Graves (1983) calls "receiving." By this he means responding to what the writer is saying or letting the writer know that his or her message has come across. Teachers can show students how to receive each other's writing by modeling the process with an anonymous piece of student writing that can be duplicated or displayed on the overhead projector. (To protect the feelings of the writer, we recommend that you not use writing from any member of the class.) The teacher can begin by rephrasing the main points of the piece and commenting on its strengths and then move on to one or two questions for the writer or suggestions for possible revision. Observations and questions from the class should be invited. Once class members have discussed what would and would not be helpful comments for the writer, they might collectively establish some ground rules for peer responses. We suggest some variation of three basic rules:

1. *Be positive.* Respond to what the writer is trying to say and what the writer does well. Tearing down another person's work will only result in discouragement and hurt feelings.
2. *Be helpful.* Do your best to make comments that will be useful to the writer.
3. *Be specific.* Talk about specific words, phrases, or paragraphs.

To facilitate peer conferences, you might consider using instructions similar to the guidelines for peer review in Figure 10.11. You might also prepare a checklist or a *peer review guide* similar to the one in Figure 10.11. Such a form gives you a way to monitor peer conferences, and it could be included in a portfolio as part of the record of how a writing project developed.

Successful peer conferences depend on successful peer relations, which of course are not always conducive to helpful cooperation. Timothy Lensmire (1994) has described how social relations among students play themselves out in writing workshop activities, sometimes to the detriment of students with low social status. He concludes that teachers should recognize peer culture and social relations and

---

PEER REVIEW

Writer: _____

Reviewer: _____

Topic/Title: _____

1. Read your partner's draft.

2. Which words or phrases struck you most? (Write them here.)

3. What do you feel the author was trying to say? Summarize it here in one sentence.

4. What are the main strengths of the draft?

5. What questions do you have for the author?

6. What one suggestion would you make to the author?

FIGURE 10.11   **A peer review guide**

take positive steps to sustain what he calls an "engaged, pluralistic classroom community" in which the voices of all students are valued and students learn to be considerate of their peers. It is unrealistic to expect that a teacher can heal all peer conflicts and maintain perfect harmony for a 45-minute period, despite whatever exchanges may be occurring in the hallways, on the street, or over the telephone. However, thoughtful modeling, guidance, and assignment of working groups can help to nourish civil and productive academic relationships.

Teacher Conferences

Teachers can respond to work in progress. In a short conference lasting two to five minutes, a teacher can read or listen to what a student is working on, ask a question or two, and respond to the writer's concerns. The goal of this kind of conference is to be helpful without being prescriptive. Teachers should confer without a pen or pencil in hand; marking a student author's draft voids the author's ownership and responsibility for the piece. Specific suggestions for adding, deleting, or altering the content of a draft may also diminish the writer's control and what Murray (1984) calls "the satisfaction of the writer's own learning, the joy and surprise of finding what [one has] to say" (p. 4). Instead, the teacher should try to adapt generic questions such as the following to each piece of writing:

What do you think you will do next with this?
What do you like best about this piece so far?
What problem or difficulty are you having?
Could you tell me more about X?
What is the connection between X and Y?

Questions such as these generate talk that can help writers work out problems and make their own discoveries.

There are several benefits to in-process teacher conferences. First, conferences can help students develop their general writing skills. Teacher guidance and feedback can improve the actual written products. Conferencing also pays off when the time comes for teachers to make a formal evaluation of students' writing. The better the writing is, the easier it will be to read. Also, reading and responding will go faster when the teacher has been involved in the development of a piece of writing.

Formal Evaluation

All writing by students need not be subjected to formal evaluation. Learning logs, informal written reflections, and other unfinished writing can be read quickly and given a simple check mark to indicate completion of the assignment, with a brief written acknowledgment or response if appropriate. Assigning formal grades to such writing defeats the purpose of informal writing-to-learn activities, in which the process of writing (and thinking) is more important than the product.

In those pieces that are polished and handed in for grading, teachers should respond first to the content. When a teacher uses the red pencil to mark each and every mechanical or stylistic miscue, it sends two unfortunate messages to the writer. First, it signals that form is more important than content. Second, it implies that there is little hope of mastering a skill so technical and arcane. A paper covered with red marks is discouraging to a writer. Where could one possibly begin to improve such a mess?

If students are writing to show what they have learned, grades and written comments should be based primarily on content. There is no question that spelling and other mechanics are important or that numerous mechanical errors detract severely from the effectiveness of writing. However, if students are writing to show what they have learned, the information presented and the quality of the reflection and thinking should merit more weight than spelling and other mechanical aspects. If necessary, a teacher might point out one or two mechanical problems that are repeated or are especially troublesome for a reader, and it is reasonable to expect that students learn how to spell the technical vocabulary of a subject area.

Mechanics should account for a portion of a grade, and we have no quarrel with rigorous academic expectations. However, "three wrong and it's a C" requirements seem too stringent for developing writers, at least for content area assignments in which the emphasis is on mastery of ideas, not mastery of conventions.

Dialect features in writing represent a particularly sensitive, complex, and controversial aspect of evaluating student writing. As we said in our earlier discussion of dialect, there is no question that all students need to be fluent with Standard English writing conventions. However, standard conventions need to be modeled and taught in a context that recognizes the legitimacy and power of diverse language forms and the importance of an individual's voice. This implies that in some situations, nonstandard stylistic features may be appropriate. In writing for which Standard English is expected, the marking of dialect miscues should be done with consideration of the age of the writer, the instruction in standard forms that he or she may have received, and the relative importance of content versus form in the writing task.

For assignments such as inquiry projects whose development is complex and time-consuming, you might consider some variation on portfolio assessment, as suggested in Chapter 5. Along with the finished product, students may hand in notes, outlines, early drafts, journal entries, and conference records. Self-evaluation should also be part of the portfolio. In fact, self-evaluation can be factored into the final grade on any formal written assignment.

SUMMARY

Writing is a rigorous kind of thinking; it can be hard work even for the most adept. Teachers who understand writing processes know that students need guidance, reassurance, and plenty of practice. When teachers thoughtfully assign, guide, and respond to student writing in content areas, students benefit in many ways. They gain increased content knowledge and understanding. When students write, they learn. Whether it is a short note reflecting on a new concept or a term paper involving several weeks of effort, writing helps them to connect and clarify their thinking. Regular informal writing activities prepare students for the more formal demands of writing papers and examinations. However, perhaps more important, writing empowers. In a world of expanding information and technology, the ability to express oneself clearly in writing is likely to become more, not less, of a social, professional, and economic determinant.

SUGGESTED READINGS

Baines, L., & Kunkel, A. (Eds.) (2000). *Going Bohemian: Activities that engage adolescents in the art of writing well.* Newark, DE: International Reading Association.

Bright, R. (1995). *Writing instruction in the intermediate grades: What is said, what is done, what is understood.* Newark, DE: International Reading Association.

Burns, M. (1995). *Writing in math class.* Sausalito, CA: Math Solutions.

English Journal (1999, September). Special issue on "research revisited," *89.* Champaign-Urbana, IL: National Council of Teachers of English.

Freedman, R. (1999). *Science and writing connections.* White Plains, NY: Seymour.

Perry, T., & Delpit, L. (Eds.) (1998). *The real Ebonics debate: Power, language, and the education of African-American children.* Boston: Beacon.

Studying and
Study Strategies

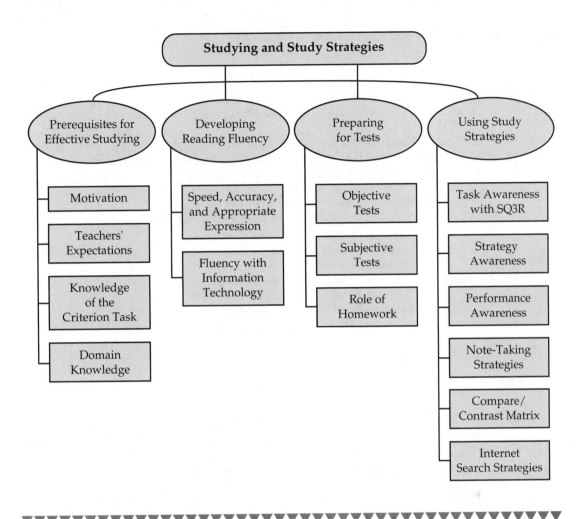

Reading. Period.*

"Once upon a time," the story began
and the world reached deeper into the horizon
than it had the last time he stretched out
into the printed lines of his book.
The bottom edge of the hard back binding
twirled slightly on the table top
as the black ink on white paper spun itself—
and him—from the pages
to another place far from where he leaned forward,

_____

*Allan A. De Fina, "Reading. Period." Copyright (C) 1997 by Allan A. De Fina.

but not far from where he sat.
He did not feel himself moving
though he knew he was descending through the ocean waters.
He could hear his breath
and he could feel the weight of the suit and the layers of sea,
and he stared at the fish which circled around him slowly and quietly,
as he dropped further into the increasingly dim depths.
Finally, he was there on the bottom, amidst the wreck and treasures.
His breathing slowed; occasionally he allowed a bubble
to gurgle free upwards. He was there. It was his. It was beau . . .

He heard a voice, at first far away and then closer.
He struggled upward for less than a second
before the waters drained away and the lamp, overhead again,
burned a hole brightly into that spot on the page
where last he stood with dry throat and wide eyes.
Was it time already? Did he really have to put the book away?

He sat upright and folded his hands dutifully.
The teacher was saying something in the front of the room.
He tried to listen. It was, after all, *now* time to learn.

▼▼▼▼▼▼

When Donna first heard the poet Allan De Fina read this poem at a forum on adolescent literacy sponsored by the International Reading Association in New York City in the fall of 1999, she remembered thinking how much it reminded her of the contrasts between reading and studying. While reading for pleasure, we slip effortlessly into print and out again as the writer's words work their magic on us, much as they did on the boy in the poem. However, while studying, that magic seems absent, or at best, it slips away too quickly. We lose our power to concentrate. Studying is hard work; it demands that we sit upright, so to speak, and pay attention to what writers have to say so that we can regurgitate their messages at a later time. However, is this really studying?

Not so, according to Paulo Freire and Donaldo Macedo (1987), two literacy educators who want their students to read the world as well as the word. To Freire and Macedo's way of thinking, "to study is not easy, because to study is to create and recreate and not to repeat what others say" (p. 77). We prefer their definition of what makes studying difficult. In fact, we think it aptly summarizes the intent of this chapter on studying and study strategies. We view studying as an active process—one born of creative and critical thinking, not of passive acceptance and mindless copying.

In this chapter, we describe several prerequisites for effective studying and the development of reading fluency. We also provide some tips on preparing students to take tests. Finally, we present several study strategies that are designed to help students develop the metacognitive and self-regulatory processes necessary for effective studying.

PREREQUISITES FOR EFFECTIVE STUDYING

To be effective in their studying, students need to develop a certain metacognitive awareness of the task and of themselves as readers; that is, they need to check their comprehension periodically for loss of meaning, apply appropriate fix-up strategies, monitor the effectiveness of those strategies, and evaluate their efforts to learn from studying (Baker & Brown, 1984). They also need to pay attention to what motivates them to learn. Beyond that, they can benefit from knowing their teachers' expectations of them as learners, understanding the nature of the criterion task, and possessing adequate domain knowledge.

Motivation

Students generally find studying a worthwhile activity only when they see real and meaningful purposes for doing it (Brozo & Simpson, 1995) or when a reward structure is sufficient for the goals they hold as learners (e.g., studying to make good grades so they can go on to college, so they can play high school sports, be a member of the marching band, and so on).

Motivating students to study in a way that makes clear what is in it for them is of primary importance. Although it is fairly easy to teach students new study strategies, it is something else to get them to apply those strategies on their own if they find no reason to do so. The strategies we introduce in this chapter will be most effective if taught at a time when students can use them to complete an assignment in one of their content area classes.

Teachers' Expectations

Teachers expect students to study the content of various subject matter specialties and to pass their courses. Because studying is mostly a self-directed activity (Thomas & Rohwer, 1986), teachers are aware of the need to teach students how to be effective studiers. Just knowing that their teachers expect them to master the content is sometimes motivation enough for students to value the study strategies they are taught (Nolen & Haladyna, 1989). However, when this is not the case, it may be useful to let them experience the difference a good study strategy can make. For example, students might find that by previewing a chapter they are able to reduce the time it actually takes them to read it. Even better, as Richardson and Morgan (2000) pointed out, teacher-guided previewing can help students reduce uncertainty about a reading assignment, especially when they discover that they do know something (however little) about the material. Reassuring students in this way can create a sense of shared responsibility in that they become aware of what they know and do not know (and thus need to study) at the same time that their teacher senses the difficulties a particular assignment will entail. When a teacher's expectations for effective studying are made explicit and easy-to-use strategies are demonstrated, as in the previewing example just given, a more relaxed and productive learning environment becomes possible.

Knowledge of the Criterion Task

Test-taking skills depend on a great deal more than students' ability to comprehend textual material. For example, there is considerable evidence that instruction in study skills is effective when students' knowledge of the criterion task enables them to study in a manner that ensures a match between the study technique and the items on a test (Alvermann & Moore, 1991; Anderson & Armbruster, 1984). This being the case, why don't more teachers tell students about the criterion task so that they can study more effectively? As Otto (1990) so aptly puts it, "teachers, themselves, often don't have a clear notion of the criterion task or its importance for studying, so they can't or don't make it clear to students" (p. 369). Faced with a lack of evaluation data on which study strategies work best for which types of learners and tasks, teachers often find themselves left with but one choice: to teach a variety of such strategies in the hope that at least one of them will be applied by their students. This hit-or-miss approach to strategy instruction is complicated further by the fact that even with a clearly set criterion task, there is no guarantee that students will use an appropriate study strategy. The mismatch between task and strategy is made worse when students do not possess adequate content area, or domain, knowledge.

Domain Knowledge

Many students lack the prerequisite knowledge to study effectively. Excessive absences or inattentiveness in class contribute to this knowledge deficit and make studying particularly difficult. Students who know little about a topic will find that their strategic knowledge cannot compensate for their lack of domain knowledge. To complicate matters further, Young, Arbreton, and Midgley (1992) observed that "all content areas may not be created equal" (p. 1). That is, students' ability to acquire knowledge in a specific domain (e.g., social studies, science, mathematics, or English) may rest partially on their motivational orientation to learning. According to Young, Arbreton, and Midgley, the middle-grade students they studied were more likely to enjoy learning for its own sake in mathematics and science than in English and social studies.

In classrooms of the twenty-first century, being literate in a particular domain is not limited by what students are able to access from printed texts using conventional study strategies. Instead, it is becoming increasingly common for readers who struggle with their content area textbooks to turn to electronic study aids to help them organize their thinking around a set of domain-specific tasks. Consider, for example, the case of Andrew Sheehan (Sheehan & Sheehan, 2000), a ninth grader whose writing disability and attention deficit disorder have been partially compensated for by the use of adaptive equipment such as

Adaptive Equipment for Readers Struggling to Acquire Domain Knowledge

Electronic organizers

If memory is the library of the mind . . . I've lost my card catalog! I use an electronic pocket organizer for day-to-day survival. I type in my homework, notes, reminders, phone numbers, et cetera. . . . I can jot something down before I forget it, and all my important messages stay in one place. Handwriting is not necessary, nor is organization on a page. . . . This is far superior to having notes to myself scattered all across the globe. (Sheehan & Sheehan, 2000, p. 27)

Portable keyboards

For daily notetaking I use a product called Alpha Smart (made by Intelligent Peripheral Devices, Inc., 20380 Town Center Lane, Suite 270, Cupertino, CA 95014; alphasmart.com). The Alpha Smart is like an overgrown organizer. This device is nearly a full-sized keyboard with an LCD screen and eight files. Each file can be used for a different school subject. Even though keyboarding is necessary, I can get down enough information in classes to serve as notes. Then I can send this information to a word processor on a Macintosh or PC and edit and print the notes. The new Alpha Smart 2000 model has a built-in spell checker, which is a big help. This device runs on three AA batteries and fits in my backpack. (Sheehan & Sheehan, 2000, p. 28)

a voice-to-text computer software program, an electronic pocket organizer, and a portable keyboard. In the box above are Andrew's own words and some ideas that teachers may find useful in helping other students like him acquire crucial domain knowledge through special study aids.

DEVELOPING READING FLUENCY

One definition of fluent readers focuses on their ability to comprehend texts of various types with speed, accuracy, and appropriate expression (National Reading Panel, 2000). Another less well-known definition is that which focuses on students' fluency with information technology (American Association of University Women Educational Foundation, 2000). The assumptions and recommended instructional practices pertaining to both definitions of reading fluency are discussed here.

Speed, Accuracy, and Appropriate Expression

The underlying assumption of fluency instruction defined in terms of a reader's speed, accuracy, and appropriate expression is that teachers will view it as a means to comprehension and not as an end in itself. Because adequate comprehension is essential for effective studying to occur, it is clear that fluency plays a pivotal role overall. The National Reading Panel (2000), while acknowledging that fluency instruction is often neglected in day-to-day classroom instruction, found sufficient research evidence to suggest that guided oral reading procedures have a positive impact on students' fluency and comprehension across a range of grade levels and in a variety of regular and special education classrooms. Although the jury is still out on whether or not independent silent reading has a similar effect, we include it as a part of this discussion because of its long-standing intuitive appeal in the field.

Guided oral reading procedures.   Repeated reading, shared reading, paired reading, and any number of other similar procedures make up what are generally referred to as guided oral reading procedures. These procedures share several key characteristics. They typically involve students in rereading the same text over and over again until a specified level of proficiency is reached. They also tend to rely on one-to-one instruction through tutoring (including peer tutoring and cross-age tutoring), audiotapes, or some other means of guided oral reading practice. Unlike whole-class, round-robin oral reading in which individuals read aloud for only a brief period of time, the guided oral reading procedures just named maximize the amount of time any one student spends practicing fluency.

Attaining a level of fluency such that difficulties with word recognition and slow, choppy reading do not interfere with comprehension and studying is a goal toward which all students need to work. However, it is an especially important goal for students who are learning English as a second language. Although the National Reading Panel (2000) did not address issues relevant to second-language learning, a growing body of research on guided oral reading procedures used with Latina/o students tends to support the panel's findings that such procedures do indeed improve reading.

For example, Robert Jiménez and Arturo Gámez (2000) were successful in their efforts to build reading fluency and improved attitudes toward reading among a group of middle school Latina/o students who, without such instruction and opportunities for guided oral rereading, might have been viewed simply as at risk for school failure. Similar results were found for a fluency procedure called "cooperative" repeated readings used with a group of African American eighth graders who struggled with reading and who were considered at risk of school failure (Tatum, 2000). As Jiménez and Gámez noted, too often the at-risk label is applied to students who "may possess untapped potential for success in literacy" (p. 81) if given appropriate instruction.

Independent silent reading.   The assumption here is that by encouraging students to read on their own, we influence the amount of time they spend practicing their literacy skills. Although procedures such as sustained silent reading, drop everything and read, and a number of incentive programs (e.g., Million Minutes and Pizza Hut's Book It) are thought to motivate students to read more, the relationship between increased voluntary reading time and reading achievement is still murky. As the National Reading Panel (2000) took pains to point out in their report, the data connecting time spent reading and reading achievement are correlational rather than causative in nature. Thus, it could be the case that reading more makes an individual a better reader, or it could be simply the fact that better readers opt to read more. The lack of conclusive evidence in support of independent silent reading does not mean that teachers should cease to encourage it. On the contrary, as Saunders and Goldenberg (1999), researchers with the Center for Research on Education, Diversity and Excellence, are quick to note, pleasure reading and teacher read-alouds are designed "to expose students to the language of expert writers and the fluency of an expert reader" (p. 5).

Fluency with Information Technology

One of several new terms to make its way into the field of reading education as a result of the information explosion associated with today's computer age is *information literacy*. It refers to what is generally defined as the ability to access, evaluate, organize, and use information culled from a variety of sources. Not to be confused with *computer literacy*, which reflects a technological know-how in manipulating software packages, information literacy requires, among other things, knowing how to formulate a search strategy for zeroing in on needed information. The topic of Internet search strategies will be discussed later. For now, it is sufficient to link information literacy to fluency with information technology.

In a report focused on how to educate girls in the computer age so that they become tech savvy and capable of participating fully in e-culture (American Association of University Women Educational Foundation, 2000), the argument is made that fluency with information technology is much more than static listings of how to become more proficient at word processing or e-mailing. Instead, the authors of the report note that, "fluency goals must allow for change, enable adaptability, connect to personal goals, and promote lifelong learning" (p. xi).

Technology Tip

A useful set of nonprint media standards for helping students achieve fluency with information technology is available through the National Research Center on English Learning and Achievement (CELA). Developed at CELA by Karen Swan, the nonprint media standards are divided into basic skills, critical literacies, and construction skills for each of three grade levels: elementary, middle, and high school. A complete listing of these standards for achieving information literacy is available at http://cela.albany.edu/standards/index.html. A pdf file of the standards is located at http://cela.albany.edu/publication/brochure/standards.pdf

These goals will require that all students become fluent in skills such as designing a home page, organizing a database, communicating with others whom they may never meet in person, and evaluating personal privacy concerns.

PREPARING FOR TESTS

By relieving some students' natural anxiety about taking tests, teachers may help them improve their performance. Teachers can minimize the weighting of test grades in a student's overall course grade and reduce the demands associated with testing. Providing students with information about the criterion task and selecting test items that students have practiced beforehand are examples of how teachers reduce the demands of testing. This type of help lessens students' need to second-guess what the teacher thinks is important and unimportant. Students are also less anxious about taking tests when they know in advance that the tests will consist of objective items (multiple-choice, true/false, fill-in-the-blank) or subjective items (short answer and opinion essay). Because objective and subjective exams place different demands on students, teachers usually find it helpful to provide a separate set of test-taking tips for each type of exam.

Objective Tests

Objective tests evaluate students' recall or recognition of information. Fill-in-the-blank items require students to recall information, and multiple-choice, true/false, and matching items require them to choose from among two or more options. Although students typically find it easier to recognize a correct answer than to recall it, there are exceptions. For example, the student for whom English is a second language generally finds recognition tasks difficult because each option presents the possibility that vocabulary meaning will be distorted. Consequently, foils (incorrect answers) are double jeopardy for such a student.

Tips on helping students prepare for objective tests include teaching them to use mnemonic devices. For example, the first letter of each word in the sentence "George Everett's old grandfather rode a pig home yesterday" will help them recall and spell the word *geography*. Similarly, HOMES is a mnemonic for the names of the Great Lakes and ROY G BIV for the colors in the spectrum. In addition, imagery (such as visualizing where the Ohio River joins the Mississippi River) may help students recognize the meaning of a word (such as *confluence*) in a matching test.

Sometimes words such as *always* and *never* are included in a list of foils; when students see them, they can be almost certain that these are not the correct answers. Exceptions, of course, are instances in which the inclusive term describes a generally accepted fact, as in "All carrots are vegetables."

Objective test items may have more than one correct answer. When this occurs, it is possible that a mistake has been made, and students should check with the teacher. If the items are correctly written and students believe that more than one answer is correct, they may bring the matter up with the teacher after the test has been marked, or teachers may give students the option of justifying their answers to objective test items as part of the examination process. Doing this, of course, greatly increases the amount of time required to grade the exam.

Subjective Tests

Subjective tests, such as short-answer tests and opinion essays, evaluate students' abilities to organize, analyze, synthesize, and integrate ideas. They are easier to construct than objective tests, but they take longer to grade and are open to more dispute regarding the correctness of answers. Both holistic and analytic scoring methods have been used successfully with essays. As its name implies, *holistic scoring* is based on the overall impression a teacher has of an essay after reading it for the general meaning of its message. Unlike holistic scoring, *analytic scoring* enables a teacher to grade separate components of an essay (its content, form, argument, grammar, and so on). The analytic scoring method is time-consuming, but it gives students a clear idea of how teachers arrive at a grade.

Tips on helping students prepare for subjective tests include providing them with information on what should be included in an essay and what the point distribution will be if analytic scoring is to be used. Letting students know whether grammar, spelling, and punctuation will be taken into consideration is also helpful.

Prompts, such as the planning cues for opinion essays listed in Figure 11.1, are useful in assisting students to think substantively about what they want to say. These cues should be used as prompts for the conceptualization of an essay, not as parts of statements in the essay itself.

Scaffolded instruction, or instruction that begins with the teacher modeling a particular process and gradually turning the responsibility for the task over to students, can be used to teach students how to write essays. Based on the ideas of Wood, Bruner, and Ross (1976), "the metaphor of a scaffold has been proposed to describe this process since a scaffold is erected at the outset of construction and gradually withdrawn as a building becomes self-supporting" (Pressley, El-Dinary, & Brown, 1992, p. 106). To provide scaffolded instruction in writing essays, teachers can show students model essays that have prompts written in the margins to indicate the types of information that should be included. A model also provides students with an idea of the form a finished product should take.

Role of Homework

Historically, opinions about the value of homework have fluctuated widely, and to our knowledge very little research exists on the role of homework in preparing students for exams. Intuitively, of course, it would seem that the more conscientious a student is in completing her or his homework, the better that student

New idea

An even better idea is . . .
An important point I haven't considered yet is . . .
A better argument would be . . .
A whole new way to think of this topic is . . .
No one will have thought of . . .

Improve

I'm not being very clear about what I just said, so . . .
A criticism I should deal with in my paper is . . .
I really think this isn't necessary because . . .

Putting it together

If I want to start off with my strongest idea, I'll . . .
I can tie this together by . . .
My main point is . . .

Elaborate

An example of this . . .
This is true, but it's not sufficient, so . . .
My own feelings about this are . . .
I'll change this a little by . . .
The reason I think so is . . .
Another reason that's good is . . .
I could develop this idea by adding . . .
Another way to put it would be . . .
A good point on the other side of the
    argument is . . .

Goals

A goal I think I could write is . . .
My purpose is . . .

FIGURE 11.1   Planning cues for opinion essays   (*Source:* B. Rosenshine & C. Meister, The use of scaffolds for teaching higher-level cognitive strategies, *Educational Leadership, 49*(7), 29. Reprinted with permission of B. Rosenshine and the Association for Supervision and Curriculum Development. Copyright © 1985 by ASCD.)

will do academically. Overall, the research literature on assigning homework supports the view that the amount of time spent doing homework is associated with students' academic achievement. For example, in a booklet distributed by the U. S. Department of Education (Paulu, 1995), we learn that

> In the *early elementary grades,* homework can help children develop . . . [good] habits and attitudes. . . . From *fourth through sixth grades,* small amounts of homework, gradually increased each year, may support improved academic achievement. In *seventh grade and beyond,* students who complete more homework score better on standardized tests and earn better grades, on the average, than students who do less homework. The difference in test scores and grades between students who do more homework and those who do less increases as children move up through the grades. (p. 5)

The nature of homework varies according to the purpose for giving the assignment. Generally, there are three types of assignments: practice, preparation, and extension (LaConte, 1981). When homework is given for the purpose of reinforcing new learning, it is thought of as a *practice assignment.* Research on expert and novice teachers indicates that the experts assign homework only after they have monitored and guided students' practice in class, but the novices are likely to assign material that they were unable to find time to teach in class (Leinhardt, 1983).

As their name implies, *preparation assignments* are meant to provide students with the background information they will need in order to understand new information when it is introduced in their textbook or in class discussion. The assumption is that students will acquire "hooks" on which to hang new information if they have the appropriate background knowledge. Unlike practice and preparation assignments, *extension assignments* are given to encourage students to move beyond their textbooks in acquiring, synthesizing, and using the information they find. Increasingly, with greater access to the World Wide Web, extension assignments are becoming popular with both teachers and students. Although this development has its upside, there is a downside as well. Unfortunately, too often students are left to flounder when it comes to completing an extension assignment for which they must develop their own search strategies. Some of the problem lies no doubt with teachers' own sense of feeling unprepared. According to a report by the National Center for Education Statistics (2000), only 20 percent of the teachers surveyed felt prepared to integrate educational technology into their teaching methods. Approximately the same percentage felt competent in using technology to address the needs of students with disabilities (21 percent) and students whose first language is other than English (20 percent).

USING STUDY STRATEGIES

Reading to learn specific information for the purpose of performing some criterion task is what defines studying and sets it apart from merely comprehending the information (Anderson & Armbruster, 1984). This type of reading, or studying, requires students to think about and control their own learning processes (Zimmerman, 1994). However, before students can become metacognitively aware of what these learning processes are, they must know the following (Wade & Reynolds, 1989, p. 6):

1. What to study in a particular learning situation, or *task awareness*
2. How best to learn it, or *strategy awareness*
3. Whether and to what extent they have learned it, or *performance awareness*

Thus, before students can actively monitor their own studying, they need to learn about and develop task, strategy, and performance awareness. Sufficient research exists on the subject of metacognitive awareness to merit basing instruction on its findings. The instructional activities for developing these three areas of awareness discussed in this section are derived from the research literature on metacognition. They have also been field-tested by Wade and Reynolds (1989).

Task Awareness with SQ3R

Helping students locate information that is important according to external criteria (although not necessarily interesting to them) is the first step in developing their task awareness. Ways of doing this include having students brainstorm about the important ideas in a short selection they have read. After recording their responses on the chalkboard, ask them to give reasons why the ideas are important, based on external criteria. External criteria imply that information is relevant if it is one of the the main ideas put forth by the author of a selection. This does not mean that internal criteria, such as students' interests, are unimportant. However, for the purpose of developing task awareness, external rather than internal criteria are employed.

To point out the importance of task awareness in answering an essay question, show students what information they would need to answer a sample question satisfactorily. As a follow-up to this activity, show students how to arrange the needed information in a hierarchical manner. Selectively focusing attention on relevant material also teaches students to self-question. For example, students might ask themselves why they placed a particular piece of information in a position subordinate to another piece of information.

Deciding what to study in a particular reading assignment is at the core of task awareness. An effective way to focus students' attention on important information is to introduce them to SQ3R—an acronym that stands for Survey, Question, Read, Recite, and Review (Robinson, 1961). This study system has been in use for several decades and for good reason. It works if introduced and practiced under teacher guidance, though not perfectly for every student in every study setting. As a systematic way of previewing, questioning, and reviewing information that is read, SQ3R offers students a chance to be proactive in developing task awareness as they study expository text. In Figure 11.2, we describe the five steps in SQ3R, and then we show how these steps relate to locating and remembering information that is considered important in a selection.

Strategy Awareness

After students have analyzed information to determine its most important points, the next step is to develop their awareness of the type of strategy that is needed to meet the requirements of the assessment or criterion task. For example, if the assessment consists of taking a true/false test, fewer cognitive resources will be called into play than if the task is writing an essay.

Step	Description of Step	Relation to Task Awareness
Survey	Preview a selection by reading titles, headings, subheadings, captions accompanying illustrations, and a summary if one is available.	Enables a reader to locate information that the author of a selection thought important enough to highlight structurally or to illustrate through examples.
Question	Turn each title, heading, and caption into a question.	Makes clear to a reader what he or she already knows (or doesn't know) about the assigned informational text.
Read	Actively read to answer questions posed in Step 2.	Focuses attention on what author believes is important and worth remembering.
Recite	Close the text and orally summarize what you just read; then make notes using your own words.	Improves memory and aids attention span after initial reading of the selection.
Review	Study your notes periodically, and refresh your memory of the text by using its main headings to cue your recall of the subheadings.	Keeps relevant information foremost in mind and reinforces relationships between important ideas and the evidence that supports them.

FIGURE 11.2   **The SQ3R study system**

One way of developing strategy awareness is to show students how to read and study a short selection by modeling the process yourself. First, as you read aloud, describe the study strategies you are using. List them on the chalkboard under one of the two headings in Figure 11.3: Observable Study Methods and In-the-Head Study Methods (Wade & Reynolds, 1989, p. 10). Ask the students to construct a similar list using a different short selection. After the students have exhausted their list of methods, they can compare their list with the list in Figure 11.3. A discussion might follow in which students tell why they sometimes, always, or never use a particular study strategy. At this point, it is important to remind students that not every strategy meets everyone's needs, nor should they feel compelled to adopt a particular strategy. Research has demonstrated that students who are effective studiers use the strategies that work for them (Swafford, 1988).

Performance Awareness

According to Wade and Reynolds (1989), "a strategy can be considered effective only when it has a strong, positive effect on learning" (p. 11). Developing students' performance awareness enables them to monitor whether or not they have understood the task and used the appropriate study strategy. If they have

OBSERVABLE STUDY METHODS

Highlight or underline

Copy—Write down information either on note paper or in the margins exactly as it is written in the text.

Write down in your own words—Either on note paper or in the margins.

Outline—Organize ideas on paper in categories or under headings to show which are the main ideas and which are supporting ideas or examples.

Draw a diagram—Organize ideas on paper in diagrams that show how they relate to each other.

IN-THE-HEAD STUDY METHODS

Look over before reading—This is a very fast type of reading. It involves either reading for the main ideas in order to get an overview of the passage, or moving very quickly over unimportant information.

Read at your usual rate—This is right for some materials.

Read slowly—Slow down your reading for better comprehension or concentration.

Go back and read again—Read certain parts of the text a second time, usually when information is confusing or you want to understand it better.

Pay special attention—Concentrate on specific information in order to remember it. This includes mentally reciting material, concentrating on specific information, memorizing, reading aloud, and going back over notes or underlinings.

Put together ideas in your head—Stop to get the whole picture, to summarize the information in your head, or to connect ideas.

Relate ideas to what you already know—Create associations between a new idea and something you already know or have experienced.

Make a picture in your mind—Imagine a picture of a place, object, or event.

Question or test yourself—Think of questions and answer them as you read along; test your comprehension and memory as you go over your notes or underlinings.

Guess what will happen—Make predictions about what will happen next or what the reading will be about.

Other—Anything you do when reading or studying that is not listed above.

FIGURE 11.3   Strategy definition sheet   (*Source:* Figure 2 from Suzanne E. Wade and Ralph E. Reynolds, Developing metacognitive awareness, *Journal of Reading,* October 1989. Reprinted with permission of Suzanne Wade and The International Reading Association.)

done both, their performance on the criterion task should reflect it. Research has shown that metacognitively aware readers know when their learning breaks down and how to adjust the strategies they are using (or adopt new ones) to remedy the problem (Ghatala, 1986).

A good way to develop performance awareness among students is to have them determine whether the strategies they use to study a selection are effective. Ask students to read a short selection, and then have them record the strategies they used on a separate sheet of paper. Next, ask them to respond to ten objective questions on the selection they have just read without looking back at the text. Finally, grade answers to the questions as a class activity, and encourage students to discuss why they think the strategies they used were or were not appropriate for the task.

Note-Taking Strategies

Both research and practical experience emphasize the importance of direct instruction in teaching students how to take notes. Such instruction should explain the purpose of note taking, and it should take place over a reasonable period of time. Brozo and Simpson (1995, p. 284) provide the following criteria for helping students develop expertise in using study strategies:

1. Strategy explanations and rationales (i.e., steps, tactics, advantages)
2. Strategy modeling and talk-throughs by the teacher
3. Examples from real texts and tasks that students will encounter
4. Guided practice with real texts, followed by specific, qualitative feedback
5. Debriefing sessions that deal with questions, student doubts, and fix-up strategies
6. Frequent independent practice opportunities across appropriate texts
7. Guidelines on how to evaluate a strategy's success or failure.

Split-page note taking.   Another activity, more complex than the one involving the data collection cards, is the *Directed Notetaking Activity* (Spires & Stone, 1989). It includes two instructional components that can be introduced over a period of time using minilessons to teach students how to

1. Take notes using the split-page method (Palmatier, 1973)
2. Use self-questioning to monitor levels of involvement in note taking before, during, and after hearing a lecture

An example of the split-page method for taking notes is shown in Figure 11.4. Examples of some questions that students might ask themselves before, during, and after taking notes include the following (Spires & Stone, 1989, p. 37):

Planning (before taking notes)
How interested am I in this topic?
If my interest is low, how do I plan to increase [it]?
Do I feel motivated to pay attention?
What is my purpose for listening to this lecture?

Definition of social control	Ways of conditioning or limiting actions of individuals in order to motivate them to conform to social norms.
Two types of social control	(1) internalized
	(2) externalized
Internal control	Individuals accept norms of group or society as part of own personality (for example, refrain from stealing not because afraid of arrest but because believe stealing is wrong).
	Most effective means of socially controlling deviant behavior.
External control	Set of social sanctions (informal or formal) found in every society.
Informal sanctions	Applied through actions of people the individual associates with every day (that is, the *primary* group).
	May range from gesture of disapproval to rejection by primary group.
Formal sanctions	Applied by agents given that function by society (such as law enforcement officials).

FIGURE 11.4   **An example of the split-page method of note taking based on a lecture titled "Social Control"**   (*Source:* Figure 1 from Hiller A. Spires and Diane P. Stone, The Directed Notetaking Activity: A self-questioning approach, *Journal of Reading,* October 1989. Reprinted with permission of Hiller A. Spires and the International Reading Association.)

Monitoring (while taking notes)
Am I maintaining a satisfactory level of concentration?
Am I taking advantage of the fact that thought is faster than speech?
Am I separating main concepts from supporting details?
What am I doing when comprehension fails?
What strategies am I using for comprehension failure?

Evaluation (after taking notes)
Did I achieve my purpose?
Was I able to maintain satisfactory levels of concentration and motivation?
Overall, do I feel that I processed the lecture at a satisfactory level?

Palmatier's (1973) split-page method of note taking gives students a systematic approach to organizing and studying their class notes. Using this method, teachers instruct students to

1. Use only one side of an 8½-by-11-inch sheet of paper that has been divided lengthwise by folding it into two parts. The left column should be about one-third of the paper; the right column, about two-thirds of the paper.
2. Record the lecture notes in the right column, using both subordination of ideas and spacing to indicate the importance of information.

Read Aloud/Note-Taking Method for Readers Who Struggle

To prepare her self-contained eighth-grade reading class for the New York State English Language Arts exam, Rebecca Meyers* engaged in an action research project to determine if her students would improve their listening and note-taking skills as a result of participating in an eight-week direct-instruction approach to the split-page method of note taking. All participants were enrolled in the school's special education program and attended inclusion classes for their core academic courses.

Ms. Meyers began the project by interviewing students about note taking. Then, after obtaining a baseline measure of their note-taking skills, she read aloud a short expository passage while the students listened for important information but did not take notes. Before reading aloud the same passage for a second time, Rebecca taught her students how to set up their papers for the split-page method of note taking. On the second read-aloud, students jotted down facts in the right-hand column of their papers. The class worked as a group to classify the facts (details) they had identified into main idea topics, which were listed in the left-hand column of their papers. In the weeks that followed, Ms. Meyers taught her students how to abbreviate words or draw stick figures that would convey their understanding of the important information they heard as she read aloud from a variety of expository and informational texts.

By scaffolding her explicit instruction of the split-page method of note taking, Rebecca was able to assist the class in moving from almost total dependence on her for structuring their notes to independence in note taking. She was also able to shorten the time that she paused between paragraphs as she read aloud from the passages. After only six sessions of explicit instruction in this method, Rebecca noted an increase in the number of facts they wrote down. She also learned from poststudy interview data that all students felt comfortable taking notes using the split-page method, although not all were comfortable using abbreviations. One girl said she could not always remember what her abbreviations stood for when she reviewed her notes.

*Used with permission of Rebecca Meyers, Wilson Middle School, Wilson, New York.

3. Review and organize the notes by first reading over the information in the right column to obtain a sense of the major concept and then placing that concept in the left column opposite the related information in the right column.
4. If the notes are unclear or sketchy, refer to the textbook or the source that was the basis for the lecture. Additional information may be added to the back of the paper if no space remains on the front.
5. Study the notes by folding the paper so that only the left column is visible. The labels in that column serve as a focal point for recalling information found in the right column.

Spires and Stone (1989) suggest a way to use videotapes to provide instruction in the split-page method of note taking. Teachers' lectures can be taped and played back as students view the tapes and practice applying the split-page method. Initially, the practice sessions should be no longer than 15 minutes. As students' comfort level with the method increases, so too should the time allotted to practice sessions.

Compare/Contrast Matrix

This study strategy assists students in organizing information as they read their content area assignments. It simultaneously involves them in summarizing that information in a compare/contrast pattern (Santa, 1988). Developing a sense of a text's organizational structure enables students to recall information more fully and efficiently. Thus, the compare/contrast matrix illustrated in Figure 11.5 is a natural tool for students to use with reading assignments that present information that differs along various attributes. For example, in Figure 11.5, Victoria Ridgeway, our colleague at Clemson University, uses six attributes

	anarchy	monarchy	democracy	dictatorship	oligarchy	fascism	theocracy
Who governs?							
How do you get power?							
How is power maintained?							
How is power transferred?							
How are laws made?							
Essential elements?							
Example:							

FIGURE 11.5 Compare/contrast matrix: Social studies—forms of government (*Source:* From V. Ridgeway's adaptation of C. M. Santa, *Content reading including study systems*, pp. 75–83, Dubuque, IA: Kendall/ Hunt, 1988.)

(stated in the form of questions) to demonstrate to the students in her content literacy course how seven different types of government differ. She also asks them to include an example of each type of government (e.g., the United States is an example of a democracy).

When using the compare/contrast matrix the first few times with your classes, we recommend that you model the procedure. This might consist of partially filling in each column and row while referring to the text. Also, you might want students to predict what they think they will find in their reading, using their predictions to fill in some of the columns and rows. Then, after reading the material, they could check the accuracy of their predictions. After students become more familiar with the compare/contrast matrix, they may begin to construct similar matrices on their own.

If using the compare/contrast matrix for the first time with students who find reading a struggle, it is advisable to have them listen for signal words such as *however, but, different from*, and *while* as you read aloud a passage from their textbook and model how you would fill in the matrix. As noted by at least one middle school teacher of considerable classroom experience, readers who have difficulty comprehending will find it frustrating if they have to divide their attention between learning a new study strategy and perceiving the organizational structure of their texts (Marlene Willis, personal communication, April 11, 2000).

Internet Search Strategies

Although we included information on planning for student involvement with the Internet in Chapter 4, we add a brief section here to highlight the importance of teaching students strategies for searching for information that will supplement their textbooks when they are studying or attempting to complete an assignment. Based on several months of firsthand observations of middle and high school students in a public library as they searched for Web sites for which they had no specific URLs (Web site addresses), we concluded that their lack of a search strategy often led to their giving up or becoming distracted by irrelevant Web site information (Alvermann et al., 2000).

In helping these students develop independent search strategies, we began with an introduction to *Ask Jeeves for Kids!* at *http://www.ajkids.com*. This user-friendly Web site does not teach a strategy per se, but through using it kids learn to narrow their questions, which is the first step in helping them become more efficient in their searches. For example, if one types in the question, "Where can I learn about ants?" on the Web site's home page, the reply is "Jeeves knows these answers":

Where can I learn about the insect?
Where can I see photographs of ants?
Where can I find a concise encyclopedia article on ants?
Where can I learn about ant interactions in a tropical rain forest?

A Response from Our Readers

Alison Pinyan,* a graduate student enrolled in Donna's content literacy course at the University of Georgia, wrote the following response after reading about the compare/contrast matrix:

> I have always had a hard time making myself read or study something that does not interest me because I'm a terrible note taker. I know that I am not alone in this. I'm sure that many children feel the same way. . . . I really liked the compare/contrast matrix. It

was a way to make a quick reference guide without having to go back and read a bunch of notes. It seems as though it would be an easy way for anyone to understand difficult concepts. I only wish my teachers knew about this method when I was in [high] school.

*Adapted with permission of Alison Pinyan.

If none of these answers prove satisfactory, kids are given the option to check out links from the Web site's metasearch partners or to ask a new question.

After the students we were observing in the public library became fairly comfortable with the *Ask Jeeves for Kids!* format, we introduced them to subject matter Web sites, such as the *History Channel* (*http://www.historychannel.com/home/index.html*). Here, they were able to further hone their search strategies by deciding what types of information would satisfy their needs. At this Web site students have the option of searching a particular topic by century (and then decade). They can also participate in a quick poll, find out what happened in history on the day they were born, and so on. One drawback to this Web site is the overabundance of options, most of which are unrelated to the topic the student types in to begin the search. Even so, we took advantage of this potentially distracting Web site to discuss with them the importance of staying focused (a skill we ourselves often find difficult to master).

For those students who were ready for more advanced Internet search strategies, we introduced them to some of the more popular search engines and subject directories. Yahoo quickly became their favorite, so much so in fact that we noticed kids teaching other kids some strategies for searching Yahoo that they had figured out on their own (mostly in relation to music Web sites). However, these self-taught strategies seemed to transfer well across topics and domains.

Finally, we showed them how to avoid too many listings on a topic of their choice. For example, we took the advice of experts on teaching with the Internet (Leu & Leu, 1999) and cautioned against using words such as *the, of,* or *a* as part of the search question. We also paired less proficient navigators of the Web with more proficient ones, being careful of course to avoid pairings that might aggravate a problem rather than solve it.

SUMMARY

Being personally motivated to learn, valuing study strategies, knowing something about the criterion task, and possessing adequate domain knowledge are all factors that help students become effective studiers. Preparing for exams is made easier for them when teachers take individual differences into account and reduce the demands associated with taking tests. Test taking is also made easier for students when they become knowledgeable about the differences in objective and subjective tests. Finally, learning how to study is facilitated by developing an awareness of the task, choosing potentially useful strategies, and identifying performance criteria needed to complete the task successfully.

Like learning to study, acquiring proficiency in Internet searches takes time, effort, and specialized knowledge.

SUGGESTED READINGS

Manzo, A. V. (1985). Expansion modules for the ReQuest, CAT, GRP, and REAP reading/study procedures. *Journal of Reading, 28,* 498–502.

Rekrut, M. D. (2000). Peer and cross-age tutoring: The lessons of research. In D. W. Moore, D. E. Alvermann, & K. A. Hinchman (Eds.), *Struggling adolescent readers: A collection of teaching strategies* (pp. 290–295). Newark, DE: International Reading Association.

Riemberg, R. (1996). Reading to write: Self-regulated learning strategies when writing essays from sources. *Reading Research and Instruction, 35,* 365–383.

Sakta, C. G. (1999). SQRC: A strategy for guiding reading and higher level thinking. *Journal of Adolescent & Adult Literacy, 42,* 265–269.

Samuels, S. J. (1979). The method of repeated readings. *The Reading Teacher, 32,* 403–408.

Taylor, B. M. (1986). Teaching middle grade students to summarize content textbook material. In J. F. Baumann (Ed.), *Teaching main idea comprehension* (pp. 195–209). Newark, DE: International Reading Association.

Developing Lifetime Readers: Literature in Content Area Classes

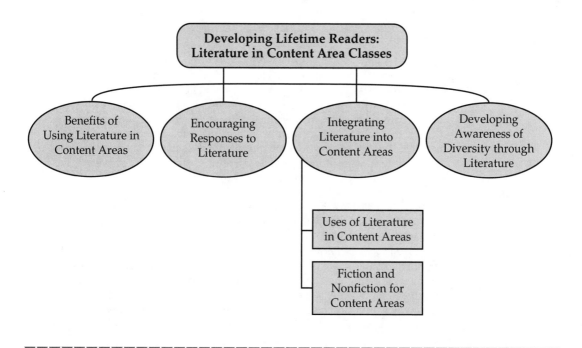

So far in this book, we have talked almost exclusively about school reading, or reading for academic purposes. In this chapter, we will take a look at the bigger picture and consider what people do with reading beyond school. At work or at leisure, several million people in this country each day turn to a book, a magazine, a newspaper, or the Internet and read for information, for personal gain, or for pleasure. In the following anecdote, Marie Saladino, a high school history teacher, reflects on her life as a reader.* As you share her thoughts, consider your own uses of reading and how you have evolved as a lifetime reader.

▼▼▼▼▼▼▼

I love to read. I can remember being four years old and demanding that my mother read to me and let me try to read parts of stories. I am certain that since reading was encouraged and worked on in my home, I had an easier time of learning in school.

I often wonder what has changed since my early days of reading. Up until eighth grade I used to read at least three books per week just for my own enjoyment. Once I entered high school, and then later in college, I never had enough time to read for personal satisfaction. In high school there was just too much going on, and in college there was so much subject matter reading.

I remember that reading was never really stressed when I was starting high school. We never read any literature except in English class, and I really did not

---

*Used with permission of Marie Saladino.

care for the novels we had to read. I always wanted to read books related to my social studies classes. The only book we ever read in four years of social studies, besides textbooks, was *The Jungle* by Upton Sinclair. I learned that I really enjoyed reading books that were fictional yet based on real-life historical events.

Now that I am teaching I have even less time to read for pleasure than I did in college. I do try to read books that deal with the subject matter I teach. Presently the most reading I get to do is a few novels or books per year, some magazines, Sunday newspapers, and a ton of African, Asian, and American government books.

Please do not think that I never read for enjoyment. I like fictional books that deal with controversy in society. This summer I read *The Handmaid's Tale* by Margaret Atwood, *The Godfather* by Mario Puzo, *Twins* by Roxanne Pulitzer, and *Sleeping with the Enemy* by Nancy Price. All of these books were very different, but I learned a great deal from each of them. The authors got me thinking and then criticizing the direction society seems to be going. I guess the major benefit I get from reading is my thinking power. While reading I am always learning new things, analyzing what I am reading, and forming my own opinions about new topics. There is always so much to learn in the world.

▼▼▼▼▼▼

This anecdote touches on several themes that will be developed in this chapter. First, it illustrates how an appreciation for reading develops over a lifetime, as the contexts, subjects, and various externally and internally imposed imperatives change. Marie mentions how the pressures of adolescence and early adulthood militated against reading for enjoyment and how she wished she had been given more opportunities to read (and enjoy reading) literature related to her content area studies. The anecdote also gives a fairly common picture of the reading activities of a professional adult, who must read extensively for work, bemoans the lack of time to read for pleasure, and yet finds great satisfaction and significance in the reading that does occur. Finally, there is social significance in what Marie reveals when she tells us her reading gets her "thinking and then criticizing the direction society seems to be going." The founders of this country guaranteed freedom of the press in order that citizens might have free access to the information they need to govern themselves. There was no more passionate believer in the necessity of an informed public than Thomas Jefferson, who said, "If a nation expects to be ignorant and free, in a state of civilization, it expects what never was and never will be." All the advances in telecommunications and mass media have not usurped the role of reading as a means for in-depth learning, reflection, and decision making.

Of course, not all adults become readers like Marie Saladino. Jim Trelease (1989), in his testament to the benefits of reading aloud, bemoans the current state of literacy and leisure reading among both adults and teenagers. Among many depressing statistics, he noted that the best-selling weekly magazines in the United States at the time were *TV Guide* and the *National Enquirer*. Still, bookstores, libraries, and publishers flourish. Many newspapers and news magazines enjoy healthy circulations. The Internet has become a major source of information, entertainment, communication, and commerce. Casual observation reveals people from all walks of life reading at home, at bus stops, on lunch or coffee breaks, at the beach—wherever they have a few minutes to themselves.

With adolescents, outside-of-school reading must compete for attention with television, video games, sports, and social activities. However, recent research contradicts the popular conception that most adolescents would rather watch "The Lawrence Welk Show" than be caught reading a book. In a canvas of 400 students in five central Illinois high schools, Moffit and Wartella (1992) found that 78 percent claimed to read books for leisure. Although reading was not a primary leisure time activity, it was ranked third by females (after sports and being with friends) and tied for fifth place with talking on the telephone and watching television among males (who listed sports, friends, music, and "solitary activities" as their top four). More females than males claimed to read, and academically proficient students were more likely to be readers than students who received poor grades.

Two separate surveys of sixth graders showed that early adolescents are also engaged readers. Worthy, Moorman, and Turner (1999) queried more than 400 students about their reading preferences. Almost every one was able to cite a favorite title, type of reading, or author, evidence that their attitudes toward reading were not as negative as is often suggested. Ivey and Broaddus (1999) elicited reading preferences from 1,700 sixth graders. Highly rated materials in both studies included scary stories, humor, popular magazines, sports, and nonfiction about varied topics. The authors of both surveys were especially impressed by the wide range of reading materials that students enjoyed reading. However, in both studies, students' stated reading preferences did not match what they found in school. Although students reported a variety of reading interests outside of school to Ivey and Broaddus, they reported a much narrower selection of in-school titles, mostly award-winning fiction read by a whole class at the same time. Similarly, Worthy, Moorman, and Turner found that the most popular reading materials were not readily available in school, especially the preferred reading of boys and struggling readers. Teachers and librarians cited lack of money, inappropriate or objectionable content, lack of academic merit, and the fact that popular materials were either always checked out or tended to "walk away" or become lost. In both studies, students were more likely to obtain their preferred reading materials outside of school.

Given time and appropriate materials, adolescents are surprisingly complex and multidimensional readers who are willing to read when it satisfies their personal needs (Ivey, 1999). Like many adults, they especially enjoy light reading on topics that are pleasing and important to them. Indeed, it is likely that students do not lose interest in reading as they progress through school; they just lose interest in school reading (Bintz, 1993). Adolescents' experiences with reading in school may very well influence what they read, their reasons for reading, and how often they read outside of school. If you believe that it is important for students to continue their development as readers after their school years, you will find many suggestions in this chapter that can help you expand their experiences with literature in school. In this chapter, we use the word *literature* in a broad sense to mean reading materials other than textbooks. These include fiction and nonfiction books and periodicals that students might read as part of their content area studies.

BENEFITS OF USING LITERATURE IN CONTENT AREAS

If students have positive reading experiences beyond their textbooks, their chances for becoming lifetime readers increase. There are more immediate benefits, too. Reading from fiction and nonfiction sources can enhance content area knowledge as well as readers' overall reading and thinking abilities. There are many reasons for using literature, both fiction and nonfiction, in content areas:

1. Reading increases vocabulary, including content-specific terms. (The role of wide reading in vocabulary development was cited in Chapter 8.) Through content-related literature, students increase their exposure to the language of a discipline. The examples are as diverse as the literature available. Readers of *The Hunt for Red October* (Clancy, 1984) will find many words specific to the technology of nuclear energy. David Macaulay's books, such as *Castle* (1977) and *City: A Story of Roman Planning and Construction* (1974), illustrate many terms specific to architecture and civic planning as well as vocabulary that describes the people and social institutions of the respective eras.

2. Literature is often more up-to-date than textbooks. A textbook may be several years in development; one with a 1997 copyright may only reflect information available in the late 1980s or early 1990s. Timely written accounts of developments in science and social studies may be available only in recent periodicals and books.

3. Although textbooks tend to pile up facts, dates, and concepts in a didactic avalanche, trade books can present much of the same information in a more appealing context (Beck & McKeown, 1991). (The term *trade books* is used for books written for the general public, as distinguished from textbooks, which are designed for classroom use.) Readers incidentally learn and store away countless facts as they enjoy books.

4. Literature goes beyond the facts. Readers get a sharper understanding of the issues and of the various stands they might adopt by sharing the experiences of fictional characters or reading nonfiction reportage and analysis. Through literature, students can begin to understand some of the uses and abuses of science, statistics, and political power. The social and emotional implications of topics as far-ranging as racism, immigration, war, nuclear energy, genetic engineering, ecology, and computer technology can be explored in works of fiction and nonfiction.

5. Literature allows readers to experience other times, other places, other people, and other cultures with empathy. For example, Spears-Bunton (1991) describes

the reaction of Courtney, a white high school student in an Ohio River town in Kentucky, to the events in Harriet Jacobs's (1987) account of her life as a slave girl. When asked what she would have done in Harriet's place when the elderly slave owner made his sexual desires clear, Courtney "turned her blue eyes toward the river and replied, 'I would have run, and I would have taken my children' " (pp. 12–13).

6. Trade books can be a powerful catalyst for thoughtful analysis (Bean, Kile, & Readence, 1996; McGowan & Guzzetti, 1991). When students read about the same topic presented from multiple perspectives, they learn to exercise critical thinking. As they compare two or more views, they will find discrepancies, contradictions, and differences of interpretation; they must decide which source is most compelling, complete, or accurate. *Johnny Tremaine* (Forbes, 1943), *My Brother Sam Is Dead* (Collier & Collier, 1974), *Sarah Bishop* (O'Dell, 1980), and *Bloody Country* (Collier & Collier, 1984), for instance, present events in the Revolutionary War from the points of view of characters of different genders, ages, races, and social standings.

7. Good experiences with reading breed motivation to seek other reading experiences. This is particularly important for reluctant readers or students who have difficulty with reading. When a teacher can help a troubled reader make a connection with an interesting and readable piece of literature, that reader gains the practice and confidence necessary to read further. Many adolescents who find reading a "turnoff" surprise themselves when they find the right material.

ACTIVITY   The following is an excerpt from *Catherine, Called Birdy* (Cushman, 1994),* a young adult novel told from the point of view of a 12-year-old girl living in thirteenth-century England. As you read it, look for vocabulary, facts, and concepts about the Middle Ages, and see what you can tell about Birdy, the narrator.

> Just three days to the feast of Saint Edward, my brother Edward's saint day. When Edward was still at home, we celebrated this day each year with feasting and dancing and mock battles in the yard. Now our celebrations include my father's face turning purple, my mother tightening her eyes and her mouth, and the cook swinging his ladle and swearing in Saxon. The cause of all the excitement is this: On this day each year, since Edward went to be a monk, my mother takes wagons full of gifts to his abbey in his honor. My father shouts that we may as well pour his precious stores in the cesspit (one day his angry liver will set him afire and I will toast bread on

him). My mother calls him Pinch-Fist and Miser. The cook boils and snarls as his bacon and flour and Renish wine leave home. But each year my mother stands firm and the wagons go. This year we send:

460 salted white herring
3 wheels of cheese, a barrel of apples
4 chickens, 3 ducks, and 87 pigeons
4 barrels of flour, honey from our bees
100 gallons of ale (for no one drinks more ale than monks, my father says)
4 iron pots, wooden spoons, and a rat trap for the kitchen
goose fat for the making of everyday candles and soap (lots of candles and little
    soap, I wager, seeing that they are monks)
40 pounds of beeswax candles for the church
a chest of blankets, linens, and napkins
horn combs, for those who have hair
goose quills, down, and a bolt of woven cloth (black) (pp. 23–24)

A check of three randomly selected samples of this book with the Fry readability formula (see Chapter 4) estimates that it is at the seventh-grade reading level, and the cover of the book recommends it for ages 12 and up. Do you think this book might be easier to read than a typical textbook intended for sixth or seventh grade? Why might it be more motivating to learn about the Middle Ages by reading a book like this than by reading a typical middle-grade history textbook?

Throughout this chapter, we will suggest ways to complement a full curriculum with literature, from short read-alouds to the use of novels and other full-length books. Consider carefully the potential understanding and appreciation that can come from literature; it is well worth including in a busy schedule.

ENCOURAGING RESPONSES TO LITERATURE

Some people are troubled by the idea of using trade books, especially fiction, to enhance students' understanding of content area concepts. They recall all too clearly how teachers "ruined" perfectly good novels by assigning questions and papers and by wringing out, chapter by chapter, every last bit of significance and interpretation, demolishing any possibility of enjoying a book purely for the personal and emotional responses it evokes. But surely, you are thinking, there are less heavy-handed ways to use literature as a basis for understanding content area information.

How should students respond to literature? How much should students' response be influenced by a teacher? The literary theory of Louise Rosenblatt (1978) suggests some possible answers. She describes reading as a complex transaction between reader and text. How a reader responds and what meaning a reader constructs from a text are influenced by the stance or purpose that the reader chooses. Rosenblatt (1985) defines two possible stances, the *efferent* and the *aesthetic:*

> The difference between the two kinds of reading lies in the reader's "selective attention" to what is being stirred up in the experiential reservoir. The predominantly efferent reader focuses attention on public meaning, abstracting what is to be retained after reading—to be recalled, paraphrased, acted on, analyzed. In aesthetic reading, the reader's selective attention is focused primarily on what is being personally lived through, cognitively and affectively, *during* the reading event. The range of ideas, feelings, associations activated in the reservoir of symbolizations is drawn upon. . . . Any text . . . can be read either way. (pp. 101–102)

Rosenblatt (1982) makes it clear that neither teachers nor readers have to make an "all-or-nothing" choice between efferent and aesthetic purposes for reading. She maintains that any reading act falls somewhere on a continuum between efferent and aesthetic, with most reading somewhere in the middle. She also recognizes the need for both kinds of reading and the need to teach students to read for both efferent and aesthetic purposes, although she cautions that greater emphasis needs to be placed on aesthetic reading.

Cynthia Lewis (2000) argues that the aesthetic stance is too often limited strictly to personal identification and interpretation. She suggests that aesthetic reading also encompasses a social or critical dimension, especially when readers are reading about cultures or experiences that are quite different from their own. She cites as an example *The Watsons Go to Birmingham—1963* (Curtis, 1995), a novel about an African American family at the time of the Civil Rights movement. The interactions of this close-knit family would have a personal aesthetic appeal to all readers, who could identify with the humor, warmth, and varied personalities. However, in the details of the Watsons' experiences with and resistance to white racism, European American readers are clearly positioned as outsiders. In this instance, the aesthetic experience is not one of close personal identification but rather understanding how the characters' lives are different from one's own.

How does a teacher translate theory into practice? That is, how can you "teach" a novel and leave room for students to experience it aesthetically? First, teachers need to be receptive to students' stances. That means that teachers should listen carefully for students' reactions—whether efferent or aesthetic, positive or negative. Students need the freedom to determine their own purposes for reading and their own reactions to reading.

Obviously, the very fact that a book is assigned for reading limits student choice and suggests an efferent purpose. Therefore, teachers must be careful how assignments and questions are posed if they wish to retain the possibility of aesthetic response. Rosenblatt (1982) warns that requests for verbal responses from students are especially liable to get in the way of aesthetic reading. In their questions, adults often telegraph what the "correct" response should be or steer students toward what the adult finds pertinent or interesting. This creates the following situation (Rosenblatt, 1982):

> The reader is often hurried away from the aesthetic experience and turned to efferent analysis by questions such as those appended to stories in various . . . anthologies and by teachers' questions or tests "checking whether the student has read the text." Questions that call for the traditional analysis of character, setting, and plot are often premature or routine, contributing to shallow, efferent reading. (p. 276)

To encourage aesthetic reading and response, teachers can begin discussion of literature by asking for the readers' responses first. Rosenblatt (1982) suggests questions such as "Did anything especially interest . . . annoy . . . puzzle . . . frighten [or] please [you or] seem familiar [or] weird?" (p. 276). Knowledge of students, their interests and their outlooks, helps a teacher choose questions that allow them to connect with other texts, other ideas, and other experiences. It is also useful to let students connect with each other, to let them see the similarities and differences in their points of view, perhaps by using some of the ideas presented in Chapter 9, such as reading for different purposes or the discussion web, or one of the strategies discussed later in this chapter.

Although consensus on how best to use trade books may never be reached, it is important to avoid creating this false dichotomy: textbooks are for school, trade books are for fun. Such a narrow view places unnecessary limits on the potential and power of literature. Drawing on the cognitive resources of literature does not necessarily obviate the aesthetic experience. Although there are differ-

Teens for Literacy

Would you be interested in making a professional commitment that would encourage lifelong literacy in students and help to make a long-term contribution to the teaching profession? Allen Berger and Elizabeth Shafran (2000) describe a program begun in 1989 to help urban adolescents improve their reading and writing. Called Teens for Literacy, the program has three goals: to involve students directly in promoting literacy and literacy awareness, to encourage them to pursue education beyond high school, and to acquaint urban adolescents with teaching as a possible career. Under the guidance of teacher sponsors, adolescents tutor other stu-

dents, plan literacy events and promotions, and visit local universities, libraries, or businesses. Student participants gain a new sense of confidence in their literacy abilities and expand their academic and vocational horizons.

In their book, Berger and Shafran explain how to establish a Teens for Literacy program, what kinds of activities could be undertaken, the many positive outcomes of the program, and how to select student participants. Teens for Literacy would be a most worthwhile and satisfying investment of time for teachers who would like to extend their professional development beyond the classroom.

ences between trade books and textbooks and between efferent and aesthetic purposes for reading, drawing sharp distinctions may well lead teachers to miss many of the ways in which literature can enhance content learning and the development of lifetime reading.

Throughout this text, we have stressed the need for students to take the initiative in seeking meaning from their reading. We have tried to present teaching strategies that provide for an interplay of teacher guidance and student independence. Professional wisdom dictates when and how much direction by the teacher is needed to facilitate the "unique coming-together of a particular personality and a particular text at a particular time and place under particular circumstances" (Rosenblatt, 1985, p. 104). The goal, however, is always to move students toward self-sufficiency, toward making their own decisions and discovering their own power as readers.

INTEGRATING LITERATURE INTO CONTENT AREAS

This section describes several uses of literature in content areas and suggests some resources that should facilitate your search for pertinent books.

Uses of Literature in Content Areas

Literature can complement any content area. For English teachers, of course, literature study represents a sizeable segment of the curriculum. Although they are likely to be familiar with a wide variety of literature, English teachers may still be able to broaden the selection of books in their curriculum, perhaps by including more young adult fiction or titles that represent cultural diversity. English teachers who work in a team with teachers from other disciplines may also be able to help integrate literature across content areas. Many social studies teachers have traditionally included literature in their classrooms. Literature complements the study of history and contemporary social issues by dramatizing and personalizing issues and events. Although literature is less likely to be associated with content areas such as science and math, there are numerous nontextbook resources that provide an added dimension to these subjects.

Read-alouds and book talks. As literate adults, teachers can be significant models, both positive and negative. In a study of high school students' perceptions of reading, Rieck (1977) found that students who reportedly did not read their content area assignments were unsure of whether their teachers were readers. When asked "Does your teacher like to read?" their responses were 20 percent "yes," 33 percent "no," and 47 percent "don't know." It is little wonder these students did not read their assignments, when 80 percent of their teachers were apparently unable to set an example!

By talking about books and reading aloud from books in class, teachers demonstrate that serious adults—experts in a content area—enjoy reading and actively pursue reading related to their field. Furthermore, such teacher modeling can be contagious. Teachers who actively promote reading and share what they read create interest on the part of students and illustrate the range of reading materials available. Equally important, hearing a teacher read high-quality sources can enhance the receptive language and broaden the conceptual scope of students from diverse linguistic and cultural backgrounds.

Reading aloud to students is one of the best ways to share a love of books. Read-alouds can be anywhere from 5 to 20 minutes or more in length and might be a daily or weekly occurrence in most any content area classroom. Short read-alouds can be used to develop interest and motivation, to introduce a new topic, to illustrate practical applications of content area concepts, and to inject a measure of humor into the classroom.

Consider this example.   In *Life on the Mississippi* (1961), Mark Twain writes about his experiences living and working on the great river in a book that is part travelogue, part natural history, and part tall tale. In one short passage, he describes how the river often cuts through a narrow neck of land, thereby shortening the course of the river by many miles. Using statistics creatively (but accurately), he calculates that in exactly 742 years, the Lower Mississippi will be only a mile and three-quarters long. He ends the passage with a typical Twain epigram: "One gets such wholesale returns of conjecture out of such a trifling investment of fact" (p. 120). Mark Forget describes how he uses this passage in his algebra class, first reading it aloud and then plugging Twain's numbers into an algebraic formula, calculating the slope of the line, and plotting it on a graph (Richardson, 2000). Forget also points out that this passage would be an ideal read-aloud for a geography class, with its accurate descriptions of how the river works its will and its many citations of places readily found on different kinds of maps.

The following are some dos and don'ts for reading aloud (Trelease, 1989; Richardson, 2000; Sanacore, 2000).

1. Choose a selection that you enjoy and that you think students will like as well. It should be something that will encourage discussion and further inquiry. Your listeners will appreciate humor, strong emotion, action, or the unusual.
2. Preview the material. Look for parts you might want to shorten, eliminate, or discuss.
3. Reader and audience should get comfortable. Sit or stand where your audience can see you easily, with your head above the heads of your listeners so your voice can carry; make frequent eye contact with your audience.
4. Practice. Be expressive with your reading and do not rush; vary your intonation to heighten the action or indicate different characters.

5. Encourage predictions, questions, and discussion during reading, but do not impose your own point of view or lecture as you read. Inferential and critical thinking questions can be used to follow up a read-aloud session.

6. Once you start a book or story, follow through unless it turns out to be universally unpopular. Students may not seem to be enjoying a book but will howl in protest if you decide not to finish it.

Appendix B is a list of books that contain short read-aloud selections pertinent to a variety of topics, historical events, and dates. A teacher could begin a class by reading about the physics of a curveball, what happened 100 years ago on a given day, or how dirty tricks were used in early presidential campaigns. A book-loving colleague especially recommends collections of weird and curious facts, for which he uses the delightful word *gallimaufry* (which originally meant a kind of hash made up of leftovers). In this type of book, you can learn how crickets chirp, how Beethoven was able to compose even though he was deaf, and how the *Mariner I* space probe was lost because a minus sign was omitted from instructions fed into a computer. Such tidbits augment textbook information and add appeal to content area studies. Students also enjoy browsing through these books, even reluctant readers who would never consider the idea of reading a whole book cover to cover.

Judith Richardson (2000) illustrates suggested read-aloud selections for a wide range of content areas, including English as a second language. For ELLs, read-alouds provide exposure to intonational and syntactic patterns, vocabulary, idioms, and important cultural and conceptual information. Among the read-aloud selections that Richardson recommends is *Grab Hands and Run* (Temple, 1993), a story of a Salvadoran family waiting for Canadian citizenship. This book treats issues of politics, immigration, assimilation, language differences, and language learning, many of which are pertinent to the experiences of ELLs.

Book talks are another medium through which a teacher can promote content-related literature. When a teacher does a five- or ten-minute "show-and-tell" with a book, whether it is an old favorite or a current page-turner, students see a reader who takes pleasure from books. Book talks can also create interest for a particular author or title. A teacher may even recommend titles for specific students, just like a recommendation between friends. It is a powerful incentive to a student to have a teacher hand him or her a book and say something such as "I know something about you, and I think you'll like this—try it!"

Free reading time.   Many teachers have successfully instituted a regular time when everybody in the class simply reads. This activity, sometimes called *S.S.R.* (Sustained Silent Reading) or *D.E.A.R.* (Drop Everything and Read) time, has only two simple requirements. First, everybody reads, including the teacher. (We have seen schoolwide free reading times during which everybody reads, including the principal, secretaries, custodians, and cafeteria workers.) Second, school reading is not allowed; students must read something other than their textbooks (and the teacher is not supposed to grade papers). This second requirement might be modified in content area classes by restricting students to reading related to the subject area. That is, students in science class should be reading something relevant to science.

In secondary-level content area classrooms, time is probably the biggest obstacle to implementing free reading time. As little as 15 minutes of free reading once or twice a week can be significant for students who otherwise might do no reading at all beyond the bare minimum required for school. Even if it is impractical to schedule free reading throughout the year, teachers can institute silent reading time when students are working on outside reading projects, especially at the beginning, when they need to make a selection and get a good head start on reading it.

In-school free reading also requires that students have access to reading materials. Some students will bring their own books to read, especially if they know independent reading will take place at a regular time. Those who do not have their own books will need to select something from the classroom library. Sanacore (1990) suggests that content area teachers stock their classroom libraries with materials that represent a variety of reading levels, lengths, and formats. Many of the titles listed in Appendix B make excellent S.S.R. resources, along with paperbacks, periodicals, and newspapers.

The purpose of S.S.R. is to give students an opportunity to practice lifetime reading skills, to read for their own purposes and pleasure. Independent reading is not a "for credit" activity. Students are not graded, nor are they expected to produce anything as a result of their reading. It might be helpful to use a part of free reading time for book talks by the teacher or by student volunteers, but otherwise it is devoted simply to reading for the sake of reading.

Independent reading is an essential component in the language development of ELLs. Reading interesting, ability-appropriate materials provides ELLs with "comprehensible input" (Krashen, 1985). Opportunities to read without academic pressure can help ELLs make a transition from easier to more difficult materials. Furthermore, reading exposes ELLs to a wider range of topics, concepts, syntactic patterns, and vocabulary than they are likely to encounter in their oral language interactions.

Janice Pilgreen (2000) describes a successful S.S.R. program established for high school ELLs. She lists eight factors that will influence the success of such a program:

1. Access: Students will need a wide variety of reading materials at suitable levels.
2. Appeal: Magazines, comic books, and series books will be especially popular.
3. Conducive environment: Posters, artwork, and comfortable places to sit make it pleasant to read. Silent reading time should also be free of interruptions and distractions.
4. Encouragement: Teachers can model their own enjoyment of reading during free reading time and explain the benefits of reading for students' language development.

5. Distributed time to read: Students need regularly scheduled times for free reading throughout the week. Daily practice is optimal.

6. Nonaccountability: Free reading should involve no book reports, journal entries, or comprehension assessments.

7. Follow-up activities: Students should have opportunities to share information with each other about their reading on a voluntary basis.

8. Staff training: Teachers need to understand the substantial benefits of free reading time as well as how to implement a formal free reading program.

High school ELL students were asked to comment on the free reading program. The following samples indicate their enthusiasm (Pilgreen, 2000):

> "My vocabulary is better, and I have noticed that my understanding of English has improved."

> "When I began reading, I didn't want to stop, even for a minute. Now I want to read the harder books."

> "The things I read now are harder than the things I read in September because I can read not a lot faster and understand more."

> "Sometimes when I read I get excited, and I don't want to stop reading so I take the book home."

> "I like a lot when you allowed us to read newspapers and magazines because I could get information about modern things."

> "I always choose books that are very thick because it makes me feel that I can do it, and I can."

> "The books are getting harder and longer now than before because I used to read short easy books." (pp. 82–85)

Complementary readings.   Literature can be used in a variety of ways to complement textbooks. Some teachers may have a whole class reading a single book or story during a thematic unit. For instance, a social studies class might read *Roll of Thunder, Hear My Cry* (Taylor, 1976) as part of a unit on the Great Depression. When teachers work in a team, the English teacher often complements study in another content area by having the class read an appropriate book; for example, *The Red Badge of Courage* (Crane, 1895/1964) might accompany study of the Civil War. Many of the prereading, comprehension, writing, and vocabulary strategies presented in earlier chapters are appropriate when the whole class is reading the same book. To maximize students' involvement and self-direction, we especially recommend anticipation guides and K-W-L (Chapter 6), ReQuest and self-questioning (Chapter 7), vocabulary self-selection (Chapter 8), thinking matrixes and discussion webs (Chapter 9), and learning logs (Chapter 10).

Whole-class study of a single book requires enough copies of the book for every student to have one, which can stretch a tight school budget. There is also the problem that some students may find a particular text uninteresting or too challenging. An alternative strategy is to select several titles, all related to a single topic. (A school librarian can be a useful ally in choosing books. Many librarians or media specialists are knowledgeable and willing coteachers who are glad to present book talks and assist students with book selection. You will also find books related to specific themes suggested in Appendixes B, C, and D.) When several different books are available, students have a choice of what to read. Multiple titles also present the possibility of offering several different cooperative-learning arrangements and tasks. If students are grouped with others reading the same book, they may work cooperatively on developing a book talk, a poster or visual display, a read-aloud, or some other presentation based on the book. Students in a group all reading different books may do book talks within their group, or the group may develop some cooperative project such as a compare-and-contrast book review or a compendium of topical facts or vocabulary.

Complementary reading does not need to be focused on a particular topic or theme. Content teachers often assign outside reading projects, for which students are allowed to choose their own books. For example, a high school honors biology class completed a book project in which they read a nonfiction book related to science and kept a response journal, which they shared with the teacher (Reynolds & Pickett, 1989). The teacher kicked off the project by giving several book talks to introduce titles and authors she thought students might find interesting. She then asked students to check their selections with her and offered extra credit for particularly difficult selections. Students were asked to make a minimum of ten entries in their response journals. In their first entry they introduced the author and title and told a little about why they chose the book and what they expected from it. The following suggestions were made for subsequent reactions (Reynolds & Pickett, 1989, p. 437):

> *Reactions to characters:* "I am amazed at _____ because _____."
> *Questions you are left with, and possible answers:* "I wonder _____.
>   Perhaps _____."
> *New ideas or new angles on old ideas:* "I never thought about _____."
> *Major point of a chapter or section, and why it was included.*
> *Relationships with something you already knew:* "This reminded me of _____."

As a result of this project, students enjoyed reading scientific nonfiction, increased their scientific literacy, and related new knowledge to their personal experiences. Many were pleasantly surprised to find they could read and understand material they had anticipated would be too difficult. Reynolds and Pickett (1989) report that variations of this book project have been successful in other science classes with all levels of students. Low-ability students, for instance, read current events articles and short selections from books, and their response journals were shorter and more structured. Similar book projects could easily be adapted to other content areas.

Social studies teacher Edwin Biloff (1996) took a more focused approach to complementary trade book reading with his eleventh-grade American history class. During their study of the Civil War, he assigned the reading of *The Killer Angels* (Shaara, 1974), a novel about the Battle of Gettysburg. Over a period of seven weeks, students read the novel, chose one of three major characters from the novel, conducted outside research in nonfiction resources on this person, and then wrote an essay that analyzed the man's character and leadership. In the essay, they were to compare the novelized treatment of their subject with the information found in the nonfiction sources.

Fiction and Nonfiction for Content Areas

One major difference between lifetime readers and school readers is the matter of choice. Young people and adults who enjoy reading as a regular pastime choose their reading materials from among many genres, authors, and subjects; in school, readers are limited for the most part to what they are assigned or what is available in the school library. However, these school reading materials are not reflective of the wide range of adolescent reading preferences (Ivey & Broaddus, 1999; Worthy, Moorman, & Turner, 1999). Lack of choice in school reading is one reason frequently cited by secondary students who are willing readers outside of school but resist assigned reading (Bintz, 1993). Aliterate students, those who can read but choose not to, cited "choosing their own books" as the number one thing that would motivate them to read more (Beers, 1996). The choices teachers can offer students are constrained by time, curriculum, and resources. However, teachers recognize the importance of selecting books and readings that will appeal to readers.

It is difficult to assess what adolescent readers are likely to enjoy because their tastes are as varied as those of adult readers. In their study of Illinois high school students, Moffit and Wartella (1992) found a preference for romance among females and for fantasy, science fiction, and sports among males. When Bank (1986) surveyed students in grades 6–12 in the New York metropolitan area, their interests ranged across a total of 58 different topics. The top ten topics were young people, mystery, humor, adventure, love, sex, movies, famous people, romances, and horror, but preferences varied widely by grade level, ethnicity, native language, and other student characteristics. Earlier in this chapter, we cited studies of sixth graders by Ivey and Broaddus (1999) and Worthy, Moorman, and Turner (1999) that revealed similar breadth in reading choices.

The annual survey of young adult choices in literature conducted by the International Reading Association and published in the November issue of the *Journal of Reading* confirms this interest in a wide range of topics, authors, and genres. When students in grades 7–12 wrote about *why* they liked a particular book, they cited the subject matter most frequently, although the actual subjects mentioned were extremely diverse (Samuels, 1989). It is important to remember, too, that nonfiction may account for as much as half of adolescents' leisure reading (Abrahamson & Carter, 1991). Nonfiction is especially effective in increasing readers' awareness of cultural diversity because it "documents what has actually occurred, establishing the record of a group's experiences and contributions to human culture" (Pugh & Garcia, 1990, p. 20).

With so many interests and so many available titles, it is difficult to pick a winner every time. Knowing your students and the available literature increases the possibility that you will make good choices, however. Appendixes C and D suggest some books that have been recommended to us by colleagues and teachers. These selections are far from exhaustive. To give you an idea of the range of options, we have tried to pick books that are of general interest as well as some that pertain to specific topics. In cases in which the title alone does not suggest the subject matter, we offer brief annotations. We also designate books written for young adults with a *YA*. This is tricky because so-called young adult books vary considerably in their format and content. Many are quite suitable for high school readers, but others are likely to be rejected as too immature. At the same time, many middle-grade students avidly read books intended for adult audiences. Ultimately, the teacher's judgment and a bit of trial and error will be necessary to match books and students.

Those who are looking for a trade book to complement a particular unit of study might find guidelines suggested by Biloff (1996) useful:

1. The reading should match students' reading levels, be interesting, represent content area concepts accurately, and complement curricular goals.
2. If choosing a novel, look for action, crisp dialogue, and empathic characters.
3. Select material for which you have special interest or expertise.
4. Consider piloting the material with a representative student sample.
5. Readings that can be coordinated with audiovisuals are especially useful.
6. Look for material that could be used in varied and interesting ways from year to year.

Picture books for content areas.   Many wonderful picture books—fiction, non-fiction, and poetry—tell stories and illustrate concepts from literature, science, social studies, and mathematics (Miller, 1998). A wide range of subjects have been treated in contemporary picture books: the environment, families, ethnic heritage, relationships, war, love, social problems, and historical events and people are just a few. Many picture books present exceptional examples of artistic and literary accomplishment.

You may think of picture books as being suitable only for elementary grades, but there are in fact many uses of picture books in the middle and secondary grades as well. They can be used to introduce abstract topics, develop technical vocabulary, provide information for inquiry projects, prompt writing, and provide both visual and conceptual experiences with people from diverse cultures.

Judith Neal and Kay Moore (1991–92) point out that the themes of many picture books have appeal that transcends age levels. Picture books also may be written at a fairly advanced conceptual and maturity level. For example, Neal and Moore cite *Rose Blanche* (Innocenti, 1985), a graphic story of the Holocaust,

Picture Books and Struggling Readers

The availability of picture books for both independent and content-specific reading helps to establish them as "acceptable" for *all* students (Miller, 1998). This is especially helpful for struggling readers, who can get pleasure and useful content from picture books but who might be embarrassed if they felt they were being targeted to read "kids' books." High-quality picture books with challenging ideas and interesting content can provide struggling readers with much-needed practice and confidence.

and *The Wall* (Bunting, 1990), which tells the story of the Vietnam Veterans' Memorial, as two picture books that address sophisticated and emotional topics in a realistic fashion. The short format of picture books makes them especially well suited to complement the short class periods in most middle and high schools. A picture book can be read in its entirety during the period, with time left for discussion or other activities.

Picture books can help make visual and verbal connections for students who are learning English. Nancy Hadaway and Jane Mundy (2000) outline a unit on weather that they developed for high school ELLs. They decided to emphasize the seasons, weather phenomena, and weather disasters. Students used informational picture books, newspaper weather reports, national weather maps, and books with weather experiments as their texts. During the course of the unit, they wrote poetry that featured weather vocabulary, created their own graphic organizers of weather concepts, wrote about their weather experiments and observations in weather journals, and made a weather collage of words and pictures. To culminate the unit, students researched weather-related disasters such as floods, tornadoes, and hurricanes. Their inquiry was scaffolded with picture books before they moved to the school library to consult standard reference materials.

Integrating popular culture.   In Chapter 9 we raised the question of how popular culture might be incorporated into school curricula. An expanded conception of adolescent literacies must take into account both the pleasure and the utility that adolescents find in such popular media as movies, television, music CDs, phones and pagers, magazines, electronic games, and the Internet. Whether we bid them to or not, adolescents bring these literacies into school. Lorri Neilsen (1998) tells the story of her son David, a high school junior who downloaded parts of the filmscript to the movie *Pulp Fiction* from the Internet. David and his friends memorized long passages of the movie dialogue and produced their own videotaped versions of favorite scenes. David also directed scenes from the movie for a school drama project. Neilsen explains that a movie such as *Pulp Fiction* can become a "touchstone text" for adolescents, texts that help adolescents to "make and shape meaning in their lives through literacy" (p. 4). She goes on to consider the implications of these texts for teachers and teaching. She says that adolescents like her son remind her

> that their ongoing curriculum is the lives they lead; that they teach one an-
> other and can teach their teachers; and that they will explore learning, grow in
> their literacy, and dream their dreams in settings often much more influential
> than school settings. What important paths to learning are we blocking off at
> the school door? How can we learn to listen to that learning and bring it into
> school settings and curricula? (p. 22)

In an intergenerational conversation, Tom Bean and his adolescent daughters explored the many functions of text and media for the two girls both in school and out (Bean, Bean, & Bean, 1999). Both girls had teachers who encouraged them to make connections between home, school, and peer cultures. Sixteen-year-old Shannon's social studies teacher allowed students to express their understanding of historical periods through artwork, models, and rap songs. For a science project on animals, twelve-year-old Kristen used her home computer to write about dogs, specifically the cocker spaniel that she has trained and shown. In each case, the girls were able to use their multiple literacies and interests in the service of school-based learning. If we expand our conception of literacy and text to incorporate popular media and culture, we will find many ways to help make such connections.

Finding suitable literature for content classrooms.   It takes time and money to compile a good collection of reading materials, whether in a school library or a classroom. In times of budget restrictions, the amount of discretionary money available for books may be limited. Although many teachers generously share their own personal libraries with students, it is not feasible for most to set up an extensive classroom collection. Publishers sometimes help by offering reduced prices. Parent–teacher associations, community book clubs, and other service groups may also be willing to donate books or funds.

Teachers can find books for classroom use in school and local libraries, in bookstores, and at garage sales. Sometimes good books are recommended by colleagues, friends, or students. There are also many sources of booklists and book reviews; see Suggested Readings at the end of the chapter for a sampling.

Periodicals are another excellent source of classroom reading material. Weekly news magazines, *Psychology Today*, *National Geographic*, *Scientific American*, and *Popular Science* are just a few examples of publications that regularly feature articles appropriate to content area studies. Some teachers have their own subscriptions, and parents may be willing to donate back issues.

Censorship.   A discussion of using literature in content areas would not be complete without considering the problem of censorship. When community

Finding Good Literature on the Internet

Amazon.com and Barnes and Noble are two well-known commercial Web sites that are excellent resources for finding content-related fiction and nonfiction. Both can be searched by using subject descriptors or author names, and both provide capsule reviews of books and "additional suggestions" once you have identified an interesting title. Their full Internet addresses are http://www.amazon.com and http://www.barnesandnoble.com. Other Internet sites that can help you identify good titles include

- Internet School Library Media Center http://falcon.jmu.edu/~ramseyil
- The Children's Literature Web Guide http://www.acs.ucalgary.ca/~dkbrown
- Young Adult Library Services Association http://www.ala.org/yalsa

groups or parents exert pressure to remove reading materials from the school library or classroom, school boards and administrators often acquiesce, with the result that an entire class or school may be denied the right to read a particular text. The potential threat of external protests as well as personal objection to certain works of literature may also lead teachers to self-censorship. As we are preparing this edition, the Harry Potter series has prompted numerous protests by people who object to the alleged promotion of witchcraft and magic in the books. (This has in turn engendered a Web site to defend the series against censorship, *http://www.mugglesforharrypotter.org*. In case you do not know what a Muggle is, you are one and you need to read one of the books.) Other books that are regularly the object of censorship attempts include *The Catcher in the Rye, Huckleberry Finn, The Diary of Anne Frank*, and *I Know Why the Caged Bird Sings.*

In interviews with five experienced high school English teachers, Jane Agee (1999) found that all wanted to include diverse, rich, contemporary literature in their curriculum, but all had found themselves at one time or another in risky territory because of their book choices. In very real terms, teachers who want their students to read a wide range of texts may be putting their careers in jeopardy. When schools have formal policies and procedures for handling book challenges, active book screening committees, collegial discussions of potential texts, and supportive administrators and colleagues, they are less likely to succumb to the pressures of censors. Even in the best of circumstances, however, books are banned and teachers learn to be cautious about what they bring into the classroom.

The teachers that Agee (1999) interviewed detailed many strategies for introducing potentially controversial texts into their curricula, and they also practiced some form of self-censorship. One defense is to carefully weigh the maturity and family backgrounds of students and decide how much of a fight a particular book is worth. Another is to communicate carefully with parents about what students will be reading and why. For instance, at the beginning of the year one teacher sent home a list of 30 films she *might* show during the year, although in practice she only used five or so a semester. Students and parents could review the list, and if there were potential problems, students could drop the class. Sometimes teachers offer to provide alternative readings if there is isolated objection to a proposed assignment.

Another proactive strategy is to include censorship issues as part of the curriculum, thus engaging students directly in the debate over their right to read. For example, to prepare for the reading of *Huckleberry Finn*, teachers often discuss the history of censorship attempts on the book. This prepares both European American and African American students to critically consider the racial issues prompted by Twain's portrayal of Huck and Jim and his use of the vernaculars of the place and time in which the story is set. Although such preparation does not settle all the controversies, it helps to diffuse them and set the stage for critical but civil discussion in which students of different backgrounds and beliefs are better prepared to understand diverse points of view.

The potential of censorship will always shadow teachers' attempts to expand students' reading beyond the "safe" confines of approved textbooks. The best defense against censorship is to be prepared. For more information on censorship in schools, visit our companion Web site at *http://www.ablongman.com/alvermann3e*.

DEVELOPING AWARENESS OF DIVERSITY THROUGH LITERATURE

It is estimated that one in every three American students will come from a home outside the traditional white, European American culture by the year 2010, a fact that challenges the very notion of a "mainstream" or "majority" culture. In many large urban centers, linguistically or culturally diverse children often comprise half or more of the school population. African American and Hispanic students represent the largest cultural minorities in schools, but they are by no means the only representatives of culturally diverse groups.

To cite one example, Grover Cleveland High School in Buffalo, New York, has approximately 1,000 students, of whom approximately 38 percent are Hispanic, 24 percent are African American, 18 percent are Asian, and 20 percent are of European origin. However, that does not tell the whole story because nearly half of these students are classified as having limited English proficiency, and their numbers encompass students from 19 different language groups, including Spanish, Vietnamese, Cambodian, Russian, Ukrainian, and Arabic. Labels such as "Hispanic" and "Asian" obscure the true diversity of these students, who include native-born Americans as well as immigrants from Puerto Rico, El Salvador, Mexico, Venezuela, Honduras, Ethiopia, Somalia, China, Japan, Korea, Vietnam, Thailand, Cambodia, and Laos. The specific demographics and ethnic mixes would differ, but most large cities would have selected schools with similar diversity.

This diversity poses both challenges and opportunities. For the students, there are the challenges and dilemmas of alienation, assimilation, and acculturation. For schools whose expectations, curricula, and methods are based on mainstream culture, there are the challenges of reaching out to an increasingly diverse student population and of fostering tolerance and understanding among all students. There is also the opportunity to celebrate this diversity, to use the varied talents of people from many cultures, and to break down the barriers between "us" and "them," while adding to the rich texture of this country's cultural tapestry.

Advantages of using multicultural literature.   Literature provides a vehicle for both meeting these challenges and realizing the potential of cultural diversity. First, there are several positive effects when students read about their own culture. Culturally relevant literature validates students' cultural identity and projects a positive image of them and their culture. In a review of African American children's literature, for instance, Bishop (1990) notes five important positive themes:

1. Warm and loving human relations, especially in the family
2. A sense of community among African Americans
3. African American history, heritage, and culture
4. A sense of continuity
5. Physical and psychological survival in the face of overwhelming odds

When such personal validation comes from books read at school, students' positive identification with the school itself is strengthened.

Culturally relevant literature can also be an important tool for developing student literacy. Stories that "do not shrink or hide from the fact that the people in the story are different from standard American characters in standard American settings" (Gonzales, 1990, p. 19) allow readers to form a more intimate link between their own experiences and the text, thus enhancing both motivation and comprehension. The personal appeal of reading about culturally familiar subjects can be especially effective with students who are otherwise turned off by books.

The value of reading stories by and about people of various cultures extends to all students, however, regardless of ethnic or cultural affiliation (Spears-Bunton, 1998). From a strictly curricular standpoint, reading culturally diverse literature can increase students' knowledge of history and geography and expand their understanding of literary technique (Norton, 1990). More important, readers can gain a greater understanding and appreciation of cultures other than their own when they identify with the characters in a novel. The literature of different cultures helps to break down some of the myths and stereotypes that people believe. For example, when high school juniors in a racially mixed classroom read and discussed African American literature, both African American and European American students "crossed perceptual, gender, and cultural lines as they engaged in the world of the text" (Spears-Bunton, 1990, p. 573). The portrayals of African American perspectives drew out conflicts and contradictions of class, race, and gender. As a community of readers, these students were able to challenge some of the sociocultural assumptions held within and outside their own cultural groups.

Resistance to multicultural literature.   Unfortunately, there is recent evidence of resistance to the use of multicultural literature on the part of some students, teachers, administrators, community members, and politicians (McCarty, 1998). Some object on the grounds that schools should focus on traditionally recognized and accepted "great works" that transmit values and ideas common to the mainstream culture (Bloom, 1994; Hirsch, 1987). Administrators may feel that using multicultural literature will not be accepted by parents, will interfere with a more skills-based approach to literacy, or will unfairly focus attention on particular ethnic or cultural groups (Godina, 1996).

Teachers' concerns fall into two general categories (Jordan & Purves, 1993). First, they see institutional constraints: whether literature should be used to foster cultural identity or to develop critical understanding, whether multicultural literature should bump the so-called classics from the curriculum, and whether a teacher from one cultural background can effectively teach multicultural literature to students of another culture. Second, they may feel constrained by the reactions and attitudes of their students. A teacher in an affluent suburb said, "Our students can feel superior to the literature of others as long as it deals with the suffering of others, but when it presents a point of view that they can't feel sorry for, then it is not welcome" (p. 10). In contrast, another teacher felt that her students could not relate to multicultural literature "because nothing we read at school makes them feel important. The school's lower middle-class whites get nothing from multicultural literature" (p. 100).

The apparent resistance of some students to multicultural literature is confirmed by Richard Beach (1997), who suggests that some of the high school readers he interviewed resisted a stance that acknowledged institutional racial or gender bias and instead adopted a stance of "individual prejudice." That is, they rejected the notion that they might be prejudiced and instead attributed bias to other individuals rather than to the society as a whole. Thus, mainstream readers may deny ethnic or gender differences, profess a lack of relevant cultural knowledge, resist feelings of guilt or complicity, and contest challenges to their privileged status in society. At the same time, Beach found other readers who adopted alternative stances that allowed them to empathize with people of other cultures and to reflect on their own status in society.

These are complex issues that do not have easy answers. It is our feeling that the very resistance to multicultural literature is an argument for its inclusion in the curriculum. The United States is a pluralistic society, and the more we understand about each other the better off we will be. There is much in multicultural literature that reinforces basic beliefs and aspirations that are common across our society, while still pointing out important differences in the way people can think, act, live, and feel. It is important that we understand where our similarities and differences lie, even if our differences cannot always be easily reconciled.

Insistence that student readers must be limited to a narrow corpus of "great works" simply does not make good sense. First, it assumes the impossible, which is that we could ever agree on what should be included in such a body of work. It ignores the fact that "greatness" is a fluid concept that changes with time, location, and those who define it. Insisting that there are certain works that students must read in school is to assume that they would or could never read anything else, that their reading will be limited exclusively to what they get in school (Hughes, 1993). Finally, there is a high degree of artistic and intellectual merit in the best of multicultural fiction and nonfiction so that inclusion of such works does not displace an emphasis on reading works of quality.

There are ways that a teacher can help to reduce students' resistance to reading about other cultures. It is important, first of all, to understand why some students may be uncomfortable with what they perceive as challenges to their position or to the beliefs of their peers and family members. As models and facilitators, teachers can set a tone of tolerance and nonconfrontational dialogue. Before introducing a multicultural text in class, a teacher should prepare by learning some biographical details of the author, reviewing the historical setting of the story and the period when the author wrote, and making "cultural footnotes" on things that may be unfamiliar to students (Willis & Palmer, 1998). This will allow teachers to share factual background information, clarify potential cultural misunderstandings, and prepare students to react to the story, characters, and action, not just to the "culture" (Jordan & Purves, 1993). To that end, many of the prereading activities in Chapter 6 could be employed.

Finally, it is important to show mainstream students that there is hope, that one can have pride and confidence in one's own heritage without necessarily being oppressive to others. To that end, Beach (1997) suggests that we give students examples of people who have transcended bias in their lives. Such people can be found in most communities, and their stories are recorded in the popular media and in biographies and autobiographies. Best of all, we can strive to be such models ourselves.

Choosing and using multicultural literature.   Locating suitable multicultural literature, planning for instruction, and actually teaching it requires a considerable investment of time (Willis & Palmer, 1998). Nevertheless, the results are worth the investment. Athanases (1998) reported on a year-long study of two urban tenth-grade classrooms in which teachers committed themselves to an exploration of diverse texts. During the year the classes read short stories, poems, autobiographical pieces, plays, and novels by a diverse groups of authors including Amy Tan, Maya Angelou, Maxine Hong Kingston, Shakespeare, Sophocles, Langston Hughes, and Albert Camus. Both teachers encouraged students to develop their own literary responses and exploratory thinking through collaborative projects and presentations, journal writing, and open-ended questioning by both teachers and students that emphasized analysis, synthesis, and speculation over literal recall. Most important, both teachers encouraged students to explore racial issues openly and to use their personal and community knowledge to help them interpret what they were reading.

The students represented diverse academic levels, ethnic backgrounds, and language communities. African American, Chinese American, Filipino, European American, Puerto Rican, Mexican, and Central American heritages were all represented in significant numbers. Half of each class spoke a language at home other than English, and one-fourth of the students had been formally identified as "at risk" for school failure. During the course of the year, Athanases (1998) documented responses over a wide range of categories:

- Family and adolescent concerns
- Pride of culture and place
- Developing cultural identities
- Developing gender and sexual identities
- Learning from new experiences and ideas about cultures
- Rethinking stereotypes

Of course, there was also resistance to challenging ideas and portrayals in the literature as well as occasional tensions and conflicts during discussions. Nevertheless, the varied texts and the exploratory talk in these classes helped students make connections and discoveries that many of them recalled vividly two years afterward. In his summary of the study, Athanases (1998) notes that simply introducing diversified texts into the classroom is not enough; he says we need to "move beyond debates on *what* should be taught, to analyses of *how*—an essential step, because changing course materials alone has not historically yielded humanistic benefits" (p. 293).

For the teacher, however, deciding what should be taught is the first step. Teachers who are not familiar with or a little overwhelmed by the growing body of multicultural literature might start by reading works that fit their particular interests or curricular needs and teaching what they are learning (Spears-Bunton, 1998). It is important to make a distinction between world literature (i.e., stories about people in Africa or Latin America) and ethnic American literature (stories about African Americans or Latino/a Americans). Selecting literature that is representative of diverse cultural backgrounds also requires sensitivity to potential cultural and gender bias.

One issue is whether the author is writing from the perspective of an "insider" or an "outsider" (Harris, 1991). Some earlier works by outsider authors tended to be paternalistic or patronizing in their portrayals of culturally diverse groups. Although many authors write with sensitivity about cultures other than their own, being an insider may give an author more license to interpret a particular ethnic group's experience. There is also a need to avoid lumping different cultures together into "cultural conglomerates" (Reimer, 1992). As we pointed out earlier, "Hispanic" does not mean just Mexican or Puerto Rican, and a term such as "Asian" or "European" encompasses many different cultures. Also, teachers should not make the mistake of assuming that all members of a particular cultural group will enjoy the same books. To do so can lead to stereotyping and damaging overgeneralization.

The following guidelines, adapted from Hansen-Krening and Mizokawa (2000) and Pang et al. (1992), can help to avoid stereotypes and choose books that accurately portray people of varying cultural identities. Good multicultural literature should have

- *An authoritative author:* If the author is not a member of the portrayed ethnic group, he or she must have some knowledge or experience that allows for credibility.
- *A culturally pluralistic theme:* Cultural diversity should be valued and issues of cultural assimilation should be treated sensitively. Also, the work should transcend the "food, festival, and folktale" approach to multicultural literature.
- *A good plot and characterization:* An interesting plot and compelling characters are what make a book enjoyable. However, plot and characters may not necessarily adhere to traditional European American literary traditions.
- *Positive and accurate portrayals:* Characters from diverse cultures should be seen as empowered people and not be stereotyped. Ethnic Americans should be accurately portrayed, but it must be clear that they are at the same time American, not foreign. Many Asian Americans and Hispanic Americans are native born and may actually represent families whose history in the United States precedes that of many immigrants from the British Isles and Europe.
- *Accurate illustrations:* If there are pictures, they should not stereotype people's physical features, dress, and mannerisms.
- *Historical accuracy:* Books should be carefully researched by their authors.

For teachers who wish to broaden the cultural scope of their students' reading, there is both good news and bad news. The good news is that there are many diverse authors from diverse backgrounds turning out excellent works. The bad news is that many ethnic groups, most notably Hispanics, who are the fastest-growing ethnic group in the United States, are not proportionately represented in literature (Barry, 1998). Also, in the competitive literary marketplace, many titles quickly go out of print and may be difficult to find. With this caution in mind, we offer in Appendix D a bibliography of titles that reflect some of the diverse cultures in today's schools. We intend this list to be representative, not exhaustive. Several of the authors listed have published numerous outstanding books, and there are many other authors we did not include due to space limitations. In addition, many of the articles and reviews cited in this chapter and in the Suggested Readings include excellent lists of culturally diverse literature. We especially recommend *Teaching and Using Multicultural Literature in Grades 9–12*, edited by Arlette Willis (1998), which has chapters on the literature of the African American, Puerto Rican, Asian/Pacific American, Native American, Mexican American, and Caribbean American communities.

SUMMARY

A local video outlet advertises with the slogan "So many movies, so little time." That is how we feel about books. For a lifetime reader, there is both joy and frustration in the great wealth of reading material available. In this chapter, we have tried to show how literature can accomplish two important purposes. First, good literature can present content area facts, concepts, and issues in a form that is often more palatable and memorable than textbooks. Second, and perhaps more important, exposure to good literature can cultivate in students a passion for lifetime reading.

SUGGESTED READINGS

Adamson, L. (1997). *Literature connections to American history, 7–12: Resources to enhance and entice.* Englewood, CO: Libraries Unlimited.

Adamson, L. (1999). *World historical fiction: An annotated guide to novels for adults and young adults.* Phoenix, AZ: Oryx Press.

Allen, J. (1995). *It's never too late: Leading adolescents to lifelong literacy.* Portsmouth, NH: Heinemann.

American Library Association. *Best books for young adults, High-low books for young adults,* and *Booklist: Young adult editors' choices.* Write to ALA, Young Adult Services Division, 50 East Huron, Chicago, IL 60611.

Barry, A. (1998). Hispanic representation in literature for children and young adults. *Journal of Adolescent & Adult Literacy, 41,* 630–637.

Brozo, W., & Schmelzer, R. (1997). Wildmen, warriors, and lovers: Reaching boys through archetypal literature. *Journal of Adolescent & Adult Literacy, 41,* 4–11.

International Reading Association. Young adults' choices. Annotated bibliography of newly published books appears each fall in the *Journal of Adolescent and Adult Literacy.*

National Council for the Social Studies/Children's Book Council. Notable children's trade books in the field of social studies. Appears each spring in *Social Education.*

National Science Teachers Association/Children's Book Council. Outstanding science trade books for children. Appears each spring in *Science and Children.*

The New Advocate, English Journal, Hornbook, and *School Library Journal* are journals that regularly review books for children and adolescents.

Rand, D., Parker, T., & Foster, S. (1998). *Black books galore! Guide to great African American children's books.* New York: Wiley.

Richardson, J. (2000). *Read it aloud! Using literature in the secondary content classroom.* Newark, DE: International Reading Association.

Sprague, M., & Keeling, K. (2000). A library for Ophelia. *Journal of Adolescent & Adult Literacy, 43,* 640–647. (Novels that examine critical issues faced by girls)

Willis, A. (Ed.) (1998). *Teaching and using multicultural literaure in grades 9–12: Moving beyond the canon.* Norwood, MA: Christopher Gordon.

Word Lover's Booklist

Ammer, Christine (1989). *Fighting words: From war, rebellion, and other combative capers.* New York: Dell.

Amner, Christine (1997). *The American heritage dictionary of idioms.* New York: Houghton Mifflin.

Blumenfeld, Warren (1989). *Pretty ugly: More oxymorons and other illogical expressions that make absolute sense.* New York: Putnam.

Bowler, P. (1994). *The superior person's second book of weird and wondrous words.* New York: Laurel.

Burchfield, Robert, & Fowler, Henry W. (2000). *The new Fowler's modern English usage,* 3rd ed. New York: Oxford University Press.

Carver, C. (1991). *A history of English in its own words.* New York: HarperCollins.

Cutler, C. (1994). *O brave new words: Native American loan words in current English.* Norman: University of Oklahoma Press.

Dunkling, Leslie (1990). *A dictionary of epithets and terms of address.* New York: Routledge.

Elster, Charles (1988). *There is no zoo in zoology and other beastly mispronunciations.* New York: Collier Books.

Flexner, S. (1993). *Wise words and wives' tales: The origins, meanings, and time-honored wisdom of proverbs and folk sayings.* New York: Avon.

Freeman, M. (1993). *Hue and cry and humble pie: The stories behind the words.* New York: Plume.

Garrison, Webb (2000). *What's in a word? Fascinating stories of more than 300 everyday words and phrases.* Nashville, TN: Rutledge Hill.

Green, Jonathan (1991). *Neologisms: New words since 1960.* London: Bloomsbury.

Hendrickson, R. (1994). *Grand slams, hat tricks, and alley-oops: A sports fan's book of words.* New York: Prentice Hall.

Lederer, Richard (1989). *Anguished English.* New York: Pocket Books.

Major, Clarence (Ed.) (1994). *Juba to jive: A dictionary of African-American slang.* New York: Viking.

Mills, J. (1993). *Womanwords: A dictionary of words about women.* New York: Henry Holt.

Neaman, Judith, & Silver, Carole (1990). *Kind words: A thesaurus of euphemisms.* New York: Avon.

Randall, Bernice (1991). *When is a pig, a hog? A guide to confoundingly related English words.* Englewood Cliffs, NJ: Prentice Hall.

Rawson, Hugh (1989). *Wicked words: A treasury of curses, insults, put-downs, and other formerly unprintable terms from Anglo-Saxon times to the present.* New York: Crown.

Rovin, J. (1994). *What's the difference? A compendium of commonly confused and misused words.* New York: Ballantine.

Sheehan, Michael (2000). *Word parts dictionary: Standard and reverse listings of prefixes, suffixes, and combining forms.* Jefferson, NC: McFarland.

Smitherman-Donaldson, G. (1994). *Black talk: Words and phrases from the hood to the amen corner.* Boston: Houghton Mifflin.

Urdang, Laurence, Hunsinger, Walter, & LaRoche, Nancy (1991). *A fine kettle of fish and other figurative expressions.* Detroit: Visible Ink Press.

Read-Aloud Books for Content Areas

History and Social Studies

Boardman, Barrington (1988). *Flappers, bootleggers, "Typhoid Mary" & the bomb: An anecdotal history of the United States from 1923–1945.* New York: Harper & Row.

Boller, Paul (1984). *Presidential campaigns.* New York: Oxford University Press.

Davis, Kenneth (2001). *Don't know much about the presidents.* New York: HarperCollins.

Garraty, John (1989). *1,001 things everyone should know about American history.* New York: Doubleday.

Garrison, Webb (1988). *A treasury of Civil War tales.* New York: Ballantine.

Hay, Peter (1988). *All the presidents' ladies: Anecdotes of the women behind the men in the White House.* New York: Viking.

Hoose, Phillip (1993). *It's our world, too! Stories of young people who are making a difference.* Boston: Little, Brown. (Young social activists, including those from Revolutionary War, abolitionists, labor, and civil rights)

Hopkins, Lee, & Arenstein, Misha (1990). *Do you know what day tomorrow is? A teacher's almanac.* New York: Scholastic.

Kane, Joseph, Anzovin, Steven, & Podell, Janet (1997). *Famous first facts: A record of first happenings, discoveries and inventions in American history* (5th ed.) New York: Wilson.

Shenkman, Richard (1988). *Legends, lies, and cherished myths of American history.* New York: Morrow.

Spinrad, Leonard, Spinrad, Thelma, Miller, Anistatia, & Brown, Jared (1999). *On this day in history.* Paramus, NJ: Prentice Hall.

Wagman, John (1990). *On this day in America: An illustrated almanac of history, sports, science, and culture.* New York: Gallery Books.

Science and Mathematics

Adair, Robert (1990). *The physics of baseball.* New York: Harper & Row.

Aschenbach, Joel (1996). *Why things are & why things aren't.* New York: Ballantine.

Berry, A. (1993). *The book of scientific anecdotes.* Buffalo, NY: Prometheus.

Bragdon, Alan (1989). *Ingenious inventions of domestic utility.* New York: Harper & Row.

Flaste, Richard (Ed.) (1991). *The New York Times book of science literacy: What everyone needs to know from Newton to the knuckleball.* New York: HarperCollins.

Flatow, Ira (1992). *They all laughed: From the lightbulb to the laser.* New York: HarperCollins.

Goldberg, Philip (1990). *The Babinski reflex and 70 other useful and amusing metaphors from science, psychology, business, sports and everyday life.* Los Angeles: Tarcher.

MacEachern, Diane (1990). *Save our planet: 750 everyday ways you can help clean up the earth.* New York: Dell.

McGervey, John (1989). *Probabilities in everyday life.* New York: Ivy Books. (The lottery, bingo, casino games, sports betting, card games, risks of alcohol, tobacco and drug abuse, uses and abuses of statistics)

Murphree, Tom, & Miller, Mary (1998). *Watching weather (Accidental scientist series).* New York: Henry Holt.

Park, Robert (2000). *Voodoo science: The road from foolishness to fraud.* New York: Oxford University Press.

Paulos, John A. (1999). *Once upon a number: The hidden mathematical logic of stories.* New York: Basic Books.

Ray, C. (1997). *The New York Times science questions and answers.* New York: Anchor.

Seff, Philip, & Seff, Nancy (1996). *Petrified lightning and more amazing stories from "Our Fascinating Earth."* Chicago: NTC/Contemporary.

Tahan, M. (1993). *The man who counted: A collection of mathematic adventures.* New York: Norton.

Waldbauer, Gilbert (2000). *Millions of monarchs, bunches of beetles: How bugs find strength in numbers.* Cambridge, MA: Harvard University Press.

Gallimaufry

Bathroom Readers' Institute (1998). *Uncle John's great big bathroom reader.* Ashland, OR: Bathroom Readers' Press.

Craughwell, Thomas (1999). *Alligators in the sewer and 444 other absolutely true stories that happened to a friend of a friend of a friend.* New York: Black Dog & Leventhal.

Drimmer, Frederick. (1988). *Born different: Amazing stories of very special people.* New York: Bantam.

Dunn, Jerry (Ed.) (1991). *Tricks of the trade: Over 79 experts reveal the secrets behind what they do.* Boston: Houghton Mifflin.

Goldberg, M. Hirsch (1984). *The blunder book: Colossal errors, minor mistakes and surprising slipups that have changed the course of history.* New York: Morrow.

Kohn, Alfie (1990). *You know what they say: The truth behind popular beliefs.* New York: HarperCollins.

Seuling, Barbara (1991). *You can't count a billion dollars! And other little known facts about money.* New York: Ballantine.

Tuleja, Tad (1999). *Fabulous fallacies: More than 300 popular beliefs that are not true.* New York: BBS.

Dead Ends

Donaldson, Norman, & Donaldson, Betty (1989). *How did they die?* New York: St. Martin's.

Forbes, Malcolm (with Jeff Block) (1988). *They went that-away.* New York: Ballantine.

Panati, Charles (1988). *Extraordinary endings of practically everything and everybody.* New York: Harper & Row.

Shushan, E. R. (1990). *Grave matters.* New York: Ballantine.

Silverman, Stephen (1991). *Where there's a will.* New York: HarperCollins.

Slee, Christopher (1990). *The Chameleon book of lasts.* Huntingdon, UK: Chameleon.

Trade Books for Science, Math, and Social Studies

Discoverers and Discoveries

Adair, Gene (1989). *George Washington Carver.* Broomall, PA: Chelsea House. (YA)

Billings, Charlene (1989). *Grace Hopper: Navy admiral and computer pioneer.* Hillsdale, NJ: Enslow. (YA)

Brooks, P. (1989). *The house of life: Rachel Carson at work.* Boston: Houghton Mifflin.

Crick, F. (1988). *What mad pursuit: A personal view of scientific discovery.* New York: Basic Books.

Feynman, Richard (1988). *What do you care what other people think? Further adventures of a curious character.* New York: Norton. (Includes an account of the commission that investigated the Challenger disaster)

Kass-Simon, G., & Farnes, P. (1993). *Women in science: Righting the record.* Bloomington: Indiana University Press.

Kidd, R., Kessler, J., Kidd, J., & Morin, K. (1995). *Distinguished African American scientists of the 20th century.* Phoenix: Oryx Press.

Peat, F. David (1989). *Cold fusion: The making of a scientific controversy.* Chicago: Contemporary Books.

Smith, Jane (1990). *Patenting the sun: Polio and the Salk vaccine.* New York: Morrow.

Vare, Ethlie, & Ptacek, Greg (1989). *Mothers of invention: From the bra to the bomb, forgotten women and their unforgettable ideas.* New York: Morrow.

Disasters

Ballard, Robert (with Rick Archbold) (1987). *The discovery of the Titanic.* New York: Warner/Madison.

Fuller, John. (1987). *Tornado watch #211*. New York: Morrow.

Gale, Robert, & Hauser, Thomas (1988). *Final warning: The legacy of Chernobyl*. New York: Warner.

Lauber, Patricia (1986). *Volcano: The eruption and healing of Mt. St. Helens*. New York: Bradbury.

Petroski, Henry (1985). *To engineer is human*. New York: St. Martin's.

Preston, Richard (1994). *The hot zone*. New York: Random House. (Outbreak of the ebola virus)

Ritchie, David (1988). *Superquake! Why earthquakes occur and when the big one will hit Southern California*. New York: Crown.

Ward, Kaari (Ed.) (1989). *Great disasters*. Pleasantville, NY: Reader's Digest.

Ecology and the Environment

Bash, B. (1990). *Urban roosts: Where birds nest in the city*. San Francisco: Sierra Club Books.

Commoner, Barry (1989). *Making peace with the planet*. New York: Pantheon.

Gribbin, John (1988). *The hole in the sky: Man's threat to the ozone layer*. New York: Bantam.

LaBastille, Anne (1991). *Woodswoman*. New York: Dutton. (Autobiographical story of a woman who lived alone in the Adirondacks, showing both the beauties and stark realities of nature)

McPhee, John (1989). *The control of nature*. New York: Farrar, Straus & Giroux.

Naar, Jon (1990). *Design for a liveable planet: The eco-action guide to positive ecology*. New York: HarperCollins.

Paulsen, Gary (1994). *Father Water, Mother Woods: Essays on hunting and fishing in the North Woods*. New York: Delacorte.

Quammen, David (1988). *The flight of the iguana: A sidelong view of science and nature*. New York: Doubleday.

Mathematics

Boyer, Carl (1991). *The history of mathematics* (revised by Uta Merzbach). New York: Wiley.

Devlin, Keith (2000). *The math gene: How mathematical thinking evolved and why numbers are like gossip*. New York: Basic Books.

Hoffman, Paul (1988). *Archimedes' revenge: The joys and perils of mathematics*. New York: Fawcett.

Pappas, Theoni (1991). *Math talk: Mathematical ideas in poems for two voices*. San Carlos, CA: Wide World/Tetra.

Paulos, John (1990). *Innumeracy: Mathematical illiteracy and its consequences*. New York: Random House.

Thomas, David (1995). *Math projects in the computer age*. New York: Watts.

Physics and Chemistry

Aschenbach, Joel (1999). *Captured by aliens: The search for life and truth in a very large universe.* New York: Simon & Schuster.

Caglioti, Luciano (1990). *The two faces of chemistry.* Boston: MIT Press.

Jaffa, Bernard (1976). *Crucibles: The story of chemistry from ancient alchemy to nuclear fission* (4th ed.). New York: Dover.

Van Cleave, Janice (1989). *Chemistry for every kid: 101 easy experiments that really work.* New York: Wiley.

Walker, Jearl (1975). *The flying circus of physics.* New York: Wiley.

Science Fiction and Fiction about Science

Adams, Douglas (1979). *Hitchhiker's guide to the galaxy.* New York: Harmony. (The first of a series; "Hitchhiker" fans are legion)

Adams, Richard (1976). *Watership Down.* New York: Avon. (Life, death, and survival from the point of view of rabbits)

Asimov, Isaac (1987). *Fantastic voyage.* New York: Bantam. (Based on the screenplay; a journey inside the human body)

Clancy, Tom (1991). *The sum of all fears.* New York: Putnam. (Terrorists plant a nuclear bomb)

Cook, Robin (1997). *Chromosome 6.* New York: Berkley. (Scientists researching apes in Africa venture into cloning)

Crichton, Michael (1990). *Jurassic Park.* New York: Knopf. (Scientists use fossil DNA to clone dinosaurs for a theme park)

Defelice, Cynthia (1998). *The ghost of Fossil Glen.* New York: Avon. (YA fiction; a girl is pursued by a ghost after a near-death experience while fossil hunting)

Hesse, Karen (1996). *The music of dolphins.* New York: Scholastic. (YA fiction; child is lost at sea and adopted by dolphins; after her rescue, she is sent to a center for scientific research, where she is taught human language but yearns for her dolphin family)

Klass, David (1994). *California blue.* New York: Scholastic. (YA fiction; battle between environmentalists and community dependent on a local mill)

Lawrence, Louise (1985). *Children of the dust.* New York: Harper & Row. (Mutant and nonmutant survivors of a nuclear holocaust)

Swindells, Robert (1985). *Brother in the land.* New York: Holiday House. (Survivors' tale after nuclear war)

Slavery Times

Armstrong, J. (1992). *Steal away . . . to freedom.* New York: Scholastic. (Story of two girls, one white, one black, and the Underground Railroad)

Clark, Margaret (1980). *Freedom crossing.* New York: Scholastic. (Underground Railroad story set in Lewiston, NY)

Cosner, Sharon (1991). *The Underground Railroad.* New York: Venture.

Hamilton, V. (1993). *Many thousand gone: African-Americans from slavery to freedom.* New York: Knopf. (African American folk tales and stories, including stories of escape from slavery)

Lester, Julius (1968). *To be a slave.* New York: Scholastic. (True narratives of the lives of slaves)

Myers, Walter Dean (1991). *Now is your time: The African-American struggle for freedom.* New York: Scholastic.

Rappaport, D. (1991). *Escape from slavery: Five journeys to freedom.* New York: HarperCollins.

Wisler, G. Clifton (1996). *Caleb's choice.* New York: Dutton. (YA fiction; set in Texas, the story of a white youth's entanglement in the area's sharp divisions over the Fugitive Slave Law)

Civil War

Chang, Ina (1991). *A separate battle: Women and the Civil War.* New York: Scholastic.

Clapp, Patricia (1986). *Tamarack tree.* New York: Lothrop, Lee & Shepard. (YA fiction; the siege of Vicksburg)

Freedman, R. (1987). *Lincoln: A photobiography.* Boston: Houghton Mifflin.

Hunt, Irene (1964). *Across five Aprils.* New York: Berkley. (YA fiction; life on an Illinois farm during the Civil War)

Marrin, Albert (1994). *Unconditional surrender: U.S. Grant and the Civil War.* New York: Atheneum. (Biography, illustrated with photographs)

Marrin, Albert (1994). *Virginia's general: Robert E. Lee and the Civil War.* New York: Atheneum. (Biography, illustrated with photographs)

Rinaldi, Ann (1993). *In my father's house.* New York: Scholastic. (YA fiction; story of a Southern family during the Civil War)

Shaara, Michael (1974). *The killer angels.* New York: Ballantine. (Fiction; the Battle of Gettysburg)

Immigration

Ashabranner, Brent (with Melissa Ashabranner) (1987). *Into a strange land; Unaccompanied refugee youth in America.* New York: Putnam.

Bode, Janet (1989). *New kids on the block: Oral histories of immigrant teens.* New York: Watts.

Conover, Ted (1987). *Coyotes.* New York: Vintage. (The lives of Mexicans who illegally cross the U.S. border)

Denenberg, Barry (1997). *Dear America: So far from home, the diary of Mary Driscoll, an Irish mill girl.* New York: Scholastic. (YA fiction)

Mays, Lucinda (1979). *The other shore.* New York: Atheneum. (Fiction about Italian Americans)

Paulsen, Gary (1987). *The crossing.* New York: Dell. (YA fiction; an orphaned 14-year-old attempts to cross the U.S.–Mexican border)

Rolvaag, Ole (1991). *Giants in the earth.* New York: Harper. (A story of Norwegian families who settled in the Dakotas)

Wartski, Maureen (1982). *Long way from home.* New York: Dutton. (YA fiction; a young Vietnamese refugee tries to establish himself in America)

Contemporary Issues

Ashabranner, Brent (1988). *Always to remember: The story of the Vietnam veterans' memorial.* New York: Dodd, Mead.

Kuklin, Susan (1996). *Irrepressible spirit: Conversations with human rights activists.* New York: Putnam.

MacDonald, John D. (1985). *Condominium.* New York: Fawcett. (Mystery fiction; the ecological consequences of building on barrier islands in Florida)

Reuter, Mark (1988). *Sparrows Point: Making steel—The rise and ruin of American industrial might.* New York: Summit.

Seeger, Pete, & Reiser, Bob (1989). *A history of the civil rights movement in songs and pictures.* New York: Norton.

Shuman, Len (1990). *The good, the bad, and the famous: Celebrities playing politics.* New York: Stuart.

Terkel, Studs (1992). *Race: How blacks and whites think and feel about the American obsession.* New York: Norton.

Williams, Juan (1987). *Eyes on the prize.* New York: Viking. (History of the civil rights movement)

Culturally Conscious Trade Books

African American

Busby, Margaret (Ed.) (1992). *Daughters of Africa: An international anthology of words and writings by women of African descent from the ancient Egyptian to the present.* New York: Pantheon.

Campbell, Bebe Moore (1998). *Singing in the comeback choir.* New York: Putnam.

Giovanni, Nikki (1974). *Ego-tripping and other poems for young people.* Chicago: Hill. (YA)

Giovanni, Nikki (1994). *Racism 101.* New York: Quill. (Essays on race relations)

Hamilton, Virginia (Ed.). (1985). *The people could fly: American black folktales.* New York: Knopf.

Haskins, James (1987). *Black music in America: A history through its people.* New York: Crowell.

Hudson, Wade (Ed.) (1993). *Pass it on: African-American poetry for children* (Floyd Cooper, Illust.). New York: Scholastic. (Illustrated collection of poetry by such African American poets as Langston Hughes, Nikki Giovanni, Eloise Greenfield, and Lucille Clifton)

Hurston, Zora Neale (1937). *Their eyes were watching God.* New York: Harper & Row. (Story of an independent African American woman in the rural South)

Lester, Julius (1987). *The tales of Uncle Remus: The adventures of Brer Rabbit.* New York: Dial.

Malcolm X (with Alex Haley) (1964). *The autobiography of Malcolm X.* New York: Ballantine.

McCall, Nathan (1994). *Makes me wanna holler: A young black man in America.* New York: Random House.

McKissack, Patricia (1989). *Jesse Jackson.* New York: Scholastic. (Critically acclaimed biography)

Morrison, Toni (1971). *Beloved.* New York: Knopf. (Freed slave and her family; life before and after Civil War)

Myers, Walter Dean (1999). *Monster.* New York: HarperCollins. (YA fiction by prolific novelist, poet, and biographer; 16-year old boy accused of a violent crime)

Njeri, Itabari (1990). *Every good-bye ain't gone.* New York: Random House. (A series of essays about growing up in New York City during the 1950s and 1960s by a writer of African American, East Indian, Native American, English, and French descent)

Parks, Van Dyke (1989). *Jump on over! The adventures of Brer Rabbit and his family.* New York: Harcourt Brace Jovanovich.

Schroeder, Alan (1989). *Ragtime Tumpie.* Boston: Little, Brown. (YA; biography of entertainer Josephine Baker)

Taylor, Mildred (1976). *Roll of thunder, hear my cry.* New York: Dial. (YA fiction; first in a series of three novels about the struggles of a black family in Mississippi in the 1930s)

Terry, Wallace (Ed.) (1985). *Bloods: An oral history of the Vietnam War by black veterans.* New York: Ballantine.

Thomas, Joyce Carol (2001). *The blacker the berry.* New York: HarperCollins. (Poems by well-known young adult author)

Wideman, John E. (1985). *Brothers and keepers.* New York: Oxford University Press. (An African American college professor explores the painful contrasts between his life and that of his brother in prison)

Asian American

Crew, Linda (1989). *Children of the river.* New York: Dell. (YA fiction; story of a Cambodian American high school student in Oregon)

Hamanaka, Sheila (1990). *The journey: Japanese Americans, racism, and renewal.* New York: Orchard. (A picture book suitable for third grade through high school)

Huynh, Quang Nhuong (1986). *Land I lost: Adventures of a boy in Vietnam.* New York: Harper & Row.

Kingston, Maxine Hong (1977). *Woman warrior: Memoirs of a girlhood among ghosts.* New York: Random House. (The struggle to keep a Chinese identity while assimilating into American society)

Lee, Marie (1992). *Finding my voice.* Boston: Houghton Mifflin. (YA fiction; Ellen Sung, a Korean American, goes to Harvard as a freshman)

Namioka, Lensey (1994). *April and the dragon lady.* San Diego: Harcourt Brace Jovanovich. (YA fiction; conflict in Chinese American family over interethnic dating and traditional versus contemporary roles)

Sone, Monica (1979). *Nisei daughter.* Seattle: University of Washington Press. (A Japanese American tells of growing up in Seattle in the 1930s and relocation during World War II)

Tan, Amy (1989). *The joy luck club.* New York: Random House. (Fiction)

Uchida, Yoshiko (1981). *A jar of dreams.* New York: Atheneum. (YA fiction; the first in a trilogy of books about an 11-year-old Japanese American girl)

Yep, Lawrence (1977). *Child of the owl.* New York: Harper & Row. (YA fiction; child struggles to balance her Chinese roots and her identity with mainstream America)

Hispanic

Anaya, Rudolfo (1976). *Bless me Ultima.* Berkeley, CA: Tonatiuh. (Fiction about a Chicano boy)

Bernardo, Anilu (1996). *Jumping off to freedom.* Houston: Pinata. (YA fiction; family leaves Cuba on a raft for the United States)

Burke, David (1999). *Street Spanish: Slang dictionary and thesaurus.* New York: Wiley.

Carlson, Lori (Ed.) (1994). *Cool salsa: Bilingual poems on growing up in the United States.* New York: Henry Holt.

Cisneros, Sandra (1986). *The house on Mango Street.* Houston: Arte Publico. (A collection of Mexican American stories)

Chavez, D. (1994). *Face of an angel.* New York: Warner. (Story of a family in rural New Mexico)

Cruz, Victor Hernandez (1989). *Rhythm, content & flavor.* Houston: Arte Publico Press. (Poetry; Puerto Rican)

Day, F. A. (1997). *Latino and Latina voices in literature for children and teenagers.* Portsmouth, NH: Heinemann.

Gonzales, B. D. (1995). *Sweet fifteen.* Houston: Piñata Books. (A girl's quinceaños celebration is changed by the death of her father just before her 15th birthday)

Mohr, Nicholasa (1979). *Felita.* New York: Dial. (YA fiction; a family faces prejudice when they move from a predominantly Hispanic neighborhood)

Ortiz Cofer, Judith (1995). *An island like you: Stories of the barrio.* New York: Orchard.

Poniatowska, Elene, & Stellweg, Carla (1992). *Frida Kahlo: The camera seduced.* San Francisco: Chronicle. (Photos and essays about the great Mexican artist)

Rodriquez, Luis (1993). *Always running: La vida loca: Gang days in L.A.* New York: Touchstone.

Santiago, E. (1994). *When I was Puerto Rican.* New York: Prentice Hall. (Autobiographical stories of a young woman's acculturation to the mainland United States)

Santiago, R. (1995). *Boricuas: Influential Puerto Rican writings—An anthology.* New York: Ballantine.

Soto, Gary (2000). *Nickel and dime.* Albuquerque: University of New Mexico Press. (Story of three Mexican American men and street life in Oakland, California)

Thomas, Piri (1967). *Down these mean streets.* New York: Vintage. (Puerto Rican)

Velasquez, Gloria (1994). *Juanita fights the school board.* Houston: Piñata Press. (YA fiction)

Islam

Idilibi, Ulfat (1998). *Grandfather's tale.* (Peter Clark, Trans.). London: Quartet. (A young boy's pilgrimage to Mecca, growth into adulthood, and fulfillment of his family duties)

Staples, Suzanne (1989). *Shabanu: Daughter of the wind.* New York: Knopf. (YA fiction; story of a young Pakastani girl in an arranged marriage)

Jewish

Adler, David (1982). *A picture book of Passover.* New York: Holiday House.

Brooks, Jerome (1990). *Naked in winter.* New York: Orchard. (YA fiction; a 16-year-old boy copes with moving to a new neighborhood, family troubles, and sexual awakening)

Grossman, Mendel, & Dabba, Frank (2000). *My secret camera: Life in the Lodz ghetto.* New York: Harcourt.

Klein, G. W. (1995). *All but my life.* New York: Hill & Wang. (Holocaust survivor's story; film version won documentary Oscar in 1996)

Mazer, Norma Fox (1999). *Good night Maman.* New York: Harcourt. (YA fiction)

Singer, Isaac B. (1980). *The power of light: Eight stories for Hannukah.* New York: Farrar, Straus & Giroux.

Native American

Bouchard, D. (1997). *The elders are watching.* Vancouver, BC: Raincoast.

Esbensen, Barbara J. (1989). *Ladder to the sky: How the gift of healing came to the Ojibway Nation.* Boston: Little, Brown.

Fleischman, Paul (1990). *Saturnalia.* New York: HarperCollins. (YA fiction; a Narrangansett boy is sold as a slave to a Boston family in the 1660s)

Hernandez, I. (1992). *Heartbeat drumbeat.* Houston: Arte Publico Press. (YA fiction; story of a girl with a Chicano father and Navajo mother)

Norman, Howard (1989). *How Glooskap outwits the ice giants and other tales of the Maritime Indians.* Boston: Little, Brown.

Thomasma, Kenneth (1984). *Soun Tetoken: Nez Perce boy.* Grand Rapids, MI: Baker. (YA fiction; the story of the Nez Perce tribe before and during the war of 1877)

Thorn, James (1989). *Panther in the sky.* New York: Ballantine. (A fictional account of Tecumseh, leader of the Shawnee tribe in the late eighteenth century)

Diverse Cultures

Lynch, Chris (1996). *Blue-eyed son: A trilogy.* New York: HarperCollins. (YA fiction; three books about Mick, the younger son in an Irish American family, and his struggles to come to terms with his heritage, his family, racism, and alcoholism)

McBride, James (1996). *The color of water: A black man's tribute to his white mother.* New York: Riverhead.

Mead, Alice (1996). *Adem's cross.* New York: Farrar, Straus & Giroux. (YA fiction; the violence and brutality of war in the former Yugoslavia, as seen in the story of a minority Albanian boy in Serb-controlled territory)

Meyer, Carolyn (1996). *Gideon's people.* San Diego: Harcourt Brace/Gulliver Books (YA fiction; family and ethnic conflicts around the relationship of Isaac, son of immigrant Jews, and his Amish friend Gideon)

References

Abrahamson, R., & Carter, B. (1991, January). Nonfiction: The missing piece in the middle. *English Journal, 79,* 52–58.

Adams, P. (1995). Teaching *Romeo and Juliet* in the non-tracked English classroom. *Journal of Reading, 38,* 424–432.

Adamson, H. D. (1993). *Academic competence: Theory and classroom practice, preparing ESL students for content courses.* New York: Longman.

Agee, J. (1999, November). "There it was, that one sex scene": English teachers on censorship. *English Journal, 89,* 61–69.

Agnew, E. J. (1985). *The grading policies and practices of high school teachers.* Paper presented at the American Educational Research Association, Chicago. (ERIC No. ED 259 022)

Alexander, P. A., & Jetton, T. L. (2000). Learning from text: A multidimensional and developmental perspective. In M. L. Kamil, P. B. Mosenthal, P. D. Pearson, & R. Barr (Eds.), *Handbook of reading research: Volume 3* (pp. 285–310). Mahwah, NJ: Erlbaum.

Allan, C. (1999). Poets of comrades: Addressing sexual orientation in the English classroom. *English Journal, 88*(6), 97–101.

Allen, J. (1995). *It's never too late: Leading adolescents to life-long literacy.* Portsmouth, NH: Heinemann.

Allen, J., & Gonzalez, K. (1998). *There's room for me here: Literacy workshop in the middle school.* York, ME: Stenhouse.

Allington, R. L., & McGill-Franzen, A. (2000, Winter). Looking back, looking forward: Excerpts from a conversation about teaching reading in the 21st century. *English Update: A Newsletter from the Center on English Learning & Achievement,* (pp. 4–5).

Alvermann, D. E. (1987). The role of textbooks in teachers' interactive decision making. *Reading Research and Instruction, 26,* 115–127.

Alvermann, D. E. (1992). The discussion web: A graphic aid for learning across the curriculum. *The Reading Teacher, 45,* 92–99.

Alvermann, D. E. (1995–96). Peer-led discussions: Whose interests are served? *Journal of Adolescent & Adult Literacy, 39,* 282–289.

Alvermann, D. E. (2000). Classroom talk about texts: Is it dear, cheap, or a bargain at any price? In B. M. Taylor, M. F. Graves, & P. Van Den Broek (Eds.), *Reading for meaning* (pp. 136–151). New York: Teachers College Press.

Alvermann, D. E., & Commeyras, M. (1998). Feminist poststructuralist perspectives on the language of reading assessment: Authenticity and performance. In C. Harrison, M. Bailey, & A. Dewar (Eds.), *New paradigms in reading assessment* (pp. 50–60). London: Routledge.

Alvermann, D. E., & Hagood, M. C. (2000). Critical media literacy: Research, theory, and practice in "new times." *Journal of Educational Research, 93,* 193–205.

Alvermann, D. E., & Moore, D. W. (1991). Secondary school reading. In R. Barr, M. L. Kamil, P. Mosenthal, & P. D. Pearson (Eds.), *Handbook of reading research: Volume 2* (pp. 951–983). New York: Longman.

Alvermann, D. E., Commeyras, M., Young, J., Hinson, D., & Randall, S. (1996a). *The gendered language of texts and classrooms: Teachers and students exploring multiple perspectives and interpretations* (Instructional Resource No. 23). Athens: University of Georgia, National Reading Research Center.

Alvermann, D. E., Dillon, D. R., & O'Brien, D. G. (1987). *Using discussion to promote reading comprehension.* Newark, DE: International Reading Association.

Alvermann, D. E., Hagood, M. C., Heron, A., Hughes, P., & Williams, K. (2000). *Critical literacy practices in after-school media clubs.* Final report submitted to the Spencer Foundation, Chicago, September 30.

Alvermann, D. E., Hagood, M. C., Heron, A., Hughes, P., & Williams, K. (2000). *The media club study.* Paper presented at the annual meeting of the College Reading Association, St. Petersburg Beach, FL.

Alvermann, D. E., Moon, J. S., & Hagood, M. C. (1999). *Popular culture in the classroom: Teaching and researching critical media literacy.* Newark, DE: International Reading Association and the National Reading Conference.

Alvermann, D. E., O'Brien, D. G., & Dillon, D. R. (1990). What teachers do when they say they're having discussions of content reading assignments: A qualitative analysis. *Reading Research Quarterly, 25,* 296–322.

Alvermann, D. E., Young, J. P., Green, C., & Wisenbaker, J. M. (1999). Adolescents' perceptions and negotiations of literacy practices in after-school read and talk clubs. *American Educational Research Journal, 36,* 221–264.

Alvermann, D. E., Young, J. P., Weaver, D., Hinchman, K. A., Moore, D. W., Phelps, S. F., Thrash, E. C., & Zalewski, P. (1996). Middle and high school students' perceptions of how they experience text-based discussions: A multicase study. *Reading Research Quarterly, 31,* 244–267.

Alvermann, D., Olson, J., & Umpleby, R. (1993). Learning to do research together. In S. Hudelson & J. Lindfors (Eds.), *Delicate balances: Collaborative research in language education* (pp. 112–124). Urbana, IL: National Council for Teachers of English.

Alvermann, D., Smith, L., & Readence, J. (1985). Prior knowledge activation and the comprehension of compatible and incompatible text. *Reading Research Quarterly, 20,* 420–436.

American Association of University Women Educational Foundation (2000). *Tech-savvy: Educating girls in the new computer age.* Washington, DC: American Association of University Women Educational Foundation.

Amit-Talai, V., & Wulff, H. (Eds.) (1995). *Youth cultures: A cross-cultural perspective.* New York: Routledge.

Anders, P., & Bos, C. (1986). Semantic feature analysis: An interactive strategy for vocabulary development and text comprehension. *Journal of Reading, 29,* 610–616.

Anderson, C. W. (1992). Strategic teaching in science. In M. K. Pearsall (Ed.), *Scope, sequence, and coordination of secondary school science: Relevant research* (Vol. 2, pp. 221–236). Washington, DC: National Science Teachers Association.

Anderson, R. C. (1984). Role of the reader's schema in comprehension, learning, and memory. In R. C. Anderson, J. Osborn, & R. J. Tierney (Eds.), *Learning to read in American schools: Basal readers and content texts* (pp. 243–258). Hillsdale, NJ: Erlbaum.

Anderson, R. C., Hiebert, E., Scott, J., & Wilkinson, I. (1985). *Becoming a nation of readers: The report of the Commission on Reading.* Washington, DC: National Institute of Education.

Anderson, R. C., Reynolds, R. E., Schallert, D. L., & Goetz, E. T. (1977). Frameworks for comprehending discourse. *American Educational Research Journal, 14,* 367–382.

Anderson, T. H., & Armbruster, B. B. (1984). Studying. In P. D. Pearson, R. Barr, M. Kamil, & P. Mosenthal (Eds.), *Handbook of reading research (pp. 657–679).* New York: Longman.

Anderson, T., & Armbruster, B. (1984). Content area textbooks. In R. C. Anderson, J. Osborn, & R. Tierney (Eds.), *Learning to read in American schools: Basal readers and content texts* (pp. 193–226). Hillsdale, NJ: Erlbaum.

Anderson, V., & Hidi, S. (1988/1989). Teaching students to summarize. *Educational Leadership, 4,* 26–29.

André, M., & Anderson, T. (1978/1979). The development and evaluation of a self-questioning study technique. *Reading Research Quarterly, 14,* 605–623.

Andrews, S. E. (2000). Writing to learn in content area reading class. In D. W. Moore, D. E. Alvermann, & K. A. Hinchman (Eds.), *Struggling adolescent readers: A collection of teaching strategies* (pp. 217–219). Newark, DE: International Reading Association.

Anyon, J. (1979). Ideology and United States textbooks. *Harvard Educational Review, 49,* 361–386.

Applebee, A. N., Langer, J. A., & Mullis, I. V S. (1987). *Literature and U.S. history: The instructional experience and factual knowledge of high school juniors.* Princeton, NJ: Educational Testing Service.

Applebee, A., Langer, J., Mullis, I., Latham, A., & Gentile, C. (1994). *NAEP 1992 writing report card.* Washington, DC: U.S. Department of Education, Office of Educational Research and Improvement.

Ardizzone, P. (1992, November). The journal—A tool in the ESL classroom. *Writing Teacher, 6,* 31–33.

Armbruster, B., Anderson, T., & Ostertag, J. (1987). Does text structure/summarization instruction facilitate learning from expository text? *Reading Research Quarterly, 22,* 331–346.

Arthur, B. (1991). Working with new ESL students in a junior high school reading class. *Journal of Reading, 34,* 628–631.

Aschbacher, P. R. (1991). Humanitas: A thematic curriculum. *Educational Leadership, 49* (2), 16–19.

Athanases, S. (1998). Diverse learners, diverse texts: Exploring identity and difference through literary encounters. *Journal of Literacy Research, 30,* 273–296.

Atwell, N. (1987). *In the middle: Writing, reading, and learning with adolescents.* Portsmouth, NH: Boynton/Cook.

Atwell, N. (1998). *In the middle: New understandings about writing, reading and learning* (2nd ed.). Portsmouth, NH: Heinemann.

Au, K. (1998). Social constructivism and the school literacy learning of students of diverse backgrounds. *Journal of Literacy Research, 30,* 297–319.

Au, K. H. (1980). Participation structures in reading lessons: Analysis of a culturally appropriate instructional event. *Anthropology and Education Quarterly, 11,* 91–115.

August, D., & Hakuta, K. (1997). *Improving schooling for language minority children: A research agenda.* Washington, DC: National Academy Press.

Ausubel, D. (1968). *Educational psychology: A cognitive view.* New York: Holt, Rinehart & Winston.

Baines, L. (2000). Same facts, different audience. In L. Baines & A. Kunkel (Eds.), *Going Bohemian: Activities that engage adolescents in the art of writing well,* (pp. 78–80). Newark, DE: International Reading Association.

Baker, L., & Brown, A. L. (1980). *Metacognitive skills and reading* (Tech. Rep. No. 188). Urbana: University of Illinois, Center for the Study of Reading.

Baker, L., & Brown, A. L. (1984). Metacognitive skills and reading. In P. D. Pearson, R. Barr, M. Kamil, & P. Mosenthal (Eds.), *Handbook of reading research* (pp. 353–394). New York: Longman.

Balajthy, E. (1990). Hypertext, hypermedia, and metacognition: Research and instructional implications for disabled readers. *Reading, Writing and Learning Disabilities, 6,* 183–190.

Bank, S. (1986). Assessing reading interests of adolescent students. *Educational Research Quarterly, 10*(3), 8–13.

Barnes, D. (1976). *From communication to curriculum.* Toronto: Penguin Education.

Barron, R. (1969). The use of vocabulary as an advance organizer. In H. Herber & P. Sanders (Eds.), *Research in reading in the content areas: First year report* (pp. 29–39). Syracuse, NY: Syracuse University Reading and Language Arts Center.

Barry, A. (1998). Hispanic representation in literature for children and young adults. *Journal of Adolescent & Adult Literacy, 41,* 630–637.

Bauer, E., & Garcia, G. (1997). Blurring the lines between reading assessment and instruction: A case study of a low-income student in the lowest reading group. In C. Kinzer, K. Hinchman, & D. Leu (Eds.), *Inquiries in literacy theory and practice* (pp. 166–176). 46th Yearbook of the National Reading Conference. Chicago, IL: National Reading Conference.

Bauer, E. (1999). The promise of alternative literacy assessments in the classroom: A review of empirical studies. *Reading Research & Instruction, 38,* 153–168.

Baumann, J. (1984). The effectiveness of a direct instruction paradigm for teaching main idea comprehension. *Reading Research Quarterly, 20,* 93–115.

Baumann, J., & Kameenui, E. (1991). Research on vocabulary instruction: Ode to Voltaire. In J. Flood, J. M. Jensen, D. Lapp, & J. R. Squire (Eds.), *Handbook of research on teaching the English language arts* (pp. 604–632). New York: Macmillan.

Beach, R. (1997). Stances of resistance and engagement in responding to multicultural literature. In T. Rogers & A. Soter (Eds.), *Reading across cultures: Teaching literature in a diverse society* (pp. 69–94). New York: Teachers College Press.

Bean, T. (1992). Combining writing fluency and vocabulary development through writing roulette. In E. Dishner, T. Bean, J. Readence, & D. Moore (Eds.), *Reading in the content areas: Improving classroom instruction* (3rd ed., pp. 247–254). Dubuque, IA: Kendall/Hunt.

Bean, T., & Bishop, A. (1992). Polar opposites: A strategy for guiding students' critical reading and discussion. In E. Dishner, T. Bean, J. Readence, & D. Moore (Eds.), *Reading in the content areas: Improving classroom instruction* (3rd ed.) (pp. 247–254). Dubuque, IA: Kendall/Hunt.

Bean, T., Bean, S., & Bean, K. (1999). Intergenerational conversations and two adolescents' multiple literacies: Implications for redefining content area literacy. *Journal of Adolescent & Adult Literacy, 42,* 438–448.

Bean, T., Kile, R., & Readence, J. (1996). Using trade books to encourage critical thinking about citizenship in high school social studies. *Social Education, 60,* 227–230.

Beane, J. A. (1990). *A middle school curriculum from rhetoric to reality.* Columbus, OH: National Middle School Association.

Beck, I., & McKeown, M. (1991). Social studies texts are hard to understand: Mediating some of the difficulties. *Language Arts, 68,* 482–490.

Beck, I., McKeown, M., Hamilton, R., & Kucan, L. (1997). *Questioning the author: An approach for enhancing student engagement with text.* Newark, DE: International Reading Association.

Beers, K. (1996). No time, no interest, no way! The three voices of aliteracy. *School Library Journal, 42,* 110–113.

Berenson, S., & Carter, G. (1995). Changing assessment practices in science and mathematics. *School Science & Mathematics, 95,* 182–186.

Berger, A., & Shafran, E. (2000). *Teens for literacy: Promoting reading and writing in schools and communities.* Newark, DE: International Reading Association.

Bergeron, B., & Rudenga, E. (1996). Seeking authenticity: What is "real" about thematic literacy instruction? *The Reading Teacher, 49,* 544–551.

Berlin, D. F., & White, A. L. (1994). The Berlin–White integrated science and mathematics model. *School Science & Mathematics, 94,* 2–4.

Berliner, D., & Biddle, B. (1995). *The manufactured crisis: Myths, frauds, and the attack on America's public schools.* Reading, MA: Addison-Wesley.

Bernhardt, E. B. (2000). Second-language reading as a case study of reading scholarship in the 20th century. In M. L. Kamil, P. B. Mosenthal, P. D. Pearson, & R. Barr (Eds.), *Handbook of reading research: Volume 3* (pp. 791–811). Mahwah, NJ: Erlbaum.

Bigelow, B. (1994). Getting off the track: Stories from an untracked classroom. In B. Bigelow, L. Christensen, S. Karp, B. Miner, & B. Peterson (Eds.), *Rethinking our classrooms.* Milwaukee, WI: Rethinking Schools.

Biloff, E. (1996). *The Killer Angels:* A case study of historical fiction in the social studies curriculum. *Social Studies, 87,* 19–23.

Bintz, W. P. (1993). Resistant readers in secondary education: Some insights and implications. *Journal of Reading, 36,* 604–615.

Bishop, J. H. (1989). Why the apathy in American high schools? *Educational Researcher, 18*(1), 6–10, 42.

Bishop, R. (1990). Walk tall in the world: African American literature for today's children. *Journal of Negro Education, 59,* 556–565.

Blachowicz, C. (1986). Making connections: Alternatives to the vocabulary notebook. *Journal of Reading, 29,* 543–549.

Blachowicz, C. (1991). Vocabulary instruction in content classes for special needs learners: Why and how? *Reading, Writing, and Learning Disabilities, 7,* 297–308.

Blachowicz, C., & Fisher, P. (2000). Vocabulary instruction. In M. Kamil, P. Mosenthal, P. D. Pearson, & R. Barr (Eds.), *Handbook of Reading Research, Vol. 3* (pp. 503–523). Mahwah, NJ: Lawrence Erlbaum.

Blachowicz, C., & Zabroske, B. (1990). Context instruction: A metacognitive approach for at-risk readers. *Journal of Reading, 33,* 504–508.

Blackman, J. A. (1992). Confronting Thomas Jefferson, slave owner. *Phi Delta Kappan, 74,* 220–222.

Blake, M., & Majors, P. (1995). Recycled words: Holistic instruction for LEP students. *Journal of Adolescent & Adult Literacy, 39,* 132–137.

Bloom, H. (1994). *The western canon: The books and school of the ages.* New York: Harcourt Brace.

Bloome, D. (1992, April). Researching language: Languaging research. *Newsletter of the Reading & Writing Program.* Amherst: University of Massachusetts, School of Education.

Bloome, D., & Green, J. L. (1992). Educational contexts of literacy. *Annual Review of Applied Linguistics, 12,* 49–70.

Bolter, D. J. (1992). Literature in the electronic writing space. In M. Tuman (Ed.), *Literacy online: The promise (and peril) of reading and writing with computers.* Pittsburgh, PA: University of Pittsburgh Press.

Bond, L., & Roeber, E. (1995). *The status of state student assessment programs in the United States.* Washington, DC: Council of Chief State School Officers/North Central Regional Educational Laboratory.

Boorstin, D., & Kelley, B. (1996). *A history of the United States.* Needham, MA: Prentice Hall.

Bormuth, J. (1968). Cloze test readability: Criterion referenced scores. *Journal of Educational Measurement, 5,* 189–196.

Bos, C., Anders, P., Filip, D., & Jaffe, L. (1989). The effects of an interactive instructional strategy for enhancing reading comprehension and content area learning for students with learning disabilities. *Journal of Learning Disabilities, 22,* 384–390.

Boyd, D. (1996). Dominance concealed through diversity: Implications of inadequate perspectives on cultural pluralism. *Harvard Educational Review, 66,* 609–630.

Bransford, J. D. (1979). *Human cognition: Learning, understanding, and remembering.* Belmont, CA: Wadsworth.

Bransford, J. D., & McCarrell, N. S. (1974). A sketch of a cognitive approach to comprehension. In W. B. Weimer & D. S. Palermo (Eds.), *Cognition and the symbolic processes.* Hillsdale, NJ: Erlbaum.

Brautigan, R. (1971). *Revenge of the lawn.* New York: Simon & Schuster.

Britzman, D. P. (1987). Cultural myths in the making of a teacher: Biography and social structure in teacher education. In M. Okazawa–Rey, J. Anderson, & R. Traver (Eds.), *Teachers, teaching, and teacher education* (pp. 220–233). Cambridge, MA: Harvard University Press.

Brock, C. H., & Gavelek, J. R. (1998). Fostering children's engagement with texts: A sociocultural perspective. In T. E. Raphael & K. H. Au (Eds.), *Literature-based instruction: Reshaping the curriculum* (pp. 71–94). Norwood, MA: Christopher-Gordon.

Brodkey, L., (1989). On the subjects of class and gender in "The Literacy Letters." *College English, 51,* 125–141.

Bromley, K. (1993). *Journaling: Engagements in reading, writing, and thinking.* New York: Scholastic.

Brown, A. L., & Campione, J. C. (1994). Guided discovery in a community of learners. In K. McGilly (Ed.), *Classroom lessons: Integrating cognitive theory and classroom practice* (pp. 229–270). Cambridge, MA: MIT Press.

Brown, A. L., & Palincsar, A. S. (1989). Guided, cooperative learning and individual knowledge acquisition. In L. B. Resnick (Ed.), *Knowing, learning, and instruction: Essays in honor of Robert Glaser* (pp. 393–451). Hillsdale, NJ: Erlbaum.

Brown, J. S., & Duguid, P. (1996). Stolen knowledge. In H. McLellan (Ed.), *Situated learning perspectives* (pp. 47–56). Englewood Cliffs, NJ: Educational Technology Publications.

Brown, J. S., Collins, A., & Duguid, P. (1989). Situated cognition and the culture of learning. *Educational Researcher, 18*(l), 32–42.

Brown, T. (1988). *High impact teaching: Strategies for educating minority youth.* Lanham, MD: University Press of America.

Brozo, W. (2000). Hiding out in secondary classrooms: Coping strategies of unsuccessful readers. In D. Moore, D. Alvermann, & K. Hinchman (Eds.), *Struggling adolescent readers: A collection of teaching strategies* (pp. 51–56). Newark, DE: International Reading Association.

Brozo, W., & Simpson, M. (1995). *Readers, teachers, learners: Expanding literacy in secondary schools* (2nd ed.). Columbus, OH: Merrill.

Bruner, J. S. (1986). *Actual minds, possible worlds.* Cambridge, MA: Harvard University Press.

Buckingham, D. (1993). Just playing games. *The English & Media Magazine, 28,* 21–25.

Buckingham, D., & Sefton-Green, J. (1994). *Cultural studies goes to school: Reading and teaching popular media.* London: Taylor & Francis.

Buehl, D. (1998, April). Questioning the author. *WEAC News & Views, 33*(8), 17. (Available at *http://www.weac.org/News/1997–98/APRIL98/read.htm*)

Buikema, J., & Graves, M. (1993). Teaching students to use context clues to infer word meanings. *Journal of Reading 36,* 450–457.

Bulgren, J., & Scanlon, D. (1997/1998). Instructional routines and learning strategies that promote understanding of content area concepts. *Journal of Adolescent & Adult Literacy, 41,* 292–302.

Bunting, E. (1990). *The Wall.* (R. Himler, Illust.). New York: Clarion.

Burns, B. (1998). Changing the classroom climate with literature circles. *Journal of Adolescent and Adult Literacy, 42,* 110–113.

Bussert-Webb, K. (1999). To test or teach: Reflections from a holistic teacher–researcher in south Texas. *Journal of Adolescent and Adult Literacy, 42,* 582–585.

Bussert-Webb, K. (2000). Did my holistic teaching help students' standardized test scores? *Journal of Adolescent and Adult Literacy, 43,* 572–573.

Byars, B. (1976). *The TV kid.* New York: Viking.

Cadenhead, K. (1987). Reading level: A metaphor that shapes practice. *Phi Delta Kappan, 68,* 436–441.

Cairney, T. H. (2000). Developing parent partnerships in secondary literacy learning. In D. W. Moore, D. E. Alvermann, & K. A. Hinchman (Eds.), *Struggling adolescent readers: A collection of teaching strategies* (pp. 58–65). Newark, DE: International Reading Association.

Cambourne, B., & Turnbill, J. (1990). Assessment in whole-language classrooms: Theory into practice. *Elementary School Journal, 90,* 337–349.

Campbell, L., & Campbell, B. (1999). *Multiple intelligences and student achievement: Success stories from six schools.* Alexandria, VA: Association for Supervision & Curriculum Development.

Canales, J. A. (1996, September). *Making English in the content areas comprehensible for language minority students.* Paper presented at the Denver Public Schools Secondary Literacy Conference, Denver, CO.

Carnegie Council on Adolescent Development (1989). *Turning points: Preparing American youth for the 21st century.* New York: Carnegie.

Carnegie Council on Adolescent Development (1996). *Great transitions: Preparing adolescents for a new century* (Abridged Version). New York: Carnegie.

Carr, E., & Ogle, D. (1987). K-W-L Plus: A strategy for comprehension and summarization. *Journal of Reading, 30,* 626–631.

Carroll, P. (2000). Journal to the third power. In L. Baines & A. Kunkel (Eds.), *Going Bohemian: Activities that engage adolescents in the art of writing well* (pp. 5–9). Newark, DE: International Reading Association.

Carver, C. (1991). *A history of English in its own words.* New York: HarperCollins.

Cazden, C. (1988). *Classroom discourse: The language of teaching and learning.* Portsmouth, NH: Heinemann.

Cazden, C. B. (2000). Taking cultural differences into account. In B. C. Cope & M. Kalantzis (Eds.), *Multiliteracies: Literacy learning and the design of social futures* (pp. 249–266). New York: Routledge.

Cena, M., & Mitchell, J. (1998). Anchored instruction: A model for integrating the language arts through content area study. *Journal of Adolescent & Adult Literacy, 41,* 559–561.

Centre for Educational Research and Innovation (1999). *Education policy analysis.* Paris: Organisation for Economic Cooperation and Development.

Cholden, H., & Gertz, B. (1996). Freedom and oppression: Opposing ideas lead to integrated knowledge. *Social Education, 60,* 139–140.

Christensen, L. (1994). Discipline: No quick fix. In B. Bigelow, L. Christensen, S. Karp, B. Miner, & B. Peterson (Eds.), *Rethinking our classrooms* (pp. 56–57). Milwaukee, WI: Rethinking Schools.

Christian, D. (1994). *Two-way bilingual education: Students learning through two languages* (Educational Practice Report No. 12). Santa Cruz: University of California, The National Center for Research on Cultural Diversity and Second Language Learning.

Ciardiello, A. (1998). Did you ask a good question today? Alternative cognitive and metacognitive strategies. *Journal of Adolescent & Adult Literacy, 42,* 210–219.

Cisneros, S. (1989). *The house on Mango Street.* New York: Vintage/Random House.

Clancy, T. (1984). *The hunt for Red October.* Annapolis, MD: Naval Institute Press.

Coble, C., Rice, D., Walla, K., & Murray, E. (1993). *Earth science.* Englewood Cliffs, NJ: Prentice Hall.

Coley, R., J., Crandler, J., & Engle, P. (1997). *Computers and classrooms: The status of technology in U.S. schools.* Princeton, NJ: Educational Testing Service, Policy Information Center.

Collier, J., & Collier, C. (1974). *My brother Sam is dead.* New York: Four Winds.

Collier, J., & Collier, C. (1985). *The bloody country.* New York: Four Winds.

Columbia University Teachers College (2000, Winter). *Teachers College Reports, 2.*

Commeyras, M., & Alvermann, D. E. (1996). Reading about women in world history textbooks from one feminist perspective. *Gender and Education, 8*(l), 31–48.

Conrad, P. (1985). *Prairie song.* New York: Harper & Row.

Cook-Gumperz, J. (Ed.) (1986). *The social construction of literacy.* Cambridge, UK: Cambridge University Press.

Cooper, C. R., & Petrosky, A. R. (1976). A psycholinguistic view of the fluent reading process. *Journal of Reading, 20,* 184–207.

Cooper, J. D. (1997). *Literacy: Helping children construct meaning* (3rd ed.). Boston: Houghton Mifflin.

Cope, B., & Kalantzis, M. (Eds.) (2000). *Multiliteracies: Literacy learning and the design of social futures.* London: Routledge.

Cormier, R. (1974). *The chocolate war.* New York: Dell.

Corno, L., & Snow, R. E. (1986). Adapting teaching to individual differences among learners. In M. C. Wittrock (Ed.), *Handbook of research on teaching* (3rd ed., pp. 605–629). New York: Macmillan.

Cowan, J. (1976). Reading, perceptual strategies and contrastive analysis. *Language Learning, 26,* 95–109.

Crafton, L. (1983). Learning from reading: What happens when students generate their own background information? *Journal of Reading, 26,* 586–593.

Crane, S. (1964). *The red badge of courage.* New York: Bantam. (Original work published 1895)

Crichton, M. (1990). *Jurassic Park.* New York: Knopf.

Cullinan, B., & Fitzgerald, S. (1985, January). IRA, NCTE take stand on readability formula. *Reading Today, 2,* 1.

Cummins, J. (1994). Knowledge, power and identity in teaching English as a second language. In E. Genesee (Ed.), *Educating second language children* (pp. 33–58). Cambridge, UK: Cambridge University Press.

Cummins, J. (1994). The acquisition of English as a second language. In K. Spangenberg-Urbschat & R. Pritchard (Eds.), *Kids come in all languages: Reading instruction for ESL students.* Newark, DE: International Reading Association.

Cummins, J. (1999). Alternative paradigms in bilingual education research: Does theory have a place? *Educational Researcher, 28*(7), 26–32, 41.

Cunningham, J. (1982). Generating interactions between schemata and text. In J. Niles & L. Harris (Eds.), *New inquiries in reading research and instruction, Thirty-first Yearbook of the National Reading Conference* (pp. 42–47). Washington, DC: National Reading Conference.

Cunningham, J., & Moore, D. (1993). The contribution of understanding academic vocabulary to answering comprehension questions. *Journal of Reading Behavior, 25,* 171–180.

Curtis, C. (1995). *The Watsons go to Birmingham—1963.* New York: Delacorte.

Cushman, K. (1994). *Catherine, called Birdy.* New York: HarperCollins.

Dalji, H., & Miner, B. (1998). "Listen to your students": An interview with Oakland high school English teacher Hafeezah AdamaDavia Dalji. In T. Perry & L. Delpit (Eds.), *The real Ebonics debate: Power, language, and the education of African-American children* (pp. 105–115.) Boston: Beacon.

Dalrymple, K. (1989). "Well, what about his skills?" Evaluation of whole language in the middle school. In K. Goodman, Y. Goodman, & W. Hood (Eds.), *The whole language evaluation book* (pp. 111–130). Portsmouth, NH: Heinemann Books.

Dalton, S. S. (1998). *Pedagogy matters: Standards for effective teaching practice.* (Research Report No. 4). Santa Cruz, CA: Center for Research on Education, Diversity, and Excellence.

Daniels, H. (1994). *Literature circles: Voice and choice in the student-centered classroom.* York, ME: Stenhouse.

Davey, B. (1988). How do classroom teachers use their textbooks? *Journal of Reading, 31,* 340–345.

Deal, D. (1999, December). *Writing in the lab: Five research scientists talk about their use of writing in pursuit of scientific inquiry.* Paper presented at the National Reading Conference, Orlando, FL.

DeLorenzo, R. (1999). When hell freezes over: An approach to develop student interest and communication skills. *Journal of Chemical Education, 76,* 503.

Delpit, L. (1988). The silenced dialogue: Power and pedagogy in educating other people's children. *Harvard Educational Review, 58,* 280–298.

Delpit, L. (1995). *Other people's children: Cultural conflict in the classroom.* New York: The New Press.

Delpit, L. (1998). What should teachers do? Ebonics and culturally responsive instruction. In T. Perry & L. Delpit (Eds.), *The real Ebonics debate: Power, language, and the education of African-American children* (pp. 17–26). Boston: Beacon.

Dickens, C. (1991). *Hard times.* New York: Bantam.

Dolan, T., Dolan, E., Taylor, V., Shoreland, J., & Harrison, C. (1979). Improving reading through group discussion activities. In E. Lunzer & K. Gardner (Eds.), *The effective use of reading.* London: Heinemann Educational Books.

Dole, J. A., Duffy, G. G., Roehler, L. R., & Pearson, P. D. (1991). Moving from the old to the new: Research on reading comprehension instruction. *Review of Educational Research, 61,* 239–264.

Dolly, M. (1990). Integrating ESL reading and writing through authentic discourse. *Journal of Reading, 35,* 360–365.

Donahue, P., Voelkl, K., Campbell, J., & Mazzeo, J. (1999). *The NAEP 1998 reading report card for the nation and the states.* Washington, DC: U.S. Department of Education, Office of Educational Research and Improvement.

Drake, S. (1998). One teacher's experiences with student portfolios. *Teaching History, 23,* 60–76.

Dufflemeyer, E. (1994). Effective anticipation guide statements for learning from expository prose. *Journal of Reading, 37,* 452–457.

Dufflemeyer, E., & Baum, D. (1992). The extended anticipation guide revisited. *Journal of Reading, 35,* 654–656.

Dufflemeyer, F., Baum, D., & Merkley, D. (1987). Maximizing reader-text confrontation with an extended anticipation guide. *Journal of Reading, 31,* 146–151.

Duncan, B. (1996). *Mass media and popular culture* (2nd ed.). Toronto, Canada: Harcourt Brace.

Durkin, D. (1978/1979). What classroom observations reveal about reading comprehension instruction. *Reading Research Quarterly, 14,* 481–533.

Eanet, M., & Manzo, A. (1976). R.E.A.P.—A strategy for improving reading/writing study skills. *Journal of Reading, 19,* 647–652.

Echevarria, J., Vogt, M., & Short, D. (2000). *Making content comprehensible for English language learners. The SIOP model.* Boston: Allyn & Bacon.

Egenberger, P. (1999). Integration through video: Seeing beyond the literary work into history and science. *Cyber Briefs, 1*(4), 55–58.

Ehlinger, J., & Pritchard, R. (1994). Using Think Alongs in secondary content areas. *Reading Research & Instruction, 33,* 187–206.

Eisenhart, M., Finkel, E., & Marion, S. F. (1996). Creating the conditions for scientific literacy: A re-examination. *American Educational Research Journal, 33,* 261–295.

Elbow, P. (1973). *Writing without teachers.* New York: Oxford University Press.

Estes, T., & Vaughan, J. (1985). *Reading and learning in the content classroom* (2nd ed.). Boston: Allyn & Bacon.

Evans, E., & Engelberg, R. (1985). *A developmental study of student perceptions of school grading.* Paper presented at the biennial meeting of the Society for Research in Child Development, Toronto, Ontario, April. (ERIC No. ED 256 482)

Ezell, H., Hunsicker, S., Quinque, M., & Randolph, E. (1996). Maintenance and generalization of QAR reading comprehension strategies. *Reading Research & Instruction, 36,* 64–81.

Fecho, B. (1998). Crossing boundaries of race in a critical literacy classroom. In D. Alvermann, K. Hinchman, D. Moore, S. Phelps, & D. Waff (Eds.), *Reconceptualizing the literacies in adolescents' lives* (pp. 75–101). Mahwah, NJ: Erlbaum.

Fecho, B. (2000). Critical inquiries into language in an urban classroom. *Research in the Teaching of English, 34,* 368–395.

Feldhusen, J. (1989). Issue: The sorting of students into ability groups has come under increasing fire recently. Should schools end the practice of grouping students by ability? *ASCD Update,* 31(1), 1–8.

Feldman, A., Alibrandi, M., & Kropf, A. (1998). Grading with points: The determination of report card grades by high school science teachers. *School Science & Mathematics, 98,* 140–148.

Fetterly, J. (1978). *The resisting reader.* Bloomington: Indiana University Press.

Field, M., & Aebersold, J. (1990). Cultural attitudes toward reading: Implications for teachers of ESL/bilingual readers. *Journal of Reading, 33,* 406–410.

Finn, P. J. (1999). *Literacy with an attitude: Educating working-class children in their own self-interest.* Albany: State University of New York Press.

Fitzgerald, J. (1995). English-as-a-second-language learners' cognitive reading processes: A review of research in the United States. *Review of Educational Research, 65,* 145–190.

Fitzgerald, J., & Cummins, J. (1999). Bridging disciplines to critique a national research agenda for language-minority children's schooling. *Reading Research Quarterly, 34,* 378–390.

Flavell, J. H. (1979). Metacognition and cognitive monitoring: A new area of cognitive–developmental inquiry. *American Psychologist, 34,* 906–911.

Flood, J., & Lapp, D. (2000). Reading comprehension instruction for at-risk students: Research-based practices that can make a difference. In D. W. Moore, D. E. Alvermann, & K. A. Hinchman (Eds.), *Struggling adolescent readers: A collection of strategies* (pp. 138–147). Newark, DE: International Reading Association.

Floriani, A. (1993). Negotiating what counts: Roles and relationships, texts and contexts, content and meaning. *Linguistics and Education, 5,* 241–273.

Focused Reporting Project (1999, Fall). *Changing schools in Long Beach: Independent reporting on the growth and achievement of young adolescents.* Atlanta: Edna McConnell Clark Foundation.

Fogarty, R. (1994, March.) Thinking about themes: Hundreds of themes. *Middle School Journal, 25,* 30–31.

Forbes, E. (1945). *Johnny Tremaine.* Boston: Houghton Mifflin.

Foster, S., & Padgett, C. (1999). Authentic historical inquiry in the social studies classroom. *The Clearing House, 72,* 357–363.

Frager, A., & Thompson, L. (1985). Conflict: The key to critical reading instruction. *Journal of Reading, 28,* 676–683.

Freebody, P., Luke, A., & Gilbert, P. (1991). Reading positions and practices in the classroom. *Curriculum Inquiry, 21,* 435–457.

Freeman, Y., & Freeman, D. (1989). Evaluation of second-language junior and senior high school students. In K. Goodman, Y. Goodman, & W. Hood (Eds.), *The whole language evaluation book* (pp. 141–150). Portsmouth, NH: Heinemann.

Freire, P., & Macedo, D. (1987). *Literacy: Reading the word and the world.* Hedley, MA: Bergin & Garvey.

Fretzin, L. (1992, November). Double-entry journals. *Writing Teacher, 6,* 36–37.

Fry, E. (1977). Fry's readability graph: Clarifications, validity, and extension to level 17. *Journal of Reading, 21,* 242–252.

Fry, E. (1989). Reading formulas—maligned but valid. *Journal of Reading, 32,* 292–297.

Gabay, J. (1991). Issue: Motivation. ASCD *Update, 33,* 7.

Gadsden, V. (2000). Intergenerational literacy within families. In M. L. Kamil, P. Mosenthal, P. D. Pearson, & R. Barr (Eds.), *Handbook of reading research: Vol. 3* (pp. 871–887). Mahwah, NJ: Erlbaum.

Galbraith, M., Hennelly, J., & Purves, A. (1994). *Using portfolios to negotiate a rhetorical community.* Albany, NY: National Research Center on Literature Teaching & Learning.

Garcia, E., Rasmussen, B., Stobbe, C., & Garcia, E. (1990). Portfolios: An assessment tool in support of instruction. *International Journal of Education, 14,* 431–436.

Garcia, G. E. (2000). Bilingual children's reading. In M. L. Kamil, P. B. Mosenthal, P. D. Pearson, & R. Barr (Eds.), *Handbook of reading research: Volume 3* (pp. 813–834). Mahwah, NJ: Erlbaum.

Garcia, G., & Pearson, P. D. (1994). Assessment and diversity. *Review of Research in Education, 20,* 337–391.

Gardner, H. (1983). *Frames of mind: The theory of multiple intelligences.* New York: Basic Books.

Gardner, H. (1991). *The unschooled mind: How children think and how schools should teach.* New York: Basic Books.

Gardner, H. (1999). *Intelligence reframed: Multiple intelligences for the 21st century.* New York: Basic Books.

Gardner, S., Benham, H., & Newell, B. (1999, September). Oh, what a tangled web we've woven! Helping students evaluate sources. *English Journal, 89,* 39–44.

Garner, R., & Alexander, P. (1989). Metacognition: Answered and unanswered questions. *Educational Psychologist, 24,* 143–158.

Garner, R., & Gillingham, M. (1987). Students' knowledge of text structure. *Journal of Reading Behavior, 29,* 247–259.

Gavelek, J. R., & Raphael, T. E. (1996). Changing talk about text: New roles for teachers and students. *Language Arts, 73,* 182–192.

Gavelek, J., Raphael, T., Biondo, S., & Wang, D. (2000). Integrated literacy instruction. In M. Kamil, P. Mosenthal, P. D. Pearson, & R. Barr (Eds.), *Handbook of reading research: Vol. 3* (pp. 587–607). Mahwah, NJ: Erlbaum.

Gearhart, M., & Herman, J. (1995, Winter). Portfolio assessment: Whose work is it? In *Evaluation Comment.* Los Angeles: UCLA Center for the Study of Evaluation & The National Center for Research on Evaluation, Standards, and Student Testing.

Gee, J. P. (1988). Legacies of literacy: From Plato to Freire through Harvey Graff. *Harvard Educational Review, 58,* 195–212.

Gee, J. P. (1996). *Social linguistics and literacies: Ideology in discourses* (2nd ed.). London: Taylor & Francis.

Gee, J. P. (1999). Reading and the new literacy studies: Reframing the National Academy of Sciences report on reading. *Journal of Literacy Research, 31,* 355–374.

Gee, J. P. (2000). Teenagers in new times: A new literacy studies perspective. *Journal of Adolescent & Adult Literacy, 43,* 412–420.

Genesee, E. (1994). *Integrating language and content: Lessons from immersion* (Educational Practice Report No. 11). Santa Cruz: University of California, National Center for Research on Cultural Diversity and Second Language Learning.

Gergen, K. (1999). *An invitation to social construction.* Thousand Oaks, CA: Sage.

Ghatala, E. S. (1986). Strategy-monitoring training enables young learners to select effective strategies. *Educational Psychologist, 21,* 43–54.

Gilles, C., Bixby, M., Crowley, P., Crenshaw, S., Henrichs, M., Reynolds, E., & Pyle, D. (Eds.) (1988). *Whole language strategies for secondary students.* New York: Richard C. Owen.

Gillespie, C. (1990). Questions about student-generated questions. *Journal of Reading, 34,* 250–257.

Glatthorn, A. (1991). Secondary English classroom environments. In J. Flood, J. M. Jensen, D. Lapp, & J. R. Squire (Eds.), *Handbook of research on teaching the English language arts* (pp. 438–456). New York: Macmillan.

Goatley, V. J., Brock, C. H., & Raphael, T. E. (1995). Diverse learners participating in regular education Book Clubs. *Reading Research Quarterly, 30,* 352–380.

Godina, H. (1996). The canonical debate—Implementing multicultural literature and perspectives. *Journal of Adolescent & Adult Literacy, 39,* 544–549.

Goerss, B. (1996). Interdisciplinary planning within cooperative groups. *Journal of Adolescent and Adult Learning, 40,* 110–116.

Goldman, S., & Rakestraw, J. (2000). Structural aspects of constructing meaning from text. In M. Kamil, P. Mosenthal, P. D. Pearson, & R. Barr (Eds.), *Handbook of reading research, Vol. 3* (pp. 311–335). Mahwah, NJ: Erlbaum.

Gonzales, R. (1990, January). When minority become majority: The changing face of English classrooms. *English Journal, 79,* 16–23.

Gonzalez, O. (1999). Building vocabulary: Dictionary consultation and the ESL student. *Journal of Adolescent and Adult Literacy, 43,* 264–270.

Goodlad, J. I. (1984). *A place called school.* New York: McGraw–Hill.

Goodman, K. (1986). *What's whole in whole language?* New York: Scholastic.

Goodman, K. (1989). Preface. In K. Goodman, Y. Goodman, & W. Hood (Eds.), *The whole language evaluation book* (pp. xi–xv). Portsmouth, NH: Heinemann.

Goodman, Y. (1985). Kidwatching: Observing children in the classroom. In A. Jagger & T. Smith-Burke (Eds.), *Observing the language learner* (pp. 9–18). Newark, DE: International Reading Association.

Gordon, C. (1990, Winter). Contexts for expository text structure use. *Reading Research & Instruction, 29,* 55–72.

Grady, M. (1998). *Qualitative and action research: A practioner handbook.* Bloomington, IN: Phi Delta Kappa.

Graves, D. (1983). *Writing: Teachers and children at work.* Portsmouth, NH: Heinemann.

Graves, M. (1986). Vocabulary learning and instruction. *Review of Research in Education, 13,* 49–89.

Graves, M., & Prenn, M. (1986). Costs and benefits of various methods of teaching vocabulary. *Journal of Reading 29,* 596–602.

Graves, M., & Slater, W. (1996). Vocabulary instruction in content areas. In D. Lapp, J. Flood, & N. Farnan (Eds.), *Content area reading and learning: Instructional strategies.* Boston: Allyn & Bacon.

Green, B. (1991). Reading "readings": Towards a postmodernist reading pedagogy. In C. D. Baker & A. Luke (Eds.), *Towards a critical sociology of reading pedagogy.* Philadelphia: Benjamins.

Greenbaum, V. (1994). Literature out of the closet: Bringing gay and lesbian texts and subtexts out in high school English. *English Journal, 83*(5), 71–74.

Greene, J. (1998). *A meta-analysis of the effectiveness of bilingual education.* Claremont, CA: Tomas Rivera Policy Institute.

Greene, M. (1991). The literacy debate and the public school: Going beyond the functional. *Educational Horizons, 69,* 129–134, 164–168.

Greenlaw, M. J. (1987). Science fiction as moral literature. *Educational Horizons, 65,* 165–166.

Greenwald, E., Persky, H., Campbell, J., & Mazzeo, J. (1999). *The NAEP 1998 writing report card for the nation and the states.* Washington, DC: U.S. Department of Education, Office of Educational Research and Improvement.

Grossman, P. L., & Stodolsky, S. S. (1995, November). Content as context: The role of school subjects in secondary school teaching. *Educational Researcher, 24,* 5–23.

Gumperz, J. J., Cook-Gumperz, J., & Szymanski, M. H. (1999). *Collaborative practices in bilingual cooperative learning classrooms* (Research Report No. 7). Santa Cruz: University of California, Center for Research on Education, Diversity & Excellence.

Gunderson, L. (2000). Voices of the teen-aged diasporas. *Journal of Adolescent & Adult Literacy, 43,* 692–706.

Guzzetti, B. (2000, March). *Strategies for addressing gender disparity in texts and talk.* Paper presented at the Adolescent Literacy Forum, Tucson, AZ.

Guzzetti, B. J., & Williams, W. D. (1996). Changing the pattern of gendered discussion: Lessons from science classrooms. *Journal of Adolescent & Adult Literacy, 40,* 38–47.

Guzzetti, B., & Hynd, C. (1998). *Theoretical perspectives on conceptual change.* Mahwah, NJ: Erlbaum.

Guzzetti, B., & Williams, W. (1996). Gender, text, and discussion: Examining intellectual safety in the science classroom. *Journal of Research in Science Teaching, 33,* 5–20.

Guzzetti, B., Snyder, T., Glass, G. V., & Gamas, W. S. (1993). Promoting conceptual change in science: A comparative meta-analysis of instructional interventions from reading education and science education. *Reading Research Quarterly, 28,* 116–159.

Hadaway, N., & Mundy, J. (2000). Children's informational picture books visit a secondary ESL classroom. In D. Moore, D. Alvermann, & K. Hinchman (Eds.), *Struggling adolescent readers: A collection of teaching strategies* (pp. 83–95). Newark, DE: International Reading Association.

Haggard, M. (1982). The vocabulary self-collection strategy: An active approach to word learning. *Journal of Reading, 26,* 203–207.

Haggard, M. (1985). An interactive strategies approach to content reading. *Journal of Reading, 29,* 204–210.

Haggard, M. (1986). The vocabulary self-collection strategy: Using student interest and world knowledge to enhance vocabulary growth. *Journal of Reading, 29,* 634–642.

Hall, S., & Whannel, P. (1998). The young audience. In J. Storey (Ed.), *Cultural theory and popular culture; A Reader* (2nd ed.), (pp. 61–67). Athens: University of Georgia Press.

Haller, E. P., Child, D. A., & Walberg, H. J. (1988). Can comprehension be taught? A quantitative synthesis of metacognitive studies. *Educational Researcher, 17*(9), 5–8.

Haney, G., & Thistlethwaite, L. (1991). A model critical reading lesson for secondary high-risk students. *Reading, Writing and Learning Disabilities, 7,* 337–354.

Hansen-Krening, N., & Mizokawa, D. (2000). Exploring ethnic-specific literature: A unity of parents, families, and educators. In D. Moore, D. Alvermann, & K. Hinchman (Eds.), *Struggling adolescent readers: A collection of teaching strategies* (pp. 96–106). Newark, DE: International Reading Association.

Hantula, J., Flickema, T., Farah, M., Karls, A., Johnson, E., Thuermer, K., Resnick, A., & Lemmo, J. (1988). *Global insights: Africa, China, Japan, India, Latin America.* Columbus, OH: Merrill.

Hardin, L. F. (1999, Fall/Winter). Netting the past: Putting our town's history on the web. *Bread Loaf Rural Teacher Network Magazine,* 7–9.

Hare, V., & Borchardt, K. (1984). Direct instruction of summarization skills. *Reading Research Quarterly, 20,* 62–78.

Hare, V., Rabinowitz, M., & Schieble, K. (1989). Text effects on main idea comprehension. *Reading Research Quarterly, 24,* 72–88.

Hargreaves, A. (1989). *Curriculum assessment and reform.* Philadelphia: Open University Press.

Hargreaves, D. H. (1967). *Social relations in a secondary school.* London: Routledge & Kegan Paul.

Harmon, J. (1998). Constructing word meanings: Strategies and perceptions of four middle school learners. *Journal of Literacy Research, 30,* 561–599.

Harmon, J. M. (2000). Vocabulary teaching and learning in a seventh-grade literature-based classroom. In D. W. Moore, D. E. Alvermann, & K. A. Hinchman (Eds.), *Struggling adolescent readers: A collection of teaching strategies* (pp. 174–188). Newark, DE: International Reading Association.

Harris, V. (1991). "Have you heard about an African Cinderella story?": The hunt for multiethnic literature. *Publishing Research Quarterly, 7*(3), 23–36.

Heath, S. B. (1983). *Ways with words: Language, life, and work in communities and classrooms.* Cambridge, UK: Cambridge University Press.

Heath, S. B. (1986a). Sociocultural contexts of language development. In *Beyond language: Social and cultural factors in schooling language minority students* (pp. 145–186). Los Angeles: California State University, Evaluation, Dissemination and Assessment Center.

Heath, S. B. (1986b). The functions and uses of literacy. In S. DeCastell, A. Luke, & K. Egan (Eds.), *Literacy, society, and schooling: A reader* (pp. 15–26). London: Cambridge University Press.

Heath, S. B. (1991). The sense of being literate; Historical and cross-cultural features. In R. Barr, M. L. Kamil, P. Mosenthal, & P. D. Pearson (Eds.), *Handbook of reading research: Volume 2* (pp. 3–25). New York: Longman.

Helfeldt, J., & Henk, W. (1990). Reciprocal question-answer relationships: An instructional technique for at-risk readers. *Journal of Reading, 33,* 509–514.

Helms, J. (1992). Why is there no study of cultural equivalence in standardized cognitive ability testing? *American Psychologist, 47,* 1083–1101.

Hemphill, L. (1999). Narrative style, social class, and response to poetry. *Research in the Teaching of English, 33,* 275–302.

Henze, R. C., & Hausser, M. E. (1999). *Personalizing culture through anthropological and educational perspectives* (Educational Practice Report No. 4). Santa Cruz, CA: Center for Research on Education, Diversity and Excellence.

Herber H. (1978). *Teaching reading in content areas* (2nd ed.). Englewood Cliffs, NJ: Prentice Hall.

Herber, H. L. (1970). *Teaching reading in content areas.* Englewood Cliffs, NJ: Prentice Hall.

Herber, H. L., & Nelson-Herber, J. (1987). Developing independent learners. *Journal of Reading, 30,* 584–588.

Herrell, A. (2000). *Fifty strategies for teaching English language learners.* Columbus, OH: Merrill.

Hidi, S., & Anderson, V. (1986). Producing written summaries: Task demands, cognitive operations, and implications for instruction. *Review of Educational Research, 56,* 473–494.

Hill, H. (1989). *Effective strategies for teaching minority students.* Bloomington, IN: National Educational Service.

Hill, M. (1991). Writing summaries promotes thinking and learning across the curriculum—But why are they so difficult to write? *Journal of Reading, 34,* 536–539.

Hinchey, P. H. (1998). *Finding freedom in the classroom: A practical introduction to critical theory.* New York: Peter Lang.

Hinchman, K. (1987). The textbook and three content-area teachers. *Reading Research and Instruction, 26,* 247–263.

Hinchman, K., & Zalewski, P. (1996). Reading for success in a tenth-grade global-studies class: A qualitative study. *Journal of Literacy Research, 28,* 91–106.

Hirsch, E. D. (1987). *Cultural literacy.* Boston: Houghton Mifflin.

Hodgkinson, H. L. (1992). *A demographic look at tomorrow.* Washington, DC: Center of Demographic Policy.

Hoffman, J. (1992). Critical reading/thinking across the curriculum: Using I-charts to support learning. *Language Arts, 68,* 121–127.

Hoffman, J. V. (1979). The intra-act procedure for critical reading. *Journal of Reading, 22,* 605–608.

Hoffman, L. (1999). Key statistics on public elementary and secondary schools and agencies. *Education Statistics Quarterly, 1*(4), 67–70.

Hofstadter, R. (1970). *Anti-intellectualism in American life.* New York: Knopf.

Hopkins, G., & Bean, T. (2000). Vocabulary learning with the verbal–visual word association strategy in a Native American community. In D. Moore, D. Alvermann, & K. Hinchman (Eds.), *Struggling adolescent readers: A collection of teaching strategies* (pp. 107–115). Newark, DE: International Reading Association.

Hruby, G. G. (2001). Sociological, postmodern, and new realism perspectives in social constructionism: Implications for literacy research. *Reading Research Quarterly, 36,* 48–62.

Hudelson, S. (1999, May/June). ESL writing: Principles for teaching young writers. *ESL Magazine, 2,* 8–10, 12.

Huey, E. B. (1968). *The psychology and pedagogy of reading.* Cambridge, MA: MIT Press. (Original work published 1908)

Hughes, R. (1993). *Culture of complaint.* New York: Oxford University Press.

Hynd, C., McNish, M., Lay, K., & Fowler, P. (1995). *High school physics: The role of text in learning counterintuitive information* (Technical Report No. 46). Athens, GA: National Reading Research Center.

Idol, L., Jones, B. F., & Mayer, R. (1991). Classroom instruction: The teaching of thinking. In L. Idol & B. F. Jones (Eds.), *Educational values and cognitive instruction: Implications for reform.* Hillsdale, NJ: Erlbaum.

Indrisano, R., & Paratore, J. R. (1991). Classroom contexts for literacy learning. In J. Flood, J. M. Jensen, D. Lapp, & J. R. Squire (Eds.), *Handbook of research on teaching the English language arts* (pp. 477–488). New York: Macmillan.

Innocenti, R. (1985). *Rose Blanche.* London: Jonas Cape.

Inos, R. H., & Quigley, M. A. (1995). *Research review for inclusive practices.* November Newsletter (pp. 1–6). Honolulu, HI: Pacific Region Educational Laboratory.

International Reading Association (1982). Misuse of grade equivalents. *The Reading Teacher, 35,* 464.

International Society for Technology in Education (2000). *National educational technology standards for students: Connecting curriculum & technology.* Eugene, OR: International Society for Technology in Education.

Irvine, J. (1990). Transforming teaching for the 21st century. *Educational Horizons, 69*(1), 16–21.

Ivey, G. (1999a). A multicase study in the middle school: Complexities among young adolescent readers. *Reading Research Quarterly, 34,* 172–192.

Ivey, G. (1999b). Reflections on teaching struggling middle school readers. *Journal of Adolescent & Adult Literacy, 42,* 372–381.

Ivey, G. (2000). Reflections on teaching struggling middle school readers. In D. W. Moore, D. E. Alvermann, & K. A. Hinchman (Eds.), *Struggling adolescent readers: A collection of teaching strategies* (pp. 27–38). Newark, DE: International Reading Association.

Ivey, G., & Broaddus, K. (1999, December). *1700+ students speak out about middle school reading.* Paper presented at the National Reading Conference, Orlando, FL.

Jacobs, H. (1987). The perils of a slave woman's life. In M. E. Washington (Ed.), *Invented lives: Narratives of black women, 1860–1960* (pp. 16–69). New York: Anchor.

Jenkins, J., Matlock, B., & Slocum, T. (1989). Two approaches to vocabulary instruction: The teaching of individual word meanings and practice in deriving word meaning from context. *Reading Research Quarterly, 24,* 215–235.

Jervis, K. (1996). "How come there are no brothers on that list?": Hearing the hard questions all children ask. *Harvard Educational Review, 66,* 546–576.

Jiménez, R. T., & Gámez, A. (2000). Literature-based cognitive strategy instruction for middle school Latina/o students. In D. W. Moore, D. E. Alvermann, & K. A. Hinchman (Eds.), *Struggling adolescent readers: A collection of teaching strategies* (pp. 74–82). Newark, DE: International Reading Association.

Jiménez, R. T., Moll, L. C., Rodriguez-Brown, F. V., & Barrera, R. B. (1999). Latina and Latino researchers interact on issues related to literacy learning. *Reading Research Quarterly, 34,* 217–230.

Jiménez, R., Garcia, G., & Pearson, P. D. (1996). The reading strategies of bilingual Latina/o students who are successful English readers: Opportunities and obstacles. *Reading Research Quarterly, 31,* 90–112.

Jiminez, R., & Gamez, A. (1996). Literature-based cognitive strategy instruction for middle school Latino/a students. *Journal of Reading, 40,* 84–91.

Johnson, D., & Pearson, P. D. (1984). *Teaching reading vocabulary* (2nd ed.). New York: Holt, Rinehart and Winston.

Johnston, P. (1987). Teachers as evaluation experts. *The Reading Teacher, 40,* 744–748.

Johnston, P. H., & Winograd, P. N. (1985). Passive failure in reading. *Journal of Reading Behavior, 17,* 279–301.

Jones, B. F., Pierce, J., & Hunter, B. (1988/1989). Teaching students to construct graphic representations. *Educational Leadership, 46*(4), 20–25.

Jones, B., Palincsar, A., Ogle, D., & Carr, E. (Eds.) (1987). *Strategic teaching and learning: Cognitive instruction in the content areas.* Alexandria, VA: Association for Supervision and Curriculum Development.

Jordan, S., & Purves, A. (1993). *Issues in the responses of students to culturally diverse texts: A preliminary study.* Albany, NY: National Research Center on Literature Teaching and Learning.

Jurdak, M., & Abu Zein, R. (1998). The effect of journal writing on achievement in and attitudes toward mathematics. *School Science & Mathematics, 98,* 412–419.

Just, M., & Carpenter, P. (1987). *The psychology of reading and language comprehension.* Boston: Allyn & Bacon.

Kaiser Family Foundation (1999). *Kids & media.* Menlo Park, CA: The Henry J. Kaiser Foundation (*http://www.kff.org*)

Kamler, B. (1999, November). *The politics of teaching writing and the changing nature of teachers' work.* Paper presented at the annual meeting of the National Council of Teachers of English, Denver.

Kamler, B., & Comber, B. (1996). Critical literacy: Not generic—not developmental—not another orthodoxy. *Changing Education, 3*(1), 1–9.

Kehaus, M. (2000). Working with teen writers online: Policies, procedures, and possibilities. *Journal of Adolescent & Adult Literacy, 44,* 179–183.

Kennedy, M., Fisher, M., & Ennis, R. (1991). Critical thinking: Literature review and needed research. In L. Idol & B. F. Jones (Eds.), *Educational values and cognitive instruction: Implications for reform* (pp. 11–40). Hillsdale, NJ: Erlbaum.

Keys, C. (1999). Revitalizing instruction in scientific genres: Connecting knowledge production with writing to learn in science. *Science Education, 83,* 115–130.

Kibby, M. (1993). What reading teachers should know about reading proficiency in the U.S. *Journal of Reading, 37,* 28–41.

Kibby, M. (1995). The organization and teaching of things and the words that signify them. *Journal of Adolescent & Adult Literacy, 39,* 208–223.

Kim, Y., & Pearson, P. D. (1999). An LEP student's view of progress in the context of portfolio assessment: A case study. In T. Shanahan & F. Rodriquez-Brown (Eds.), *NRC Conference Yearbook 48* (pp. 258–265). Chicago: National Reading Conference.

Kirby, D., & Kuykendall, C. (1991). *Mind matters: Teaching for thinking.* Portsmouth, NH: Boynton-Cook.

Klare, G. (1984). Readability. In P. D. Pearson (Ed.), *Handbook of reading research* (pp. 681–744). New York: Longman.

Klingner, J. K., & Vaughan, S. (1996). Reciprocal teaching of reading comprehension strategies for students with learning disabilities who use English as a second language. *Elementary School Journal, 96,* 275–293.

Knoblauch, C. H. (1990). Literacy and the politics of education. In A. A. Lunsford, H. Moglen, & J. Slevin (Eds.), *The right to literacy* (pp. 74–80). New York: Modern Language Association of America.

Knowles, J. (1960). *A separate peace.* New York: Macmillan.

Koki, S. (2000, February). Bullying in Pacific schools—Should we be concerned? *Pacific Education Updates,* 1–12.

Konopak, B., Martin, M., & Martin, S. (1987). Reading and writing: Aids to learning in the content areas. *Journal of Reading, 31,* 109–117.

Konopak, B., Martin, S., & Martin, M. (1990). Using a writing strategy to enhance sixth-grade students' comprehension of content material. *Journal of Reading Behavior, 22,* 19–38.

Konopak, B., Sheard, C., Longman, D., Lyman, B., Slaton, E., Atkinson, R., & Thames, D. (1987). Incidental versus intentional word learning from context. *Reading Psychology, 8,* 7–21.

Krashen, S. (1985). *The input hypothesis: Issues and implications.* New York: Longman.

Krashen, S. (1989). *Language acquisition and language education.* New York: Prentice Hall.

Krashen, S. D. (1988). Do we learn to read by reading? The relationship between free reading and reading ability. In D. Tannen (Ed.), *Linguistics in context: Connecting observation and understanding* (pp. 269–298). Norwood, NJ: Ablex.

Kreidler, W. J. (1984). *Creative conflict resolution.* Glenview, IL: Scott, Foresman.

Kuykendal, C. (1992). *From rage to hope: Strategies for reclaiming Black and Hispanic students.* Bloomington, IN: National Educational Service.

LaBerge, D., & Samuels, S. J. (1976). Toward a theory of automatic information processing in reading. In H. Singer & R. Ruddell (Eds.), *Theoretical models and processes of reading* (3rd ed., pp. 689–718). Newark, DE: International Reading Association.

LaConte, R. T. (1981). *Homework as a learning experience: What research says to the teacher.* Arlington, VA: ERIC Document Reproduction Service. (ED 217 022)

Ladson-Billings, G. (1994). *The dreamkeepers.* San Francisco: Jossey-Bass.

Langer, J. (1986). Learning through writing: Study skills in the content areas. *Journal of Reading, 29,* 400–406.

Langer, J. (1989). Literate thinking and schooling. *Literacy Research Newsletter, 5*(l), 1–2.

Lankshear, C., & McLaren, P. (Eds.). (1993). *Critical literacy: Politics, praxis, and the postmodern.* Albany, NY: State University of New York Press.

Laursen, B., Hartup, W. W., & Koplas, A. L. (1996). Towards understanding peer conflict. *Merrill–Palmer Quarterly, 42*(1), 76–102.

Lave, J., & Wenger, E. (1991). *Situated learning.* Cambridge, UK: Cambridge University Press.

Lebauer, R. (1985). Nonnative English speaker problems in content and English classes: Are they thinking or reading problems? *Journal of Reading, 29,* 136–142.

Lee, O. (1997). Scientific literacy for all: What is it, and how can we achieve it? *Journal of Research in Science Teaching, 34,* 219–222.

Lehr, F. (1984). ERIC/RCS: Cooperative learning. *Journal of Reading, 27,* 458–461.

Leinhardt, G. (1983, April). *Routines in expert math teachers' thoughts and actions.* Paper presented at the annual meeting of the American Educational Research Association, Montreal.

Lemke, J. (1990). *Talking science: Language, learning and values.* Norwood, NJ: Ablex.

Lemke, J. L. (1995). *Textual politics: Discourse and social dynamics.* London: Taylor & Francis.

Lensmire, T. (1994). *When children write: Critical re-visions of the writing workshop.* New York: Teachers College Press.

Leu, D., & Leu, D. (1998). *Teaching with the Internet: Lessons from the classroom.* Norwood, MA: Gordon.

Levin, H. (1998). Educational performance standards and the economy. *Educational Researcher, 27,* 4–11.

Lewis, C. (1998). Rock 'n' roll and horror stories: Students, teachers, and popular culture. *Journal of Adolescent & Adult Literacy, 42,* 116–120.

Lewis, C. (2000). Limits of identification: The personal, pleasurable, and critical in reader response. *Journal of Literacy Research, 32,* 253–266.

Lewis, C., Ketter, J., & Fabos, B. (in press). Reading race in a rural context. *International Journal of Qualitative Studies in Education.*

Luke, A. (1988). *Literacy, textbooks, and ideology.* London: Falmer.

Luke, A., & Elkins, J. (1998). Reinventing literacy in new times. *Journal of Adolescent & Adult Literacy, 42,* 4–7.

Luke, A., & Freebody, P. (1997). Critical literacy and the question of normativity: An introduction. In S. Muspratt, A. Luke, & P. Freebody (Eds.), *Constructing critical literacies* (pp. 1–18). Cresskill, NJ: Hampton.

Luke, C. (1997). Media literacy and cultural studies. In S. Muspratt, A. Luke, & P. Freebody (Eds.), *Constructing critical literacies: Teaching and learning textual practice* (pp. 19–49). Cresskill, NJ: Hampton Press.

Luke, C. (2000). Cyber-schooling and technological change: Multiliteracies for new times. In B. Cope & M. Kalantzis (Eds.), *Multiliteracies: Literacy learning and the design of social futures* (pp. 69–91). London: Routledge.

Lyman, B. G., & Collins, M. D. (1990). Critical reading: A redefinition. *Reading Research and Instruction, 29*(3), 56–63.

Lytle, S. (2000). Teacher research in the contact zone. In M. Kamil, P. Mosenthal, P. D. Pearson, & R. Barr, (Eds.), *Handbook of reading research, Vol. 3.* (pp. 691–718) Mahwah, NJ: Erlbaum.

Macaulay, D. (1973). *Cathedral.* New York: Houghton Mifflin.

Macaulay, D. (1974). *City: A story of Roman planning and construction.* Boston: Houghton Mifflin.

Macaulay, D. (1977). *Castle.* Boston: Houghton Mifflin.

Madaus, G., & O'Dwyer, L. (1999). A short history of performance assessment: Lessons learned. *Phi Delta Kappan, 80,* 688–695.

Malcolm X (with A. Haley) (1965). *The autobiography of Malcolm X.* New York: Ballantine.

Mandler, J., & Johnson, N. (1979). Rememberance of things parsed: Story structure and recall. *Cognitive Psychology, 9,* 111–151.

Manzo, A. (1969). The ReQuest procedure. *Journal of Reading, 13,* 23–26.

Manzo, A., & Casale, U. (1985). Listen–read–discuss: A content heuristic. *Journal of Reading, 28,* 732–734.

Marshall, N. (1996). The students: Who are they and how do I reach them? In D. Lapp, J. Flood, & N. Farnan (Eds.), *Content area reading and learning* (2nd ed., pp. 79–93). Boston: Allyn and Bacon.

Martin, M., & Konopak, B. (1987). An instructional investigation of students' ideas generated during content area writing. In J. Readence & R. S. Baldwin (Eds.), *Research in literacy: Merging perspectives* (pp. 265–271). Rochester, NY: National Reading Conference.

Martin, S. (2000). Tabloid expose'. In L. Baines & A. Kunkel (Eds.), *Going Bohemian: Activities that engage adolescents in the art of writing well* (pp. 123–124). Newark, DE: International Reading Association.

Marzano, R., & Kendall, J. (1996). *The fall and rise of standards-based education* (National Association of State Boards of Education *Issues in Brief*). Aurora, CO: Mid-Continent Regional Educational Laboratory.

May, K. (1994, October). The case of the cavity. *Science Scope, 18,* 23–27.

McCarthy, C. (1998). Multicultural education, minority identities, and the challenge of curriculum reform. In A. Willis (Ed.), *Teaching and using multicultural literature in grades 9–12: Moving beyond the canon* (pp. 1–16). Norwood, MA: Christopher Gordon.

McCombs, B. L. (1995, Winter). Understanding the keys to motivation to learn. In *What's noteworthy on learners, learning, schooling* (pp. 5–12). Aurora, CO: Mid-Continent Regional Educational Laboratory.

McGowan, T., & Guzzetti, B. (1991). Promoting social studies understanding through literature-based instruction. *Social Studies, 82,* 16–21.

McIntosh, M., & Draper, R. (1995). Applying the question–answer relationship strategy in mathematics. *Journal of Reading, 39,* 120–131.

McKenna, M. C., & Robinson, R. D. (1990). Content literacy: A definition and implications. *Journal of Reading, 34,* 184–186.

McKeown, M. (1985). The acquisition of word meaning from context by children of high and low ability. *Reading Research Quarterly, 20,* 482–496.

McMahon, S. I., & Raphael, T. E. (Eds.). (1997). *The book club connection.* New York: Teachers College Press.

Mehan, H. (1991). *Sociological foundations supporting the study of cultural diversity* (Research Report No. 1). Santa Cruz: University of California, National Center for Research on Cultural Diversity and Second Language Learning.

Meier, T. (1998a). Kitchen poets and classroom books: Literature from children's roots. In T. Perry & L. Delpit (Eds.), *The real Ebonics debate: Power, language, and the education of African-American children* (pp. 94–104). Boston: Beacon.

Meier, T. (1998b). Teaching teachers about black communications. In T. Perry & L. Delpit (Eds.), *The real Ebonics debate: Power, language, and the education of African-American children* (pp. 117–125.) Boston: Beacon.

Meskill, C., Mossop, J., & Bates, R. (2000, Winter). E-texts in ESL classes. *English Update: A Newsletter of the Center on English Learning & Achievement*, pp. 2–3. (Full report No. 12012 available on-line at *http://cela.albany.edu*)

Met, M. (1994). Teaching content through a second language. In F. Genesee (Ed.), *Educating second language children* (pp. 159–182). Cambridge, UK: Cambridge University Press.

Metzger, E. (1992). Plate tectonics within a thematic approach to science teaching. *Journal of Geological Education*, 40, 89–91.

Middleton, J. (1991). Student-generated analogies in biology. *The American Biology Teacher*, 53, 42–46.

Mike, D., & Rabinowitz, J. (1998). Collaborative projects on the Internet. *Language & Literacy Spectrum*, 8, 48–60.

Miller, G., & Gildea, P. (1987). How children learn words. *Scientific American*, 257, 94–99.

Miller, K., & George, J. (1992). Expository Passage Organizers: Models for reading and writing. *Journal of Reading*, 35, 372–377.

Miller, T. (1998). The place of picture books in middle-level classrooms. *Journal of Adolescent & Adult Literacy*, 41, 376–381.

Minami, M., & Ovando, C. J. (1995). Language issues in multicultural contexts. In J. A. Banks & C. A. McGee Banks (Eds.), *Handbook of research on multicultural education* (pp. 427–444). New York: Macmillan.

Moffit, M., & Wartella, E. (1992). Youth and reading: A survey of leisure reading pursuits of female and male adolescents. *Reading Research and Instruction*, 31, 1–17.

Moje, E. B., Willes, D. J., & Fassio, K. (2001). Constructing and negotiating literacy in a seventh-grade writer's workshop. In E. B. Moje & D. G. O'Brien (Eds.), *Constructions of literacy: Studies of teaching and learning in secondary classrooms and schools*. Mahwah, NJ: Erlbaum.

Moje, E., Brozo, W., & Haas, J. (1994). Portfolios in a high school classroom: Challenges to change. *Reading Research and Instruction*, 33, 275–292.

Moll, L. (1991). Literacy research in community and classrooms: A sociocultural approach. In C. Baker & A. Luke (Eds.), *Towards a critical sociology of reading pedagogy* (pp. 211–245). Philadelphia: John Benjamins.

Moore, D. W. (1996). Contexts for literacy in secondary schools. In D. J. Leu, C. K. Kinzer, & K. A. Hinchman (Eds.), *Literacies for the twenty-first century: Research and practice* (pp. 15–46). Chicago: National Reading Conference.

Moore, D. W., Alvermann, D. E., & Hinchman, K. A. (Eds.) (2000). *Struggling adolescent readers: A collection of teaching strategies*. Newark, DE: International Reading Association.

Moore, D. W., Bean, T. W., Birdyshaw, D., & Rycik, J. R. (1999). Adolescent literacy: A position statement. *Journal of Adolescent & Adult Literacy*, 43, 97–112.

Moore, D. W., Readence, J. E., & Rickelman, R. J. (1983). A historical exploration of content area reading instruction. *Reading Research Quarterly*, 18, 419–438.

Moore, D., & Moore, S. (1992). Possible sentences: An update. In E. Dishner, T. Bean, J. Readence, & D. Moore (Eds.), *Reading in content areas: Improving classroom instruction* (3rd ed., pp. 196–201). Dubuque, IA: Kendall/Hunt.

Moran, C. E., & Hakuta, K. (1995). Bilingual education: Broadening research perspectives. In J. A. Banks & C. A. McGee Banks (Eds.), *Handbook of research on multicultural education* (pp. 445–462). New York: Macmillan.

Moran, C., & Selfe, C. L. (1999). Teaching English across the technology/wealth gap. *English Journal*, 88(6), 49–54.

Morgan, W. (1997). *Critical literacy in the classroom*. New York: Routledge.

Moulton, M. (1999). The multigenre paper: Increasing interest, motivation, and functionality in research. *Journal of Adolescent & Adult Literacy*, 42, 528–539.

Murray, D. (1984). *Writing to learn*. New York: Holt, Rinehart and Winston.

Muth, K. D., & Alvermann, D. E. (1999). *Teaching and learning in the middle grades* (2nd ed.). Boston: Allyn & Bacon.

NAEP 1994 reading report card published. (1996, August/September). *Reading Today*, 14, 24.

Nagy, W., & Herman, P. (1987). Breadth and depth of vocabulary knowledge: Implications for acquisition and instruction. In M. McKeown & M. Curtis (Eds.), *The nature of vocabulary acquisition* (pp. 19–35). Hillsdale, NJ: Erlbaum.

Nagy, W., & Scott, J. (2000). Vocabulary processes. In M. Kamil, P. Mosenthal, P. D. Pearson, & R. Barr (Eds.), *Handbook of Reading Research, Vol. 3* (pp. 269–284.). Mahwah, NJ: Erlbaum.

Nagy, W., Herman, P., & Anderson, R. C. (1985). Learning words from context. *Reading Research Quarterly*, 20, 233–253.

Naipaul, V. S. (1984). *A house for Mr. Biswas*. New York: Vintage.

National Center for Education Statistics (2000). Teachers' feelings of preparedness. *Education Statistics Quarterly*, 2(1), 51.

National Reading Panel (2000). *Report of the National Reading Panel: Teaching children to read*. Washington, DC: National Institute of Child Health and Human Development.

Neal, J., & Moore, K. (1991/1992). *The Very Hungry Caterpillar* meets *Beowulf* in secondary classrooms. *Journal of Reading*, 35, 290–296.

Neilsen, A. (1991). Examining the forces against change: Fulfilling the promise of professional development. *Reflections on Canadian Literacy*, 9(2), 66–69.

Neilsen, J. (1990). *Hypertext and hypermedia.* Boston: Academic Press.

Neilsen, L. (1991). Of parachutes, mockingbirds, and bat-poets: A new paradigm for professional growth. *The Reading Teacher, 45,* 64–66.

Neilsen, L. (1998). Playing for real: Performative texts and adolescent identities. In D. Alvermann, K. Hinchman, D. Moore, S. Phelps, & D. Waff (Eds.), *Reconceptualizing the literacies in adolescents' lives* (pp. 3–26). Mahwah, NJ: Erlbaum.

Nelson, B. (1996). *Learning English: How school reform fosters language acquisition and development for limited English proficient elementary school students.* Santa Cruz, CA: National Center for Research on Cultural Diversity and Second Language Learning.

New London Group. (1997). A pedagogy of multiliteracies: Designing social futures. *Harvard Educational Review, 66,* 60–92.

Newmann, F. M. (1988). Can depth replace coverage in the high school curriculum? *Phi Delta Kappan, 69,* 345–348.

Nicholson, T. (1984). Experts and novices: A study of reading in the high school classroom. *Reading Research Quarterly, 19,* 436–451.

Nieto, S. (1994). Lessons from students on creating a chance to dream. *Harvard Educational Review, 64,* 392–426.

Nilsen, A. P., & Nilsen, D. L. F. (2000). Language play in Y2K: Morphology brought to you by Pokémon. *Voices from the Middle, 7*(4), 32–37.

Nolan, T. (1991). Self-questioning and prediction: Combining metacognitive strategies. *Journal of Reading, 35,* 132–138.

Nolen, S. B., & Haladyna, T. M. (1989, March). *Psyching out the science teacher: Student motivation, perceived teacher goals and study strategies.* Paper presented at the annual meeting of the American Educational Research Association, San Francisco.

Norton, D. (1990). Teaching multicultural literature in the reading curriculum. *The Reading Teacher, 44,* 28–40.

Nystrand, M., Gamoran, A., & Heck, M. J. (1992, April). *Using small groups for response to and thinking about literature.* Paper presented at the annual meeting of the American Educational Research Association, San Francisco.

O'Brien, D. G., & Stewart, R. A. (1990). Preservice teachers' perspectives on why every teacher is not a teacher of reading: A qualitative analysis. *Journal of Reading Behavior, 22,* 101–129.

O'Dell, S. (1980). *Sarah Bishop.* Boston: Houghton Mifflin.

O'Hear, M., & Aikman, C. (1996). Main ideas in best-sellers: A new look at an old problem. *Reading Research & Instruction, 35,* 315–322.

O'Neil, W. (1998). If Ebonics isn't a language, then tell me, what is? (pace James Baldwin, 1979). In T. Perry & L. Delpit (Eds.), *The real Ebonics debate: Power, language, and the education of African-American children* (pp. 38–47). Boston: Beacon.

Oakes, J. (1985). *Keeping track: How schools structure inequality.* New Haven, CT: Yale University Press.

Oakes, J. (1986). Keeping track, Part I: The policy and practice of curricular inequality. *Phi Delta Kappan, 68,* 12–17.

Offner, S. (1992). Teaching biology around themes: Teach proteins & DNA together. *The American Biology Teacher, 54,* 93–101.

Ogle, D. (1986). K-W-L: A teaching model that develops active reading of expository text. *The Reading Teacher, 39,* 563–570.

Ohanian, S. (1985). On stir-and-serve recipes for teaching. *Phi Delta Kappan, 66,* 696–701.

Oldfather, P., & Thomas, S. (1996). *"The changer and the changed": Student-initiated research on literacy motivation and schooling* (Research Report No. 61). Athens: University of Georgia, National Reading Research Center.

Orner, M. (1992). Interrupting the calls for student voice in "liberatory" education: A feminist poststructuralist perspective. In C. Luke & J. Gore (Eds.), *Feminisms and critical pedagogy* (pp. 74–89). New York: Routledge.

Otto, W. (1990). Getting smart. *Journal of Reading, 33,* 368–370.

Palincsar, A. S. (1986). The role of dialogue in providing scaffolded instruction. *Educational Psychologist, 21,* 73–98.

Palincsar, A. S., & Brown, A. L. (1984). Reciprocal teaching of comprehension-fostering and comprehension-monitoring activities. *Cognition and Instruction, 1,* 117–175.

Palmatier, R. A. (1973). A notetaking system for learning. *Journal of Reading, 17,* 36–39.

Palmer, D. (1991, April). *Group discussion in science: Two classrooms, two worlds for sense making.* Paper presented at the annual meeting of the American Educational Research Association, Chicago.

Pang, V., Colvin, C., Tran, M., & Barba, R. (1992). Beyond chopsticks and dragons: Selecting Asian-American literature for children. *The Reading Teacher, 46,* 216–224.

Paris, S. G., Lipson, M. Y., & Wixson, K. K. (1983). Becoming a strategic reader. *Contemporary Educational Psychology, 8,* 293–316.

Paris, S., Wasik, B., & Turner, J. (1991). The development of strategic readers. In R. Barr, M. Kamil, P. Mosenthal, & P. D. Pearson (Eds.), *Handbook of reading research, Vol. 2* (pp. 609–640). New York: Longman.

Patterson, A., Mellor, B., & O'Neill, M. (1994). Beyond comprehension: Poststructuralist readings in the English classroom. In B. Corcoran, M. Hayhoe, & G. M. Pradl (Eds.), *Knowledge in the making* (pp. 61–72). Portsmouth, NH: Boynton/Cook.

Patterson, N. (1999, September). Making connections: Hypertext and research in a middle school classroom. *English Journal, 89,* 69–73.

Paulu, N. (1995). *Helping your child with homework.* Washington, DC: U.S. Department of Education, Office of Educational Research and Improvement.

Pearson, P. D. (1998). Standards and assessment: Tools for crafting effective instruction? In J. Osborn and F. Lehr (Eds.), *Literacy for all: Issues in teaching and learning* (pp. 264–288). New York: Guilford.

Pearson, P. D., & Fielding, L. (1991). Comprehension instruction. In R. Barr, M. Kamil, P. Mosenthal, & P. D. Pearson (Eds.), *Handbook of reading research: Volume 2* (pp. 815–860). New York: Longman.

Pearson, P. D., & Gallagher, M. C. (1983). The instruction of reading comprehension. *Contemporary Educational Psychology, 8*, 317–344.

Pearson, P. D., & Johnson, D. (1978). *Teaching reading comprehension.* New York: Holt, Rinehart & Winston.

Peltz, C., Powers, M., & Wycoff, B. (1994, March). Teaching world economics: An interdisciplinary approach for the middle-level classroom. *Middle School Journal, 25*, 23–25.

Peralta-Nash, C., & Dutch, J. A. (2000). Literature circles: Creating environment for choice. *Primary Voices K–6, 8*(4), 29–37.

Perry, T., & Delpit, L. (Eds.) (1998). *The real Ebonics debate: Power, language, and the education of African-American children.* Boston: Beacon.

Phelps, S. (1984). A first step in content area reading instruction. *Reading World, 23*, 265–269.

Phelps, S. F., & Weaver, D. (1999). Public and personal voices in adolescents' classroom talk. *Journal of Literacy Research, 31*, 321–354.

Phelps, T. (1992). Research of three-search? *English Journal, 81*(2), 76–78.

Phillips, D. C. (Ed.). (2000). *Constructivism in education: Opinions and second opinions on controversial issues.* Chicago: University of Chicago Press.

Pierce, L. (1988). *Facilitating transition to the mainstream: Sheltered English vocabulary development* (Program Information Guide Series No. 6). Wheaton, MD: National Clearinghouse for Bilingual Education.

Pilgreen, J. (2000). *The SSR handbook: How to organize and manage a sustained silent reading program.* Portsmouth, NH: Boynton/Cook.

Powell, R. (1997). Classroom management in an integrative middle school: An exploratory study. *Research in Middle Level Education Quarterly, 20*(4), 1–35.

Powell, R., & Skoog, G. (1995). Students' perspectives of integrative curricula: The case of Brown–Barge Middle School. *Research in Middle Level Education Quarterly, 19* (1), 85–115.

Powell, R., Skoog, G., & Troutman, P. (1996). On streams and odysseys: Reflections on reform and research in middle level integrative learning environments. *Research in Middle Level Education Quarterly, 19*(4), 1–30.

Pressley, M. (1998). Comprehension strategies instruction. In J. Osborn & F. Lehr (Eds.), *Literacy for all: Issues in teaching and learning* (pp. 113–133). New York: Guilford.

Pressley, M. (2000). What should comprehension instruction be the instruction of? In M. L. Kamil, P. B. Mosenthal, P. D. Pearson, & R. Barr (Eds.), *Handbook of reading research: Volume 3* (pp. 545–561). Mahwah, NJ: Erlbaum.

Pressley, M., El-Dinary, P. B., & Brown, R. (1992). Skilled and not-so-skilled reading: Good information processing and not-so-good information processing. In M. Pressley, K. R. Harris, & J. T. Guthrie (Eds.), *Promoting academic competence and literacy in school* (pp. 91–127). San Diego: Academic Press.

Pressley, M., Hogan, K., Wharton-MacDonald, R., Mistretta, J., & Ettenberger, S. (1996). The challenges of instructional scaffolding: The challenges of instruction that supports student thinking. *Learning Disabilities Research & Practice, 11*, 138–146.

Pugh, S., & Garcia, J. (1990). Portraits in black: Establishing African American identity through nonfiction books. *Journal of Reading, 34*, 20–25.

Purves, A. C. (1998). *The web of text and the web of God: An essay on the third information transformation.* New York: Guilford.

Rakow, S., & Gee, T. (1987, February). Test science, not reading. *The Science Teacher, 54*, 28–31.

Randall, S. N. (2000). Information charts: A strategy for organizing student research. In D. Moore, D. Alvermann, & K. Hinchman (Eds.), *Struggling adolescent readers: A collection of strategies* (pp. 198–205). Newark, DE: International Reading Association.

Raphael, T. (1982). Question–answering strategies for children. *The Reading Teacher, 36*, 186–191.

Raphael, T. (1984). Teaching learners about sources of information for answering comprehension questions. *Journal of Reading, 27*, 303–311.

Raphael, T. (1986). Teaching question–answer relationships, revisited. *The Reading Teacher, 39*, 516–522.

Raphael, T. E., & McKinney, J. (1983). An examination of fifth- and eighth-grade children's question–answering behavior: An instructional study in metacognition. *Journal of Reading Behavior, 15*(3), 67–86.

Raphael, T., & Gavelek, J. (1984). Question-related activities and their relationship to reading comprehension: Some instructional implications. In G. Duffy, L. Roehler, & J. Mason (Eds.), *Comprehension instruction: Perspectives and suggestions* (pp. 234–250). New York: Longman.

Raphael, T., & Pearson, P. D. (1982). *The effect of metacognitive awareness training on children's question answering behavior,* Technical report #238. Urbana, IL: Center for the Study of Reading.

Ratekin, J., Simpson, M., Alvermann, D., & Dishner, E. (1985). Why teachers resist content reading instruction. *Journal of Reading, 28*, 432–437.

Rawls, J., & Weeks, P. (1985). *Land of liberty.* New York: Holt, Rinehart and Winston.

Readence, J. E., Moore, D. W., & Rickelman, R. J. (2000). *Prereading activities for content area reading and learning* (3rd ed.). Newark, DE: International Reading Association.

Reif, L. (1990). Finding the value in evaluation: Self-assessment in a middle school classroom. *Educational Leadership, 47*, 24–29.

Reimer, K. M. (1992). Multiethnic literature: Holding fast to dreams. *Language Arts, 69*, 14–21.

Reinking, D., McKenna, M., Labbo, L., & Kieffer, R. (1998). *Handbook of literacy and technology.* Mahwah, NJ: Erlbaum.

Reis, R., & Spekman, N. J. (1983). The detection of reader-based versus text-based inconsistencies and the effects of direct training of comprehension monitoring among upper-grade poor comprehenders. *Journal of Reading Behavior, 15*(2), 49–60.

Rekrut, M. (1997). Collaborative research. *Journal of Adolescent & Adult Literacy, 41,* 26–34.

Rekrut, M. (1999). Using the Internet in classroom instruction: A primer for teachers. *Journal of Adolescent & Adult Literacy, 42,* 546–557.

Rekrut, M. D. (1994). Peer and cross-age tutoring: The lessons of research. *Journal of Reading, 37,* 356–362.

Reppen, R. (1994/1995, Winter). A genre-based approach to content writing instruction. *TESOL Journal, 4,* 32–35.

Resnick, D. P., & Goodman, M. (1994). American culture and the gifted. In P. O. Ross (Ed.), *National excellence: A case for developing America's talent: An anthology of readings* (pp. 109–121). Washington, DC: U.S. Department of Education, Office of Educational Research and Improvement.

Reyes, M. L., & Molner, L. A. (1991). Instructional strategies for second-language learners in the content areas. *Journal of Reading, 35,* 96–103.

Reynolds, F., & Pickett, I. (1989). Read! Think! Write! The reading response journal in the biology classroom. *The American Biology Teacher, 51,* 435–437.

Reynolds, R., Taylor, M., Steffensen, M., Shirey, L., & Anderson, R. (1982). Cultural schemata and reading comprehension. *Reading Research Quarterly, 17,* 353–366.

Rhodes, L. K., & Shanklin, N. L. (1993). *Windows into literacy.* Portsmouth, NH: Heinemann.

Richardson, J. (2000). *Read it aloud! Using literature in the secondary content classroom.* Newark, DE: International Reading Association.

Richardson, J. S., & Morgan, R. F. (2000). *Reading to learn in the content areas* (4th ed.). Belmont, CA: Wadsworth/Thompson Learning.

Richgels, D., McGee, L., Lomax, R., & Sheard, C. (1987). Awareness of four text structures: Effects on recall of expository text. *Reading Research Quarterly, 22,* 177–196.

Rieck, B. (1977). How content teachers telegraph messages against reading. *Journal of Reading, 20,* 646–648.

Rinaldi, A. (1993). *The fifth of March.* New York: Harcourt Brace.

Rinaldi, A. (1995). *A ride into morning.* New York: Harcourt Brace.

Robinson, F. P. (1961). *Effective study I* (Rev. ed.). New York: Harper & Row.

Rosenblatt, L. (1978). *The reader, the text, the poem: The transactional theory of the literary work.* Carbondale, IL: Southern Illinois University Press.

Rosenblatt, L. (1982). The literary transaction: Evocation and response. *Theory into Practice, 21,* 268–277.

Rosenblatt, L. (1985). Transaction versus interaction—A terminological rescue operation. *Research in the Teaching of English, 19,* 96–107.

Rosenshine, B., & Meister, C. (1992). The use of scaffolds for teaching higher-level cognitive strategies. *Educational Leadership, 49*(7), 26–33.

Rosenshine, B., & Meister, C. (1994). Reciprocal teaching: A review of the research. *Review of Educational Research, 64,* 479–530.

Roskos, K., & Walker, B. J. (1994). *Interactive handbook for understanding reading diagnosis: A problem-solving approach* (pp. 5–7). New York: Merrill.

Rothenberg, S. S., & Watts, S. M. (2000). Students with learning difficulties meet Shakespeare: Using a scaffolded reading experience. In D. W. Moore, D. E. Alvermann, & K. A. Hinchman (Eds.), *Struggling adolescent readers: A collection of teaching strategies* (pp. 148–156). Newark, DE: International Reading Association.

Ruddell, M. (1996). Engaging students' interest and willing participation in subject area learning. In D. Lapp, J. Flood, & N. Farnan (Eds.), *Content area reading and learning: Instructional strategies* (2nd ed., pp. 95–110). Boston: Allyn & Bacon.

Ruddell, M. R. (1997). *Teaching content reading and writing* (2nd ed.). Boston: Allyn & Bacon.

Ruddell, R., Ruddell, M., & Singer, H. (1995). *Theoretical models and processes of reading* (4th ed.). Newark, DE: International Reading Association.

Salinger, J. D. (1951). *The catcher in the rye.* Boston: Little, Brown.

Samuels, B. (1989). Young adults' choices: Why do students "really like" particular books? *Journal of Reading, 32,* 714–719.

Sanacore, J. (1990). Creating the lifetime reading habit in social studies. *Journal of Reading, 33,* 414–419.

Sanacore, J. (2000). Promoting the lifetime reading habit in middle school students. *The Clearinghouse, 73,* 157–161.

Sanders, M. (1994). Technological problem-solving activities as a means of instruction: The TSM integration program. *School Science & Mathematics, 94,* 36–43.

Santa, C. M. (1988). *Content reading including study systems.* Dubuque, IA: Kendall/Hunt.

Santa, C., Havens, L., & Harrison, S. (1996). Teaching secondary science through reading, writing, studying, and problem-solving. In D. Lapp, J. Flood, & N. Farnan (Eds.), *Content area reading and learning: Instructional strategies* (2nd ed., pp. 165–180). Boston: Allyn & Bacon.

Sarroub, L., Pearson, P. D., Dykema, C., & Lloyd, R. (1997). When portfolios become part of the grading process: A case study in a junior high setting. In C. Kinzer, K. Hinchman, & D. Leu (Eds.), *Inquiries in literacy theory and practice* (pp. 101–113). Chicago: National Reading Conference.

Saunders, W. M., & Goldenberg, C. (1999). *The effects of instructional conversations and literature logs on the story comprehension and thematic understanding of English proficient and limited English proficient students.* Santa

Cruz, CA: Center for Research on Education, Diversity & Excellence.

Scanlon, D., Deshler, D., & Schumaker, J. (1996). Can a strategy be taught and learned in secondary inclusive classrooms? *Learning Disabilities Research & Practice, 11*, 41–57.

Schallert, D., & Roser, N. (1996). The role of reading in content area instruction. In D. Lapp, J. Flood, & N. Farnan (Eds.), *Content area reading and learning* (2nd ed., pp. 27–38). Englewood Cliffs, NJ: Prentice Hall.

Schatz, E., & Baldwin, S. (1986). Context clues are unreliable predictors of word meanings. *Reading Research Quarterly, 21*, 439–453.

Schell, L. (1988). Dilemmas in assessing reading comprehension. *The Reading Teacher, 42*, 12–16.

Schimberg, A., & Grant, H. (1998, Fall). Who-dun-it? A mystery thematic unit. *Science Activities, 35*, 29–35.

Schoenbach, R., Greenleaf, C., Cziko, C., & Hurwitz, L. (1999). *Reading for understanding: A guide to improving reading in middle and high school classrooms.* San Francisco: Jossey-Bass.

Schraer, W., & Stoltze, H. (1993). *Biology: The study of life* (5th ed.). Englewood Cliffs, NJ: Prentice Hall.

Schultz, K., & Fecho, B. (2000). Society's child: Social context and writing development. *Educational Psychologist, 35*, 51–62.

Schwartz, R. (1988). Learning to learn vocabulary in content area textbooks. *Journal of Reading, 32*, 108–118.

Schwartz, R., & Raphael, T. (1985). Concept of definition: A key to improving students' vocabulary. *The Reading Teacher, 39*, 198–205.

Scott, J. C. (1990). *Domination and the arts of resistance.* New Haven, CT: Yale University Press.

Sefton-Green, J. (1999). Young people, creativity and new technologies: The challenge of digital arts. London: Routledge and the Arts Council of England.

Sewall, G. (1988). American history textbooks: Where do we go from here? *Phi Delta Kappan, 69*, 553–558.

Shaara, M. (1974). *The killer angels.* New York: Ballantine.

Shanahan, T. (1995). Avoiding some of the pitfalls of thematic units. *The Reading Teacher, 48*, 718–719.

Shealy, A. (2000, Spring/Summer). On becoming a teacher and writer. *Bread Loaf Rural Teacher Network Magazine*, 10–11.

Sheehan, A. D., & Sheehan, C. M. (2000). Lost in a sea of ink: How I survived the storm. *Journal of Adolescent & Adult Literacy, 44*, 20–32.

Shefelbine, J. (1990). Student factors related to variability in learning word meanings from context. *Journal of Reading Behavior, 22*, 71–97.

Simmons, J. (1990, March). Adapting portfolios for large-scale use. *Educational Leadership, 47*, 28.

Singer, H., & Donlan, D. (1982). Active comprehension: Problem-solving schema with question generation for comprehension of complex short stories. *Reading Research Quarterly, 17*, 166–186.

Singer, H., & Donlan, D. (1989). *Reading and learning from text.* Hillsdale, NJ: Erlbaum.

Sjostrom, C., & Hare, V. (1984). Teaching high school students to identify main ideas in expository text. *Journal of Educational Research, 78*, 114–118.

Slavin, R. E. (1983). *Cooperative learning.* New York: Longman.

Slavin, R. E. (1984a). Students motivating students to excel: Cooperative incentives, cooperative tasks, and student achievement. *Elementary School Journal, 85*, 53–63.

Slavin, R. E. (1984b). Team assisted individuation: Cooperative learning and individualized instruction in the mainstrearned classroom. *Remedial and Special Education, 5*(6), 33–42.

Smith, C., & Bean, T. (1980). The guided writing procedure: Integrating content reading and writing improvement. *Reading World, 19*, 290–298.

Smith, F. (1971). *Understanding reading: A psycholinguistic analysis of reading and learning to read.* New York: Holt, Rinehart and Winston.

Smith, F. R., & Feathers, K. M. (1983a). Teacher and student perceptions of content area reading. *Journal of Reading, 26*, 348–354.

Smith, F. R., & Feathers, K. M. (1983b). The role of reading in content classrooms: Assumption vs. reality. *Journal of Reading, 27*, 262–267.

Smolen, L., Newman, C., Wathen, T., & Lee, D. (1995). Developing student self-assessment strategies. *TESOL Journal, 5*, 22–27.

Spalding, E. (2000). Performance assessment and the New Standards Project: A story of serendipitous success. *Phi Delta Kappan, 81*, 758–764.

Spears-Bunton, L. (1990). Welcome to my house: African American and European American students' responses to Virginia Hamilton's *House of Dies Drear. Journal of Negro Education, 59*, 566–576.

Spears-Bunton, L. (1991, December). *Literature, literacy and resistance to cultural domination.* Paper presented at the meeting of the National Reading Conference, Palm Springs, CA.

Spears-Bunton, L. (1998). All the colors of the land: A literacy montage. In A. Willis (Ed.), *Teaching and using multicultural literature in grades 9–12: Moving beyond the canon* (pp. 17–36). Norwood, MA: Christopher Gordon.

Spires, H. A., & Stone, P. D. (1989). The directed notetaking activity: A self-questioning approach. *Journal of Reading, 33*, 36–39.

Stahl, S., & Clark, C. (1987). The effects of participatory expectations in classroom discussion on the learning of science vocabulary. *American Educational Research Journal, 24*, 541–556.

Stahl, S., & Kapinus, B. (1991). Possible sentences: Predicting word meanings to teach content area vocabulary. *The Reading Teacher, 45*, 36–43.

Stake, R. E., & Easley, J. (1978). *Case studies in science education*, Vol. 2: *Design, overview and general findings.* Washington, DC: U.S. Government Printing Office.

Stanovich, K. E. (1980). Toward an interactive-compensatory model of individual differences in the development of reading fluency. *Reading Research Quarterly, 16,* 32–71.

Stauffer, R. (1969). *Directing reading maturity as a cognitive process.* New York: Harper & Row.

Stauffer, R. (1976). *Teaching reading as a thinking process.* New York: Harper & Row.

Steffensen, M., Joag-Dev, C., & Anderson, R. (1979). A cross-cultural perspective on reading comprehension. *Reading Research Quarterly, 15,* 10–29.

Stein, N., & Glenn, C. (1979). An analysis of story comprehension in elementary school children. In R. O. Freedle (Ed.), *New directions in discourse processing.* Norwood, NJ: Ablex.

Steinbeck, J. (1989). *The pearl.* In R. Anderson, J. Brinnin, J. Leggett, & D. Leeming (Eds.), *Elements of literature* (pp. 674–712). Austin, TX: Holt, Rinehart & Winston.

Sternberg, R. J. (1987). Teaching critical thinking: Eight easy ways to fail before you begin. *Phi Delta Kappan, 68,* 456–459.

Sternberg, R. J., & Grigorenko, E. L. (2000). *Teaching for successful intelligence.* Arlington Heights, IL: Skylight.

Sternberg, R. J., Grigorenko, E. L., Jarvin, L., Clinkenbeard, P., Ferrari, M., & Torff, B. (2000, Spring). The effectiveness of triarchic teaching and assessment. *The National Center on the Gifted and Talented Newsletter,* pp. 3–8.

Stiggins, R., Frisbie, D., & Griswold, P. (1989). Inside high school grading practices: Building a research agenda. *Journal of Educational Measurement, 8,* 5–14.

Stodolsky, S. S. (1988.) *The subject matters.* Chicago: University of Chicago Press.

Street, B. V. (1995). *Social literacies: Critical approaches to literacy in development, ethnography, and education.* New York: Longman.

Strother, D. B. (1985). Adapting instruction to individual needs: An eclectic approach. *Phi Delta Kappan, 67,* 308–311.

Survey finds students, teachers show bias (2000, May). *The Council Chronicle,* p. 13.

Swafford, J. (1988, December). *The use of study strategy instruction with secondary school students: Is there a research base?* Paper presented at the annual meeting of the National Reading Conference, Tucson, AZ.

Swanson, P., & de la Paz, S. (1998). Teaching effective comprehension strategies to students with learning and reading disabilities. *Intervention in School and Clinic, 33,* 209–218.

Taba, H. (1967). *Teacher's handbook for elementary social studies.* Reading, MA: Addison-Wesley.

Tatum, A. W. (2000). Breaking down barriers that disenfranchise African American adolescent readers in low-level tracks. *Journal of Adolescent & Adult Literacy, 44,* 52–64.

Taylor, B., & Beach, R. (1984). The effects of text structure instruction on middle-grade students' comprehension and production of expository text. *Reading Research Quarterly, 19,* 134–146.

Taylor, D., & Dorsey-Gaines, C. (1988). *Growing up literate: Learning from inner-city families.* Portsmouth, NH: Heinemann.

Taylor, M. (1976). *Roll of thunder, hear my cry.* New York: Dial.

Taylor, T. (1984). *The hostage.* New York: Bantam.

Taylor, W. (1953). Cloze procedure: A new tool for measuring readability. *Journalism Quarterly, 30,* 415–433.

Temple, F. (1993). *Grab hands and run.* New York: Orchard.

Tharp, R., & Gallimore, R. (1988). *Rousing minds to life: Teaching, learning, and schooling in social context.* Cambridge, UK: Cambridge University Press.

Tharp, R., Dalton, S. S., & Yamauchi, L. (1994). Principles for culturally compatible Native American education. *Journal of Navajo Education, 11*(3), 33–39.

Thomas, H. K. (1999). The social construction of literacy in a high school biology class. In T. Shanahan & F. V. Rodriguez-Brown (Eds.), *48th Yearbook of the National Reading Conference.* Chicago: National Reading Conference.

Thomas, J. W., & Rohwer, W. D. (1986). Academic studying: The role of learning strategies. *Educational Psychologist, 21,* 19–41.

Thomas, W. (1986, February). Grading—Why are school policies necessary? What are the issues? *NASSP Bulletin, 70,* 22–26.

Tierney, R., Clark, C., Fenner, L., Herter, R., Simpson, C., & Wiser, B. (1998). Portfolios: Assumptions, tensions and possibilities. *Reading Research Quarterly, 33,* 474–486.

Tierney, R., Readence, J., & Dishner, E. (2000). *Reading strategies and practices: A compendium* (5th ed.). Boston: Allyn & Bacon.

Tierney, R., Soter, A., O'Flahavan, J., & McGinley, W. (1989). The effects of reading and writing upon thinking critically. *Reading Research Quarterly, 24,* 134–173.

Trelease, J. (1989). *The new read-aloud handbook.* New York: Penguin.

Trujillo, L. (2000, March 12). Latino or Hispanic? *The Arizona Republic,* pp. A1, A22.

Twain, M. (1961). *Life on the Mississippi.* New York: New American Library.

Tyson-Bernstein, H. (1988). *A conspiracy of good intentions: America's textbook fiasco.* Washington, DC: Council for Basic Education.

U.S. Department of Education (1992). *Hard work and high expectations: Motivating students to learn* (Announcement PIP92-1500a). Washington, DC: Superintendent of Documents (Stock No. 065-00496-8).

U.S. Department of Education (1998). *Pocket projections: Projections of education statistics to 2008* (NCES Report No. 98-017). Washington, DC: National Center for Education Statistics.

U.S. Department of Education (1999). *Student computer use* (Report No. NCES 1999-011). Washington, DC: National Center for Education Statistics, Office of Educational Research and Improvement.

U.S. Department of Education (2000). *Teacher use of computers and the Internet in public schools* (Report No.

NCES 2000-090). Washington, DC: National Center for Education Statistics, Office of Educational Research and Development.

Valencia, S., & Wixson, K. (2000). Policy-oriented research on literacy standards and assessment. In M. Kamil, P. Mosenthal, P. D. Pearson, & R. Barr (Eds.), *Handbook of reading research, Vol. 3* (pp. 909–935). Mahwah, NJ: Erlbaum.

Van Slyck, M., & Stern, M. (1999). A developmental approach to the use of conflict resolution interventions with adolescents. In L. R. Forcey & I. M. Harris (Eds.), *Peacebuilding for adolescents: Strategies for educators and community leaders* (pp. 177–193). New York: Lang.

Vande Steeg, M. (1991). A new challenge for teachers. *The American Biology Teacher, 53,* 20–21.

Vygotsky, L. (1986). *Thought and language.* Cambridge, MA: MIT Press.

Vygotsky, L. S. (1978). *Mind in society: The development of higher psychological processes.* Cambridge, MA: Harvard University Press.

Wade, S. E., & Moje, E. B. (2000). The role of text in classroom learning. In M. L. Kamil, P. B. Mosenthal, P. D. Pearson, & R. Barr (Eds.), *Handbook of reading research: Volume 3* (pp. 609–627). Mahwah, NJ: Erlbaum.

Wade, S. E., & Reynolds, R. E. (1989). Developing metacognitive awareness. *Journal of Reading, 33,* 6–14.

Waggoner, D. (1999). Who are secondary newcomer and linguistically different youth? In C. Faltis & P. Wolfe (Eds.), *So much to say: Adolescents, bilingualism, and ESL in the secondary school* (pp. 13–41). New York: Teachers College Press.

Walpole, S. (1998/1999). Changing texts, changing thinking: Comprehension demands of new science textbooks. *The Reading Teacher, 52,* 358–369.

Walvoord, B., & Anderson, V. (1998). *Effective grading: A tool for learning and assessment.* San Francisco: Jossey-Bass.

Warger, C. L., & Rutherford, R. B., Jr. (1997). Teaching respect and responsibility in inclusive classrooms: An instructional approach. *Reclaiming Children and Youth, 6*(3), 171–175.

Watson, B., & Konicek, R. (1990). Teaching for conceptual change: Confronting children's experience. *Phi Delta Kappan, 71,* 680–685.

Weaver, C. (1988.) *Reading process and practice: From sociopsycholinguistics to whole language.* Portsmouth, NH: Heinemann.

Weber, A. (2000). Playful writing for critical thinking: Four approaches to writing. *Journal of Adolescent & Adult Literacy, 43,* 562–568.

Webster's New World Dictionary of American English (Third College Edition) (1991). New York: Prentice Hall.

Weiner, B. (1986). *An attributional theory of motivation and emotion.* New York: Springer-Verlag.

Welner, K. G., & Oakes, J. (1996). (Li)ability grouping: The new susceptibility of school tracking systems to legal challenges. *Harvard Educational Review, 66,* 451–470.

Wenger, E. (1998). *Communities of practice: Learning, meaning, and identity.* Cambridge, UK: Cambridge University Press.

Wertsch, J. V. (1985). *Vygotsky and the social formation of mind.* Cambridge, MA: Harvard University Press.

Wertsch, J. V. (1991). *Voices of the mind.* Cambridge, MA: Harvard University Press.

Westera, J., & Moore, D. W. (1995). Reciprocal teaching of reading comprehension in a New Zealand high school. *Psychology in the Schools, 32,* 225–232.

White, R. M. (1995). How thematic teaching can transform history instruction. *The Clearinghouse, 68,* 160–162.

White, T., Graves, M., & Slater, W. (1990). Growth of reading vocabulary in diverse elementary schools: Decoding and word meaning. *Journal of Educational Psychology, 82,* 281–289.

White, T., Power, M., & White, S. (1989). Morphological analysis: Implications for teaching and understanding vocabulary growth. *Reading Research Quarterly, 24,* 283–304.

Wigfield, A., Wilde, K., Baker, L., Fernandez-Fein, S., & Scher, D. (1996). *The nature of children's motivations for reading, and their relations to reading frequency and reading performance.* (Research Report No. 63). Athens: University of Georgia, National Reading Research Center.

Wiggins, G. (1993, Fall). Assessment to improve performance, not just monitor it: Assessment reform in the social sciences. *Social Science Record, 30,* 5–12.

Wiggins, G. (1998). *Educative assessment: Designing assessments to inform and improve student performance.* San Francisco: Jossey-Bass.

Willinsky, J. (1990). *The new literacy: Redefining reading and writing in the schools.* New York: Routledge.

Willis, A., & Palmer, M. (1998). Negotiating the classroom: Learning and teaching multicultural literature. In A. Willis (Ed.), *Teaching and using multicultural literature in grades 9–12: Moving beyond the canon* (pp. 215–250). Norwood, MA: Christopher Gordon.

Willis, S. (1993). Are letter grades obsolete? *ASCD Update, 35,* 1, 4, 8. [Chapter 11]

Wineburg, S. (1991). On the reading of historical texts: Notes on the breach between school and academy. *American Educational Research Journal, 28,* 495–519.

Winne, P., Graham, L., & Prock, L. (1993). A model of poor readers' text-based inferencing: Effects of explanatory feedback. *Reading Research Quarterly, 28,* 53–66.

Winograd, P. N. (1984). Strategic difficulties in summarizing texts. *Reading Research Quarterly, 19,* 404–425.

Wolf, K., & Siu-Runyan, Y. (1996). Portfolio purposes and possibilities. *Journal of Adolescent & Adult Literacy, 40,* 30–37.

Wolf, S., Edmiston, B., & Enciso, P. (1997). Drama worlds. In J. Flood, D. Lapp, & S. B. Heath (Eds.), *Handbook of research on teaching literacy through the communicative and visual arts* (pp. 492–505). New York: Macmillan.

Wolfe, R. R. (2000). Protein supplements and exercise. *The American Journal of Clinical Nutrition, 72,* 551–557.

Wong, B. (1997). Research on genre-specific strategies for enhancing writing in adolescents with learning disabilities. *Learning Disability Quarterly, 20,* 140–159.

Wong, B. Y. L. (1985). Self-questioning instructional research: A review. *Review of Educational Research, 55,* 227–268.

Wong, B., Butler, D., Ficzere, S., & Kuperis, S. (1997). Teaching adolescents with learning disabilities and low achievers to plan, write, and revise compare-and-contrast essays. *Learning Disabilities Research & Practice, 12,* 2–15.

Wood, D., Bruner, J. S., & Ross, G. (1976). The role of tutoring in problem solving. *Journal of Child Psychology and Psychiatry, 17,* 89–100.

Wood, K. (1986). The effect of interspersing questions in text: Evidence for "slicing the task." *Reading Research & Instruction, 25,* 295–307.

Woods 100 helps to restore self-respect. (1978, December 30). *The Australian* (No. 4497).

Woodward, A., & Elliott, D. L. (1990). Textbook use and teacher professionalism. In D. L. Elliott & A. Woodward (Eds.), *Textbooks and schooling in the United States* (Eighty-ninth Yearbook of the National Society for the Study of Education, Part I, pp. 179–193). Chicago: University of Chicago Press.

Worthy, J., Moorman, M., & Turner, M. (1999). What Johnny likes to read is hard to find in school. *Reading Research Quarterly, 34,* 12–27.

Wu, S., & Rubin, D. (2000). Evaluating the impact of collectivism and individualism on argumentative writing by Chinese and North American college students. *Research in the Teaching of English, 35,* 148–178.

Wysocki, K., & Jenkins, J. (1987). Deriving word meanings through morphological generalization. *Reading Research Quarterly, 22,* 66–81.

Young, A. J., Arbreton, A. J., & Midgley, C. (1992, April). *All content area may not be created equal: Motivational orientation and cognitive strategy use in four academic domains.* Paper presented at the annual meeting of the American Educational Research Association, San Francisco.

Young, J. P. (2000). Critical literacy: Young adolescent boys talk about masculinities within a homeschool context. *Reading Research Quarterly, 35,* 312–337.

Young, J. P., Mathews, S. R., Kietzmann, A. M., & Westerfield, T. (2000). Getting disenchanted adolescents to participate in school literacy activities: Portfolio conferences. In D. W. Moore, D. E. Alvermann, & K. A. Hinchman (Eds.), *Struggling adolescent readers: A collection of teaching strategies* (pp. 302–316). Newark, DE: International Reading Association.

Zimmerman, B. J. (1994). Dimensions of academic self-regulation: A conceptual framework for education. In D. H. Schunk & B. J. Zimmerman (Eds.), *Self-regulation of learning and performance* (pp. 3–21). Hillsdale, NJ: Erlbaum.

Author Index

Subject Index